LATE MEDIEVAL DEVOTION TO SAINTS
FROM THE NORTH OF ENGLAND

MEDIEVAL CHURCH STUDIES

VOLUME 48

Editorial board under the auspices of the
Department of History, University of Nottingham.

Ross Balzaretti, Peter Darby, Rob Lutton, Claire Taylor

Previously published volumes in this series
are listed at the back of the book.

Late Medieval Devotion to Saints from the North of England

New Directions

Edited by
CHRISTIANIA WHITEHEAD,
HAZEL J. HUNTER BLAIR,
and DENIS RENEVEY

BREPOLS

British Library Cataloguing in Publication Data
A catalogue record for this book is available from the British Library

© 2022, Brepols Publishers n.v., Turnhout, Belgium.

All rights reserved. No part of this publication may be reproduced,
stored in a retrieval system, or transmitted, in any form or by
any means, electronic, mechanical, photocopying, recording,
or otherwise without the prior permission of the publisher.

ISBN: 978-2-503-58851-3
e-ISBN: 978-2-503-58852-0
DOI 10.1484/M.MCS-EB.5.119568
ISSN: 1378-868X
e-ISSN: 2294-8449

Printed in the EU on acid-free paper.

D/2022/0095/3

Table of Contents

List of Illustrations	9
Abbreviations	13
Acknowledgements	15
Introduction Christiania WHITEHEAD	17

PART I
Northern Sanctity and Northern Identity

I.1
Textual Culture: Hagiography, Legendary, Suffrage

Aelred of Rievaulx and the Saints of Durham, Galloway, and Hexham
Denis RENEVEY
35

The Production of Northern Saints' Lives at Holm Cultram Abbey in Cumbria
Christiania WHITEHEAD
53

Flower of York: Region, Nation, and St Robert of Knaresborough in Late Medieval England
Hazel J. HUNTER BLAIR
75

Praying to Northern Saints in English Books of Hours
Cynthia TURNER CAMP
99

I.2
Material Culture: Space, Oil, Image

Space, It's About Time Too: Architecture and Identity in Medieval Durham
Euan MCCARTNEY ROBSON
129

TABLE OF CONTENTS

**Holy Geysers? Oily Saints and Ecclesiastical Politics
in Late Medieval Yorkshire and Lincolnshire**
John JENKINS   147

**Art and Northern Sanctity in
Late Medieval England**
Julian LUXFORD   165

PART II
New Case Studies of Northern Saints and Their Cults

II.1
The Eremitic Life

**The Context for and Later Reception of
Reginald of Durham's *Vita sancti Godrici***
Margaret COOMBE   199

**Robert of Knaresborough, Religious Novelty,
and the Twelfth-Century Poverty Movement**
Joshua S. EASTERLING   217

Hermit Saints and Human Temporalities
Catherine SANOK   237

II.2
Female Networks and Locations:
Coldingham, Ely, Whitby

**Beyond the *Miracula*: Practices and Experiences
of Lay Devotion at the Cult of St Æbbe, Coldingham**   263
Ruth J. SALTER

**Ætheldreda in the North: Tracing Northern
Networks in the *Liber Eliensis* and the
*Vie de seinte Audree***   285
Jane SINNETT-SMITH

**Conflicting Memories, Confused Identities,
and Constructed Pasts: St Hilda and the
Refoundation of Whitby Abbey**
Daniel TALBOT   305

TABLE OF CONTENTS　7

Remembering St Hilda in the Later Middle Ages
Christiane KROEBEL　321

II.3
Beyond the North:
Southern, European, and Post-Medieval Perspectives

The French *Life* of St Godric of Finchale, or
Adventures for Thirteenth-Century Nuns
Anne MOURON　343

The Reception of St Oswine in Later
Medieval England
James G. CLARK　361

Northern Saints' Names as Monastic Bynames in
Late Medieval and Early Tudor England
David E. THORNTON　387

Northern Lights on Southern Shores:
Rewriting St Oswald's Life in
Eighteenth-Century Friuli
Claudia DI SCIACCA　409

Manuscript Index　433

Index　437

List of Illustrations

Christiania Whitehead

Figure 2.1.   London, British Library, MS Cotton Faustina
              B.IV, fol. 65v 'Incipit vita Wulfrici'.   60

Figure 2.2.   London, British Library, MS Cotton Claudius
              A.V, fol. 160v 'Incipit vita Wulfstani'.   60

Cynthia Turner Camp

Table 4.1.   Books of Hours with suffrages to northern saints.   102

Figure 4.1.   Miniature of St John of Beverley, from his suffrage
              in the Hours of William Porter. New York,
              The Morgan Library & Museum, MS M.105,
              fol. 51r. Rouen, France, *c.* 1420–1425.   117

Julian Luxford

Figure 7.1.   The common seal of Haltemprice Priory (made
              1322), reverse side.   173

Figure 7.2.   Ceiling bosses of the nails and five wounds of
              Christ and the badge (or 'arms') of the Virgin
              Mary, now in the priory dining room at Durham.   175

Figure 7.3.   Chillingham (Northumberland): tomb of Sir
              Ralph Grey (d. 1443) and Elizabeth FitzHugh
              (d. 1445), from the north-east.   181

Figure 7.4.   Penwork initial in a fifteenth-century cartulary
              from Beverley Minster (Oxford, University
              College, MS 82, fol. 7r).   182

Figure 7.5.   Impression of a seal from Durham Cathedral
              Priory incorporating an antique gem (London,
              British Library, Egerton charter 523).   183

Figure 7.6.   Mutilated, partially reconstructed image of
              St Cuthbert holding the head of St Oswald,
              now in the feretory at Durham Cathedral.   184

10   LIST OF ILLUSTRATIONS

Figure 7.7. Thirteenth-century vault boss in the episcopal chapel at Girona Cathedral (Catalonia) sculpted with an image of St William of York. 185

Ruth J. Salter

Table 11.1. Social categorizations of the *Vita Æbbe*'s cure-seekers. 269

Table 11.2. Distance between the starting location of the *Vita Æbbe*'s cure-seekers and Coldingham. 271

Table 11.3. Afflictions suffered by Æbbe's cure-seekers. 273

Table 11.4. Location of the *Vita Æbbe*'s cure-seekers at the time of their miraculous cure. 276

Table 11.5. Æbbe's appearances to and interactions with her cure-seekers. 280

Jane Sinnett-Smith

Figure 12.1. 'Saint Ætheldreda of Ely', London, British Library, MS Additional 70513, fol. 100v, 1275–1300. 299

Christiane Kroebel

Figure 14.1. Churches and hermitages dedicated to St Hilda within pre-1974 county boundaries. 324

David E. Thornton

Table 17.1. Distribution of surnames of monks and canons before 1537. 392

Table 17.2. Some English hagionymic bynames of northern provenance. 394

Table 17.3. Distribution of northern hagionymic bynames by county, *c.* 1300–1540. 397

Table 17.4. The hagionymic byname Cuthbert. 397

Table 17.5. Monastic bynames at Glastonbury, derived from saints and other figures (first attested *after* 1450). 399

Table 17.6. Hagionymic bynames from Durham, *c.* 1420–1540. 402

LIST OF ILLUSTRATIONS   11

Figure 17.1.   Toponymic/topographical and hagionymic
surnames in the diocese of Worcester
(as percentage by decade).   393

Figure 17.2.   Hagionymic bynames according to monastic
order (percentage of total).   395

Figure 17.3.   Most common hagionyms (total numbers).   396

Abbreviations

AASS	*Acta Sanctorum*, ed. by Jean Baptiste Carnandet and others (Paris: Victorem Palmé, 1863-)
BHL	*Socii Bollandiani, Bibliotheca Hagiographica Latina antiquae et mediae aetatis,* Subsidia Hagiographica, 6 (Brussels: Société des Bollandistes, 1898–1901)
BL	British Library
Bodl. Lib.	Bodleian Library
BnF	Bibliothèque nationale de France
CCCM	Corpus Christianorum Continuatio Medievalis
CVMA	Corpus Vitrearum Medii Aevi
EETS	Early English Text Society o.s. Original Series e.s. Extra Series
JEGP	*Journal of English and Germanic Philology*
NCE	*New Catholic Encyclopedia*, ed. by Berard L. Marthaler, 2nd edn, 15 vols (Detroit, MI, and Washington, DC: Thomson/Gale and Catholic University of America, 2003)
SS	Surtees Society
STC	Short Title Catalogue

Acknowledgements

The publication of *Late Medieval Devotion to Saints from the North of England: New Directions*, would not have been possible without the generous support and collaboration of several institutions and individuals. This book is one of the major outcomes of the project 'Region and Nation in Late Medieval Devotion to Northern English Saints' at the University of Lausanne, which was funded by the Swiss National Science Foundation for an initial period of three years, with additional half-year (senior researcher) and one-year (SNSF doctoral student) extensions (2016–2021). Hazel J. Hunter Blair, the doctoral student, also received a SNSF mobility grant for a six-month research stay as Departmental Visiting Student at the Faculty of English Language and Literature, University of Oxford. As a research team, we are grateful to the SNSF and the University of Lausanne for providing ideal financial and logistical support for the smooth running of the project.

Other institutions welcomed members of the project who were able to present aspects of their research to international audiences. Denis Renevey and Christiania Whitehead gave guest lectures at Shizuoka and Keio Universities in Japan in 2017. This was followed by a presentation of the project by Hazel, Christiania, and Denis at the CUSO doctoral workshop in Medieval and Early Modern English Studies, University of Geneva and the University of Lausanne, six months later. Christiania and Hazel presented aspects of their own research linked to the project at the 2018 International Anchoritic Society Conference at the University of East Anglia, Norwich. Further discussions and presentations took place at the 2018 Leeds International Medieval Congress, where the team organized two sessions and a roundtable. We are grateful to the participants of these sessions, and especially to our respondent, Professor Jocelyn Wogan-Browne, from Fordham University, as the ideas circulated during these exchanges helped us shape the development of our research project in important ways. Christiania and Hazel presented further research results at the Research Day in Medieval English Studies hosted by Károli Gáspár University of the Reformed Church and Pázmàny Péter Catholic University in Budapest in October 2018. The team then went north to present some aspects of the project at the University of St Andrews, the University of Glasgow, and the University of Lancaster.

Team members individually presented work related to the project at the following venues: the 2017 Medieval Translator Conference, Austrian Academy of Sciences, Vienna; the 2017 Women and the Medieval Literary Canon Conference, University of Bergen, Norway; the 2018 Medieval Insular Romance Conference, Cardiff University; the 2018 ESSE Conference, University of Brno, Czech Republic; the 2019 Ecclesiastical History Society Summer Conference,

University of Durham; the 2019 Leeds International Medieval Congress; and the Medieval English Research Seminar, University of Warwick. In 2018, Hazel J. Hunter Blair also delivered a public lecture on Robert of Knaresborough, as part of a series of locally organized events held to commemorate the 800th anniversary of his death, in Knaresborough, England. All these presentations helped finesse our thinking about late medieval northern sanctity in England, and beyond. We are grateful to the individuals who welcomed us within their academic homes and at international conferences.

However, without the lively presentations and exchanges which took place at the Lausanne conference organized by our 'Region and Nation' research team, *Northern Lights: Late Medieval Devotion to Saints from the North of England*, in March 2019, this volume would simply not exist. Although not all the presentations given at the conference are included here, they all stimulated further reflections and helped to shape the volume as it stands. We are grateful to our participants for their enthusiastic contribution to the debates that emerged during the sessions and in response to the four plenary presentations. Olena Danylovych, Andrea Grütter, and Ana Rita Parreiras Reis, students from the English department, provided invaluable support during the conference. Eva Suarato, secretary of the English department helped us with the logistical preparations for many weeks beforehand. Subsequently, we would like to thank our contributors who have responded promptly and courteously to the many queries we have sent their way. It is a pleasure to collaborate with Guy Carney, our main contact at Brepols. We are also grateful to the anonymous reviewer who offered useful suggestions about the volume. We would like to thank our excellent copy-editor, Katharine Bartlett, for her scrupulous work on the text, and Tatiana Ronan for her meticulous preparation of the volume index. Last, but not least, our thanks to the board members of the Brepols Medieval Church Series for offering a prestigious home to our volume.

The Editors

CHRISTIANIA WHITEHEAD

Introduction

This volume explores a range of northern English saints' cults in the late medieval period, from *c.* 1150 to 1500, focusing on the later development of significant pre-Conquest cults, such as those of Oswald of Northumbria, Hilda of Whitby, and John of Beverley; the 'recovery' of the cults of further pre-Conquest holy men and women, including Oswine of Tynemouth, Æbbe of Coldingham, and Bega of Copeland; and the establishment and development of a number of new cults, including those of Godric of Finchale, Robert of Knaresborough, William of York, and Archbishop Richard Scrope. Taking an interdisciplinary approach, it draws upon a variety of textual sources including some previously overlooked material such as suffrages to saints in late medieval Books of Hours, and lists of monastic bynames. In addition, it also pays attention to the artistic and material dimensions of these cults, analysing fabric donations in relic lists, the architectural spaces within which medieval veneration took place and their relation to the landscape, the spread of church and chapel dedications, and the surprising extrusion of holy oil from a cluster of Yorkshire episcopal tombs. Finally, this volume analyses patterns of devotion to northern saints *beyond* the region: the development of northern cults in southern England and continental Europe are detailed and considered, while the less-studied phenomenon of the pressure of continental and universal sanctity upon indigenous cultures of devotion is also rendered visible.

The focus of interest sounds straightforward enough, but in actuality it opens a door onto some long-standing conundrums of scholarly debate. First, was there such a thing as 'the North' in the late Middle Ages? Did it have a distinct regional identity recognizable both to those who inhabited it and others further afield? Second, dependent on some sort of affirmative response to these initial questions, does it make sense to refer to a coherent northern English sanctity or should we rather give priority to the disparate agendas governing individual cults, or to more localized clusters and networks?

Christiania Whitehead (Christiania.whitehead@unil.ch) is an Honorary Professor of Middle English Literature at the University of Warwick and a Senior Research Fellow on the SNSF-funded project 'Region and Nation: Late Medieval Devotion to Northern English Saints' at the University of Lausanne, Switzerland.

Late Medieval Devotion to Saints from the North of England: New Directions, ed. by Christiania Whitehead, Hazel J. Hunter Blair, and Denis Renevey, MCS 48 (Turnhout: Brepols, 2022), pp. 17–32

BREPOLS ❧ PUBLISHERS   10.1484/M.MCS-EB.5.124342

Was there a medieval 'North of England'? The answer looks rather different depending upon whether we place ourselves in the mid-twelfth century or at the beginning of the sixteenth, and what tradition of historical or literary scholarship we use to inform our perspective. At the beginning of the period under scrutiny, the Anglo-Scottish border was by no means set irrevocably in its final form, the York archdiocese was in contention with the Scottish church over its sphere of jurisdiction, and the memory of the seventh-century kingdom of Northumbria extending from the Humber to the Forth still carried considerable cultural force. Writing around 1180, Adam of Dryburgh famously described the area of former northern Northumbria between the Tweed and the Forth as 'the land of the English [...] in the kingdom of the Scots'.[1] Building on this acknowledgement of extensive cross-border contact, enacted across a range of monastic, ecclesial, and secular institutions and economies, the term 'middle Britain' has recently been coined to describe the lands to either side of the border and the common cultures shared between them.[2] This perception of a common cause was undoubtedly assisted by the spread of the reformed monastic orders: the Yorkshire Cistercians expanded north from Rievaulx to Melrose in Roxburghshire, and then turned west to found daughter houses at Dundrennan in Galloway and Holm Cultram just south of the border in Cumbria.[3] Following similar trajectories, the Premonstratensian canons expanded from Alnwick to Dryburgh, and from Cockersand to Tongland, additionally establishing houses at Soulseat and Whithorn in Galloway.[4] Even the traditionally less mobile Benedictines participated in this migration: Coldingham in Berwickshire was acquired by Durham Benedictine Priory at the end of the eleventh century, while St Mary's York sent monks west to found the priories of St Bees and Wetheral in northern Cumbria, early in the twelfth. A medieval 'North of England' in 1160 or in 1220 would have a good claim to incorporate Galloway, Melrose and Coldingham within its field of vision, and several of the essays in this volume engage specifically with this expanded understanding of the North, addressing the cults of St Æbbe at Coldingham, St Ninian in Galloway, and scrutinizing the cross-border contacts shared between Holm Cultram Abbey and its northern monastic neighbours.[5]

---

1 Quoted in Stringer, 'Introduction', p. 11.
2 McGuigan, 'Neither Scotland nor England: Middle Britain'; Stringer, 'Introduction'.
3 The administrative county of Cumbria was created in 1974, replacing the historic counties of Cumberland and Westmoreland. The modern term is retained throughout this volume for ease of reference, nonetheless it is important to acknowledge that it had a distinctively different resonance in the medieval period; see further, Whitehead's essay in this volume, 'Production of Northern Saints' Lives', pp. 53–74 (53).
4 Burton, 'Dioceses, Saints' Cults', pp. 189–92.
5 See the essays in this volume by Ruth J. Salter, Jane Sinnett-Smith, Denis Renevey and Christiania Whitehead.

INTRODUCTION 19

This inclusive definition of the 'North' loses traction from the 1290s and through the two centuries that follow, due to the onset of the Anglo-Scottish wars. These wars harden the border, confirm the perception of England and Scotland as two distinct unitary kingdoms, and remake much of 'middle Britain' as a militarized zone, severing family and institutional networks and undermining previous cross-border cultures of devotion. From this point on, were we taking a principally church-oriented view, a medieval 'North of England' might viably be equated with the northern ecclesiastical province of York, comprising the dioceses of York, Carlisle, and Durham.[6] However, a very similar determination can be achieved by adopting a more secular and adminstrative point of view. From the 1250s forward, the River Trent was widely perceived as the boundary between north and south for purposes of royal administration, while the heraldic province of the Norroy ('north men') King of Arms, which comes into view from 1276, is similarly located north of the Trent.[7] *De facto*, for the majority of essays in the volume, our 'North of England' covers approximately the same geographical expanse.

Did this late medieval North think of itself as distinct region? And was it regarded in this way from an external perspective? The publications of the AHRC Research Centre for North-East English History (2000–2005), set up to investigate this question over the *longue durée*, usefully remind us that, according to cultural rather than physical paradigms, a region is an 'imagined' community or social identity which only begins to exist when those inhabiting it start consciously to experience themselves in this way.[8] Pitched somewhere between the local and the national in scale, and constantly adjusting its self-perception with reference to those termini, what is thought of as 'the northern region' mutates subtly in social character and geography over time and according to place. To this we might add that different communities are capable of imagining the North very differently within a single temporality — the eremitic North may have a wholly different colour to the administrative or archdiocesan North — and that definitions will certainly differ significantly in accordance with the bodies of textual or material evidence under survey: an assembly of saints' lives in a Durham manuscript compilation opens a different window on the North from a cluster of suffrages in a Book of Hours. The linguistic and dialectal North is another thing again, and the editors of the recent volume *Revisiting the Medieval North of England: Interdisciplinary Approaches* set out a tradition of scholarship on northern textual and manuscript production stretching from Carl Horstmann to Ralph Hanna which follows a largely

---

6 Additionally, Whithorn persists as a suffragan diocese of York until the mid-fourteenth century.

7 Holford, 'Locality, Culture and Identity', pp. 50–52. See Luxford's essay, p. 167, n. 10.

8 Green and Pollard, 'Introduction: Identifying Regions', pp. 9, 15–17; Pollard, 'Introduction', p. 8. Underpinning this approach, see further the seminal work of Benedict Anderson on 'imagined communities', and of Barbara Rosenwein on 'emotional communities': Anderson, *Imagined Communities*; Rosenwein, *Emotional Communities*.

independent trajectory to the historiographic conversation on regionalism.[9] Without again reproducing William of Malmesbury's jaded observation in the twelfth century that the language of Northumbrians and Yorkshiremen is uncouth and unintelligible to southerners (the remark survives intact through John Trevisa's translation of Higden's *Polychronicon* (1385) to William Caxton's *Description of England* (1480)), it is nevertheless suggestive to learn that texts were frequently 'translated' from northern English into midland and southern dialects for ease of reading during the late medieval period, but more seldom the other way.[10] Book history and historical linguistics offer clear evidence of a regional distinction and hierarchy between north and south.

Taking the land north of the Trent as a working definition for the *partes boreales,* to what extent is it viable to view this 'North' as a unified terrain, superseding the force of individual county or diocesan boundaries, or other physical subdivisions premised on topography or land use? Many scholars have felt more secure highlighting the *divided* north and emphasizing it as an amalgam of communities driven by disparate agendas. R. B. Dobson, one of the founding fathers of northern medieval church history, albeit of a northern church somewhat tilted toward the Durham and York cathedral archives, writes that 'regional, social and ecclesiastical divisions *within* the province of York were often greater than those which separated it from the southern province'.[11] Keith Stringer, Julian Luxford and others have pinpointed the Pennines as a fundamental physical barrier, separating a North East facing primarily towards the east and south, distinguished by more major commercial centres, impressive historic cities, and better arable land, from a poorer North West oriented in a completely different direction towards the Irish Sea world.[12] On a smaller scale, Matthew Holford, Andy King, and Christian Liddy remind us that while it is easy to think of Northumberland and Durham as a single north-eastern territorial unit arousing memories of the ancient kingdom of Northumbria, in reality, the River Tyne acted as an important political boundary, segregating the powers of the bishop of Durham from those of the earl of Northumberland. To the south, the citizens of the bishopric enjoyed enviable rights of exemption from royal taxation and military service, while those north of the Tyne participated in none of these privileges, and felt the impact of the wars against the Scots far more keenly.[13]

All these internal divisions need to be treated seriously. Nonetheless, without disavowing their validity, it is still possible to derive considerable mileage from Matthew Holford's far-reaching research on the potency of the 'idea of the North' within late medieval discourse. Remarking on the frequency with

---

9   Auer, Renevey, Marshall and Oudesluijs, 'Introduction'.
10 Auer, Renevey, Marshall and Oudesluijs, 'Introduction', p. 1.
11 Dobson, *Church and Society,* p. xii. My italics.
12 Stringer, 'Introduction', p. 20; Julian Luxford's and Christiania Whitehead's essays in this volume.
13 Holford, King and Liddy, 'North-East England in the Late Middle Ages'.

which 'the north country' and 'northern parts' were used within a variety of national narratives (markedly more than the other cardinal points), he argues that this 'idea' carried more power nationally than the characteristics and identities of the individual northern counties, in particular, in the fifteenth and early sixteenth centuries.[14] Arising from its proximity to Scotland and prolonged involvement in the Scottish wars, Holford demonstrates that the North was viewed as a militarized country occupied by hardy, battle-ready men, whose fieriness could easily degenerate into rashness. Nonetheless, it was also territorially vulnerable by virtue of its location, and related depictions emphasize its exposure, susceptibility to pillage, and consequent impoverishment. Both these representations led to a third imagination of the North as a site of treachery, rebellion and infraction.[15] This imagination seems to have held true from at least the early thirteenth century — the opponents of King John are identified as 'northerners' — but it carries most sway toward the end of the medieval period. Thomas Malory recasts King Arthur's early campaigns against the Scots and Picts in Geoffrey of Monmouth's *Historia regum brittanniae*, as wars against northern kings.[16] Those involved in the Lancastrian deposition in 1461 and revolt of 1469, seminal episodes in the Wars of the Roses, are characterized by agitated southerners as 'pepill in þe northe' and, deploying biblical prophetic imagery associated with the devil, as 'a whirlwind [coming] from the north'.[17] The Tudor monarchs continue to view the North in similar terms, and the perception achieves its fullest expression (and becomes a self-perception) during the 'Pilgrimage of Grace' of 1536–1537, in which the rebel army, characterizing itself as 'the barons and commonalty of the North', demands the recovery of lost sanctuaries and liberties attached to the minsters and cathedrals of Yorkshire and Durham, and the establishment of a separate parliament for those *ultra Trent*.[18]

Sanctity and the North

St Cuthbert's banner travels in the vanguard of the 'Pilgrimage' of 1536–1537, giving him a late link to the North, imagined as a single entity, and positioning him as its spiritual patron. This might seem a powerful argument in favour of a coherent, unitary notion of northern sanctity, but again, it needs to be

---

14 Holford, 'Locality, Culture and Identity', pp. 44–48, 50–74.
15 Holford, 'Locality, Culture and Identity', pp. 63–73.
16 Geoffrey of Monmouth, *History*, trans. by Thorpe, pp. 218–21; Malory, *Works*, ed. by Vinaver, pp. 76–81.
17 Holford, 'Locality, Culture and Identity', pp. 69–70. The quotations are drawn respectively from the *Paston Letters* and the *Croyland Chronicle*. The whirlwind from the north derives from Eziekiel 1. 4; patristic and medieval commentary on this verse commonly interpreted this whirlwind as the turbulence of the devil.
18 Holford, 'Locality, Culture and Identity', pp. 104–06.

opened to further interrogation. Not dissimilar to the focus in regional history on north-eastern England, the modern lineage of scholarship on northern medieval sanctity has tended to be weighted very heavily in favour of the *familia* of Anglo-Saxon saints associated with Lindisfarne and Durham, in particular, Cuthbert and Oswald.[19] In large part, this is an effect of the groundbreaking work of David Rollason and R. B. Dobson upon these saints and locations; other cults in the ecclesial North have simply not been studied with comparable levels of detail and authority. In part, it is also an effect of the propaganda drive of Durham Benedictine Priory: through the fifteenth century, it was keen to extend Cuthbert's influence west and south, and to have him acknowledged as the region's premier saint, a desire which crystallized in unforeseen ways in 1536.[20] The move to epitomize northern sanctity as a simplified culture of devotion to Cuthbert and his regal auxiliary, Oswald of Northumbria, also influenced perceptions south of the Trent, where they became the only northern saints to be listed in the Sarum calendar (John of Beverley was duly added as a third in the early fifteenth century). The same preoccupation with ancient Northumbria seems to have governed the selection of northern saints in the *South English Legendary* (again, just Cuthbert and Oswald), and its fifteenth-century derivatives.[21]

A veritable library of monographs and essay collections prioritize Cuthbert and his auxiliaries, but the scholarly landscape is beginning to shift. The Yorkshire episcopal saints have become recent, individual topics of interest, Richard Rolle has long generated analysis and editorial work in literary circles, and Keith Stringer has done invaluable work in giving the religious cultures of medieval Cumbria and Galloway greater visibility.[22] This volume extends that momentum, conducting further explorations into the pre- and

---

19 See, in particular, Dobson, *Durham Priory*; Bonner, Rollason, and Stancliffe ed., *Cuthbert, His Cult*; Rollason, Harvey, and Prestwich ed., *Anglo-Norman Durham*; Stancliffe and Cambridge ed., *Oswald: Northumbrian King*; Aird, *St Cuthbert and the Normans*; Rollason ed., *Symeon of Durham*; Symeon of Durham, *Libellus de exordio*, ed. and trans. by Rollason; Liddy, *Bishopric of Durham*; Brown ed., *Durham Cathedral*; Coombe, Mouron, and Whitehead ed., *Saints of North-East England*.

20 See Whitehead, *Afterlife of St Cuthbert*, pp. 216–23.

21 In fact, Oswald's legend is excluded from the supplementary English saints' legends in the *Gilte Legende* and Caxton's *Golden Legend*, leaving Cuthbert as the solitary representative of northern sanctity. It should be said that the situation is very different in late medieval *Latin* legendaries of insular saints, notably John of Tynemouth's *Sanctilogium Anglie*. Northern saints remain well represented in this collection, although it is again possible to detect something of a bias towards the Lindisfarne–Durham *familia*. Whitehead, *Afterlife of St Cuthbert*, pp. 179–83.

22 See Wilson, *Life and After-Life*; Norton, *St William of York*; Higham ed., *Wilfrid: Abbot, Bishop, Saint*; Watson, *Richard Rolle*; Renevey, *Language, Self and Love*; Hanna ed., *Richard Rolle: Uncollected Prose and Verse*; Hanna, *English Manuscripts of Richard Rolle*; Hanna ed., *Richard Rolle: Unprinted Latin Writings*; Karáth, *Richard Rolle: The Fifteenth-Century Translations*; Albin, *Richard Rolle's Melody of Love*; Stringer, *Reformed Church in Medieval Galloway and Cumbria*.

post-Conquest episcopal cults of the Yorkshire Ridings and Lincoln, and tracing new constellations of affinity and devotion.[23] It also identifies new strains of eremitic sanctity relatively independent of the Cuthbertine model,[24] and opens a window onto uncharted female networks of sanctity — again, relatively independent of the Lindisfarne–Durham *familia* — threading up and down the east coast from Coldingham to Ely.[25] Jocelyn Wogan-Browne remarked, in an early response to a number of the essays in this volume, that Ninian of Whithorn might well prove to be 'the North West's Cuthbert figure, existing on the same latitude, but in a different topography, and within different communication networks with many of Britain's islands'.[26] We explore Ninian's part in a series of Cistercian configurations of northern sanctity that either ignore or significantly decentre Cuthbert, and pay adjacent attention to the apparent dearth of local saints within the Cumbrian North West and the strategies used to compensate for this.[27] At different times, hagiographers within Cumbria turn north then south in their search for their insular exemplars of holiness; however, they also construct their one 'local' saint, Bega of Copeland, in terms that show a competitive, even pugnacious, awareness of her place in relation to other northern cults. During her life, Bega befriends then surpasses Hilda of Whitby in her contemplative vocation, and after her death, she chases off scoundrels from Galloway (a statement about loosening ties between the regions), and heals supplicants whom Oswine of Tynemouth and Thomas of Canterbury prove incapable of helping.[28] Although this particular cure looks like a two-pronged geographical riposte, directed east and south-east against a saint of ancient Northumbria and the southern archiepiscopate, in the light of James G. Clark's essay in this volume outlining St Albans' control of Oswine's cult, perhaps we should re-evaluate it as a more binary confrontation between north and south. If so, Bega ambitiously places herself on a par with the challenge to Thomas of Canterbury's spiritual power posed by Cuthbert and detailed by Reginald of Durham.[29] Could it be she rather than Ninian who has the best claim (in her hagiographer's eyes at least) to be seen as the 'Cuthbert figure' of the North West? A later poetic fragment preserved at Glastonbury pushes her to even greater heights. Appearing in a vision to Reinfrid, one of the soldiers

---

23 See Cynthia Turner Camp's and John Jenkins's essays.

24 See Catherine Sanok's essay on John of Beverley, and Joshua Easterling's and Hazel J. Hunter Blair's essays on Robert of Knaresborough.

25 See Jane Sinnett-Smith's and Ruth J. Salter's essays.

26 Jocelyn Wogan-Browne, unpublished 'Response' to two sessions and a roundtable organized by the 'Region and Nation: Late Medieval Devotion to Northern English Saints' Project, Leeds International Medieval Congress, July 2018. I am grateful to Professor Wogan-Browne for sharing the script of this response with us.

27 See Denis Renevey's and Christiania Whitehead's essays.

28 *Vita Bege*, ed. by Wilson, Miracles 1 and 9; Whitehead, 'Bega's Bracelet'. See also, Whitehead's essay, p. 66, n. 60, in this volume.

29 Reginald of Durham, *Libellus de admirandis*, ed. by Raine, chaps 112, 114–16, 126.

in William the Conqueror's army, in the ruins of Hackness Priory, she urges him to become a monk to carry out penance for the devastation caused by the Harrying. Reinfrid subsequently becomes one of the three legendary Benedictines who ride north from Evesham to re-establish proper monastic observance in the North.[30] The ramifications of this are considerable, indicating that, in the late Middle Ages in the south, a story existed claiming that Bega of Copeland was the supernatural protagonist behind the whole re-emergence of monastic observance in the north of England.

The *Vita Bege* shows Bega working alongside St Aidan (who ordains her as a nun), and St Hilda of Whitby. This east–west network complements Jane Sinnett-Smith's discernment of Hilda's genealogical links with Æbbe of Coldingham and Ætheldreda of Ely. Elsewhere, John Jenkins links William of York, John of Beverley, Robert of Knaresborough, and Hugh and Robert Grosseteste of Lincoln, on the basis of the miraculous effusion of oil from their shrines, identifying a broader and more creative constellation of related sanctities, crossing county and archdiocesan boundaries, than the clerically imposed penitential pilgrimage between the minsters of York, Beverley, and Ripon.[31] Later, drawing in the fifteenth-century saints John of Bridlington and Richard Scrope, Cynthia Turner Camp unearths more *contemporary* configurations of Yorkshire sanctity in the suffrages of prayer books intended for upper-class devotion. These and other groupings of saints (the Hexham saint-bishops with Wilfrid and Cuthbert; Oswine with Edmund of East Anglia and Edward the Confessor)[32] enable us to propose a visualization of northern sanctity as an indefinitely expandable series of dynamic networks projected from different institutional and personal perspectives — simultaneously less rigid than the segregations imposed by the categories of 'county' and 'diocese', and more open to productive exchanges beyond the region.

Here, we plot a series of geographical diagrams premised on *lateral* connections between individual saints (based on consanguinity, myroblytic prowess,[33] or whatever else); however, it is also very relevant to think in terms of vertical *scalar* relations upwards and downwards. Catherine Sanok's recent monograph does important work in demonstrating how saints can function as icons of corporate identity on local, regional and national scales, moving perhaps from one principal scale to another over time, or signifying on

---

30 Rigg, 'Latin Poem on St Hilda'; Whitehead, 'Bega's Bracelet'; see also Kroebel's essay, 'Remembering St Hilda', pp. 322, 328, in this volume.

31 In the fifteenth century, additional stops at the shrines of John of Bridlington and Archbishop Richard Scrope were added. This pilgrimage itinerary, however, was not as far-reaching as that proposed by William Ecopp, rector of Heserlton, which also took in Yorkshire shrines at Doncaster, Pontefract, Hackness, Scarborough, Guisborough, and Newburgh, before heading further afield to Carlisle, Whithorn, and Galway: *Testamenta Eboracensia*, ed. by Raine and Clay, III, pp. 200–01, quoted in Holford, 'Locality, Culture and Identity', p. 218.

32 See Denis Renevey's and James G. Clark's essays in this volume.

33 A myroblyte is a saint whose shrine is reputed to exude holy oil.

several scales simultaneously.[34] In this volume, Hazel J. Hunter Blair excavates references to the neglected Yorkshire hermit Robert of Knaresborough in monastic chronicles from St Albans to Lanercost which elucidate the ways his holy life was utilized on a regional, national, and international stage in addition to its more localized meanings. Used to thinking of national English saints as southern, and either regal or episcopal, it can come as a shock to realize that Matthew Paris selects Robert alongside two southern bishops to create a triumvirate of 'English' sanctity set against Elizabeth of Hungary, and Hildegard of Bingen.[35] Cynthia Turner Camp similarly uses an examination of suffrages (short intercessory prayers) to northern saints in Books of Hours to show that John of Bridlington and John of Beverley are put to work on two different scales depending on context and readership. In some Books of Hours, grouped with other northern and York episcopal saints, they function as icons of York's civic spiritual identity, signifying on a municipal and regional scale.[36] In other Books, they are selected by devout southern aristocrats because of their *Lancastrian* affiliations — both were particular favourites of Henry V, while John of Beverley retains a supplementary association with royalty stretching back to his supernatural assistance to English troops in earlier wars against Scotland.[37] Here, the scale of operation and identity is national.

Both constructions of northern sanctity — those based on fluid lateral networks and those emphasizing scalar relations — can readily but mistakenly be co-opted to wholly *indigenous* definitions of the sanctities in question: northern saints lived, died, and remained posthumously serviceable to their local communities in the north of England. Julian Luxford's essay in this volume offers an important corrective to this assumption, emphasizing the role of international cults in northern sanctity, the melding of local devotions with universal ones in iconography and material culture, and the contemporary perception, which must have existed, of their fundamental complementarity. Not only did northern saints habitually sit alongside international ones in large-scale visual programmes such as the fifteenth-century glazing of York Minster or the wood panel paintings of Carlisle Cathedral; their iconography was also formed with reference to image-types imported from continental Europe, further challenging unexamined assumptions about the validity of any form of 'closed' regional expression. Moreover, not only does the international seep into the regional, colouring its distinctive articulations, but there is also ample evidence of reverse traffic. Northern saints maintain a visual, textual,

---

34 Sanok, *New Legends of England*.

35 See Hazel Blair's essay, pp. 82–83.

36 In the Bolton Hours, for example, John of Bridlington is grouped with Richard Scrope, William of York, John of Beverley, and Cuthbert, as a northern saint within a conceptualization of sanctity centred on the York archiepiscopate.

37 Sharpe, 'Banners of the Northern Saints', pp. 281–84. For John of Bridlington, John of Beverley, and William of York as both local and regional icons, see further Holford, 'Locality, Culture and Identity', pp. 196–201, 211–14, 216.

and devotional presence in the south: Euan McCartney Robson describes how, as early as the 1050s, Bishop Ælfwold of Sherbourne derives comfort on his deathbed by singing antiphons to Cuthbert, and David E. Thornton examines how the pre-Conquest deposit of northern saints' relics at Glastonbury leads, many centuries later, to a secondary efflorescence of northern bynames in the monastic house. Further afield, Claudia Di Sciacca's scholarly essay traces the early movement of Oswald of Northumbria's relics to the Low Countries and German-speaking lands, and the later diffusion of his devotion to the Carnian Alps in north-east Italy, where it continued to generate new *vitae* and exposition into the eighteenth century. Oswald and Cuthbert may have been decentred on their home soil in favour of the later Yorkshire worthies, but these ancient Northumbrian figureheads, charged with idealized imaginations of the synthesis of church and crown, seem to have continued to find a warm reception in the Catholic regions of post-Reformation Europe.

* * *

Divided into two main parts, *Late Medieval Devotion to Saints from the North of England: New Directions* opens with a selection of essays addressing the volume's main conceptual themes of northern sanctity and identity, internally partitioned between those that prioritize textual sources and those focused on material culture. The Cistercian monasteries of northern England have long attracted significant scholarly attention.[38] The first two essays in 'Textual Culture: Hagiography, Legendary, Suffrage' address them from a less familiar angle, pursuing their interest in, and hagiographical production of, northern saints' lives. Denis Renevey untangles the complicated web of familial, institutional, and Yorkshire loyalties that determine Aelred of Rievaulx's attitude to his hagiographical subjects, Ninian and the Hexham saint-bishops. Meanwhile, Christiania Whitehead concentrates on Cistercian hagiographers and copyists on the other side of the country, at Holm Cultram Abbey in northern Cumbria, highlighting the abbey's production of two singularly early collections of insular saints: BL, MS Cotton Faustina B.IV and MS Cotton Claudius A.V, and exploring the criteria which underpinned their selection of saints. The Yorkshire Cistercians also displayed an early interest in Hazel J. Hunter Blair's subject, the cave-dwelling hermit Robert of Knaresborough, subsequently appropriated to a Trinitarian milieu. Blair anatomizes Robert in relation to the centrifugal scales of locality, region, and nation, exploring the local concerns that initially shape his *vitae* set against later references co-opting him to regional and national agendas. While hagiographies remain fundamental tools for assessing schemas of northern identity, it emerges that they are not the only textual resources available. Defining and analysing a previously untouched archive of information — suffrages to northern saints

---

38 See, most recently, Jamroziak, *Survival and Success on Medieval Borders*; Burton and Kerr, *Cistercians in the Middle Ages*; Carter, *Art and Architecture of the Cistercians*.

in late medieval Books of Hours — Cynthia Turner Camp reveals how these saints are variously invoked to index local civic identities, broader northern affinities, or Lancastrian affections, and notes a devotional emphasis in the prayer lives of the fifteenth-century upper-class laity directed *not* towards the ancient Northumbrian worthies celebrated by Bede, but towards more contemporary saints affiliated with Yorkshire and York Minster.

In 'Material Culture: Space, Oil, Image' we turn from the textual evidence for northern sanctity to a series of more physical and architectural expressions. Euan McCartney Robson meditates on Durham Cathedral (the posthumous home of Cuthbert and his Northumbrian *familia*) as a richly multifaceted, constantly rewritten conceptual space, drawing on descriptions of its contents and practices from the late Old English *De situ Dunelmi* to the sixteenth-century *Rites of Durham*. John Jenkins links the more southerly cathedrals and churches of York, Beverley, Knaresborough, and Lincoln (shown here within the sphere of influence of York Minster), on the basis of the shared emission of holy oil from their patron saints' shrines. Jenkins speculates on the reasons for this singular outbreak, largely an *episcopal* phenomenon, within an eighty-mile radius of York, and concludes that it was driven by primarily regional and capitular concerns, enabling cathedral chapters to control and interpret the expression of episcopal authority in contradistinction to the agendas of living incumbents. Finally, recalibrating the idea of northern sanctity in relation to broader frames of visual reference, Julian Luxford's essay reminds us that international cults made much of the spiritual running in the North, alongside local cults, by the late Middle Ages, and explains how images of the northern saints were mainly informed by iconographic types developed outside the region.

The second main part changes tack from broader questions of northern identity to a selection of focused case studies showcasing new research on individual saints and their cults. The twelfth and thirteenth centuries saw a flowering of eremitic sanctity in the North East of England, possibly influenced by renewed institutional interest in Cuthbert's eremitic sojourn on Farne.[39] In 'The Eremitic Life', Margaret Coombe and Joshua Easterling discuss two of these 'new' hermits, Godric of Finchale and Robert of Knaresborough. Coombe's essay explores the local political agendas that determined Reginald of Durham's initial portrayal of Godric, and the later uses to which the saint was put by other orders and within wider geographies. On a larger scale still, Easterling reads Robert's singular option for the poor and decision to associate with 'poremen' in relation to the contemporary poverty movements emerging

---

39 See Whitehead, *Afterlife of St Cuthbert*, pp. 99–138. Four out of six hermit saints active in England during this period were based in the North East: as well as Godric and Robert, we should note Bartholomew of Farne and Henry of Coquet Island. See Licence, *Hermits and Recluses*. Although Bega of Copeland is a much older, quasi-mythical figure, her *Vita* emphasizing her strongly eremitic life was composed in the early thirteenth century, adding an eremitic cast to the North West.

in Italy and France (the Franciscans, the *Humiliati*, etc.). Turning in a different direction, Catherine Sanok re-reads the late medieval vernacular hermit legends of Cuthbert and John of Beverley (extant only in a sixteenth-century Dutch playscript) in the light of new research on premodern temporalities. Complicating any simple binary between secular time and sacred atemporality, she explores how these northern hermits express a primary creaturely temporality at the border of both social times and institutional devotions.

'Female Networks and Locations: Coldingham, Ely, Whitby' foregrounds three female saints from the north-east coastline: Æbbe, Ætheldreda, and Hilda, unearthing the familial links and narrative parallels that connect them in their *vitae*, and placing each within her local and regional landscapes of devotion. Ruth J. Salter discusses the distinctive characteristics of Æbbe's cult at Coldingham, setting out her ministry to female pilgrims, her repertoire of cures, and her unusual 'doubled' presence within the landscape, both at Coldingham Benedictine Priory and at Kirk Hill, the reputed site of her seventh-century monastery. Jane Sinnett-Smith approaches this same landscape from the south, utilizing two twelfth- and thirteenth-century narratives about Ætheldreda, the powerful spiritual patron of Ely, to highlight her hitherto-neglected associations with a range of Northumbrian worthies: Æbbe, Hilda, Wilfrid, and Cuthbert. Sinnett-Smith argues that these associations, enacted through material spaces and objects, enable Ætheldreda to benefit from the spiritual authority of the early Northumbrian saints while also assimilating them to the narrative of her own sanctity. The fact that one of these narratives, the *Vie de seinte Audree*, was written by a woman and utilized by women readers, brings an additionally gendered dimension to this discussion. Daniel Talbot and Christiane Kroebel shift the focus from Coldingham and Ely to the monastic lands and churches stamped with the impress of Hilda's saintly presence. Talbot conducts a close examination of a twelfth-century record narrating the refoundation of Whitby Abbey, *The Memorial of the Benefactions of Whitby Abbey*, to ascertain Hilda's meaning and importance for the young Benedictine house. Starting from this monastic hub, Kroebel pursues the diffusion of Hilda's cult into the northern landscape, enumerating her medieval church dedications from Islekirk in Cumbria to Rudfarlington west of York, and accounting for them by reference to secular patronage networks. Research into the post-Conquest cult of St Hilda is hampered by the non-survival of the early *vita* which must have been written at Whitby to promote her cult. As such, it is tremendously exciting to uncover a new attestation to the existence of such a *vita* in late fourteenth-century Yorkshire legal records.[40]

The final sub-section, 'Beyond the North: Southern, European and Post-Medieval Perspectives', recalibrates the idea of northern sanctity in relation to broader geographical and temporal frames of reference. Although many English saints' lives were translated into Anglo-Norman in the twelfth and

---

40 Kroebel, 'Remembering St Hilda', pp. 321–39 in this volume.

thirteenth centuries, northern sanctity seems to have lagged behind in this respect. Anne Mouron examines the single Anglo-Norman *vie* to survive from the north, the late twelfth-century *French Life* of Godric of Finchale, scrutinizing its interest and didactic value for the Franciscan nuns of Longchamp near Paris who were its only known readers.[41] While northern hermits were finding favour in Parisian convents, a number of Northumbrian saint-kings also became subjects of veneration in southern England and further afield. James G. Clark conducts a masterly examination of the development of the cult of Oswine of Deira in late medieval England. Enshrined at Tynemouth Priory, a dependent house of St Albans Abbey, the martyred king generated devotional responses up and down the realm and across the St Albans family of monasteries, from the thirteenth to the sixteenth centuries, leading ultimately to his appropriation by the Tudors to assist in the construction of their imperial authority. Similarly focused on a southern Benedictine response to northern sanctity, David E. Thornton draws our attention to a fascinating new field of study — the late fifteenth-century phenomenon of monastic bynames derived from the names of saints (*hagionyms*), and uses the information derived from this study to ask important questions about the prevalence of northern hagionyms at Glastonbury Benedictine Abbey. Meanwhile, another Northumbrian king-martyr, Oswine's predecessor, Oswald, was garnering attention beyond English shores. Claudia Di Sciacca traces the diffusion of Oswald's cult to the Low Countries and southern Germany in the first instance, and then across the Alps into north-east Italy, where a relic of the king's thumb enshrined in the village church at Sauris attracted pilgrims and continued to generate healings and the local composition of new *vitae* well into the eighteenth century. While the more contemporary Yorkshire saints found short-term favour with Lancastrian kings and aristocrats through the fifteenth century, within a longer timescale, the ancient Northumbrian king-martyrs proved unexpectedly symbolically durable both at home and abroad.

At the beginning of the introduction, we alluded to '*our* North of England'. This volume is just that: a discernment of a number of new constellations of northern sanctity that acknowledges not only the conceptual multiplicity of the North, but also our own situatedness as scholars and editors, positioned some fifteen years after the outputs of the AHRC Research Centre on North-Eastern History within a Europe actively rethinking the relation of region to nation, and at the intersection of specific historiographical and textual conversations. In time, these 'new constellations' will be superseded by still newer ones, projected from as yet unimaginable critical perspectives. For now, we hope to have elucidated the character of the northern medieval sky as it appears within our field of vision in 2022.

---

41 *Reginald of Durham's Life of St Godric*, ed. by Coombe, Hunt, and Mouron.

Works Cited

Manuscripts and Archival Sources

London, British Library, MS Cotton Faustina B.IV
——, MS Cotton Claudius A.V

Primary Sources

Geoffrey of Monmouth, *The History of the Kings of Britain*, trans. by Lewis Thorpe (Harmondsworth: Penguin, 1966)

Malory, Sir Thomas, *Works*, ed. by Eugène Vinaver (Oxford: Oxford University Press, 1971)

Reginald of Durham, *Libellus de admirandis beati Cuthberti virtutibus*, ed. by James Raine, Surtees Society, 1 (London: J. B. Nichols and Son, 1835)

Reginald of Durham's Life of St Godric: An Old French Version, ed. by Margaret Coombe, Tony Hunt, and Anne Mouron (Oxford: Anglo-Norman Text Society, 2019)

Symeon of Durham, *Libellus de exordio atque procursu istius, hoc est Dunhelmensis ecclesie*, ed. and trans. by David Rollason (Oxford: Clarendon Press, 2000)

Testamenta Eboracensia, ed. by James Raine and John William Clay, 6 vols, Surtees Society (London: J. B. Nichols and Son, 1836–1902)

Vita S Bege, in *The Register of the Priory of St Bees*, ed. by James Wilson, Surtees Society, 126 (Durham: Andrews & Co., 1915), pp. 497–520

Secondary Works

Aird, William, *St Cuthbert and the Normans: The Church of Durham, 1071–1153* (Woodbridge: Boydell, 1998)

Albin, Andrew, *Richard Rolle's Melody of Love: A Study and Translation with Manuscript and Musical Contexts* (Toronto: Pontifical Institute of Mediaeval Studies, 2018)

Anderson, Benedict, *Imagined Communities: Reflections on the Origin and Spread of Nationalism* (London: Verso, 1983)

Auer, Anita, Denis Renevey, Camille Marshall, and Tino Oudesluijs, 'Introduction: Setting the Scene: Indisciplinary Perspectives on the Medieval North of England', in *Revisiting the Medieval North of England: Interdisciplinary Approaches*, ed. by Anita Auer and others (Cardiff: University of Wales Press, 2019), pp. 1–12

Bonner, Gerald, David Rollason, and Clare Stancliffe, ed., *Cuthbert, His Cult and His Community to AD 1200* (Woodbridge: Boydell and Brewer, 1989)

Brown, David, ed., *Durham Cathedral: History, Fabric and Culture* (New Haven: Yale University Press, 2015)

Burton, Janet, and Julie Kerr, *The Cistercians in the Middle Ages* (Woodbridge: Boydell, 2011)

Burton, Janet, 'Dioceses, Saints' Cults and Monasteries', in *Northern England and Southern Scotland in the Central Middle Ages*, ed. by Keith Stringer and Angus Winchester (Woodbridge: Boydell, 2017), pp. 173–96

Carter, Michael, *The Art and Architecture of the Cistercians in Northern England, c. 1300–1540* (Turnhout: Brepols, 2019)

Coombe, Margaret, Anne Mouron, and Christiania Whitehead, ed., *Saints of North-East England, 600–1500* (Turnhout: Brepols, 2017)

Dobson, R. B., *Durham Priory, 1400–1450* (Cambridge: Cambridge University Press, 1973)

——, *Church and Society in the Medieval North of England* (London: Hambledon, 1996)

Green, Adrian, and A. J. Pollard, 'Introduction: Identifying Regions', in *Regional Identities in North-East England, 1300–2000*, ed. by Adrian Green and A. J. Pollard (Woodbridge: Boydell, 2007), pp. 1–26

Hanna, Ralph, ed., *Richard Rolle: Uncollected Prose and Verse with Related Northern Texts*, EETS OS 329 (Oxford: Oxford University Press, 2007)

——, *The English Manuscripts of Richard Rolle: A Descriptive Catalogue* (Exeter: University of Exeter Press, 2010)

——, ed., *Richard Rolle: Unprinted Latin Writings* (Liverpool: Liverpool University Press, 2019)

Higham, N. J., ed., *Wilfrid: Abbot, Bishop, Saint* (Donington: Shaun Tyas, 2013)

Holford, Matthew, 'Locality, Culture and Identity in Late Medieval Yorkshire, c. 1270–c. 1540' (unpublished doctoral dissertation, University of York, 2001)

Holford, Matthew, Andy King, and Christian Liddy, 'North-East England in the Late Middle Ages: Rivers, Boundaries and Identities, 1296–1461', in *Regional Identities in North-East England, 1300–2000*, ed. by Adrian Green and A. J. Pollard (Woodbridge: Boydell, 2007), pp. 27–48

Jamroziak, Emilia, *Survival and Success on Medieval Borders: Cistercian Houses in Medieval Scotland and Pomerania from the Twelfth to Late Fourteenth Century* (Turnhout: Brepols, 2011)

Karáth, Tamás, *Richard Rolle: The Fifteenth-Century Translations* (Turnhout: Brepols, 2018)

Licence, Tom, *Hermits and Recluses in English Society, 950–1200* (Oxford: Oxford University Press, 2011)

Liddy, Christian, *The Bishopric of Durham in the Late Middle Ages: Lordship, Community and the Cult of St Cuthbert* (Woodbridge: Boydell, 2008)

McGuigan, Neil, 'Neither Scotland nor England: Middle Britain c. 850–1150' (unpublished doctoral dissertation, University of St Andrews, 2015)

Norton, Christopher, *St William of York* (Woodbridge: York Medieval, 2006)

Pollard, A. J., 'Introduction', in *North-East England in the Later Middle Ages*, ed. by Christian Liddy and R. H. Britnell (Woodbridge: Boydell, 2005), pp. 1–12

Renevey, Denis, *Language, Self and Love: Hermeneutics in the Writings of Richard Rolle and the Commentaries on the Song of Songs* (Cardiff: University of Wales Press, 2001)

Rigg, A. G., 'A Latin Poem on St Hilda and Whitby Abbey', *Journal of Medieval Latin*, 6 (1996), 12–43

Rollason, David, ed., *Symeon of Durham: Historian of Durham and the North* (Stamford: Shaun Tyas, 1998)

Rollason, David, Margaret Harvey, and Michael Prestwich, ed., *Anglo-Norman Durham 1093–1193* (Woodbridge: Boydell, 1994)

Rosenwein, Barbara, *Emotional Communities in the Early Middle Ages* (Ithaca: Cornell University Press, 2006)

Sanok, Catherine, *New Legends of England: Forms of Community in Late Medieval Saints' Lives* (Philadelphia: University of Pennsylvania Press, 2018)

Sharpe, Richard, 'The Banners of the Northern Saints', in *Saints of North-East England, 600–1500*, ed. by Margaret Coombe, Anne Mouron, and Christiania Whitehead (Turnhout: Brepols, 2017), pp. 245–303

Stancliffe, Clare, and Eric Cambridge, ed., *Oswald: Northumbrian King to European Saint* (Stamford: Paul Watkins, 1995)

Stringer, Keith, *The Reformed Church in Medieval Galloway and Cumbria: Contrasts, Connections and Continuities* (Whithorn: Friends of Whithorn Trust, 2003)

——, 'Introduction: "Middle Britain" in Context, *c.* 900–*c.* 1300', in *Northern England and Southern Scotland in the Central Middle Ages*, ed. by Keith Stringer and Angus Winchester (Woodbridge: Boydell, 2017), pp. 1–29

Watson, Nicholas, *Richard Rolle and the Invention of Authority* (Cambridge: Cambridge University Press, 1991)

Whitehead, Christiania, *The Afterlife of St Cuthbert: Place, Texts and Ascetic Tradition, 690–1500* (Cambridge: Cambridge University Press, 2020)

——, 'Bega's Bracelet', in *Women, Reading, and Piety in Medieval England*, ed. by Filip Krajnik and Klara Petrikova (Brno: Masaryk University Press, forthcoming 2022)

Wilson, Susan, *The Life and After-Life of St John of Beverley* (Aldershot: Ashgate, 2006)

PART I

Northern Sanctity and Northern Identity

1.1 Textual Culture:
Hagiography, Legendary, Suffrage

DENIS RENEVEY

Aelred of Rievaulx and the Saints of Durham, Galloway, and Hexham

Aelred and the North of England

Aelred of Rievaulx spread Cistercian spirituality in the North of England, first as a novice master at Rievaulx, then as abbot of the newly founded monastery of Saint Laurence of Revesby, Lincolnshire from 1143 to 1147. In 1147 he returned to Rievaulx, serving as abbot there up until his death in 1167.[1] Rievaulx was the motherhouse of five other Cistercian daughter houses in England and southern Scotland.[2] Aelred, who had received some of his training at the court of King David of Scotland, was able to use his skills as court diplomat and steward for the benefit of these Cistercian houses. Rievaulx became a spiritual and economic powerhouse during the time of his abbacy, doubling in size, both in terms of personnel (monks, *conversi*, laymen) and material possessions (farms, lands, and equipment).[3] Aelred travelled extensively in the first decade of his Rievaulx abbacy, undertaking a trip to Rome with prelates from the North of England in 1142.[4] He must also have travelled annually in Galloway, more specifically to the Cistercian abbey of Dundrennan, the fourth daughter house, founded by Fergus, First Lord of Galloway,[5] and was clearly familiar with Galloway and keen to promote the Christian faith in the south-west of Scotland.

Even if we must assume Aelred did not always have the perfect writing conditions, he was a prolific writer, emulating Bernard of Clairvaux (1090–1153), the second and most charismatic founder of the Cistercian order. Aelred

---

1 *Oxford Dictionary of Saints*, ed. by Farmer.
2 Rievaulx's daughter houses were Melrose Abbey (Scotland), Warden Abbey (Bedfordshire), Revesby (Lincolnshire), Rufford Abbey (Nottinghamshire) and Dundrennan (Scotland); see *History of Rievaulx Abbey*.
3 Daniel, *Life of Aelred*, trans. by Powicke, p. 31 (hereafter cited as *Life of Aelred*).
4 *Life of Aelred*, p. 34.
5 Aelred, *Lives of the Northern Saints*, trans. by Freeland, ed. by Dutton, p. 11.

Denis Renevey (denis.renevey@unil.ch) is Professor of Middle English Literature, and Director of the SNSF-funded project 'Region and Nation: Late Medieval Devotion to Northern English Saints' at the University of Lausanne, Switzerland.

Late Medieval Devotion to Saints from the North of England: New Directions, ed. by Christiania Whitehead, Hazel J. Hunter Blair, and Denis Renevey, MCS 48 (Turnhout: Brepols, 2022), pp. 35–51
BREPOLS ☙ PUBLISHERS   10.1484/M.MCS-EB.5.124343

however differed from Bernard and other Cistercian writers by showing an interest in historical writings. He was best known in the medieval period for his *Vita et miraculis Edwardi Regis et Confessoris* (*Life of Saint Edward, King and Confessor*) the most popular work during his own lifetime. He also wrote a life of King David of Scotland, the *Eulogium Davidis*, and a genealogy of the kings of England, the *Genealogia regum Anglorum*. In addition, the substantial number of letters written to some of the most important political and religious figures of the time attests to his interest in the politics of the twelfth century. Aelred is nowadays better known for his spiritual writings, such as the *Speculum caritatis* (*Mirror of Charity*), *De spirituali amicitia* (*On Spiritual Friendship*), and *De institutione inclusarum*,[6] and for more than two hundred sermons. However, alongside these spiritual writings which were initially aimed at the Cistercian community throughout Europe, it is clear that he also showed an interest in more regional and local religious and political affairs, in some of which his ancestors had participated actively.

Aelred was born in Hexham, the son of Eilaf, a Hexham priest at the church of St Andrew, and the grandson of Eilaf, who was a cathedral canon treasurer of the church of St Cuthbert at Durham until 1083. Following the injunction from the new bishop of Durham, William of Saint-Calais, obliging the secular clerks to choose between their wives or their positions at the cathedral, Eilaf gave up his Durham position to take up a benefice in the church of St Andrew at Hexham. However, Aelred's family ties with Durham went still further back in time as he was also a great-grandson of Elfred, son of Westou, sacristan of Durham and guardian of the shrine of St Cuthbert. Hence, devotion to Cuthbert seems to have been a family affair to which Aelred may possibly have contributed textually via a now lost eulogy devoted to the saint.[7] Aelred must have shown great abilities, for he was given an education that went beyond the means of the son of a parish priest. He was taught at Hexham in his early years, and then possibly received further education in Durham before joining the court of David I of Scotland in 1124. His experience working at a prestigious secular court contributed to his success as a Cistercian abbot, whose position required diplomatic skills and leadership abilities, among other things.

Aelred's strong roots in the north of England, the interest he showed in Galloway and, most importantly, his childhood in Hexham, account for his compositions of the *Vita S Niniani* (*The Life of Saint Ninian*) and the *De miraculis Hagustaldensis ecclesiae* (*On the Miracles of the Church of Hexham*) in the mid-twelfth century. With these writings, Aelred appears as a significant contributor to a robust culture of devotion to northern English saints.

This essay assesses the role played by Aelred in the construction of a network of northern sanctity in which he functions both as a subject and a contributor. Aelred takes part in the composition and transmission of northern sanctity by

---

6   Aelred, *Historical Works*, trans. by Freeland, ed. by Dutton, p. 20.
7   Bell, 'Ailred of Rievaulx', *ODNB*.

disseminating knowledge of Cuthbert, Ninian, and the ancient saint-bishops of the church of Hexham. This exercise reveals the complexity of constructing a corporate body of saints that distributes saintly agency cautiously among different regions from the North. Following his death, Aelred himself becomes the subject of hagiographic memorialization, with his life, the *Vita Aelredi*, written by Walter Daniel soon after his death in 1167. This chapter considers first the way in which Walter Daniel's *Vita Aelredi* (*Life of Aelred of Rievaulx*) contextualizes Aelred as a northern religious figure imitating Cuthbert and Bede as models for proper monastic conduct, and Ninian as missionary model. Second, it argues that regional sanctity is sanctioned by Aelred himself in his *De miraculis Hagustaldensis ecclesie*, devoted to the five Hexham bishop-saints, Eata, Acca, Alchmund, Frethbert, and Tilbert.

Aelred, Cuthbert, and Bede

Walter Daniel's *Vita Aelredi* survives in one manuscript, Cambridge, Jesus College, MS Q.B. 7 (fols 63^v–74^r). The manuscript is from the late fourteenth century, and probably from Durham.[8] Walter Daniel spent seventeen years at Rievaulx, under the abbacy of Aelred. His *Vita Aelredi*, written at the request of an 'Abbot H', whose identity is otherwise unknown, seemed to have been designed to ward off criticism of Aelred, who was regarded as ambitious and overly involved in the affairs of the world. The *Vita* therefore strategically avoids references to Aelred's religio-political influence and focuses instead on his interactions with the Rievaulx monks. With his health having deteriorated in the last decade of his life, from 1157 onwards, the *Vita*'s representation of Aelred lovingly instructing his Rievaulx monks may not be too far away from the reality of his final years. Also, Walter Daniel's intimate knowledge of Aelred's illness supports the possibility that he officiated within the infirmary precincts, the place from which Aelred gave instructions to his monks and ran the monastic foundation, as his authorized scribe and *medicus*.

The *Vita* depicts Aelred as a champion of humility and charity in order to combat the criticism that emerged immediately following his death in 1167.[9] Hence, even his early years, followed by the time spent at the court of King David, depict a young man already touched by divine love. Daniel presents each moment of his early life as a preparation for his entry into the Cistercian community, showcasing the acquisition of gifts and experiences that will allow him to accomplish great things for Rievaulx. Succeeding events, such Aelred's departure from David's court and his discovery of Rievaulx, are fashioned with narrative flair by Daniel, who relies for this part of Aelred's life

---

8 *Life of Aelred*, p. 8.

9 I am summarizing and paraphrasing Dutton, in Daniel, *Life of Aelred*, trans. by Powicke, intro. by Dutton, pp. 9–40.

on the testimony of other Cistercian monks, such as Simon, former novitiate master of Rievaulx, and current abbot of Sartis, also called Wardon Abbey, in Bedfordshire.[10] Although dependent on first-hand witnesses for these early years, he nevertheless shows complete authorial control in selecting particular events designed to eulogize Aelred. The following moment is worth quoting in full:

> Nec pretereundum quomodo in probatorio casellam testeam ad modum paruule cisterne sub terra fabricauerat, cui per occultos riuulos aqua influebat. Os autem eius lapide latissimo claudebatur ne a quoquam cerneretur. In quam Alredus machinam intrans, si quando secretum silencium reperisset, et aqua frigidissima totum corpus humectans calorem in sese omnium extinxit uiciorum.

>> (I should not omit to tell you he had built a small chamber of brick under the floor of the novice house, like a little tank, into which water flowed from hidden rills. Its opening was shut by a very broad stone in such a way that nobody would notice it. Aelred would enter this contrivance, when he was alone and undisturbed, and immerse his whole body in the icy cold water, and so quench the heat in himself of every vice.)[11]

Aelred, at this time novice-master at Rievaulx, seems to be shown emulating Cuthbert in this ascetic practice. If Cuthbert immerses himself more spectacularly in the cold waters of the North Sea near Coldingham, nonetheless he does so with the same level of secrecy and with the same desire to discipline the flesh as described in Aelred's *Vita*.[12] Both are consequently caught engaging in an impressive ascetic exercise that becomes a public demonstration of their zeal for self-discipline. Although there is no direct reference to Cuthbert, Walter Daniel certainly chose this particular event with a view to aligning Aelred with Cuthbert and other northern English saints.

Indeed, the *Vita Aelredi* attests to the importance of northern figures in constructing Aelred's sanctity.[13] The connection of Rievaulx with Durham, as well as the references to Cuthbert and Bede, in the context of the description of Maurice, second abbot of Rievaulx, in chapter twenty-five, is further evidence of Daniel's intention:

---

10 *Life of Aelred*, pp. 96–101.

11 Daniel, *Life of Ailred*, ed. by Powicke, p. 25 (cited hereafter as *Vita Ailredi*); *Life of Aelred*, p. 108; see also Whitnah, 'Aelred of Rievaulx and the Saints of Hexham', p. 29. Whitnah mentions the fact that Reginald of Durham addresses his collection of Cuthbert's miracles to Aelred.

12 *Life of Aelred*, p. 108; Bede, Prose *Vita Sancti Cuthberti*, 10, ed. and trans. by Colgrave, pp. 188–91.

13 On the relationship between Aelred and his biographer, see Heffernan, *Sacred Biography*, pp. 72–122. Walter Daniel's *Vita* combines his intimate knowledge of Aelred with reference to ancillary texts of sacred biography in which the biographer plays a role as a character.

AELRED OF RIEVAULX AND THE SAINTS OF DURHAM, GALLOWAY, AND HEXHAM

Huic successit Mauricius magne sanctitatis uir et preclare prudencie utpote qui potauerat a puero uinum leticie spiritalis in claustro Dunolmensi, et ex pane Cuthberti uiri Dei refectus creuerat in sublime ita ut a sociis secundus Beda cognominaretur; cui reuera erat in tempore suo tam uite quam sciencie prerogatiua secundus.

> (Maurice succeeded him (i.e. William, first abbot), a man of great sanctity and of outstanding judgement, befitting one who from boyhood had drunk the wine of spiritual gladness in the cloister at Durham, and, refreshed by the bread of Cuthbert, that man of God, had climbed so high as to be called by his companions a second Bede; and truly in his day, by his pre-eminence both in life and learning he alone could be compared with Bede.)[14]

As mentioned earlier, Aelred was probably educated at Durham between his initial schooling in Hexham and his ten-year stay at the court of David I.[15] It is interesting to see that his familial and educational ties with Durham are matched in his *Vita* with a spiritual association with two of the major figures linked to Durham Cathedral, that is Cuthbert and Bede, Bede's relics having passed into the possession of the Durham monks after their translation from Jarrow to Durham by Elfred Westou in the mid-eleventh century. Interestingly then, the narrative of the appointment of Aelred as third abbot of Rievaulx is represented as taking place under the auspices of his predecessors William and Maurice, in the light of their resemblances to both Cuthbert and Bede.[16] In my view, this move was carefully conceived by Walter Daniel in order to create a spiritual lineage for Aelred, linking Rievaulx to the towering figures of Cuthbert and Bede based in Durham. The fact that Daniel's *Vita* must have been conceived for a local audience to deflect charges of ambition, pride and excessive interest in the affairs of the world, may also have played a role in the prominence given to these northern saints. With that audience in mind, and in order to strengthen Aelred's spiritual roots with the north of England, Daniel carefully chose Aelred's models from among the most influential of the northern saints.

If Daniel worked under the request of 'Abbot H', with the intention of offering a defence of Aelred's spiritual and monastic achievements, he was, as Aelred's scribe and close companion, and the second most prolific writer at Rievaulx, the best person to fulfil this task.[17] Although the *Vita* explicitly omits to mention Aelred's extensive travels in England and on the continent in order to highlight his achievements as the spiritual leader of a monastic

---

14 *Vita Ailredi*, p. 33; *Life of Aelred*, pp. 114–15.
15 See Dutton, 'Aelred of Rievaulx', *Oxford Bibliographies*; Dutton mentions Hexham and Durham as possible venues for Aelred's education before his move to the court of King David.
16 *Oxford Dictionary of Saints*, ed. by Farmer.
17 *Life of Aelred*, p. 89.

community, Daniel nevertheless offers a brief report of Aelred's visit to Galloway, reinforcing his northerness. Daniel's unflinching and aggressive account of the barbarity of the men from Galloway contrasts with Aelred's peaceful intentions:

Est autem terra illa fera et homines bestiales et barbarum omne quod gignit. Veritas ibi non habet ubi caput suum reclinet, quia a planta pedis usque ad uerticem non est in terra illa ulla sapiencia. Nam neque fides neque uera spes neque caritas constans perdurat in ea longo tempore. Ibi castitas tociens patitur naufragium quociens libido uoluerit, nec est inter castam et scortum ulla distancia nisi quod castiores inibi per menses uiros alternent et uir pro una bucula uendat uxorem [...]

Quam, ut dictum est, uisitans pater inuenit principes illius prouincie dissencientes inter se, quorum odia et rancores animorum et tirranidem ad inuicem nec rex Scocie humiliare potuit nec episcopus mitigare suffecit, set filii in patrem consurgentes et pater in filios et frater in fratrem et e conuerso multo sanguine infelicem terrulam polluerunt cotidie. Quos omnes conueniens Alredus pacificus uerbis pacis et uirtutis natos iratos firmissima pace federauit in unum dileccionis uinculum.

(It is a wild country where the inhabitants are like beasts, and is altogether barbarous. Truth there has nowhere to lay her head, and 'from the sole of the foot even unto the head there is no wisdom in it'.[Isaiah 1:6] For neither faith nor true hope nor loyal charity for long lasts in it. There chastity founders as often as lust wills, and the pure is only so far removed from a harlot that the more chaste will change their husbands every month and a man will sell his wife for a heifer [...]

As I have said, our father on a visit to the place found the princes of the province quarrelling among themselves. The king of Scotland could not subdue, nor the bishop pacify, their mutual hatreds, rancor and tyranny. Sons were against father, father against sons, brother against brother, daily polluting the unhappy little land with bloodshed. Aelred the peacemaker met them all and, with words of peace and goodness, bound together the angry sons by a firm peace in a single bond of affection.)[18]

This depiction of the moral laxity and degeneracy of the Gallowegians is designed to make it appear that their Christianization is far from complete in the mid-twelfth century. As a result, it requires Aelred's peaceful holiness and benign influence upon the king and princes of Galloway to procure stability within the North West. This narrative moment roots Aelred firmly

---

18 *Vita Ailredi*, pp. 44–46; *Life of Aelred*, pp. 124–25.

Missionary Zeal: Aelred and Ninian

The reference to Aelred helping Fergus, First Lord of Galloway, by settling a dispute between him and his sons, shows the extent of his close ties with that province, which he travelled through on the occasion of his annual visits to Dundrennan. That long-standing acquaintance with the religious and political figures of the area prompted the writing of his *Vita Niniani* (*Life of St Ninian, Apostle of the Southern Picts*), probably his first hagiographical composition, written around 1154–1160. The *Vita Niniani* probably addresses Christian, bishop of Whithorn, the Scottish see founded by Ninian himself, supposedly in the fourth century.[19] In the same fashion as Bede, Aelred presents the saint as a significant local Northumbrian and Brittonic figure who undertakes a mission to the Picts of Southern Scotland. Following his pilgrimage and several years stay in Rome where Ninian deepens his spiritual understanding and experiences the grace of contemplation, the pope sends him back to Galloway, close to his native land where, according to Aelred, his father was king. There, he offers orthodox faith to those who had previously only heard it from heretics, or continued with pagan practices. Ninian returns to Galloway via Tours, where his encounter with St Martin introduces him to the life of sanctity. In addition, Ninian seems to be impressed by the architectural feats of the Tours architects, so much so that he brings two stonemasons to Whithorn to build the White House, a church devoted to St Martin, built of stone, a practice then unknown in the British Isles:

> Elegit autem sibi sedem in loco qui nunc Witerna dicitur; qui locus super litus occeani situs, dum se ipsum mare longius porrigit ab oriente, occidente, atque meridie, ipso pelago clauditur a parte tantum aquilonali, via ingredi, volentibus aperitur. Ibi igitur jussu viri Dei cementarii, quos secum adduxerat, ecclesiam construunt; antequam nullam in Brittania de lapide dicunt esse constructam.
>
> > (Ninian chose for his see a place now called Whithorn, situated on the ocean shore. Extending quite a way into the sea on the east, the west, and the south, it is enclosed by the woven waves themselves; only on the north is there a passage-way for those wishing to

---

19 See Aelred, *Life of Ninian*, trans. by Freeland, ed. by Dutton, p. 31 n. 1; Whitehead, 'Translating the Northern English Saints', pp. 38, 39 n. 65. More probably, Ninian, if he ever existed, was active in the sixth century.

enter. There, by order of the man of God, the masons whom he had brought with him built a church. Before this, they say, none in Britain had been built of stone.)[20]

Ninian's interest in new architectural techniques imported from Roman Gaul may have been perceived by Aelred as a productive precursor to the later Cistercian importation of European Gothic architecture to northern England and southern Scotland.[21] This enthusiasm is preceded in the *Vita Niniani* by a lexical field linked to agricultural work. Ninian enters his mission-field as an assiduous labourer, rooting out what was badly planted, scattering what was badly gathered, and tearing down what was badly built, in order to lay the new foundations of a sound faith, then building upon them 'aurum sapiencie et sciencie argentum, bonorumque operum lapides' (the gold of wisdom, the silver of knowledge, and the stones of good works).[22] Aelred offers an example of Christianization that precedes the somewhat difficult spread of Cistercian spirituality in that area. Walter Daniel may not have been too far from the reality when describing the difficulties of establishing a solid Christian foundation in Galloway. Aelred's *Vita Niniani* first presents Ninian as a missionary, a builder of churches, but also as a man labouring to establish deep-seated Christian values in that area. The Galloway episode in Daniel's *Vita Aelredi* therefore presents his abbot as the missionary successor of Ninian in Galloway.

Aelred of Rievaulx was of course aware of the complex pulls of powerful religious northern centres such as York and Durham. Whithorn had become a suffragan see of York in *c.* 1125, but Aelred, rather than highlighting possible tensions, presents Ninian mainly as a local Northumbrian saint who shares some characteristics with Cuthbert.[23] With the *Vita Niniani*, his first hagiographical piece, Aelred displays religious and political acumen by contextualizing Ninian as a local Northumbrian saint in an area now to the north of the Anglo-Scottish border.

Aelred at Home: the Hexham Saints

De sanctis ecclesiae Haugustaldensis, et eorum miraculis libellus, known in English as *The Saints of the Church of Hexham and Their Miracles*, shows a similar preoccupation with rooting sanctity locally, in this case in Hexham, Aelred's

---

20 Aelred, *Lives of S. Ninian and S. Kentigern*, ed. by Forbes, pp. 143–44; Aelred, *Life of Ninian*, trans. by Freeland, ed. by Dutton, p. 44. The reference to Ninian's importation of Tours' stone masons is originally found in Bede, *Ecclesiastical History*, trans. by Sherley-Price, p. 148.

21 Wilson, 'Cistercians as "Missionaries of Gothic"'.

22 Aelred, *Lives of S. Ninian and S. Kentigern*, ed. by Forbes, p. 143; Aelred, *Life of Ninian*, trans. by Freeland, ed. by Dutton, p. 44.

23 Whitehead, 'Translating the Northern English Saints', p. 38.

native town, which he constructs as a bastion of collective sanctity within his broader vision of a united northern saintly family.[24] Hexham's veneration of its saint-bishops dated to long before Aelred's contribution to its revivification in the twelfth century. Hexham was initially a monastery of the kingdom of Northumbria, founded in around 674, and offered as a gift by Queen Ætheldreda to Bishop Wilfrid. When the Northumbrian see was divided into three new sees, Hexham became one of them, with a succession of thirteen bishops, four of whom are relatively well known to us: Eata (678–81 and 685–85/6), John of Beverley (687–706), Wilfrid (706–09), and Acca (703–31). This bishopric ceased to exist from the beginning of the ninth century. It was only in the course of the eleventh century, when married priests ran the church, that Hexham reappeared on the map as a Durham possession. These arrangements were terminated in 1113 when Augustinian canons were brought in by Thomas II, Archbishop of York, to curate the church at Hexham.[25] Apart from William of York, there was no cult of bishop-saints in York, and apart from Cuthbert, who was venerated as hermit, monk, and bishop, there was nothing at Durham. It may be that the cult of bishop-saints at Hexham was linked to its desire to acquire more political and jurisdictional freedom from its subordination to the church of Durham before it was reformed as a Benedictine abbey in 1083.[26] Hexham's move from the hands of one diocese (Durham) to another (York), with the consequent loss of significant land for Durham, must have created additional tensions between these two sees.[27] Although according to Rollason these tensions seem to have abated by the middle of the twelfth century, the revivification of devotion to the bishop-saints of Hexham by Aelred in 1155 was certainly due in part to Hexham's desire to stand on its own feet, identifying a corporate body of local saints with which Durham and York could not compete. If this ambitious desire for emancipation was designed to be done without unnecessarily offending its weighty religious neighbours, then no one was capable of serving the needs of Hexham as well as Aelred. His long-standing family ties with Durham on the one hand, and his close contacts with the archbishopric of York and Walter Espec, founder of Rievaulx, on the other, gave him the best tools not to hurt the sensibilities of either. However, Durham and York could not come out completely unscathed if he was going to be successful in his attempt to restore Hexham's reputation as a significant centre of corporate local sanctity.

This is one of the pervasive themes of *De sanctis ecclesiae Haugustaldensis*. The five saints celebrated by Aelred are part of a broader perspective, focused

---

24 Aelred, *De sanctis ecclesiae Haugustaldensis*, ed. by Raine, pp. 173–203 (cited hereafter as *DSH*). For a translation, see Aelred, *Saints of the Church of Hexham*, trans. by Freeland, ed. by Dutton (cited hereafter as *SCH*).

25 *Life of Aelred*, p. 20.

26 I am summarizing Rollason, 'The Hexham Bishop-Saints', pp. 177–86.

27 For more details about these ongoing tensions, see Rollason, 'The Hexham Bishop-Saints', pp. 187–90.

upon communities in general. These saints, although rarely individualized in the reports of the miracles taking place in Hexham, are Eata, Acca, Alchmund, Frethbert, and Tilbert. *De sanctis ecclesiae Haugustaldensis* was initially composed as a homily designed for the celebration of the translation of bishop-saints' relics on 3 March 1155 by the Augustinian canons of Hexham. In the prologue, the narrator characterizes himself as a part of the community celebrating the five bishop-saints buried in the church of St Andrew. Although the homily was most probably delivered by Aelred on the occasion of the translation, the text's inclusion of a narrative voice speaking from the standpoint of the community would have been welcomed by the canons as a performance script for later annual celebrations of the translation. We recall that Aelred's emotional bond with the Hexham community was the result of his strong family attachments with the church of Saint Andrew, where he spent his boyhood and where his father officiated as a married priest before the arrival of the canons.[28] Thus one should not be surprised that Aelred would have been able to assume a narrative voice speaking as a part of the Augustinian community he addresses:

> Audientes, fratres karissimi, Sanctos istos ereptum caecis lumen suis precibus reddidisse, si forte mentis nostrae occulos insipientiae caligo fuscaverit, ad eorum secure fugiamus auxilium, ut sanctissimis eorum meritis verum sapientiae lumen caecicate detersa reseratis hauriamus.

> (When we hear, dearest brothers, that by their prayers these saints restored lost light to the blind, if perhaps a cloud of foolishness has darkened the eyes of our mind, let us fly to them fearlessly for help. Then, with their holy merits revealed and our blindness removed, we may drink in the true light of wisdom.)[29]

The narrative voice invites the primary audience of Augustinian canons to reflect on the benevolence of the bishop-saints towards Hexham. It also incorporates a broader audience consisting of Hexham citizens, thus representing a mixed community of secular and religious centred around the church of St Andrew in Hexham. The church is shown to work as a spiritual rallying point for the entire community, but Aelred goes further in showing its protective role as a physical space in his description of an episode in which Malcolm, king of the Scots, lays waste to Northumbria. If the venerated church of Hexham had been preserved from his savagery during his previous raids, his intent on this occasion was to plunder the church. Aelred describes the turmoil created by this imminent attack by Malcolm and his Gallowegian men, on the people of Hexham gathered in the church:

---

28 Whitnah, 'Aelred of Rievaulx and the Saints of Hexham', pp. 1–9, discusses Aelred's authorship of the treatise.

29 *DSH*, p. 175; *SCH*, p. 66.

Quibus regressis ad ecclesiam, et referentibus quae audierant, tumultus miserabilis oritur, clamor ingens, ploratus, et ululatus multus. Mulieres detecto capite propriis manibus crines lacerant, pectus diverberant, ejulatumque dirae vocis emittentes, horribile spectaculum intuentibus praebuerunt. Viri prostati solo, moderatius Sanctorum auxilium precabantur.

> (As soon as they returned to the church and related what they had heard, a pitiful tumult broke out, a great outcry, weeping and much wailing. Women bared their heads, tore their hair with their own hands, and beat their breasts; uttering dreadful shrieks in anguished voices, they presented a horrible spectacle to the onlookers. Prostrate on the ground, the men, with more moderation, begged the help of the saints.)[30]

The people of Hexham participate as a community in the terror of the anticipated raid and the prospect of their destruction as they stand hopeless in the church. Their only defence, as Aelred points out, is the weapon of prayer, which they address to a community of saints. Some address prayers and appeals to Wilfrid, the founder of Hexham; others appeal to Cuthbert who received the Hexham see, according to Bede, following the deposition of Tunbert in 684.[31] Even if Cuthbert only officiated for about a year (if at all) before taking the bishopric of Lindisfarne, Hexham would nonetheless have been keen to associate him as an adjunct to their bishop-saints, and of course Aelred would have been happy to incorporate a saint whose shrine had been looked after by his great-grandfather to his hometown at Hexham. The other two saints that are called upon are Acca and Alchmund, whose relics were being translated on the day Aelred delivered his homily.[32] As mentioned above, in 1155 Hexham was under the tutelage of York, Durham having lost its hold on Hexhamshire. Although Cuthbert is undeniably the main contender to lead this northern saintly corporation, Aelred uses his skills as a writer to give prominence to additional saintly figures within a northern family of saints. Such a project clearly requires an understanding of the political tensions at play between Durham and York. In proposing a more prominent role for Hexham by highlighting the miracles performed by its bishop-saints, Aelred performs a delicate balancing act.

Following the appeal from the Hexham people for support against Malcolm, two figures on horseback appear in a vision to a Hexham priest, comforting him with information about a thick fog spreading from the source of the River Tyne that will make it impossible for the king and his Gallowegian soldiers to find their way to Hexham. As the priest asks about the identity of the apparitions

---

30 *DSH*, p. 179; *SCH*, p. 71.
31 Whitnah, 'Aelred of Rievaulx and the Saints of Hexham', p. 16; Bede, *Ecclesiastical History*, trans. by Sherley-Price, p. 259.
32 Wilfrid (634–709) became bishop of York from 664 to 678, and then bishop of Hexham from *c.* 686 to 688 and 705 to 709, after the division of the diocese in 678; see *SCH*, p. 67 n. 2.

who bear such good news, one of them replies: 'Wilfridus vocor, et ecce hic mecum est Sanctus Cuthbertus, quem transiens per Dunelmum adduxi'. ('I am called Wilfrid, and see, here with me is Saint Cuthbert. I brought him with me as I passed Durham').[33] The relegation of Cuthbert, the great saint of the North, to an afterthought by Wilfrid: 'I brought him with me as I passed Durham', reveals a complex understanding of local devotion, particularly at Hexham. The moderate reference to Cuthbert attests to the recent, possibly difficult, transfer of affiliation of Hexham from Durham to York. Hexham was in the gift of the bishop of Durham until the death of Bishop Æthelwine in 1071, when it passed into the hands of Thomas, archbishop of York.[34] At the same time, Aelred's great-grandfather's involvement with the cult of Cuthbert at Durham testifies to the intricacy of regional saintly networks, within which it was possible to maintain a simultaneous commitment to saints from several churches and locations. Considering that the text was written as a homily to celebrate the translation of the Hexham bishop-saints' relics, the presence of Cuthbert, however subdued, attests to his importance within the North as a whole.

The long-standing dependence of Hexham upon the powerful religious centres of Durham and York stands as an unresolved issue for Aelred. Two significant episodes in his homily testify to his desire to contribute to the lasting reputation of Hexham as a religious centre. One of these episodes is made more poignant for the fact that it shows Aelred's great-grandfather, Elfred Westou, custodian of the shrine of Saint Cuthbert, intent upon translating relics from Hexham to Durham. However, the translation of the relics of Acca is cancelled, due to a last-minute change of heart by Elfred:[35]

> Hic Divina revelatione commonitus, per sacra loca quae saevitia barbarorum vastaverat discurrens, multorum Sanctorum reliquias de tumulis eruens ad Dunelmensem transtulit ecclesiam. Veniens vero ad sanctam Haugustaldensem ecclesiam, cum sanctissimi Accae reliquias sustulisset, praevidens forte in spiritu (nam et spiritum prophetiae dicitur habuisse) quid religionis, quid honoris ea ipsa ecclesia erat habitura; sacras illas reliquias absportare noluit, vel non potuit; sed eas intra ecclesiam honeste recondens, venerationi locorum, devotioni praesentium, profectui futurorum, Divina gratia disponente, consulit.

> (Prompted by divine revelation, as he passed through the sacred places laid waste by the savagery of the barbarians, he took the relics of many saints from their burial places and transferred them to the church at Durham. He came to the holy church of Hexham and took up the relics of Saint Acca. But foreseeing (perhaps in spirit, for he

---

33 *DSH*, p. 179; *SCH*, p. 72.
34 *SCH*, p. 89 n. 24.
35 *SCH*, p. 88 n. 19.

is also said to have had the spirit of prophecy) what sacredness and honor this church was to have, he was unwilling, or unable, to take away these sacred relics.)[36]

The explanation for the failure in the removal of the relics from the church of Hexham is vague. Was Elfred wise enough to decide not to move the relics, or was divine intervention necessary to prevent their theft? The episode reveals Aelred's ambiguous relationship to his ancestor Elfred Westou and the role he played in the cult of Cuthbert in Durham, as well as to his possible initial intention of depriving Hexham of its spiritual treasures. We are told that Elfred is wise and has the gift of prophecy, and so are invited to favour unwillingness rather than inability, but the fact that the latter is left as an option may conceal complex issues linked to Durham as a centre of regional spiritual power with Hexham as a subsidiary entity. However, as Aelred has been commissioned to celebrate the robust faith of Hexham via its bishop-saints, he has no intention of demeaning its status despite his own emotional links to Durham and Cuthbert. On the contrary, the second episode reviles both Elfred, Aelred's ancestor, and the Durham community that he represents, for their disrespectful greed towards the Hexham relics.

The episode involves Collan, possibly Elfred's brother-in-law, and Elfred, Aelred's forebear and the guardian of Cuthbert's shrine.[37] Collan, a simple thane known for his faith rather than his knowledge, receives a vision from Bishop Alchmund asking him to convey to Elfred that he would like his relics moved to a more suitable place in the church of Hexham. However, after locating the relics of Alchmund, Elfred decides to secretly bring a part of Alchmund's body to Durham:

> Caeteris itaque alto sopore depressis, accessit ad loculum, et unum ex ossibus, quibus intervenientibus per certos articulos nervis digitus fuerat arte creatrice compactus, auferens, sibi reponere et reservare curavit.

> (And so while the others lay deep in sleep, he approached the casket. Taking up one of the bones, a finger that through the Creator's art had been joined by certain tendons with the interveinal nerves, he took care to lay it aside to keep it for himself.)[38]

As can be expected, Elfred fails once again to bring the relic to Durham. When the casket containing the now incomplete relic of Alchmund cannot be moved, Collan receives another vision of Alchmund who demands his

---

36 *DSH*, p. 190; *SCH*, p. 88. This account contrasts markedly with the account given earlier in the century by Symeon of Durham, the monastic historian of Durham Benedictine Priory. In Symeon's *Libellus de exordio*, Acca's and Alchmund's relics are removed successfully from Hexham by Elfred with no hint of any moral hesitation. Symeon of Durham, *Libellus de exordio*, ed. and trans. by Rollason, III. 7.

37 *SCH*, p. 95.

38 *DSH*, p. 197; *SCH*, pp. 97–98.

finger to be restored to him so that his body can repose in its integrity in the Hexham church. As in the previous attempt, this account shows how Aelred confects a narrative of Hexham's combative and agentive saintly relics in order to present Hexham successfully resisting Durham's attempt to exercise control over its cults, and its broader stranglehold upon northern relics.

The attachment of the Hexham saints to their locality is exemplary, and their refusal to comply with the parturition of their bodies gives the church authority as an independent and self-contained locale for saintly devotion. The last attempt at removing relics from Hexham, in this particular case the relics of blessed Eata, comes from the York clergy, declared by Aelred to be 'jam exaltati et dilatati' (still overbearing and proud in these days):[39]

> aegre ferentes nullius se episcoporum suorum habere memoriam, cum Paulinum Roffensis, Wilfridum Ripensis, Joannem Beverlacensis ecclesia possideret, et aliquem illorum transferre populis obsistentibus esset impossibile.
>
> > (They could hardly bear the fact that they had no memorial of any of their bishops when this church [i.e. Hexham] possessed Paulinus of Rochester, Wilfrid of Ripon, and John of Beverley, but to remove any of these over the people's objections would be impossible.)[40]

The Augustinian brothers have only their prayers to offer against the York clergy, described as 'thieves' by Aelred, until Bishop Eata appears to Thomas the Young, Archbishop of York, who leads the York clergy, and strikes him twice on the shoulder. To the great dismay of the clergy, Thomas decides against translating Eata's relics from Hexham to York and, once healed by Eata, he leaves Hexham.

The abrupt ending of the narrative, devoid of an envoi by Aelred, leaves a powerful image of Hexham as an inviolate church, successfully preserving the integrity of the relics of its five local saints. The Augustinian brothers who pray in front of the casket ask blessed Eata not to leave the place he had cherished when alive. Representing the Hexham community, their persuasive prayers move the saint to choose Hexham against York. Aelred, despite his own links to Durham and York, but as a native of Hexham where he received his first education, constructs Hexham as a haven for its local saints, one that even the superpowers of Durham and York are unable to destabilize.

---

39 Aelred refers to Thomas's archiepiscopy at York (1070–1100). It is interesting to see Aelred showing hesitation in relating this event: 'de quo quid modernis acciderit temporibus, huic operi inserendum putavimus'. (I think I ought to insert in this work a modern incident concerning him); *DSH*, p. 202; *SCH*, p. 105.

40 *SCH*, p. 105.

Conclusion

Both the *Vita Niniani* and *De sanctis ecclesiae Haugustaldensis* were commissioned to reinvigorate the local religious centres of Whithorn and Hexham, whose influence must have been difficult to maintain within a northern English orbit in the middle of the twelfth century. While St Martin was widely represented and acknowledged as the patron saint of the Frankish kingdom, the different lives of Cuthbert aimed to represent him in a similar role as the leader of a united Northumbria.[41] However, even if contestation of Cuthbert as the premier northern saint could have been hard to imagine, in his lives of Ninian and the Hexham bishop-saints, Aelred constructed interesting acolytes who seem ready to share even a small portion of the fame usually given to Cuthbert. The episode of Ninian's encounter with St Martin, however chronologically implausible, and his initiative in building a Frankish-style White Church at Whithorn, indicates Aelred's desire to represent him as a plausible St-Martin alternative for the North of England.

In *De sanctis ecclesiae Haugustaldensis* Aelred chooses instead to present a collective of saints working on behalf of the local community of Hexham, giving Cuthbert only a minimal role in renewing the faith of the locality. Also, by preventing the aggressive Yorkshire clergy from despoiling Hexham of its relics via a translation to York, the bishop-saints play a key role in reinstating Hexham as a strong spiritual centre, despite its official religious affiliation to York.

So, without disputing the prominence of Cuthbert as the premier northern English saint, Aelred cautiously offers an alternative to his dominance. Instead of envisaging an exclusive 'St Martin of the North of England', he confects a northern community of saints rooted in specific locales where they can contribute most effectively to the growth of the faith. If these texts do not highlight Aelred's Cistercian spirituality, nonetheless they reveal his skilful political acumen and sensibility towards local communities, acquired first at the court of David of Scotland, and developed later as abbot of the most powerful English Cistercian house in the twelfth century.

---

41 Rollason, 'Hagiography and Politics', pp. 105–07.

Works Cited

Manuscripts and Archival Sources

Cambridge, Jesus College, MS Q.B. 7

Primary Sources

Aelred of Rievaulx, *De sanctis ecclesiae Haugustaldensis, et eorum miraculis libellus*, in *The Priory of Hexham: Its Chronicles, Endowments, and Annals*, ed. by James Raine, SS, 44 (Durham: Andrews and Co., 1864) (cited as *DSH*)
——, *Lives of S. Ninian and S. Kentigern. Compiled in the Twelfth Century*, ed. by Alexander Penrose Forbes (Edinburgh: Edmonston and Douglas, 1874)
——, *The Historical Works*, trans. by Jane Patricia Freeland, ed. by Marsha L. Dutton, Cistercian Fathers Series, 56 (Kalamazoo: Cistercian Publications, 2005)
——, *The Life of Ninian*, in *The Lives of the Northern Saints*, trans. by Jane Patricia Freeland, ed. by Marsha L. Dutton, Cistercian Fathers Series, 71 (Kalamazoo: Cistercian Publications, 2006), pp. 35–63
——, *The Lives of the Northern Saints*, trans. by Jane Patricia Freeland, ed. by Marsha L. Dutton, Cistercian Fathers Series, 71 (Kalamazoo: Cistercian Publications, 2006)
——, *The Saints of the Church of Hexham*, in *The Lives of the Northern Saints*, trans. by Jane Patricia Freeland, ed. by Marsha L. Dutton, Cistercian Fathers Series, 71 (Kalamazoo: Cistercian Publications, 2006), pp. 65–107 (cited as *SCH*)
Bede, Prose *Vita Sancti Cuthberti*, in *Two Lives of Cuthbert: A Life by an Anonymous Monk of Lindisfarne and Bede's Prose Life*, ed. and trans. by Bertram Colgrave (Cambridge: Cambridge University Press, 1940, repr. 1985)
——, *Ecclesiastical History of the English People*, trans. by Leo Sherley-Price (London: Penguin Books, 1990)
Daniel, Walter, *The Life of Ailred of Rievaulx*, ed. by F. M. Powicke (Oxford: Clarendon Press, 1978) (cited as *Vita Ailredi*)
——, *The Life of Aelred of Rievaulx, and The Letter to Maurice*, trans. by F. M. Powicke, intro. by Marsha Dutton, Cistercian Fathers Series, 57 (Kalamazoo: Cistercian Publications, 1994) (cited as *Life of Aelred*)
Symeon of Durham, *Libellus de exordio atque procursu istius, hoc est Dunhelmensis ecclesie*, ed. and trans. by David W. Rollason (Oxford: Oxford University Press, 2000)

Secondary Works

Heffernan, Thomas J., *Sacred Biography: Saints and their Biographers in the Middle Ages* (Oxford: Oxford University Press, 1992)
Rollason, David, 'Hagiography and Politics in Early Northumbria', in *Holy Men and Holy Women: Old English Prose Saints' Lives and Their Contexts*, ed. by Paul E. Szarmach (Albany: State University of New York Press, 1996), pp. 95–114

——, 'The Hexham Bishop-Saints: Cults, History, and Power', in *Saints of North-East England, 600–1500*, ed. by Margaret Coombe, Anne Mouron, and Christiania Whitehead, Medieval Church Studies, 39 (Turnhout: Brepols, 2017), pp. 177–95

Whitehead, Christiania, 'Translating the Northern English Saints within Late Medieval Vernacular Legendaries: Oswald, Cuthbert, Ninian', *Viator*, 49 (2018), 25–45

Whitnah, Lauren L., 'Aelred of Rievaulx and the Saints of Hexham: Tradition, Innovation, and Devotion in Twelfth-Century Northern England', *Church History*, 87 (2018), 1–30

Wilson, Christopher, 'The Cistercians as "Missionaries of Gothic" in Northern England', in *Cistercian Art and Architecture in the British Isles*, ed. by Christopher Norton and David Park (Cambridge: Cambridge University Press, 1986), pp. 88–116

Online Publications

Bell, David, 'Ailred of Rievaulx', *Oxford Dictionary of National Biography*, <https://www.oxforddnb.com/view/10.1093/ref:odnb/9780198614128.001.0001/odnb-9780198614128-e-8916;jsessionid=B451D3C1F9E16AFEA1801E2406E07691> [accessed 2 November 2018]

Dutton, Marsha, 'Aelred of Rievaulx', *Oxford Bibliographies*, <https://www.oxfordbibliographies.com> [accessed 2 November 2018]

History of Rievaulx Abbey, <https://www.english-heritage.org.uk/visit/places/rievaulx-abbey/history-and-stories/history/> [accessed 1 July 2018]

The Oxford Dictionary of Saints, ed. by David Hugh Farmer, 5th rev. edn (Oxford: Oxford University Press, 2011), <https://www.oxfordreference.com/view/10.1093/acref/9780199596607.001.0001/acref-9780199596607> [accessed 1 July 2018]

CHRISTIANIA WHITEHEAD

The Production of Northern Saints' Lives at Holm Cultram Abbey in Cumbria[*]

Holm Cultram Cistercian Abbey was founded in 1150, close to Carlisle and the Solway, as a daughter house of Melrose Abbey (itself founded in 1136 as a daughter of Rievaulx in Yorkshire).[1] Both Melrose and Holm Cultram were founded under the supervision of King David I of Scotland, and Holm Cultram's foundation in particular seems to have been intended to buttress the Scottish occupation of northern Cumbria between 1141 and 1157.[2] It should be noted at the outset that in 1150 there was still nothing pre-determined about the national identity of Cumbria. Part of the Brittonic kingdom of Cumbria/ Strathclyde until the early eleventh century, it appears to have come under the control of Malcolm III, King of Scots, in the 1060s, before falling to William II of England in 1092.[3] The Anglo-Norman regime remained in power there during the first decades of the twelfth century, but lost its footing during the sixteen-year period in which David I extended his rule south. The region was finally brought back under English control in 1157 by Henry II, and that control was maintained in the face of occasional incursions up until the Treaty of York (1237), when Alexander II agreed to renounce in perpetuity Scottish claims to the counties of Northumberland, Cumberland, and Westmorland, and the national border was fixed between the Solway and the Tweed.[4]

---

[*] The administrative county of Cumbria was created in 1974, replacing the historic counties of Cumberland and Westmoreland. I use the modern term for ease of reference throughout this essay, while recognizing that the term had a different signification in the eleventh and twelfth centuries as specified in my opening paragraph.

[1] Melrose's other daughter houses were Newbattle (1140), Kinloss (1150), and Coupar Angus (1164). Rievaulx founded a daughter house north of the Solway, Dundrennan, in 1142.

[2] Stringer, 'Introduction', p. 14.

[3] Edmonds, 'Emergence and Transformation'; Stringer, 'Introduction', pp. 1–2.

[4] Stringer, 'Introduction', p. 2.

Christiania Whitehead (Christiania.whitehead@unil.ch) is an Honorary Professor of Middle English Literature at the University of Warwick and a Senior Research Fellow on the SNSF-funded project 'Region and Nation: Late Medieval Devotion to Northern English Saints' at the University of Lausanne, Switzerland.

Late Medieval Devotion to Saints from the North of England: New Directions, ed. by Christiania Whitehead, Hazel J. Hunter Blair, and Denis Renevey, MCS 48 (Turnhout: Brepols, 2022), pp. 53–74
BREPOLS ❧ PUBLISHERS   10.1484/M.MCS-EB.5.124344

Despite Holm Cultram's speedy appropriation to English soil, its cross-border affiliations remained vigorous and ongoing. Emilia Jamroziak writes that until the 1290s, the decade of the onset of extended Anglo-Scottish hostilities, the abbey probably regarded itself less as either English or Scottish, and more as a principally Cumbrian institution.[5] In addition to its filial relationship with Melrose further east, the abbey maintained strong economic and territorial contacts with Galloway, counting the lords of Annandale, Nithsdale, and Galloway among its patrons, and obtaining property in Dumfries, a saltwork and fishery north of the Solway, and, perhaps most importantly, a substantial grange at Kirkgunzeon in 1185.[6] These contacts offer a particular instance of a much more widespread regional tendency in which, through the late twelfth and thirteenth centuries, religious houses in northern England and southern Scotland continued to maintain institutional relationships, and manage properties and industries on both sides of the border.[7] The externally imposed political border clearly remained of much less day-to-day consequence than the cross-border networks created by the geographical expansion of the religious orders, in particular the Cistercians.

While Holm Cultram's principal economic affiliations seem to have been with Galloway, the abbey also cultivated strong contacts to the west. It maintained important trade links with the Isle of Man and Ireland, owning property to facilitate these links in Drogheda, and appears to have enjoyed benefactions from Anglo-Norman lords newly arrived in northern Ireland.[8] Strengthening these economic links by means of institutional ties, in 1193 it was granted a daughter house (Grey Abbey) in County Down by Affreca, the Manx wife of Sir John de Courcy who had spearheaded the Norman colonizing drive from Cumbria into Ulster.[9] This affinity between the de Courcys and the northern Cistercians was reinforced by the appointment of William de Courcy as abbot of Holm Cultram in 1214 (he was subsequently transferred to Melrose, then Rievaulx).[10]

It would be erroneous to overlook Holm Cultram's contacts with eastern England. As a large-scale wool producer it nurtured lucrative trade links with Flemish textile manufacturers, and owned premises in the port towns of Newcastle, Hartlepool, and Boston to facilitate the export of its wool to

---

5 Jamroziak, 'Holm Cultram Abbey', p. 28.

6 Stringer, 'Introduction', p. 15; *Register and Records*, ed. by Grainger and Collingwood, pp. 117–26.

7 Jamroziak, 'Holm Cultram Abbey', p. 36; Burton, 'Dioceses, Saints' Cults', pp. 189–93.

8 Stringer, *Reformed Church*, pp. 23–34. The lords in question were Hugh de Lacy, lord of Meath (1172–1186) and Richard de Clare, lord of Leinster (1171–1176).

9 Other Cumbrian monasteries were also granted daughter establishments in Ireland by the de Courcys during these decades; St Bees Priory was given Nendrum Abbey (1178) while Furness Abbey was granted Inch Abbey, County Down (1180). Duffy, 'First Ulster Plantation', pp. 1–27.

10 *Register and Records*, ed. by Grainger and Collingwood, pp. 131–36; Jamroziak, 'Holm Cultram Abbey', p. 32.

the ports of Flanders.[11] However, in general it would seem that the Pennines posed a stronger conceptual divide (in this case, between western and eastern England) than either the Anglo-Scottish border or the Irish Sea, and that the energies of this peripheral abbey were mainly directed to the north and west.

Keith Stringer, who has carried out some of the most extensive recent work on Holm Cultram from the perspectives of economic and regional history, defines the abbey as a 'transnational' institution, deeply engaged with northern England, eastern Scotland, Galloway, and Anglo-Norman Ireland. He also emphasizes its 'European' character: the product of a current that transmitted European architecture and intellectual and institutional structures along Cistercian pathways into northern Cumbria.[12] This essay will examine the abbey's character through a new, more textual lens. Focusing upon the surprisingly large number of saints' lives likely composed within the abbey or copied in its scriptorium in the late twelfth and thirteenth centuries, it will argue that there are also two distinctively 'Celtic' and south-west English angles to this story, demonstrating that Holm Cultram initially sought to connect itself to the early Irish 'mission' saints before making a surprise turn south-west toward the Celtic peripheries of England. These experimental turns north then south bear witness to the different cult milieux east and west of the Pennines. Throughout the high Middle Ages, north-eastern England was defined spiritually by the towering figure of St Cuthbert (634–687), associated with Lindisfarne and Farne, enshrined at Durham, and attended by a series of auxiliary Northumbrian saints and their relics (Oswald, Aidan, Boisil, Æthelwold, etc.). The North West however lacked any local saint of even vaguely comparable *potentia*. Consequently, the religious houses were forced to look *beyond* the immediate locality in their search for saintly inspiration, and the direction of their gaze and objects of their interest provide a new way of gauging their spiritual self-definition.

Looking North

Holm Cultram seems to have had an extensive library and active scriptorium, neither of which has received the attention it deserves. This library included late twelfth-century copies of Philippe de Thaon's Anglo-Norman *Bestiary* and *Computus*, possibly produced at the abbey;[13] satirical and rhetorical

---

11 Stringer, *Reformed Church*, p. 10.

12 Stringer, 'Introduction', p. 14; Burton, 'Dioceses, Saints' Cults', p. 194; Wilson, 'Cistercians as "Missionaries of Gothic"'. For European influences on northern material cultures of devotion, see further Julian Luxford's essay in this volume.

13 BL, MS Cotton Nero A.V (s.xii²ᐟ²). This manuscript and those in notes 14–18 contain the Holm Cultram *ex libris* inscription. *Medieval Libraries of Great Britain* database, <http://mlgb3.bodleian.ox.ac.uk/mlgb/?search_term=holm+cultram&page_size=500> [accessed 8 June 2020].

works by Horace, Persius, Geoffrey of Vinsauf, and John of Garland;[14] biblical homilies in Greek;[15] part of Aelred of Rievaulx's *De institutione inclusarum*, and numerous biblical commentaries and sermons.[16] Mary Curruthers has drawn scholarly attention to Huntington Library, MS HM 19915 (s.xii$^{2/2}$), a copy of Augustine's *Enchiridion* produced at the abbey, which includes a series of ingenious, high-quality marginal images apparently intended to serve as mnemonic cues.[17] Ovid's *Remedia amoria* and a fragment of Thomas's Anglo-Norman *Tristan et Iseult*, recycled to form the flyleaves of the abbey's late thirteenth-century cartulary, afford us tantalizing glimpses of more secular and romantic enthusiasms amongst the monks, the second, tellingly, an enthusiasm with a distinctively Irish strain to it.[18]

The picture which emerges from these library survivals — of a sophisticated, classically informed, literary reading community, adept in several languages — belies the marginality we may tend to impose erroneously and retrospectively upon a religious community so far north and west. It also helps to form an intellectual context for the remarkable number of saints' lives gathered and possibly also produced within the abbey. We will begin with the shadowy trio that look north. There is an infuriatingly inconclusive thread of references suggesting that the first abbot of Holm Cultram, Everard (1150–1192), may have authored the Lives of Cumméne and Adomnán, seventh-century abbots of Iona, and a Life of Waltheof, abbot of Melrose (1148–1159), all now lost. References to Everard's Lives of Cumméne and Adomnán occur in two seventeenth-century historical works but can be traced no earlier.[19] Nonetheless, I take seriously Keith Stringer's judgement that it is 'just possible' they may be correct.[20] Such hagiographies would certainly correlate with the interest in Ionan sanctity discernible in north-east England in the late twelfth century, when Adomnán's Life of Columba was copied into a manuscript of northern hagiographies at Durham Benedictine Priory.[21] If Everard *did* write these two Lives as the founding abbot of a new Cistercian foundation in Cumbria, it would seem to suggest that he was proposing a saintly model and monastic anchor for his new community in the early Irish spiritual traditions of Iona.

We have slightly stronger evidence for Everard's composition of some sort of Life of Waltheof, first abbot of Melrose Cistercian Abbey (d. 1159).

---

14 Cambridge, Trinity College, MS R.3.29 (s.xiii).

15 BL, MS Additional 17511 (s.xiii).

16 Oxford, Bodl. Lib., MS Hatton 101 (s.xiii/xiv).

17 Carruthers, *Book of Memory*, pp. 309–14. I am grateful to Julian Luxford for drawing my attention to these images and Carruthers's interpretation of them.

18 Cambridge, Trinity College, MS R.3.29; Benskin, Hunt and Short, 'Un nouveau fragment'.

19 Dempster, *Historia ecclesiastica*, ed. by Irving, V.479, p. 260; Denton, *Accompt*, ed. by Ferguson, p. 93; Sharpe, *Handlist of Latin Writers*, p. 114.

20 Stringer, 'Introduction', p. 16.

21 BL, MS Additional 35110, fols 96^v–143^r; Whitehead, 'Durham Manuscript Compilations'. See further, a reference to a chapel of St Columba on Lindisfarne in Geoffrey of Durham's *Vita sancti Bartholomaei*, ed. by Arnold, p. 322.

Everard and Waltheof were close friends, beginning their monastic careers as Augustinian canons at Kirkham and converting jointly to the Cistercian habit. When Waltheof was appointed abbot of Melrose in 1148, Everard joined him there as his chaplain and confessor up until his own appointment as the abbot of Holm Cultram in 1150.[22] Jocelin of Furness, Waltheof's early thirteenth-century Cistercian hagiographer, cites Everard as his major source of information about Waltheof.[23] Helen Birkett considers this indicative of some kind of written account by Everard, with a copy held at Furness, while Robert Bartlett thinks Jocelin may just have been drawing on oral testimony.[24] Although it seems impossible, given the ambiguity of Jocelin's references, to be quite certain whether Everard ever put pen to parchment to celebrate his saintly friend, nonetheless, we should not overlook the fact that Jocelin uses his *Vita Waldevi* to eulogize Everard in terms that certainly leave room for hagiographical scholarship: 'cui praefuit interius ad magnae religionis culmen erexit, & exterius praediis & possessionibus ditatam in altum pervexit' (he brought [the house] to a peak of spiritual perfection and material wealth).[25]

Working from admittedly scanty and unsatisfactory evidence, it would seem that three saints' lives *may* have been produced at Holm Cultram in the second half of the twelfth century which turn their gaze north toward the early Irish monasticism of Iona and Northumbrian-inflected monasticism of Melrose. These putative lives should be considered in relation to other northern Cistercian productions demonstrating similar interests: Jocelin's hagiographies of Waltheof, Kentigern, and Patrick, generated from Furness Abbey in southern Cumbria during the same decades, and Aelred of Rievaulx's Life of Ninian of Whithorn in Galloway, compiled in 1164. It also seems relevant to note that Aelred's Life of Ninian was commissioned by Bishop Christian of Whithorn, a close friend of Abbot Everard, who spent much of his episcopal career filling in as Bishop of Carlisle during a long vacancy in that see, before retiring to Holm Cultram where he was finally buried in 1196.[26] Ecclesial links if not textual evidence draw Ninian into the orbit of Holm Cultram. Here then, in the second half of the twelfth century, we see a *spread* of Cistercian hagiographers from Cumbria and Yorkshire opting to record the lives of the fifth- and sixth-century Irish and Brittonic evangelists whose

---

22 Birkett, *Saints' Lives*, p. 132.
23 Jocelin's *Vita Waldevi* explicitly represents as Waltheof the spiritual heir of St Cuthbert (Cuthbert initially entered the monastic life at Old Melrose) — one small way in which the north-western Cistercian monasteries *may* have associated themselves with the sanctity of north-east England. But of course, we have no idea whether Everard would have pursued this parallel which seems mainly to have come to the fore after the discovery of Waltheof's incorruption in 1206. Birkett, *Saints' Lives*, pp. 209–10.
24 Birkett, *Saints' Lives*, pp. 132–34; Bartlett, 'Cults of Irish, Scottish and Welsh Saints', p. 83 n. 49.
25 Jocelin of Furness, *Vita Waldevi*, 4.49, p. 261B.
26 Jamroziak, 'Holm Cultram Abbey', pp. 29–31.

mission fields they were now busily populating with monastic colonies. Current scholarship on the principal formative influences underpinning early Cistercian spirituality tends to light on the example of the desert fathers.[27] However this flurry of northern hagiographical writing suggests a parallel (potentially even more pressing) interest in local forms of early mission sanctity, arising from their ability to serve as helpful precedents and templates for the northern Cistercian expansion into Cumbria, Galloway, and northern Ireland. It seems tenable, then, to propose that these lives may signify an attempt to present the Cistercian movement in the North West as a *renewal* of those early acts of evangelism, enacted on pristine religious soil. If so, what changed with regard to the saintly exemplars on offer in the early decades of the thirteenth century?

Looking South: The Insular *vitae* of Faustina B.IV and Claudius A.V

We will now turn to three extant collections of saints' lives held in Holm Cultram's medieval library and almost certainly produced in its scriptorium between 1175 and 1225. The first can be dealt with relatively briefly. Cambridge, MA, Harvard College, MS Lat. 27 (s.xii), bearing the Holm Cultram *ex libris* inscription, is a *vitae sanctorum* containing the lives of Anselm of Bec, and the continental Cluniac saints, Maiolo, Odilo, and Odo, who spearheaded Benedictine reforms in the late tenth and eleventh centuries. Holm Cultram's interest in this gathering of saints makes perfect sense given that Robert de Molesme, the founder of the Cistercian order, commenced his spiritual career as a Cluniac monk. The other two collections, British Library, MS Cotton Faustina B.IV and British Library, MS Cotton Claudius A.V, merit closer investigation. Both are now composite manuscripts formed from three or four sections bound together by Sir Robert Cotton; however, in both cases, we shall just be concerned with a single relevant section. Fols 3–179 of Faustina B.IV, copied in a neat Gothic textura bookhand, contain William of St Alban's double Lives of Alban and Amphibalus, John of Ford's Life of Wulfric of Haselbury, the anonymous Life of Bega of Copeland, Faricius's Life of Aldhelm, and Folcard's Life and William Ketell's Miracles of John of Beverley.[28] Fols 135–99 of Claudius A.V, copied in an almost identical hand,

---

27 Jamroziak, *Cistercian Order*, pp. 18–19; Bruun, 'Cistercian Rethinking'.

28 This gathering is now bound with a Life of Alexis (s.xii), originating from Byland Abbey, Alcuin's epistolae (s.xv), a record of an inquest at Bury St. Edminds (s.xiv), letters and tracts by Stephen of Tournai and others, and some sermons of Bernard of Clairvaux (s.xii). British Library Manuscript Catalogue online description available at: <https://searcharchives.bl.uk/primo_library/libweb/action/display. do;jsessionid=E9BC40781B5CF4BEB779718 E81CA7DCF?tabs=details Tab&ct=displ ay&fn=search&doc=IAMS040-001103882&indx=2&recIds=IAMS040-001103882&rec

contain the Life of Erkenwald, the anonymous Life and Miracles of Wenefred of Wales, the 'later' Latin Life of Neot, and William of Malmesbury's Life of Wulfstan.[29] Frustratingly, this manuscript does not include a Holm Cultram *ex libris* (possibly because the section in question was taken from the centre of another manuscript), nonetheless, Neil Ker, and Michael Winterbottom and Rodney Thomson, the editors of the Life of Wulfstan from Claudius A.V, concur that the script, decoration, and punctuation of the section point to the Cistercian scriptorium of Holm Cultram where it was certainly housed by the fourteenth century.[30]

It may be possible to take Ker's, and Winterbottom's and Thomson's observations a step further. Reviewing the two manuscripts side by side, one is immediately struck by the degree of similarity between the two sections.[31] Both comprise a page size of *c.* 250 × 170 mm, with a text space of *c.* 215 × 145 mm divided into two ruled columns of identical dimensions, and alternate red and green illuminated capitals with doubled verticals (see Figs 2.1 and 2.2).

A light hand makes occasional notes and draws light crosses in the margins of both manuscripts. Both sections contain repetitions of chapter rubrics in a tiny hand at the base of the bottom margin to assist collation (although the tiny hand is not the same in the two manuscripts).[32] The Gothic textura bookhands of the two sections look superficially identical, but closer inspection reveals that they are the work of different scribes. Unfortunately, further physical evidence in the form of uniform catchwords, foliation markings, etc., is wanting. Did these two sections once piece together to form two parts of a larger, single, insular saints' legendary? Without stronger codicological

---

Idxs=1&elementId=1&renderMode=poppedOut&displayMode=full&frbrVersion=&frbg=&&dsc
nt=0&scp.scps=scope%3A%28BL%29&mode=Basic&vid=IAMS_
VU2&srt=rank&tab=local&vl(freeTexto)=Cotton %20Faustina%20B.%20
4&dum=true&dstmp=1649856558556 [accessed 13 April 2022].

29 British Library Manuscript Catalogue online description available at <https://searcharchives.
bl.uk/primo_library/libweb/action/dlDisplay.do?docId=IAMS040-001102440&vid=IAMS_
VU2&indx=1&dym=false&dscnt=1&onCampus=false&group=ALL&institution=BL&ct=se
arch&vl(freeTexto)=040-001102440&submit=search> [accessed 13 April 2022]. This gathering
is preceded by a copy of the Peterborough Chronicle (s.xiv), and the first recension of William
of Malmesbury's *Gesta pontificum* (s.xii) from the Benedictine priory of Belvoir (Lincs.).
William of Malmesbury's Saints' Lives, ed. by Winterbottom and Thomson, p. 3.

30 Ker, *Medieval Libraries*, p. 102; *William of Malmesbury's Saints' Lives*, ed. by Winterbottom
and Thomson, pp. xxv, 3; Winterbottom, 'Faricius of Arezzo's Life of St Aldhelm', pp. 109–11;
Medieval Libraries database: <http://mlgb3.bodleian.ox.ac.uk/mlgb/book/3236/?search_
term=holm%20cultram&page_size=500>: 'evidence from the style of script or illumination'.

31 *Medieval Libraries* database: <http://mlgb3.bodleian.ox.ac.uk/mlgb/book/3236/?search_
term=holm%20cultram&page_size=500>: 'script and decoration very like Faustina B.IV, fols 3–179'.

32 Cambridge, Camb. Uni. Lib., MS Addit. 3037, a contemporary Cistercian manuscript
of possible Suffolk provenance, containing the lives of William of Norwich, Wulfric of
Haselbury, and Godric of Finchale, includes similar instructions regarding rubrication at the
base of many of its folios. Ringrose, *Summary Catalogue*, pp. 50–51. See n. 37 below.

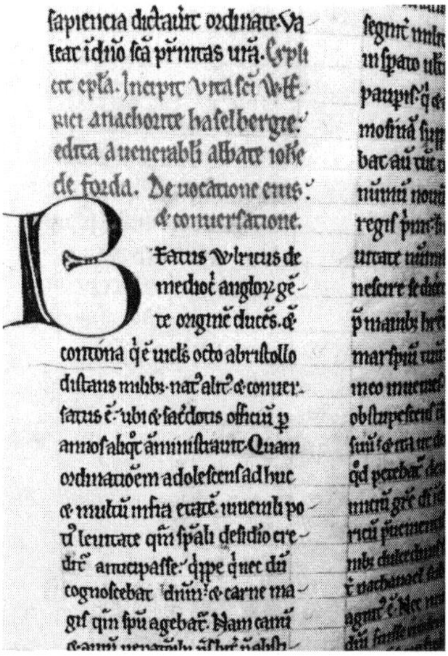

FIGURE 2.1. London, BL, MS Cotton Faustina B.IV, fol. 65v 'Incipit vita Wulfrici'. Reproduced by permission of the British Library Board.

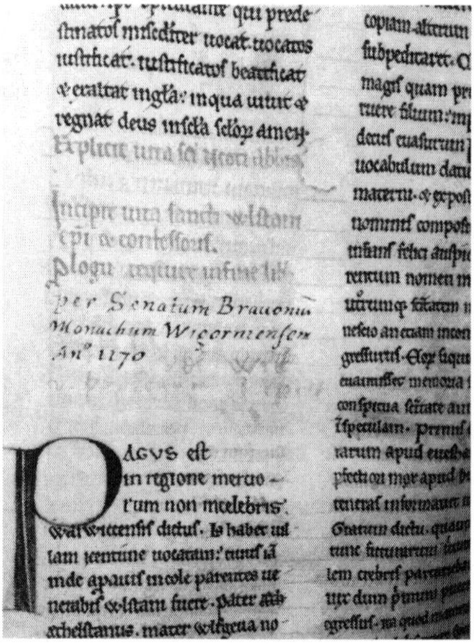

FIGURE 2.2. London, BL, MS Cotton Claudius A.V, fol. 160v 'Incipit vita Wulfstani'. Reproduced by permission of the British Library Board.

evidence it is impossible to state that with certainty. What we *can* conclude is that these two runs of saints' lives were produced at Holm Cultram during the same decades, and that, together, they would appear to represent parallel small-scale gestures toward a native saints' legendary.

In the present state of scholarship, the earliest Latin legendaries organized around the principle of nationality or insularity, containing solely English or British saints, are generally understood to derive from the fourteenth century. British Library, MS Lansdowne 436, a legendary of forty-three English saints, was compiled *c.* 1300 in Hampshire, while British Library, MS Cotton Tiberius E.1, the earliest surviving copy of John of Tynemouth's *Sanctilogium Angliae, Walliae, Scotiae et Hiberniae*, a legendary of 156 English, Welsh, Scottish, and Irish saints, dates from the third quarter of the fourteenth century and is closely associated with St Albans Abbey.[33] While the two Holm Cultram gatherings, totalling ten native saints, are on nothing like this scale, I would argue that they do force a reconsideration of the field, driving the date at which saints were selected upon insular or national principles back by almost one hundred years, and shifting the sphere of energy associated with these selections to the north-west rim of the country.[34] The second half of this essay

33 See further James G. Clark's essay in this volume, pp. 374–75.

34 It is necessary to stress that these gatherings, as also Lansdowne 436 and Tiberius E.1,

Principles of Saintly Selection

Returning to the saints' lives in the two relevant manuscript sections — William of St Albans' Lives of Alban and Amphibalus, John of Ford's Life of Wulfric of Haselbury, the Life and Miracles of Bega of Copeland, Faricius's Life of Aldhelm, Folcard's Life and Ketell's Miracles of John of Beverley, the Life of Erkenwald, the anonymous Life and Miracles of Wenefred of Wales, the 'later' Latin Life of Neot, and William of Malmesbury's Life of Wulfstan — some potential points of commonality begin to emerge. First, it is possible to detect an interest in insular hermit saints. Neot and Wulfric were hermits in ninth-century Cornwall and twelfth-century Devon respectively, while Bega, a mythical ninth-century Irish princess fleeing an unwanted marriage, made landfall at Copeland in Cumbria where she lived for some time as a hermit before journeying east to become abbess of Hartlepool.[35] It is well known that the Cistercian order showed a significant interest in the eremitic vocation deriving from their commitment to 'desert' monasticism. Indeed Wulfric's biographer, John (c. 1150–1214), was a monk at Ford Cistercian abbey, not far from Haselbury, who later became its abbot. Two other manuscripts of John's Life of Wulfric juxtapose it with the Life of Godric of Finchale (d. 1170), a twelfth-century hermit living north of Durham.[36] Not dissimilar to Wulfric, who posthumously became the object of a tussle between the Cistercians and Benedictines, the Cistercian order initially seems to have been keen to control Godric's cult (although it quickly lost ground to the Durham Benedictines), implying that manuscripts which pair the two hermits may well constitute attempts to make Cistercian claims on their sanctity.[37] Given these codicological contexts, we should perhaps be surprised to find Wulfric travelling *without* his eremitic partner, Godric, in Faustina B.IV. However, this does add ballast to my supposition (developed further below) that north-eastern saints associated with the Durham Cuthbertine *familia* were deliberately de-selected from these Holm Cultram manuscripts.

---

operate very differently from large-scale cathedral *vitae sanctorum* of the twelfth and thirteenth centuries, such as Lincoln Cathedral, MS 149 (s.xii^2), MS 150 (s.xii$^{med.}$), and Gloucester Cathedral, MS 1 (s.xiii). These legendaries indeed include many insular saints, but they are intermingled with universal saints, and the principle of ordering is calendrical.

35 *Vita S Bege*, ed. by Wilson.

36 Cambridge, Camb. Uni. Lib., MS Additional 3037 (s.xii$^{4/4}$); BL, MS Harley 322 (s.xiii$^{3/4}$). John of Ford, *Wulfric*, ed. by Bell, pp. lxxviii–lxxx.

37 Licence, 'The Benedictines, the Cistercians'.

Second, it is possible to identify a focus on the west and south-west of England, and an engagement with Cistercian monasteries and networks located on that side of the country. We have already commented upon the south-west provenances of Neot and Wulfric, and noted John of Ford's association with Ford Cistercian Abbey in Dorset. In addition, the anonymous Life of Wenefred, offering a specifically *Welsh* construction of the saint, was probably written by a monk from Basingwerk Cistercian Abbey near Holywell in North Wales.[38] Aldhelm's cult was centred on Malmesbury in Wiltshire and Sherborne in Dorset, while Wulfstan was venerated at his episcopal see at Worcester. William's miracles of Alban feature a number of stories located on the western side of the country, from Chester, to stories related to crossing the Irish Sea, to Bristol, Glastonbury, and Cornwall, despite the fact that St Alban's Abbey held no property in the west.[39]

Third, several of these Lives take pains to emphasize the more 'Celtic' qualities of the saints that they celebrate. The anonymous 'later' Latin Life of Neot locates him solely in the south-west, showing a detailed knowledge of the legends and sites of that area, and makes no mention of the translation of his relics to Huntingdonshire in the late tenth century.[40] Mary Richards opines that its author must have been based in Exeter where Neot was also venerated. Borrowing from the Cornish saints' lives, this 'later' Life celebrates the Celtic elements in Neot's wonderworking, including the magical replenishment of food, miraculous opening of locked doors, and taming of wild animals. Very similar motifs dominate the early part of the Life of Bega, which probably originated at St Bees Priory, a few miles south-west of Holm Cultram in northern Cumbria.[41] Bega escapes from her palace in Ireland with the aid of a magic bracelet which miraculously opens locked doors, sails across the Irish Sea, and then lives as a forest hermit and healer in Copeland, taming the wild animals in her vicinity.[42] As we have seen, the anonymous version of the Life of Wenefred in Claudius A.V furnishes us with a Welsh version of the saint, showing a knowledge of local place names and oral traditions, and confining her wonderworking to Holywell in Flintshire. As with Neot, no mention is made of the controversial translation of her relics to Shrewsbury

---

38 Winward, 'Lives of St Wenefred', pp. 90, 95, 98–100; 'The Life of St Winifred', ed. and trans. by Gregory.

39 I am grateful to James G. Clark for this information. Clark suggests that these miracle locations may reflect a conscious effort on the part of the abbey to promote St Alban *beyond* their own domain.

40 Richards, 'Medieval Hagiography', p. 273. The 'earlier' Latin life, extant in four manuscripts, and probably written by a monk from St Neot's priory, Huntingdonshire, celebrates the Priory's possession of Neot's relics and the miracles attributed to them there. An eleventh-century Old English homily about Neot was composed by a monk from Croyland, Lincs., which also seems to have held his relics at various points.

41 St Bees, a Benedictine daughter house of St Mary's Abbey, York, held the wonderworking bracelet of Bega, the focus of her north-western cult. Whitehead, 'Bega's Bracelet'.

42 *Vita S Bege*, ed. by Wilson, pp. 503–04.

Benedictine Abbey in 1138, and her subsequent construction there as an exemplary English abbess.[43]

Fourth, turning again to these western saints, the Lives of Bega and Wulfric are both notable for their extensive resort to images and analogies drawn from the Song of Songs. Bega's bracelet is construed as a spiritual adornment readying her for her marriage to Christ, while her life of contemplation at Copeland grants her sensory access to Christ's sweetness: 'Ibi ergo dilectus suus sibi, et ad eam conversacio eius inter ubera sua commorantis, currensque in odore unguentorum eius, ab eo post eum tracta, et in amore eius liquefacta' (For there was her beloved, his conversation with her abiding between her breasts; and running in the odour of his ointments, she is drawn by him after him, melted in his love).[44] Wulfric's cell is similarly interpreted as the nuptial bedchamber of the bride and bridegroom, a place of 'sacra et secreta voluptas' (sacred and secret rapture), from which he removes himself only reluctantly to offer spiritual counsel to others.[45] Keeping a vigil of love there through the night, he is party to Christ's amorous words to his soul, confirming: 'Dilectus meus mihi et ego illi' (My beloved is mine and I am his).[46] The interpretation of the nuptial dialogue of the Song of Songs as an allegory for contemplative rapture was a hallmark of Cistercian writing throughout the twelfth century.[47] Indeed, John of Ford made a significant contribution to this exegetical focus, composing 120 sermons on the Song of Songs intended to complete the famous sermon series initiated by Bernard of Clairvaux and continued by Gilbert of Hoyland. While the Life of Bega is more likely to have originated from St Bees Benedictine Priory, its inclusion of images from the Song of Songs could suggest, *either*, that it contains Cistercian interpolations potentially added when it was copied into Faustina B.IV, *or*, that its author was influenced by the contemplative interests of the neighbouring Cistercian houses.

Fifth, offsetting the eremitic and Celtic focus, there is clearly also a more institutional and episcopal pre-Conquest flavour to these collections. John of Beverley, Erkenwald of London, Wulfstan of Worcester and Aldhelm of Malmesbury were all venerated as model bishops who were simultaneously associated with seminal pre-Conquest monastic foundations, either as their founders or, in Aldhelm's case, as their first abbot. St Alban was of course Britain's proto-martyr, and a premier object of English devotion during the

---

43 Wenefred is rendered as an English saint in the *Vita* and *translatio* composed by Prior Robert of Shrewsbury in 1138, extant in three manuscripts. Winward suggests a tentative date for the anonymous, Basingwerk *Vita* in the second half of the twelfth century: Winward, 'Lives of St Wenefred', p. 128. Like Wulfric, Wenefred's cult was an object of contention between the Basingwerk Cistercians, and the English Benedictines of Shrewsbury and Chester Abbeys.

44 *Vita S Bege*, ed. by Wilson, p. 503; *Life and Miracles*, trans. by Tomlinson, p. 12. See further, *Vita S Bege*, ed. by Wilson, p. 506; *Life and Miracles*, trans. by Tomlinson, p. 16.

45 John of Ford, *Wulfric*, ed. by Bell, chaps 7–8, pp. 20–21.

46 John of Ford, *Wulfric*, ed. by Bell, chap. 31, p. 48. Song of Songs 2. 16.

47 Aelred of Rievaulx draws upon the same bank of imagery to describe Ninian's deathbed in his *Vita S Niniani*.

high Middle Ages. These Cistercian choices, generated we should recall from an abbey with strong Anglo-Norman affiliations, suggest a desire to tie their monasticism to mainstream icons of pre-Conquest spiritual authority.

The degree of deliberation underpinning these choices is supported by a couple of further realizations. First, where more than one version of a Life is available, the compilers appear to have opted for the version designed to make sense to audiences *beyond* the immediate sphere of the saint's shrine and cult. Faricius's Life of Aldhelm, composed at Malmesbury, 1093–1099, suppresses almost all local references to the abbey and the miracles performed there, seeming to have envisaged a more far-flung readership.[48] Similarly, the Lives of Wenefred and Neot selected for inclusion are *not* the ones which celebrate the relic holdings of a particular house and work to promote pilgrimage to that site. Instead, they offer a less focused, more 'Celticized' reading. Second, it is imperative to note that an appreciable proportion of the insular saints' lives in Faustina B.IV and Claudius A.V represent either the only copy or the earliest extant copy of these lives that we retain. To elaborate: Faustina B.IV contains the only extant copy of the Life of Bega, while its copy of William of St Albans' Lives of Alban and Amphibalus uniquely includes the invention and miracles of Amphibalus and the only early extant version of the miracles of Alban.[49] Its full-length copies of Folcard's Life and Ketell's Miracles of John of Beverley are significantly earlier than any other manuscript witness,[50] while its copy of Faricius's Life of Aldhem represents a distinct, shortened version, suppressing local references. In Claudius A.V, the anonymous Life of Wenefred, the anonymous 'later' life of Neot,[51] and William of Malmesbury's Life of Wulfstan,[52] all represent the sole surviving copies of these texts. The hagiographical compilers of Holm Cultram seem to have cast their nets very widely indeed and gone to considerable trouble convening the exemplars that lie behind these copies. It seems especially likely that some kind of textual contact was established with Exeter (Neot), Malmesbury (Wulfstan and Aldhelm), Basingwerk (Wenefred) and St Bees. Again, this all combines to strengthen the impression of a purposefully selected collection of Lives.

---

48 Faricius of Arezzo, 'An Edition of Faricius, *Vita S Aldhelmi*', ed. by Winterbottom, p. 94; Winterbottom, 'Faricius of Arezzo's Life', p. 123.

49 Gordon-Taylor, 'Hagiography of St Alban', p. 28. William's Life of Alban, *without* these additions, is extant in two other slightly earlier twelfth-century manuscripts. A later, variant copy of Alban's miracles is extant in BL, MS Cotton Claudius E.IV (pt 1), (after 1396); I am grateful to James G. Clark for this information in a private correspondence.

50 Folcard's Life is also extant in the fourteenth-century Beverley Cartulary and in two sixteenth/seventeenth-century manuscripts. Wilson, *Life and After-Life*, p. 60.

51 The 'later' life of Neot also exists in a versified version in Oxford, Magdalen College, MS 53 (s.xiv). Richards, 'Medieval Hagiography', p. 272.

52 William's Life of Wulfstan also exists in a late twelfth-century abridgement, surviving in two copies from Worcester and Reading. *William of Malmesbury's Saints' Lives*, ed. by Winterbottom and Thomson, p. xxv.

SAINTS' LIVES AT HOLM CULTRAM ABBEY   65

Before proceeding further, a brief digression is in order. Cambridge, Corpus Christi College, MS 161 (s.xii$^{3/4}$–s.xiii$^{1/4}$), possibly assembled at the Cluniac monastery at Faversham in Kent, contains sixteen English and continental saints' lives. Seven of these lives — an abridged version of Faricius's Aldhelm, Erkenwald, Neot (an abridgement of the 'early' Life), a heavily abridged adaptation of Folcard's John of Beverley for liturgical use, Odilo, Maiolo, and Odo — correspond to lives in the three collections associated with Holm Cultram.[53] These two monasteries could not be further apart from one another geographically, and it seems imprudent to hypothesize any form of textual contact or influence, nonetheless, the *differences* between the two sets of saints' lives, compiled at roughly the same time in Cluniac and Cistercian institutions at opposite corners of the country, generate food for thought. The Cluniac collection demonstrates the strong pre-Conquest institutional adherence we noted earlier, celebrating the model bishops Aldhelm, Erkenwald, and John of Beverley, strengthened in this instance by the additional inclusion of Dunstan, Swithun, and Ithamar. It adds a regal interest in the form of Aelred's and Osbert's Lives of Edward the Confessor, and includes additional Cluniac and continental saints: Hugh, Martial, and Nicholas. The Holm Cultram manuscripts manifest no commitment to regal saints (does this arise from the shifting allegiances of northern Cumbria?).[54] Instead, tellingly, they innovate the lives of Wenefred, Bega, and Wulfric, significantly *feminizing* the insular canon and adding a strong western and eremitic focus. We have already defined these interests as strikingly Cistercian ones, but this is a new angle from which to generate that realization. Indeed, one might argue on the basis of the difference between these collections, that it is the inclusion of these three in the Holm Cultram manuscripts that effectively refashions a late twelfth-century Cluniac collection of institutional insular saints as a more contemplative *Cistercian* one.

Returning to Faustina B.IV and Claudius A.V, it is also necessary to consider their omissions. Despite Holm Cultram's northern provenance, the gaze east across the Pennines does not play a strong role in their collections; the gaze south and west is much more pervasive. To excavate this further,

---

53 To place these parallels in context: one other full-length thirteenth-century copy of Faricius's Life of Aldhelm is known (Gloucester Cathedral, MS 1, fols 182^r–192^r); CCC, MS 161 comprises the only other extant twelfth/thirteenth-century copy of the Life of Erkenwald; the full-length 'early' Latin life of Neot survives in three further late eleventh- and twelfth-century manuscripts, and the same Folcardian abridgement is also extant in BL, MS Cotton Tiberius D.III (s.xii): Wilson, *Life and After-Life*, pp. 13–14, 64. The lives of the three Cluniac abbots are also extant in one other manuscript of medieval English provenance: Oxford, Bodl. Lib., MS Rawlinson A.416 (s.xii$^{mid.}$), and are further attested in the early thirteenth-century library catalogue of the Augustinian canons of Bridlington Priory (A 4.47: 'vita iiii abbatum de Cluniaco'), while Peter Damien's Life of Odilo receives further attestations in two fourteenth-century English library catalogues: *Medieval Libraries* database [accessed 17 June 2020].

54 See pp. 68–69, detailing further Scottish incursions in the early thirteenth century.

such attention as there is to the east focuses almost entirely on Yorkshire. John of Beverley's cult is centred in the East Riding. Bega becomes abbess of Hartlepool, but her allegiances are all further south. She forms a close friendship with Hilda of Whitby and experiences a vision of her death from Whitby's daughter house in Hackness. Later, several centuries after her own death, her bones are transferred to Whitby. Bega's cult was clearly celebrated by the Benedictines at both Whitby and St Mary's Abbey, York, in addition to St Bee's, Copeland (a dependency of St Mary's), during the Middle Ages,[55] and there is some evidence that her veneration also reached one of St Mary's southern dependencies, Rumburgh Priory in Suffolk.[56] Given John of Beverley's early links with Whitby (he reputedly studied there under Hilda's headship),[57] it may well be that Holm Cultram's gaze east is principally focused on the cults associated with Whitby Abbey and St Mary's.[58] This, in turn, might be explained by its proximity to St Bees Priory, and by evidence suggesting some degree of textual and devotional collaboration between the Cistercians at Holm Cultram and their Benedictine neighbours.[59]

The hagiographical compilers of Holm Cultram show some awareness of Yorkshire devotional cultures. However, they remain obstinately silent about the cluster of Northumbrian cults, centred upon Cuthbert, celebrated at Durham Cathedral some seventy miles north.[60] It seems impossible that they should have been unaware of this influential cluster, ticking so many of the

---

55 For details about Bega's cult at Whitby, see Carter, 'The Whitby Missal'; I am grateful to Dr Carter for sharing this unpublished work with me. A fifteenth-century Book of Hours and Psalter belonging to St Mary's, York, include Bega in their calendars. The Book of Hours also includes a hymn that would have been sung on her feast day, 7 November. Todd, 'St Bega: Cult, Fact and Legend', p. 24.

56 See Heale, 'Rumburgh Priory'. An image of Bega, 'money box of St Bega the Virgin', and a book of hymns and prayers to St Bega are recorded in fifteenth-century inventories of the Priory. I am grateful to Julian Luxford for alerting me to this reference.

57 Bede, *Historia ecclesiastica*, ed. and trans. by Colgrave and Mynors, IV. 23.

58 It should also be noted that Holm Cultram acquired a 'hermitage of St Hilda' at Islekirk in 1215: *Register and Records*, ed. by Grainger and Collingwood, pp. 126–27. Did this strengthen their interest in Whitby and its saints? See further, Christiane Kroebel's essay in this volume, pp. 332–33.

59 When Bega's wonderworking bracelet is stolen in a Scottish raid in 1216, the Chronicle of St Mary's Abbey, York, records that it was a *conversus* from Holm Cultram who killed the soldiers involved and retrieved the bracelet: *Chronicle*, ed. by Craster and Thornton, p. 76. If written at St Bees, the *Vita Bege* was presumably loaned temporarily to Holm Cultram to be copied into Faustina B.IV.

60 The final miracle in the *Miracula Bege* does include St Oswine of Tynemouth in a cameo role: a French pilgrim seeking healing for his two disabled boys is sent northwards by Thomas of Canterbury. Arriving at Tynemouth he experiences a further vision in which Oswine directs him west to Bega's shrine at St Bees. Here, Oswine's inclusion is purely intended to demonstrate the inferiority of his thaumaturgical force compared to Bega: the Cumbrian west wins out over the Northumbrian east. It should also be noted that Oswine was *not* one of Cuthbert's satellites controlled by Durham, but was, rather singularly, under the control of St Albans Abbey. (See further, James G. Clark's essay in this volume).

boxes of pre-Conquest episcopal, monastic, and eremitic spiritual authority that they clearly cherished. Nonetheless, they chose not to incorporate any into their own collections, and we can only speculate that this may either have followed from the topographical barrier posed by the northern Pennines, the fact that the Cumbrian abbeys looked principally toward their mother and grandmother institutions in Yorkshire or, conceivably, from some level of rivalry between the Yorkshire cults, whom they acknowledged, and Durham. Certainly, at an episcopal level, Durham and York remained at loggerheads with one another for much of the twelfth and early thirteenth centuries,[61] and Yorkshire saints' lives never figure in the institutional compilations generated by the Durham scriptorium.[62]

Not only do the collections in Faustina B.IV and Claudius A.V eschew any reference to the Northumbrian pre-Conquest saints; they also veer away from that elusive gaze north toward the saints of Iona, Whithorn, Glasgow, and Melrose that we noted in the second half of the twelfth century during Everard's abbacy. Why were the saints of Scotland exchanged for a largely south-western gaze directed towards North Wales, Malmesbury, and Devon, at some point between the 1180s, and the 1220s? The final section of this essay will propose some speculative answers to this question.

Bega and the Man from Galloway

Although manuscript catalogues tend to place Faustina B.IV within a broad date range between 1175 and 1225, I will suggest that it was compiled close to the end of this date spectrum, and that this may provide some clues about Faustina's (and Claudius's) curious turn south-west. As noted in the introduction to this essay, the religious houses of North Cumbria and Galloway enjoyed extremely close links throughout the twelfth century. Both Holm Cultram and St Bees Priory cultivated benefactors, and administered granges and industries north of the Solway,[63] and we will recall that Bishop Christian of Whithorn in Galloway retired to Holm Cultram and was eventually buried there. However, the only reference to Galloway in the entire collection, in the first miracle of Bega, transpires to be an unexpectedly negative one. We are told that a layabout from Galloway, designated a 'man of the devil', derides the reputed power of the saint, and attempts to steal horses from her priory land, but is rewarded by an arrow up his backside. After this, declares Bega's hagiographer, the people of Galloway no longer attempt any liberties with the saint.[64] What accounts for this sudden downturn in sentiment?

---

61 Burton, 'Dioceses, Saints' Cults', pp. 180–81; Stringer, *Reformed Church*, p. 21.

62 Whitehead, 'Durham Manuscript Compilations'.

63 Stringer, *Reformed Church*, p. 22.

64 *Vita S Bege*, ed. by Wilson, pp. 509–10. The cultural stereotype of the the 'barbarous' Gallowegian appears periodically through the Middle Ages in northern English hagiography

In 1216, during the rebellion against King John, Alexander II of Scotland (leading Scottish and Gallowegian troops) took advantage of the situation to invade Cumbria and occupy Carlisle. In the course of this push south, both Holm Cultram and St Bees Priory were plundered. More traumatic still, according to the Chronicle of St Mary's, York, St Bees' most treasured possession, Bega's bracelet, was temporarily taken captive at Eaglesfield (suggesting that it must have been carried into battle against the Scots), but heroically retrieved by a *conversus* (lay brother) from Holm Cultram who killed the Scottish soldiers.[65] This is a telling statement about the level of local Cistercian involvement in Bega's cult by the early thirteenth century, all the more so since it comes from a Benedictine chronicle. Both Holm Cultram and St Bees must have struggled to reorient their identity in the aftermath of these attacks. Institutional and economic allegiances across the border had suddenly been jeopardized, and previous patrons had turned into political foes. To make matters more complex still, Melrose Abbey, Holm Cultram's mother house in Roxburghshire, was patronized by Alexander II and cultivated close relations to the Scottish crown. The Chronicle of Melrose attempts to negotiate this delicate situation in its entry for 1216 by distancing Alexander from the violations and blaming them instead on barbaric Gallowegians and Scots north of the Forth who had got out of hand.[66] It is likely that this strategic allocation of blame filtered through to Holm Cultram and St Bees. If it did, that would help to explain the negative depiction of the Gallowegian in Bega's miracle. Indeed, if we allow that the raids of 1216 form the historical backdrop to the narrative, then it is perfectly feasible to interpret the miracle as an encoded retelling of this incursion within a compensatory frame of reference in which the saint makes a successful riposte. A dastardly Gallowegian crosses the Solway and violates Bega's possessions and territory, but is suitably repaid by a sexualized act of violation (the arrow), leading his compatriots to resolve to leave her lands alone in the future.

If this miracle responds to Alexander's incursion of 1216 and the plundering of St Bees Priory, then it would seem that Faustina B.IV must have been copied some time toward the end of its date-range spectrum, between 1216 and *c.* 1225. A date of compilation during these years may help us understand the reasoning lying behind the selection of saints' lives that make up this manuscript and its putative partner Claudius A.V. In a north-west Cistercian milieu in which economic and ecclesial relationships with Galloway, and more

---

and romance. Early examples can be found in Aelred of Rievaulx's Life of Ninian (1164), and in anecdotes about his visitations to the Rievaulx daughter house of Dundrennan: Daniel, *Life of Aelred*, trans. by Powicke, pp. 124–25. There, however, the wish is to show the Cistercians (and their Brittonic saintly predecessor) bringing Christian civility to a previously barbarous populace. Here I would argue that the stereotype (tilted towards devilry) is deployed in a markedly more short-term, politically reactive way.

65 *Chronicle*, ed. by Craster and Thornton, p. 76; Todd, 'St Bega: Cult, Fact and Legend', p. 25.
66 Jamroziak, 'Cistercian Identities', p. 181.

abstract authorizing connections with Scottish and Ionan Christianity, have been thrown into disarray by the Scottish raids, what would be more natural than that Holm Cultram should downplay its northern connections, and opt for saints' lives drawn from the west and south, transferring its spiritual allegiances to the southern English ecclesial pantheon exemplified by Alban, Erkenwald, Aldhelm, and Wulfstan. 'Celtic' fascination remains in play, but this is now a 'Celtic' fascination channelled through an Irish Bega, a Welsh Wenefred, and a Cornish Neot. It is not a 'Celtic' fascination filtering down from Whithorn and Iona.

Conclusion

This new south-west leaning construction of insular sanctity in Faustina B.IV and Claudius A.V was a sign of things to come. In 1296, hostilities were renewed between England and Scotland — the beginning of nearly three centuries of intermittent conflict — hardening the border and making it difficult for Holm Cultram to access its mother house at Melrose. The Bishop of Carlisle's manors were ravaged by Scottish troops in 1301, while in 1306 the Bishop of Whithorn's estates received similar treatment from English soldiers. Edward I ('the hammer of the Scots') made a series of visits to Holm Cultram in the 1300s clearly aimed at strengthening English regnal authority in the North West, and co-opting the region into his military push against Scotland. Dying in the course of one of these campaigns, his entrails were buried at Holm Cultram in 1307, turning the abbey into something of a commemorative shrine to anti-Scottish militarism in the North.[67] Holm Cultram seems to have continued as an English base, supplementing the garrison city of Carlisle, for military expeditions against Scotland through the first half of the fourteenth century. In 1319, the threat of Scottish aggression was so high that the abbey had to be disbanded, and the monks temporarily sent to houses in safer parts of England, and in 1322 it was plundered once again by King Robert the Bruce. The border Cistercian abbeys experienced a further period of trauma in the 1380s when an English army destroyed Melrose Abbey, and in retaliation Holm Cultram was menaced by the army of Earl James Douglas.[68]

This narrative of disruption and of hardening relations between England and Scotland enables us to position the saintly productions of Holm Cultram at a turning point within the spiritual history of the abbey and the region more broadly. After a heyday of cross-border collaboration through the twelfth century, encouraging the Cumbrian Cistercians to look north to Cumméne, Adomnán, Ninian, and Waltheof in their search for abbatial models, in the early years of the thirteenth century, galvanized by the incursions of 1216, those

---

67 Jamroziak, 'Holm Cultram Abbey', p. 34.

68 Stringer, *Reformed Church*, pp. 34–36; Jamroziak, 'Holm Cultram Abbey', pp. 33–35; Downham, 'St Bega: Myth, Maiden, or Bracelet?'.

shadowy connections with Scottish saints vanish. Their place is taken by the saints of Faustina B.IV and Claudius A.V, a predominantly *English* pantheon prioritizing western and southern cults. 'Nationalizing' saints' legendaries, that is, those that convene specific saints to create an image of spiritual nationhood, are generally supposed to have appeared in England from the 1270s. The vernacular *South English Legendary* mixes English saints with universal ones, perhaps with a series of more regional agendas in mind, to assert the adequacy of native saints upon a European stage.[69] BL, MS Lansdowne 436, assembled in Hampshire shortly after, *c.* 1300, confines itself to English saints' lives, pairing Anglo-Saxon bishops, kings, and monastic founders with a handful of twelfth-century saints who demonstrate more eremitic sensibilities.[70] Later legendaries such as the *Scottish Legendary* (s.xiv$^{2/2}$), blending a small number of Scottish saints with many more universal ones, Camb. Univ. Lib., MS Additional 2604 (s.xv), a vernacular collection of east and south-eastern English female saints' lives, and the supplementary English saints' lives of the *Gilte Legende*, a fifteenth-century translation of the *Legenda aurea*, carry various constructions of Scottish and English sanctity forward into the late Middle Ages. However, the twin witnesses of Faustina B.IV and Claudius A.V, convening saints according to the criteria that they are English (or Welsh) but *not* Scottish, means that we need to revise this well-established chronology. Compiled in all probability in the 1220s, these manuscript sections push back the date at which a national perception of sainthood became apparent by over fifty years. More astonishing still, they locate that perception, not in the southern heartlands of the Plantagenet regime but at its margins: in a corner of Cumbria that must have felt itself particularly vulnerable to Scottish pressure at the beginning of the thirteenth century, and responded to that pressure by creating for itself, for its spiritual reading and consolation, a reactively *English* representation of native sanctity.

---

69 Breckenridge, 'Mapping Identity'.

70 The twelfth-century saints in question are Godric of Finchale, Wulfric of Haselbury, and Robert of Newminster. In fact, Lansdowne 436 makes some controversial decisions about the spiritual borders of England. Wenefred of Wales and Æbbe of Coldingham are both co-opted into the collection as *English* founding-abbesses. Other communities and *vitae* would interpret their allegiances very differently.

Works Cited

Manuscripts and Archival Sources

Cambridge, MA, Harvard College, MS Lat. 27
Cambridge, Corpus Christi College, MS 161
——, Trinity College, MS R.3.29
——, Cambridge University Library, MS Additional 2604
——, Cambridge University Library, MS Additional 3037
Gloucester Cathedral, MS 1
Lincoln Cathedral, MS 149
——, MS 150
London, British Library, MS Additional 17511
——, MS Additional 35110
——, MS Cotton Claudius A.V
——, MS Cotton Claudius E.IV (pt. 1)
——, MS Cotton Faustina B.IV
——, MS Cotton Nero A.V
——, MS Cotton Tiberius D.III
——, MS Cotton Tiberius E.I
——, MS Harley 322
——, MS Lansdowne 436
Los Angeles, Huntington Library, MS HM 19915
Oxford, Bodleian Library, MS Hatton 101
——, MS Rawlinson A.416
Oxford, Magdalen College, MS 53

Primary Sources

Bede, *Bede's Ecclesiastical History of the English People*, ed. and trans. by Bertram
 Colgrave and R. A. B. Mynors (Oxford: Clarendon Press, 1969) (cited as
 Historia ecclesiastica)
The Chronicle of St Mary's Abbey, York, ed. by H. H. E. Craster and Mary Thornton,
 SS, 148 (Durham: Andrews & Co., 1934)
Daniel, Walter, *The Life of Aelred of Rievaulx, and The Letter to Maurice*, trans.
 by F. M. Powicke, intro. by Marsha Dutton, Cistercian Fathers Series, 57
 (Kalamazoo: Cistercian Publications, 1994)
Dempster, Thomas, *Historia ecclesiastica gentis Scotorum* (1627), ed. by D. Irving,
 2 vols (Edinburgh: Bannatyne Club, 1829)
Denton, John, *An Accompt of the County of Cumberland* (1610), ed. by Richard
 Ferguson (Kendal: T. Wilson, 1887)
Faricius of Arezzo, 'An Edition of Faricius, *Vita S Aldhelmi*', ed. by Michael
 Winterbottom, *Journal of Medieval Latin*, 15 (2005), 93–147
Geoffrey of Durham, *Vita Sancti Bartholomaei Farnensis*, in *Symeonis monachi
 opera omni*, ed. by Thomas Arnold, Rolls Series, 2 vols (London: Longman,
 1882–1885), I, pp. 295–325

Jocelin of Furness, *Vita S Waldevi*, 'Vita auctore Jordano vel Joscelino, monacho Furnesiensi', in *AASS, Augusti I*, pp. 249D–278E

John of Ford, *Wulfric of Haselbury by John, Abbot of Ford*, ed. by Maurice Bell, Somerset Record Society, 47 [London: printed for subscribers only, 1933]

The Life and Miracles of Sancta Bega, ed. and trans. by George Tomlinson, Carlisle Historical Tracts, 8 (Carlisle: n. pub., 1842)

The Register and Records of Holm Cultram, ed. by Francis Grainger and W. G. Collingwood, Cumberland and Westmoreland Antiquarian and Archaeological Society, Record Series, 7 (Kendal: Titus Wilson & Son, 1929)

Vita S Bege, in *The Register of the Priory of St Bees*, ed. by James Wilson, SS, 126 (Durham: Andrews & Co., 1915), pp. 497–520

'The Life of St Winifred. The *Vita S Wenefrede* from BL Lansdowne 436', ed. and trans. by James Ryan Gregory, *Medieval Feminist Forum*, Subsidia Series, 4 (2016), 1–57

William of Malmesbury's Saints' Lives, ed. by Michael Winterbottom and Rodney M. Thomson (Oxford: Oxford University Press, 2002)

Secondary Works

Bartlett, Robert, 'Cults of Irish, Scottish and Welsh Saints in Twelfth-Century England', in *Britain and Ireland 900–1300: Insular Responses to Medieval European Change*, ed. by Brendan Smith (Cambridge: Cambridge University Press, 1999), pp. 67–86

Benskin, Michael, Tony Hunt, and I. Short, 'Un nouveau fragment du *Tristan* de Thomas', *Romania*, 113 (1992–1995), 289–319

Birkett, Helen, *The Saints' Lives of Jocelin of Furness: Hagiography, Patronage and Ecclesiastical Politics* (Woodbridge: York Medieval, 2010)

Breckenridge, Sara, 'Mapping Identities in the *South English Legendary*', in *Rethinking the South English Legendaries*, ed. by Heather Blurton and Jocelyn Wogan-Browne (Manchester: Manchester University Press, 2011), pp. 329–46

Bruun, Mette B., 'The Cistercian Rethinking of the Desert', *Cîteaux*, 53 (2002), 193–212

Burton, Janet, 'Dioceses, Saints' Cults and Monasteries', in *Northern England and Southern Scotland in the Central Middle Ages*, ed. by Keith Stringer and Angus Winchester (Woodbridge: Boydell, 2017), pp. 173–95

Carruthers, Mary, *The Book of Memory: A Study of Memory in Medieval Culture*, 2nd edn (Cambridge: Cambridge University Press, 2008)

Carter, Michael, 'The Whitby Missal: Material Evidence of Memory' (unpublished paper delivered at Leeds International Medieval Congress, July 2019)

Downham, Clare, 'St Bega: Myth, Maiden, or Bracelet? An Insular Cult and its Origins', *Journal of Medieval History*, 33 (2007), 33–42

Duffy, Seán, 'The First Ulster Plantation: John de Courcy and the Men of Cumbria', in *Colony and Frontier in Medieval Ireland: Essays Presented to J. F. Lydon*, ed. by Terence Barry, Robin Frame, and Katharine Simms (London: Hambledon, 1995), pp. 1–27

Edmonds, Fiona, 'The Emergence and Transformation of Medieval Cumbria', *Scottish History Review*, 93 (2014), 195–216

Gordon-Taylor, Benjamin, 'The Hagiography of St Alban and St Amphibalus in the Twelfth Century', (unpublished Masters thesis, Durham University, 1991)

Heale, Martin, 'Rumburgh Priory in the Later Middle Ages: Some New Evidence', in *Proceedings of the Suffolk Institute of Archaeology and History*, 40.1 (2001), 8–20

Jamroziak, Emilia, 'Holm Cultram Abbey: A Story of Success?', *Northern History*, 45.1 (2008), 27–36

——, 'Cistercian Identities in Twelfth- and Thirteenth-Century Scotland: The Case of Melrose Abbey', in *New Perspectives on Medieval Scotland, 1093–1286*, ed. by Matthew Hammond (Woodbridge: Boydell, 2013), pp. 175–82

——, *The Cistercian Order in Medieval Europe 1090–1500* (London: Routledge, 2013)

Ker, Neil, *Medieval Libraries of Great Britain*, 2nd edn (London: Royal Historical Society, 1964)

Licence, Tom, 'The Benedictines, the Cistercians, and the Acquisition of a Hermitage in Twelfth-Century Durham', *Journal of Medieval History*, 29 (2003), 315–29

Medieval Libraries of Great Britain database (Bodleian Libraries, University of Oxford, 2015), <http://mlgb3.bodleian.ox.ac.uk> [accessed 8 June 2020]

Richards, Mary, 'The Medieval Hagiography of St Neot', *Analecta Bollandiana*, 99 (1981), 259–78

Ringrose, Jayne, *Summary Catalogue of the Additional Medieval Manuscripts in Cambridge University Library Acquired before 1940* (Woodbridge: Boydell, 2009)

Sharpe, Richard, *A Handlist of the Latin Writers of Great Britain and Ireland before 1540* (Turnhout: Brepols, 1997)

Stringer, Keith, *The Reformed Church in Medieval Galloway and Cumbria: Contrasts, Connections and Continuities* (Whithorn: Friends of the Whithorn Trust, 2003)

——, 'Introduction: Middle Britain in Context, *c*. 900–*c*. 1300', in *Northern England and Southern Scotland in the Central Middle Ages*, ed. by Keith Stringer and Angus Winchester (Woodbridge: Boydell, 2017), pp. 1–30

Todd, John M., 'St Bega: Cult, Fact and Legend', *Transactions of the Cumberland and Westmoreland Antiquarian and Archaeological Society*, 2nd series, 80 (1980), 23–36

Whitehead, Christiania, 'Bega's Bracelet', in *Women, Reading and Piety in Medieval England*, ed. by Filip Krajnik and Klara Petrikova (Brno: Masaryk University Press, forthcoming 2022)

——, 'Durham Manuscript Compilations of Northern Saints' Lives: The Cuthbertine *Familia* Post-Conquest', *Medium Aevum* (forthcoming 2022)

Wilson, Christopher, 'The Cistercians as "Missionaries of Gothic" in Northern England', in *Cistercian Art and Architecture in the British Isles*, ed. by Christopher Norton and David Park (Cambridge: Cambridge University Press, 1986), pp. 88–116

Wilson, Susan, *The Life and After-Life of St John of Beverley: The Evolution of the Cult of an Anglo-Saxon Saint* (Aldershot: Ashgate, 2006)

Winterbottom, Michael, 'Faricius of Arezzo's Life of St Aldhelm', in *Latin Learning and English Lore: Studies in Anglo-Saxon Literature for Michael Lapidge*, ed. by Katherine O'Brien O'Keeffe and Andy Orchard, 2 vols (Toronto: University of Toronto Press, 2005), I, pp. 109–31

Winward, Fiona, 'The Lives of St Wenefred (BHL 8847–51)', *Analecta Bollandiana*, 117 (1999), 89–132

HAZEL J. HUNTER BLAIR

Flower of York: Region, Nation, and St Robert of Knaresborough in Late Medieval England[*]

Matthew Paris counted Robert Flower of Knaresborough (*c.* 1160–1218) among the most remarkable saints of the thirteenth century.[1] Born in York, the hermit lived much of his life in a cave-chapel by the River Nidd in Knaresborough, where he became famous for his asceticism and charitable concern for the poor. As well as attracting pilgrims, Robert's holy life and miracles inspired Anglo-Latin and Middle English hagiographic writing between the thirteenth and fifteenth centuries, but these texts have attracted less scholarly attention than other contemporary hagiographies.[2] Robert features in none of the

---

[*] Thank you to Christiania Whitehead, Denis Renevey, and Robin Hughes for their suggested revisions to this essay. An earlier version of this work was presented at the 2018 Leeds International Medieval Congress, and an abbreviated version was delivered as part of a travelling SNSF project presentation to audiences at the universities of St Andrews, Glasgow, and Lancaster. I would like to thank all these audiences for their thought-provoking feedback, which has helped with the revision of this research for publication. The article's title was inspired by Mark Pallant's 2013 cantata 'Flower of York (Scenes from the Life of St Robert of Knaresborough)', <https://markpallant.wordpress.com/tag/knaresborough/> [accessed 05/03/2021].

[1] Paris, *Chronica majora*, ed. by Luard (cited hereafter as *CM*), III, p. 521; IV, p. 378; V, p. 195.

[2] Grosjean, ed., 'Vitae Roberti Knaresburgensis'; *Metrical Life*, ed. by Bazire; *Chronicon de Lanercost*, ed. by Stevenson, pp. 25–27; Golding, 'Hermit and the Hunter'; Easterling, 'A Norbert for England'; Clay, *Hermits and Anchorites*, pp. 40–44; Dauphin, 'L'Érémitisme'; Holdsworth, 'Hermits', 57; Alexander, 'Hermits, Hagiography and Popular Culture', pp. 26, 39, 59, 142–43; Easterling, '*Singulare Propositum*', pp. 118–86; Licence, *Hermits and Recluses*, pp. 173–96; Slater, 'Recreating the Judean Hills?', 619–25; Hanna, ' "So to interpose a little ease": Northern Hermit-lit', pp. 77–79; Macht, 'Changing nature of Monastic Historical Writing' (I thank Claire for sharing with me extracts from her thesis prior to its publication); Hunter Blair, 'Trinitarian Hagiography'. 'See also, in this volume, the essays by Joshua Easterling (pp. 217–35) and by John Jenkins (pp. 147–63).

> **Hazel J. Hunter Blair** (Hazel.blair@unil.ch) is currently completing her doctoral thesis on St Robert of Knaresborough and the Trinitarian Order in Medieval England at the University of Lausanne. She is a member of the SNSF-funded project 'Region and Nation: Late Medieval Devotion to Northern English Saints'.

Late Medieval Devotion to Saints from the North of England: New Directions, ed. by Christiania Whitehead, Hazel J. Hunter Blair, and Denis Renevey, MCS 48 (Turnhout: Brepols, 2022), pp. 75–98

BREPOLS ❧ PUBLISHERS   10.1484/M.MCS-EB.5.124345

great national legendaries of late medieval England, but this should not automatically relegate him to the position of a peripheral figure. As Frank Bottomley has emphasized, 'his significance is not merely local but national, even international.'[3] Robert's sanctity, moreover, was documented and defined by people writing with their own local, regional, national, and literary agendas in mind. Working chronologically, then, this essay analyses the late medieval impetus to memorialize Robert as a figure of significance at various territorial[4] levels, tracing the complexity and fluidity of his textual identity as this was constructed and reconstructed over time in various hagiographies, poems, chronicles, and *miracula*.

Frameworks of Locality

This examination of St Robert's hagiographic corpus is indebted to previous work pertaining to regional, local, and institutional history, which has highlighted the importance of regionally sympathetic approaches in understanding the diversity of past cultures, and particularly to Matthew Holford's work on locality, culture, and identity in medieval Yorkshire and northern England.[5] Holford examines 'the paradigms through which locality was organised and understood in late medieval English culture.'[6] In so doing, he traces 'discourses of locality' which, he argues, were imagined according to various frameworks in the late medieval period. Holford's thesis emphasizes the complex multiplicity of factors (geographical, historical, territorial, ethnographic, etc.) at play in the construction of any one localized identity, but his study is nevertheless divided into three parts, exploring the national, regional, and local frameworks within which the identities and perceptions of late medieval Yorkshire might be constructed:

> By national frameworks of locality I mean those perceptions of the units and parts into which the kingdom was divided which were shared, broadly speaking, in all parts of late-medieval England and also across a relatively wide social spectrum.[7]

---

3 Bottomley, *Yorkshire's Spiritual Athletes*, p. 110 (quoted) and chap. 13, pp. 145–55 at p. 145.
4 I use the term 'territorial' loosely.
5 Ellis, 'Region and Frontier'; Eßer and Ellis, 'Conclusion'; Sarnowsky, *Mendicants, Military Orders, and Regionalism*, pp. 1–15 and 283–88; Brodman, 'Crisis in Charity'; Jamroziak, *The Cistercian Order*, pp. 108–11 and 311–13 (ebook pages, cited here, may differ from the printed version); Easterling, 'A Norbert for England', p. 82; Holford, 'Locality'; Holford, 'The North'.
6 Holford, 'Locality', p. 1. Although many of Holford's key ideas about northern regional identity were published in 'The North', in this essay I have referred mainly to Holford's PhD thesis, 'Locality', which as well as focusing specifically on evidence from Yorkshire, has sections on the geographical extent of miracles (pp. 193–201) and on saints as local and regional figures (pp. 210–20).
7 Holford, 'Locality', p. 25.

Explaining how urban centres, counties, dioceses, and wider territories (such as 'the north' or the province of York) could be recognized as being distinct parts of a wider English whole, Holford demonstrates how Yorkshire and its inhabitants were often conceived of nationally in relation to their northernness. Thus, in several late medieval records 'Yorkshire' is synonymized with 'the north country', while a northern aesthetic is frequently invoked in descriptions of the county's characteristics (e.g. as wild, poor, militarized, and vulnerable to attack)[8]. Moreover, as Holford highlights in his examination of petitionary literature, 'national' perceptions of Yorkshire could be referenced by both northerners and southerners alike.[9]

Regional frames of reference, by contrast, were generally produced by institutions with interests in particular 'substantial areas' (such as dioceses, counties, ridings, or even 'the north' more generally).[10] As Holford explains, saints' cults frequently became vehicles of institutional power at a regional level:

> The primary function of *miracula* very often entails an assertion of the territorial extent of a saint's power, usually centred in an area around the shrine, but extending widely beyond it. Miracle collections assert their saints' patronage of a range of particular locations, usually chosen with some care, through which a sense of the saints' 'country' is built up, and the power and prestige of the institution associated with the saint is asserted.[11]

He recognizes that national, regional, and local frameworks often overlapped, but the latter category might still be distinguished as relating to those discourses which pertained to subdivisions of a given region; in an ecclesiastical context this might refer to the site occupied by a religious community and its relationship with its immediate surrounds and possessions.[12]

Holford highlights that ecclesiastical institutions often served 'as focal points for different levels of locality', and argues that 'emblematic or iconic figures and institutions [...] provided a loose and flexible framework through which individual or institutional identities could be related to a range of wider regional attachments'.[13] His examination of saints' cults and locality is focused regionally on Yorkshire, but there is a broader relevance to his conclusion that saints could be both local and regional, and that locally and regionally associated saints could be interpreted in myriad ways.[14] Moreover, Holford's observation that the 'local associations' of individual saints were 'only one

---

8   Holford, 'Locality', p. 45. These characteristics are discussed in detail all throughout
    Holford's work. See also Holford, 'The North', p. 304.
9   Holford, 'Locality', pp. 89–96. See also Holford, 'The North', p. 307.
10 Holford, 'Locality', p. 120.
11 Holford, 'Locality', p. 192.
12 Holford, 'Locality', pp. 12, 162 and 291.
13 Holford, 'Locality', pp. 202, 204. For a more recent literary and theoretically inflected
    approach to overlapping 'forms of community' in fifteenth-century Middle English
    hagiography, see Sanok, *New Legends*.
14 Holford, 'Locality', p. 201 and 219.

part of these figures' identities, and not always the most important part' is an insight upon which the following analysis of Robert's sanctity is built.[15] Reading the hagiography of a single English cult according to Holford's general framework, then, the remainder of this essay facilitates a multifaceted reading of representations of Robert's local, regional, and national identities as these developed over time and space in relation to the needs and expectations of various medieval writers and their audiences.[16]

Early Hagiographies (i) The 'Cistercian' *vita*

The earliest life of St Robert of Knaresborough likely dates to the first half of the thirteenth century.[17] This early Latin prose text is attributed to someone called Richard Studley, and it creates a spiritual topography for Robert that exists, primarily, within a small corner of the old West Riding of Yorkshire. The only extant manuscript copy of this text — British Library, MS Harley 3775 — is damaged, so this *vita* survives incomplete: one folio has been lost near the beginning (taking with it details of Robert's youth), while the second half of the document is missing such that the remaining narrative breaks off mid-way through.[18] Nevertheless, a significant portion of text remains, detailing Robert's life in search of divine perfection — a pursuit which is thwarted time and again by several vocational false starts and then by a series of unfortunate events that lead to multiple changes of residence. The extant text thus presents Robert as he negotiates his place in the world (or, rather, away from it), and follows him as he oscillates between community and solitary living in various northerly locations. We first see Robert as a Cistercian at Newminster Abbey in Northumberland and then as a religious solitary in a series of sites around the West Riding of Yorkshire, after which he re-joins the coenobium as a member of the Benedictine priory at Headley. Robert is rejected by the black monks, and so he returns to one of his former hermitages — a chapel dedicated to St Hilda near Rudfarlington, three miles south of Knaresborough — where he cultivates a small community dedicated to manual labour and poor relief. Here, William de Stuteville, constable of Knaresborough Castle, persecutes the saint for trespassing on his land and his men destroy Robert's chapel. The text breaks off at this point, but not before Robert vows to rebuild his hermitage next to William's castle.

What emerges from this earliest extant articulation of the hermit's holiness is that Robert was imagined in intensely local terms. Nevertheless, his local

---

15 Holford, 'Locality', p. 220.

16 The 'geography' outlined in Part III of Campbell's *Landscape* indirectly complements Holford's model and there is a useful map of England on p. xiii.

17 *Vita sancti Roberti heremite*, ed. by Grosjean, pp. 365–74 (cited hereafter as *VA*). Licence, *Hermits and Recluses*, p. 193; Holdsworth, 'Hermits', p. 73 n. 12.

18 BL, MS Harley 3775, fols 74^r–77^r.

spiritual topography is described metaphorically as a desert ('in heremo iuxta Knaresburgum').[19] Studley also describes Robert's eremitic wilderness as an existence 'in loco horroris et vaste solitudinis' (in a place of horror and vast solitude) and, based on the *vita*'s integration of this *topos* (and further internal evidence), Tom Licence has suggested that this early hagiography may have been written by a Cistercian, perhaps from the abbey of Fountains (located around ten miles north-west of Knaresborough).[20] Licence writes that this early hagiographer's purpose was primarily 'edificatory', and indeed Robert's experience in the wilderness would have been of interest to an audience of Cistercians whose own identity was tightly bound up with desert ideologies.[21] There is no evidence that Robert accepted any kind of support from the Fountains community during his lifetime, but — as Licence has demonstrated elsewhere — hermitages and their associated lands were sought-after by religious institutions keen to expand their monastic estates.[22] Later iterations of Robert's legend do include scenes in which the monks of Fountains are accused of trying to appropriate Robert's relics against the saint's will.[23] Thus might Studley's *vita* have been written in anticipation of, or to help facilitate the extension of, Cistercian authority in the West Riding via the acquisition of Robert's relics and/or hermitage?[24]

Yet, despite its localism, this text also presents Robert's sphere of sanctity extending northward into Northumbria. The Newminster episode in this text is damaged in the manuscript (and the 'monasterium' is not explicitly named), but later versions of Robert's legend state that the abbot there held Robert up as a holy example for the brothers to emulate: 'O religiosi, celi volatilia attendite quomodo huic obediunt, et quomodo Robertus carnem macerat, mundi cuncta declinans oblectamenta'.[25] (Monks, pay attention to the way that the birds of the air are obedient to this man and notice how Robert vexes his flesh and turns aside from all worldly pleasures).[26] This depiction of Robert's ascetic ability to command birds echoes the Anonymous *Vita Sancti Cuthberti*'s depiction of the hermit St Cuthbert to whom the 'birds of the sky' (*aues coeli*) were 'obedient' (*obedierunt ei*).[27] The Cistercians were interested in Cuthbert's sanctity, even if they did not possess his relics,[28] and it is likely that this characterization of Robert would have been present in Studley's

---

19 *VA*, chap. 1, p. 366.

20 *VA*, chap. 4, p. 369; Licence, *Hermits and Recluses*, pp. 193–94.

21 On the desert and Cistercian 'spiritual topography', see Bruun, 'Cistercian Rethinking'.

22 Licence, 'The Benedictines, the Cistercians and the Acquisition of a Hermitage', pp. 315–29.

23 *Vita sancti Roberti iuxta Knaresburgum*, ed. by Grosjean (cited hereafter as *VR*), chap. 24, p. 398.

24 This paragraphs draws and builds on Hunter Blair, 'Trinitarian Hagiography', pp. 79–81.

25 *VR*, chap. 2, pp. 378–79.

26 *St Robert*, trans. by Bottomley, p. 4.

27 *Vita sancti Cuthberti* (Anon), ed. by Colgrave, pp. 100–01.

28 On Cistercian interest in St Cuthbert, see Lawrence-Mathers, *Manuscripts in Northumbria*, pp. 229–41.

text (even if the relevant section is now lost due to the damage sustained by the Harley manuscript). What remains of the episode in Harley constitutes Studley's rebuke of spiritual laxity at Newminster and his description of how Robert's pure-hearted eremitic aspirations were badmouthed by the monastery's hypocritical brethren.[29] Fountains was Newminster's motherhouse, and so if this is a Fountains' *vita* then it may well have served Fountains both locally and regionally, not only as an articulation of institutional interests and authority in Nidderdale and beyond, but also as an instrument of spiritual correction through which that authority might be sustained. Indeed, Robert emerges from this text as an eremitic figure reminiscent of a Cistercian founder, whose sanctity appears to have been memorialized in order to reflect, and even to justify, the specific local territorial and regional spiritual interests of Cistercians in the West Riding.[30]

Early Hagiographies (ii) The Trinitarian prose *vita*

Localism and regional potential thus seem to have been key aspects of Robert's saintly identity from its inception. Nevertheless, the second of the saint's two earliest hagiographies, composed around the middle of the thirteenth century, while retaining this local focus, envisages Robert's spiritual topography as existing on a distinctly different plane.[31] This prose hagiography is anonymous, but appears to have been written by a member of the Order of the Holy Trinity for the Redemption of Captives (Trinitarians), an order founded in France at the end of the twelfth century, which traditionally reserved one third of its income for ransoming Christians taken captive during the Crusades, and which, in England and elsewhere, came to focus on local hospital work and poor relief via alms-collecting.[32] Upon founding a priory in Knaresborough (before *c*. 1252), the Trinitarians came into possession of Robert's relics and began writing his hagiography.[33]

The Trinitarian prose *vita* lists most of the same locations as the 'Cistercian' hagiography (as far as the latter goes), but although the geographical coordinates of Robert's legend remain fairly constant between these two *vitae*,

---

29 *VA*, chap. 3, p. 368.

30 On territorial and spiritual agendas in Cistercian historical writing, see Freeman, *Narratives of a New Order*, esp. chap. 5 (Fountains' foundation history) at p. 153.

31 *VR*, pp. 375–400; Holdsworth, 'Hermits', p. 73 n. 12.

32 Brodman, *Charity and Religion*, pp. 150–62. Brodman, 'Trinitarian and Mercedarian Orders', pp. 157–58, 238–39, and 242–43.

33 *Calendar of Entries*, ed. by Bliss, I, p. 277. Extensive hagiographic writing on St Robert can be found alongside Trinitarian historical texts in London, British Library, MS Egerton 3143 — a unique collection of texts including a Latin prose life (see Grosjean [*VR*] and *Metrical Life*, ed. by Bazire, Appendix B, pp. 129–33), a Latin verse life (see *Metrical Life*, ed. by Bazire, , Appendix C, pp. 134–44), and a Middle English life (*Metrical Life*, ed. by Bazire), in addition to shorter devotional texts linked to Robert's cult.

their topographical significance is subtly altered in the Trinitarian version of events. If Studley had worked to associate Robert's spiritual topography with the desert in his bid to centralize his subject's eremitism for a Cistercian audience, then Robert's first Trinitarian hagiographer, by contrast, mutes (or at least does not emphasize) the desert landscape of Robert's legend.[34] Thus the saint is immediately localized as Robert who lived 'iuxta Knaresburgum' (by Knaresborough), and 'the desert' as a concept hardly features in this rewriting.[35] Indeed, despite the eremitic reputation of its subject, the Trinitarian prose *vita* does not label Robert a hermit until chapter 8.[36] What we are perhaps witnessing in this second thirteenth-century *vita*, then, is a Trinitarian hagiographer writing to disentangle Robert's spirituality from that of the Cistercians, and doing so, partly, by dismantling the potent desert landscape that Studley had constructed for Robert's life. Indeed, the text appears to have subtly urbanized Robert by presenting him more directly as an alms-collector; the text thus brings Robert's spiritual interests more in line with those of the Trinitarians at Knaresborough Priory, who begged alms for charitable works.[37]

Moreover, the Trinitarian prose *vita* — as Joshua Easterling has shown — reframed Robert's life to present him in the manner of a founder saint of international renown.[38] Robert's affiliation with Newminster is retained in the *vita*, but the episode ends abruptly and does not appear to have been of instructional interest for the hagiographer, who preserves Robert's reputation as a saint with Northumbrian connections, while simultaneously nationalizing him. Indeed the Trinitarian writer's interests are primarily local and national (rather than local and regional), and thus his text begins, 'Sanctus Robertus iuxta Knaresburgum, nacione Anglicus ...' ('St Robert of Knaresborough, an Englishman by birth').[39] As Kathy Lavezzo notes, the Latin *natio, nationis* is a term which 'resists definition', nevertheless its use here in the context of birth quickly anchors Robert in a broader tradition of 'English' community.[40] The precise location of Robert's birth, however, is specified as the 'city of York' (*civitate Eboracensi*).[41] Rather than underscoring Robert's flight from

---

34 This point is also noted in Hunter Blair, 'Trinitarian Hagiography', pp. 80–81.

35 *VR*, 'Prologue', p. 375.

36 *VR*, chap. 8, p. 382 (*heremita Robertus nomine*). That Robert had embraced the eremitic life before this point is certainly implied (e.g. *VR*, chap. 3, p. 379), but the Trinitarian hagiographer is not at pains to emphasize this or to reduce his identity to that of 'hermit'.

37 Hunter Blair, 'Trinitarian Hagiography', p. 80; *VR*, chap. 6, p. 381: 'Quartum utique secum tenuit perambulando patriam pro elimosinis fidelium, pauperibus et egenis, quos sibi congregavit, sollicite colligendis' (The fourth [servant] he retained by his side as he walked about the neighbourhood gathering alms from the faithful on behalf of the poor and needy who gathered round his cell). Translation adapted from *St Robert*, trans. by Bottomley, p. 6; Cf. *VA*, chap. 6, p. 372: 'Quartum servum [...] habuit occupatum in elemosinis colligendis' (A fourth servant he had [...] occupied in alms-gathering) (my translation).

38 Easterling, 'A Norbert for England', 100–03.

39 *VR*, chap. 1, p. 378; *St Robert*, trans. by Bottomley, p. 3.

40 On the implications of *natio*, see Lavezzo, *Imagining*, pp. xv–xvi.

41 *VR*, chap. 1, p. 378; *St Robert*, trans. by Bottomley, p. 3.

the world, then, by cultivating an image of his local spiritual topography imagined through wilderness *topoi*, the Trinitarian hagiographer instead contextualizes Robert's Knaresborough as one constituent part of a larger national community containing urban centres large (York) and small (Knaresborough) — the sorts of places in which English Trinitarians tended to plant houses and collect alms.[42] For the first generation of Knaresborough Trinitarians, then, Robert's inherently local identity was also self-consciously national, and even (potentially) urban. This subtle reorientation of the saint's legend is perhaps reflective of Knaresborough Trinitarians' desire to tease Robert's cult out of Cistercian hands while simultaneously consolidating their own values and authority within the local area and reinforcing their order's recent English expansion.[43]

Chronicles and *miracula*: (i) Matthew Paris

Robert's potential as a 'national' saint is further explored in contemporary depictions of him outside Yorkshire. St Albans chronicler Matthew Paris noted that, in 1238, 'Eodemque anno claruit fama sancti Roberti heremitae apud Knareburc, cujus tumba oleum medicinale fertur abundanter emisisse' (the fame of Robert the hermit at Knaresborough became evident, for his tomb was said to have emitted a large quantity of medicinal oil).[44] As John Jenkins's essay in this volume suggests, this miracle can be linked to a regional interest in northern *myroblytes*.[45] Nevertheless, as Jenkins notes, this type of miracle was more commonly associated with continental saints, and in his broader coverage Paris seems primarily interested in presenting Robert within an international framework.[46] In his summary of key events from the first half of the thirteenth century, he writes:

> Sanctus Ædmundus Cantuariensis archiepiscopus, corpore incorruptus apud Pontiniacum, sanctus quoque Robertus heremita apud Knareburg, sanctus quoque Rogerus episcopus Londoniensis, et alii plures in Anglia, et sancta Elizabeth filia regis Hungariae, et sancta Hyldegardis prophetissa in Alemannia insignibus choruscant miraculis.[47]

---

42 Trinitarian houses were usually sited near towns and main roads. See the 'gazetteer' in Gray, *Trinitarian Order*, pp. 103–27 (for the house at Knaresborough, see pp. 115–18).

43 On Robert as an English Trinitarian founder-figure, see Easterling, 'A Norbert for England', p. 105.

44 Paris, *CM*, ed. by Luard, III, p. 521, cf. Paris, *Historia Anglorum*, ed. by Madden, II, p. 415. My modification of Paris, *English History*, trans. by Giles, I, p. 158.

45 See John Jenkins's essay in this volume, pp. 147–63.

46 Bottomley, *Yorkshire's Spiritual Athletes*, p. 145.

47 Paris, *CM*, ed. by Luard, V, p. 195, cf. Paris, *Historia Anglorum*, ed. by Madden, III, p. 93. My modification of Paris, *English History*, trans. by Giles, II, p. 408.

(St Edmund, archbishop of Canterbury, [whose] uncorrupt body [is] at Pontignac [Pontigny]; St Robert, a hermit at Knaresborough; St Roger, bishop of London, and several other [saints] in England, and St Elizabeth, daughter of the King of Hungary, and St Hildegard, a prophetess in Germany, shone forth with remarkable miracles.)

Naming the hermit alongside saints Edmund 'Archbishop of Canterbury', Roger 'Bishop of London', and 'several other saints in England', Paris verbally envelops Robert within a specifically English gathering of saints — a gathering juxtaposed with and complemented by continental saints with national affiliations: Elizabeth 'daughter of the King of Hungary' and Hildegard, 'a prophetess in Germany'.[48] Paris, though making a clear link between saints and their locales, may be picking up on earlier projections of Robert as a decidedly 'English' saint. Yet he pushes further, extending the discussion transnationally so that Robert's holiness becomes a statement of English excellence on an international stage of sanctity. For Paris, Robert's eremitism and miraculously produced oil makes him a fashionable addition to England's pantheon, and proves the nation's continuing participation in the Christendom-wide production of new saints.[49]

Chronicles and *miracula*:
(ii) *Miracula Symonis de Montfort*

Another contemporary southern reference to St Robert exists in the *Miracula Symonis de Montfort*, which documents the sanctity of the rebel baron Simon de Montfort (d. 1265). The *Miracula* was likely penned at Evesham Abbey around the end of the thirteenth century.[50] Among the many miracles recounted in this collection is the cure of a deacon called Henry, who was struck blind *c.* 1280 in a bridge-chapel in Burton-on-Trent:

> Henricus, diaconus de Bourton super Trent, sedens in capella sita super pontem, ultra flumen quod vocatur Trent in eadem villa, scribens, et subito inflatu miserandi venti insoliti coecus factus, et, vanitate in cerebro percussus, cecidit in terram quasi mortuus, et sic permansit omnino coecus per triennium. Sed in misericordia Dei sperans, adductus ad Robertum de Knaresborue, et at Sanctum Thomam Cantuar', et alibi per totam Angliam, ubi ulla spes fuerit alicujus sancti.

---

48 The saints in question are Edmund of Abingdon (d. 1240); Roger Niger (d. 1241), also known as Roger of Beeleigh; Elizabeth of Thuringia (d. 1231); and Hildegard of Bingen (d. 1179).

49 Weiler, 'Matthew Paris', 269: 'Matthew understood England to be part of a greater whole, its affairs inextricably linked to those of Christendom at large'.

50 Heffernan, '"God hathe schewed ffor him many grete miracules": Political Canonization', p. 187; Robert's presence in this text is briefly noted in Thornton, *Prophecy, Politics*, p. 159 n. 64.

(Henry, a deacon from Burton-on-Trent, sitting in a chapel sited upon a bridge, over the river called Trent in that town, writing, and being unaccustomed to the sudden blow of the miserable wind, was made blind; and, having been struck with foolishness in [his] brain, he fell upon the ground as if he was dead, and thus he remained entirely blind for three years. But hoping in accordance with the mercy of God, he was led to Robert of Knaresborough, and to Saint Thomas of Canterbury, and to other places throughout all England where there was any prospect of anyone holy.)[51]

Henry found no cure at these sites, but was finally led to Evesham, where his vision was restored upon praying at de Montfort's tomb. As Diana Webb has shown, the 'competitive' *topos* was not uncommon, and could be invoked to enhance the local and regional authority of English saints, often by way of comparison with Becket.[52] Thus, Webb notes that Reginald of Durham's late twelfth-century writings on the miracles of Cuthbert and Godric, which offer examples of both competition and collaboration with Becket, reveal 'a complex interplay between these two saints of the north and the canonised saint of the south'.[53] The Evesham writer plainly envisages a country containing numerous distinct saintly locales, but the saintly topography sketched here is striking. As Holford highlights, the Trent was widely recognized as the most important late medieval boundary between north and south,[54] and here in the *Miracula* we have the story of a man struck blind right between these two areas. The conspicuous liminality of Henry's situation is underscored by the hagiographer's presentation of Henry's cure-seeking: although he visited a large number of English saints' shrines before being cured in Evesham, two saints — 'Robert of Knaresborough' and 'Saint Thomas of Canterbury' (d. 1170) — are singled out for particular attention. The miracle's verbal map thus seems bounded by Knaresborough and Canterbury, presented here as being synonymous with the northern and southern limits of Henry's trip 'throughout all England'. We are being encouraged to think of Robert and Thomas, then, as saintly articulations of north and south, respectively. Nevertheless, the author's decision to signal northernness through the figure of Robert is initially puzzling. Cuthbert, Godric, or William of York might have been more obvious candidates for such a geographically minded comparison. Adding to Webb's observations, Christiania Whitehead has shown that Reginald of Durham had already used the competition *topos* to demonstrate the superior healing powers and eremitic authority of Cuthbert and Godric in the North by contrast with Becket's southern archiepiscopal sanctity.[55] What might have prompted

---

51 *Miracula Symonis*, ed. by Haliwell, pp. 108–09. My translation.
52 On this *topos*, Becket, and his relationship with other saints, see Webb, *Pilgrimage*, pp. 52–56.
53 Webb, *Pilgrimage*, pp. 53–54, quoted at p. 53.
54 Holford, 'Locality', pp. 50–54; Holford, 'The North', p. 305.
55 Whitehead, 'Spiritual Healing', p. 175.

our Midlands writer to conceive of his north in relation to Robert of Knaresborough instead?

On closer inspection, there is perhaps more at stake in this miracle than the demonstration of de Montfort's superior healing powers: the three saints seem to be juxtaposed here primarily on account of their reputations for challenging royal authority.[56] Becket's defence of church rights against the ambitions of Henry II needs no introduction, and nor does de Montfort's championing of baronial rights in opposition to Henry III. Perhaps less familiar is Robert's rebuke of King John, who stopped by the saint's hermitage on a visit to Knaresborough to find Robert deep in prayer and unwilling to defer to his presence.[57] John went on to support Robert, and there was no real political fall-out, but Robert nevertheless made sure to remind John that his secular authority was limited in comparison to God's. Given, as Simon Walker notes, that among England's political saints, de Montfort's cult remained unusually opposed to royal authority, the miracle story seems designed to legitimize and sanctify de Montfort's rebelliousness by associating him with figures the hagiographer deems spiritual brothers-in-arms and thereby worthy competitors.[58] The monks of Evesham, then, may have been interested in Robert primarily as a figure of resistance to royal authority, a facet of his sanctity which could explain his promotion to a figure representative of 'the north' in the context of the *Miracula*.

Chronicles and *miracula*: (iii) *Lanercost Chronicle*

Interest in Robert as a regionally emblematic figure also grew in the north in the later thirteenth and fourteenth centuries. The hermit's legend was partially incorporated by an Augustinian canon into the fourteenth-century manuscript of the *Lanercost Chronicle* — a text partly based on the earlier, now lost, 'northern Franciscan chronicle' by Richard of Durham.[59] The northern Franciscan portion of the chronicle covers the years 1201 to 1297, and was written in Northumbria between *c.* 1285 and 1297.[60] It contains a mix of chronicle entries and *exempla*, which has led Antonia Gransden to suggest that it may once have served as a repository for Franciscan preaching material.[61] The entry for Robert's death (1218) focuses in detail on three of his *in vita* miracles.[62] All three feature the hermit admonishing affluent and covetous

---

56 Walker, 'Political Saints', p. 212: 'comparison [of de Montfort] with Becket's cause and martyrdom is particularly frequent'.
57 *VR*, chap. 20, pp. 393–94.
58 Walker, 'Political Saints', pp. 209, 212–13.
59 Little, 'Authorship', 48–49; Gransden, *Historical Writing*, I, pp. 494–96.
60 Gransden, *Historical Writing*, I, p. 495.
61 Gransden, *Historical Writing*, I, p. 498.
62 *Chronicon de Lanercost*, ed. by Stevenson, pp. 25–27.

men: the first episode recounts the nightmare experienced by de Stuteville after he tried to chase Robert off his land; the second is a condensed version of King John's visit to Robert's hermitage, and the third details Robert's punishment of a church rector who greedily tried to tax the poor. In every case, Robert secures gifts and goods for the poor as a result of his resistance to lay corruption or extravagance. The thematic unity of the episodes is striking and supports Franciscan authorship of the entry: concern for the poor and criticism of material excess were at the heart of the friars' spirituality. On this basis, and like his Trinitarian counterpart, the Franciscan writer would have had a vested interest in memorializing someone like Robert, through whom lessons in charity and poverty could be captivatingly galvanized. Moreover, the chronicler seems to have been familiar with Robert's shrine. Under the year 1282, he writes:

> Fratres de ordine Cruciferorum, qui aream Roberti de *Chartresburghe* incolunt et aedificia amoena exstruunt, arvali opere per medium ecclesiae facto in superiori parte, chorum sibi parabant inferiorem, ubi viri justi corpus requiescit, peregrinis relinquentis, gratia vigiliarum exercendarum et candelarum ibi accendendarum. Quod spiritus viri justi moleste tulit, et inundatione permaxima facta, qualem nemo ibi meminis, aquam de *Nith* in superiorem aream et usque in medium ecclesiae deduxit, arcuatum opus de nocte destruxit, et modo pavimento aliquantulum elevato, ut socios sibi non ut dominos eos astare permittit.[63]

> (The brothers of the order of the cross who inhabit the area of Robert of Chartresburghe [Knaresborough], and who are constructing pleasant buildings there, having carried out architectural work through the middle of the church in the upper part, were preparing for themselves a lower choir, where the body of that just man lies, leaving the lower part to pilgrims, [who come] to that place in order to perform vigils and burn candles with grace. Because the spirit of the just man resented this, and as a result of a tremendous flood such as no man there remembers, the waters of the Nith [Nidd] were directed into the upper area and all the way into the middle of the church. The vaulted work was destroyed in the night, and [St Robert] permitted [the brothers] to stand on a pavement raised only a little [above the flood], in order that they were companions to him and not masters.)

---

63 *Chronicon de Lanercost*, ed. by Stevenson, p. 108, my italics. My modified translation is based on *Chronicle of Lanercost*, trans. by Maxwell, p. 28; and Jennings, *Harrogate and Knaresborough*, p. 98. Robert's cave-chapel, where he is thought to have been buried, is located on the northern bank of the Nidd, but his relics may have been translated to the nearby priory (Gray, *Trinitarian Order*, pp. 115–18), in which case the miracle may have occurred in that building.

As H. F. Chettle noticed, the chronicler here misidentifies the Trinitarians as Crossed Friars.[64] The picture is further complicated because the Augustinian copyist appears to have rendered 'Knaresborough' as 'Chartesburghe', an error that Joseph Stevenson left uncorrected in his edition, which was carried into Herbert Maxwell's English translation.[65] Maxwell considers the passage 'obscure', but in the translation above it seems the chronicler is critiquing Trinitarian grandiosity at Knaresborough: in renovating the church and allowing Robert's shrine to be built over, the brethren had come to see themselves as superior to the saint (and the pilgrims who visited his tomb), thus undermining the humility Robert championed throughout his life. The saint punished them as a result, miraculously causing the Nidd to flood the church and destroy the architectural divide. The Franciscan chronicler's narration of these events thus portrays the Trinitarians negatively. Could this perhaps imply that there was a rivalry between these two orders committed to similar goals, or a jealousy regarding Trinitarian monopoly of Robert's cult?

On the other hand, the chronicler's description of this episode, alongside his detailed knowledge of the internal layout of the church, might indicate that he himself had visited the shrine, where he may have obtained the information about Robert's life included in the chronicle's entry for 1218. The Franciscan writer may thus have been displaying a receptiveness in that earlier entry to aspects of Robert's sanctity being celebrated contemporaneously by the Trinitarians in Knaresborough. But this is not to say that he reproduced these exactly in his own text. Rather, in curating a selection of episodes from Robert's life which he perhaps felt would be particularly relevant to the Franciscan community, the chronicler made subtle changes to Robert's saintly landscape. Thus, he locates the hermit's career in Knaresborough within the 'partes aquilonares' (northern parts) and takes care to note that Robert's sojourn in Newminster took place 'in Northumbria' — his own part of England.[66] Conversely, he does not display the same level of geographic precision in his description of Robert's birthplace. Rather than localizing this to the 'city of York' as the Trinitarian hagiographer had done, the chronicler writes more vaguely of Robert of Knaresborough 'qui de Eboracensi oriundus patria' (who was born in the country of York).[67] The word *patria* (country) could simply mean 'homeland', but could also refer to a range of 'geographically or socially cohesive areas' of various extents, which need not exclude cities.[68] Similarly, the term *Eboracensi* could mean 'York' (the city), but was also used in descriptions of the county of Yorkshire, and also in references to the diocese and province of York.[69] Coupled with *patria*, *Eboracensi* might be taking on

---

64 Chettle, 'Friars of the Holy Cross', 218.
65 BL, MS Cotton Claudius D.VII, fol. 192ʳ.
66 *Chronicon de Lanercost*, ed. by Stevenson, pp. 25–26.
67 *Chronicon de Lanercost*, ed. by Stevenson, p. 25. Cf. *VR*, chap. 1, p. 378: 'civitati Eboracensi'.
68 Holford, 'Locality', p. 11.
69 Holford, 'Locality', pp. 81, 152.

the quality of an area comprising but also extending beyond York's city walls. Ultimately, the chronicler does not make clear which York-based area he has in mind as Robert's 'homeland', though his decision to write about the hermit in broadly regional terms is clear enough.

The regional interests of the chronicle have been widely recognized by scholars, such that references to Robert in these particular terms likely represent a Franciscan desire to embrace him as an inspirational figure for friars throughout the North.[70] Indeed, the posthumous river miracle narrated for the year 1282 enhances Robert's 'regional' identity as a wonderworking hermit with control over the elements like his predecessor Cuthbert.[71] Moreover, it takes on a further Northumbrian quality in being juxtaposed in the chronicle with a miracle of St Cuthbert that occurred at Bothans Church in Lothian 'per idem tempus' (about the same time).[72] In this second miracle, Cuthbert miraculously facilitates the successful completion of woodwork being carried out in his honour. Construction miracles were a long-standing feature of Cuthbert's sanctity but not of Robert's, so the juxtaposition of these two miracles worked by saints keen to safeguard the architectural aspects of their cults seems designed to lend authority to Robert's broader northern sanctity by associating it with Cuthbert's spiritual premiership.[73]

In the thirteenth century, then, Robert's national, regional, and local affiliations were in flux. Local Cistercian interest in Robert's cult in the West Riding of Yorkshire was superseded by local Trinitarian interest in Robert at Knaresborough, with these orders extending Robert's saintly potential regionally and nationally, respectively, in accordance with their own institutional agendas. Robert's regional significance seems to have resonated particularly with the Franciscans, who absorbed stories about his commitment to poverty and charity and redeployed these as *exempla* for northern Franciscan brethren. All this implies burgeoning recognition of the saint's spiritual ties to areas in Yorkshire and Northumbria, with his attachment to the 'north parts' more generally being recognized as far south as Evesham by the end of the century; but these local and regional characteristics also sit alongside depictions of Robert as a nationally significant English saint, shared by writers both north and south of the Trent.

Robert in the Vernacular

The Trinitarians, who in the thirteeth century had primarily engaged with Robert's sanctity in local and national terms (perhaps because they were focused on establishing and consolidating their authority locally in the

---

70 Gransden, *Historical Writing*, I, pp. 496–98.
71 On Cuthbert's water miracles, see Lawrence-Mathers, 'Bede, St Cuthbert', esp. 12–14.
72 *Chronicon de Lanercost*, ed. by Stevenson, pp. 108–09.
73 Eg. Crook, 'The Architectural Setting of the Cult of St Cuthbert', p. 239.

first century since their arrival in Knaresborough), had by the turn of the fifteenth century become more engaged in expressing Robert's sanctity in regional and national terms. The Middle English *De vita et conversacione sancti Roberti iuxta Knaresburgum* (hereafter the *Life*) is an alliterative poem in 505 rhyming couplets by an anonymous Trinitarian writer, and here in the vernacular Robert's regional ties to the broader northern English landscape come strikingly to the fore.[74] The spatial concept 'the north parts' does not feature in any Trinitarian landscape of Robert's life in Latin; in Middle English, however, the poet refers — albeit very subtly — to events in relation to a secular, even militarized 'north' inhabited by knights. In one episode, a local knight called 'Sir' (e.g. l. 843) Brian de Lisle seeks out Robert's saintly blessing, having been tasked with carrying out royal business elsewhere in the kingdom. The Trinitarian Latin *vita* states that Brian stopped to see Robert on his journey *ad australes partes* (to the south parts), but in the *Life* the direction is switched such that Brian rides instead 'to the North Cuntre' (where he died).[75] Similarly, where in the Latin Robert's foe, local landowner William de Stuteville, is said to have travelled to Knaresborough *de australi parte* (from the south), soon ordering Robert to vacate his land, the *Life*, where William is styled 'Sir' (e.g. l. 411), instead reports that:

> The forsayd William Scutivyle
> Outt of the North Countre, I weyne,
> Come to Knaresburghe castell cleyne.[76]

These off-stage allusions to secular, knightly activity in the north subtly reorient Robert's legend in the way that draws the action closer to the Anglo-Scottish border. Indeed, as Holford and King point out, Yorkshire — and northern England more generally — was an area imagined nationally as being renowned for its 'military prowess':[77] one fifteenth-century poem attributing general characteristics to each of the counties of England, thus noted that 'Yorkeshir' was 'full of knights'.[78] Given the *Life*'s interest in an implicitly militarized northern landscape, then, one might interpret that Robert's regional identity

---

74 *De vita et conversacione sancti Roberti iuxta Knaresburgum* (cited hereafter as *Life*), in *Metrical Life*, ed. by Bazire. On the extended lifespan of alliteration in Yorkshire writing, see Hanna, 'Yorkshire and York', p. 273.

75 *Life*, l. 853; cf. *VR*, chap. 22, p. 396. Bazire suggests that the *Life*'s directional changes may be due to the vernacular translator writing from a more northerly geographical position than Knaresborough. Her theory, based on internal textual evidence which could equally be explained as rhetoric, is that the text was written at the Trinitarian house of Walknoll, near Newcastle (*Metrical Life*, ed. by Bazire, pp. 24–27 n. 99, 405, 836). At present, I am inclined to think that the text probably originated more locally within the orbit of Robert's shrine at Knaresborough.

76 *Life*, ll. 404–06; cf. *VR*, chap. 10, p. 384.

77 Holford, 'Locality', pp. 43 and 47; King, 'Anglo-Scottish Marches', p. 48. King notes this perception persisted even though 'most of "the North" was no more militarised than the south'.

78 'The Shires', ed. by Sisam and Sisam, no. 235, l. 15; Holford, 'Locality', pp. 43 and 47.

was manifested further by the poet's depiction of him, figuratively, as an ideal knight: a figure 'dubbed' (l. 150) with devotion, who stood 'stalworthy and wyght' (l. 54) against various enemies, including a demon named 'Sir Gerrard' (l. 698).[79] This romance-like register — more often found in stories about the lives and deeds of secular heroes — is employed throughout the poem.[80] The *Life* thus presents the hermit anew as a flower of chivalry: physically strong, skilled in battle, but nonetheless gentle, refined, and courteous. Although there is a long tradition of Christian hermits being cast as spiritual warriors or *miles christi*, in which the *Life* is participating, the image is working here on an overwhelmingly secular and chivalrous level.

The vernacular hagiographer's construction of Robert in secular, knightly terms is probably ultimately rooted in a wider Trinitarian interest in the order's crusading past.[81] Simultaneously, however, presenting Robert in this way may also have helped to focus and reflect his identity in regionally specific terms as a 'northern English' (if not a 'Yorkshire') saint. The priory's institutional responsibility had, by this time, been extended northward into Northumberland when it became responsible for the visitation of a new Trinitarian house at Walknoll, near Newcastle, founded in 1360.[82] In this context, it is perhaps not surprising to find the Trinitarians keen to depict Robert as a saint whose spiritual authority was linked, more explicitly than before, to 'the North'. But this is not to say that the *Life* is necessarily a regionally focused piece of literature. As a just and moral 'knight', Robert is implicitly imagined with bonds of loyalty linking him to the kingdom of England. Indeed, the same text simultaneously positions the hermit alongside King Arthur, Hector of Troy, and the Greek warrior Achilles as a leading national figure:

> Vhenn frendes fared well at a fest
> And glewmen gladdes þaim wyth gest,
> Of harpyng som has lyst to here
> And som of carpyng of tales sere
> Of Arthure, Ector, and Achilles—
> Princes þat wer proude in prese—
> Of kyngys and kempes, of conquerours,
> Of lordys, of ladys, of paramours,
> Þat ar bott vaine and vanite.
> Of slyke sall noght my carpyng be,

---

79 On how Robert's presentation in the vernacular compares with his presentation in a near-contemporary Trinitarian Latin verse life, see Hunter Blair, 'Trinitarian Hagiography', esp. pp. 94–95. The remainder of this section integrates and expands on that discussion.

80 *Metrical Life*, ed. by Bazire, p. 16 and n. 39.

81 The *Life* is paired in manuscript with a vernacular history of the Trinitarian order that describes the ransom of Christians held prisoner by Muslims in the Holy Land (*Metrical Life*, ed. by Bazire, pp. 72–76). On Trinitarian historical writing, see Macht, 'The Changing Nature of Monastic Historical Writing'.

82 *Confirmatio*, ed. by Brand; Gray, *Trinitarian Order*, pp. 122–24.

Bott of a better he me haste,
Fadir and Son and Haly Gaste.[83]

As well as creating an expectation of military heroism in the text, the three secular figures named in these lines evoke the genres of epic and romance.[84] As Ralph Hanna has noted, copies of Middle English religious texts at the 'interface' of instructional writing and romance — such as *Cursor Mundi* — frequently hail from Yorkshire.[85] In this sense, the *Life* may be a typically northern, Yorkshire-based production. Yet the Trinitarian hagiographer simultaneously engages a national discourse, both aligning Robert with — and setting him above — a string of classical and early British military heroes. The reference to Arthur, in particular, who had become an Anglo-centric hero by the fifteenth century, subtly underscores Robert's potential as a nationally significant 'English' saint.[86] Indeed romance has been recognized as a platform of sorts for late medieval expressions of national identity.[87] Nevertheless, as Thomas H. Crofts and Robert Allen Rouse have highlighted, the medieval English identities expressed through romance writing were never homogeneous, and multiple identities might even surface in single texts.[88] The Robert that emerges from the *Life*, indeed, is both a national hero and a saint with strong local and regional connections.

Beyond romancing Robert's legend, the vernacular hagiographer envisages his text not just as a written poem, but as a 'carpyng' (l. 44) — an *oral performance* akin to those stories of secular military heroes read aloud as entertainment at courtly events.[89] Indeed, in those early lines, the Middle English author constructs a courtly backdrop of noble feasting 'frendes' being entertained by minstrels and musicians, within which he, as narrator, prepares to commence a reading of Robert's legend. Elsewhere in the text, the narrator interjects into his telling of Robert's legend short moral appeals to 'Sirres' (l. 795) and 'myghty men' (l. 285), whose riches he juxtaposes with Robert's asceticism. The *Life*, then, bears several hallmarks of a text designed to be read — or, perhaps, even heard — by a noble, secular audience, whom the author flatters and hopes to morally instruct. Hanna has suggested that the *Life* may have been read by the Plumptons, a gentry family based near Knaresborough Priory.[90] This is a solid suggestion and offers an important local context within which to consider the text's audience. On the other hand, the audience envisioned by the hagiographer could also have extended further: the Plumptons were members of a sprawling network of literate

---

83 *Life*, ll. 35–46.
84 *Metrical Life*, ed. by Bazire, p. 83 n. 39 ff.
85 Hanna, 'Yorkshire and York', pp. 269–75.
86 Fulton, 'Arthurian Prophecy', pp. 67, 81.
87 Crofts and Rouse, 'Middle English Popular Romance'; Turville-Petre, *England the Nation*.
88 Crofts and Rouse, 'Middle English Popular Romance', pp. 82–85.
89 *Metrical Life*, ed. by Bazire, p. 83 n. 39ff; Reichl, 'Orality and Performance', pp. 132–49.
90 Hanna, *Patient Reading*, p. 204.

laypeople, while the priory's proximity to Knaresborough Castle (granted to Queen Phillipa in 1331 and part of the Duchy of Lancaster since 1372) may offer an additional, royal, context for considering the type of audience the hagiographer was hoping to reach.[91] The text's embrace of various national frames of reference also supports the idea that the poet was aiming for a broad vernacular audience: similar 'discourses of locality' can often be found in texts and documents intended for wide circulation.[92] Paradoxically, then, Robert's identity as a northerner may have been underscored for a secular audience in the vernacular precisely because the hagiographer wanted his subject's sanctity to be recognized *more widely* in English society. Construction of Robert's 'northern' identity in this case might then be interpreted as a form of translation for both regional and national audiences.[93]

Conclusion

In academic circles, Robert is not as well known as some of his saintly contemporaries, yet public interest in him is so high that a year-long series of educational, cultural, and devotional events was held in 2018 to commemorate 800 years since his death.[94] Robert's claim to the title 'patron saint of Yorkshire' has even been debated in the local press — but would Robert deserve this title if it was bestowed upon him today?[95] Despite hagiographers' engagement with Robert's northernness in a variety of ways between the thirteenth and fifteenth centuries, none of the medieval materials for the hermit's cult present him as a representative 'of Yorkshire' *per se*. It is not until the early seventeenth century that we find Robert being explicitly celebrated in county terms in the English vernacular, when he cameos in Elizabethan poet Michael Drayton's *Poly-Olbion*, an encyclopaedic 15,000-line topographical poem about England's great diversity:

> Nor in one country thus our Saints confinéd were
> But through this famous Isle disperséd here and there :
> As *Yorkshire* sent us in Saint Robert to our store,
> At *Knaresborough* most known, whereas he long before
> His blesséd time bestow'd ; then one as just as he,
> (If credit to those times attributed may be)
> Saint *Richard* with the rest deserving well a room,
> Which in that country once, at *Hampoole* had a tomb.
> Religious *Alred* so, from *Rydall* we receive,

---

91 Hanna, *Patient Reading*, pp. 203–08; Jennings, *Harrogate and Knaresborough*, pp. 37–38.
92 Holford, 'Locality', p. 74.
93 On northern texts and southern English readers, see Hanna, *Patient Reading*, pp. 180–81.
94 See 'St Robert of Knaresborough, 1160–1218', <strobertofknaresborough.org.uk>
95 'The Return of the Saint?', <www.yorkpress.co.uk/news/1701455.the-return-of-the-saint>

The Abbot, who to all posterity did leave,
The fruits of his staid faith, deliveréd by his pen.[96]

Included here in a catalogue of England's saints and positioned alongside Richard Rolle and Aelred of Rievaulx as a saint of 'Yorkshire', Robert's sanctity finally performs itself upon a national stage in explicitly county-specific terms.

In sum, despite his exclusion from medieval national legendaries, this did not preclude Robert's sanctity from being imagined as nationally significant by both northern and southern English writers. Moreover, monastic and mendicant articulations of his medieval sanctity were composed according to numerous complex and varied territorial frames of reference, including institutional and corporate landscapes that varied from one order to another. Robert's saintly identity, indeed, was continuously reformulated by medieval writers with varying regional and national agendas. It is ironic that where Robert is at his most explicitly 'northern' in Trinitarian writing (in the *Life*), he is also, arguably, at his most national; but what this drives home is that, even for long-dead saints whose bodies never left their localities, local, regional, and national identities were rarely simple or static.

---

96 Drayton, *Poly-Olbion*, ed. by Hooper, III, p. 125, Song 24, ll. 845–55. On the local and national stakes in this poem, see Adrian, *Local Negotiations*, pp. 88–95.

Works Cited

Manuscripts and Archival Sources

London, British Library, MS Egerton 3143
——, MS Harley 3775
——, MS Cotton Claudius D.VII

Primary Sources

Calendar of Entries in the Papal Registers Relating To Great Britain and Ireland, Volume 1: 1198–1304, ed. by William Henry Bliss (London: HMSO, 1893)

The Chronicle of Lanercost, 1272–1346, trans. by Herbert Maxwell (Glasgow: J. Maclehose, 1913)

Chronicon de Lanercost, ed. by Joseph Stevenson (Bannatyne Club, 1839)

Confirmatio Ordinationis Hospitalis de Walknoll, infra Villam Novi Castri (1363), ed. by John Brand, in *The history and Antiquities of the Town and County of the Town of Newcastle upon Tyne* (London, 1789), pp. 643–48. Digitised by Eighteenth-Century Collections Online <quod.lib.umich.edu/e/ecco/004896316.0001.001> [accessed 1 December 2019]

De vita et conversacione sancti Roberti iuxta Knaresburgum (Middle English) in *The Metrical Life of St Robert of Knaresborough; Together with the Other Middle English Pieces in British Museum Ms. Egerton 3143*, ed. by Joyce Bazire, EETS, 228 (London: Oxford University Press, 1953), pp. 42–81 (cited as *Life*)

Drayton, Michael, *Poly-Olbion*, in *The Complete Works of Michael Drayton*, ed. by Richard Hooper, 3 vols (London: J. R. Smith, 1876)

Grosjean, Paul, ed., 'Vitae S. Roberti Knaresburgensis', *Analecta Bollandiana*, 57 (1939), 364–400

The Metrical Life of St Robert of Knaresborough; Together with the Other Middle English Pieces in British Museum Ms. Egerton 3143, ed. by Joyce Bazire, EETS, 228 (London: Oxford University Press, 1953)

Miracula Symonis de Montfort, ed. by James Orchard Haliwell, in *The chronicle of William de Rishanger, of the barons' war, the miracles of Simon de Montfort* (London: Camden Society, 1840), pp. 67–110

Paris, Matthew, *Matthaei Parisiensis, monachi Sancti Albani, Historia Anglorum, sive, ut vulgo dicitur, Historia minor*, etc. ed. by Sir Frederic Madden, Rolls Series, 3 vols (London: Longman, 1866–1869) (cited as *Historia Anglorum*)

——, *Matthaei Parisiensis, monachi Sancti Albani, Chronica majora*, ed. by Henry Richards Luard, *Rerum Britannicarum medii aevi scriptores*, 57, 7 vols (London: Longman, 1872–1883) (cited as CM)

——, *Matthew Paris's English History: from the year 1235 to 1273*, trans. by J. A. Giles, 3 vols (London: H. G. Bohn, 1889) (cited as *English History*)

'The Shires', in *The Oxford Book of Medieval English Verse*, ed. by Celia Sisam and Kenneth Sisam (Oxford: Clarendon Press, 1970), p. 499

Vita sancti Cuthberti (Anon.), in *Two Lives of Saint Cuthbert: a Life by an Anonymous Monk of Lindisfarne and Bede's Prose Life*, ed. and trans. by Bertram Colgrave (Cambridge: Cambridge University Press, 1940, repr. 1985), pp. 59–140

Vita sancti Roberti heremiti, in Paul Grosjean, ed., 'Vitae S. Roberti Knaresburgensis', *Analecta Bollandiana*, 57 (1939), 364–400, at pp. 364–74 (cited as *VA*)

Vita sancti Roberti iuxta Knaresburgum, in Paul Grosjean, ed., 'Vitae S. Roberti Knaresburgensis', *Analecta Bollandia*, 57 (1939), 364–400, at pp. 375–400 (cited as *VR*)

St Robert of Knaresborough, trans. by Frank Bottomley (Ilkley: n. pub., 1993)

Secondary Works

Adrian, John M., *Local Negotiations of English Nationhood, 1570–1680* (New York: Palgrave Macmillan, 2011)

Alexander, Dominic, 'Hermits, Hagiography, and Popular Culture: A Comparative Study of Durham Cathedral Priory's Hermits in the Twelfth Century' (unpublished doctoral thesis, Queen Mary and Westfield College, University of London, 2000)

Brodman, James, 'The Trinitarian and Mercedarian Orders: A Study of Religious Redemptionism in the Thirteenth Century' (unpublished doctoral thesis, University of Virginia, 1974)

——, *Charity and Religion in Medieval Europe* (Washington, DC: Catholic University of America Press, 2009)

——, 'Crisis in Charity: Centrifugal and Centripetal Influences Upon Medieval Caritative Orders', *Imago Temporis: Medium Aevum*, 5 (2011), 163–73

Bruun, Mette B., 'The Cistercian Rethinking of the Desert', *Citeaux: Commentarii Cistercienses*, 53 (2002), 233–52

Bottomley, Frank, *Yorkshire's Spiritual Athletes: Hermits & Other Solitaries* (online) <https://web.archive.org/web/20160202025339/www.zurgy.org/medieval/hermits.pdf> [accessed 14 Jan 2022]

Campbell, William H., *The Landscape of Pastoral Care in Thirteenth-Century England* (Cambridge: Cambridge University Press, 2018)

Clay, Rotha Mary, *The Hermits and Anchorites of England* (London: Methuen, 1914)

Chettle, H. F., 'The Friars of the Holy Cross in England', *History*, 34 (1949), 204–20

Crofts, Thomas H., and Robert Allen Rouse, 'Middle English Popular Romance and National Identity', in *A Companion to Medieval Popular Romance*, ed. by Raluca Radulescu and Cory James Rushton (Cambridge: Brewer, 2009), pp. 79–95

Crook, John, 'The Architectural Setting of the Cult of St Cuthbert in Durham Cathedral', in *Anglo-Norman Durham, 1093–1193*, ed. by David Rollason, Margaret Harvey, and Michael Prestwich (Woodbridge: Boydell, 1994), pp. 235–50

Dauphin, Hubert, 'L'Érémitisme en Angleterre aux XIe et XIIe siècles', in *L'Eremitisimo in Occidente nei Secoli XI e XII. Settiman internazionale di studio, 2d, Passo della Mendola 1962* (Milan: Societa Editrice Vita E. Pensiero, 1962), pp. 55–76

Easterling, Joshua, '*Singulare Propositum*: Hermits, Anchorites and Regulatory Writings in Late Medieval England' (unpublished doctoral thesis, Ohio State University, 2011)

——, 'A Norbert for England: Holy Trinity and the Invention of Robert of Knaresborough', *Journal of Medieval Monastic Studies*, 2 (2013), 75–107

Ellis, Steven G., 'Region and Frontier in the English State: The English Far North, 1296–1603', in *Frontiers, Regions and Identities in Europe*, ed. by Steven G. Ellis and Raingard Eßer with Jean-François Berdah and Miloš Řezník (Pisa: Plus-Pisa University Press, 2009), pp. 77–100

Eßer, Raingard, and Steven G. Ellis, 'Conclusion: Towards an Agenda for a New Regional History', in *Frontiers, Regions and Identities in Europe*, ed. by Steven G. Ellis and Raingard Eßer with Jean-François Berdah and Miloš Řezník (Pisa: Plus-Pisa University Press, 2009), pp. 287–90

Fulton, Helen, 'Arthurian Prophecy and the Deposition of Richard II', in *Arthurian Literature*, 22, ed. by Keith Busby and Roger Dalrymple (Cambridge: Brewer, 2005), pp. 64–83

Freeman, Elizabeth, *Narratives of a New Order: Cistercian Historical Writing in England, 1150–1220* (Turnhout: Brepols, 2002)

Golding, Brian, 'The Hermit and the Hunter', in *The Cloister and the World: Essays in Medieval History in Honour of Barbara Harvey*, ed. by John Blair and Brian Golding (Oxford: Oxford University Press, 1996), pp. 95–117

Gransden, Antonia, *Historical Writing in England, Vol. I: c. 500 to c. 1307* (London: Routledge, 1974)

Gray, Margaret, *The Trinitarian Order in England: Excavations at Thelsford Priory*, ed. by Lorna Watts and Phillip Rahtz (Oxford: Tempus Reparatum, 1993)

Hanna, Ralph, 'Yorkshire and York', in *Europe: A Literary History, 1348–1418*, ed. by David Wallace (Oxford: Oxford University Press, 2016), pp. 256–78

——, *Patient Reading/Reading Patience: Oxford Essays on Medieval English Literature* (Liverpool: Liverpool University Press, 2017)

——, '"So to interpose a little ease": Northern Hermit-lit', in *Revisiting the Medieval North of England: Interdisciplinary Approaches*, ed. by Anita Auer, Denis Renevey, Camille Marshall, and Tino Oudesluijs (Cardiff: University of Wales Press, 2019), pp. 73–90

Heffernan, T. J., '"God hathe schewed ffor him many grete miracules": Political Canonization and the *Miracula of Simon de Montfort*', in *Art and Context in Late Medieval English Narrative*, ed. by Robert Edwards (Cambridge: Brewer, 1994), pp. 177–91

Holford, Matthew, 'Locality, Culture, and Identity in Late Medieval Yorkshire, c. 1270–c. 1540' (unpublished doctoral thesis, University of York, 2001) <https://etheses.whiterose.ac.uk/2446/1/DX222355.pdf > [accessed 14 Jan 2022]

——, 'The North and the Dynamics of Regional Identity in Later Medieval England', in *An Agenda for Regional History*, ed. by Bill Lancaster, Diana Newton, and Natasha Vall (Newcastle-upon-Tyne: Northumbria University Press, 2007), pp. 303–20

Holdsworth, Christopher, 'Hermits and the Powers of the Frontier', *Reading Medieval Studies*, 16 (1990), 55–76

Hunter Blair, Hazel J., 'Trinitarian Hagiography in Late Medieval England: Rewriting St Robert of Knaresborough in Latin Verse', *Studies in Church History*, 57 (2021), 74–95

Jamroziak, Emilia, *The Cistercian Order in Medieval Europe: 1090–1500* (Oxford: Routledge, 2013; ebook 2015) <https://play.google.com/books/reader?id=c7YyDQAAQBAJ&pg=GBS.PP1> [accessed 14/01/2022]

Jennings, Bernard, ed., *A History of Harrogate and Knaresborough* (Huddersfield: The Advertiser Press, 1970)

King, Andy, 'The Anglo-Scottish Marches and the Perception of "the North" in Fifteenth-Century England', *Northern History*, 49 (March 2012), 37–50

Lavezzo, Kathy, ed., *Imagining a Medieval English Nation* (Minneapolis: University of Minnesota Press, 2004)

Lawrence-Mathers, Anne, *Manuscripts in Northumbria in the Eleventh and Twelfth Centuries* (Woodbridge: Boydell, 2003)

——, 'Bede, St Cuthbert, and the Science of Miracles', *Reading Medieval Studies*, 45 (2019), 3–28

Licence, Tom, 'The Benedictines, the Cistercians and the Acquisition of a Hermitage in Twelfth-Century Durham', *Journal of Medieval History*, 29.4 (2003), 315–29

——, *Hermits and Recluses in English Society, 950–1200* (Oxford: Oxford University Press, 2011)

Little, A. G., 'The Authorship of the Lanercost Chronicle', *English Historical Review*, 32 (1917), 48–49

Macht, Claire, 'The Changing Nature of Monastic Historical Writing in Late Medieval England' (unpublished doctoral thesis, University of Oxford, 2020)

Reichl, Karl, 'Orality and Performance', in *A Companion to Medieval Popular Romance*, ed. by Raluca Radulescu and Cory James Rushton (Cambridge: Brewer, 2009), pp. 132–49

'The Return of the Saint?' (20 September 2007), *The Press* (York) <www.yorkpress.co.uk/news/1701455.the-return-of-the-saint> [accessed 14 Jan 2022]

Sanok, Catherine, *New Legends of England: Forms of Community in Late Medieval English Saints' Lives* (Philadelphia: University of Pennsylvania Press, 2018)

Sarnowsky, Jürgen, ed., *Mendicants, Military Orders, and Regionalism in Medieval Europe*, (Aldershot: Ashgate, 1999)

Slater, Laura, 'Recreating the Judean Hills? English Hermits and the Holy Land', *Journal of Medieval History*, 42.5 (2016), 603–26

'St Robert of Knaresborough, 1160–1218' <strobertofknaresborough.org.uk> [accessed 29 April 2020]

Turville-Petre, Thorlac, *England the Nation: Language, Literature, and National Identity, 1290–1340* (Oxford: Clarendon Press, 1996)

Thornton, Tim, *Prophecy, Politics, and the People in Early Modern England* (Woodbridge: Boydell, 2006)

Walker, Simon, 'Political Saints in Later Medieval England', in *Political Culture in Later Medieval England*, ed. by Michael Braddick (Manchester: Manchester University Press, 2006), pp. 198–222

Webb, Diana, *Pilgrimage in Medieval England* (London: Hambledon and London, 2000)

Weiler, Björn, 'Matthew Paris on the Writing of History', *Journal of Medieval History*, 35.3 (2009), 254–78

Whitehead, Christiania, 'Spiritual Healing: Healing Miracles Associated with the Twelfth-Century Northern Cult of St Cuthbert', in *Medieval and Early Modern Literature, Science and Medicine*, ed. by Rachel Falconer and Denis Renevey (Tübingen: Narr, 2013), pp. 173–85

CYNTHIA TURNER CAMP

Praying to Northern Saints
in English Books of Hours

On 17 August, 1415, Henry V knighted his esquire and long-time companion William Porter.[1] Porter had been instrumental in the English troops' landing outside Harfleur, and he fought alongside his king at the Battle of Agincourt.[2] Between 1417 and 1421, Porter aided Henry's subjugation of France, later becoming an executor of the king's will.[3] Some five to ten years after Agincourt, Porter ordered a Book of Hours for himself, lavishly decorated by the Fastolf Master, now New York, Pierpont Morgan Library, MS M.105.[4] That book includes sixty-seven suffrages (short intercessory prayers) for sixty-one saints — an immense number unprecedented, to the best of my knowledge, in English Books of Hours. Of those sixty-one saints, sixteen are British holy men and women. Some are commemorated in English Books of Hours regularly, like Edmund of East Anglia and Ætheldreda, and some, like Jaenbehrt of Canterbury and Richard of Chichester, receive seemingly unique prayers.

One unexpected feature of Porter's suffrage collection is commemorations of the northern saints John of Bridlington, John of Beverley, William of York, and Cuthbert. Usually, atypical suffrages can be used to provenance a manuscript, on the assumption that devotees wanted prayers for their favourite local saints. William Porter, however, had no ties to the northern counties. His landholdings were primarily in Northamptonshire, Cambridgeshire, and Suffolk, and his wife Agnes brought him property in Kent and Cambridgeshire.[5] Porter could have embraced John of Beverley after Agincourt and John of Bridlington was

---

1 This essay could not have been written without help from many individuals, including John Jenkins, Julian Luxford, Kathryn McKee, and the engaged audience at the Northern Lights conference.

2 Barker, *Agincourt*, pp. 151–53, 161; Mortimer, *1415*, pp. 326–27, 501; Wylie and Waugh, *Reign of Henry the Fifth*, II, p. 17. On Porter, see Dodd, 'Henry V's Establishment', pp. 46, 52; Woodger, 'Porter'; Wylie and Waugh, *Reign of Henry the Fifth*, I, pp. 344–45.

3 Allmand, *Henry V*, p. 177; Strong and Strong, 'Last Will', pp. 86–88, 97.

4 Driver, 'Me fault faire', p. 425.

5 Woodger, 'Porter'.

> **Cynthia Turner Camp** (ctcamp@uga.edu) is Associate Professor of English at the University of Georgia, Athens, GA, USA.

Late Medieval Devotion to Saints from the North of England: New Directions, ed. by Christiania Whitehead, Hazel J. Hunter Blair, and Denis Renevey, MCS 48 (Turnhout: Brepols, 2022), pp. 99–125
BREPOLS ❦ PUBLISHERS   10.1484/M.MCS-EB.5.124346

widely honoured, but William and Cuthbert only appear otherwise in Books of Hours firmly linked to Yorkshire. No immediate answer suggests itself as to why Porter wanted all four figures.

This surprise appearance of John of Bridlington, John of Beverley, William of York, and Cuthbert allows me to ask several interlocking questions concerning the veneration of northern saints across later medieval England. These four suffrages are unanticipated, but not unique, in Porter's hours: each saint receives at least one other suffrage elsewhere in English Books of Hours, and some were popular. Tracing the circulation of these four saints' suffrages, plus those of two more, Oswald of Northumbria and Archbishop Richard Scrope, opens a new window onto devotion to northern saints, in the North and across England. What emerges is a devotional current centred not on the Northumbrian worthies Bede praises — Cuthbert, Oswald, and Wilfrid — but on saints affiliated with Yorkshire and York Minster. It is partly informed by the Lancastrian fashion for embracing English saints, but it also operates independent of national trends. By attending to which saints appear together, I trace complex patterns of veneration that demonstrate how these saints were attractive to different communities for reasons beyond local affection.

The textual circulation of northern saints' suffrages reveals a coherent if narrow concept of northern sanctity among fifteenth-century English people, north and south. Whether or not 'the north of England' is a distinct region, visible as such to the island's denizens (in the late medieval period and beyond), and what its defining characteristics might be, is a question that scholars of the region have been pursuing since the 1990s.[6] Despite surface geographic, economic, and administrative cohesion, 'a supposedly *unitary* "north of England"' is not a meaningful unit for serious historical analysis' in the later Middle Ages.[7] Nevertheless, ideas about the North are recognizable in circulation even as its defining features (and what areas of the region are most relevant) are imagined variably by different communities.[8] That is, the north of England is a conceptual space imagined through, upon, and beyond the geographic place it purports to identify,[9] such that there were many different 'norths' of England, centred on different institutions or loyalties, envisioned variably depending on where the viewer stood. In the ways northern saints' suffrages cluster in prayerbooks, we can see one such concept of the north of England come into focus, centred on certain saints (and not others) within a tight geographic proximity. It is this conceptual image of northern sanctity that helps explain why William Porter included William of York and Cuthbert

---

6 Select studies include Jewell, *North-South Divide*; Russell, *Looking North*; Pollard, *North-Eastern England*; Green and Pollard ed., *Regional Identities*; Liddy and Britnell ed., *North-East England*.
7 Dobson, 'Politics', p. 3, emphasis added. See also Green and Pollard ed., *Regional Identities*; Liddy and Britnell ed., *North-East England*.
8 Jewell, *North-South Divide*, pp. 35–52; Taylor, 'Chaucer's Uncanny Regionalism'.
9 Green and Pollard, *Regional Identities*, pp. 15–16; Pollard, 'Introduction', pp. 8, 11; Baker and Billinge, 'Material and Imagined Geographies', p. 3.

alongside John of Beverley and John of Bridlington, while the malleability of these saints' intercessory appeal illuminates why Porter turned his spiritual interests northward in the first place.

Saints' variable devotional attraction make them useful lenses for examining the scaled affinities through which English people constructed their relationships with the country. As Catherine Sanok has recently outlined, English saints can constitute diverse religious loyalties for readers in different contexts. The Middle English legends she examines use saints 'to raise and explore questions about how different forms of community — regional, national, and supernational; religious and secular; intimate and imagined — relate to one another'.[10] Saints' ability to figure multiple, overlapping, and sometimes competing communities is not solely a feature of narrative hagiography; Felicity Riddy and Sarah Rees Jones have established how the Bolton Hours — a manuscript I consider below — and its assembly of saints tracks national religious interests and intensely local ones.[11] When northern saints appear in Books of Hours, therefore, they may be indexing identities other than, or in addition to, regional ones.

Books of Hours are an ideal genre of manuscript for studying the spiritual investments of later medieval noble and bourgeois classes. As the best sellers of the later Middle Ages, these prayerbooks would have been owned by every literate household, and elite families would have owned several. They are both aesthetic objects, often elaborately illuminated, and pragmatic collections of prayers designed to be said at certain times of the day or week.[12] It is the particular prayers included that concern us here. Although Books of Hours contain standardized texts — nearly every copy includes a calendar, the Hours of the Virgin, the Litany, and the Office of the Dead — they are also personalizable 'archives of prayer' frequently tailored to the patron's individual devotional priorities.[13] This interplay between personalization and standardization makes them challenging to work with. Long the purview of art historians, Books of Hours have been more rarely studied for their texts, and this scholarly lacuna makes it difficult to generalize about the circulation of individual prayers or to identify the rarity of particular saints.[14] That interplay, however, also makes them fruitful objects of inquiry into personal devotion, because they reveal what texts (standard and unexpected) their patrons found worth investing in. This essay therefore makes one contribution to the study of these texts by

---

10 Sanok, *New Legends*, p. 5.

11 Rees Jones and Riddy, 'Bolton Hours', pp. 250–51; Rees Jones, 'Richard Scrope', pp. 223–27.

12 Leroquais, *Les Livres d'Heures*, pp. i–lxx; Wieck, *Painted Prayers*; Wieck, *Time Sanctified*; Reinburg, *French Books of Hours*. On English Books of Hours, see Duffy, *Marking the Hours*; Morgan, 'English Books of Hours'.

13 The term is Virginia Reinburg's: Reinburg, *French Books of Hours*.

14 For example, Backhouse, *Books of Hours*; Wieck, *Painted Prayers* and Wieck, *Time Sanctified*. Exceptions include Scott-Stokes ed. and trans., *Women's Books of Hours*; Reinburg, *French Books of Hours*; Duffy, *Marking the Hours*, pp. 67–106.

detailing the circulation of suffrages for these six northern saints in Books of Hours made for use in England.[15]

A suffrage is a tripartite invocation of a saint found in nearly every Book of Hours.[16] Each suffrage consists of an antiphon or hymn, followed by a versicle with response and finally a prayer; in many manuscripts they are prefaced with a miniature of the saint holding her or his attribute. Suffrages are typically gathered together into coherent collections, organized by type of saint (apostles first, followed by martyrs, confessors, and virgins), but they can also appear singly at any point in a Book of Hours. In English *horae*, two suffrage collections commonly appear, one before the Hours of the Virgin and one integrated into it as *memoriae* at the end of the hour of Lauds; they can also appear later in the manuscript. Although suffrages for popular saints like John the Baptist, Christopher, and Katherine appear ubiquitously, among English saints Thomas Becket is the only standard inclusion. Therefore, if a Book of Hours includes a suffrage to an English saint, the original patron had to request that prayer, and the suffrage becomes diagnostic of the patron's special devotion to that individual; when an array of English saints appears in a single manuscript, it lets us devise a robust profile of the first owner's spiritual priorities as they map onto England's holy landscape.

Table 4.1. Books of Hours with suffrages to northern saints.

Manuscript	Location / Use / Date	Northern Saints' Suffrages
Percy Hours	Yorkshire / Use of York / 1275–1300	William of York
London, British Library, MS Add. 89379		
Madresfield Hours	Northern Yorkshire / Use of York / 1300–1340	Oswald of Northumbria
(private owner)		William of York
Oxford, Bodleian Library, MS lat. liturg. f. 2	Low Countries, updated in England / Use of Sarum / 1390–1410	John of Bridlington
		Richard Scrope
York Minster Library, MS Add. 54	England / Use of Sarum, updated to York / Late fourteenth century	Richard Scrope

---

15 The data in this study is drawn from a survey of ninety-five Books of Hours undertaken in 2018–2019.

16 Wieck, *Painted Prayers*, pp. 109–19; Wieck, *Time Sanctified*, pp. 111–23; Backhouse, *Books of Hours*, pp. 73–79, Reinburg, *French Books of Hours*, pp. 174–76. As Harper, 'Traces', p. 2 n. 4 notes, the suffrage originally appeared as a liturgical add-on to the Divine Office at Lauds and Vespers, and in monastic use differed in function but not form from *memoriae*. The terms are used interchangeably in studies of Books of Hours, but I distinguish them by length and position: suffrages include rhymed hymns, and *memoriae* use short antiphons and appear in Lauds of the Virgin.

Manuscript	Location / Use / Date	Northern Saints' Suffrages
Bolton Hours	York / Use of York / 1400–1425	Cuthbert
York Minster Library, MS Add. 2		John of Beverley
		John of Bridlington
		Richard Scrope
		William of York
York Minster Library, MS Add. 67	York / Use of York / 1400–1425	John of Beverley
		Richard Scrope
		William of York
Pavement Hours	York / Use of York / 1400–1425	Richard Scrope
York Minster Library, MS XVI.K.6		
Tabram Hours (private owner)	South-west England / Use of Sarum / 1401–1429	John of Bridlington
Beaufort-Beauchamp Hours	London and Bruges / Use of Sarum / 1401–1443	John of Bridlington
London, British Library, MS Royal 2.A.XVIII		
London, British Library, MS Add. 28946	Northern France, York / Use of Sarum, Use of York / 1410–1430	John of Bridlington, twice
Porter Hours	France for England / Use of Sarum / 1420–1425	Cuthbert
New York, Pierpont Morgan Library, MS M.105		John of Beverley
		John of Bridlington
		William of York
Hours of Elizabeth the Queen	London / Use of Sarum / 1420–1430	John of Bridlington
London, British Library, MS Add. 50001		
Leeds, Brotherton Collection, MS Add. 18	England, probably northern / Use of Sarum / Fifteenth century	William of York
Burnet Psalter	Low Countries for York / Use of Sarum / Fifteenth century	John of Beverley
Aberdeen University Library, MS 25		William of York
Cambridge, St John's College, MS E.26	London / Use of Sarum / Mid-fifteenth century	John of Beverley
		John of Bridlington
		Richard Scrope
London, British Library, MS Harley 955	Syon Abbey / 1450–1500	John of Beverley
		John of Bridlington

Suffrages for northern saints appear frequently in English prayerbooks made for use in northern and southern contexts (See Table 4.1). I have uncovered eleven suffrages for John of Bridlington, seven for William of York, six each for Archbishop Richard Scrope and John of Beverley, two for Cuthbert, and one for Oswald of Northumbria, all appearing in sixteen Books of Hours. As a point of comparison, Edmund King and Martyr, the most invoked English saint after Thomas Becket, has seventeen suffrages in this same corpus of manuscripts. More revealing than the number of witnesses, however, are the contexts in which these suffrages appear, the textual variations across them, and their circulation, together or singly. Viewed from these angles, these suffrages can be seen to participate in widespread and idiosyncratic patterns of veneration that reveal the multiple communities that these saints helped to imagine — including a common, flexible, yet recognizable concept of northern sanctity.

Richard Scrope

I begin with the most recent saint, Richard Scrope. Elected Archbishop of York in 1398, Scrope was executed by Henry IV in 1405 for his participation in the Yorkshire Risings.[17] His tomb in York Minster was almost immediately the site of pilgrimage, which Henry IV's supporters initially attempted to suppress but eventually accepted.[18] Although McKenna's claim that 'adherence to the cult of Richard Scrope and support of his shrine at York Minster was a touchstone of opposition to Lancastrian rule' is overstated,[19] the chapter at York Minster certainly allowed his cult in its early days against the pleasure of the crown,[20] and it was cultivated by families such as the Scropes of Masham and townspeople of York.[21] By the 1460s the House of York adopted Scrope on a low level and attempted, with limited success, to make him a partisan symbol.[22] Although Scrope had the potential to become an anti-Lancastrian figure, immediately following his death and during Edward IV's reign, it

---

17 On the Yorkshire Uprising, see Given-Wilson, *Henry IV*, pp. 267–70, 275–77; Walker, 'Yorkshire Risings'; Ormrod, 'Rebellion'. On Scrope's life and cult, see Goldberg ed., *Richard Scrope*.

18 Walker, 'Political Saints', pp. 84–85; French, 'Tomb of Archbishop Scrope', pp. 95–100; Norton, 'Richard Scrope', pp. 175–76; Piroyansky, *Martyrs*, pp. 51–52.

19 McKenna, 'Popular Canonization', p. 608, corrected in Walker, 'Political Saints', pp. 93–94.

20 Norton, 'Richard Scrope', pp. 173–76, 178–80.

21 French, 'Tomb of Archbishop Scrope', p. 97; Norton, 'Richard Scrope', pp. 176–77, 181–91, 212; Piroyansky, *Martyrs*, pp. 64–66; Rees Jones, 'Richard Scrope'; Rees Jones and Riddy, 'Bolton Hours'.

22 A window for Scrope was included in the glazing programme of Fotheringhay Church, where Richard Duke of York was reburied by Edward IV: Marks, 'Glazing of Fotheringhay', pp. 85, 96–97. Edward considered pursuing canonization for Scrope, but the chapter at York Minster declined. On this and other Yorkist uses of Scrope, see McKenna, 'Popular

is more accurate to say that the people of York deployed him as a figure of metropolitan sanctity, a *pastor* who could protect his townfolk from the afterlife as he had attempted to do in life.[23]

This tight correlation between veneration of Scrope and a York-centred identity plays out in suffrages to Scrope, which appear almost solely in Use of York Books of Hours produced in the early decades of the fifteenth century. Three of the six suffrages are integral to York *horae*, the most well studied being the Bolton Hours (York Minster Library, MS Add. 2), which also contains a remarkable two images of Scrope.[24] This manuscript was made *c.* 1405–1415 for a member of York's civic elite and stayed in that milieu throughout the century. As Rees Jones and Riddy have demonstrated, the manuscript can be located to York's Micklegate neighbourhood, where affiliations with the Scrope family were strong.[25] It also appears in York Minster Library, MS Add. 67 (fol. 102^{r-v}) and in York Minster Library, MS XVI.K.6 (fol. 27^{r-v}), in both standing alone rather than incorporated into the suffrage collection.[26] Two other suffrages were added to Sarum Books of Hours that were updated for Use of York. One appears on the flyleaves of York Minster Library, MS Add. 54.[27] The other, with a miniature (fol. 146^v), was added to Oxford, Bodleian Library, MS lat. liturg. f. 2 (fol. 147^{r-v}), which Norton argues was updated in 1406 for (and the Scrope suffrage added for) Henry, 3rd Lord Scrope of Masham (d. 1415), Archbishop Scrope's nephew and supporter.[28] All five *horae* are early witnesses to Scrope's cult, all locatable to the archdiocese (and often the city itself), and in some instances possibly owned by known supporters of the archbishop. In the case of the Bolton Hours and potentially Bodl., MS lat. liturg. f. 2, the Scrope suffrage signals intimate affiliations with civic neighbourhood and family. However, York Minster Library, MS XVI.K.6 was made for a parishioner of All Saints Pavement, across the river from Micklegate,[29] demonstrating that affection for Scrope had a wider appeal in the city. For all these patrons, a York identity and veneration of Scrope went hand in hand.

This cohesive picture is complicated by Cambridge, St John's College, MS E.26. This mid-fifteenth century Sarum *horae*, which was at Isleham, Cambridgeshire in the 1480s, was originally crafted for a London owner. Its calendar includes both St Erkenwald's feasts of 30 April and 14 November in red, and Erkenwald appears in the suffrages. Erkenwald's 14 November

---

Canonization', pp. 618–21; Walker, 'Political Saints', p. 94; Norton, 'Richard Scrope', pp. 199–202; Piroyansky, *Martyrs*, pp. 53–54, 67.

23 Piroyansky, *Martyrs*, pp. 55–56, 67–71.
24 Ker and Piper, *Medieval Manuscripts*, IV, pp. 786–91; Scott, *Later Gothic Manuscripts* no. 33, pp. 119–21; Rees Jones and Riddy, 'Bolton Hours'.
25 Rees Jones and Riddy, 'Bolton Hours', pp. 240–43, 247–49; Rees Jones, 'Richard Scrope', pp. 225–27.
26 Ker and Piper, *Medieval Manuscripts*, IV, pp. 811–13, 727–30.
27 Ker and Piper, *Medieval Manuscripts*, IV, pp. 809–11.
28 Scott, *Later Gothic Manuscripts*, pp. 89–92; Norton, 'Richard Scrope', pp. 188–90.
29 Ker and Piper, *Medieval Manuscripts*, IV, pp. 727–30.

translation feast occurs rarely in Books of Hours calendars, most commonly in books provenanced to London or in metropolitan contexts. Added to the calendar is a 1484 obit for Thomas Payton, who was a landowner in Isleham and twice served as sheriff of Cambridgeshire and Huntingdonshire.[30] A suffrage for Scrope appears in the *memoriae* in Lauds, closing the series of martyrs (fol. 55ʳ). This manuscript's features are consistent with a southern provenance — except the commemoration of Scrope, which (unlike the prayers found in the York manuscripts) was integrated with the others. Scrope's surprise appearance is difficult to account for, short of an otherwise invisible personal link to York by the original patron. It may be possible to explain this suffrage via normalization of the cult under Henry V, who approved of offerings at Scrope's tomb, or the Yorkist adoption of Scrope in the 1460s and 1470s.[31] A Middle English carol in honour of Scrope, added in a later fifteenth-century hand to Cambridge, Trinity College, MS R.4.20 (fol. 171ʳ), provides additional evidence for southern interest in Scrope.[32] In both the St John's College suffrage and the carol's addition to this southern manuscript, Scrope is detached from the tight-knit York community that originally embraced his cult to function as a generalized episcopal martyr and intercessor.

John of Bridlington

Whereas Scrope almost always marks clear-cut York civic affiliations, John of Bridlington was '[b]y the middle of the fifteenth century [...] firmly established as [an object] of royal devotion', such that his cult is frequently seen as a Lancastrian phenomenon.[33] An Augustinian canon noted for his piety and humility, even after he became prior of Bridlington, John Thweng died in 1379; within ten years of his death, the miracles done at his tomb 'stunned almost the whole of England' and he was canonized in 1401.[34] That canonization push, begun during Richard II's reign,[35] was completed by Henry IV, who had gone on pilgrimage to John's tomb in 1391 immediately upon returning from his Prussian crusading activity.[36] Lancastrian devotion

---

30 James, *Descriptive Catalogue*, pp. 162–65. I am grateful to Kathryn McKee, Archivist at St John's College, for providing me with information about this manuscript. On Payton, see Burke, *Genealogical and Heraldic History*, p. 409.

31 Piroyansky, *Martyrs*, pp. 52–54; see also above, n. 21.

32 James, *Western Manuscripts*, II, pp. 147–49. Furnivall ed., *Hymns*, p. 128; 'The Bishop Scrope', ed. by Wright. The manuscript is of the 1440s: Lydgate, *Siege of Thebes*, pp. 57–58. The poem is discussed in Wright, 'Genres of Sanctity', pp. 119–26.

33 Sanok, *New Legends*, p. 23.

34 'ut pene totam Angliam ducerent in stuporem': Walsingham, *St Albans Chronicle*, ed. and trans. by Taylor, Childs, and Watkiss, I, pp. 882–83. Purvis, *St John*, pp. 31–42 prints the canonization bull.

35 Purvis, *St John*, pp. 18, 48.

36 Given-Wilson, *Henry IV*, pp. 381, 69–70; Mortimer, *Fears of Henry IV*, pp. 379–80; Grosjean,

PRAYING TO NORTHERN SAINTS IN ENGLISH BOOKS OF HOURS 107

continued apace under Henry V, who took John as his 'special protector'.[37] Henry visited John's shrine as prince in 1408 and as king in 1421,[38] and several of his retainers, especially the Beauforts, were equally devoted to him.[39] Henry VI too spent time in Beverley during his 1448 tour through the northern counties,[40] and Bridlington Priory's charters reveal that the priory was under royal sponsorship from Richard II through to Edward IV.[41]

This narrative of royal, especially Lancastrian affiliation accords with many of John's suffrages. Six of its eleven witnesses are in southern manuscripts, four with definite Lancastrian connections. It appears at the end of a manuscript made for Henry VI, London, British Library, MS Cotton Cleopatra A.XIII. The manuscript's primary text is the *Tractatus de regimine principum ad Regem Henricum Sextum*, written for the king in the 1430s and followed by a series of prayers, including one for John of Bridlington (fols 179^r–180^v).[42] The *Tractatus* urges Henry to call upon John of Bridlington by name;[43] evidently, John was seen as a suitable spiritual patron for the young king. It also appears in the Beaufort-Beauchamp Book of Hours (London, British Library, MS Royal 2.A.XVIII).[44] The opening folios with fabulously illuminated miniatures of and prayers to saints, including John of Bridlington, were originally part of Rennes, Bibliothèque Municipale, MS 22, a *c.* 1401–1410 Book of Hours produced in London for John Beaufort (d. 1410) and Margaret Holland (d. 1439).[45] John Beaufort was the eldest of John of Gaunt's children by Katherine Swynford and crucial to the establishment of Henry IV's reign,[46] making the original suffrage a marker of loyalty to the crown as well as personal Beaufort affection. The core of the Beaufort-Beauchamp Hours was produced *c.* 1430–1440 for

---

'De S. Johanne', p. 107; Walsingham, *St Alban's Chronicle*, ed. and trans. by Taylor, Childs, and Watkiss, II, p. 410; Twemlow, 'St John', pp. 129–31. Henry also visited John's shrine in 1398 and 1401: Given-Wilson, *Henry IV*, pp. 109–10.

37 'specialis patroni sui': Walsingham, *St Alban's Chronicle*, ed. and trans. by Taylor, Childs, and Watkiss, II, pp. 526–27. Henry invokes John of Bridlington in his will of July 1415: Rymer ed., *Foedera* IV, part 2, p. 138.

38 Allmand, *Henry V*, pp. 32–33, 157–58; Doig, 'Propaganda'.

39 Thomas Beaufort was a pilgrim to Bridlington in 1417: Walsingham, *St Alban's Chronicle*, ed. and trans. by Taylor, Childs, and Watkiss, II, p. 722. John Beaufort included a suffrage for John of Bridlington in his prayerbook (below). The will of Thomas, earl of Arundel, claims he went to Bridlington with Prince Henry and vowed to pay the shrine 5 marks any year he did not visit: *Register of Chichele*, ed. by Jacob, II, p. 74. John appears in the stained glass of the Beauchamp Chapel, the funerary chapel of Richard Beauchamp, earl of Warwick (d. 1439), alongside Wenefred; Richard also left an image to John's shrine in his will: Winston, 'Painted Glass', pp. 302, 307.

40 Sanok, *New Legends* p. 23; Wolffe, *Henry VI*, p. 367; Webb, *Pilgrimage*, p. 136.

41 Purvis, *St John*, p. 49.

42 *Tractatus*, ed. by Genet, pp. 40–43.

43 *Tractatus*, ed. by Genet, p. 114.

44 Scott, *Later Gothic Manuscripts*, pp. 127–34; Rickert, 'So-Called Beaufort Hours'; Frońska, 'Beaufort/Beauchamp Hours', p. 147.

45 Frońska, 'Beaufort/Beauchamp Hours', p. 147.

46 Harriss, 'Beaufort, John, marquess of Dorset'.

Margaret Beauchamp (d. 1482), whose second husband (m. 1442) was John II Beaufort (d. 1444), son of John Beaufort and Margaret Holland, and a major player in Lancastrian attempts to hold French conquests during Henry VI's minority.[47] The miniature and suffrage for John of Bridlington, along with the other Rennes leaves, were probably added to the Beaufort-Beauchamp Hours after Margaret's marriage to John II, where it again reiterates Beaufort and Beauchamp loyalty to the Lancastrian cause.[48]

The other two manuscripts with clear Lancastrian ties demonstrate how Henry V's adoption of John of Bridlington spread further into the royal affinity. Another suffrage appears, with miniature, in the Porter Hours (fol. 52[r–v]), as well as in London, British Library, MS Harley 955, a prayerbook associated with Syon Abbey.[49] In both, John of Bridlington stands alongside other saints embraced by the king: John of Beverley and Wenefred.[50] Given Porter's high standing with Henry V and Henry's foundation of Syon Abbey,[51] these witnesses relate affection for the sainted canon to affection for the House of Lancaster.

The three other southern Books of Hours, however, indicate that devotion to John of Bridlington was not strictly a Lancastrian affair. One appears in Cambridge, St John's College, MS E.26 (fols 55[v]–56[r]), of probable London origins and, with its suffrage for Scrope, less likely to be a Lancastrian production.[52] Another (fol. 19[r]) appears in the Tabram Hours, a *c.* 1401–1429 Sarum *horae* in private hands that Julian Luxford has provenanced to Devonshire and that has no clear Lancastrian connections.[53] The final witness is the Hours of Elizabeth the Queen (London, British Library, MS Add. 50001), a *de luxe* manuscript produced in England *c.* 1420–1430, possibly for a member of the Neville family, for it includes an erased prayer (fol. 147[r]) for the soul of Cecily Neville, Duchess of Warwick (d. 1450) and niece of Cecily Neville, Duchess of York.[54] Eventually owned by (and named for) her cousin, Elizabeth of York, daughter of the Duchess of York and wife of Henry VII, the manuscript had a number of suffrages, including one to John of Bridlington (fol. 154[v]), added in the later fifteenth century. Given the manuscript's movement through the Neville family to land in Elizabeth's possession, it seems probable that the suffrage was added for Neville or Yorkist use during the Wars of the Roses. Although it might be tempting to read this added suffrage as a retrenchment of Neville or Yorkist regional distinction, it can also be understood as a sign of royal aspirations, as English kings since Richard II had patronized John's cult.

---

47 Harriss, 'Beaufort, John, duke of Somerset'.

48 Scott, *Later Gothic Manuscripts*, p. 131.

49 *Catalogue of the Harleian Manuscripts*, I, pp. 481–82; Rand, 'Syon Pardon', p. 332.

50 On Wenefred as a Lancastrian saint, see Sanok, *New Legends*, pp. 21–22.

51 Allmand, *Henry V*, pp. 274–76.

52 James, *Descriptive Catalogue*, pp. 162–65.

53 Luxford, 'Luxury and Locality', pp. 226–27, 241–44. I am grateful to Julian for supplying me with the John of Bridlington suffrage from this manuscript.

54 Drimmer, 'Hours of Elizabeth the Queen', p. 155; Scott, *Later Gothic Manuscripts*, p. 175.

John of Bridlington's suffrages also appear four times in three Use of York *horae*. In the Bolton Hours, John of Bridlington becomes a decisively northern saint, paired as he is with Archbishop Scrope, William of York, John of Beverley, and Cuthbert. John of Bridlington's suffrage also appears in Bodl. Lib., MS Lat. liturg. f. 2 (fol. 143[r]), the Book of Hours updated to Use of York that contains a prayer for Scrope.[55] These books celebrate John alongside Scrope as the two most recent English saints, both hailing from Yorkshire. Finally, London, British Library, MS Add. 28946 is a composite Book of Hours, *c.* 1410–1430, produced by the Augustinian Friars of York, that interleaves quires from both a Sarum Book of Hours and a York Book of Hours.[56] The hand associated with the York material wrote two different suffrages to John of Bridlington (fols 100[r]–101[r]), back to back, to open a collection of suffrages late in the manuscript. Although John of Bridlington was an Augustinian canon and so not of the same orders as the friars, this doubled veneration of John may derive from their shared status as learned and pious members of the Yorkshire clerical ranks. In all four instances, John's northern origins are foregrounded by pairing him with other northern holy men, saints, and clerics, within a York liturgical book.

John of Beverley

Like John of Bridlington, John of Beverley is often seen as co-opted to the Lancastrian machine.[57] English kings had adopted him as their protector since the thirteenth century, especially when heading into battle against Scotland; this royal patronage escalated under Henry IV and Henry V.[58] Henry IV visited Beverley during his 1408 tour of the North, and it was claimed that John's tomb seeped oil when Henry returned from exile.[59] But it was English success at the Battle of Agincourt on 25 October 1415 — the date of John's translation feast, as well as the feast of Crispin and Crispian — that cemented Lancastrian devotion to the northern bishop. Early in 1416, Archbishop Chichele decreed that the southern province should recognize John's feast on 7 May; later that year he also ordered England to celebrate 25 October as a high feast day in nine lessons (three for John of Bridlington) to honour the Agincourt victory, a liturgical elevation designed to affirm God's approval of Henry V's military

---

55 Scott, *Later Gothic Manuscripts*, pp. 89, 91–92.

56 Friedman, 'Richard de Thorpe'.

57 Barker, *Agincourt*, pp. 342–43; Wilson, *Life and After-Life*, pp. 123–24; Sanok, *New Legends*, pp. 20, 24.

58 Wilson, *Life and Afterlife*, pp. 120–24. Kings since Henry I carried John's banner into battle: Sharpe, 'Banners'.

59 Mortimer, *Fears of Henry IV*, pp. 379–80; Raine ed., *Historians of the Church of York*, III, p. 288. On John of Beverley's oil, particularly the extensive relationship between his oil and the Lancastrian kings, see Jenkins' essay in this volume, pp. 156–59.

successes.[60] Henry also included Beverley along with Bridlington in his 1421 progress through northern England.[61]

As with John of Bridlington, the suffrage evidence both supports and complicates this narrative of Lancastrian patronage. Two of John of Beverley's six suffrages show up in Lancastrian contexts, alongside John of Bridlington and Wenefred: the Porter Hours (fol. 51^{r-v}) and MS Harley 955 (fol. 55^v), the Syon prayerbook. He also appears with John of Bridlington and Scrope in the London *horae* St John's College, MS E.26 (fol. 55^r–56^r). However, in three others he operates as a northern more than Lancastrian figure: the Bolton Hours, York Minster Library, MS Add. 67 (fols 125^{r-v}), and the Burnet Psalter (Aberdeen, Aberdeen University Library, MS 25, fols 259^v–260^r).[62] The former two are Use of York manuscripts with a civic focus, as suggested by their Scrope suffrages, and Rogers posits that the Burnet Psalter was produced for a merchant of York. In all three, John also appears alongside William of York, a grouping that indicates a sustained interest in northern saints to which I will return. John of Beverley does at times track Lancastrian associations, but in other contexts — most notably the Bolton Hours and York Minster Library, MS Add. 67 — he stands alongside holy archbishops of York as an ancient Yorkshire bishop who grounds a lineage of northern sanctity in the early English past.[63] This construction of northern holiness may stand against a broadly English notion of sanctity, if the inclusion of Scrope does denote regional resistance to royal prerogative, or it may simply reflect a civic pride in the Minster's episcopal saints.[64]

William of York, Cuthbert, Oswald

The last three — William of York, Cuthbert, and Oswald the King — appear almost solely in Books of Hours with northern associations. William of York, Archbishop of York 1143–1147 and again 1153–1154, was canonized in 1226, after which point he was 'greeted by an almost universal lack of interest'.[65] Never enjoying an expansive cult, even in the North, William nevertheless received seven suffrages, four in Use of York *horae* and two in Books of Hours otherwise

---

60 *Register of Chichele*, ed. by Jacob, III, pp. 14, 28–29; Pfaff, *Liturgy*, p. 439; Allmand, *Henry V*, p. 101.

61 Allmand, *Henry V*, p. 158; Doig, 'Propaganda', p. 170.

62 James, *Catalogue*, pp. 25–35; Rogers, 'Patrons and Purchasers', pp. 1173–76.

63 Although John was Bishop of York, he is frequently given archiepiscopal status in York Minster contexts: French and O'Connor, *York Minster*, p. 15. York was made an archbishopric in 735.

64 Neither manuscript includes suffrages for southern English saints save Becket. York Minster Library, MS Add. 67 includes a suffrage for St Ninian, making the volume look north rather than south for additional holy figures.

65 Norton, *St William*, p. 202. On William's cult in fourteenth- and fifteenth-century York, see Rentz, 'Castles for St William', and see Jenkins in this volume.

interested in northern saints, plus the Porter Hours.[66] Cuthbert was, of course, the premier saint of ancient Northumbria, his reputation having been established by Bede in his *Historia ecclesiastica* and his two *vitae* of Cuthbert, and extended by Durham Priory in the years after its 1083 refoundation.[67] Despite his widespread fame, Cuthbert only received two suffrages. One is in the Bolton Hours, where Cuthbert's presence suggests a desire for a comprehensive collection of northern saints; the other (fols 54^{r-v}) is in the Porter Hours, where William (fols 53^{r-v}) also appears. Finally, Oswald, the Northumbrian king celebrated by Bede for his holiness who was killed at Maserfeld by Penda of Mercia,[68] is even more rarely attested than Cuthbert. He receives only one suffrage, in the fourteenth-century Madresfield Hours which is provenanced to the far north of Yorkshire, where he accompanies William (fols 52^v–53^v).[69]

Grouping the Northern Saints

As I have been indicating, these northern saints tend to appear in Books of Hours *in groups*, often clustered together. This frequent juxtaposition suggests how they could collectively constitute a concept of northern holiness, even when those saints were adopted by patrons (like William Porter) outside the North. This is a different concept of northern sanctity than one 'focused, first of all, on Monkwearmouth-Jarrow and Lindisfarne and, later, on the bishopric of Durham, linked in time and space by the cult of St Cuthbert';[70] it is centred instead on the archbishopric of York and, secondarily, the East Riding. It does not praise holy kings like Edwin or abbesses like Hilda, but rather York's bishops and archbishops from the eighth century to the fifteenth. Its centripetal force incorporates John of Beverley from his monastic foundation and burial site of Beverley back to the cathedral community where he served much of his career, and it also draws in John of Bridlington, who had no connection to York.[71] Cuthbert and Oswald play a supporting, not defining role. This concept of northern sanctity takes York Minster and its holy archbishops as

---

66 The four York Hours are the Bolton Hours (fols 184^{r-v}); York Minster Library, MS Add. 67 (fols 120^{r-v}); the Madresfield Hours, a *c.* 1330 manuscript from northwest Yorkshire (Backhouse, *Madresfield Hours*, pp. 25–26 and pl. 29–30) (fols 54^{r-v}); and BL, MS Add. 89379, a Use of York *horae* owned by the Percy family 1275–1300 (fol. 42^v). The two others — the Burnet Psalter (fol. 260^r) and Leeds, Leeds University, Brotherton Collection, MS Add. 18 (fols 153^{r-v}) — emphasize northern saints throughout. Rogers, 'Patrons and Purchasers', pp. 1173–76 proposes a York merchant as the first owner of the Burnet Psalter. Brotherton, MS Add. 18 is a Sarum manuscript *c.* 1404–1425 that includes Wilfrid, William of York, and Oswin King and Martyr in its calendar, saints who rarely appear in southern contexts. Pickering, 'Brotherton Collection MS 18', pp. 223–26.

67 Piper, 'First Generation of Durham Monks'; Tudor, 'Cult of St Cuthbert'.

68 Bede, *Ecclesiastical History*, ed. and trans. by Colgrave and Mynors, III.2–3, 6, 9–13.

69 Backhouse, *Madresfield Hours*, pl. 26–28.

70 Coombe and Whitehead, 'Introduction', p. 6.

71 Wilson, *Life and After-Life*, pp. 27–34.

the core to which other northern spiritual figures can be added to refine its image of regional holiness.

The frequency with which northern saints appear together is worth pausing over, because it is unusual. Suffrages to English saints do not cluster in regular patterns. For instance, despite the high number of suffrages to the two East Anglian saints Edmund King and Martyr (seventeen) and Ætheldreda (eight), they only appear together in two Books of Hours: New Haven, Beineke Library, Osborn MS a44 (c. 1390–1420) and the Wollaton Prayerbook.[72] Similarly, suffrages for English nun-virgins occasionally circulate together, with Ætheldreda as the consistent figure. She appears alongside Frideswide and Cuthburga in the Wollaton Prayerbook and alongside Wenefred in Oxford, Bodleian Library, MS Auct. D.inf.2.11 and London, British Library, MS Harley 955,[73] and both Frideswide and Ætheldreda were added (albeit by different hands) to Cambridge, Cambridge University Library, MS Ii.6.2.[74] Finally, Wenefred appears with John of Bridlington and John of Beverley in the two *horae* with probable Lancastrian connections that I have been discussing.[75] So although southern saints' suffrages can track conceptions of sanctity that align with regional, royal, and/or professional identities, they do so with little regularity.

In comparison, two or more northern saints appear in eight of the sixteen manuscripts under consideration here, and four include three or more northern saints. A deeper analysis of when these saints appear together, and when they appear singly, reveals some of the identities these northern saints can index. It also elucidates the nuanced ways that northern sanctity was constituted in these prayer archives.

John of Bridlington, Archbishop Scrope, and William of York all appear occasionally as the only northern saint in a suffrage collection. When John of Bridlington does so, it is primarily in Sarum *horae* created for consumption in elite southern contexts: the Beaufort-Beauchamp Hours, the Hours of Elizabeth of York, and the Tabram Hours. The exception is BL, MS Add. 28946, the Use of York manuscript affiliated with the Augustinian Friars of York, where the paired suffrages to John may track a professional, Yorkshire-centred interest. A similar pattern holds for manuscripts that include only Archbishop Scrope[76] or only William of York.[77] In these cases, the appearance of a single northern saint seems to indicate York affinities, as these four manuscripts are either Use of York or have rare northern saints in their calendars.

Because John of Bridlington and John of Beverley were adopted by the Lancastrian regime, one might expect their pairing in Books of Hours to

---

72 I exclude the Porter Hours from my tallies here because of its unique position in my corpus. It includes suffrages for all saints named here. Nottingham, University of Nottingham, MS WLC/LM/LL: Hanna and Turville-Petre, *Wollaton Manuscripts*, pp. 102–03.

73 On Oxford, Bodl. Lib., MS Auct. D. inf. 2.11 (c. 1440–1450), see Driver, 'Me fault faire', p. 441.

74 Duffy, *Marking the Hours*, pp. 83–96.

75 The Porter Hours and MS Harley 955, discussed above.

76 York Minster Library, MS Add. 54 and York Minster Library, MS XIV.K.6, discussed above.

77 The Percy Hours and Brotherton Collection, MS Add. 18, discussed above.

point to a Lancastrian context. It does so only occasionally. Although this is a partial explanation for their grouping in the Porter Hours, the only other prayerbook in which this seems the case is the Syon MS Harley 955.

The other times the two Johns appear, it is alongside other northern saints to signal York affiliations. This is clearly the case in the Bolton Hours; by placing them in a devotional context that also includes Scrope, William of York, and Cuthbert, the Bolton Hours claims these two saints for a civic spiritual identity, situating these five figures within York's liturgical landscape.[78] This is also an effect of Scrope's addition to Bodl. Lib., MS Lat. liturg. f. 2; while John of Bridlington's suffrage was included when the manuscript was updated for the Use of York, Scrope's suffrage is in a different hand and may have been a slightly later addition.[79] By first including the canon during the liturgical personalization, the original owners incorporate the Bridlington saint into the liturgical ambit of the Minster; by later adding the archbishop, they incrementally mark the book as distinctively York- and possibly family-centric. When John of Beverley appears with William, that pairing too integrates John of Beverley into a York-centred conception of sanctity. This is certainly the case in the Bolton Hours and York Minster Library, MS Add. 67. But it also operates in the Porter Hours (as I will elaborate below) and the Burnet Psalter. Even St John's College, MS E.26, the southern manuscript which adopts Scrope as a newly popular archbishop, positions him in the *memoriae* alongside the northern (arch)bishops John of Beverley and William as well as two southern ones, Thomas Becket and Erkenwald. Here, English episcopal holiness is lauded, but it is also weighted north.

This gradual absorption of the East Riding saints into the Minster's ambit would have been reinforced by their different groupings within the Yorkshire landscape. The association of John of Beverley with William as icons of York Minster's episcopal sanctity, despite the fact that John's shrine was thirty miles away in Beverley, was bolstered by the West and East Windows in York Minster, where they appear together as holy archbishops.[80] As John Jenkins demonstrates in this volume, John of Beverley's tomb exuded oil frequently as a method of associating the Beverley saint with the *myroblyte* William.[81] York clergy in the later fourteenth and fifteenth centuries were frequently enjoined to do penance by going on pilgrimage to some combination of John of Beverley, John of Bridlington, William of York, and/or Wilfrid of Ripon's tombs, emphasizing via travel the interconnectedness of these northern holy men.[82] John of Bridlington's association with the York Minster luminaries was undoubtedly informed by the pilgrimage route that linked Beverley,

---

78 Rees Jones, 'Richard Scrope', pp. 223–27.
79 Scott, *Later Gothic Manuscripts*, p. 92.
80 French and O'Connor, *York Minster: A Catalogue*, pp. 29, 35; French, *York Minster: The Great East Window*, pp. 11, 141.
81 See Jenkins' essay in this volume, pp. 156–59.
82 York, York Minster Library, MS M2(1)f. I am grateful to John Jenkins for this reference.

Bridlington, and occasionally York. The two Johns were so frequently visited together that a pilgrim's badge portraying both was struck.[83] The pilgrim experience of physically travelling to and through the East Riding would have accentuated the sense that these two saints belonged particularly to Yorkshire, their sometime national appeal notwithstanding.

This centripetal concept of Yorkshire sanctity even incorporates the far northern saints Cuthbert and perhaps Oswald.[84] Despite his international fame, Cuthbert only appears in the most expansive suffrage collections, never attracting devotional attention in his own right. Rather, he appears as an adjutant to William and John of Beverley, his ancient sanctity shoring up a northern episcopal holiness focused otherwise on York. Only in the Madresfield Hours, a manuscript first used in the fourteenth century by one Matilda, daughter of Roger de Lascelles and linked to north-west Yorkshire and County Durham, is York not the centre of gravity.[85] This manuscript leans further north through its provenance and through the presence of the Northumbrian martyr Oswald, whose head famously rested at Durham Cathedral. In this instance, William and Oswald geographically bookend a northern sanctity that stretches from York to Durham.

Textual Variation, Conceptual Cohesion

This expansive notion of a Yorkshire sanctity is *conceptual*, rather than *textual*. That is, these suffrages cluster not because scribes found them together in their exemplars and copied them together by rote. Were this true, we would find the same prayers circulating in common groupings — especially for William and John of Beverley, and/or John of Beverley and John of Bridlington, who each appear together four times. But we don't. Rather, they appear in discrete textual combinations in eight independent prayerbooks because these saints went together in the imaginations of patrons and bookmakers alike. Those patrons and bookmakers would have sought or devised suffrages for these saints, as the textual evidence also suggests that scribes sometimes had difficulty accessing common versions of these prayers.

The evidence indicates modest standardization of these suffrages, and that they never circulated together. William of York evinces the most textual stability. His seven suffrages have the same prayer, from Vespers for William's feast in the York Breviary, four with the same antiphon.[86] This suffrage's earliest

---

83 The early fifteenth-century badge, now in the Museum of London (item ID 88.84), can be viewed online at <https://collections.museumoflondon.org.uk/online/object/31330.html>. On pilgrimage to the two shrines, plus William of York, see Webb, *Pilgrims and Pilgrimage*, pp. 143, 145–46.

84 Although Oswald had a cult centre at Gloucester, no suffrages for him appear in Gloucester or southern English contexts.

85 Backhouse, *Madresfield Hours*, pp. 25–26.

86 The prayer is 'Deus qui nos beati wilelmi confessoris': *Breviarium ad usum insignis ecclesie*

PRAYING TO NORTHERN SAINTS IN ENGLISH BOOKS OF HOURS   115

attestation, in the Percy Hours (1275–1300) only fifty years after William's canonization in 1226, corroborates other evidence that William's cult was tightly centred on York Minster itself. John of Beverley and John of Bridlington have some degree of standardization. While each has two common suffrages, each also has nonce suffrages: suffrages apparently independently composed.[87] The two extant suffrages for Cuthbert differ. Finally, as one might expect for a new-come saint, there are five completely different Scrope suffrages among the six witnesses, demonstrating almost no uniformity.[88] Although there is some evidence that scribes could acquire standardized suffrages, especially for William, it appears as though they and their patrons were sometimes left to their own devices in compiling these prayers.

More importantly, none of these Books of Hours contain the same groupings of suffrage texts. We might expect the four Use of York manuscripts produced 1400–1425 to share prayers; however, they do not. While York Minster Library, MS Add. 67 and the Bolton Hours contain identical prayers for William of York, their suffrages for John of Beverley and Scrope differ. Similarly, the Bolton Hours and BL, MS Add. 28946 contain different suffrages for John of Bridlington, even though both were made within York. All four include unique prayers for Scrope, despite being produced at the epicentre of his early cult. Only the Bolton Hours (made in York) and the Burnet Psalter (made in the Low Countries for a probable York patron) contain identical prayers for John of Beverley as well as nearly the same prayer for William of York — but the fact that they were made in different locales and the textual differences in the William *memoriae* argue against the likelihood that the suffrages circulated together.[89] The one place textual uniformity obtains is in the three southern Books of Hours that contain only a suffrage for John of Bridlington.[90] The Beaufort-Beauchamp Hours, the Hours of Elizabeth the Queen, and the Tabram Hours contain identical texts, suggesting that this suffrage was widely available in southern England in the early fifteenth century.[91]

Eboracensis, ed. by Lawley, II, col. 297. The shared antiphon is 'O Willelme pastor'.

87   The suffrage printed in Grosjean, 'De S. Johanne', pp. 109–10 appears in three manuscripts; two others begin 'Salue sancte prior'. There are four nonce suffrages. John of Beverley's suffrage 'Inclite doctor ave preceptor' appears three times, and the suffrage 'Ave doctor nobilis presul eboraci', which is also attested in John of Tynemouth's *Sanctilogium*, appears once: Harper, 'Traces of Lost Medieval Offices?', p. 18. There is one nonce suffrage.

88   The one common suffrage appears in Cambridge, St John's College, MS E.26 and York Minster Library, MS Add. 54. Four suffrages are printed in *Horae Eboracenses*, pp. 181–83.

89   The shared suffrage for John of Beverley is 'Inclite doctor ave preceptor'. While the Bolton Hours contains the standard suffrage for William, the Burnet Psalter includes a variant versicle, 'Magnificauit eum'.

90   Grosjean, 'De S. Johanne', pp. 109–10.

91   The Hours of Elizabeth the Queen and the relevant sections of the Beaufort-Beauchamp Hours were produced in London, and Luxford has tentatively assigned the Tabram Hours to south-west England: Scott, *Later Gothic Manuscripts*, pp. 171, 127; Luxford, 'Luxury and Locality', pp. 238–41.

Appearing in wildly varied textual combinations, these suffrages demonstrate the strength, and the flexibility, of the conceptual northern sanctity that unites them. While each saint can represent other communities and other modes of holiness, their frequent clustering in prayerbooks reinforces their geographic proximity and regional association. These suffrages therefore participate in the 'kaleidoscopic mosaics which made up whatever the fifteenth-century north was',[92] their various groupings demonstrating a coherent focus on York and its Minster even as each assembly nuances a different facet of Yorkshire sanctity.

William Porter's Northern Saints

We now have a firmer foundation for assessing these four northern saints' appearance in William Porter's prayerbook. Produced *c.* 1420–1425 in France, with miniatures by the Fastolf Master and border decoration by a French artist, the Porter Hours differs from most manuscripts containing northern saints, almost all made or updated in England.[93] The conditions of its creation help illuminate the circulation of these northern saints' prayers in early fifteenth-century England, which in turn speaks to Porter's investment in these saints.

Like every other saint in the manuscript, all four receive three-quarter page miniatures that open the suffrage. This is uncommon among these sixteen *horae*, but not unprecedented; the other *de luxe* manuscripts illustrate their saints.[94] In the Porter Hours, some other saints' miniatures encapsulate an element of their narratives, but that is not true for these four figures, who are depicted as ecclesiasts in standard ways. John of Beverley (fol. 51^r) (see Fig. 4.1), William (fol. 53^r), and Cuthbert (fol. 54^r) are garbed as bishops with crosiers and often books,[95] while John of Bridlington is dressed as a sober Augustinian canon, with a white habit and grey shoulder cape and stole (fol. 52^r).[96]

The suffrage texts too are uncommon but not unprecedented, their unusual features a product of the manuscript's construction. Of the four suffrages, only John of Beverley's is unique; the other three are variants on commendations witnessed elsewhere. In each case, the antiphon and often versicle are new, but the prayer is commonly attested. The French scribe therefore had access

---

92 Dobson, 'Politics and the Church', p. 3.

93 Only the Burnet Psalter contains *memoriae* for northern saints penned on the continent.

94 The Bolton Hours includes miniatures for its northern saints, albeit not adjacent to their suffrages, and the Madresfield Hours opens its *memoriae* with small miniatures of all its saints, including William and Oswald. The Beaufort-Beauchamp Hours and Bodl. Lib., MS lat. liturg. f. 2 also include miniatures for John of Bridlington and, in the latter, Scrope.

95 Porter's motto, 'aultre ne vuel mes', appears in a banderole in the margins next to John of Beverley and Cuthbert's miniatures. However, it features regularly in the manuscript and does not seem to indicate any particular favour for the saints it accompanies.

96 Fizzard, 'Shoes', p. 257. On his visual portrayal, see Sanok, 'John of Bridlington', pp. 153–57.

FIGURE 4.1. Miniature of St John of Beverley, from his suffrage in the Hours of William Porter. New York, The Morgan Library & Museum, MS M.105, fol. 51ʳ. Rouen, France, c. 1420–1425. Purchased by J. Pierpont Morgan (1837–1913) in 1902. Photo: The Morgan Library & Museum, New York.

to standard English texts, although he replaced the opening antiphons (if he ever had them) with shorter utterances, presumably so the whole suffrage could fit on the recto and verso of a single leaf below the miniature. The presence of these standard English prayers in the hands of a French scribe, albeit not in combinations attested elsewhere, suggests that Porter himself (or his confessor) had collected these prayers.

The notion that Porter gathered these prayers helps pinpoint how he came to embrace all four northern saints. We will start with the two Lancastrian saints, John of Bridlington and John of Beverley. John of Bridlington's prayer in the Porter Hours, 'Deus qui beatum iohannem', also appears in the three southern manuscripts that include only a suffrage for him: the Beaufort-Beauchamp Hours, the Hours of Elizabeth the Queen, and the Tabram Hours. The fact this suffrage only appears in southern contexts suggests that this version was circulating among John's southern devotees; Porter probably gathered it through his close connections with the crown. Porter's prayer for John of Beverley, 'Deus qui presentem diem', is taken from the Vespers prayer for John of Beverley's 7 May feast in the Sarum breviary, making that prayer also readily available.[97] If Porter wanted these prayers because of a shared Lancastrian affection for the two Johns, he easily could have done so from his English landholdings in the Midlands and south-east. The Cuthbert prayer also comes from the Sarum breviary.[98] Whatever may have drawn Porter's attention to Cuthbert, he or his confessor could have confected this prayer from readily available liturgical elements.

The prayer for William of York, however, was not available in the south. It does not appear in the printed Sarum breviary and that suffrage only circulated in northern *horae*. Given its textual stability across its seven witnesses and its early appearance in the Percy Hours and Madresfield Hours, it is probable that it was purposefully constructed at York Minster after William's canonization and disseminated locally. Moreover, the nonce antiphon that opens Porter's suffrage is taken from the antiphons for Lauds for William's 7 May feast in the York Breviary.[99] To lay hands on this prayer and antiphon, then, Porter would have needed to travel north.

And he did, shortly before he commissioned this manuscript. In February 1421, Porter returned to England with Henry V for the coronation of Katherine of Valois. In March, Henry and his wife went on a tour of the North, stopping (among other places) at York; Katherine stayed in York while Henry continued to Bridlington and Beverley.[100] Porter accompanied the royal couple.[101] Given his close relationship with the king, Porter probably went with him to honour the two northern saints, reinforcing the southern knight's affection for them while also cementing for him their position within Yorkshire's landscape. Had he first visited York Minster — and it's hard to imagine he wouldn't have — Porter would have seen his favoured John of Beverley alongside William as archbishops of York in the lowest register of the great East Window as well as in the second tier of the West Window, and the entire story of William's life laid out in the newly completed St William Window.[102] Although the St Cuthbert Window would not be installed until after Porter's death, Porter knew its patron, Thomas Langley, Bishop of Durham and Henry V's chancellor, very well. Porter and Langley were both part of Henry V's January 1415 embassy to France,[103] and Langley was with Porter and the king for part of their northern tour, including their days in York.[104] Porter may therefore

---

97 *Breviarium ad usum insignis ecclesiae Sarum*, ed. by Procter and Wordsworth, III, col. 285.

98 The prayer opens Matins for Cuthbert's 20 March feast: *Breviarium ad usum insignis ecclesiae Sarum*, ed. by Procter and Wordsworth, III, col. 217.

99 *Breviarium ad usum insignis ecclesie Eboracensis*, ed. by Lawley, II, col. 303.

100 Allmand, *Henry V*, pp. 156–58; Wylie and Waugh, *Reign of Henry the Fifth*, III, pp. 267–71.

101 Woodger, 'Porter', p. 120.

102 French, *York Minster: The Great East Window*, p. 141; French and O'Connor, *York Minster*, pp. 15–16, 29, 35; French, *York Minster: The St William Window*, pp. 1, 17–21.

103 Wylie and Waugh, *The Reign of Henry the Fifth*, I, p. 435; Storey, *Thomas Langley*, pp. 31–32.

104 Henry and his entourage were there from 2 April to 7 or 8 April; Langley was present on at least 5–6 April: Wylie and Waugh, *The Reign of Henry the Fifth*, III, pp. 271–72; Storey, *Thomas Langley*, pp. 43, 234–35; Doig, 'Propaganda', p. 170.

have come to appreciate Cuthbert through his association with the Durham saint's greatest early fifteenth-century devotee.

The presence of these four northern saints in William Porter's Hours can be attributed, therefore, to a complex matrix of personal, professional, and devotional investments. Porter probably came to John of Bridlington through Henry V's influence, and the royal pilgrimage through the North would have reinforced that connection. The same is true for John of Beverley; as one of the saints celebrated as influential in the Agincourt victory, Porter's affection for him would be natural, intensified by the 1421 pilgrimage. In the Porter Hours miniatures, the faces of both the Johns have been smeared by what appears to be water damage, hinting at Porter's deep affection for them. He has kissed their features away.

On that 1421 pilgrimage, Porter would have experienced the two Johns as positioned within a different conception of sanctity, one located in the geography of the East Riding and centred on York Minster and its holy archbishops. In adding William and Cuthbert to his personal pantheon of intercessors, Porter commemorates his northern progress, includes Cuthbert as the heavenly protector of one of his earthly protectors, and adds associates of John of Beverley, a saint who had already protected him so well. And in collecting William of York's suffrage during his time in the North, Porter also gains his name-saint as an intercessor, an intimate affiliation independent of ties to region or crown.

These four saints in the Porter Hours speak to the strength of this conceptual northern sanctity. Porter seems to have associated these saints, juxtaposed as they are in his prayerbook, despite his varied attachments to them. Although Porter has constructed his personal conception of northern holiness differently from the northern *horae* — the absence of Scrope, after Porter encountered the archbishop's cult in York Minster, is telling — it nevertheless closely resembles them. It was York Minster's bishops and archbishops, and the East Riding's spiritual worthies, who most commonly found their way into the prayer lives of the English laity, not the conversion-era holy men and women lauded by Bede. It is a concept of holiness more contemporary than ancient, informed by royal patronage, and typically limited to the geography from York to the eastern coast — but not confined to any of these categories. It is recognizably consistent from book to book, yet never identical, speaking to both the coherence of this notion of northern sanctity as well as its flexibility, personalization, and broad appeal.

Works Cited

Manuscripts and Archival Sources

Aberdeen, Aberdeen University Library, MS 25 (Burnet Psalter). <https://www.abdn.ac.uk/burnet-psalter/>

Cambridge, Cambridge University Library, MS Ii.6.2 <https://cudl.lib.cam.ac.uk/view/MS-II-00006-00002/1>

——, St John's College, MS E.26

——, Trinity College, MS R.4.20 <https://mss-cat.trin.cam.ac.uk/Manuscript/R.4.20> [accessed 14 Jan 2022]

Leeds, Leeds University, Brotherton Collection, MS Add. 18 <https://explore.library.leeds.ac.uk/special-collections-explore/372699/horae_beatae_mariae_virginis>

London, British Library, MS Add. 28946

——, MS Add. 50001 (Hours of Elizabeth the Queen) <https://www.bl.uk/manuscripts/FullDisplay.aspx?ref=Add_MS_50001>

——, MS Add. 89379 (The Percy Hours) <http://www.bl.uk/manuscripts/FullDisplay.aspx?ref=Add_MS_89379>

——, MS Cotton Cleopatra A.XIII

——, MS Harley 955

——, MS Royal 2.A.XVIII (Beaufort-Beauchamp Hours) <https://www.bl.uk/manuscripts/FullDisplay.aspx?ref=Royal_MS_2_A_XVIII>

New Haven, Beineke Library, MS Osborn a44 <https://brbl-dl.library.yale.edu/vufind/Record/3729204>

New York, Pierpont Morgan Library, MS M.105 (Porter Hours)

Nottingham, University of Nottingham, MS WLC/LM/LL

Oxford, Bodleian Library, MS Auct. D. inf. 2.11 <https://digital.bodleian.ox.ac.uk/inquire/p/b47aba38-e226-4dc7-9943-698293d73d2f>

——, MS lat. liturg. f. 2

Rennes, Bibliothèque Municipale, MS 22

York, York Minster Library, MS M2(1)f

——, MS Add. 2 (Bolton Hours)

——, MS Add. 54

——, MS Add. 67

——, MS XVI.K.6 (Pavement Hours)

Primary Sources

Bede, *Bede's Ecclesiastical History of the English People*, ed. and trans. by Bertram Colgrave and R. A. B. Mynors (Oxford: Clarendon Press, 1969)

'The Bishop Scrope that Was so Wise', ed. by Stephen K. Wright, in *Richard Scrope: Archbishop, Rebel, Martyr*, ed. by P. J. P. Goldberg (Donington: Shaun Tyas, 2007), p. 113–14

Breviarium ad usum insignis ecclesiae Eboracensis, ed. by Stephen Willoughby Lawley, 2 vols, SS, 71, 75 (Durham: Andrews, 1880–1883)

Breviarium ad usum insignis ecclesiae Sarum, ed. by Francis Procter and Christopher Wordsworth, 3 vols (Cambridge: Alma Matric Academiae, 1882–1886)

Furnivall, Frederick J., ed., *Hymns to the Virgin and Christ*, EETS, o.s., 24 (London: Early English Text Society, 1867)

Horae Eboracenses: The Prymer or Hours of the Blessed Virgin Mary, According to the Use of the Illustrious Church of York, SS, 132 (Durham: Andrews, 1920)

Lydgate, John, *Lydgate's Siege of Thebes. Part II*, ed. by Axel Erdmann and Eilert Ekwall, EETS, e.s., 125 (London: Early English Text Society, 1930)

Raine, James, ed., *The Historians of the Church of York and its Archbishops*, Rolls Series, 71, vol. III (London: Her Majesty's Stationery Office, 1894)

The Register of Henry Chichele, Archbishop of Canterbury, 1414–1443, ed. by E. F. Jacob, 4 vols (Oxford: Clarendon Press, 1938)

Rymer, Thomas, ed., *Foedera, conventiones, litterae, et cujuscunque generis acta publica, inter reges Angliae et alios quosvis imperatores, reges, pontifices, principes, vel communitates*, vol. IV (Hagae Comitis: Neaulme, 1739)

Tractatus de regimine principum ad Regem Henricum Sextum, in *Four English Political Tracts of the Later Middle Ages*, ed. by Jean-Philippe Genet, Camden Society, 4th series, 18 (London: Royal Historical Society, 1977), pp. 40–173

Walsingham, Thomas, *The St Albans Chronicle: The Cronica maiora of Thomas Walsingham*, ed. and trans. by John Taylor, Wendy R. Childs, and Leslie Watkiss, 2 vols (Oxford: Clarendon Press, 2003)

Secondary Works

Allmand, Christopher, *Henry V* (Berkeley: The University of California Press, 1992)

Backhouse, Janet, *The Madresfield Hours: A Fourteenth-Century Manuscript in the Library of Earl Beauchamp* (Oxford: Roxburghe Club, 1975)

——, *Books of Hours* (London: The British Library, 1985)

Baker, Alan R. H., and Mark Billinge, 'Material and Imagined Geographies of England', in *Geographies of England: The North-South Divide, Material and Imagined*, ed. by Alan R. H. Baker and Mark Billinge (Cambridge: Cambridge University Press, 2004), pp. 1–14

Barker, Juliet, *Agincourt: Henry V and the Battle that Made England* (New York: Little, Brown and Co., 2006)

Burke, John, *A Genealogical and Heraldic History of the Extinct and Dormant Baronetcies of England, Ireland, and Scotland*, 2nd edn (London: Scott, Webster, and Geary, 1844)

A Catalogue of the Harleian Manuscripts in the British Museum, 4 vols (London, 1808–1812)

Coombe, Margaret, and Christiania Whitehead, 'Introduction', in *Saints of North-East England, 600–1500*, ed. by Margaret Coombe, Anne Mouron, and Christiania Whitehead (Turnhout: Brepols, 2017), pp. 1–16

Dobson, R. B., 'Politics and the Church in the Fifteenth-Century North', in *The North of England in the Age of Richard III*, ed. by A. J. Pollard (New York: St Martin's, 1996), pp. 1–17

Dodd, Gwilym, 'Henry V's Establishment: Service, Loyalty and Reward in 1413', in *Henry V: New Interpretations*, ed. by Gwilym Dodd (York: York Medieval, 2013), pp. 35–76

Doig, James A., 'Propaganda and Truth: Henry V's Royal Progress in 1421', *Nottingham Medieval Studies*, 40 (1996), 167–79

Drimmer, Sonja, 'The Hours of Elizabeth the Queen', in *Royal Manuscripts: The Genius of Illumination*, ed. by Scot McKendrick, John Lowden, and Kathleen Doyle (London: The British Library, 2011), pp. 154–55

Driver, Martha W., '"Me fault faire": French Makers of Manuscripts for English Patrons', in *Language and Culture in Medieval Britain: The French of England c. 1100–c. 1500*, ed. by Jocelyn Wogan-Browne, Carolyn Collette, Maryanne Kowalski, Linne Mooney, Ad Putter, and David Trotter (York: York Medieval, 2009), pp. 420–43

Duffy, Eamon, *Marking the Hours: English People and their Prayers 1240–1570* (New Haven: Yale University Press, 2006)

Fizzard, Allison D., 'Shoes, Boots, Leggings, and Cloaks: The Augustinian Canons and Dress in Later Medieval England', *Journal of British Studies*, 46 (2007), 245–62

French, T. W., 'The Tomb of Archbishop Scrope in York Minster', *Yorkshire Archaeological Journal*, 61 (1989), 95–102

French, Thomas, *York Minster: The Great East Window*, CVMA Great Britain Summary Catalogue, 2 (Oxford: British Academy, 1995)

——, *York Minster: The St William Window*, CVMA Great Britain Summary Catalogue, 5 (Oxford: British Academy, 1999)

French, Thomas, and David O'Connor, *York Minster: A Catalogue of Medieval Stained Glass*, CVMA Great Britain, 3, York Minster fascicule, 1 (Oxford: British Academy, 1987)

Friedman, John B., 'Richard de Thorpe's Astronomical Kalendar and the Luxury Book Trade at York', *Studies in the Age of Chaucer*, 7 (1985), 137–60

Frońska, Johanna, 'The Beaufort/Beauchamp Hours', in *Royal Manuscripts: The Genius of Illumination*, ed. by Scot McKendrick, John Lowden, and Kathleen Doyle (London: The British Library, 2011), p. 147

Given-Wilson, Chris, *Henry IV* (New Haven: Yale University Press, 2016)

Goldberg, P. J. P., ed., *Richard Scrope: Archbishop, Rebel, Martyr* (Donington: Shaun Tyas, 2007)

Green, Adrian, and A. J. Pollard, ed., *Regional Identities in North-East England, 1300–2000* (Woodbridge: Boydell, 2007)

Grosjean, P., 'De S. Johanne Bridlingtoniensi Collectanea', *Analecta Bollandiana*, 53 (1935), 101–29

Hanna, Ralph, and Thorlac Turville-Petre, ed., *The Wollaton Medieval Manuscripts: Texts, Owners and Readers* (York: York Medieval, 2010)

Harper, Sally, 'Traces of Lost Medieval Offices? The *Sanctilogium Angliae, Walliae, Scotiae, et Hiberniae* of John of Tynemouth (fl. 1350)', in *Essays on the History of English Music in Honour of John Caldwell: Sources, Style, Performance, Historiography*, ed. by Emma Hornby and David Maw (Cambridge: Boydell, 2010), pp. 1–21

Harriss, G. L., 'Beaufort, John, duke of Somerset (1404–1444)', *Oxford Dictionary of National Biography* 4 October 2008 <https://doi.org/10.1093/ref:odnb/1862> [accessed 31 May 2019]

——, 'Beaufort, John, marquess of Dorset and marquess of Somerset (*c.* 1371–1410)', *Oxford Dictionary of National Biography* 19 May 2011 <https://doi.org/10.1093/ref:odnb/1861> [accessed 31 May 2019]

James, M. R., *The Western Manuscripts in the Library of Trinity College, Cambridge: A Descriptive Catalogue*, 3 vols (Cambridge: Cambridge University Press, 1900–1902)

——, *A Descriptive Catalogue of the Manuscripts in the Library of St John's College, Cambridge* (Cambridge: Cambridge University Press, 1913)

——, *A Catalogue of the Medieval Manuscripts in the University Library, Aberdeen* (Cambridge: Cambridge University Press, 1932)

Jewell, Helen M., *The North-South Divide: The Origins of Northern Consciousness in England* (Manchester: Manchester University Press, 1994)

Ker, N. R., and A. J. Piper, *Medieval Manuscripts in British Libraries*, 4 vols (Oxford: Clarendon Press, 1969–2002)

Leroquais, Abbé V., *Les Livres d'Heures: Manuscrits de la Bibliothéque nationale*, 2 vols (Paris: n. pub., 1927)

Liddy, Christian D., and Richard H. Britnell, ed., *North-East England in the Later Middle Ages* (Woodbridge: Boydell, 2005)

Luxford, Julian, 'Luxury and Locality in a Late Medieval Book of Hours from South-West England', *The Antiquaries Journal*, 93 (2013), 225–47

Marks, Richard, 'The Glazing of Fotheringhay Church and College', *Journal of the British Archaeological Association*, 131 (1978), 79–109

McKenna, J. W., 'Popular Canonization as Political Propaganda: The Cult of Archbishop Scrope', *Speculum*, 45 (1970), 608–23

Morgan, Nigel, 'English Books of Hours, *c.* 1240–*c.* 1480', in *Books of Hours Reconsidered*, ed. by Sandra Hindman and James H. Marrow (Turnhout: Brepols, 2013), pp. 65–95

Mortimer, Ian, *The Fears of Henry IV: The Life of England's Self-Made King* (London: Vintage, 2008)

——, *1415: Henry V's Year of Glory* (London: Bodley Head, 2009)

Norton, Christopher, *St William of York* (York: York Medieval, 2006)

——, 'Richard Scrope and York Minster', in *Richard Scrope: Archbishop, Rebel, Martyr*, ed. by P. J. P. Goldberg (Donington: Shaun Tyas, 2007), pp. 138–213

Ormrod, W. Mark, 'The Rebellion of Archbishop Scrope and the Tradition of Opposition to Royal Taxation', in *The Reign of Henry IV: Rebellion and Survival, 1403–1413*, ed. by Gwilym Dodd and Douglas Biggs (York: York Medieval, 2008), pp. 162–79

Pfaff, Richard W., *The Liturgy in Medieval England: A History* (Cambridge: Cambridge University Press, 2009)

Pickering, Oliver, 'Brotherton Collection MS 18 and its Riddling Middle English Verses', in *The Medieval Book and a Modern Collector: Essays in Honour of Toshiyuki Takamiya*, ed. by Takami Matsuda, Richard A. Linenthal, and John Scahill (Cambridge: D. S. Brewer, 2004), pp. 223–32

Piper, A. J., 'The First Generation of Durham Monks and the Cult of St Cuthbert', in *St Cuthbert, His Cult and His Community to AD 1200*, ed. by Gerald Bonner, David Rollason, and Clare Stancliffe (Woodbridge: Boydell, 1989), pp. 437–46

Piroyansky, Danna, *Martyrs in the Making: Political Martyrdom in Late Medieval England* (New York: Palgrave Macmillan, 2008)

Pollard, A. J., *North-Eastern England During the Wars of the Roses: Lay Society, War, and Politics 1450–1500* (Oxford: Clarendon Press, 1990)

——, 'Introduction', in *North-East England in the Later Middle Ages*, ed. by Christian D. Liddy and Richard H. Britnell (Woodbridge: Boydell, 2005), pp. 1–12

Purvis, J. S., *St John of Bridlington*, Journal of the Bridlington Augustinian Society, 2 (Bridlington: Bridlington Augustinian Society, 1924)

Rand, Kari Anne, 'The Syon Pardon and Sermon: Contexts and Texts', in *Preaching the Word in Manuscript and Print in Late Medieval England: Essays in Honour of Susan Powell*, ed. by Martha W. Driver and Veronica O'Mara (Turnhout: Brepols, 2013), pp. 317–49

Rees Jones, Sarah, 'Richard Scrope, the Bolton Hours, and the Church of St Martin in Micklegate: Reconstructing a Holy Neighbourhood in Later Medieval York', in *Richard Scrope: Archbishop, Rebel, Martyr*, ed. by P. J. P. Goldberg (Donington: Shaun Tyas, 2007), pp. 214–36

Rees Jones, Sarah, and Felicity Riddy, 'The Bolton Hours of York: Female Domestic Piety and the Public Sphere', in *Household, Women, and Christianities in Late Antiquity and the Middle Ages*, ed. by Anneke B. Mulder-Bakker and Jocelyn Wogan-Browne (Turnhout: Brepols, 2005), pp. 215–60

Reinburg, Virginia, *French Books of Hours: Making an Archive of Prayer, c. 1400–1600* (Cambridge: Cambridge University Press, 2012)

Rentz, Ellen K., 'Castles for St William: The Late Medieval Commemoration of York's Local Saint', *Viator*, 43 (2012), 111–30

Rickert, Margaret, 'The So-Called Beaufort Hours and York Psalter', *The Burlington Magazine*, 104.7 (1962), 238–46

Rogers, Nicholas, 'Patrons and Purchasers: Evidence for the Original Owners of Books of Hours Produced in the Low Countries for the English Market', in *'Als Ich Can': Liber Amicorum in Memory of Professor Dr Maurits Smeyers*, ed. by Bert Cardon, Jan van der Stock and Dominique Vanwijnsberghe, 3 vols (Leuven: Peeters, 2002), pp. 1165–81

Russell, Dave, *Looking North: Northern England and the National Imagination* (Manchester: Manchester University Press, 2004)

Sanok, Catherine, *New Legends of England: Forms of Community in Late Medieval Saints' Lives* (Philadelphia: University of Pennsylvania Press, 2018)

——, 'John of Bridlington, The Mitred Prior and Model of the Mixed Life', in *Religious Men and Masculine Identity in the Middle Ages*, ed. by P. J. Cullum and Katherine J. Lewis (Woodbridge: Boydell, 2019), pp. 143–59

Scott-Stokes, Charity, ed. and trans., *Women's Books of Hours in Medieval England: Selected Texts* (Cambridge: Brewer, 2006)

Scott, Kathleen L., *Later Gothic Manuscripts, 1390–1490*, vol. VI parts 1–2 of *A Survey of Manuscripts Illuminated in the British Isles* (London: Harvey Miller, 1996)

Sharpe, Richard, 'Banners of the Northern Saints', in *Saints of North-East England, 600–1500*, ed. by Margaret Coombe, Anne Mouron, and Christiania Whitehead (Turnhout: Brepols, 2017), pp. 245–303

Storey, R. L., *Thomas Langley and the Bishopric of Durham 1406–1437* (London: SPCK, 1961)

Strong, Patrick, and Felicity Strong, 'The Last Will and Codicils of Henry V', *English Historical Review*, 96 (1981), 79–102

Taylor, Joseph, 'Chaucer's Uncanny Regionalism: Rereading the North in The Reeve's Tale', *JEGP*, 109 (2010), 468–89

Tudor, Victoria, 'The Cult of St Cuthbert in the Twelfth Century: The Evidence of Reginald of Durham', in *St Cuthbert, His Cult and His Community to AD 1200*, ed. by Gerald Bonner, David Rollason, and Clare Stancliffe (Woodbridge: Boydell, 1989), pp. 447–67

Twemlow, J. A., 'St John of Bridlington', in *A Miscellany Presented to J. M. MacKay* (Liverpool: Liverpool University Press, 1914), pp. 128–31

Walker, Simon, 'Political Saints in Later Medieval England', in *The McFarlane Legacy: Studies in Late Medieval Politics and Society*, ed. by R. H. Britnell and A. J. Pollard (New York: St Martin's Press, 1995), pp. 77–106

——, 'The Yorkshire Risings of 1405: Texts and Contexts', in *Henry IV: The Establishment of the Regime, 1399–1406*, ed. by Gwilym Dodd and Douglas Biggs (York: York Medieval, 2003), pp. 161–84

Webb, Diana, *Pilgrimage in Medieval England* (London: Hambledon, 2000)

——, *Pilgrims and Pilgrimage in the Medieval West* (London: I. B. Tauris, 2001)

Wieck, Roger S., *Time Sanctified: The Book of Hours in Medieval Art and Life* (New York: George Brazillier, 1988)

——, *Painted Prayers: The Book of Hours in Medieval and Renaissance Art* (New York: George Brazillier, 1997)

Wilson, Susan E., *The Life and After-Life of St John of Beverley: The Evolution of the Cult of an Anglo-Saxon Saint* (Aldershot: Ashgate, 2006)

Winston, Charles, 'The Painted Glass in the Beauchamp Chapel at Warwick', *Archaeological Journal*, 21 (1864), 302–18

Wolffe, Bertram, *Henry VI* (London: Eyre Methuen, 1981)

Woodger, L. S., 'Porter, William II', in *The History of Parliament: The House of Commons 1386–1421*, ed. by J. S. Roskell, Linda Clark, and Carole Rawcliffe, vol. IV (Stroud: Alan Sutton, 1992), pp. 118–21

Wright, Stephen K., 'Genres of Sanctity: Literary Representations of Archbishop Scrope', in *Richard Scrope: Archbishop, Rebel, Martyr*, ed. by P. J. P. Goldberg (Donington: Shaun Tyas, 2007), pp. 115–37

Wylie, James Hamilton, and William Templeton Waugh, *The Reign of Henry the Fifth*, 3 vols (Cambridge: Cambridge University Press, 1914–1929)

1.2 Material Culture:
Space, Oil, Image

EUAN McCARTNEY ROBSON

Space, It's About Time Too

Architecture and Identity in Medieval Durham

Shortly after 2.33am, on 1 May 1942, air-raid sirens rang out across the city of Durham. A fleet of Luftwaffe bombers had been spotted approaching the coast and were only minutes away from flattening its 800-year-old cathedral. Describing what happened next, an operative on duty with the Royal Observer Corps recorded: 'I shall believe to the end of my days that I witnessed a miracle.'[1] With an uncanny haste a thick white mist rose up from the River Wear, shielding the entire peninsula from view. The Germans circled blindly overhead several times before unleashing a torrent of incendiaries. Moments later, as the planes retreated, the mysterious mist vanished, revealing the building to be entirely unscathed. Thus, the 'Mist of St Cuthbert' was added to the miraculous tradition of the cathedral's stalwart guardian, more than twelve hundred years after his death.

Sceptics, then as now, protested. And yet to doubt — however reasonably — the innate capacity of a building to defend itself is to stand at odds with a persistent tradition of architectural ekphrasis that stretches back well over two millennia.[2] In antiquity, the *genius loci* was the protector, the spirit, and the instinctive animation of built space. Its existential status as a living character meant that its presence and the products of its agency could be seen and felt by its occupants. As such, its favour (not unlike a Christian saint) could be courted: locally in the *vicus* by votive means or, more grandly, in the imperial cults of the Roman Emperors, with Augustus often being depicted as a *genius* of Rome in its entirety. Many of these tropes persisted in the medieval world long after the Empire's decline. In fact, even as late as the thirteenth century, stone personifications of ancient *genii* were still being incorporated directly into English ecclesiastical fabrics (as, for example, in the south wall of the nave

---

1 See Dufferwiel, *A-Z of Curious County Durham*, p. 78.
2 Ekphrasis is a rhetorical device involving the verbal description of a visual work of art.

Euan McCartney Robson (euan.robson.14@ucl.ac.uk) defended his PhD at University College London in 2019. He is a Research Fellow at the Paul Mellon Centre for Studies in British Art.

Late Medieval Devotion to Saints from the North of England: New Directions, ed. by Christiania Whitehead, Hazel J. Hunter Blair, and Denis Renevey, MCS 48 (Turnhout: Brepols, 2022), pp. 129–146
BREPOLS ❦ PUBLISHERS   10.1484/M.MCS-EB.5.124347

at St Giles in Tockenham, Wiltshire).[3] So powerful, in fact, and so widespread was the belief in the intrinsic animation of stones that the Dominican friar Albertus Magnus (d. 1280) felt compelled to write a lengthy rebuttal — his *De mineralibus* — explaining why, in essence, they did not possess souls.[4]

Nowhere, indeed, were the spontaneous and often almost impetuous actions of medieval masonry any better attested than in the north of England. In chapter 92 of his *Libellus de admirandis*, Reginald of Durham (d. *c.* 1190) tells the story of a young man healed by St Cuthbert of a nasty head wound. But it begins in unusual fashion with the root cause of the 'impetus furore' (furious attack). In admonishment for his irresponsible and possibly drunken behaviour at Whitsun, 'plectrum unius mirae magnitudinis' (one of the astonishingly large clappers) from the bell of Durham's north tower shot through the crowded cathedral 'cerebri interiora denudando proferebat' (laying bare the inner parts of his brain).[5] Several chapters later, Reginald also details the story of an agnostic knight who, having had the audacity to approach the cathedral door, was suddenly flung from his horse and rolled repeatedly back and forth in the mud.[6] In fact, the Second World War was not even the first time that inclement northern weather had been wielded at Durham to thwart an invader. No lesser threat than the Conqueror himself had been repelled by 'Cuthbert's Mist' while trying to sack the old pre-Conquest cathedral, a structure which, in the simple assessment of one his own men, 'ab omni adversitate praesidium' (always protected them from their adversities).[7]

To our modern instincts, the living presence of the dead in old ashlar and mortar might seem much less strongly embodied. Plato's theory of Forms notwithstanding, the ascription of human agency and animation to otherwise inanimate phenomena has been suspect at least since John Ruskin's 'pathetic fallacy'.[8] As Catherine Ingraham — the author of *Architecture, Animal, Human* — recently wrote, many of the modern edifices we live with today seem largely to resist our investments of personal saga, anecdote, and the now 'disjunctive narratives of the present postmodern condition'.[9] But, even if not literally true, the rising of 'Cuthbert's Mist' can be read just as usefully as an indicator of the latent and powerful human attachment (even in the twentieth century) to non-human agencies. This, the unique causal disposition, or 'spirit' of built space, was compellingly described by Christian Norberg-Schulz as a type of 'existential foothold'.[10] (Not for no reason, incidentally, does the *genius loci*

---

3 It was once thought that this relief depicted Asclepius. Jocelyn Toynbee, however, has argued convincingly that it is a *genius loci*: Toynbee, 'Two Romano-British Genii', pp. 329–30.
4 Albertus Magnus, *Book of Minerals*, trans. by Wyckoff.
5 Reginald, *Libellus de admirandis*, ed. by Raine, pp. 202–03.
6 Reginald, *Libellus de admirandis*, ed. by Raine, pp. 272–73.
7 Aird, 'The Origins and Development', p. 96.
8 Ruskin, *Works*, p. 205.
9 Ingraham, *Architecture, Animal, Human*, p. 33. See also Ingraham, 'Architecture as Evidence', pp. 61–81.
10 Norberg-Schulz, *Genius Loci: Towards a Phenomenology of Architecture*, p. 5.

feature prominently in the title of his often-neglected Modernist work on phenomenology.) Buildings offer shelter but humans only 'dwell' at length, he argued, when they can connect and identify themselves in meaningful ways with the fabric. Often the most profound and efficient structures are the ones that quickly make 'sites' become 'places': the ones we see something of ourselves in, the ones that provide the 'horizon', to borrow from Juhani Pallasmaa, for 'confronting the human existential condition'.[11]

Seen in this way, the ultimate historical significance of a building like Durham Cathedral lies beyond itself. It has, of course, always been a visibly very seductive structure; it has long drawn our attention inward, towards its unique shape and arrangement. More than that though, it has borrowed, adapted, and reflected meanings of our own making right back at us: back out into our own sense of Self and being in the world. In keeping with the new directions sought from this volume, this essay is in effect one long attempt to reverse-engineer something of that process. It begins and ends, not with Durham, nor with its particular and extraordinary surviving forms, but with historically and culturally contingent medieval men and women. To dwell, as it were, in Durham Cathedral today is to be suspended in numberless of their Geertzian 'webs' of society and selfhood, the oldest silks of which are often frayed, intertwined, or missing entirely.[12] A precious few, however, are so integral to the fabric that they remain unbroken to this day.

A Mysterious Sweetness

Bishop Ælfwold's (d. 1058) devotion to Durham and especially to the holy father Cuthbert was so profound that he frequently found himself brought to tears, William of Malmesbury stressed, at the mere mention of either name.[13] As the 'amor' (love) he felt for the saint's cult increased day by day, eventually the 'bona flamma' (good flame) within him could contain itself no longer. And so Ælfwold set out on a pilgrimage from his home in faraway Sherborne, in Dorset, to seek out the cathedral. Having arrived in the east end, the bishop then took an even bolder decision: 'reuulso sepulchri operculo cum eo quasi cum amico fideliter collocutus' (he tore away the cover of the tomb and talked with [the saint], as with an old friend to whom he was loyal). Then, 'xeniolum in perpetui pignus amoris deposuit' (leaving a small gift as a token of his lasting affection), he went on his way.[14] Years later, as he began to recognize that his days were almost at an end, Ælfwold could be repeatedly heard singing his favourite antiphon:

---

11 Pallasmaa, *The Eyes of the Skin*, p. 13.
12 Geertz, *The Interpretation of Cultures*, p. 5.
13 William, *Gesta Pontificum*, ed. and trans. by Winterbottom and Thomson, p. 283.
14 William, *Gesta Pontificum*, ed. and trans. by Winterbottom and Thomson, p. 284.

Sanctus antistes Cuthbertus,
uir perfectus in omnibus,
in turbis erat monachus,
digne cunctis reuerendus.[15]

> (Holy Bishop Cuthbert,
> A man perfect in all things,
> Was a monk amid such crowds
> And worthy of respect from all.)

Later still, when his speech began to fade, he implored others to sing it into his ear instead. And thus, William affirmed, 'ita inditium amoris quem in Sanctum habebat cum extremo flatu emisit' (to his very last breath he showed the love he felt for the saint).[16]

This rather touching account speaks directly to the main themes of this essay, to space and to time, as well as to a very human conflation of architecture and identity. In an attempt to consider, on a par, both object and subject, both cause and effect, evidence for the analyses that follow has been sought out in just these kinds of atypical histories. William here focuses on the meanings body and building generated together, as dynamic and mutually enhancing agents. How the cathedral complex at Durham thrilled, attracted, persuaded, frightened or even annoyed, these (and more) functions were all corroborated by contemporary sources. Just as critical here, however, is the historically contingent medieval viewer, for whom, in their particularity, such impressions neither sprang consistently, nor without mediation. Building throughout on the innate political and cultural alterity of the medieval world, a mixture of viewing communities is therefore emphasized along regional, social, and professional lines. Over and above the conclusions it provides, these embodied perspectives are key: not just insofar as they might differ from, but ultimately complement and augment, existing architectural scholarship.

William describes 'in eius pectore dulce incrementum' (a mysterious sweetness slowly growing inside [the bishop's] chest).[17] Implicitly positive and yet incendiary, vivid but invisible, what was this 'bona flamma'? What work did William mean for it to do in his account? We know from many sources (both past and present) that medieval pilgrimage served a number of collective and individual needs. Many pilgrims had the hope of divine favour or prophecy in mind, and still more the relief from illness, hardship, and a wide range of other workaday problems. None, though, seem to have been the case here for Ælfwold. Everyone agreed: 'Constat eum reuerentissimae uitae fuisse' (he [the bishop] was a man of the most respectable life). He disregarded the 'profusissimos conuiuiorum apparatus' (the lavish accompaniments of banqueting), ate from a wooden dish, took no rich food, and always washed his

---

15 William, *Gesta Pontificum*, ed. and trans. by Winterbottom and Thomson, p. 284.
16 William, *Gesta Pontificum*, ed. and trans. by Winterbottom and Thomson, p. 285.
17 William, *Gesta Pontificum*, ed. and trans. by Winterbottom and Thomson, p. 283.

cup out to 'omnis sapor ceruisiae dilueretur' (remove the taste of any beer).[18] He wanted for nothing; he was abstemious and he wasn't sick. Indeed, his final and unspecified illness seems only to have caught up with him long after his pilgrimage to Durham. This, though, was likely the point. That William didn't expand on what he meant by the 'bona flamma', except incidentally, suggests either that its meaning was implicit in the twelfth century and/or that Ælfwold was less the subject here than Cuthbert himself. In either event, crucially, the saint and his cult were flattered.

In his *Libellus de admirandis*, Reginald of Durham collated the testimonies of many pilgrims who benefitted from Cuthbert's cures. And yet, almost as equally, he mentioned the large number of clerics, nobles and even royalty, who, like Ælfwold, journeyed 'non sibi' (not for themselves) to offer gifts 'ab imo pectore' (sincerely, from the heart, or out of affection). The extent to which Cuthbert was said to be loved unconditionally, without agenda or ulterior motive, a claim evidenced here by the bishop's repeated selflessness, was a useful *topos*. For both William and Ælfwold, Cuthbert's sanctity, his miracle-working and his curative powers, while far from incidental, were nonetheless secondary to what we can take — pretty much literally — to mean a kind of *burning desire* for proximity in space. That the bishop could no longer be satisfied simply by bringing the saint to mind, that he yearned for a more physical communion, that he tore away at the cover of Cuthbert's tomb, these instincts all speak to a profound sense of somatic and material urgency.

This is an essential reality to note of a cult site like Durham because, writing from the ancient Near East, Clement of Alexandria (d. 215) had been absolutely adamant that 'it was impossible to draw [the divine] near to us in our eyes, or to grasp [Him] with the hands'.[19] Like many other early Christian theologians, Clement believed that real-world conferences with the divine, even of the intercessory type that William described here, were either nonsense or delusion. Actually, he argued, He dwelt only 'in the light which no man can approach unto [... and] whom no man hath seen, nor can see' (a clear reference to 1 Timothy 6. 16).[20] No single place or space on earth, in other words, was any more likely to have been holier, in the ancient world, than any other. And yet, a wealth of documentary sources like this attest to the fact that large numbers of medieval men and women, like Ælfwold, had begun to make often very long journeys in order, conversely, to shorten this very same gap between themselves and a whole series of sacred and site-specific loci.

A steady and increasing stream of medievalists interested in pilgrims and pilgrimage have annexed the generative promise of Yi-Fu Tuan's *Space and Place: The Perspective of Experience* into an impressively broad catalogue of inquiries, since it was first published. Tuan's repeated retreat, however, to just this same sense (indeed, *yearning*) to travel to be right there, *in situ* and

---

18   William, *Gesta Pontificum*, ed. and trans. by Winterbottom and Thomson, p. 283.
19   Clement, *Stromateis*, trans. by Ferguson, p. 236.
20   Clement, *Stromateis*, trans. by Ferguson, p. 236.

in space, remains foundational. Even insofar as Ælfwold's 'small gift' might be construed as indicating a diplomatic mission of some kind, or an intent to curry favour for his bishopric, William, like Tuan, was clear that it did not preclude the fundamental gravitational allure — often described by sociologists of modern tourism today — of an authentic first-hand experience. This is key too because, just as the bishop prepared himself for the saint, so too, in effect, did the saint and his community prepare themselves for him. As Ælfwold approached the limits of Durham Cathedral, both were already poised for him to enter. Adopting something of Alfred Gell's brilliant phrasing, we might say that the building was about to perform an 'abduction of agency'; it was about to exploit a relationship already long in the making.[21]

Of course, before he could reach to tear away the cover of Cuthbert's tomb — the climactic finale of his own pilgrimage at least, if not everyone's — Ælfwold would first have had to negotiate the cathedral's lengthy preamble: initially, the crowds — other pilgrims, traders, and the local community outside, the noise and the muddle of Durham's cramped urban peninsula (more on which below); then, a liminal moment, the transition to the inner sanctum. For at least the first thirty years after its completion the great west door would have been the main thoroughfare for visitors, before it was blocked by the new Galilee Chapel, and even more pointedly by Bishop Langley's chantry tomb after 1437. However they arrived though, passing beyond the start of the main northern wall, or beneath the enormous two-storey porch above it (now lost), a calmer scene would doubtless have ensued: not quite the hush and solemnity often enforced today (because the medieval nave could still be a loud and raucous place), but an immediate and deliberate shift in atmosphere and expectation.

Pilgrims would doubtless have had some freedom to move as they liked (if much less than today), but a clear sense of direction and purpose — augmented by the unique modes and forms of the cathedral — would nonetheless have seen them along the right path. Durham's large arresting piers, its high gallery and windows, its many altars, and the warm and lambent tongues of candle-light — all would have caught the eye and the ear, scattering their thoughts away towards countless digressions, but collectively and progressively towards one main objective. Around the choir they would head, past the tall figures on the rood, beneath the rose window, through the Nine Altars and behind the presbytery: all guiding them incrementally closer to the ultimate threshold of Cuthbert's feretory. Then the *scopus*, the final chapter itself, the image to which the bishop's entire journey, from Sherborne to Durham, had been devoted: Cuthbert's tomb and shrine.

Writing in the late sixteenth century, William Claxton, author of the *Rites of Durham* began with this space, the cathedral's 'highest part', its holiest places, in the east end, the 'Nine Altars', 'St Cuthberts feritorye' and the 'Quire'. It is not just the lavish description of Cuthbert's final resting place, 'one of the most

---

21 Gell, *Art and Agency*.

sumptuous monuments in all England', but its 'foure seates or places' reserved directly beneath it for 'lame or sicke men', that again immediately reinforces that sense of a powerful 'gravitational allure'. It is a feeling that the cathedral was not so much built for but around the saintly body.[22] Stand next to the shrine today (or what survived of it past the First and Second Suppression Acts of the late 1530s) and you will also notice that, like elsewhere in England, some of the flagstone flooring has been worn away. John Crook will tell you that this attests to the shuffling feet of countless generations of pilgrims, all huddled and clambering for communion with Cuthbert's *corpus*.[23] On most days (though by no means all) visitors to this part of the cathedral can now expect a rather hushed and tranquil spectacle. In the twelfth century, however, Reginald of Durham described packed throngs, whose enthusiasm was sometimes so great that stewards with wooden beams had to be brought in to keep good order.[24] 'Men of every rank, age and profession, the secular and the spiritual', the *Capitula de miraculis* recorded, '[they] all hastened to be present'.[25]

Sarah Blick and Laura D. Gelfand stress this idea even more pointedly in their introduction to *Push Me, Pull You*.[26] Based on the 'Pushmi-Pullyu' (an animal with two heads that is only able to move when both are in agreement) in Hugh Lofting's Dr Dolittle books, their title epitomises an approach focused on the reciprocal and cooperative relationship between viewer and object. Consider how Ælfwold's attention and especially his emotions (both encapsulated in the heat of his 'bona flamma') shifted back and forth: from Sherborne to Durham, from his own inner monologue to that with the saint, and eventually from outside to inside his cathedral. Each spoke to one another, they cooperated. And, as his flame grew, so their respective distances shortened. William of Malmesbury's narrative, in other words, was defined by the way that a relationship was advanced over time and eventually compressed across space: the unique push and pull of Ælfwold and Cuthbert working in tandem.

Put another way: inasmuch as a building can be thought of as cognisant, the corollary question might now be less *why* William of Malmesbury's Ælfwold travelled so far to commune with Cuthbert, than how Durham Cathedral played on and with that decision in aesthetic terms.

De situ Dunelmi

Despite being squeezed, somewhat precariously, between a cliff above the River Wear to its west and an abrupt land slope to the east, the cathedral complex at Durham was built almost to the largest dimensions its site would

---

22 *Rites of Durham*, ed. by Fowler, pp. 1–19.
23 Crook, 'Architectural Setting', pp. 237–38.
24 Reginald, *Libellus de admirandis*, ed. by Raine, p. 100.
25 Symeon, *Capitula de miraculis*, ed. by Arnold, I, 251.
26 Blick and Gelfand ed., *Push Me, Pull You*, pp. xxxvii–lii.

permit. With walls exceeding three metres in thickness and a final length of more than four hundred feet, it can be counted among the largest and most ambitious structures, not only of its generation, but almost of any following the decline of the Roman Empire. Between the late fourth and early twelfth centuries only three buildings in the entirety of Latin Christendom could rival the size of Old St Peter's in Rome (begun 318). In England, however, ground was broken on nine such giants, including Durham, in less than a generation after 1066.[27] If, like many of its southern counterparts, this massive chassis was intended to function as something like 'hard' Norman power — forcing, boasting, eclipsing, and thereby conquering — then a number of other documents also hint at a much 'softer', more nuanced, kind of projection. From a bishop-pilgrim looking in, now we can turn to a poet (in all likelihood a monk, living, working, possibly even building on site) looking out.

Writing in or around 1104 (the year of Cuthbert's *translatio*), the anonymous author of the Old English poem *De situ Dunelmi* blended space and time with landscape and nostalgia:

> Is ðeos burch breome   geond Breotenrice,
> steppa gestaðolad   stanas ymbutan
> wundrum gewæxen.   Weor ymbeornad,
> ea yðum stronge   and ðer inne wunað
> 5 feola fisca kyn   on floda gemonge.
> And ðær gewexen   is wudafæstern micel;
> wuniad in ðem wycum   wilda deor monige,
> in deope dalum   deora ungerim.[28]

> (The city is famous throughout the kingdom of Britain,
> built on high, the rocks around it
> wondrously grown up. The Wear runs round it,
> a stream strong in waves, and within it dwell
> 5 many kinds of fish in the thronging of the waters.
> And there has grown up a great woodland-enclosure;
> dwelling in the place are many wild beasts,
> in the deep dales, beasts without number.)

With these first eight of twenty-one relatively brief lines, our monk-poet brings an ambitious and abundant image of Durham into view. It is unclear whether

---

27 Those continental buildings are the abbey church at Cluny, and the cathedrals of Mainz and Speyer. The Norman buildings are the cathedrals of Westminster, Canterbury St Augustine's, St Albans, Winchester, York, Ely, Bury, Durham and Norwich. See Fernie, *The Architecture of Norman England*, p. 299.

28 *De situ Dunelmi* survived the medieval period in two manuscripts, both from the twelfth century: Cambridge, Camb. Uni. Lib., MS Ff. 1. 27 and BL, MS Cotton Vitellius D.XX (V). The latter was very badly damaged in the Cottonian fire of 1731. The poem has also been widely transcribed. See, in particular, 'Durham', in *Anglo-Saxon Minor Poems*, ed. by Dobbie, p. 27, used here throughout.

the 'Oceani insula' (island in the [Atlantic] ocean) Bede first described in his *De situ Britanniae* as 'fluuiis quoque multum piscosis ac fontibus praeclara copiosis, et quidem praecipue issicio abundat, et anguilla' (remarkable for its rivers abounding in fish, salmon, eels and plentiful springs) is being consciously evoked here; it does seem likely.[29] In any case, not only is the *situ* here inseparable from the city, our author seems very obviously to be investing the poem, right away, with a series of strong visual connections to the northern past. The natural protection afforded to Durham through its combination of 'stanas' (rocks), 'floda' (water) and 'wudafæstern' (woodland) — not to mention, of course, Cuthbert's 'mist' — was essential throughout its early medieval years (not least when a much less powerful pre-Norman community had to deal with the repeated threats of Scandinavians and, to no lesser degree, the Scots). But the specific and persistent praise of the landscape here was also very probably indicative of some of the long literary traditions associated with Cuthbert's Hiberno-Saxon heritage.

In early medieval Northumbria, southern Scotland and certain parts of eastern Ireland, it was more than customary for new monastic foundations to seek remote locations, but also specifically wooded ones too. St Patrick (d. mid-fifth century), one of Cuthbert's primary missionary ancestors, founded his 'ecclesia super siluam Fochluth' (great church in the wood of Fochloth).[30] The hermit Marbán (d. late seventh century) lived alone in his 'cleit' (bothy) in the wood.[31] Guthlac of Crowland (d. 714) took to the Land of the Fens and, as the Exeter Book describes it, a remote island in a wood revealed to him by God.[32] St Deglan (d. mid-eighth century) built a secluded cell for himself next to the sea with 'arboribus circa finem' (trees close about it).[33] Cedd (d. 664), a major influence at the Synod of Whitby, chose a site among some steep and remote hills.[34] And, even as late as the twelfth century, Geoffrey of Burton recorded in his *Vita sancte Moduenne*, that the saint had sought out a secluded hermitage for herself, specifically on an island in the River Trent, full of woods, wild animals and desolation.[35]

The extent to which *De Situ Dunelmi* also brings not just Durham's '[v]erdure mellows' — as Pevsner once described them — but its 'floda gemonge' (thronging waters) to mind, its 'feola fisca kyn' (many kinds of fish) and 'deora ungerim' (beasts without number), makes for a certain sense of region-specificity too.[36] A number of recent studies in ecocriticism have unpacked the ways

---

29 Bede, *Ecclesiastical History*, ed. and trans. by McClure and Collins, p. 9. *De situ Britanniae* is the first chapter of Book 1 of Bede's *Historia ecclesiastica*.
30 Cusack, *The Sacred Tree*, p. 78.
31 Hooke, *Trees in Anglo-Saxon England*, p. 86.
32 Hooke, *Trees in Anglo-Saxon England*, p. 85.
33 Hooke, *Trees in Anglo-Saxon England*, p. 87.
34 Pickles, *Kingship, Society, and the Church*, p. 140.
35 Geoffrey, *Life and Miracles of St Modwenna*, ed. and trans. by Bartlett, p. 14.
36 Pevsner, *Buildings of England: County Durham*, p. 159.

by which many medieval sources made a habit of masking the relationship and cooperative potentials of human and non-human environments.[37] This was done either by mitigating descriptions of the landscape through the use of topoi or otherwise mundane and formulaic prose, or, more commonly, by emphasizing the essential Otherness and danger of 'animality' beyond civilized borders.[38] By contrast, our poet here seems not only to actively court but to eulogize the natural and perhaps even numinous phenomena of the cathedral's surroundings. First and seemingly foremost, these were the attributes that made Durham 'breome geond Breotenrice' (famous throughout the kingdom of Britain).[39]

The poem goes on:

> Is in ðere byri eac　　bearnum gecyðed
> 10　ðe arfesta　　eadig Cudberch
> 　and ðes clene　　cyninges heafud,
> 　Osuualdes, Engle leo,　　and Aidan biscop,
> 　Eadberch and Eadfrið,　　æðele geferes.
> 　Is ðer inne midd heom　　Æðelwold biscop
> 15　and breoma bocera Beda,　　and Boisil abbot,
> 　ðe clene Cudberte　　on gecheðe
> 　lerde lustum,　　and he his lara wel genom.
> 　Eardiæð æt ðem eadige　　in in ðem minstre
> 　unarimeda　　reliquia,
> 20　ðær monia wundrum gewurðað,　　ðes ðe writ seggeð,
> 　midd ðene drihnes wer　　domes bideð.[40]

> (There is also in the city, well-known to men,
> 10　the gracious, blessed Cuthbert
> 　and the head of the pure king,
> 　of Oswald, the lion of the English, and Bishop Aidan,
> 　Eadberht and Eadfrith, noble companions.
> 　Inside there with them is Bishop Æthelwold
> 15　and the famous writer Bede, and Abbot Boisil,
> 　who taught Cuthbert the pure in his youth
> 　with pleasure, and Cuthbert well received his teaching.
> 　Living beside the blessed one in the minster
> 　are uncounted relics —

37　See, for example, Steel, *How To Make a Human*; Rudd, *Greenery: Ecocritical Readings*; Hanawalt and Kiser ed., *Engaging with Nature*.

38　Although Alfred K. Siewers does demonstrate that descriptions of the Welsh and Irish worlds would more readily infuse human narratives with wild and bestial agencies, he still concludes on the generally 'alienating and allegorical descriptions of nature' that defined most early medieval literature: Siewers, *Strange Beauty: Ecocritical Approaches*, p. 134.

39　*Anglo-Saxon Minor Poems*, ed. by Dobbie, p. 27.

40　*Anglo-Saxon Minor Poems*, ed. by Dobbie, p. 27.

20 Where many things are accomplished wondrously, as the writing says, with the man of the Lord, they await the Judgment.)

Here we can note another kind of abundance, the 'unarimeda reliquia' (uncounted relics) of Durham's most revered historical figures.[41] At the heart of the descriptions, as at the heart of the new cathedral complex, sat the physical remains of Durham's most renowned holy characters. Cuthbert, the 'arfesta' (gracious) and most 'eadig' (blessed), flanks an extraordinary cast including Oswald, Aidan, and Bede, many of whom also resided (quite literally) within the saint's embrace, inside his tomb.[42] Thus, a repeated interest in containment seems to emerge: successively, the kingdom of Britain, the River Wear, the woodland, the city, Cuthbert, and finally Durham's relic collection. In summarizing this peculiarity of structuring, Seth Lerer has argued that it signifies a concern with 'patterns of echo and interlace' as well as the alliterative structural traditions of early elegiac poetry.[43] Taking it a step further, Heather Blurton has suggested that each consecutive layer of enshrinement might almost function like a kind of precious written reliquary for the last.[44] In each case it is the special relation and play between site and frame that interests us here. Landscapes are often viewed in their narrowest sense, as literal and physical vistas, but in this instance each successive space can be thought of as a kind of socio-cultural construct: from nation to region to city to saint, an ever reducing, ever richer, distillation of a felt 'place' is brought together.

Durham Cathedral, this is to say, is viewed from within as being inextricably tied to the spaces that surround it; it appears to aspire to the uncanny potential, to borrow from Pallasmaa once more, to 'revive the poetic dimensions already present in a place'.[45] Whereas so many other medieval churches become hemmed-in over time, sometimes even half-hidden by their urban surroundings, at Durham nature here provides the theatrical stage that Pevsner also famously deemed comparable only to 'Avignon and Prague'.[46] Indeed, our anonymous poet was far from the only medieval source to single these spaces out for special appraisal.

Symeon's *Libellus de exordio*

Writing not much later on the subject of Durham's foundation, Symeon of Durham (d. 1129) was at repeated pains to stress just how remote and uninhabitable the first multitude found this little hill-island — the 'Dun-holm'

---

41 *Anglo-Saxon Minor Poems*, ed. by Dobbie, p. 27.
42 *Anglo-Saxon Minor Poems*, ed. by Dobbie, p. 27.
43 Lerer, 'Old English and its Afterlife', p. 21.
44 Blurton, '*Reliquia*: Writing Relics', pp. 39–56.
45 Pallasmaa, *The Eyes of the Skin*, p. 14.
46 Pevsner, *Buildings of England: County Durham*, pp. 159–60.

as it was known before being Latinized to 'Dunelm' after the Conquest, and eventually 'Durham' — to be. There is every reason to suspect that Durham had long been inhabited prior to 995: the peninsula had unique natural defences, unrivalled views of the surrounding area and — although Symeon would not, of course, have known it — a record of human archaeology that stretched back nearly four millennia.[47] And yet he repeatedly made claims to the effect that the landscape was wild, unkempt and 'quoniam densissima undique silua totum occupauerat' (covered on all sides by very dense forest).[48] Initially this extended and corroborated one of his original insinuations that the ground was unspoiled and therefore, by reason, pristine upon discovery. Unaffected by human hands, the extent to which the discovery of this site was thus attributed — by reverse implication — to theophany, to a unique intercession of Cuthbert's will and therefore to a very special kind of providence and legitimacy, was strongly insinuated. It also threw the 'people' of St Cuthbert's flight from Lindisfarne into dramatic relief. Fleeing servitude at the hands of the Vikings and ultimately forsaking the world, society and culture, the resolve and special deliverance of the faithful was made to evoke a kind of latter-day Exodus.[49] These two inferences were both, of course, among the most common in foundation stories of the period, but they also seem to have been very consciously allied to a third.

In his much earlier *Historia ecclesiastica* — with which we know Symeon was intimately familiar — Bede had already presented the islands of Farne as the culmination in a sequence of the saint's own ever more extreme withdrawals into the wild.[50] Bede described those islands as being 'aquae prorsus et frugis et arboris inops [... et] humanae habitationi minus accommodus' (utterly lacking in water, corn and trees [... and] ill-suited for human habitation).[51] That is, of course, until Cuthbert arrived and laboured to transform the site until it was made 'habitabilis per omnia factus est' (in all respects habitable).[52] 'Condidit ciuitatem' (He built a city there), our monk will also have read in Bede's prose *Vita Cuthberti*, 'suo aptam imperio' (fitted for his rule).[53] Symeon, then, likely provided a calculated and propitious analogue when he recounted at length how the first multitude at Durham, marshalled by Bishop Ealdhun, likewise found their own island to be 'sed non facile habitabilem inuenit' (not

---

47 It was in 995 that Cuthbert's body was brought to Durham for the first time. It was held in the *Ecclesia alba* (or 'White Church'), a small whitewashed structure made from timber. For the archaeological record see Carver, 'Early Medieval Durham', pp. 11–19.

48 Symeon, *Libellus de exordio*, ed. and trans. by Rollason, p. 148.

49 Symeon, *Libellus de exordio*, ed. and trans. by Rollason, p. 148.

50 That Symeon pulled at will from both Bede's *Historia ecclesiastica* as well as his prose *Vita sancti Cuthberti* — often *verbatim* — is well attested. For a full analysis of the *Libellus de exordio*'s many written and oral influences, see Symeon, *Libellus de exordio*, ed. and trans. by Rollason, pp. lxviii–lxxvii.

51 Bede, *Ecclesiastical History*, ed. and trans. by McClure and Collins, p. 225.

52 Bede, *Ecclesiastical History*, ed. and trans. by McClure and Collins, p. 225.

53 Bede, *Two Lives*, ed. and trans. by Colgrave, pp. 215–16.

easily habitable) until with the help of all the people and 'amore Christi et sancti Cuthberti feruens' (a burning love for Christ and St Cuthbert) they built 'de uirgis ecclesiola' (a little church made from branches).[54] Durham's earliest community was being portrayed in the self-same image of intense labour and humility with which Cuthbert was associated, and from which the special space and topography of the site, in turn, became inseparable.

Nor did the exacting details of struggle and industry end there. Later on, Symeon recorded that an even larger gathering of the faithful, from the whole area between the River Coquet and the River Tees, came to aid voluntarily in the construction of a second church made of stone. 'Totam extirpans siluam succidit' (they uprooted and cut down the whole forest); 'arando' (ploughing), and 'seminando' (sowing),[55] and persevered devotedly, he explained, until it was finished. Then 'ecclesiam honesto nec paruo opere inchoauit' (they began to build a church of noble workmanship and by no means small in scale).[56] Each of these narratives will have made for tacit allusions to the meagre and labour-intensive provisions of an eremitic life too, but also, in the repeated invocation of timber, to an already widespread region-specific tradition. In this one story alone, Durham's first two churches were presented as the latest in an ancient and legitimizing line of sacred wilderness retreats. With Symeon's remote wildwood peninsula performing a variation on the classic *locus amoenus* (less the 'pleasant place' of Virgil's imagining perhaps, than a kind of labour-intensive haven for ascetic comfort), the builders of its third and final church were therefore strategically poised for a very special kind of spatial inheritance.

Both Symeon and our anonymous poet of the *De situ Dunelmi* seem to have been quite conscious of how they really wanted to set their cathedrals apart, of what gave the site its lustre and ought to drive its fame in earnest. In short, it was their *mises en scène*: a socially constructed series of interdependent material and abstract spaces that, working together over time, embodied all the hallmarks of what Benedict Anderson would once have termed an 'imagined community'.[57] Another account of the 'Origins and Progress of this Church' might have described a region beset by recurrent trauma and upheaval: by repeated Viking invasions, by Conquest, by the near-genocidal Harrying of the North and, most recently, by the sudden and radical dismissal of the old community of lay clerks in 1083. To the contrary, however, both scribes were clearly making the case (very possibly directly to visitors like Bishop Ælfwold) for something like stability and continuity. Symeon, in particular, offers an almost seamless teleological narrative within which the rule of the new Norman aliens is merely the logical restoration of a natural order.[58]

---

54 Symeon, *Libellus de exordio*, ed. and trans. by Rollason, pp. 146–47.

55 Symeon, *Libellus de exordio*, ed. and trans. by Rollason, pp. 148–49.

56 Symeon, *Libellus de exordio*, ed. and trans. by Rollason, pp. 148–49.

57 Anderson, *Imagined Communities*.

58 On this last point, see also Meehan, 'Outsiders, Insiders, and Property', pp. 45–58 and Foster, 'Custodians of St Cuthbert', pp. 53–65. Both have argued that Symeon and his retinue were

Conclusion

The cathedral complex at Durham has long been seen as both a canonical and superlative example of early medieval engineering: put tersely, a kind of brilliant late-Romanesque lynchpin, linking with and preempting the nascent proto-Gothic style. It is 'justly recognized', wrote John Bilson, 'as the culminating achievement of the Norman Romanesque'.[59] Thus, analyses and descriptions of the cathedral can very often be found, either opening or closing chapters, in a variety of survey texts on medieval art and architecture.[60] On account of its sheer precision, its scale, its vaulting and — in particular — its precocious pointed ribs, Durham has come to represent a sparkling apogee, not only to the first generation of post-Conquest building, but to a continent-wide narrative of 'progressive' structural experimentation. It has not been my intention to disagree with any of these assessments, simply for the sake of it, nor do I think them particularly disagreeable in themselves. And yet, I have wanted to take this essay in a different and effectively opposite direction.

While neither an exhaustive nor definitive collection *per se*, many of the accounts, histories, poems, and stories employed above perhaps invite us to consider an alternative set of conclusions. And, wrapping things up himself, William of Malmesbury may lend us one final hand. In the climactic last section to Book 3 of his *Gesta pontificum*, he describes the final heady days leading to Cuthbert's *translatio* into Durham Cathedral in 1104. In the dead of night, Bishop Ralph Flambard was awoken by a loud sound. The timber scaffolding supporting the cathedral's new roof-vault had collapsed to the ground prematurely. Fearing for the vault, and especially for the expensive new altar and floor beneath it, Ralph rushed to the presbytery. As he stood surveying the scene with several of his monks, he and they were overwhelmed by *timor* (a mixture of reverence and fear). Somehow no harm had come to any part of the building, and not even to the timber props themselves, despite having fallen from a great height. William, however, did not attribute the vault's remarkable survival to the advanced talents of any mason, to the building's innate structural integrity, or to a dynamic chronology of trial and error. He said nothing about design, load, lateral thrust, or counter resistance. He attributed it, rather, to the miraculous intervention of St Cuthbert, whom he then begged, for the sake of his own soul, to remember his narration kindly.[61]

It is impressive to realize that nearly eighty years have now passed since Richard Krautheimer first argued that the 'problems of construction, design and function' fundamental to the study of buildings in other periods, were

---

particularly keen to consolidate their rights to property and power at Durham after 1083 following the radical decision to establish a new Benedictine assembly.

59 Bilson, 'Durham Cathedral', p. 101. See further, Bony, 'Stonework Planning', p. 33; Fernie, 'Romanesque Cathedral', p. 141.

60 A notable example is Conant, *Carolingian and Romanesque Architecture*.

61 William, *Gesta Pontificum*, ed. and trans. by Winterbottom and Thomson, pp. 418–19.

simply 'differently emphasised [...] in the medieval conception of architecture'. 'As a matter of fact', he went on, 'no medieval source ever stresses the design of an edifice or its construction'. Rather, it was the 'religious implications' of buildings that were 'uppermost in the minds of its contemporaries'.[62] Reasonable exceptions to this latter rule might include Procopius's *De aedificiis*, Gervase of Canterbury's *De combustione et reparatione* and Guillaume Durand's *Rationale divinorum officiorum*. But the larger point still stands.

It was not just that the structural merits of Durham's ingenious new transverse arches were ignored in the twelfth-century account, nor that Bishop Flambard's reaction was an emotional and thus, frankly, immaterial process either. Rather, it is the fact that feeling not form, indeed feeling over and above the evidence of form, won out in the end. The community's response to the collapsing scaffolding was the hinge upon which the entire story opened up. The bishop's sentiments alone confirmed the miracle. Nothing, in fact, even needed to be said: *timor* sufficed. What was felt was enough, even to the extent that (nearly three hundred miles away in his abbey in Wiltshire) William himself was moved to beg Cuthbert for his mercy.

By adopting space as an analytical category in this essay I have wanted to make an implicit point of emphasizing time too. Much of the original stone fabric at Durham Cathedral survives intact, and yet the spaces it contains have been made, unmade, and remade incessantly. The quantifiable form of any medieval building — its shape and dimensions, its geometry, its style relative to others, its basic lithic reality — are all always likely to be instructive (and interesting) to architectural historians. Big old buildings, in particular, offer us the rare comfort that big old histories might be saved and remembered. Durham's remarkable survival as an object, its hard and fast factuality, its sheer *thereness*, all strengthen the belief (indeed, the *hope*) that meaning might wait, patiently and protected, in a close examination of its stones. And yet, because generation after generation of people have perceived and created the world simultaneously, because the relationship between bodies and buildings is mediated through both the physical and cogno-cultural spaces that surround us, no stone can simply be an end in itself.

---

62 Krautheimer, 'Introduction to an "Iconography of Medieval Architecture"', p. 1.

144 EUAN MCCARTNEY ROBSON

Works Cited

Manuscripts and Archival Sources

Cambridge, Cambridge University Library, MS Ff.1.27
London, British Library, MS Cotton Vitellius D.XX (V)

Primary Sources

Albertus Magnus, *Book of Minerals*, trans. by Dorothy Wyckoff (Oxford: Clarendon Press, 1967)

The Anglo-Saxon Minor Poems, ed. by Elliott Van Kirk Dobbie, Anglo-Saxon Poetic Records, 6 (New York: Columbia University Press, 1946)

Bede, *The Ecclesiastical History of the English People. The Greater Chronicle. Bede's Letter to Egbert*, ed. and trans. by Judith McClure and Roger Collins (Oxford: Oxford University Press, 2008)

——, *Two Lives of Saint Cuthbert: A Life by an Anonymous Monk of Lindisfarne and Bede's Prose Life*, ed. and trans. by Bertram Colgrave (Cambridge: Cambridge University Press, 1940, repr. 1985)

Clement of Alexandria, *Stromateis, Books 1–3*, trans. by John Ferguson, The Fathers of the Church, 85 (Washington, DC: Catholic University of America Press, 1991)

Geoffrey of Burton, *Life and Miracles of St Modwenna*, ed. and trans. by Robert Bartlett (Oxford: Clarendon Press, 2002)

Reginald of Durham (attrib.), *Libellus de admirandis beati Cuthberti virtutibus quae novellis patratae sunt temporibus*, ed. by James Raine, SS, 1 (London: J. B. Nichols and Son, 1835)

The Rites of Durham, ed. by Joseph T. Fowler, SS, 107 (Durham: Andrews & Co., 1903)

Ruskin, John, *The Works of John Ruskin. Vol. 5: Modern Painters III*, ed. by Edward Cook and Alexander Wedderburn (Cambridge: Cambridge University Press, 2010)

Symeon of Durham (attrib.), *Capitula de miraculis et translationibus Sancti Cuthberti*, in *Symeonis monachi opera omnia*, ed. by Thomas Arnold, 2 vols (London: Longman, 1882–1885), I

Symeon of Durham, *Libellus de exordio atque Procursu istius hoc est Dunhelmensis ecclesie. Tract on the Origins and Progress of this the Church of Durham*, ed. and trans. by David Rollason (Oxford: Clarendon Press, 2000)

William of Malmesbury, *Gesta Pontificum Anglorum = The History of the English Bishops*, ed. and trans. by Michael Winterbottom and Rodney Thomson (Oxford: Clarendon Press, 2007)

Secondary Works

Aird, William, 'The Origins and Development of the Church of St Cuthbert, 635–1153, with special reference to Durham in the period circa 1071–1153' (unpublished doctoral thesis, University of Edinburgh, 1991)

Anderson, Benedict, *Imagined Communities: Reflections on the Origin and Spread of Nationalism* (London: Verso, 1991)

Bilson, John, 'Durham Cathedral: The Chronology of its Vaults', *Archaeological Journal*, 79 (1922), 101–60

Blick, Sarah, and Laura D. Gelfand, ed., *Push Me, Pull You: Imaginative and Emotional Interaction in Late Medieval and Renaissance Art* (Leiden: Brill, 2011)

Bony, Jean, 'The Stonework Planning of the First Durham Master', in *Medieval Architecture and its Intellectual Context*, ed. by Paul Crossley and Eric Fernie (London: Hambledon, 1990), pp. 19–34

Blurton, Heather, '*Reliquia*: Writing Relics in Anglo-Norman Durham', in *Cultural Diversity in the British Middle Ages: Archipelago, Island, England*, ed. by Jeffrey Jerome Cohen (Basingstoke: Palgrave Macmillan, 2008), pp. 39–56

Carver, M. O. H., 'Early Medieval Durham: The Archaeological Evidence', in *Medieval Art and Architecture at Durham Cathedral*, ed. by Nicola Coldstream and Peter Draper (Leeds: The British Archaeological Association, 1980), pp. 11–19

Conant, Kenneth, *Carolingian and Romanesque Architecture, 800–1200*, 2nd rev. edn (Harmondsworth: Penguin, 1978)

Crook, John, 'The Architectural Setting of the Cult of St Cuthbert in Durham Cathedral (1093–1200)', in *Anglo-Norman Durham, 1093–1193*, ed. by David Rollason, Margaret Harvey and Michael Prestwich (Woodbridge: Boydell, 1994), pp. 235–50

Cusack, Carole M., *The Sacred Tree: Ancient and Medieval Manifestations* (Cambridge: Cambridge Scholars, 2011)

Dufferwiel, Martin, *The A-Z of Curious County Durham* (Stroud: History Press, 2014)

Fernie, Eric, *The Architecture of Norman England* (Oxford: Oxford University Press, 2000)

——, 'The Romanesque Cathedral, 1093–1133', in *Durham Cathedral: History, Fabric and Culture*, ed. by David Brown (New Haven: Yale University Press, 2015), pp. 131–41

Foster, Meryl, 'Custodians of St Cuthbert: The Durham Monks' Views of their Predecessors, 1083–c. 1200', in *Anglo-Norman Durham, 1093–1193*, ed. by David Rollason, Margaret Harvey and Michael Prestwich (Woodbridge: Boydell, 1994), pp. 53–65

Geertz, Clifford, *The Interpretation of Cultures: Selected Essays* (New York: Basic Books, 1973)

Gell, Alfred, *Art and Agency: An Anthropological Theory* (Oxford: Clarendon Press, 2013)

Hanawalt, Barbara A., and Lisa J. Kiser, ed., *Engaging with Nature: Essays on the Natural World in Medieval and Early Modern Europe* (Notre Dame, IN: University of Notre Dame Press, 2008)

Hooke, Della, *Trees in Anglo-Saxon England* (Woodbridge: Boydell, 2010)

Ingraham, Catherine T., 'Architecture as Evidence', in *Drifting: Architecture and Migrancy*, ed. by Stephen Cairns (London: Routledge, 2004), pp. 61–81

——, *Architecture, Animal, Human: The Asymmetrical Condition* (London: Routledge, 2006)

Krautheimer, Richard, 'Introduction to an "Iconography of Medieval Architecture"', *Journal of the Warburg and Courtauld Institutes*, 5 (1942), 1–33

Lerer, Seth, 'Old English and its Afterlife', in *The Cambridge History of Medieval Literature*, ed. by David Wallace (Cambridge: Cambridge University Press, 1999), pp. 7–34

Meehan, Bernard, 'Outsiders, Insiders, and Property in Durham around 1100', *Studies in Church History*, 12 (1975), 45–58

Norberg-Schulz, Christian, *Genius Loci: Towards a Phenomenology of Architecture* (London: Academy Editions, 1980)

Pallasmaa, Juhani, *The Eyes of the Skin: Architecture and the Senses* (Chichester: Wiley, 2012)

Pevsner, Nikolaus, *The Buildings of England: County Durham*, ed. by Nikolaus Pevsner and Elizabeth Williamson (New Haven: Yale University Press, 2002)

Pickles, Thomas, *Kingship, Society, and the Church in Anglo-Saxon Yorkshire* (Oxford: Oxford University Press, 2018)

Rudd, Gillian, *Greenery: Ecocritical Readings of Late Medieval English Literature* (Manchester: Manchester University Press, 2010)

Siewers, Alfred K., *Strange Beauty: Ecocritical Approaches to Early Medieval Landscape* (New York: Palgrave Macmillan, 2009)

Steel, Karl, *How To Make A Human: Animals and Violence in the Middle Ages* (Columbus: Ohio State University Press, 2011)

Toynbee, J. M. C., 'Two Romano-British Genii', *Britannia*, 9 (1978), 329–30

Tuan, Yi-Fu, *Space and Place: The Perspective of Experience* (Minneapolis: University of Minnesota Press, 1977, repr. 2001)

JOHN JENKINS

Holy Geysers? Oily Saints and Ecclesiastical Politics in Late Medieval Yorkshire and Lincolnshire

In 1223, Matthew Paris recorded that 'prorupit oleum lucidissimum in magnus ecclesia apud Eboracum de tumba beati Willelmi' (the clearest oil burst forth in the great church at York from the tomb of St William).[1] Fifteen years later, in the same chronicle, it was noted that from the tomb of Robert of Knaresborough 'oleum medicinale fertur abundanter emisisse' (medicinal oil was abundantly discharged).[2] At the 1280 translation of St Hugh in Lincoln Cathedral, the Peterborough Chronicle reported that 'in cujus sepulcro inventa est olei quantitas non modica, et per ipsius merita plurima ibidem fiunt miracula' (large quantities of oil were found in the tomb, and through its merits many miracles were performed there).[3] In 1288 Oliver Sutton, Bishop of Lincoln, wrote in a letter promoting the cause of the canonization of Robert Grosseteste of 'the dripping [...] of the most pure oil flowing from the tomb of this eminent man of God'.[4] In 1312 the Beverley Cartulary relates that 'oil flowed from the tomb of St John, Archbishop and confessor, which was smeared on the eyes of some boys who had not been able to see properly for three months. Immediately they began to see more clearly'.[5] Over the course of almost ninety years, five men, three of them within thirty miles of York and the other two in Lincoln, were the only recorded cases in England of bodies posthumously producing miraculous oil. The phenomenon started at York with St William and ended as a nationally celebrated aspect of the cult of St John of Beverley.

---

1 Paris, *Matthaei Parisiensis, Monachi Sancti Albani Chronica maiora*, ed. by Luard, III, p. 77 (cited hereafter as *Chronica maiora*)
2 Paris, *Chronica maiora*, ed. by Luard, III, p. 521.
3 Gerald of Wales, *Opera*, ed. by Brewer, Dimock, and Warner, VII, pp. 221–22.
4 Cole, 'Proceedings Relative to the Canonisation', p. 11.
5 Wilson, *Life and After-Life*, p. 221.

> **John Jenkins** (john.jenkins@york.ac.uk) is a Research Associate and Teaching Fellow at the University of York.

Late Medieval Devotion to Saints from the North of England: New Directions, ed. by Christiania Whitehead, Hazel J. Hunter Blair, and Denis Renevey, MCS 48
(Turnhout: Brepols, 2022), pp. 147–163
BREPOLS ❧ PUBLISHERS   10.1484/M.MCS-EB.5.124348

The effusion of oil from saints' bodies has received little more than passing comment until very recently.[6] Holy oil has always had a central place in Christianity. Initially, the 'oil of saints' functioned and was produced in much the same way as holy water: being blessed at a saint's tomb or by contact with the saint's body or bones.[7] There were, however, also occasional references in both Western and Eastern hagiography of the early Middle Ages to spontaneous outpourings of oil from relic caskets and tombs. This was a potential identifying characteristic of saintly bodies, along with the 'odour of sanctity' and a tendency to remain incorrupt. The seemingly miraculous outpouring of oil served to confirm the sanctity of the body and the satisfaction of the saint with their location (especially after a translation or *furta sacra*), and provided a healing oil that was the catalyst for miracles.[8] The right to consecrate holy oil was reserved to the episcopate, and used for baptisms, confirmations, and the anointing of the sick. Given the close association of this sacramentally central oil with the episcopal office, it was a short stretch to the understanding that holy oil might be produced by contact with, or emanation from, the body of a sainted bishop.

Sylvia Mullins, building on the observations of Caroline Walker Bynum, has traced the history of oil-producing saints (*myroblytes*) in Western Europe. Earlier examples of this phenomenon tended to be male and the later examples were mostly female, with the eleventh and twelfth centuries being the 'ambiguous' crossover point. The chief exemplars for male and female myroblytes were, respectively, St Nicholas of Myra and St Catherine of Alexandria. John the Deacon's *Vita* of St Nicholas, a largely mythical fourth-century bishop of Myra near Ephesus, was one of the most popular hagiographies of tenth-century Western Europe.[9] It contained an addition, seemingly of the later ninth century, which noted that

> the tomb in which his venerable corpse was enclosed never ceased to distil an oily liquid, even to this day. To the spot come multitudes of weak, lame, blind, withered, deaf and dumb, and ones who are vexed by unclean spirits. When they are anointed with that holy liquor, they are restored to their original state of health.[10]

Between the mid-ninth and mid-twelfth centuries, there are at least twelve accounts of individuals expressing oil from their corpses or tombs, of which the majority were bishops.[11] St Nicholas himself was taken from Myra and

---

6 I am very grateful to Sylvia Mullins for providing me with a copy of her PhD dissertation ('Myroblytes').

7 Mullins, 'Myroblytes', pp. 176–86.

8 Vauchez, *Sainthood*, pp. 427–31; Mullins, 'Myroblytes', pp. 187–205.

9 Burnett, 'The Cult of St Nicholas', pp. 26–33; Mullins, 'Myroblytes', pp. 107, 118–21, 208, 211–23.

10 Jones, *Saint Nicholas of Myra*, p. 66.

11 Besides those noted by Mullins (Bishops Willebrord of Utrecht; Gundechar of Eichstätt; Eligius of Noyon; Martin of Tours; and Sabinus of Canosa; the Frankish Abbots Babolenus

OILY SAINTS AND ECCLESIASTICAL POLITICS   149

re-interred in a shrine in Bari in 1087. His contentment with this new situation was proved by his characteristic oil flowing even more abundantly than before.[12] From the later eleventh century, and with the addition of oil production to the cult of St Catherine of Alexandria, later medieval myroblytes were almost exclusively female. The oil evidenced a new female sanctity in its symbolism of nourishment, purity, and peace, and myroblytes were particularly concentrated in the Italian Peninsula and the Low Countries.[13]

The five northern English saintly figures named at the start of this chapter notably buck the prevailing European trend, in that they were male and mostly bishops at a time when the vast majority of new myroblytes were female mystics and nuns. While Mullins considered the symbolic and theological aspects of the production of oil by saintly relics, in studying these northern male saints I will look more closely at the political and practical aspects of the phenomenon. Unlike most other characteristics of saintly corpses, oil emanating from a tomb on a regular basis required a high degree of stage-management: for the oil to come out it had to have been poured in. The strong regional flavour of this phenomenon in England, and its isolation from any other examples, make it particularly ripe for a study of its origins, spread, and function.

St William of York

There is no evidence of the phenomenon in England before Matthew Paris's account of St William of York in 1223.[14] After a turbulent career as archbishop, William died on 8 June 1154, although miracles only started occurring at his tomb on the anniversary of his death in 1177.[15] For most of the twelfth century the archbishops of York, including St William, had fought a losing battle with Canterbury, England's other metropolitan see, over the rights and honour due to each.[16] The 1170 murder of Thomas Becket, archbishop of Canterbury, and his rapid canonization ensured that Canterbury Cathedral had sudden possession of the country's most popular saint. Given the temporal proximity of William's first miracles and his outpourings of oil to the 1170 martyrdom and 1220 translation of Thomas Becket, it is tempting to see them as a direct response to Canterbury by the canons of York, and thus as a continuation of

---

and Bercharius; and the Italian confessor-saints Fantinus and Venerius) there are also Paul, Bishop of Verdun; Perpetuus, Bishop of Maastricht; and Reverianus, Bishop of Autun. Mullins, 'Myroblytes', pp. 194–99, 220–29, 262; *AASS*, Feb. II, col. 174; June, I, cols 40–41, Nov. II, col. 295.

12 Jones, *Saint Nicholas of Myra*, pp. 205–06.
13 Bynum, *Holy Feast, Holy Fast*, pp. 211, 274, 391–92; Mullins, 'Myroblytes', pp. 244–305; Jones, 'The Norman Cult', pp. 216–30.
14 Paris, *Chronica maiora*, ed. by Luard, III, p. 77.
15 Norton, *St William of York*.
16 Haines, *Ecclesia Anglicana*, pp. 78–83.

the primacy dispute.[17] The oil, in particular, looks to be an echo of the Water of St Thomas (Becket's blood mixed with water and doled out at his tomb for use as medicine), so characteristic of the early cult.[18]

Yet it was probably more local northern concerns that were foremost in the need to be creative in the promotion of William's cult. It has been well-noted that York's metropolitan status suffered throughout the Middle Ages from an inability to assert control over its disparate province.[19] In the 1170s, prior to St William's miracles, the Minster (the seat of the archbishop) did not have a resident saint at a time when Durham and St Andrews were promoting their spiritual patrons. This threatened to weaken York's status in the North, and the archbishops were already losing their claims to primacy over the Scottish sees. At the nearby Cistercian abbey of Fountains the monks were also promoting the sanctity of their former abbot Aelred.[20] At the time of the first flowing of oil in the 1220s, nearby Ripon and Beverley, both minsters with ancient rights and influence within the local area, were the focus of renovations around the shrines of their saints — eighth-century archbishops of York, Wilfrid and John.[21]

Although Christopher Norton felt that Canterbury was the key rivalry driving St William's cult, the history of William's oil shows that while it was 'aimed at reasserting the authority of the church of York', this was with a focus decidedly more provincial and capitular than national. While much has been made of the 'Becket model' in post-1170s English hagiography, it is barely evident in William's *Vita* of the 1220s.[22] Indeed, the most 'Becket' element of William's cult, his supposed murder by poisoned communion wine while celebrating Mass, is not included in the *Vita*.[23] Rather, it is more concerned with generic pastoral-episcopal descriptions of William's generosity and his instruction, correction, comforting, and protection of his flock, drawn from well-known episcopal exemplars, in particular the *Vita* of St Nicholas.[24] The symbolism of the oil continues these pastoral ideas: 'de sacro sarcophago oleum quo unxit pugilem suum infernalis claustri propugnator, ad caecorum lumen, ad debilium robur, ad tristium exhilarationem [...] et ad aegrorum sanitatem, saepius effluit abundanter' (from the holy sarcophagus oil often abundantly flowed, which anointed the boxer as his champion in the infernal ring, brought light to the blind, strength to the weak, cheer to the sorrowful [...] and health to

---

17 Norton, *St William of York*, pp. 161–62, 193–96.

18 Koopmans, '"Water Mixed with the Blood"', pp. 535–58.

19 Dobson, *Church and Society*, pp. 4–5, 177; Brentano, *York Metropolitan Jurisdiction*, pp. 23–41.

20 Norton, *St William of York*, pp. 160–62; Brentano, *York Metropolitan Jurisdiction*, p. 28.

21 Brown, *'Our Magnificent Fabrick'*, p. 13; Horrox, 'The Later Medieval Minster', p. 37; *Historians of the Church of York*, ed. by Raine, III, pp. 124–25.

22 Vauchez, *Sainthood*, pp. 167–73.

23 Norton, *St William of York*, pp. 144–48.

24 'Anonymous Life of St William', *Historians of the Church of York*, ed. by Raine, II, pp. 276–77; *Old English Life*, ed. by Traherne, p. 186.

the sick).[25] The anointing of fighters is a theme taken from early Christianity, particularly from John Chrysostom, relating to the use of oil in baptismal and confirmation ceremonies preparing the catechumen for their struggle against sin in the life ahead.[26] Combined with the curative properties of St William's oil, these functions correspond to the oil and chrism produced by a bishop for use in baptism, confirmation, and the anointing of the sick. The oil thus contained within it clear episcopal and pastoral symbolism, distinct from the Water of St Thomas's quasi-Eucharistic cure-all.

The derivation of the oil miracle from St Nicholas's exemplar is clearest in the description of the oil in William's liturgy, probably composed at around the same time as the *Vita*.[27] In Nicholas's liturgy the phenomenon is described as 'Ex ejus tumba marmorea sacrum resudat oleum' (Holy oil exudes from the marble tomb [of St Nicholas]). William's liturgy clearly borrows both imagery and terminology directly, with 'resudat oleum' slightly modified to 'corpus […] oleum […] resudabat': 'Quod sanctissimum corpus ejus de quo per lapidis duriciem oleum frequentius resudabat' (That most holy body [of St William] frequently exuded oil through the hard stone).[28] St William was being promoted as a bishop not in the new mould of the Becket martyr-bishop but mainly as a Nicholas-style pastoral bishop for his archdiocese. Thus it is likely that the widely reported tale of his poisoning was written out of the *Vita* because it was supposedly perpetrated by one of his own archdeacons. Whatever hagiographic potential there was in this vivid story could not be exploited as it ran counter to the main thrust of the cult — that William was the model of a good, active, pastoral diocesan, and beloved for it by his lay and clerical flocks alike.

There was not, as far as can be ascertained, a continuous flow of oil. Instead it coincided with significant events in the calendar. The two firmly datable occasions of oil production occurred in 1223, when William's feast (8 June) fell on the Thursday before Pentecost/Whitsun, and in 1308 on Corpus Christi Thursday in Whitweek two days before William's feast.[29] This was a time when, across Western Christendom, parishioners in every diocese were supposed to visit their cathedral *en masse* in order to collect the oil and chrism that had been blessed by the bishop for that year. Christopher Brooke cast doubt on the idea that, particularly in such massive English sees as York, the custom ever resulted in the presence of the entire diocesan population in the cathedral even over the course of the entire week, but nevertheless concluded that 'the Pentecostal custom in fact brought great throngs' to the cathedral.[30] By the

---

25 'Anonymous Life of St William', *Historians of the Church of York*, ed. by Raine, II, p. 280.

26 Mullins, 'Myroblytes', pp. 55–62.

27 Norton, *St William of York*, p. 201.

28 *Breviarium*, ed. by Lawley, I, col. 180; II, col. 105.

29 Paris, *Chronica Maiora*, ed. by Luard, III, p. 77; 'Tables of the Vicars Choral', *Historians of the Church of York*, ed. by Raine, II, pp. 537–38.

30 Brooke, *Churches and Churchmen*, pp. 186–87; Edwards, *English Secular Cathedrals*, pp. 100–01.

later thirteenth century the period between Rogationtide and Whitweek was an extremely important time in York's ecclesiastical and civic calendar, with processions, fairs, and the parading of relics, including that of the head shrine of St William on Whit Monday.[31] Between 1310 and 1464 York Minster's vicars-choral staged an elaborate annual performance over Whitsuntide, outside the Minster gates and clearly intended for large crowds.[32] The oil was thus a part of, and quite probably an important factor in the development of, these major and well-attended festivities. The combination of episcopal feast, diocesan gathering, civic ritual and the miraculous emanation of oil with its echoes of the model pastoral bishop St Nicholas, was designed to place St William's tomb in the nave of York Minster at the heart of the regional, and indeed the northern, Church.

Such periodic outflowings indicate that the curators of the tomb at York were pouring the oil in as a form of pious fraud. It was a highly stage-managed method of cultic promotion. In this sense, we can see the purpose of oil in confirming the continued vitality of a cult, or in providing evidence of the legitimacy of a new cultic setting. Between the translation of some of St William's bones to a shrine behind the high altar in 1283 and the subsequent major redevelopment of the nave, the east end of which was completed in around 1300, the tomb was largely inaccessible.[33] Two days before his feast in 1308, on the Thursday of Pentecost (6 June), the tomb once again exuded a healing oil. The laity reported it to the Minster canons who, expressing doubt that it was oil, 'lichino inde facto et accenso, mirabilis flammae inde procedentes, ac si oleum fuisset, commune mirum cernetibus intulerunt' (made a lamp of it and set it alight, the miraculous flames which came forth, as if it were oil, bringing wonder to all who saw). Then psalms were sung and the bells were rung throughout the city to celebrate, and the spread of the fame of the miracle caused many people from the city and beyond to come to the Minster and be healed by anointing themselves.[34]

As well as proving the continued functionality of the tomb site following the translation and renovation of the nave, the centrality of the canons of York to the process was reaffirmed by the oil as they were the arbiters of its authenticity. The oil miracle was celebrated and widely advertised, and allowed for direct interaction between the laity and the sainted archbishop. An undated miracle tells how, on one occasion when the oil began to flow, the laity at the tomb ran to find drinking vessels and one ended up eating rose petals he had dipped in the healing liquid.[35] Yet two surviving *ampullae* from York, very similar in form to those sold at Canterbury to hold the Thomas Water and possibly dating to the 1220s and the early fourteenth century, show that there was enough of a

---

31 Rees Jones, *York*, pp. 262, 266–68.
32 Rentz, 'Castles for St William', pp. 111–20.
33 Brown, *'Our Magnificent Fabrick'*, pp. 88–90.
34 'Tables of the Vicars Choral', *Historians of the Church of York*, ed. by Raine, II, pp. 537–38.
35 'Tables of the Vicars Choral', *Historians of the Church of York*, ed. by Raine, II, p. 540.

periodic flow to warrant a souvenir trade in containers. Both *ampullae* show St William in full archiepiscopal regalia, blessing the viewer and flanked by SS Peter and Paul as symbols of his Rome-derived authority.[36] The canons would have known when the oil would appear and could thus prepare articles for its collection. The tomb with its oil became the lay-devotional focus and site of miracles, while the shrine in the retrochoir became the liturgical focus for the canons and vicars-choral.[37] The oil also served to validate the site of the tomb, following the translation, as a continued site of proper devotion: it effectively confirmed that the tomb was not now 'empty'.[38]

While the cult had a decidedly episcopal flavour, this was not primarily for the benefit of the archbishops. Individual archbishops such as Walter de Grey (1215–1255) might be prominent in patronizing large-scale architectural remodellings of the Minster centred on St William, but the management of the cult lay with the cathedral chapter. It was, most probably, a canon who wrote the *Vita*, and it would have been the decision of the canons to pour oil into the tomb in order for it to flow out.[39] The nature of the cult was carefully organized by the chapter for a particular purpose, in similar fashion to the way that the monastic community at Canterbury utilized Becket's body to emphasize their control over archiepiscopal election and thus their importance within the province.[40] The oil was certainly intended to draw the laity to the tomb of St William, but more importantly it was part of a cultic narrative. It highlighted the York canons' custodianship of the saintly archbishop. This then mirrored and emphasized the chapter's control, through the power of election, over his successors, which in the thirteenth century they usually exercised by electing one of their own number.[41] When the oil flowed again in 1308, it may be notable in this context that the archbishop at the time, William Greenfield, was the first since Walter Giffard in 1266 not to have been a member of the Minster chapter prior to his election.[42] The oil also reinforced the independence of the canons from the archbishop, who had no right to sit in chapter and was limited in his powers of visitation.[43] The presence of an active, if dead, archbishop within the Minster made up for the routine absence of the current incumbent, and was far more easily controlled.[44] Hence the notably episcopal flavour of St William's cult. The oil drew the laity to the shrine, confirmed William

---

36 Boertjes, 'Pilgrim Ampullae', pp. 52–56.

37 Jenkins, 'Replication or Rivalry?', pp. 41–42.

38 Jenkins, 'Replication or Rivalry?', p. 38; Phillips and Atkinson, *The Cathedral of Archbishop Thomas*, pp. 125–27.

39 Norton, *St William of York*, p. 201.

40 Jenkins, 'Replication or Rivalry?', pp. 29–38.

41 Dobson, 'The Later Middle Ages', pp. 78–79; Dobson, *Church and Society*, pp. 168–71.

42 Dobson, *Church and Society*, pp. 168–70.

43 Edwards, *English Secular Cathedrals*, pp. 101–11, 129–30; Brentano, *York Metropolitan Jurisdiction*, pp. 29–30.

44 Edwards, *English Secular Cathedrals*, pp. 104–05.

as *the* sainted archbishop of York, and placed the Minster and its cathedral chapter at the heart of the province.

The oil of St William thus had a number of functions within the Minster, the city, and the diocese: as a healing fluid, a miraculous sign, a symbol of episcopality, and as a mechanism of capitular control of the cult, amongst others. The phenomenon was replicated from the cult of St Nicholas, with a nod towards the fluid-relics of St Thomas Becket. Yet it also had a further history of regional replication, in a process we can hopefully be excused from calling a 'trickle-down effect'.

Oil at Knaresborough, Lincoln, and Beverley

Robert of Knaresborough, a York-born hermit of the late twelfth century who had associations with the Cistercians and Trinitarians, was the next English myroblyte, and is something of a mystery. His oil is least explicable as he was not a bishop, and it was never mentioned again after 1238.[45] The oil first flowed twenty years after his death, but at a time when the status of his cult is otherwise unclear. A later medieval account suggests that the site of his cult at Knaresborough was briefly acquired by the Premonstratensian canons of Coverham Abbey around this time, and if this is the case then the oil would be explicable as marking Robert's posthumous approval of the transfer of ownership.[46] Knaresborough was only seventeen miles from York, where Robert's family (Flur/Flower) were prominent citizens. They also provided the chapel which was to become the main site of the cult.[47] The oil looks to have been a replication of a particularly local phenomenon, borrowed directly from the cult of St William, in order to testify St Robert's acquiescence in a change of ownership of the relics and site. Given the relationship between William's oil and the nascent civic rituals of York in which the Flower family would have been closely involved, and which Sarah Rees Jones notes were developing from the late twelfth century, saintly oil production may quickly have become associated with the city of York.[48] Was the production of oil, in this instance, considered something that a 'York saint' such as Robert would do, and that pilgrims from York might come expecting? We can do no more than speculate on the limited evidence.

More understandable is the discovery of oil in St Hugh of Lincoln's tomb at his 1280 translation. Not only was his body found in a pool of fragrant oil, during the ceremony itself St Hugh's head released more: 'Cumque sanctissimum

---

45 Paris, *Chronica maiora*, ed. by Luard, III, p. 521.

46 *Metrical Life*, ed. by Bazire, p. 73; Bottomley, *St Robert of Knaresborough*, p. 39; Easterling, 'A Norbert for England', pp. 86–87; Golding, 'Hermit and the Hunter', p. 103.

47 Rees Jones, *York*, pp. 279–80; Bottomley, *St Robert of Knaresborough*, pp. 36–39; *Metrical Life*, ed. by Bazire, p. 57.

48 Rees Jones, *York*, pp. 266–69.

caput [...] Oliverus Lincolniensis episcopus in manibus reverenter teneret, ex ejus maxilla non parum olei distillavit' (And when Oliver [Sutton], Bishop of Lincoln, reverently held the most holy head in his hands, no small amount of oil dripped from its jaw).[49] There is a prosaic explanation for this in that Hugh, having died abroad, was embalmed.[50] In the twelfth and thirteenth centuries this took the form of removing the internal organs, including from the skull, and pumping the body full of heavy oils such as myrrh.[51] These evaporate extremely slowly, so much so that a modern excavation at St Bees Priory, Cumbria, found one medieval stone grave with an occupant swimming in a 'fragrant soup'.[52] It is thus believable that not only would St Hugh have been found in a puddle of his own embalming oil, but that the many cavities of the skull might suddenly eject oil when it was handled. The experience of having St Hugh's oily head disgorge itself over his hands may have also been the spark for Bishop Oliver Sutton's letter in support of his predecessor Robert Grosseteste's canonization at Lincoln eight years later, where he claimed that oil had dripped from Robert's tomb.[53]

In the case of both St Hugh and Grosseteste, the ease with which the production of oil could be interpreted as a saintly episcopal attribute surely owes much to the presence of St William in the neighbouring diocese. The proximity of York's myroblyte had to an extent normalized the phenomenon in the region and made it available both as an interpretation of St Hugh's unexpected discharging of oil and as a viable saintly characteristic in a canonization attempt. The association of the oil with Whitweek, not a factor in either of the thirteenth-century outpourings at Lincoln, was clear in a further emanation from St Hugh in the fifteenth century, apparently his first since the translation. In 1445, a letter sent by John Percy, subdean of the cathedral, to the Carthusians' Grande Chartreuse stated that oil had flowed from the tomb of St Hugh on the eve of Pentecost (14 May) that year, and enclosed some in a small golden phial: 'de marmoreis tumba [...] miraculosum et verissimum liquore et odore sapore et vuctuolitate [*recte* unctuositate] et in copiosa quantitate fluere et manare cepit et usque in presens non cessat per plura ac diversa loca fluere et manare oleum'. (from the marble tomb [...] oil, miraculous and most true in fluidity, odour, taste, and oiliness, began to flow in great quantity, and up to the present time has not ceased to flow from many places).[54]

The bishop and chapter of Lincoln were assiduous in promoting Pentecostal diocesan processions and donations to the cathedral throughout the Middle Ages, and as at York it is possible to see St Hugh's oil as a centrepiece to these

---

49 Gerald of Wales, *Opera*, ed. by Brewer, Dimock, and Warner, VII, pp. 221–22.

50 Gerald of Wales, *Opera*, ed. by Brewer, Dimock, and Warner, VII p. 114.

51 Georges, 'Mourir c'est pourrir un peu', pp. 372–79.

52 Gilchrist and Sloane, *Requiem*, pp. 109, 119.

53 Cole, 'Proceedings Relative to the Canonisation', p. 11.

54 Farmer, 'The Cult and Canonization', p. 87.

rites.[55] As will be discussed below, the oil of St John at Beverley was notable for flowing throughout the fifteenth century, offering a current and powerful regional model for resurrecting this phenomenon at Lincoln. In a more immediate context, the cathedral had been riven for decades by a series of high-profile feuds between the eccentric and debt-ridden absentee Dean John Mackworth and his chapter, which the bishops of Lincoln were frequently called upon to adjudicate. In one episode in 1435, crowds of pilgrims and worshippers in the cathedral church witnessed the dean and his armed retinue attacking the chancellor. By this time the funds and fabric of the cathedral were said to be gravely suffering.[56] That the author of the letter to the Grand Chartreuse was the subdean, a noted antagonist of the dean at this point, suggests that as at the Yorkshire sites the oil was being produced to make a point about the chapter's ownership of the sainted corpse and of the cathedral in which it sat, as well as providing an impetus for the laity of the diocese to return to their mother church at Pentecost following what must have been an off-putting violent episode. This may have been the only outpouring of oil at Lincoln subsequent to the thirteenth century, but as elsewhere it highlights the phenomenon as predominantly an ecclesio-political act.

This is particularly exemplified in the cult of St John of Beverley, an eighth-century archbishop of York whose tomb and shrine was at Beverley Minster, around thirty miles from York. Just four years after the major oil miracle of St William in 1308, on 11 June 1312, three days after the feast of St William and in a year when Whitweek had fallen almost a full month before, oil began to flow from the tomb of St John. The purpose looks to have been similar, in that a new liturgically focused shrine behind the high altar had been completed in 1308 and the relics translated to it, while the devotionally focused and accessible 'empty' tomb was validated by the emanation of oil.[57] That the occasion was stage-managed to reaffirm the tomb's significance is also suggested by the presence of the Bishops of Norwich and Bath and Wells to witness it. The oil appeared in the morning and increased in flow throughout the day 'to the quantity of one spoonful' by the end of Vespers, continuing to be produced until 9am the following day. It proved to be miraculous when it healed two boys of blindness.[58] The success of this venture in popularizing the tomb is shown in an archiepiscopal injunction of 1314 to take down a recently erected altar at its head as it was now impeding the access of the faithful, pointing to an upturn in devotion at the site.[59]

The date of the first emanation of oil, close to St William's feast but respecting no other major event in the Beverley calendar, indicates a desire on the part of the canons of Beverley to link the two in the popular mind.

---

55 Owen, 'Historical Survey', pp. 131–32.
56 Thompson, *English Clergy*, pp. 90–97.
57 Wilson, *Life and After-Life*, pp. 113–16; Horrox, 'The Late Medieval Minster', p. 39.
58 'Beverley Cartulary', trans. in Wilson, *Life and After-Life*, pp. 219–29 (221).
59 *Memorials of Beverley*, ed. by Leach, II, pp. 303–04.

OILY SAINTS AND ECCLESIASTICAL POLITICS   157

Subsequent occurrences fitted with the pattern found at York. Later in the fourteenth century a woman of Nunkeeling, around eleven miles north-east of Beverley, came to the tomb on the day following Ascension Day to find that oil was flowing from the tomb.[60] As at York, Rogationtide was one of the most important points in Beverley's ritual calendar. St John's shrine was taken out and paraded around the town for three days, returning to the Minster for Mass on Ascension Day.[61] It was a fitting time to remind the laity of the functionality of both shrine and tomb.

The regional importance of Beverley Minster in the fourteenth century should not be understated. Barrie Dobson called it 'the wealthiest institution in the wealthiest part of Yorkshire'.[62] The Archbishop of York was lord of Beverley and had extensive rights of jurisdiction within the liberty.[63] Yet while he theoretically held the ninth seat in the Minster chapter, as at York the canons were largely successful in resisting his adoption of this right, and the Minster has been described as something of a 'spiritual republic' as well as 'peculiar and unique' in terms of the complexities of the jurisdictional relationship between archbishop and chapter.[64] While for the most part relations were friendly, there were nonetheless long-standing underlying tensions over the extent of the archbishop's authority.[65] This is shown most clearly in the 'clerical strike' of 1381–1388, when a dispute between Archbishop Neville over his capitular rights, which had started at York Minster before being applied to Beverley, resulted in the mass walkout of the canons and vicars-choral at the latter.[66] While this was an extraordinary sequence of events, it reveals the potential for conflict, and the need on the part of the canons for powerful symbols of their own rights and liberties.

The subordination of any living archbishop to the sainted St John was made clear by the canons in a miracle recorded in the later twelfth century, wherein the congregation of the Minster refused to listen to Archbishop Gerard's (1100–1108) attempts to interpret one of the saint's miracles.[67] As with the chapter at York, the canons of Beverley had operational control over St John and his cultic sites within their church. In another fourteenth-century account of oil flowing from St John's tomb on the feast of his translation (25 October), the clergy 'closed the openings of his tomb' from which it flowed in order to get further proof of its veracity which they did by 'vigorously rubbing it on their hands, then by the other usual customs'.[68] As at York, the centrality of the canons to the process of verifying the miracle emphasized their control

---

60 'Beverley Cartulary', trans. in Wilson, Life and After-Life, p. 224.
61 Horrox, 'Medieval Beverley', pp. 10–11.
62 Dobson, 'Beverley in Conflict', p. 149.
63 Horrox, 'Medieval Beverley', pp. 11–16.
64 Dobson, 'Beverley in Conflict', pp. 152–55; Sharp, 'The Minster Churches', pp. 74–76.
65 Sharp, 'The Minster Churches', pp. 192–93.
66 Dobson, 'Beverley in Conflict'.
67 Wilson, Life and After-Life, pp. 75, 181–82.
68 'Beverley Cartulary', trans. in Wilson, Life and After-Life, p. 222.

over the cult, particularly through their ability to regulate the flow of oil. Spigot-type 'openings' can be seen on images of the tomb of St William in the early fifteenth-century glass at York Minster, suggesting that at Beverley the tomb also had a superstructure of this type.[69] The otherwise obscure 'usual customs' may well have been the practice of making the oil into a lamp as seen at York four years previously, suggesting a local understanding of how to test whether the oil of saints was genuine.

The chapter of Beverley thus took the model of cultic management provided by York Minster and adapted it to their own ends. We should not necessarily see this as a rivalry, and as far as can be ascertained the chapters were generally on good terms. Furthermore, York Minster's Court of Audiences routinely linked itself to Beverley and Ripon, a similar distance to the west, through penitential pilgrimages imposed on clergy and laity of the region so the cultic settings of all three would have been familiar to many within the area.[70] Rather, we should see the replication of the oil phenomenon as an adoption of best practice provided by the preeminent Minster of the diocese, which would have been explicable in the fundamentals of its symbolism to local observers.[71]

For most of the fourteenth century oil now seeped from the tombs of St William and St John, thirty miles apart, and yet apparently from nowhere else in England or indeed the British Isles. Yet despite St William's cult having introduced this practice to the country, it was St John whose oil became nationally renowned. St John's banner had long been a feature of campaigns against the Scots, but Henry IV made particular use of his cult as a popular saint in a potentially rebellious region.[72] His son Prince Henry visited the shrine in 1408 after the execution of Richard Scrope, Archbishop of York, had prompted the rise of a troublesome cult based on his perceived political martyrdom.[73] According to one account the tomb exuded oil for sixty-one days following Henry IV's return from exile on the day after Pentecost in order to seize the throne, thus linking the cult to the king's legitimacy from the earliest possible opportunity.[74] The story was recorded much later in the fifteenth century and is highly suspect, as in 1399 Pentecost fell on 18 May and Henry was in France until mid-June, landing at Ravenspur around 30 June.[75] Yet St John's feast (7 May) fell four days before Rogationtide that year, unusually so thanks to the particularly early Easter, so would have been a perfect occasion for oil production. The compilation in which the story survives post-dates the Battle of Agincourt and contains a number of

---

69 French, *York Minster*, pp. 69, 80, pl. 12.

70 York Court of Audiences, York, York Minster Library, MS M2(1)f, fols 7ᵛ, 9ʳ, 15ᵛ, 16ᵛ, 19ʳ, 20ʳ, 30ʳ, 32ᵛ, 33ʳ, 34ᵛ, 35ᵛ, 37ᵛ, 40ʳ, 41ᵛ, 42ᵛ, 44ᵛ, 51ᵛ.

71 Sharp, 'The Minster Churches', pp. 172–75.

72 Sharpe, 'Banners of the Northern Saints', pp. 281–84.

73 Wilson, *Life and After-Life*, pp. 122–23; Piroyansky, *Martyrs in the Making*, pp. 49–73.

74 'An Account of the Proceedings against Archbishop Scrope', *Historians of the Church of York*, ed. by Raine, III, p. 288.

75 Given-Wilson, *Henry IV*, pp. 125–27, 542.

OILY SAINTS AND ECCLESIASTICAL POLITICS 159

dubious or fanciful tales, and the emanations of 1399 may have been elided in the popular imagination with the arrival of the future king a month and a half later and with subsequent Lancastrian devotion to St John.

Most famously, in 1415 the Battle of Agincourt coincided with the feast of his translation, when 'stillantibus guttis ad modum sudaris emanavit oleum' (oil flowed like drops of sweat) from his tomb, following which Henry Chichele, Archbishop of Canterbury, instituted both his feast and translation as nationally celebrated feast days.[76] The tomb was undergoing refurbishment, presumably to reflect this new national status, in 1419.[77] In 1421 Henry V visited the shrine of St John as part of a thanksgiving tour including St William of York and St John of Bridlington, and adopted him as a patron saint of the royal family, transforming him from a local figure in the shadow of St William and York Minster to 'a patron of England on a par with St George' and Thomas Becket for the remainder of the fifteenth century at least.[78] The continued political importance of Beverley and St John's oil to the North was shown again in 1443 during the course of a regional clash between John Kemp, Archbishop of York, and the Percy Earls of Northumberland. In the context of increasingly violent Percy resentment at the independent archiepiscopal jurisdiction within liberties such as Beverley, Archbishop Kemp pointedly granted a hundred days' indulgence to anyone visiting St John's tomb, connecting it to the cults of William of York and Wilfrid of Ripon as each important in their cities and throughout the diocese, then singling it out for the abundant supply of curative oil it produced in ever more quantities, and noting its royal patronage.[79]

Conclusion

So what does all this oil tell us? Firstly, that it appears as a northern English phenomenon centred on York. Subsequent occurrences at Knaresborough, Beverley, and Lincoln are directly derivative. While we may not think of

---

76 *Register of Henry Chichele*, ed. by Jacob, III, pp. 28–29. In the eighteenth century Drake credited 'Walsingham' as saying that blood also flowed from the tomb on that day, Drake, *Eboracum*, p. 109. While this has been repeated by many historians it does not appear anywhere in Thomas Walsingham's works. Walsingham does, however, refer to the emanation of blood in 1359 from the tomb of Thomas, earl of Lancaster, the 'political martyr' buried at Pontefract in the West Riding of Yorkshire, around twenty-five miles south of York. A further emanation of blood occurred in 1466, and both outpourings are discussed by Diana Piroyansky in the context of regional and national political events, Piroyansky, 'Bloody Miracles'. Although the author of this present essay came upon Thomas of Lancaster's bloody emanations too late for them to be incorporated into the main argument, they should clearly be seen as of a piece with, and as a response to, the ongoing oily emanations at nearby York, Beverley, and Lincoln.

77 Horrox, 'Later Medieval Minster', p. 40.

78 Kingsford, *English Historical Literature*, p. 290; Wilson, *Life and After-Life*, p. 94.

79 Register of Archbishop Kemp, York, Borthwick Institute of Historical Research, Register 19, fols 85ᵛ–86ʳ; Griffiths, *Reign of King Henry VI*, pp. 577–79.

Lincoln as being part of the 'northern hermeneutic', it was certainly within the sphere of influence of York Minster and this points to the fuzziness of the boundaries of the medieval 'North'. Previous analysis, particularly of St William, has assumed that the oil was a direct response to the cult of Becket and the primacy dispute with Canterbury. Yet by studying it on its own terms the chief exemplar can be shown as the archetypal 'good bishop' St Nicholas, and the production of oil looks to be driven far more by regional and capitular concerns than the question of national primacy. The oil was a symbol of episcopal authority, and its production was controlled by the Minster chapter. While the archbishops themselves could, and did, patronize the cult for its resonance for their own authority, it was ultimately and symbolically managed and interpreted by the canons.

While the oil had several devotional functions, including the promotion of the cult to the laity and the provision of healing and anointing fluid to devotees, its political and practical uses have been hitherto overlooked. These are thrown into sharp relief by the use of the oil in this northerly region of England. Beverley directly appropriated the use of oil from York seemingly as a 'best-practice' model to delineate devotional and liturgical sites within the Minster, to confirm the ongoing validity of an 'empty' tomb site after a translation, and as a potent weapon in a long-running (if rarely erupting) contest over diocesan rights and liberties. The borrowing was not primarily about competing with York's archiepiscopal cult, but about providing a symbol of the Minster's independence from the archbishop. It was Beverley's good fortune that *the* major national triumph of the fifteenth century coincided with one of these expressions of oil, firmly establishing St John's ascendance until the end of the Middle Ages and ensuring that his oil-producing powers would be co-opted for use on a larger political stage.

The regionality of the oil is striking, so why did it not spread further? We can only speculate, but as it was essentially an ongoing form of pious fraud it required, the thirteenth-century case of St Hugh of Lincoln aside, an active decision on the part of shrine managers to instigate the practice and to believe that doing so would complement and enhance the cultic narrative of their saint. At Lincoln in 1445 this was a decision taken in extreme circumstances by a beleaguered chapter in conflict with their own dean. This drew on the political and ecclesiastical symbolism of Pentecostal oil production at York and Beverley Minsters, where both were the custodians of sainted archiepiscopal bodies and both had complex independent relationships with their living archbishop in ways that were largely if not entirely restricted to the archdiocese. The ability for 'spiritual republics' such as those characteristic of the archdiocese of York to produce its own episcopal oil, hallowed by production from an ancient archbishop's body, was a useful tool in asserting its ancient rights.

Works Cited

Manuscripts and Archival Sources

York, Borthwick Institute of Historical Research, Register 19
——, York Minster Library, MS M2(1)f

Primary Sources

Breviarium ad usum insignis ecclesie Eboracensis, ed. by Stephen Lawley, SS, 71, 75, 2 vols (Durham: Andrews & Co., 1880–1883)

Gerald of Wales, *Giraldi Cambrensis Opera*, ed. by J. S. Brewer, James F. Dimock, and George F. Warner, Rerum Britannicarum Medii Aevi Scriptores, 21, 7 vols (London: Longman, 1861–1891)

The Historians of the Church of York and its Archbishops, ed. by James Raine, Rerum Britannicarum Medii Aevi Scriptores, 71, 3 vols (London: Longman, 1879–1894)

Memorials of Beverley Minster: The Chapter Act Books of the Collegiate Church of S. John of Beverley A.D. 1286–1347, ed. by Arthur F. Leach, SS, 98, 108, 2 vols (Durham: Andrews & Co., 1898–1903)

The Metrical Life of St Robert of Knaresborough: together with the other Middle English pieces in British Museum Ms. Egerton 3143, ed. by Joyce Bazire, EETS, o.s., 228 (London: Oxford University Press, 1953)

The Old English Life of St Nicholas with the Old English Life of St Giles, ed. by Elaine M. Traherne, Leeds Texts and Monographs, n.s., 15 (Leeds: Leeds Studies in English, 1997)

Paris, Matthew, *Matthaei Parisiensis, Monachi Sancti Albani Chronica maiora*, ed. by Henry Richards Luard, Rerum Britannicarum Medii Aevi Scriptores, 57, 7 vols (London: Longman, 1872–1883) (cited as *Chronica maiora*)

The Register of Henry Chichele, Archbishop of Canterbury 1414–1443, ed. by E. F. Jacob, Canterbury and York Society, 42, 45–47, 4 vols (Oxford: Oxford University Press, 1937–1947)

Secondary Works

Boertjes, Katja, 'Pilgrim Ampullae of York and the Healing Oil of the Shrine of St William', in *Beyond Pilgrim Souvenirs and Secular Badges: Essays in Honour of Brian Spencer*, ed. by Sarah Blick (Oxford: Oxbow, 2007), pp. 48–63

Bottomley, Frank, *St Robert of Knaresborough* (Ruddington: Adlard, 1993)

Brentano, Robert, *York Metropolitan Jurisdiction and Papal Judges Delegate, 1279–1296* (Berkeley: University of California Press, 1959)

Brooke, Christopher N. L., *Churches and Churchmen in Medieval Europe* (London: Hambledon, 1999)

Brown, Sarah, *'Our Magnificent Fabrick': York Minster: An Architectural History c. 1220–1500* (Swindon: English Heritage, 2003)

Burnett, Sarah, 'The Cult of St Nicholas in Medieval Italy' (unpublished doctoral thesis, University of Warwick, 2009)

Bynum, Caroline Walker, *Holy Feast, Holy Fast: The Religious Significance of Food to Medieval Women* (Berkeley: University of California Press, 1987)

Cole, R. E. G., 'Proceedings Relative to the Canonisation of Robert Grosseteste, Bishop of Lincoln', *Associated Architectural Societies' Reports*, 33 (1915), 1–34

Dobson, Barrie, 'The Later Middle Ages, 1215–1500', in *A History of York Minster*, ed. by G. E. Aylmer and Reginald Cant (Oxford: Clarendon Press, 1977), pp. 44–110

——, 'Beverley in Conflict: Archbishop Alexander Neville and the Minster Clergy, 1381–8', in *Medieval Art and Architecture in the East Riding of Yorkshire*, ed. by Christopher Wilson, British Archaeological Association Conference Transactions, 9 (Leeds: W. S. Maney, 1989), pp. 149–64

——, *Church and Society in the Medieval North of England* (London: Hambledon, 1996)

Drake, Francis, *Eboracum, or, The History and Antiquities of the City of York* (Wakefield: EP Publishing, 1978)

Easterling, Joshua, 'A Norbert for England: Holy Trinity and the Invention of Robert of Knaresborough', *Journal of Medieval Monastic Studies*, 2 (2013), 75–107

Edwards, Kathleen, *The English Secular Cathedrals in the Middle Ages: A Constitutional Study with Special Reference to the Fourteenth Century*, 2nd edn (Manchester: Manchester University Press, 1967)

Farmer, David H., 'The Cult and Canonization of St Hugh', in *Saint Hugh of Lincoln*, ed. by Henry Mayr-Harting (Oxford: Oxford University Press, 1987), pp. 75–87

French, Thomas, *York Minster: The Saint William Window*, CVMA: Great Britain, Summary Catalogue, 5 (Oxford: Oxford University Press, 1999)

Georges, Patrice, 'Mourir c'est pourrir un peu … Intentions et techniques contre la corruption des cadavres à la fin du Moyen Age', *Micrologus*, 7 (1999), 359–82

Gilchrist, Roberta, and Barney Sloane, *Requiem: The Medieval Monastic Cemetery* (London: Museum of London Archaeology Service, 2005)

Given-Wilson, Chris, *Henry IV* (New Haven: Yale University Press, 2016)

Golding, Brian, 'The Hermit and the Hunter', in *The Cloister and the World: Essays on Medieval History in Honour of Barbara Harvey*, ed. by John Blair and Brian Golding (Oxford: Clarendon Press, 1996), pp. 95–117

Griffiths, Ralph A., *The Reign of King Henry VI: The Exercise of Royal Authority, 1422–1461* (Berkeley: University of California Press, 1981)

Haines, Roy Martin, *Ecclesia Anglicana: Studies in the English Church of the Later Middle Ages* (Toronto: University of Toronto Press, 1989)

Horrox, Rosemary, 'Medieval Beverley', in *A History of the County of York: East Riding Volume VI: The Borough and Liberties of Beverley*, ed. by Keith John Allison, The Victoria History of the Counties of England (Oxford: Oxford University Press and the University of London, 1989), pp. 2–62

——, 'The Later Medieval Minster', in *Beverley Minster: An Illustrated History*, ed. by Rosemary Horrox (Beverley: Friends of Beverley Minster, 2000), pp. 37–49

Jenkins, John, 'Replication or Rivalry? The "Becketization" of Pilgrimage in English Cathedrals', *Religion*, 49.1 (2019), 24–47

Jones, Charles W., 'The Norman Cult of Saints Catherine and Nicholas', in *Hommages à André Boutemy*, ed. by Guy Cambier (Brussels: Latomus, 1976), pp. 216–30

——, *Saint Nicholas of Myra, Bari, and Manhattan: The Biography of a Legend* (Chicago: University of Chicago Press, 1978)

Kingsford, Charles Lethbridge, *English Historical Literature in the Fifteenth Century* (Oxford: Clarendon Press, 1913)

Koopmans, Rachel, '"Water Mixed with the Blood of Thomas": Contact Relic Manufacture Pictured in Canterbury Cathedral's Stained Glass', *Journal of Medieval History*, 42.5 (2016), 535–58

Mullins, Sylvia Elizabeth, 'Myroblytes: Miraculous Oil in Medieval Europe' (unpublished doctoral dissertation, Georgetown University, 2016)

Norton, Christopher, *St William of York* (Woodbridge: York Medieval, 2006)

Owen, Dorothy, 'Historical Survey, 1091–1450', in *A History of Lincoln Minster*, ed. by Dorothy Owen (Cambridge: Cambridge University Press, 1994), pp. 112–63

Phillips, Derek, and R. J. C. Atkinson, *The Cathedral of Archbishop Thomas of Bayeux: Excavations at York Minster II* (London: HMSO, 1985)

Piroyansky, Diana, 'Bloody Miracles of a Political Martyr: The Case of Thomas Earl of Lancaster', *Studies in Church History*, 41 (2005), 228–38

——, *Martyrs in the Making: Political Martyrdom in Late Medieval England* (Basingstoke: Palgrave Macmillan, 2008)

Rees Jones, Sarah, *York: The Making of a City 1068–1350* (Oxford: Oxford University Press, 2013)

Rentz, Ellen K., 'Castles for St William: The Late Medieval Commemoration of York's Local Saint', *Viator*, 43.2 (2012), 111–30

Sharp, Ian Stuart, 'The Minster Churches of Beverley, Ripon, and Southwell, 1066–*c*. 1300' (unpublished doctoral thesis, University of Hull, 2009)

Sharpe, Richard, 'Banners of the Northern Saints', in *Saints of North-East England, 600–1500*, ed. by Margaret Coombe, Anne Mouron, and Christiania Whitehead (Turnhout: Brepols, 2017), pp. 245–304

Thompson, A. Hamilton, *The English Clergy and their Organization in the Later Middle Ages* (Oxford: Clarendon Press, 1947)

Vauchez, André, *Sainthood in the Later Middle Ages* (Cambridge: Cambridge University Press, 1997)

Wilson, Susan E., *The Life and After-Life of St John of Beverley: The Evolution of the Cult of an Anglo-Saxon Saint* (Aldershot: Ashgate, 2006)

JULIAN LUXFORD

Art and Northern Sanctity in Late Medieval England

True to the project from which it arises, this essay represents an opportunity to ponder the manifestation of English regional identity through culture. For an art historian, the largest advantage of this is the access it promises to the problem of *Kunstlandschaft*, something that has provoked little interest with respect to England, probably because, unlike France, Germany or Italy, the geography of the country after the Norman Conquest was and is not usually considered in terms of culturally distinctive regions (or provinces).[1] Rather, the tendency is to think in terms of counties, or dioceses, or simply an urban/rural binary. The late medieval discourse on regions, as opposed to anything more local, is vague except in redescriptions of Roman and Anglo-Saxon England like those offered in Ranulf Higden's *Polychronicon*.[2] There is, however, something for art historians to explore. East Anglia as the domain of object-classes that are almost exclusive to it (e.g. architectonic and iconographic flint flushwork, angel roofs, fonts carved with the seven sacraments) suggests this, as do the marches of Scotland and Wales, where formal and typological interpenetration produced distinctive-looking art from the later fourteenth century onwards. Architecture, which, unlike portable objects, could not usually be shipped from London or some other centre, was particularly susceptible to regional variation. It thus seems reasonable to ask whether there was anything distinctive about northern English art in the period. A positive finding would enrich medieval art history conceptually, while the process of investigation alone would advertise a domain largely occluded in existing literature by what survives in southern England. As things

---

1 Compare Le Patourel, 'Northern History', pp. 5–8. For *Kunstlandschaft* see e.g. Engel, 'Kunstlandschaft und Kunstgeschichte'. The term has no suitable English equivalent: 'geography of art' (*Kunstgeographie*) comes close but has nationalistic connotations that *Kunstlandschaft* sidesteps. See DaCosta Kaufmann, *Towards a Geography of Art*, pp. 53–54, 87–88.

2 *Polychronicon Ranulphi Higden*, ed. by Babington and Lumby, II, pp. 30–35, 96–109.

Julian Luxford (jml5@st-andrews.ac.uk) is Professor of Medieval Art History at the University of St Andrews.

Late Medieval Devotion to Saints from the North of England: New Directions, ed. by Christiania Whitehead, Hazel J. Hunter Blair, and Denis Renevey, MCS 48 (Turnhout: Brepols, 2022), pp. 165–195
BREPOLS ❧ PUBLISHERS   10.1484/M.MCS-EB.5.124349

stand, excepting the enclaves of Durham and York, a place for northern art in the art of late medieval England is barely recognized.[3]

These are the larger stakes. The business of this essay is to make some advance on them, mainly by pursuing the underpinning problem of regional definition and the relationship of image-focused devotion to this. At the end, brief attention will be paid to the representation of northern saints in southern England, because this seems germane to any concept of the North informed by the perception and iconography of sanctity. Conversely, relatively little will be said about images of Cuthbert and other northern saints in the cathedral priory at Durham, as this subject tends to give an unbalanced impression of how sanctity was generally represented in northern English art. This Durham imagery is in any case adequately addressed by available scholarship.[4]

Geography and the North

Definitions can be vexing to medievalists, in part because they imply precision about things for which evidence is fragmentary and often ambiguous. Formulating them can thus seem like an exercise in bad faith. Yet, of course, vagueness about one's premises tends to result in lack of control over a subject. Fortunately, one can often assume a working definition of a given phenomenon (e.g. Canterbury, sheriff, monastery, charter) by relying on received wisdom. The idea of a specifically 'northern' sanctity depends on such an assumption. It is nevertheless worth asking how an assumed definition which relies on geography works. A good way of doing this is to examine the nature of the distinctions it implies. How does one distinguish the north of England from the rest of the country? Various attempts have been made at this question, mostly by historians of the North East: this alone suggests it is worth asking. But the fact that all of them leave the matter open will hopefully help to manage the reader's expectations of what follows.

The most obvious and useful starting point is geography, or rather, since 'north' is a relative term, perceptions of geography. Here, already, a difficulty arises. While one's reflex is to identify medieval texts that state or imply ideas about the north of England (the classic one being Bede's *Historia ecclesiastica*), it is naturally impossible to see such ideas undistorted by the modern and

---

3 The index of the only recent, broad survey of late medieval English art, *Gothic: Art for England*, ed. by Marks and Williamson, is indicative here. Along with very large numbers of entries for London and Westminster there are thirty-seven for Canterbury, twenty-seven for York, twenty for Bury St Edmunds, seventeen for Bristol, fourteen for Norwich, five for Durham and three for Chester. Effectively, the north is represented by York and its hinterland.

4 Apart from publications, three excellent theses have recently been completed: Turner, 'Image and Devotion'; Robson, 'A Cathedral Encountered'; Harrison, 'Illuminating Narrative'.

contemporary accretions they have collected. This problem, which has been discussed in detail by David Lowenthal, cannot be allowed to detain the current essay: the best one can do is take it as an encouragement to vigilance about the contaminating effects of retrospection on what has been called 'conceptual hygiene'.[5] However, there remains a need to acknowledge the peculiarity and discrepancies in what medieval evidence there is. Peculiarity here refers to both the specificity of use (as in 'Council of the North', 'Norroy', etc.) and the fact that a concept of northern Englishness was presumably uncommon in the Middle Ages (although some literate people certainly had one). It seems safe to think that, wherever they lived, most late-medieval people were geographically near-sighted and predominantly local in outlook. Even if this is wrong, the relationship of whatever mental geography they had to modern, map-based concepts is obscure.[6] It is telling that ideas about routes, distance, and thus relative location differed greatly among the experienced travellers called in 1361 to testify about the amount of time needed to get from Durham to York.[7]

Faced with such imponderables, one may choose to assume a historical notion of insular geography formally similar to what is shown on the Gough Map (probably made some time between 1375 and 1425), supplemented, perhaps, by the description of England in the *Polychronicon*.[8] However, this inevitably provokes the question 'north in relation to what?' The undertones here are vaguely imperialistic in ways much explored by scholars of the relationship between a Westminster-centred England and the 'peripheral' countries of Ireland, Scotland, and Wales.[9] Indeed, while a hasty answer might be, 'the other parts of England', a more reflective one would specify the south-east, particularly the triangle defined by London and the university towns. North makes less sense in relation to, say, Leicestershire, which is in fact the geographical centre of England. Northern Leicestershire borders on the Trent, the river that defined the southern limit of the 'northern' ecclesiastical province of York. The country between the Trent and the Scottish border was also, from Edward I's reign, a separate heraldic province, 'ruled' by the Norroy (literally 'north men') king of arms.[10] And from the reign of Edward IV it was the domain of the Council

---

5   Lowenthal, *The Past is a Foreign Country Revisited.* 'Conceptual hygiene' is used by the editors of a recent book concerned with similar issues of definition to those raised here: see Crooks, Green, and Ormrod, 'Empire and the English Identity', p. 23.

6   Compare Bartlett, 'Heartland and Border', p. 31.

7   Harvey, 'Travel from Durham'. There were forty-four deponents.

8   See *Polychronicon Ranulphi Higden*, ed. by Babington and Lumby, II, pp. 30–142. The Gough map (Oxford, Bodl. Lib., MS Gough Gen. Top. 16), whose dating is contested, shows Britain and peripheral islands. A digital reproduction and commentary are available at <http://www.goughmap.org/> [accessed 01 November 2019].

9   See, for example, the essays and literature cited in Crooks, Green, and Ormrod ed., *Plantagenet Empire.*

10 'Of the Norreis' (north-men) rather than, as one might think, 'king of the north' (i.e. north-roy): see Godfrey and Wagner, 'Norroy King of Arms'.

'in the North Parties', whose president replaced royal lieutenants of other designations who had administered territories referred to as *ultra Trentam* by Westminster bureaucrats since the thirteenth century.[11] Thus, to spell it out, the heart of England was almost in the jurisdictional north, which effectively means the conceptual north as viewed from London or Oxford. An alternative would be to identify the North specifically with the Anglo-Saxon kingdom of Northumbria, whose name embodies northernness in relation not to London but to the River Humber (which from a modern point of view looks a more sensible terminus than the Trent). Some encouragement to do this arises from the enduring reputation of Bede as a historian in later medieval England, and also the tendency — largely dependent on Bede's testimony — of religious communities to identify themselves with pre-Conquest origins through material objects and texts.[12] But this would hardly suit the period from the mid-fourteenth century to the Reformation, not least because of the need to account for a large part of southern Scotland and its culture. The late medievalist wants to draw a line at or close to the River Tweed. Obviously, Durham and York represented points south for anyone travelling overland to London from the northern limits of the historical Northumbria.

According to Barrie Dobson, the archdiocese of York 'was notoriously by no means coterminous with what we now regard as the North'.[13] Others have been more sanguine about this.[14] From any angle other than an excessively rigid (and anachronistic) one based on county lines, the Midlands are a complicating factor, particularly Midland cults of Northumbrian saints (e.g. Alchmund, Chad) and the 'feel' of much of Derbyshire, Nottinghamshire, and (north) Lincolnshire. If judgements about regional definition are to be made instinctively, as one is inclined to do after worrying the problem for long enough, then there are reasonable grounds for identifying these parts of England as northern on the basis of topography, architectural style, and population density. They seem as peripheral to a centre located in and around London as much of Yorkshire does. At the same time, there was a marked historical disparity between different parts of England that are indisputably northern. The Pennines were more economically and thus culturally influential than any river.[15] On the whole, the land to the east was better for arable farming, better served by navigable rivers, and closer to southern England and continental Europe. It is no coincidence that the North East had old, tradition-rich religious houses while the North West did not. Carlisle was England's poorest diocese,

---

11 Reid, *King's Council*, pp. 485–90, for the dates given here; *First Report of the Deputy Keeper*, pp. 127, 139, 142; Pollard, *North-Eastern England*, pp. 9–10. For the medievalist, 'ultra Trentam' is a reasonable alternative to 'northern England'.

12 Gransden, 'Bede's Reputation', especially pp. 419–25.

13 Dobson, 'Northern Province', p. 53.

14 See, for example, Newton, 'Borders and Bishopric', p. 61.

15 See Christiania Whitehead's essay on Cumbria and the importance of the east–west divide, in this volume.

Durham among its richest: the very creation of the diocese of Carlisle in 1133 was effectively an acknowledgement of the difference between the two sides of the North. The point of rehearsing these familiar facts is to underline their relationship to sanctity, art, and the architecture used to frame and rationalize both. The North West is England's poorest region in terms of both written evidence for medieval art and surviving objects. Moreover, it never appears to have been a coherent domain of indigenous sanctity, although many saintly people — hermits rather than martyrs or evangelists — probably lived and died in it unrecorded.[16] Little evidence arises from the country between the shrine of St Werburgh at Chester and that of St Ninian at Whithorn. There was the cult of the Irish émigré-saint Bega at St Bees in Cumbria, which centred on a miracle-working arm-ring; but overall, more documentary evidence seems to exist for the relics and furniture of a single chapel in a Cumbrian parish church, at Brigham, than for most monasteries in the region.[17]

Indigenous Northern Sanctity

There is an alternative to this complicated picture which is better aligned with the aims of the current volume, although it will be subjected to some pressure in this essay. This is simply that northern England can be conceptualized with reference to the indigenous character of its saints. This would of course be a circular (not to say eccentric) way of defining the North for general purposes (i.e. the north is so because its saints were northern), but that hardly matters if one relaxes any boundary-angst and confines the focus to the late medieval reception of sanctity and the cultural production arising from this. Implicit reasoning of this kind commonly underlies the parameters assumed for domains of sanctity elsewhere. However, the vision of northernness arising from indigenous sanctity is scarcely more coherent than that which emerges from geography. The problem here is not dubious parameters but lack of connective tissue. For, in effect, the native cults adhered to a limited number of monastic and collegiate churches, to which may be added — if one cares for the notion — a few 'sacred landscapes' such as the Farne Islands and the corridor along the River Wear leading from Chester-le-Street to Durham.[18] The bulk of northern English churches — those of parochial and mendicant status, plus most of the secular collegiate and non-Benedictine monastic ones — did not have an observable or necessary stake in them. While there were church and altar dedications to Cuthbert and Oswald, and (no doubt)

---

16 Individuals like Herbert, the solitary of Derwentwater, recorded only because he befriended Cuthbert: Bede, *Ecclesiastical History*, ed. by Colgrave and Mynors, p. 440.

17 Fletcher, 'Brigham Church', pp. 164–65, 173–77. None of the relics or images was of a northern English saint. On Bega, Begu and the distinction between them see Morgan ed., *English Monastic Litanies*, III, p. 79.

18 For a case-study of one of these see Wells, '"… he went round the holy places".

numerous images also, this should not be taken uncritically as evidence of late medieval enthusiasm for these saints. Indeed, the indigenous quality of northern sanctity was old-fashioned as well as elite (this was part of its appeal to monks). The later Middle Ages witnessed a great, transnational growth of saint-devotion and cults, yet, like Edward the Confessor, Dunstan, or Swithun in the south, the old saints of the North had very little stake in this. Even Cuthbert, whose devotional relevance the Durham monks tried to refresh in the twelfth and thirteenth centuries through miracle stories, and in the fourteenth with a new shrine, had limited appeal outside the see of Durham in the period addressed here.[19] It is perhaps telling that Margery Kempe, so avid a seeker after saints, did not extend her pilgrimages to St John at Bridlington and St William at York to include St Cuthbert at Durham.[20] Thus, in short, a northernness rooted in native sanctity yields a patchy as well as variegated picture.

This is not to downplay unduly the sacred credentials of the so-called patrimony of St Cuthbert, even if these credentials were routinely pressed to serve realpolitik in the period.[21] (*Haliwerfolc*, as its denizens were known collectively, is a political designation rooted in religion but not implying personal piety.) Apart from north-east Kent, and possibly Cornwall, this was the most coherent domain of indigenous sanctity in medieval England, although, as at Canterbury, it was largely concentrated in one place in the late Middle Ages. In fact, the coherence was largely due to the historical efforts of the Durham community to define their Anglo-Saxon endowment according to sacred and moral criteria, which they did, *inter alia*, by translating relics from churches within the patrimony to Durham Cathedral. The main evidence for this is found in Symeon of Durham's *Libellus de exordio*, and also in the Durham relic lists, which date from the twelfth and thirteenth centuries (a third list is dated 1383).[22] Specifically, relics were obtained from Coldingham, Hexham, Lindisfarne, Melrose, Tynemouth, and elsewhere. The saints in question included the Lindisfarne bishops Aidan, Eadfrith, and Æthelwold; the Hexham bishops Alchmund and Frithbert; Northumbrian kings Ceolwulf, Edwin, Oswald, and Oswin; abbot Boisil of Melrose plus the abbesses Æbbe of Coldingham and Ælfflæd of Whitby (in Yorkshire); the Venerable Bede and the hermit Bilfrith, recorded as illuminator of the Lindisfarne Gospels. The Gospels themselves were also kept at Durham. To this collection of raw and confected materials the monks later added relics

---

19 Crumplin, 'Modernizing St Cuthbert'; Hope, 'On the Early Working', p. 225.

20 Noted by Pollard, *North-Eastern England*, p. 24. Compare *Book of Margery Kempe*, ed. by Windeatt, pp. 87–90 (to Bridlington in 1413), and 241–57 (to York and Bridlington in 1417).

21 This is perhaps an effect of how they have been studied. See the illuminating discussion in Liddy, *Bishopric of Durham*, particularly pp. 1–24, 175–235; also Holford, 'Durham'; Pollard, *North-Eastern England*, pp. 9–30 and throughout.

22 Symeon, *Libellus*, ed. and trans. by Rollason, pp. 161–67; Thomas, 'Cult of Saints' Relics', pp. 73–88, 342–43.

of St Margaret of Scotland, the archbishops of York William and Wilfrid (the latter, like Boisil, had a Lindisfarne pedigree), the hermit Godric of Finchale and, eventually, Thomas of Lancaster and John of Bridlington.[23] These later acquisitions may be thought to indicate a more diffuse interest in northern sanctity, although more likely they were collected for their sanctity alone, as the relics of many non-northern saints were. With this in mind, it is worth noting that Durham's monks do not seem to have aimed at regional completeness in their relic collecting. None of their three relic lists includes Benedict Biscop or Ceolfrith, abbots of Monkwearmouth-Jarrow, nor for that matter John of Beverley, although relics of all three were claimed by Glastonbury in Somerset from at least the twelfth century, and by other southern monasteries too.[24]

After Durham, the part of northern England most readily associated with native sanctity is the southern and central part of Yorkshire that includes the Vale of York and what is now the East Riding. One should not draw too rigid a distinction here, of course, if only because important Northumbrian saints were remembered for their careers in this more southerly domain. In 1541, for instance, the antiquary John Leland saw inscriptions on the new wall ('in novo muro') of the Lady Chapel at Ripon minster declaring that saints Cuthbert and Eata, as well as Wilfrid (who was culted at Ripon), had once been monks of the place.[25] However, the saints of the area around York were often of high or later medieval date, and only saintly in the extended sense for which public enthusiasm was sufficient. Along with the early, episcopal saints John of Beverley, William of York, and Wilfrid, one counts Aelred of Rievaulx (d. 1167), Robert of Newminster (d. 1159) and Robert of Knaresborough (d. 1218), Richard Rolle (d. 1349) and Richard Scrope (executed 1405), Thomas of Lancaster (executed 1322), John of Bridlington (d. 1379), and others. Thus, unlike the country north of the River Tees, Yorkshire continued to produce popular, documented saints into the late Middle Ages, some of whom emerged from Cistercian and Augustinian settings.[26] This suggests a more innovative, if not necessarily more vital, devotional climate, where established cults alone did not satisfy either metaphysical cravings or the embodied, therapeutic needs

---

23 This is to mention only those saints cited in the relic lists (Symeon mentions others). See Thomas, 'Cult of Saints' Relics', pp. 73–88, 358 (Aidan), 359 (Alchmund), 369 (Bede), 372 (Bilfrith), 373 (Boisil), 378 (Ceolwulf), 384 (Cuthbert), 389 (Æbbe), 390 (Eadfrith), 392 (Edwin), 393 (Ælfflæd), 396 (Æthelwold), 402 (Frithbert), 407 (Godric), 417 (John of Bridlington), 428 (Margaret of Scotland), 442 (Oswald), 443 (Oswine), 466 (Thomas of Lancaster), and 474 (Wilfrid; William of York).

24 Thomas, 'Cult of Saints' Relics', pp. 370 (Benedict Biscop), 378 (Ceolfrith), 417 (John of Beverley).

25 Leland, *Itinerary*, ed. by Smith, v, p. 143. (My thanks to James Carley for the date of Leland's visit to Ripon).

26 See, broadly and readably, Hughes, *Pastors and Visionaries*, pp. 298–346; also, Cynthia Turner Camp's essay in this volume.

that are mocked in the *Compendium compertorum*.[27] The difference between
the regions may be partially a matter of perception rather than anything
sounder: inequalities of demographic, quantity of religious houses and
surviving documentation have to be taken into account. But the impression
of a difference nevertheless persists, and with it the hint of a subtler variance
in regional culture within the north of England than that starkly determined
by the Pennines. The impression is coloured by the distinctive iconographies
and pilgrimage apparatus devoted to the Yorkshire saints (e.g. the cave of
Robert of Knaresborough and scenes of his life in stained glass supposed to
come from Dale Abbey in Derbyshire; the artistic and architectural evidence
for the cult of Richard Scrope at York Minster), although, as presumably with
regional hagiography, what remains of this material in any region is relatively
slight and statistically unreliable.[28]

Clearly, there is no requirement to conjure with regional identity in relation
to northern English sanctity. A specific site of activity like Durham or York
can be singled out, or else some category of saint identified according to a
given characteristic like royalty or inclusion by Bede.[29] In this case, the terms
of reference may be broad: for example, one might explore the contribution
of the Northumbrian kings, especially Oswald and his cousin Oswine, to the
devotional and political phenomenon of sacred kingship in late medieval
England, which has left artistic as well as textual traces.[30] Manifest possibilities
here include female sanctity, solitaries, or the cadre of never-canonized
individuals of holy reputation for whom, as far as anyone knows, biographies
were never written. Tombs rather than sumptuous shrines seem to have been
the normal focus of their cults. As suggested above, the popular interest in
these figures is reasonably seen as an integral rather than collateral aspect of
late medieval sanctity. They emerge from the Northumbrian age — Herebald,
supposed abbot of Tynemouth (d. 745), whose grave or tomb was in the
post-Conquest priory, is an example — but are mostly known through late
medieval documents.[31] As elsewhere in England, founder-status was often a
factor in their reputations. William, first abbot of Rievaulx (d. 1145), is one such
individual for whom part of a later monument survives.[32] A secular founder's
tomb that served local devotion was at the Augustinian priory of the Holy Cross
at Haltemprice on the outskirts of Hull. Here, the *Compendium compertorum*
reports a pilgrimage: 'Huc fit peregrinatio ad Thomam Wake pro febri' (to

---

27 That is, the dossier on monastic obedience to the Crown compiled in 1536 on behalf of
Henry VIII (now Kew, TNA, SP 1/102, fols 91^r–114^r). An English translation of most of it is
printed in *Letters and Papers*, ed. by Gairdner, pp. xl–xlii, 137–44 (no. 364).

28 On Robert's cave see Slater, 'Recreating the Judean Hills?'; some of the glass survives in
the north aisle at Morley parish church (also Derbyshire). For Scrope's cult and its material
apparatus see Norton, 'Richard Scrope'; Brown, 'Archbishop Richard Scrope's Lost Window'.

29 For Bede as a criterion see, for example, Foot, 'Bede's Northern Saints'.

30 For such traces see e.g. Luxford, 'Sacred Kingship'.

31 For Herebald see Luxford, 'Manuscripts, History', pp. 195, 210 n. 8.

32 Illustrated and discussed in Carter, *Art and Architecture*, pp. 117–18.

FIGURE 7.1. The common seal of Haltemprice Priory (made 1322), reverse side. © The Trustees of the British Museum.

Thomas Wake for [relief from] fever).[33] As the term 'pilgrimage' is sparingly used in this document, significant activity seems to be indicated. The tomb is mentioned together with relics of the True Cross and an arm of St George (the chivalric relic *par excellence*), which Wake, a knight who served his king against the Scots and died in 1349, may have given to the canons as part of their primary endowment, and which were probably linked to his spiritual reputation.[34] The example is useful for indicating how local history, when intelligently curated, could serve as a devotional resource for both laypeople and a convent with perpetual obligations to its founder's reputation. In this case, the convent had no pretensions to either antiquity or wider celebrity, but was not debarred by this from the economy of pilgrimage. Material objects including but not limited to tombs and relics surely played their part in the interest and effectiveness of figures like Abbot William and Thomas Wake. The common seal of Haltemprice, made in 1322, presents a sort of visual epitome of the priory's foundation, including Wake and his wife kneeling in elevated positions on either side of a church where prior, canons, angels and saints worship the crucified Christ (Fig. 7.1).[35] Such imagery is a possible source of posthumous reputation.

---

33 A parallel case is that of Joan of Acre (d. 1307), a daughter of Edward I and Eleanor of Castile, whose tomb at the church of the Austin friars at Clare (Suffolk) was visited by local people for relief from fever: *Cartulary of the Augustinian Friars*, ed. by Harper-Bill, p. 90 (no. 158).

34 Wake was respectfully noticed by the Lanercost chronicler: *Chronicon de Lanercost*, ed. by Stevenson, pp. 266, 291. Haltemprice's canons also had 'the girdle of St Mary which is thought to be helpful in childbirth': *Letters and Papers*, ed. by Gairdner, p. 139.

35 Cherry, 'Seal of Haltemprice'.

International Northern Sanctity

Northern sanctity can also be usefully approached by acknowledging the share of international cults within it. If this suggestion appears to conflate things better kept apart, then it must be remembered that the sanctity of any given man or woman is impossible to separate out from those of Christ, the Virgin Mary, and other formative saints, for distinctive reasons as well as the obvious generic ones. It need hardly be said that the psychology and behaviour of each saint who lived and died in northern England — except for laymen like Thomas of Lancaster and Thomas Wake — were constantly infused by the elemental sanctity of his or her religion. Reginald of Durham's account of St Godric of Finchale gives a vivid sense of this in its exemplification of devotion by visionary experience (sometimes mediated by sculpture and painting) that arose from prayer and self-mortification.[36] The colours given to international cults by local practice are suggested, again, in the *Compendium compertorum*, whose compilers paid special attention to 'superstitious' objects in active use at the time of visitation. Most of what is recorded under this heading does not relate to indigenous saints. The Benedictine nuns of Wallingwells (Nottinghamshire) venerated an image of the Virgin Mary discovered when their nunnery was founded, the Cistercian monks of Roche (Yorkshire) a crucifix which had similarly been found on site, and the secular brethren of St Leonards hospital in York a special image of St Leonard. Belt-relics associated with the Virgin and other saints were kept at monasteries as large as Fountains (Cistercian) and Selby (Benedictine) in Yorkshire, and as small as Calder (Cistercian) and Wetheral (Benedictine) in Cumbria, where they were used by local women in childbirth. Benedictine Tynemouth had a finger of St Bartholomew and a belt of St Margaret of Antioch (the patron saint of women in labour), and the Augustinian canons of Lanercost (Cumbria) a belt of Mary Magdalene. The canons of Newburgh (Yorkshire), who also followed the rule of St Augustine, had an arm of another doctor of the Church, St Jerome (a sort of ecclesiastical equivalent to Haltemprice's arm of St George). Pieces of the True Cross were more widely distributed than any other sort of relic. Devotion to later saints is noticed as well: an image of St Bridget of Kildare at the Benedictine nunnery of Arden (Yorkshire) was supplicated for lost and sick cows, St 'Sytha' — either Sitha (Zita) of Lucca or the Mercian princess Osyth — was worshipped in nunneries of the same order at Wykeham (Yorkshire) and York, the Yorkshire Cistercian houses of Kirkstall, Meaux and Sinningthwaite had relics of St Bernard of Clairvaux (at Meaux it was a belt, 'lent to pregnant women'), and there were relics of Thomas Becket at Premonstratensian Hulne (Northumberland), Augustinian Carlisle (the sword that killed him), and in the Benedictine nunnery at Chester.[37] It is

---

36 Reginald, *Libellus de vita et miraculis S. Godrici, heremitae de Finchale*, ed. by Stevenson, pp. 99–101, 154–55, 157–59 (visions involving art) (cited hereafter as *Vita Godrici*).

37 See *Letters and Papers*, ed. by Gairdner, pp. 138–42.

FIGURE 7.2. Ceiling bosses of the nails and five wounds of Christ and the badge (or 'arms') of the Virgin Mary, now in the priory dining room at Durham. Photo by Janet Gunning. © Chapter of Durham Cathedral.

worth noting that devotion to relics and images of internationally popular saints may have been particularly active in the north of England. While superstitious objects and practices were reported by Henry VIII's commissioners at some twelve per cent of religious houses in the diocese of Norwich, about half of the northern houses yielded evidence of them.[38] There is, incidentally, no obvious reason to doubt the commissioners' testimony in this regard, although the tone in which it is reported is thoroughly partisan and unsympathetic.

In general, it seems safe to think that the devotional interests of religious and lay people alike in Durham, York or anywhere else in the North, would have been familiar throughout much of late medieval Europe. It seems revealing that the sculpted wooden bosses of the ceiling of what is now the Deanery dining room (originally, perhaps, from the prior's chapel) at Durham include no imagery associated with Cuthbert or any other indigenous saint but do incorporate the profusely bleeding wounds of Christ and the badge of the Virgin Mary (a winged heart impaled by a sword) (Fig. 7.2).[39]

Altogether, this late fifteenth-century ceiling has about one hundred bosses, so there was ample opportunity for reference to local saints. Evidently, however,

---

38 This is noted by Shaw, '*Compendium compertorum*', pp. 361, 446–51.
39 These bosses have not been published but are the subject of a report compiled by Norman Emery, the cathedral archaeologist. They include the arms of the priory (*a cross flory between 4 lions rampant*), which, as noted below, could also be read as those of Cuthbert, Oswald or (lacking tinctures) both.

176   JULIAN LUXFORD

such reference was thought unnecessary where there was no need to advertise cults: it thus appears that not even Cuthbert was iconographically compulsory at Durham in the way that Christ and the Virgin Mary were. Around the same time, the monks seem to have removed an image of Cuthbert in favour of another representing the fashionable saint Henry VI in the central west window of the Galilee Chapel.[40] At the heart of the cathedral, Cuthbertine relics and images were everywhere juxtaposed and valorized by those of Christ, the Virgin and other saints. The *Rites of Durham* has copious evidence for the imagery. The high altar reredos had an alabaster Virgin and Child at the centre, flanked by subordinate statues of Cuthbert and Oswald in narrower niches.[41] Among the special cult objects was the diminutive Black Rood of Scotland, a relic-cross with a religious and political history that made it a trophy of national importance.[42] This is one of three cult objects at Durham mentioned in the *Compendium compertorum*, which records its value to women in labour, something it shared with many relics kept in rural churches.[43] Another miracle-working rood of Scottish provenance, this one monumental in size, was displayed in the south choir aisle: it was plated in tarnished silver and had 'marueilous sumptuous furniture for festiuall days belonging to it'.[44] There was also a remarkable sculpture of the Virgin and Child, called Our Lady of Bolton, which opened up like a triptych below the breast to reveal an image of the Holy Trinity. It stood on an altar in the south transept, near which was a stained glass window displaying a two-dimensional version of the same image (presumably showing it in its open state). To an art historian, at least, this is tantalizing and extraordinary. The sculpture is the only recorded English example of a so-called 'shrine Madonna', an image-type found in continental art from the thirteenth century until the end of the Middle Ages.[45] As such it

---

40 See, convincingly, Lynda Rollason, 'Northern Saints', pp. 334–35. What they did with the glass is unknown, but, in any case, images of Cuthbert and Oswald were not sacrosanct. They were sometimes destroyed at Durham as a legal precaution when seals of deceased bishops were broken. In one recorded case the metal was recast as a chalice: see Hope, 'Seals of English Bishops', pp. 279–80 (note); compare Birch, *Catalogue of Seals*, I, pp. 396–99, 401, 403 (nos 2443, 2447, 2451, 2459, 2464).

41 *Rites of Durham*, ed. by Fowler, p. 7.

42 Grigg, 'Black Rood of Scotland'; also *Rites of Durham*, ed. by Fowler, pp. 25–26, 215–16.

43 See *Letters and Papers*, ed. by Gairdner, p. 142.

44 *Rites of Durham*, ed. by Fowler, pp. 18–19, 210.

45 Above 'the Ladie of Boultons alter' stood 'a marveylous lyvelye and bewtifull Image of the picture of our Ladie socalled the Lady of boultone, whiche picture was maide to open with 2 leaves from her breaste downdward. And which in ye said image was wrowghte and pictured the Image of our saviour [i.e. God the Father], merveylouse fynlie gilted houldinge vppe his hands, and holding betwixt his hands a fair & large crucifix of christ all of gold, the whiche Crucifix was to be taiken fourthe euery good fridaie [...] and euery principall Daie the said image was opened that euery man might se pictured within her, the father, the sonne, and the holy ghost, most curiouslye and finely gilted' (*Rites of Durham*, ed. by Fowler, p. 30); 'The [...] altar haith alsoe a Window with 3 lights [...] in the 2 light ye picture of our Lady of Bolton, with a golden mase [sceptre] in her hand, & a crowne of gold on her head, a

is likely to have been imported from France, Flanders, or possibly Germany. The reproduction of it in a window, curious in its own right, suggests how highly the sculpture was valued. No other window at Durham demonstrably replicated a cult-image. The recognition that such a sculpture would have a powerful devotional impact, the trouble taken to obtain it, and its elevated reproduction in glass, combine to suggest it was procured with the success of other Marian cult images in mind, particularly Our Lady of Walsingham.[46] Thinking of this sort was evidently going on at Carlisle in the mid-fifteenth century, where the prior and convent planned a sculpture of the Virgin and Child covered with gilded silver plates and set with 'gemmis, monilibus, multisque aliis ornamentis pretiosis' (gems, coins, and many other precious ornaments). They petitioned their bishop and the archbishop of York in 1451 to issue an indulgence that would encourage donations towards its making. Quite possibly they had Our Lady of Bolton in mind.[47]

One could make this point about the parallel importance of Christ and the Virgin (in particular) at Durham on literary or ritual grounds, too, and extend it a good deal. But there is no need for this, nor any reason to play down the political importance of Cuthbert and the other local saints. The point is not so much to suggest that the value of indigenous sanctity has been overemphasized for Durham, and by extension for Hexham, York, and other places, but rather that there are other ways of seeing the evidence. One of these is to recognize the complementary importance of international cults. Our Lady of Bolton or the precious image of the Virgin at Carlisle did not necessarily or even probably deflect devotional attention from native cults and their iconographies. Devotional practice could presumably be mutually reinforcing as well as self-reinforcing. William of York may have got a large new shrine in the fifteenth century in part to assert the local pre-eminence of his cult in relation to that of Richard Scrope, but the intra-mural rivalry here — such as it was — represented an unusual case.[48] As a rule, it is reasonable to think that the devotional apparatus of any one institution expressed a distinctive religious integrity that was absorbed by visitors without any attempt to disaggregate it, even if they did head for a particular object on entering a church.

---

monke vunder her feete, kneeling & praying with eleuated hands' (p. 113). On the image-type see e.g. Gertsman, *Worlds Within*.

46 On cult images of the Virgin see Marks, *Image and Devotion*, pp. 186–227.

47 *Priory of Hexham*, ed. by Raine, I, pp. xcvii–xcviii (appendix no. 76).

48 See Norton, 'Richard Scrope', pp. 207–08. As Norton's work and that of others represented in the same volume shows, Scrope's cult flourished for a period after his execution in 1405 for treason. Its popularity was bolstered by parallels between Scrope and Christ (e.g. it supposedly took five blows to sever his head, just as Christ had five principal wounds) and Thomas Becket (Scrope, like Becket, was an archbishop killed for opposition to a king). With good reason, it is thought that the popular appeal of this cult may have come at the expense of interest in St William.

Clearly, it is hard to discuss late medieval experience of devotional integration in a satisfactory way, for a subject so appealing and nebulous easily lends itself to misrepresentation. In the discussion of whole interiors, only the *Rites of Durham* and the fifteenth-century glazing of the east end of York Minster provide a reasonable basis for speculation about it, although the suggestion of these examples is reinforced by well-preserved churches elsewhere in Europe. One is obliged to take on trust much that is in the *Rites* with regard to tone and the *ductus* of ritual: at York, however, much of the glass still exists, and is being progressively restored to something like its original condition. Here, the representation of indigenously northern saints alongside non-northern and biblical ones has been characterized by Christopher Norton as a strategy for emphasizing the Minster's status in relation to the whole province of York, and also the structural and metaphysical integration of this province with the universal Church.[49] He points out the shared occupancy of windows in the north choir aisle, where the Virgin Mary and saints Peter, Paul, and Nicholas are displayed together with saints Paulinus, Chad, and John of Beverley (each an archbishop of York). Here, too, William of York is paired with Becket. Norton is also inclined to read the great narrative windows dedicated to William of York on the north side of the choir, Cuthbert standing opposite it on the south, and the Apocalypse in the east as 'a kind of giant triptych for the high altar of the Minster', which emphasizes the eschatological role of the northern saints considered preeminent at York.[50] While eschatology is implied by every representation of a saint, the main way of emphasizing it in art was by such a juxtaposition of images.

Anyone satisfied with snapshots of patronal intention will find limited but still coherent traces of devotional integration in smaller ensembles. An example is the set of seven panels from the high altarpiece of Hexham Abbey, painted in the mid-fifteenth century and now displayed on the north side of the choir. These panels have large images of saintly bishops who ruled the ancient see of Hexham in the seventh and eighth centuries: Eata, Cuthbert, John of Beverley, Wilfrid, Acca, Frithbert, and Alchmund. One figure, probably Tilbert, is evidently missing from an original set of eight, as is the central subject to which the other figures stared and gestured. The only likely candidates for this lost central image are Christ (crucified or in majesty), the Virgin and Child, or the priory's patron saint, Andrew.[51] The 'prominent' image (*figuram pretendentis*) of Andrew beheaded by the Scots in 1296 was perhaps a predecessor.[52] There are also numerous smaller paintings of Hexham's early bishops, along with others

---

49 Norton, 'Sacred Space and Sacred History'.

50 Norton, 'Sacred Space and Sacred History', pp. 170–72, 178–79. William of York and Cuthbert were represented with other saints in earlier windows at St Mary's abbey, York: see Ayers, 'Writing about Art', p. 26.

51 Luxford, 'Idol of Origins', pp. 428–30; compare Rollason, 'Hexham Bishop-Saints'.

52 *Chronicon de Lanercost*, ed. by Stevenson, p. 175. Alternatively, *pretendentis* may have been meant to indicate a sculpture on the west front of the church.

of the same period representing the Virgin Mary and apostles, on the abbey's wooden pulpitum, and it is obvious that still more have been lost from the same object.[53] This visual communion of local and international sanctity was paralleled in the north transept at Durham by the 148 painted images formerly on the wooden screen of the chapel of saints Benedict and Jerome. These were probably executed in the early fifteenth century. In this case the emphasis was different, the tie that unified the saints and saint-like figures being their status as professional or honorary Benedictine monks. Fourteen were Northumbrian, including one king (Ceolwulf, who retired to become a monk in 738) and seven monastics associated with Lindisfarne (mostly as bishops). The rest were from other parts of Britain and Europe.[54] In retrospect, the ensemble looks like a case of *Bilderpolitik* with a northern accent, conceived as part of an English Benedictine response to widespread criticism about loss of religious integrity. Other products of the reaction include treatises on the origins of monasticism, one of which was written by John Wessington, prior of Durham from 1416 to 1446.[55] The imagery of the panels is only known because Wessington copied the accompanying *tituli*.[56] But the whole also reflects an affective ambition to set local saints in a wider devotional context. This is particularly so when whatever images were displayed at the altar are factored into the whole, along with those in the chapel's window: Christ's resurrection and ascension with a kneeling monk, Catherine of Alexandria, Mary Magdalene, and the titular saints Jerome and Benedict, who were fundamental to the scheme but not shown on the painted panels recorded by Wessington.[57] By any standard, this scheme was remarkable for the quantity and integration of its imagery, and it seems likely that the Hexham panels, which were painted later, were indebted to it in some way.

The coherence of such schemes relied on spatial logic over and above simple juxtaposition. A sense of this is had by comparing the images at Durham and Hexham with the sets of paintings (made *c.* 1475–1510) on the backs of the choir stalls at Carlisle Cathedral. While the decision to make them may have been influenced by what existed at Durham, their patrons were evidently less concerned with visual integration. The narrative sequences of Cuthbert, Antony of Egypt (each seventeen scenes) and Augustine of Hippo (twenty-two scenes), and the single standing figures of the apostles interposed between Cuthbert and Antony, rise vertiginously before the viewer and are segregated from one another by great compound piers.[58] In each bay, the

---

53 Tracey, 'Pulpitum at Hexham Priory'.
54 *Rites of Durham*, ed. by Fowler, pp. 124–36, 292.
55 Dobson, *Durham Priory*, pp. 379–82.
56 Durham University Library, MS Cosin B III 30, fols 5ʳ–25ʳ.
57 *Rites of Durham*, ed. by Fowler, pp. 112–13; also Pantin, 'Some English Medieval Treatises', pp. 200–01.
58 See, among others, Park and Cather, 'Late Medieval Paintings', pp. 214–22. Two blank bays on the south side may also originally have had more saint-imagery.

images are compartmentalized and supplied with lots of text in black letter, which emphasizes their individuality: indeed, the whole scheme highlights the difficulty of transferring an artistic paradigm that worked in books, and also in stained glass (where its effects were mediated by light and there was little or no distracting text), to a medium and format not well suited to it.[59] In this case, the choice of subjects was not obviously calculated to express the intersection of local and universal sanctity: it looks more miscellaneous. While it is plausible enough to imagine a coherence based on shared monastic status, Cuthbert and Antony (if not Augustine) may have been selected simply because the canons and their artists could access the necessary illustrated models. These, as is well known, included an illuminated life of Cuthbert (Bede's *vita prosaica*) made *c.* 1200 or slightly before and borrowed from Durham.[60] This is not to deny the canons' devotional interest in Cuthbert as a specifically northern saint (there was another narrative image of him in the cathedral), or their recognition of his stake in the broader religious current, but only to note that the choir-screen paintings are a doubtful reflection of these things.[61]

Finally, an impression of how the integration discussed here was manifested in the sphere of lay experience is provided by the improbably well-preserved tomb of Sir Ralph Grey (d. 1443) and Elizabeth FitzHugh (d. 1445) in the tiny parish church of Chillingham in Northumberland (Fig. 7.3). The chest of this monument is embellished with fourteen sandstone images of saints, diminutive but full-length and each in a richly sculpted niche. There are angels holding shields between the niches and a tropical growth of foliate ornament that expresses the saints' enduring vigour. The indigenous northern figures here are Cuthbert (holding Oswald's head) and Ninian (holding his chain); the rest are apostles and familiar late medieval helper-saints including John the Baptist, Thomas Becket, Catherine, Margaret of Antioch, and Sitha of Lucca.[62] The northern accent of this ensemble is comfortably absorbed into the mainstream of late medieval iconography, where it helps to express conventional faith in the variety and multiplication of sacred imagery.

As it happens, opinions have differed over some of the saints shown on the Grey tomb. The image of Thomas Becket on the east end has been taken for St Wilfrid (even though it clearly represents an archbishop), while a

---

59 On the Cuthbert texts, and another perspective on the Carlisle paintings, see Whitehead, 'Visual and Verbal Vernacular'.

60 Colgrave, 'St Cuthbert Paintings', and Park and Cather, 'Late Medieval Paintings', pp. 220–21, suggest drawings from the Durham manuscript were sent to Carlisle rather than the manuscript itself, but this seems an unnecessary complication. The same manuscript (now British Library, MS Yates Thompson 26) was lent to the archbishop of York *c.* 1400, perhaps as a model for the Cuthbert window there (Harrison, 'Illuminating Narrative', pp. 52–53, 111–20).

61 For this image, painted on one of the crossing piers, see Park and Cather, 'Late Medieval Paintings', pp. 221–22.

62 Heslop and Harbottle, 'Chillingham Church'; Blair, *Northumbrian Monuments*, pp. 116–19 and pl. vii–ix.

FIGURE 7.3. Chillingham (Northumberland): tomb of Sir Ralph Grey (d. 1443) and Elizabeth FitzHugh (d. 1445), from the north-east. Photo by Julian Luxford.

female figure which seems intended for St Ætheldreda — a locally as well as nationally important saint — has been called St Margaret of Scotland.[63] Even the St Sitha has been called St Elizabeth of Hungary, despite her chain of keys.[64] Such confusion is due to the artistic practice of representing saints according to generic types (e.g. bishop, king, princess, nun) which are differentiated in minor formal and iconographic ways. While an image of (say) John the Baptist (holding a lamb) or St Margaret of Antioch (standing on a dragon) is immediately identifiable by unique attributes, many saints, including most later and regional ones, can be harder to tell apart. Thus, John of Beverley and King Æthelstan (d. 939) are labelled with captions in a drawing in a later fifteenth-century cartulary from Beverley Minster, so that the canons could distinguish them from any archbishop and king (Fig. 7.4).[65]

---

63   For Ætheldreda's northern and Coldingham connections, see Jane Sinnett-Smith's essay in this volume.
64   Heslop and Harbottle, 'Chillingham Church', p. 132.
65   Oxford, University College, MS 82, fol. 7^r.

FIGURE 7.4. Penwork initial in a fifteenth-century cartulary from Beverley Minster (Oxford, University College, MS 82, fol. 7ʳ). Reproduced by kind permission of the Master and Fellows of University College.

This example points up a technical approach to the place of international religion in the devotional art of northern England which can be fleshed out with reference to Durham. To the best of art historical knowledge, the generic image-types mentioned above were invented in continental Europe and imported to England. Even the representation of Cuthbert holding Oswald's head, which looks remarkable and certainly confirms the identity of figures on the Grey tomb, the gatehouse of Worksop Priory (Nottinghamshire), the seal of the Carmelites of Northallerton (Yorkshire), and elsewhere, is only a variant of the cephalophore type found earlier in northern French images of bishop-saints including Denis, Firmin, and Nicaise.[66] Before it appeared at Durham, presumably in the late thirteenth or early fourteenth century, non-narrative images of Cuthbert showed him as a bishop without a customized attribute, the late twelfth-century wall painting in the Galilee Chapel being a conspicuous example. Identification in such cases — unless there were inscriptions — depended on setting and juxtaposition with other figures, typically, as it now appears, Oswald, and sometimes Aidan.[67] The need to differentiate arose as images in general became more popular and numerous. Even then, Cuthbert must often have been represented without Oswald's head, particularly where context made his identification clear (as

---

66 Birch, *Catalogue of Seals*, I, p. 680 (no. 3734) (Northallerton seal).
67 See e.g. Park, 'Decoration of the Cathedral', pp. 166, 171.

FIGURE 7.5. Impression of a seal from Durham Cathedral Priory incorporating an antique gem (London, British Library, Egerton charter 523). Reproduced by permission of the British Library Board.

on the cenotaphs in the churches at Lindisfarne and Chester-le-Street and cloister at Durham).[68] In any case, the adoption of the cephalophore type from France made Cuthbert readily identifiable where a distinction was required. It was also versatile in allowing the reduction of two indigenous saints to a single figure and alluding to the cathedral's unique relic-cult. However, for all that, it is based on a foreign and internationally recognizable model.

As noted, the adoption of a foreign image-type was more direct where Our Lady of Bolton was concerned. In another, historically important, case it amounted to frank appropriation. This relates to an antique gem incorporated into a seal of Durham Priory (Fig. 7.5).

The seal, which was in use in the fifteenth century but probably made in the twelfth, was evidently understood as a relic of St Cuthbert in its own right, and if so then the surviving impressions of it deserve a place with the treasures of the saint now displayed at the cathedral.[69] The obverse of this seal had a cross with arms of equal length and the inscription '+ SIGILLVM CVDBERHTI PRAESVLIS SEI', while on the reverse there was the gem, engraved with a head of Jupiter Seraphis wearing a cylindrical headdress of the type known as a modius but here styled like a crown. In this case the accompa-

---

68 For these cenotaphs see Raine, *History and Antiquities*, p. 125; Leland, *Itinerary*, ed. by Smith, I, p. 74; *Rites of Durham*, ed. by Fowler, pp. 68, 74.
69 The best impression appears to be that on British Library, Egerton Charter 523.

184   JULIAN LUXFORD

FIGURE 7.6. Mutilated, partially reconstructed image of St Cuthbert holding the head of St Oswald, now in the feretory at Durham Cathedral. Photo by Janet Gunning. © Chapter of Durham Cathedral.

nying inscription read '+ CAPVT SANCTI OSWALDI REGIS'.[70] If, as it appears, this seal was considered a relic then it is possible that its Jupiter-Oswald image was thought canonical, and *ipso facto* influenced both the representation of disembodied royal heads on later Durham seals and the heads held by Cuthbert in other media.[71] Oswald's crown has the cylindrical look of that on the seal in several surviving images, including the (mutilated and restored) fourteenth-century sculpture now displayed in the feretory (Fig. 7.6).[72]

Admittedly, it is challenging to explain how such an influence got into art made (as fine sculpture of this date surely was) far from Durham. One has to suppose the use of intermediary drawings sent by the patrons to the artists. It is in any case known that Durham obtained some and perhaps most of its important Cuthbert and Oswald imagery from or via London in the late Middle Ages, including (in 1380) the figures on the high altar reredos and (in 1429) a certain linen roll with Cuthbertine narrative scenes, evidently a model for stained glass windows.[73]

---

70 Birch, *Catalogue of Seals*, I, p. 416 (no. 2511); Ellis, *Catalogue of Seals*, p. 32 (no. M305–06).
71 See e.g. Birch, *Catalogue of Seals*, I, pp. 397–98 (no. 2447), 400–01 (no. 2457), 542 (no. 3095). For a documented instance of seal imagery serving as a model for monumental images see *Testamentary Records*, ed. by Woolgar, p. 155.
72 An image (perhaps the same one, but with Oswald's head in the right rather than left hand) shown in the feretory by Raine also had this high-based crown: Raine, *Brief Account*, pp. 66–67; compare Billings, *Architectural Illustrations*, pl. xxviii.
73 Hope, 'Early Working', pp. 225–26; Wilson, 'Neville Screen'; Harrison, 'Illuminating Narrative', p. 179. As Harrison points out, the linen roll may have related to the Cuthbert window in York Minster, whose donor was a bishop of Durham (Thomas Langley). Given space, these comments about European models could be extended to the narrative imagery of Cuthbert and William of York. I thank Dr Harrison for allowing me to refer to her thesis before its publication.

FIGURE 7.7. Thirteenth-century vault boss in the episcopal chapel at Girona Cathedral (Catalonia) sculpted with an image of St William of York. Adapted from José O. Oliveras, *Las claves de bóveda de la cathedral de Gerona* (1975).

The North in the South

Devotion to northern saints in other parts of England is an open-ended topic, and the goal here is merely to insinuate its relevance to the concept of a distinctively northern sanctity. The net should of course be cast wider to this end, for the cults of Cuthbert and Oswald were not confined to English devotion and its art. Oswald's reach into continental imagery is a Renaissance and Baroque phenomenon as well as a Gothic one,[74] while for Cuthbert, the cycle of twenty-six miniatures in the Sarum breviary made in Paris in the 1420s for John, duke of Bedford must be allowed to represent all of the non-English images for the purposes of this essay. It is worth noting that most of these miniatures adhere to French rather than English models.[75] In fact, one further representative deserves mention here, in three dimensions rather than two, since it is both remarkable and effectively invisible in scholarship. This is a thirteenth-century vault boss carved (according to the small literature on it) with an image of William of York in the episcopal chapel at Girona Cathedral in Catalonia (Fig. 7.7).[76] It is paired with another boss showing (*mirabile dictu*) William of Norwich: the choice is ascribed to the idiosyncratic devotion of William of Cabanelles, who was bishop from 1227 to 1245.

---

74 Clemoes, *Cult of St Oswald*, citing other sources for Oswald's cult. See further, Claudia Di Sciacca's essay on the eighteenth-century cult of Oswald in northern Italy in this volume.
75 The breviary, now BnF, MS lat. 17294, fols 434ᵛ–437ᵛ, is viewable at <https://gallica.bnf.fr/ark:/12148/btv1b8470142p/.f.1.image.r=17294.langFR> [accessed 01 November 2019]. On its Cuthbert images see also Baker, 'Medieval Illustrations', pp. 44–46; Harrison, 'Illuminating Narrative', pp. 121–26. The manuscript has a single image of Oswald, seated before supplicating men, at fol. 533ʳ.
76 Casanovas and Planagumá, 'Apuntes históricos', p. 275; Oliveras, *Las claves de bóveda*, pp. 21–22.

Cuthbert and Oswald were also venerated in Scotland, not only because they appear in the Sarum calendar (Sarum being the normal liturgical use of the secular Church in Scotland), but also in relation to the distinctively Scottish sanctity distilled in the Aberdeen breviary, published in Edinburgh in 1509–1510. This volume includes feasts for ninety-two saints born in or linkable to Scotland, including various Irish and Northumbrian natives.[77] In addition to Cuthbert and Oswald, the latter are the Lindisfarne bishops Aidan and Finnan, and Æbbe of Coldingham. However, there is no image of any of these saints in the breviary, and Scottish devotion to Aidan, Finnan, and Æbbe, at least, presumably had little if any iconographic extension.

As Sarum saints, Cuthbert (principal feast, 20 March; translation, 4 September) and Oswald (5 August) were part of the ritual currency of secular religion in the province of Canterbury throughout the later Middle Ages. John of Beverley (7 May) was added to the Sarum calendar in the early fifteenth century, perhaps due to the personal devotion of Henry V.[78] The monastic uses of southern England also include these saints, and, often, others of northern origin. Aidan, for example, occurs in litanies from Abbotsbury (Dorset), Chertsey (Surrey), Glastonbury, and Peterborough (Cambridgeshire), while Wilfrid is found at Abingdon (Berkshire), Christ Church Canterbury, Ely (Cambridgeshire), Kirkstead (Lincolnshire), Muchelney (Somerset), Peterborough, Rochester (Kent), and Worcester.[79] Various southern monasteries possessed relics of northern saints: Glastonbury, for instance, had parts of Cuthbert, Aidan, and Bede, plus four abbots of Wearmouth-Jarrow, Cuthbert's mentor Boisil, kings Oswald and Edwin, the abbesses Æbbe, Ælfflæd, and Hilda, and (as noted earlier) John of Beverley.[80] Waltham Abbey in Essex had relics of Cuthbert, Aidan, Ceolfrith, Bede, Oswine, and Godric of Finchale.[81]

All this probably meant little in iconographic terms, and while the votive imagery that did exist was widely diffused, cumulatively it is likely to have amounted to a tiny fraction — much less than one per cent — of the original total, even if representations of Christ and the Virgin are factored out. The following examples, which are baldly suggestive and could comfortably be multiplied, are chosen to indicate the diffusion. Most of the relevant imagery will have represented Cuthbert and Oswald in the form of either single standing figures or as components of specialized cycles in painting, sculpture, or stained glass. Thus, for example, Oswald is included in a specification of 1532 for a 'royal' window at the Greyfriars, Greenwich ('make hym crowned w^t an open crowne', etc.), and among other saintly English kings in the Toppes window

---

77 *Legends of the Scottish Saints*, ed. and trans. by Macquarie and Butter; Turpie, 'North-Eastern Saints'.
78 Morgan ed., *English Monastic Litanies*, III, p. 143.
79 Morgan ed., *English Monastic Litanies*, III, pp. 64, 197–98.
80 For the use of northern monastic hagionyms at Glastonbury, possibly derived from their relic collection, see David E. Thornton's essay in this volume.
81 Thomas, 'Cult of Saints' Relics', pp. 358, 369, 370, 378, 384, 389, 392, 393, 407, 411, 413, 417, 442, 443, 459.

(*c.* 1450) at St Peter Mancroft in Norwich.[82] Oswine is also shown in this window, and both kings are likely candidates for inclusion on the dado of the rood screen at nearby Catfield, which has only royal figures on it.[83] A panel painting of Oswald was included on the rood screens at Horsham St Faith near Norwich and Woodbridge in Suffolk.[84] Cuthbert is in the glass at Wiggenhall St Mary Magdalene, a Marshland village south of The Wash, and there was a painted votive image of him in the parish church at Bugbrooke in Northamptonshire. Thorpe Malsor, in the same county, had a painted statue of John of Beverley in a tabernacle. Images of Cuthbert in stained glass and (probably) sculpture are recorded in the hostelry at St Albans abbey *c.* 1430, associated with an altar dedicated to the same saint and founded by a bishop of Durham.[85] There is a smattering of relevant imagery in illuminated manuscripts, although its range is unbalanced by the great missal made *c.* 1400 for the Benedictine abbey of Sherborne in Dorset, which has bust-length miniatures of Cuthbert (twice), Bede, Oswald, Paulinus with Aidan, and Wilfrid.[86] A luxury prayer book made around the same time, probably in London, commences with thirteen full-page miniatures of saints, all familiar, international figures plus John of Bridlington (here evidently modelled on an image of St Dominic).[87] The book's preciousness reminds one that this northern saint had prominent devotees in the south, including Richard Beauchamp, earl of Warwick (d. 1439), who bequeathed a gold image of himself holding an 'ancre' (presumably an anchor) to St John's shrine.[88] Elsewhere, there was an altar dedicated to the same saint at Launceston Priory (Augustinian) in Cornwall which may have had an image associated with it, and a rood-screen painting of him at Hempsted (Norfolk).[89]

Occasionally, something more unusual presents itself. For example, there is a parish church dedicated to St Eata at Atcham in Shropshire which probably had an image of its patron saint in its chancel, as patron-images were apparently both normal and required by ecclesiastical legislation.[90] Accounts from Rumburgh Priory in Suffolk contain evidence for a votive image of the Irish saint Bega, also culted at St Bees: both Rumburgh and St Bees were

---

82 Rogers, 'Pattern for Princes', p. 338 (quotation); King, *Medieval Stained Glass*, pp. clxxxix–cxcii, 89–91, 95–96, 97–98, 103–04, 116–17.

83 King, *Medieval Stained Glass*, p. cxci; Luxford, 'Sacred Kingship', pp. 113–14.

84 Baker, *English Panel Paintings*, pp. 149, 205–09: the Woodbridge painting is lost but known from antiquarian records.

85 Nichols, *Early Art of Norfolk*, p. 183; Serjeantson and Longden, 'Parish Churches and Religious Houses', pp. 291, 415; *Annales monasterii Sancti Albani*, ed. by Riley, I, pp. 448–49.

86 BL, MS Add. 74236, pp. 428 (Cuthbert), 456 (Bede: holding a book), 516 (Oswald: with a sword), 538 (Paulinus and Aidan), 541 (Cuthbert), 569 (Wilfrid). (Note that this is a paginated rather than foliated manuscript).

87 BL, MS Royal 2.A.XVIII, fol. 9ᵛ. This manuscript, known as the 'Beaufort-Beauchamp Hours', is also discussed in Cynthia Turner Camp's essay in this volume.

88 *Historia vitæ et regni Ricardi II.*, ed. by Hearne, pp. 246–47.

89 Orme, *Saints of Cornwall*, p. 152; Baker, *English Panel Paintings*, p. 147.

90 Marks, *Image and Devotion*, pp. 61, 73–74 (legislation).

dependencies of St Mary's Abbey at York, which, as Martin Heale notes, must explain what would otherwise be a puzzling migration. A book of St Bega — not, perhaps, illuminated — is also recorded. Money was regularly left in boxes near these objects by visitors during the fifteenth and early sixteenth centuries.[91] Wall paintings of the martyrdom of Thomas of Lancaster exist at South Newington in Oxfordshire and Longthorpe Tower on the outskirts of Peterborough, and there is a miniature that shows the same event in the Luttrell Psalter, owned and probably made in Lincolnshire.[92] These images were all made within a few decades of Thomas's death, and evidently express their patrons' positive identification with Thomas, although they would have had no clear anti-monarchical relevance in the reign of Edward III (if they had, then they would hardly have been publicly displayed on church walls). Later, Henry V is recorded to have owned a relic of Thomas of Lancaster, paired with one of 'St Cedde' (either Chad or Cedd), in a reliquary weighing 3lb 7 oz.[93] The monumental brass of Abbot Thomas de la Mare (d. 1396) at St Albans incorporates an exquisite engraving of Oswine on it, paired with an image of St Alban, which looks like an expression of personal devotion as well as institutional prerogative (Tynemouth was a dependency of St Albans), since de la Mare had been prior of Tynemouth between 1340 and 1349. Here Oswine holds the spear of his martyrdom, just as he does on Tynemouth's conventual seal.[94] Heraldry attributed to Oswine (*gules 3 crowns or*) was also displayed at St Albans, above the arch on the west wall of the presbytery (with the arms of saints Alban and Amphibalus) and in other contexts.[95] By the end of the Middle Ages, heraldry was recognized for Cuthbert (*azure, a cross flory or between 4 lions rampant*) and Oswald (*gules, a cross between 4 lions rampant or*), too, and this got into the armorial collections of the Tudor heralds.[96] Here was artistic representation at its most abstract, if not necessarily its least devout. To attribute arms to a saint was to acknowledge his or her nobility, a concept often associated with sanctity: the so-called *Boke of Saint Albans* styled Christ himself 'a gentilman of his moder behalue [who] bore cotarmure of aunseturis'.[97] It is in this light, no doubt, that the *Rites of Durham* recalls how the arms of Cuthbert and Oswald were piously coupled with those of the Virgin Mary and St George underneath images of the same saints in a window in the south choir aisle.[98]

---

91 Heale, 'Rumburgh Priory', pp. 18, 21 n. 47.

92 Rouse and Baker, 'Wall-Paintings at Longthorpe Tower', pp. 32, 37; BL, MS Add. 42130, fol. 56ʳ.

93 Kew, TNA, E101/44/26, membrane 3. On Thomas of Lancaster's image in art see McQuillen, 'Who was St Thomas of Lancaster?'.

94 Norris, *Monumental Brasses*, I, p. 31; II, pl. 37; Luxford, 'Manuscripts, History', p. 198 (image of Tynemouth seal).

95 Michael, *St Albans Cathedral*, p. 60. See further, James G. Clark's essay on Oswine's cult in late medieval England in this volume.

96 Ashley ed., *At the Roots of Heraldry*, pp. 77, 96 (Cuthbert), 77, 81, 118 (Oswald).

97 *Boke of Saint Albans*, ed. by Blades, fol. b i.

98 *Rites of Durham*, ed. by Fowler, p. 116.

Conclusion

Fascinated by the number and variety of indigenous saints in the Aberdeen breviary, the historian and Catholic priest David McRoberts postulated a nationalistic turn in late medieval Scottish devotion.[99] Once planted, this seed proved easy to grow by selective reference to the available evidence, and, as David Ditchburn has shown in a trenchant refutation, its influence on scholarship has been considerable.[100] According to Ditchburn, the problem stems not only from misplaced nationalism but also from what is passively obscured by such a focus, including the historical appetite for international cults, not least Christocentric and Marian ones.

There are particular reasons why McRoberts's ideas have proved so attractive in an independently minded but not politically sovereign country. However, the issue at stake has a clear relevance to the study of devotion in any country or region for which a strong element of indigenous sanctity can be claimed, including the north of England. It seems important to stress what historians know but do not always recognize: that the transnationalism of a cult did not disqualify the possibility of its distinctively regional articulation, nor neutralize the interest of its artistic and textual equipment, nor somehow render it typologically different from that of a native saint. Readers who consider this a matter of common sense will, I hope, forgive the way this point is spelled out here.

As noted at the outset, the ability to achieve anything in this quarter is related to one's ideas about the north of England as a region. Any argument for late medieval coherence, even if it is based on sanctity and devotion, looks weak: as A. J. Pollard noted, the North in this period is better understood as an amalgam of several regions than a cultural or political unity.[101] Whether or not one breaks the North down, geography proves a slippery criterion and texts — even medieval ones concerned with geography — insufficient yardsticks. The imagery and forms of devotional art do not appear to help much. This is not in the least to deny the value to medieval scholarship of a concept of northernness, but merely to suggest that the concept is, like the vision of 'pure Northernness' that engulfed C. S. Lewis when he discovered Wagner, more a function of spirit than reason.[102] Admittedly, this will not strike everyone as satisfactory, and may even look like a cop-out; but as a basis for investigation of sanctity and its art it is at least in sympathy with its objects.

---

99 McRoberts, 'Scottish Church and Nationalism'.
100 Ditchburn, '"McRoberts Thesis"'.
101 Pollard, *North-Eastern England*, pp. 1–6, 9–30.
102 Lewis, *Surprised by Joy*, p. 83: 'I had never heard of Wagner, nor of Siegfried. [...] Pure "Northernness" engulfed me: a vision of huge, clear spaces hanging above the Atlantic in the endless twilight of Northern summer, remoteness, severity [...]'.

Works Cited

Manuscripts and Archival Sources

Durham, Durham University Library, MS Cosin B III 30
Kew, The National Archives, E101/44/26
——, The National Archives, SP 1/102
London, British Library, MS Add. 42130
——, MS Add. 74236
——, MS Royal 2.A.XVIII
——, Egerton Charter 523
Oxford, Bodleian Library, MS Gough Gen. Top. 16, (Gough map) <http://www.
    goughmap.org/> [accessed 01/11/2019]
——, University College, MS 82
Paris, Bibliothèque nationale de France, MS lat. 17294 <https://gallica.bnf.fr/ark:
    /12148/btv1b8470142p./f.1.image.r=17294.langFR>[accessed01November2019]

Primary Sources

Annales monasterii Sancti Albani a Johannes Amundesham monacho, ed. by Henry T.
    Riley, 2 vols (London: Longman and Co., 1870–71)
Bede, *Historia ecclesiastica gentis anglorum*, ed. and trans. by Bertram Colgrave and
    Roger A. B. Mynors (Oxford: Clarendon Press, 1969)
The Boke of Saint Albans, ed. by William Blades (London: Elliot Stock, 1881)
The Book of Margery Kempe, ed. by Barry Windeatt (Cambridge: Cambridge
    University Press, 2000)
The Cartulary of the Augustinian Friars of Clare, ed. by Christopher Harper-Bill
    (Woodbridge: Boydell and Brewer, 1991)
Chronicon de Lanercost, M.CC.I–M.CCC.XLVI, ed. by Joseph Stevenson
    (Edinburgh: Bannatyne Club and Maitland Club, 1839)
Historia vitæ et regni Ricardi II. Angliæ Regis, ed. by Thomas Hearne (Oxford:
    Sheldonian Theatre, 1729)
*Legends of the Scottish Saints: Readings, Hymns and Prayers for the Commemorations
    of Scottish Saints in the Aberdeen Breviary*, ed. and trans. by Alan Macquarie and
    Rachel Butter (Dublin: Four Courts Press, 2012)
Leland, John, *Itinerary in England and Wales*, ed. by Lucy Toulmin Smith, 5 vols
    (Fontwell: Centaur, 1964)
*Letters and Papers, Foreign and Domestic, of the Reign of Henry VIII: Volume 10,
    January-June 1536*, ed. by James Gairdner (London: HMSO, 1887)
Polychronicon Ranulphi Higden Monachi Cestrensis, ed. by Churchill Babington and
    Joseph R. Lumby, 9 vols (London: Longman and Co., 1865–1886)
The Priory of Hexham: Its Chroniclers, Endowments, and Annals, ed. by James Raine,
    2 vols (Durham: Andrews & Co., 1864–1865)

Reginald of Durham, *Libellus de vita et miraculis S. Godrici, heremitae de Finchale*, ed. by
    Joseph Stevenson (London: J. B. Nichols and Son, 1847) (cited as *Vita Godrici*)
Rites of Durham, ed. by Joseph T. Fowler (Durham: Andrews & Co., 1903)
Symeon of Durham, *Libellus de exordio atque procursu istius, hoc est Dunhelmensis
    ecclesie*, ed. and trans. by David Rollason (Oxford: Clarendon Press, 2000)
Testamentary Records of the English and Welsh Episcopate 1200–1413, ed. by C. M.
    Woolgar (Woodbridge: Canterbury and York Society, 2011)

Secondary Works

Ashley, Steven, ed., *At the Roots of Heraldry: Collected Papers of John Archibald
    Goodall* (London: Harleian Society, 2018)
Ayers, Tim, 'Writing about Art: A Monastic Art of Memory at St Mary's Abbey, York,
    c. 1300', in *Word and Image: Corpus Vitrearum 27th International Colloquium, York,
    7–11 July 2014*, ed. by Richard Marks (York: CVMA, 2014), pp. 24–27
Baker, Audrey, *English Panel Paintings 1400–1558: A Survey of Figure Paintings on
    East Anglian Rood Screens* (London: Archetype, 2011)
Baker, Malcolm, 'Medieval Illustrations of Bede's Life of St Cuthbert', *Journal of the
    Warburg and Courtauld Institutes*, 41 (1978), 16–49
Bartlett, Robert, 'Heartland and Border: The Mental and Physical Geography of
    Medieval Europe', in *Power and Identity in the Middle Ages: Essays in Memory
    of Rees Davies*, ed. by Huw Pryce and John Watts (Oxford: Oxford University
    Press, 2007), pp. 23–36
Billings, Robert W., *Architectural Illustrations and Description of the Cathedral
    Church of Durham* (London: T. and W. Boone, 1843)
Birch, Walter de Gray, *Catalogue of Seals in the Department of Manuscripts in the
    British Museum*, 6 vols (London: The British Museum, 1887–1900)
Blair, Charles H. H., *Northumbrian Monuments, or, Shields of Arms, Effigies and
    Inscriptions in the Churches, Castles and Halls of Northumberland*, Newcastle upon
    Tyne Record Series 4 (Newcastle upon Tyne: Northumberland Press, 1924)
Brown, Sarah, 'Archbishop Richard Scrope's Lost Window in York Minster', in
    Saints and Their Cults in Medieval England, ed. by Susan Powell (Donington:
    Shaun Tyas, 2017), pp. 299–317
Carter, Michael, *The Art and Architecture of the Cistercians in Northern England,
    c. 1300–1540* (Turnhout: Brepols, 2019)
Casanovas, Jaime M., and José M. Marqués Planagumá, 'Apuntes históricos sobre
    el palacio episcopal de Gerona', *Anales del Instituto de Estudios Gerundenses*, 14
    (1960), 263–306
Cherry, John, 'The Seal of Haltemprice Priory', in *Studies in Medieval Art and
    Architecture Presented to Peter Lasko*, ed. by David Buckton and Sandy Heslop
    (Stroud: Alan Sutton, 1994), pp. 14–23
Clemoes, Peter, *The Cult of St Oswald on the Continent*, Jarrow Lecture 1983
    (Jarrow: St Paul's Church, 1983)
Colgrave, Bertram, 'The St Cuthbert Paintings on the Carlisle Cathedral Stalls',
    Burlington Magazine, 73 (1938), 16–21

Crooks, Peter, David Green and Mark W. Ormrod, 'Empire and the English Identity: Reflections on the King of England's *dominium*', in *The Plantagenet Empire 1259–1453*, ed. by Peter Crooks, David Green and Mark W. Ormrod (Donington: Shaun Tyas, 2016), pp. 1–34

Crooks, Peter, David Green and Mark W. Ormrod, ed., *The Plantagenet Empire 1259–1453* (Donington: Shaun Tyas, 2016)

Crumplin, Sally, 'Modernizing St Cuthbert: Reginald of Durham's Miracle Collection', in *Signs, Wonders, Miracles: Representations of Divine Power in the Life of the Church*, ed. by Kate Cooper and Jeremy Gregory (Cambridge: Cambridge University Press, 2005), pp. 179–91

DaCosta Kaufmann, Thomas, *Towards a Geography of Art* (Chicago: Chicago University Press, 2004)

Ditchburn, David, 'The "McRoberts Thesis" and Patterns of Sanctity in Late Medieval Scotland', in *The Cult of Saints and the Virgin Mary in Medieval Scotland*, ed. by Steve Boardman and Eila Williamson (Woodbridge: Boydell and Brewer, 2010), pp. 177–94

Dobson, R. Barrie, *Durham Priory 1400–1450* (Cambridge: Cambridge University Press, 1973)

——, 'The Northern Province in the Later Middle Ages', *Northern History*, 42 (2005), 49–60

Ellis, Roger H., *Catalogue of Seals in the Public Record Office: Monastic Seals* (London: HMSO, 1986)

Engel, Ute, 'Kunstlandschaft und Kunstgeschichte: Methodische Probleme und neuere Perspektiven', in *Landschaft(en): Begriffe, Formen, Implikationen*, ed. by Franz J. Felten, Harald Müller and Heidrun Ochs (Stuttgart: Franz Steiner, 2012), pp. 87–114

First Report of the Deputy Keeper of the Public Records [no ed. specified] (London: William Clowes and Sons, 1840)

Fletcher, Isaac, 'Brigham Church', *Transactions of the Cumberland and Westmoreland Antiquarian and Archaeological Society*, 4 (1878–1879), 149–77

Foot, Sarah, 'Bede's Northern Saints', in *Saints of North-East England, 600–1500*, ed. by Margaret Coombe, Anne Mouron, and Christiania Whitehead (Turnhout: Brepols, 2017), pp. 19–41

Gertsman, Elina, *Worlds Within: Opening the Medieval Shrine Madonna* (University Park: Pennsylvania University Press, 2015)

Godfrey, Walter H., and Anthony Wagner, 'Norroy King of Arms', in *The College of Arms, Queen Victoria Street*, ed. by Walter H. Godfrey, Survey of London Monograph, 16 (London: London Survey Committee, 1963), pp. 101–18

Gransden, Antonia, 'Bede's Reputation as an Historian in Medieval England', *Journal of Ecclesiastical History*, 32 (1981), 397–425

Grigg, Julianna, 'The Black Rood of Scotland: A Social and Political Life', *Viator*, 48 (2017), 53–78

Harrison, Katharine E., 'Illuminating Narrative: An Interdisciplinary Investigation of the Fifteenth-Century St Cuthbert Window, York Minster' (unpublished doctoral thesis, University of York, 2019)

Harvey, Margaret, 'Travel from Durham to York (and Back) in the Fourteenth Century', *Northern History*, 42 (2005), 119–30

Heale, Martin R. V., 'Rumburgh Priory in the Later Middle Ages: Some New Evidence', *Proceedings of the Suffolk Institute of Archaeology and History*, 40 (2001), 8–23

Heslop, David, and Barbara Harbottle, 'Chillingham Church, Northumberland: The South Chapel and the Grey Tomb', *Archaeologia Aeliana*, 5th ser. 27 (1999), 123–34

Holford, Matthew L., 'Durham: History, Culture and Identity', in *Border Liberties and Loyalties: North-East England, c. 1200 to c. 1400*, ed. by Matthew L. Holford and Keith J. Stringer (Edinburgh: Edinburgh University Press, 2012), pp. 17–57

Hope, William H. St John, 'The Seals of English Bishops', *Proceedings of the Society of Antiquaries*, 11 (1886–1887), 271–306

——, 'On the Early Working of Alabaster in England', *Archaeological Journal*, 61 (1904), 221–40

Hughes, Jonathan, *Pastors and Visionaries: Religion and Secular Life in Late Medieval Yorkshire* (Woodbridge: Boydell and Brewer, 1988)

King, David, *The Medieval Stained Glass of St Peter Mancroft, Norwich* (Oxford: Oxford University Press, 2006)

Le Patourel, John, 'Is Northern History a Subject?', *Northern History*, 12 (1976), 1–15

Lewis, C. S., *Surprised by Joy: The Shape of My Early Life* (London: HarperCollins, 2002)

Liddy, Christian D., *The Bishopric of Durham in the Late Middle Ages: Lordship, Community and the Cult of St Cuthbert* (Woodbridge: Boydell and Brewer, 2008)

Lowenthal, David, *The Past is a Foreign Country Revisited* (Cambridge: Cambridge University Press, 2015)

Luxford, Julian, 'The Idol of Origins: Retrospection in Augustinian Art during the Later Middle Ages', in *The Regular Canons in the Medieval British Isles*, ed. by Janet Burton and Karen Stöber (Turnhout: Brepols, 2011), pp. 417–42

——, 'Manuscripts, History and Aesthetic Interests at Tynemouth Priory', in *Newcastle and Northumberland: Roman and Medieval Architecture and Art*, ed. by Jeremy Ashbee and Julian Luxford (Leeds: Maney, 2013), pp. 193–213

——, 'Sacred Kingship, Genealogy and the Late Medieval Rood Screen: Catfield and Beyond', in *The Art and Science of the Church Screen in Medieval Europe: Making, Meaning, Preserving*, ed. by Spike Bucklow, Richard Marks and Lucy Wrapson (Woodbridge: Boydell and Brewer, 2017), pp. 100–22

McQuillen, John T., 'Who was St Thomas of Lancaster? New Manuscript Evidence', in *Fourteenth-Century England IV*, ed. by Jeff S. Hamilton (Woodbridge: Boydell and Brewer, 2006), pp. 1–25

McRoberts, David, 'The Scottish Church and Nationalism in the Fifteenth Century', *Innes Review*, 19 (1968), 3–14

Marks, Richard, *Image and Devotion in Late Medieval England* (Stroud: Alan Sutton, 2004)

Marks, Richard, and Paul Williamson, ed., *Gothic: Art for England, 1400–1547* (London: The Victoria & Albert Museum, 2003)

Michael, M. A., *St Albans Cathedral Wall Paintings* (London: Scala, 2019)

Morgan, Nigel J., ed., *English Monastic Litanies of the Saints after 1100*, 3 vols (Woodbridge: Boydell, 2012–2018)

Newton, Diana, 'Borders and Bishopric: Regional Identities in the Pre-Modern North East, 1559–1620', in *Regional Identities in North-East England, 1300–2000*, ed. by Adrian Green and Anthony J. Pollard (Woodbridge: Boydell and Brewer, 2007), pp. 49–70

Nichols, Ann E., *The Early Art of Norfolk* (Kalamazoo: Medieval Institute Publications, 2002)

Norris, Malcolm, *Monumental Brasses: The Memorials*, 2 vols (London: Faber and Faber, 1977)

Norton, Christopher, 'Sacred Space and Sacred History: The Glazing of the Eastern Arm of York Minster', in *Glasmalerei im Kontext Bildprogramme und Raumfunktionen*, ed. by Rüdiger Becksmann (Nuremberg: Germanisches Nationalmuseum, 2005), pp. 167–81

——, 'Richard Scrope and York Minster', in *Richard Scrope: Archbishop, Rebel, Martyr*, ed. by Jeremy Goldberg (Donington: Shaun Tyas, 2007), pp. 138–213

Oliveras, José C., *Las claves de bóveda de la catedral de Gerona* (Barcelona: Editorial Escudo de Oro, 1975)

Orme, Nicholas, *The Saints of Cornwall* (Oxford: Oxford University Press, 2000)

Pantin, William A., 'Some English Medieval Treatises on the Origins of Monasticism', in *Medieval Studies Presented to Rose Graham*, ed. by Veronica Ruffer and Arnold J. Taylor (Oxford: Oxford University Press, 1950), pp. 189–215

Park, David, 'The Decoration of the Cathedral and Priory in the Middle Ages', in *Durham Cathedral: History, Fabric and Culture*, ed. by David Brown (New Haven: Yale University Press, 2015), pp. 166–85

Park, David, and Sharon Cather, 'Late Medieval Paintings at Carlisle', in *Carlisle and Cumbria: Roman and Medieval Architecture, Art and Archaeology*, ed. by Mike McCarthy and David Weston (Leeds: Maney, 2004), pp. 214–31

Pollard, Anthony J., *North-Eastern England During the Wars of the Roses: Lay Society, War, and Politics 1450–1500* (Oxford: Clarendon Press, 1990)

Raine, James, *A Brief Account of Durham Cathedral* (Newcastle-upon-Tyne: Blackwell, 1833)

——, *The History and Antiquities of North Durham* (London: J. B. Nichols and Son, 1852)

Reid, Rachel R., *The King's Council in the North* (London: Longmans, 1921)

Robson, Euan, 'A Cathedral Encountered: Stories and Storytelling in Medieval Durham' (unpublished doctoral thesis, University of London, 2019)

Rogers, Nicholas, 'A Pattern for Princes: The Royal Window at the Greenwich Greyfriars', in *Saints and Their Cults in Medieval England*, ed. by Susan Powell (Donington: Shaun Tyas, 2017), pp. 318–38

Rollason, David, 'The Hexham Bishop-Saints: Cults, History and Power', in *Saints of North-East England, 600–1500*, ed. by Margaret Coombe, Anne Mouron, and Christiania Whitehead (Turnhout: Brepols, 2017), pp. 177–95

Rollason, Lynda, 'Northern Saints and the Painted Glass of Durham Cathedral in the Later Middle Ages', in *Saints of North-East England, 600–1500*, ed. by Margaret Coombe, Anne Mouron, and Christiania Whitehead (Turnhout: Brepols, 2017), pp. 327–43

Rouse, E. Clive, and Audrey Baker, 'The Wall-Paintings at Longthorpe Tower near Peterborough, Northants', *Archaeologia*, 96 (1955), 1–57

Serjeantson, Robert M., and Henry I. Longden, 'The Parish Churches and Religious Houses of Northamptonshire: Their Dedications, Altars, Images and Lights', *Archaeological Journal*, 70 (1913), 217–452

Shaw, Anthony N., 'The *Compendium compertorum* and the Making of the Suppression Act' (unpublished doctoral thesis, University of Warwick, 2003)

Slater, Laura, 'Recreating the Judean hills? English Hermits and the Holy Land', *Journal of Medieval History*, 42 (2016), 603–26

Thomas, Islwyn G., 'The Cult of Saints' Relics in Medieval England' (unpublished doctoral thesis, University of London, 1974)

Tracey, Charles, 'The Pulpitum at Hexham Priory', in *Newcastle and Northumberland: Roman and Medieval Architecture and Art*, ed. by Jeremy Ashbee and Julian Luxford (Leeds: Maney, 2013), pp. 152–70

Turner, Philippa, 'Image and Devotion in Durham Cathedral Priory and York Minster, *c.* 1300–*c.* 1540: New Contexts, New Perspectives' (unpublished doctoral thesis, University of York, 2014)

Turpie, Tom, 'North-Eastern Saints in the Aberdeen Breviary and the *Historia gentis Scotorum* of Hector Boece: Liturgy, History and Religious Practice in Late Medieval Scotland', in *Medieval Art, Architecture and Archaeology in the Dioceses of Aberdeen and Moray*, ed. by Jane Geddes (London: Routledge, 2016), pp. 239–47

Wells, Emma J., '"… he went round the holy places praying and offering": Evidence for Cuthbertine Pilgrimage to Lindisfarne and Farne in the Late Medieval Period', in *Newcastle and Northumberland: Roman and Medieval Architecture and Art*, ed. by Jeremy Ashbee and Julian Luxford (Leeds: Maney, 2013), pp. 214–31

Whitehead, Christiania, 'Visual and Verbal Vernacular Translations of Bede's Prose Life of St Cuthbert in Fifteenth-Century Northern England: The Carlisle Panel Paintings', in *What is an Image in Medieval and Early Modern England?*, ed. by Antoninia B. Zlatar and Olga Timofeeva (Tübingen: Narr Francke Attempto, 2017), pp. 11–37

Wilson, Christopher, 'The Neville Screen', in *Medieval Art and Architecture at Durham Cathedral*, ed. by Nicola Coldstream and Peter Draper (Leeds: Maney, 1980), pp. 90–104

PART II

New Case Studies of Northern Saints and Their Cults

II.1 The Eremitic Life

MARGARET COOMBE

The Context for and Later Reception of Reginald of Durham's *Vita sancti Godrici*[*]

It was Maundy Thursday in the year 1170, at a hermitage four miles or so north-east of the large English Benedictine cathedral monastery of Durham city. The hermitage was at Finchale, now the site of a ruined priory, and there an elderly hermit named Godric lay in pain, close to death. Many years ago, he had been granted permission by the bishop to live on this land, had farmed it and there welcomed many visitors, high-born and low, with his salmon and his singing. But now he had been bedridden for eight long years, during which time he had been cared for by Durham monks. One in particular, Reginald, who may have been a blood relative, had been his closest and most frequent visitor and carer.[1] After each visit, Reginald had kept notes of their conversation, added information gained from other, reliable people who knew the old man, and finally turned it into a book of his life story.

This essay will argue that Reginald's book, the *Vita sancti Godrici*, is a product of the turbulent political and cultural context into which its author was introduced in the 1140s. The result is a culturally flexible text, an attribute which has contributed to its long afterlife. This essay explains the contemporary unpopularity of the *Vita* and the subsequent versions which were quickly produced in its aftermath. Later commentators have largely agreed that Reginald was a poor writer, but this paper will argue that his reputation demands revision: rather, the same political agendas which rendered the *Vita*

---

[*] All references to the *Vita Godrici* in this essay are to *Reginald of Durham: The Life and Miracles of Saint Godric, Hermit of Finchale*, ed. and trans. by Margaret Coombe, Oxford Medieval Texts (Oxford: Oxford University Press, 2022) (cited hereafter as Reginald, *Vita Godrici*).

[1] Reginald, *Vita Godrici*, § 230 explains: 'erat frater quidam Dunelmensis ecclesie ei consanguinitatis coniunctus gratia atque familiaritate' (a certain monk of the church of Durham who was connected with him by blood and in friendship) was deputed to look after him in his illness. Was Reginald Godric's relative, who 'post illius depositum locum eiusdem solitudinis est adeptus' (after [Godric's] death, also attained the same place of solitude)?

Margaret Coombe (margaret.coombe@history.ox.ac.uk) is Director of Study Skills and Lecturer in Medieval History at the University of Oxford.

Late Medieval Devotion to Saints from the North of England: New Directions, ed. by Christiania Whitehead, Hazel J. Hunter Blair, and Denis Renevey, MCS 48 (Turnhout: Brepols, 2022), pp. 199–216

BREPOLS ❧ PUBLISHERS   10.1484/M.MCS-EB.5.124350

200 MARGARET COOMBE

unacceptable at the time promoted these alternative versions. It is, moreover, not the product of the pen of one man, but includes testimony from a range of sources and writers.

Agencies and Agendas Driving the Production of the *Vita sancti Godrici*

It has been said in studies of hagiography that saints' lives are often newly produced or revised at times of crisis, perhaps to legitimize the authority of one of a series of warring groups or of some newly installed individuals.[2] Reginald's context, mid-twelfth-century Durham, was marked by two overriding themes: the maintenance of the history and rights of the community of St Cuthbert, and frequent disputes between various self-interested parties. These disputes included the defence of Durham against external forces, between different internal factions over who should be bishop, and between the see and the priory over ownership of lands and resources, often leading to violence. It was said, for example, of Bishop William of Ste Barbe (1144–1153) that 'multa in episcopatu aduersa sustinens, tam propter regis Scotie exactiones non iustas quam propter uicinorum latrocinia, et depredationes non tam crebras quam pene continuas' (he had to bear many adversities in that office, as much on account of the unjust exactions of the king of Scotland, as on account of robberies committed by his neighbours, and of depredations which were not so much frequent as virtually continuous).[3] A further complication arose from the fact that the patrimony of St Cuthbert was regarded as belonging, not just to the bishop or the monks, but also to the people: 'the county community of Durham [...] was essentially an imagined community, whose coherence and sense of collective awareness were created and maintained by a distinctive cultural identity. This identity was associated with the historical traditions of the church of Durham and the concept of the *haliwerfolc*.'[4]

Strife between the monks and the bishops was never far from the surface. In the 1140s local war broke out between supporters of two claimants to the see, William Cumin and William of Ste Barbe. Ste Barbe was eventually appointed, but the next episcopal appointment, of Hugh du Puiset in 1153, was also contested. His enthronement at Durham in May 1154 gave him 'a profitable field for his energies and ambitions',[5] ambitions which brought him into almost constant dispute with the monks.[6] Although the gift back to the monks of the freedoms they had enjoyed at the start of Flambard's

---

2 For example, Hayward, 'Demystifying the Role of Sanctity', pp. 124, 127, 135.
3 Symeon, *Libellus de exordio*, ed. by Rollason, p. 321, from a section written by the continuator following Symeon's death.
4 Aird, *St Cuthbert and the Normans*, pp. 5–8, 231.
5 Scammell, *Hugh du Puiset*, p. 21.
6 Scammell, *Hugh du Puiset*, pp. 46–47, 128–66, 283–84, 300–07.

episcopate in 1099 was repeated almost verbatim by Hugh in 1154–57,[7] and reconfirmed in 1162 by Pope Alexander, subsequent disagreements came to a head in 1186–89, by which time the bishop had apparently sequestered the entire revenues of the priory. In 1188–89 he returned some power to the monks and finally restored everything on his deathbed in 1195.[8] However, arguments about land between the monks and the bishop continued until the early thirteenth century.[9]

Reginald therefore found himself within a turbulent monastic community whose identity was defended in a number of ways, including relic collecting and the custodianship of Cuthbert's reputedly incorrupt body. The community found that the best way to protect its rights was, however, through the medium of writing. Among a huge output of histories, and official and administrative papers, were many documents forged in an attempt by the monks to demonstrate that earlier bishops had granted them exemption from episcopal oversight. However, the disputes raging in Durham were reflected or even played out, not only in historical and legal texts, but also in hagiographies, demonstrating a mixture of 'loyalty and litigiousness'.[10]

Whilst the bishop and the monks remained at loggerheads, Reginald also seems to have been very unhappy with his fellow monks, and I would argue that he used the traditional monastic format of hagiography as a convenient vehicle to objectify his own grievances and promote his own agendas.[11] Reginald singled out many of his contemporaries for disdain, including an abbot, a fat and lazy monk, a wife-beating husband and some people who tried to rob him. The details of these contemporaries are contained in lengthy stories, at times in obscure terms which only an insider would fully understand. One example is his overt criticism of the Tod family. They had for centuries been monks of Durham and one or more of them had carried St Cuthbert's coffin on its long peregrinations. In his *Libellus Cuthberti*, Reginald used a very long tale of a cheese and a fox to make his point against them. In brief, the monks who carried St Cuthbert's coffin were starving during a famine. It would be no light decision to divert to themselves gifts made to their saint, but the circumstances were dire, so it was decided to open the coffin and eat from it a cheese which had been donated to the saint. However, the cheese

---

7   *Durham Episcopal Charters*, ed. by Offler, p. 114.

8   Norton, 'History, Wisdom and Illumination', p. 99.

9   They were apparently resolved in 'Le Conuenit': Symeon, *Libellus de Exordio*, ed. by Rollason, p. lxxxvi.

10 Bartlett, *England under the Norman and Angevin Kings*, p. 628.

11 Three works can be attributed to him with certainty. The *Vita sancti Oswaldi* (of King Oswald of Northumbria) was begun in 1165, the *Libellus de admirandis Beati Cuthberti* was written c. 1167–mid-1170s, and the *Vita Godrici* was largely completed before the saint died but was clearly supplemented with other material and posthumous miracles up to at least 1181. Reginald has also been credited with the *Vita* of St Æbbe and a so-called 'Irish' *De ortu* of St Cuthbert, but the evidence is against such an attribution: Coombe, 'Reginald of Durham's Latin Life', pp. 188–202.

was nowhere to be seen, until someone spotted a fox running through the clearing with the cheese in its mouth. Reginald then explained that, in the local dialect, a fox is known as a 'tod'. The inference is clear: the 'tod' was a thief and a glutton. At the time Reginald was writing, monks surnamed Tod remained very much in evidence in Durham.[12]

At the same time, Reginald also sought approbation and perhaps preferment from Bishop Hugh du Puiset. His preface to the life of Godric, with its dedication to the Bishop, is a masterpiece of flattery:

> cum ceteri per Angliam episcopi de terrenis lucris uel commodis habeant transitorie gloriari, uobis singulariter donatum est a Christo de sanctarum cetu animarum profusius gratulari, quas uestris temporibus sub uestro imperio militantes cognouistis in celestibus ab ipso coronari.
>
> > (While the other bishops throughout England might find passing glory in lucrative and comfortable earthly pursuits, it has been granted by Christ to you alone greatly to rejoice in that host of holy souls, fighting in your times and under your command, whom you knew had been crowned by him in the heavens).[13]

It is, however, in his life of St Oswald that Reginald signalled the root cause of his personal dissatisfaction. This text was poorly edited for the Rolls Series and has been little studied, yet it offers a major clue to Reginald's motive in writing and to the way in which it should be read. Research indicates that Reginald most likely arrived in Durham from Coldingham in the company of a colleague, Henry, who had been appointed sub-prior on the death of Prior Roger, probably in 1149.[14] Both Roger and Lawrence, Roger's successor as prior, had been sub-prior before promotion, but the three priors that followed Roger were not.[15] Henry seems to have remained sub-prior during all that time. Reginald was clearly not pleased when Henry was passed over for preferment on no fewer than three occasions, and when he finally put quill to parchment in 1165, the last of these occasions, to write his life of St Oswald, he set out his ambition for his colleague. The preface contains a great deal of praise for Henry, beginning with a dedicatory sentence in the form of a riddle. The

---

12 Dobson, *Durham Priory*, p. 32; Reginald, *Libellus de admirandis Beati Cuthberti*, ed. by Raine, chap. 15, pp. 21–28 (cited hereafter as *Libellus Cuthberti*).

13 Reginald, *Vita Godrici*, § 1.

14 Roger was last documented *c.* 1148: *Durham Episcopal Charters*, ed. by Offler, no. 38.

15 Roger appears as sub-prior in July 1127: *Durham Episcopal Charters*, ed. by Offler, p. 97. He succeeded Algar as prior in 1137x38 (BL, MS Cotton Claudius D.IV, fol. 73ʳ) and is said to have died in 1148x49 (BL, MS Cotton Claudius D.IV, fol. 79ʳ); certainly before 1152 (*Durham Episcopal Charters*, ed. by Offler, no. 36a). Laurence, sub-prior on 14 November 1147 (*Durham Episopal Charters*, ed. by Offler, no. 36), is said to have succeeded Roger *c.* 1149 (BL, MS Cotton Claudius D.IV, fol. 79ᵛ) and died in France between February and May 1154 (Geoffrey, *Historiae Dunelmsis scriptores tres*, ed. by Raine, p. 6; Reginald, *Vita Godrici*, § 219). Subsequent priors Absalom (1154–1158), Thomas (1158x1161–1162), and Germanus (1163–1189) are not named as sub-prior in any document.

dedication reads: 'Venerabili in Christo domino et patri Henrico quondam Dunelmensium suppriori Reginaldus suus secundi nominis caput abscidere et quod residuum fuerit temporibus felicibus obtinendo possidere'[16] (To the venerable lord and father in Christ, Henry, formerly sub-prior of Durham, his Reginald, (wishing that) he cut off the head of his second name and possess that which will then remain by getting it in happier times). Thomas Arnold, the Rolls Series editor, considered that this was Reginald's way of identifying himself as the second monk of Durham to be so called ('Reginaldus secundi nominis'), losing the intended impact of the riddle. What it in fact indicates is that the reader should delete the first part of Henry's title of sub-prior (so, delete 'sub'), leaving 'prior' which is what Reginald wished his friend might have become in 'happier times'.

Henry's influence may well extend rather further. The *Vita* frequently mentioned that a key influence on Godric was the priest who came to say Mass for him. It is likely that this was Henry and that some of the events described in Reginald's text were penned by him. This surely makes sense in the context of twelfth-century Durham. The monastery had many competent writers and it was commonplace for one writer to take up where another had left off in keeping the history of Durham up to date. It was also commonplace in twelfth-century hagiography for reliable external testimonies to be sought, especially later in the century when official canonizations began to demand more independent evidence of sanctity.

It also makes more sense of the text itself. Reginald's *Vita* of Godric has been described as internally contradictory and repetitive. Throughout the *Vita* there are two distinct writing styles, and I would suggest that some of the apparently duplicated stories represent two different versions of the same events. For example, the events surrounding Godric's death are described in detailed and emotional terms which could only have been written by someone present at the time.[17] Yet, equally emotionally, the text describes an absent monk learning in a dream about Godric's imminent death but arriving at Finchale after the burial, too late to say goodbye.[18] While it is clear that Reginald, Godric's carer, was the principal author of the life, he also collected stories, from, as he says, 'ueridicis uiris [...] qui his forte intererant, seu qui ea de illo audierant' (reliable men [...] who had either been present when the events happened or who had heard these things from him).[19] One of these reliable men was probably Henry.

As sub-prior of Durham, Henry would have had some responsibility for Durham hermits, perhaps to a greater extent than might have been usual.[20]

---

16 Symeon, *Symeonis monachi*, ed. by Arnold, I, p. 362 n. a.
17 Reginald, *Vita Godrici*, § 306, 311–13.
18 Reginald, *Vita Godrici*, § 302–04.
19 Reginald, *Vita Godrici*, § 6.
20 Tom Licence sets out in detail the question of supervision of hermits with particular reference to Godric: Licence, 'The Benedictines, the Cistercians'.

When Godric decided to live according to a religious rule, he submitted himself to the authority of the priors of Durham 'quia in proximo erant, et beati Cuthberti, quem ipse specialiter diligebat, thesaurarii, filii et ministri exsistebant', (because they were nearby and because they were the treasurers, sons and servants of blessed Cuthbert, to whom he was especially devoted).[21] Prior Germanus, quoted in a subsequent life of Godric by Geoffrey of Coldingham,[22] added that this occurred at an early date when Prior Roger was still alive. If this is accurate, then Godric had come under the guidance of the priory before 1149. The next prior, Lawrence, would have wanted to maintain contact with the hermit, but have been unable to do so from around 1152: he went to Rome in 1153 to seek papal confirmation of Hugh du Puiset's appointment as bishop, and died in France in March 1154 on his way back to Durham.[23] Although it was the bishop's legal responsibility to look after hermits in his diocese, it is likely that the sub-prior would have been charged with such duties in the absence of both bishop and prior.[24]

Cultural Ambiguity and Flexibility in the *Vita*

Although Reginald emphasized only how Godric benefitted from his submission to Durham spiritually, there may well have been other motives present in the prior's mind.[25] Licence comments:

> Anxious that the Cistercians were making inroads into the priory's long-standing monopoly of authority, Prior Roger [...] sought to prevent his rivals from using Finchale as a suitable location for founding the first Cistercian abbey in the county by taking control of the hermitage himself.[26]

I would argue that, aware of this, and thwarted in his ambitions, Reginald drafted culturally flexible hagiographies. Those of Oswald and Cuthbert, lengthy and based on traditional information, appear to have attracted little

---

21 Reginald, *Vita Godrici*, § 127.

22 Piper, 'Coldingham, Geoffrey of'. Germanus's date of death is 'c. 1189' in BL, MS Cotton Claudius D.IV, fol. 84ᵛ. See n. 30 below.

23 Rigg, 'Durham, Lawrence of'.

24 In 1228, an agreement, 'Le Convenit', was drawn up between the bishop of Durham and the prior of the monastery, defining the relationship between them. The list of the witnesses on the prior's side in 'Le Convenit' includes the then sub-prior, also a Henry who dealt with John the hermit of Yereshale; clearly matters of hermitage landholdings came or could come under the aegis of the sub-prior: *Charters of Endowment of the Priory of Finchale*, ed. by Raine, p. 279.

25 Godric adopted a rule of silence, only received those visitors allowed by the monks, and moderated his austere practices. Consequently, Prior Roger was allegedly visited in a vision by the Devil who complained that, under Roger's guidance, Godric had become much less gullible and easy to tempt: Reginald, *Vita Godrici*, §§ 127–29, 84, and the same story in Geoffrey, *Vita Godrici*, chap. 4.

26 Licence, 'The Benedictines, the Cistercians', p. 317.

local attention. That of Godric, a new saint of lowly origins with no historic links to Durham, was different. This is not to say that the life is *structurally* very different from any other hagiography. There are at the beginning many elements from the life of Christ and, later, from the life of St Anthony, which form a traditional framework for the text. There are also elements of continuity with Durham's past in the frequent references to the monastic calendar there and to St Cuthbert, and many turns of phrase from Bede. It is, however, possible to discern throughout the text signs that Godric's identity is treated flexibly, and frequent suggestions that these links with Durham's past are open to re-negotiation.

Far more so than in the *vitae* of Oswald and Cuthbert, there is a strong consciousness of Godric's local physical terrain, constructing him as a versatile figure of nature rather than culture. Some of this consciousness draws upon the pagan past: there are traces of old buildings at Finchale, and Godric is attacked by demons with English-sounding names. The natural world is similarly ambiguous. Godric's fights with wild animals, fire and flood, and his expulsion of snakes, all hint at his ability to appropriate the land to himself unaided by Durham. While attempts to prevent Godric from leading a virtuous life are an important aspect of these struggles, the attacks and his misfortunes are very clearly tied to the saint's actual location. When Godric arrives there, he finds all manner of obstructions — wolves, snakes, thorns and weeds — and later, incursion by Scots, hunters, and robbers. These suggest a struggle not merely for his soul but also for his territory. Reginald is at pains to say that Godric lived at Finchale for sixty years and left the hermitage only three times for local trips early in his career there. His territory was frequently contested but he was able to conquer it physically and spiritually by building on the land and cultivating it, and by establishing his mother, sister, and brother there. He stamped his spiritual mark on the area by receiving frequent visitations from St John the Baptist and the Virgin Mary, his two personal saintly protectors. While still alive, Godric hewed his own tomb out of solid rock at Finchale, and when he died, unlike his hermit friend, Ælric, many years before, he was buried in the hermitage, not taken to Durham as would befit a member of the community, thus establishing posthumous control of the area and giving new meaning to the land as holy ground.

The Contemporary Reception of the *Vita*

Uncertain of the way in which the *Vita* would be received, and whether he would achieve his aim of promoting himself and his companion, Reginald took care to shelter behind the words of Godric to avoid completely alienating his colleagues. This latter point can be inferred from Reginald's description of the reception Godric gave to the writing of his life story. On the day in Lent 1170 described in the opening paragraph above, Reginald had completed all his tasks and was about to go back to Durham, because all the monks had to be present for the communal feast of the Last Supper.[27] He looked in on Godric, and perhaps fearing that the old man would die before he could return, shyly asked a favour: Godric's blessing on his book, which was almost complete. Reginald thought he had successfully concealed the nature of his project so, when asked what it was, he told Godric that it was the book of the life of a holy man who would present an example to other men. The saint blessed it but revealed that he knew what Reginald had been writing, and made him swear not to share it until after Godric's death. The monk blushed, embarrassed.

Astonishment and dismay were added to embarrassment when, handing back the book, Godric said to Reginald,

> Adhuc tamen dies superuenient in quibus a nonnullis tibi emulantibus aspera et satis amara uerba pro his auditurus es. Sed cum illa hora peruenerit, memento ne pro his in aliquo mouearis, quia ueritas manum tuam in his omnibus precessit […]. Post dies uero multos […] quod predixerat impleretur.[28]

> > (The days will come in which you will hear some very harsh and sharp words from some of your rivals on account of this (i.e. Reginald's version of Godric's life). But when that hour shall come, remember that you should in no way be upset on account of these, because the truth has guided your hand in all things […]. After many days, […] that which he had predicted was fulfilled.)

Having already said that he had relied on 'reliable men' for first-hand testimony, Reginald also claimed that, at the end of every visit to Godric, he rushed away to record the exact words of the saint: 'quotidie […] membranulis commendaueram […] eadem uerba que dixerat eodem tenore quo illa explicauerat scriptis inserere contendebam' (I committed to these little pages every day […] whatever of value that I learned from his holy lips […] in the very words which he uttered).[29] Dissemination of his text after Godric's death would mean that critics would be unable to interrogate the saint, originator of the stories. Reginald would also be able to distance himself from the content of the text of Godric's life.

Godric died in May 1170, a couple of months after the blessing of the book had taken place. There is no record of what people said about Reginald in the immediate aftermath, but within a very few years another *Vita* of Godric had been written by an unidentified Walter.[30] In the preface to his text, without mentioning Reginald by name, Walter declared that he had abbreviated an existing work on Godric because it was 'operis tediosa prolixitas, ordinis

---

27 Reginald, *Vita Godrici*, §§ 298–99.

28 Reginald, *Vita Godrici*, § 299.

29 Reginald, *Vita Godrici*, § 297.

30 The *Vita* by Walter can be found in CUL, MS Add. 3037; BL, MS Harley 322, and in two copies in BnF, MS Latin 11784.

turbata peruersitas, significationum et constructionum non satis obseruata proprietas'[31] (of tedious length in its execution, of perverse disorder in its sequence, and of insufficient accuracy in its meaning and construction). Walter's writing of Godric's life suggests that he was an opponent of Reginald but was also keen to promote Godric as worthy of veneration. If so, he can perhaps be counted among those eager to establish Godric's relationship more firmly with Durham and the monks. A third version of Godric's life was later written by a Durham monk named Geoffrey who had met Godric when he was a very young boy and Godric a very old man.[32] This *Vita*, probably produced to mark the establishment of a new priory at Finchale in 1196, drew heavily on Reginald's work but also included some extracts from writings by Germanus, prior of Durham from 1163 to 1189. It seems to have sought to establish Godric almost as a lay brother of Durham, who submitted to their care and counsel at an early date. While Reginald was careful to note that this submission was Godric's choice and that he was 'exinde sibi doctores accersiens' (inviting them to be his teachers from that time forward), Geoffrey's vocabulary ('subjecit' and 'accepit') suggests that Godric felt under some obligation to seek spiritual guidance or perhaps to consider an offer from Durham to oversee his religious life.[33] Godric's early submission makes the establishment of Finchale Priory appear an obvious move rather than the controversial matter it seems to have been.

By also naming many of Godric's contacts with other religious houses such as Rievaulx, Newminster, Westminster, and Canterbury, and emphasizing his extreme asceticism, humanity, and openness to guests, Reginald wrote a life calculated to appeal widely. However, it also contains a veiled threat, warning that the men in white who surrounded Godric's deathbed would try to appropriate him: were they angels, or Cistercians?[34] Godric was after all well-known in Cistercian circles and had especially close contact with Aelred of Rievaulx. Certainly, there seems to have been sufficient doubt after Godric's death about the future ownership of his hermitage for a letter to be procured from the pope confirming the site to the Durham monks.[35] The monks also forged their own charter to the effect that Bishop Ralph Flambard had granted the land to Godric on condition that it revert to Durham after his death.[36] There was also the worry that the Augustinian canons might take it over. In

---

31 BL, MS Harley 322, fol. 36ʳ.

32 Geoffrey, *Vita Godrici*, 'Preface'. Geoffrey's *Vita Godrici* is found in BL, MS Royal 5 F.VII; Winchester Cath. Lib., MS 10; Dijon, Bibl. Publ., MS 657; BnF, MS Latin 11784 (alongside those by Walter in the same manuscript); Oxford, Bodl. Lib., MS Fairfax 6; BL, MS Cotton Galba A.XVII; BL, MS Lansdowne 436.

33 Geoffrey, *Vita Godrici*, chap. 4.

34 Reginald, *Vita Godrici*, § 306.

35 *Papsturkunden*, ed. by Holtzmann, II. p. 405; Tudor, 'Reginald of Durham and St Godric', p. 371; Tudor, 'Durham Priory', p. 77.

36 *Durham Episcopal Charters*, ed. by Offler, pp. 68–71.

1189, Henry (the natural son of Bishop Hugh du Puiset) had endowed their settlement at Baxterwood, a few miles away, and was persuaded only after his father's death in 1195 to make a new arrangement with them to transfer Baxterwood land to Finchale as a new Benedictine house.[37]

The *Vita*'s cultural flexibility can also be seen in the breadth of later responses to it, a flexibility which has perhaps been obscured by more recent comments. Practices such as pilgrimages and the visionary experiences of the saints attracted opprobrium both at the Reformation, and from classically educated Victorian scholars who were critical of credulous medieval texts and the Latin in which they were written. Reginald was dubbed a 'credulous collector of legends'[38] whose life of St Godric supported suspicions that the 'monks were not in their right minds at all',[39] and credited with a 'low scale' of intellect and a writing style 'not worse than that of his contemporaries'[40] who suffered from 'excessive credulity [...] the universal failing of the middle ages'.[41]

Since, both in the late twelfth century, and again more recently, commentators have generally agreed that Reginald's prose was poor, no one has been surprised that his *Vita* was unpopular. It is surprising, though, that Godric's original observation has attracted no attention.[42] If the unpopularity of Reginald's work really resided only in its literary style, Godric's prescient comment that it would not be well received would be astonishing. Godric could not be expected to have read its contents: Reginald was at pains to emphasize that the saint had no knowledge of Latin, apart from a couple of 'miraculous' episodes where he intuitively understood some clerics' conversation.[43] He knew the Lord's Prayer and the Creed, had picked up some hymns at the Durham boys' school and learned parts of the liturgical offices which the Durham monks performed for him at Finchale, but was certainly unable to read.[44] Godric's perception that Reginald's work would be shunned must have been due to what he knew of its content rather than because of any lack of literary value.

---

37 *English episcopal acta*, ed. by Snape, pp. 5–6; Licence, 'The Benedictines, the Cistercians'; Page and Cooke ed., *Victoria History of the County of Durham*, II. p. 109.
38 Reginald, *Libellus Cuthberti*, ed. by Raine, p. vii.
39 Kingsley, *The Hermits*, p. 314.
40 Kingsley, *The Hermits*, p. xi.
41 Kingsley, *The Hermits*, p. ix.
42 Even though it was promoted to prominence in the preface to Walter's *Vita Godrici*.
43 Reginald, *Vita Godrici*, § 170.
44 Reginald, *Vita Godrici*, §§ 103, 129, 277, 288.

The Reception of Reginald's *Vita Godrici* in Late Medieval England

That content, flexibly designed as we have seen, at least in part, to further Reginald's ambitions, was also packed with information about Godric's spirituality which enabled the text to appeal to a wide audience in the Middle Ages for many purposes. During his lifetime and posthumously Godric attracted the attention of high-ranking individuals. He corresponded with Archbishop Thomas Becket, was a friend of Aelred of Rievaulx, and was granted land in Lothian by Malcolm IV, king of Scotland.[45] He received a letter from the pope, Alexander III, late in his life (perhaps 1168x1169), requesting Godric's prayers for the then schismatic Church and offering to remember the hermit in his own prayers.[46] After his death, the Cistercian monks of Fountains Abbey included him in the history of their house written *c.* 1207, perhaps continuing to claim Godric as a saint who represented Cistercian asceticism and values.[47] He is mentioned in the *Vita* of Wulfric of Haselbury written by the Cistercian John of Ford, as a luminary of the church in England, alongside Sts Wulfric, Thomas Becket, and William of York.[48] Interestingly, all three English Cistercian monasteries for which a library list survives from this period — Meaux, Flaxley, and Fountains — had strong links with Godric. Flaxley had two copies of the life of Godric, one in Latin and one in French,[49] while an Anglo-French life, written by a cleric with firm links to Meaux, is now extant in a later copy in France.[50] According to the *Miraculis Godrici*, an exemplar was sent to Fountains to be copied there, and was decorated and illuminated in honour of the saint.[51] Locally, Godric appears to have been of great interest to a wide range of Yorkshire monastic chroniclers, not just Benedictines.[52] Further afield, he was known in Wales and Scotland. Towards the end of the twelfth century, Gerald of Wales mentions Godric in his

---

45 Reginald, *Vita Godrici*, § 327.

46 *Papsturkunden*, ed. by Holtzmann, III. p. 303.

47 *Memorials of Fountains*, ed. by Walbran, p. 60 and intro. p. xiii.

48 John, *Life of Wulfric*, trans. by Matarasso, p. 11 and intro. p. xvii.

49 Bell, *The Libraries of the Cistercians*, pp. 99 line 27, p. 101 line 71.

50 In Paris, Bibl. Mazarine, MS 1716. The Meaux Abbey library list, dating from 1410, has numerous volumes of saints' lives, but none mentions Godric by name: Bell, 'Books of Meaux Abbey'. For an edition of the French version, see Reginald, *Life of Godric: An Old French Version*, ed. by Coombe, Hunt, and Mouron.

51 Reginald, *Vita Godrici*, §§ 594–96.

52 Towards the end of the twelfth century, William of Newburgh mentions his meeting with the elderly ill saint: William, *Historia rerum Anglicarum*, ed. by Howlett, II. p. 20. Roger of Hoveden, writing after 1192, also gives a (largely inaccurate) summary of Godric's *Vita*: Roger, *Chronica*, ed. by Stubbs, I, p. 267; II, pp. 16–17. The *Chronicle* of Walter of Guisborough, using William of Newburgh as his source, and the *Vita* of St Robert of Newminster both include references to Godric: Walter, *Chronicle*, ed. by Rothwell, p. 62; Grosjean, 'Vita sancti Roberti', p. 355.

Gemma ecclesiastica, speaking admiringly of the saint's ascetic lifestyle.[53] He is also mentioned in the annals of Margam in Glamorgan, and the Chronicle of Melrose Abbey, daughter house of Rievaulx.[54]

Even more interesting is the discovery that knowledge of Godric spread to the south of England. The *Liber revelationum* of the Augustinian prior, Peter of Cornwall,[55] probably compiled 1200–1206, contains extensive, verbatim extracts from Reginald: 'Quidam monachus Raginaldus nomine de dunelmo qui et scriptor fuit uite sancti Godrici sancto uiro egrotanti ministrauit. Hic de eo ita scribit'. (A monk called Reginald of Durham, who was also the writer of the Life of St Godric, looked after the holy man when he was ill. He wrote this about him).[56] At St Albans, Roger of Wendover, writing his *Flores historiarum c.* 1215, and Matthew Paris, writing his *Chronica maiora*, appear to have used an exemplar containing Walter's version of the life of Godric. Manuscript copies of Paris's work contain many slightly different versions of the songs of Godric, whose origin is unclear. Matthew Paris's work reached Westminster Abbey before 1256, where a summary of Godric's *Vita* is thought to have been written. Godric's appeal nationally within religious houses can be seen through the wide dispersion of his secondary relics, not only to Durham, but also to Lichfield, Meaux, Waltham, St Albans, and Salisbury,[57] and his name appears in numerous liturgical calendars. Godric's fame also spread to France. He was mentioned in a chronicle of Clairvaux produced after 1192, suggesting that Clairvaux owned a copy of his *Vita*, while a manuscript of Geoffrey's *Vita Godrici* reached Cîteaux sometime after 1208.[58]

Godric's gift of foresight and his spiritual encounters with angels and devils seem to have resonated with medieval writers, some of whom, struck by Godric's fame as a visionary, gave him a fictitious role in their chronicles. In Book 3 of his *De principis instructione*, Gerald of Wales seems to have appropriated Godric to an anti-Henrician discourse: he depicts Godric

---

53 Gerald, *Opera*, ed. by Brewer, Dimock and Warner, II.

54 *Annales monastici*, ed. by Luard, I, p. 16; *Chronica de Mailros*, ed. by Stevenson, pp. 31, 38.

55 Prior of the Augustinian Priory of Holy Trinity, Aldgate, London, 1197–1221.

56 London, Lambeth Palace Library, MS Lambeth 51, fol. 181ra. In addition, the *Chronica Johannis de Oxenedes*, written in the late thirteenth century at St Benet of Hulme in Norfolk, drawing on the works of authors such as William of Malmesbury and Matthew Paris, mentions Godric: *Chronica*, ed. by Ellis, pp. 44, 62. There is also a small passage on Godric in French in *Le Livere de Reis de Britannie e le Livere de Reis de Engleterre*, a book of translated abridgements of extracts from well-known chroniclers such as Geoffrey of Monmouth and Florence of Worcester: *Livere de Reis*, ed. by Glover, p. 220.

57 For Durham relic lists, see York, York Minster Library, MS XVI.I.12; Durham, Durham Cathedral Library, MS B II 35; *Charters of Endowment*, ed. by Raine, pp. 425–35. For Lichfield: Lichfield Cathedral, MS o.1. For Meaux: BL, MS Cotton Vitellius C.V, fols 241^v–242^r. For St Albans: BL, MS Cotton Claudius E.IV fols 349^{r-v}. For Salisbury, Salisbury Cathedral Library, MS 148 fols 15^v–19^v. For Waltham: BL, MS Harley 3776, fols 31^r–35^v.

58 *Chronicon Clarevallense*, col. 1248; the Cîteaux manuscript is Dijon, Bibliothèque Publique, MS 657.

dreaming about King Henry II and his sons fouling an altar by urinating on it.[59] The thirteenth-century *Chronicon de Lanercost*, perhaps based on a chronicle by Richard of Durham, details Godric's supposed prophesy, not found in the *Vita*, that the Friars Minor would come to Newcastle.[60] It is not clear whether this arrival would have been welcomed by the Augustinian canons of Lanercost or not, but perhaps Godric was being used here to emphasize its inevitability and help legitimize the Franciscan presence in the north of England at the time.

Conclusion

This essay has agreed with the suggestion that a new cult is most commonly promoted at a time of crisis in the life of a community.[61] I argue that the Durham community suffered many crises, but that the crisis which gave rise to Reginald's *Vita Godrici* came about not so much because of the meteoric rise of the cult of Thomas Becket, momentous though that was, or because of any marked decline in the fortunes of St Cuthbert, but through the struggle for power and prestige locally in Durham. In particular, Reginald seems to have had a personal crisis arising from the thwarting of Henry's ambitions, and maybe those of Reginald himself, towards high office within the Benedictine priory. Angry with the Durham monks and friendly with the Cistercians and others, he wrote texts calculated to upset the monks and to hint at the possible establishment on Durham's doorstep of a religious house belonging to a competing order. Reginald appears to have been successful: unusually, the posthumous grant of Godric's hermitage land was made, not to the body of monks of Durham, but personally to Reginald and Henry.[62] No work which can with certainty be attributed to Reginald appears to have been written after his *Vita* of Godric, and it can be inferred that he was quite happy to lay down his quill in exchange for that living and to stay at Finchale until he died.

While Reginald then sank into relative obscurity, the cultural flexibility of his *Vita Godrici* gave Godric a wider afterlife than perhaps he might otherwise have had, appealing as it did to many later chroniclers. In his day and for a century or so after, he was lauded in many parts of England by different religious orders, had an international reach, and was appropriated to a variety of propagandist ideas. The decline in interest in him after the Reformation, apart of course from the Surtees Society's edition which nevertheless denigrates the quality of the *Vita*, simply mirrors the tastes and prejudices of those times.

---

59 Gerald, *Opera*, ed. by Brewer, Dimock, and Warner, VIII, p. 313.

60 *Chronicon de Lanercost*, ed. by Stevenson, pp. 269–79.

61 Hayward, 'Demystifying the Role of Sanctity', pp. 115–42.

62 *Charters of Endowment*, ed. by Raine, p. 21: 'dilectis filiis nostris, Reginaldo et Henrico, monachis Dunelmensibus, apud Finchale habitantibus' (Our beloved sons Reginald and Henry, Durham monks, now living at Finchale).

The twentieth century has seen a softening of the Victorian distaste for such works and it is now possible to reappraise and contextualize Godric. In the past century or so, growing popular attendances at Sunday schools and day schools have promoted the publication of compendia of stories of Jesus and the saints, emphasizing their gentleness and kindness to animals. Godric fits well within this ecological Christian ethos. The modern gate of an ancient well, a couple of late nineteenth-century schools, and a church in the Durham area are named for Godric,[63] while his role as a protector of stags and snakes, is highlighted in several books.[64] Lately, his appeal has widened to include versions for children, an association with Harry Potter, and a business version for City traders, which describes Godric as a 'twelfth-century monk reviled for his love of money', in order ultimately to compare him with Bill Gates.[65] There have even been novels[66] and, recently, a quantity of online sermons and recordings of Godric's songs.[67]

It has been said that 'saints' lives are both part of a genre of immense longevity and the products of individual circumstances'.[68] The work of Reginald of Durham, long criticized for its great length and lack of literary style, can be seen to have considerable value and importance to historians when viewed within his contemporary, frequently violent, context. Thanks to Reginald, his major subject, the poor sailor-turned-hermit Godric of Finchale, whose cult was once erroneously described as 'simple, local, unpretentious', and to whose tomb 'most people came from within forty miles of Finchale',[69] has had an extraordinarily flexible textual and musical afterlife.

---

63 The important and ancient holy well and well house are at Wolsingham, OS map ref: NZ 0766637882. The names of Godric and his hermit friend Ælric are written on the gate. There is no evidence of any connection with the hermits, who lived nearby. The schools and church are in or near Durham city and of late nineteenth-century foundation.

64 For example: Waddell, trans., *Beasts and Saints*, pp. 67–83; Gibbs and Robinson, *Saints Beyond the White Cliffs*, pp. 129–44; Ryder, *Animal Revolution*, p. 30, particularly mentions Godric of Finchdale (*sic*) releasing trapped birds; Stevens, *The One Year Book of Saints*, p. 158.

65 Godric and Harry Potter have been linked by many popular commentators, mostly online, on the basis of their relationships with stags and snakes, and the similarity between 'Godric's Hollow', the village where Harry Potter was born, and the place where Godric settled. For commercial similarities, see Means, *Money and Power*, p. 23.

66 Buechner, *Godric*; Hill, *Death's Jest-Book*.

67 Coombe, 'What a Performance', p. 219.

68 Bartlett, 'Rewriting Saints' Lives', p. 598.

69 Finucane, 'Posthumous Miracles', pp. 47–50.

Works Cited

Manuscripts and Archival Sources

Cambridge, Cambridge University Library, MS Add. 3037
Dijon, Bibliothèque publique, MS 657
Durham, Durham Cathedral Library, MS B II 35
Lichfield Cathedral, MS 0.1
London, British Library, MS Cotton Claudius D.IV
——, MS Cotton Claudius E.IV
——, MS Cotton Galba A.XVII
——, MS Cotton Vitellius C.V
——, MS Harley 322
——, MS Harley 3776
——, MS Lansdowne 436
——, MS Royal 5 F.VII
London, Lambeth Palace Library, MS Lambeth 51
Oxford, Bodleian Library, MS Fairfax 6
Paris, Bibliothèque nationale, MS Latin 11784
——, Bibliothèque Mazarine, MS 1716
Salisbury, Salisbury Cathedral Library, MS 148
Winchester, Winchester Cathedral Library, MS 10
York, York Minster Library, MS XVI.I.12

Primary Sources

Annales Monastici, ed. by Henry Richards Luard, Rolls Series, 36, 5 vols (London: Longman, 1864–9)
Buechner, Frederick, *Godric* (London: Chatto & Windus, 1981)
The Charters of Endowment, Inventories and Account Rolls of the Priory of Finchale, ed. by James Raine, SS, 6 (London: J. B. Nichols & Son, 1837)
Chronica Johannis de Oxenedes, ed. by Henry Ellis, Rolls Series, 13 (London: Longman, 1859)
Chronica de Mailros, ed. by Joseph Stevenson, Bannatyne Club (Edinburgh: Impressum Edinburgi, 1835)
Chronicon Clarevallense, in *Patrologia latina*, ed. by Jacques-Paul Migne, CLXXXV (Paris: Garnier, 1878–1890), cols 1247–52
Chronicon de Lanercost, ed. by Joseph Stevenson (Edinburgh: Typis Societatis Edinburgensis, 1839)
Durham Episcopal Charters, 1071–1152, ed. by Hilary S. Offler, SS, 179 (Gateshead: Northumberland Press, 1968)
English episcopal acta. 24, Durham, 1153–95, ed. by M. G. Snape (Oxford: Oxford University Press, 2002)
Geoffrey of Coldingham, *Vita S Godrici*, in *AASS, Maius V*, p. 68 ff.

Geoffrey of Coldingham, Robert de Graystanes, and William de Chambre, *Historiae Dunelmensis scriptores tres*, ed. by James Raine, SS, 9 (London: J. B. Nichols & Son, 1839)

Gerald of Wales, *Giraldi Cambrensis Opera*, ed. by John S. Brewer, James F. Dimock, and George F. Warner, Rolls Series, 21, 8 vols (London: Longman, 1861–1891)

Grosjean, Paul, ed., 'Vita Sancti Roberti novi monasterii in Anglia abbatis', *Analecta Bollandiana*, 56 (1938), 334–60

Hill, Reginald, *Death's Jest-Book* (London: Collins Crime, 2002)

John of Ford, *Wulfric of Haselbury*, ed. by Maurice Bell, Somerset Record Society, 47 (London: Printed for subscribers only, 1933)

——, *The Life of Wulfric of Haselbury, Anchorite*, trans. by Pauline Matarasso, Cistercian Fathers Series, 79 (Collegeville, MN: Cistercian Publications, Liturgical Press, 2011)

Le livere de reis de Brittaine e Le livere de reis de Engletere, ed. by John Glover, Rolls Series, 42 (London: Longman, 1865)

Memorials of the Abbey of St Mary of Fountains, ed. by John R. Walbran, SS, 42, 67, 130 (Durham: Andrews & Co., 1863–1918)

Papsturkunden in England, ed. by Walther Holtzmann, 3 vols (Berlin: Weidmannsche Buchhandlung, 1930–1952)

Reginald of Durham *Libellus de admirandis Beati Cuthberti virtutibus quae novellis patratae sunt temporibus*, ed. by James Raine, SS, 1 (London: J. B. Nichols & Son, 1835) (cited as *Libellus Cuthberti*)

——, *Reginald of Durham: The Life and Miracles of Saint Godric, Hermit of Finchale*, ed. and trans. by Margaret Coombe, Oxford Medieval Texts (Oxford: Oxford University Press, 2022) (cited as Reginald, *Vita Godrici*)

——, *Life of St Godric: An Old French Version*, ed. by Margaret Coombe, Tony Hunt, and Anne Mouron (Oxford: Anglo-Norman Text Society, 2019)

Roger of Hoveden, *Chronica magistri Rogeri de Houedene*, ed. by William Stubbs, Rolls Series, 51, 4 vols (London: Longman, 1868–1871)

Symeon of Durham, *Libellus de exordio procursu istius, hoc est Dunhelmensis, ecclesie*, ed. and trans. by David W. Rollason (Oxford: Clarendon Press, 2000)

——, *Symeonis monachi opera omnia*, ed. by Thomas Arnold, Rolls Series 75, 2 vols (London: Longman, 1882–1885)

Walter of Guisborough, *Chronicle of Walter of Guisborough*, ed. by Harry Rothwell, Camden Society 3rd series, 89 (London: Royal Historical Society, 1957)

William of Newburgh, *Historia rerum Anglicarum*, in *Chronicles of the Reigns of Stephen, Henry II, and Richard I*, ed. by Richard Howlett, Rolls Series, 82, 4 vols (London: Longman, 1884–1889), I

Secondary Works

Aird, William, *St Cuthbert and the Normans: The Church of Durham 1071–1153* (Woodbridge: Boydell, 1998)

Bartlett, Robert, 'Rewriting Saints' Lives: The Case of Gerald of Wales', *Speculum*, 58 (1983), 598–613

——, *England under the Norman and Angevin Kings, 1075–1225* (Oxford: Clarendon Press, 2000)

Bell, David, 'The Books of Meaux Abbey', *Analecta Cisterciensia*, 40 (1984), 25–83

——, ed., *The Libraries of the Cistercians, Gilbertines and Premonstratensians* (London: British Library, 1992)

Coombe, Margaret, 'Reginald of Durham's Latin Life of St Godric of Finchale: A Study' (unpublished doctoral thesis, University of Oxford, 2011)

——, 'What a Performance: The Songs of Godric of Finchale', in *Saints of North-East England, 600–1500*, ed. by Margaret Coombe, Anne Mouron, and Christiania Whitehead (Turnhout: Brepols, 2017), pp. 219–44

Dobson, R. B., *Durham Priory 1400–1450* (London: Cambridge University Press, 1973)

Finucane, Ronald C., 'Posthumous Miracles of Godric of Finchale', in *Transactions of the Architectural and Archaeological Society of Durham and Northumberland*, 3 (1974), 47–50

Gibbs, Margaret A., and Thomas Robinson, *Saints Beyond the White Cliffs: Stories of English Saints* (London: Hollis & Carter, 1947)

Hayward, Paul Anthony, 'Demystifying the Role of Sanctity in Western Christendom', in *The Cult of Saints in Late Antiquity and the Middle Ages: Essays on the Contribution of Peter Brown*, ed. by Paul A. Hayward and James Howard-Johnston (Oxford: Oxford University Press, 2000)

Kingsley, Charles, *The Hermits* (London: Macmillan, 1868)

Licence, Tom, 'The Benedictines, the Cistercians and the Acquisition of a Hermitage in Twelfth-Century Durham', *Journal of Medieval History*, 29.4 (2003), 315–29

Means, Howard, *Money and Power: The History of Business* (New York: Wiley, 2001)

Norton, Christopher, 'History, Wisdom and Illumination', in *Symeon of Durham, Historian of Durham and the North*, ed. by David W. Rollason (Stamford: Shaun Tyas, 1998), pp. 61–105

Page, William, and Gillian Cooke, ed., *Victoria History of the County of Durham*, 5 vols (London: Archibald Constable, 1905–)

Piper, A. J., 'Coldingham, Geoffrey of (d. *c.* 1215), Benedictine monk, chronicler, and probably hagiographer', *Oxford Dictionary of National Biography* (2004) <https://doi.org/10.1093/ref:odnb/16167> [accessed 9 Dec 2021]

Rigg, A. G., 'Durham, Lawrence of (*c.* 1110–1154)', *Oxford Dictionary of National Biography* (2004) <http://www.oxforddnb.com/view/article/16167> [accessed 16 March 2010]

Ryder, Richard, *Animal Revolution: Changing Attitudes towards Speciesism* (Oxford: Blackwell, 1989)

Scammell, Geoffrey Vaughn, *Hugh du Puiset, Bishop of Durham* (Cambridge: Cambridge University Press, 1956)

Stevens, Clifford J., *The One Year Book of Saints* (Huntington, IN: Our Sunday Visitor, 1989)

Tudor, Victoria, 'Reginald of Durham and St Godric of Finchale: A Study of a Twelfth-Century Hagiographer and his Major Subject' (unpublished doctoral thesis, University of Reading, 1979)

——, 'Durham Priory and its Hermits in the Twelfth Century', in *Anglo-Norman Durham 1093–1193*, ed. by David Rollason, Margaret Harvey, and Michael Prestwich (Woodbridge: Boydell, 1994), pp. 67–78

Waddell, Helen, trans., *Beasts and Saints* (London: Constable, 1934, repr. London: Darton, Longman and Todd, 1995)

JOSHUA S. EASTERLING

Robert of Knaresborough, Religious Novelty, and the Twelfth-Century Poverty Movement

In his *Chronica maiora* the Benedictine monk Matthew Paris (d. 1259) celebrates a number of 'new saints' who were flourishing in thirteenth-century England (*novi sancti clarent in Anglia*).[1] His naming of the Yorkshire hermit Robert of Knaresborough (d. 1218) along with other religious luminaries is especially felicitous in view of the decisive turn in the hermit's spiritual vocation. After loosening his connections with two separate monastic communities and adopting the life of a hermit, Robert began to associate with *pauperes* and beggars in charitable service to their needs — a move for which there was no real precedent within the eremitic tradition, at least in England.[2] That Robert attracted a number of devotees, who apparently remained under his guidance until his death, places the hermit both historically and ascetically alongside other charismatics across thirteenth-century religious culture. The innovations brought by such figures were exemplified most famously in the poverty movement led by Robert's contemporary Francis of Assisi (d. 1226).

Multifaceted and less ascetically uniform than the designation 'hermit' implies, Robert's turbulent career as presented in the hagiographical record expresses a cultural dialectic between religious traditions and novelty.[3] The

---

1 For the date of Robert's death, 24 Sept. 1218, see *Chronicon*, ed. by Stevenson, p. 25, and Matthew Paris, *Chronica*, pp. 378 and 195, for the years 1240 and 1250, respectively. For discussion, see Vauchez, *Sainthood*, pp. 112 and 176 n. 62.

2 Like Richard Rolle (d. 1349) after him, Robert extended the grand lineage of northern English eremitism. See esp. Burton, *Monastic Order*, pp. 23–44; Burton, 'The Eremitical Tradition', pp. 18–39, and Tudor, 'Durham Priory', pp. 67–78. See also Licence, *Hermits and Recluses*, pp. 43–66; Clay, *Hermits and Anchorites*, pp. 40–44. Extending from the hermit-bishop Cuthbert (d. 687), this northern tradition is crowned in the fourteenth century by the hermit-mystic Richard Rolle. See *Two Lives*, ed. by Colgrave, and *Officium et miracula*, ed. by Woolley, p. 23 ff. See also Clayton, 'Hermits and the Contemplative Life', pp. 152–56.

3 On the culture and reforms of monastic and eremitic life across the twelfth century, see Leyser, *Hermits*; Grundmann, *Religious Movements*, esp. pp. 1–74, 203–36; Burton, 'Reform or

---

Joshua S. Easterling (jeasterling@murraystate.edu) is Assistant Professor in the Department of English and Philosophy at Murray State University, Kentucky, USA.

Late Medieval Devotion to Saints from the North of England: New Directions, ed. by Christiania Whitehead, Hazel J. Hunter Blair, and Denis Renevey, MCS 48 (Turnhout: Brepols, 2022), pp. 217–235

BREPOLS ❧ PUBLISHERS   10.1484/M.MCS-EB.5.124351

dynamic interplay between tradition — both eremitic and monastic — and Robert's own idiosyncratic innovations is presented in the Middle English and Latin *vitae* of British Library, MS Egerton 3143 (s.xv), where the unfolding of his life appears far more deeply marked by innovation and cultural rupture than by an adherence to long-standing practices and institutions.[4] Meanwhile, across the twelfth century both religious and secular elites frequently defended established traditions often by attacking the countervailing force of 'novelties' that were introduced by hermits, wandering preachers, and others. Robert's career is centrally relevant here. In her landmark treatment of the subject, Beryl Smalley demonstrated the widespread emergence of religious novelty throughout twelfth- and thirteenth-century religious culture, as well as a concomitant hostility on the part of local elites toward such innovations.[5] At the same time, critical analyses of eremitic writings in England have yet to explore such tensions, or the implications they hold for our understanding of English hermits in their social and cultural contexts.[6]

This essay situates Robert alongside mainstream ideals that sought to negotiate the difficult terrain between tradition and unity, on the one hand, and religious 'novelty' on the other. Composed under the aegis of the Trinitarian order in England, the Latin *Vita sancti Roberti Knaresburgensis* (hereafter *Vita*) and a Middle English verse narrative *De vita et conversacione Sancti Roberti* (hereafter *Life*) show Robert's pursuit of a distinct form of asceticism that mirrors the poverty movements then emergent on the continent.[7] In this connection, Robert's varied career forms an intrinsic part of his identity as a hermit, which at the same time represents an innovative response to local ascetic traditions within the twelfth-century culture of reform and spiritual renewal. An expression of the rapid and, at times, novel currents within religious culture, the mendicant turn that marked the final decades of the twelfth century represents an important context for the local community of the socially disadvantaged, or *pauperes*, that formed around Robert. I read this investment in religious poverty alongside the like-minded culture that

---

Revolution'; Constable, *Reformation*, and Constable, *Three Studies*, pp. 1–141. See also Jestice, *Wayward Monks*.

4 On Robert and the contents of BL, MS Egerton 3143, see also Easterling, 'A Norbert for England', 75–107. Although never canonized, Robert retained the status of saint throughout the later Middle Ages. A Trinitarian priory existed at Knaresborough, where Robert was venerated, by 1255 at the latest. See *Metrical Life*, ed. by Bazire, pp. 17–21. On the Trinitarian order, see Deslandres, *L'Ordre des Trinitaires*; Gray, *The Trinitarian Order*; and, most recently, Flannery, 'Trinitarian Order', 135–44.

5 Smalley, 'Ecclesiastical Attitudes', pp. 113–31.

6 However, see Burton, 'The Eremitical Tradition'. On twelfth-century English hermits, see also Licence, *Hermits and Recluses*.

7 The Latin *Vita* and Middle English *Life* of Robert are edited in *The Metrical Life of St Robert*, ed. by Bazire, pp. 113–28 and 42–81 respectively. For discussion of these movements, see Grundmann, *Religious Movements*, pp. 31–138; Constable, *Reformation*, and Milis, 'Hermits and Regular Canons', pp. 181–246.

was emerging on the continent through Francis of Assisi and the *Humiliati* in Italy, and the early Trinitarians in France.

I argue that Robert emerges in these writings not as a founder of a new religious order, or as having abandoned the eremitic tradition, but as the embodiment of the nuanced and complex interactions between tradition and novelty, rather than a cut-and-dried image of one or the other. Robert stands as far more than a mere projection by later mendicant, and specifically Trinitarian, promoters of his cult. Even if no hagiographical text was without its elements of partisan bias, neither were medieval saints created *ex nihilo* by later devotions, which often sought in their subjects evidence of the virtues embraced by a later foundation or monastic order. The cultural and textual continuities that shaped religious currents in the long twelfth century eventually left their mark on the late fifteenth-century contents of BL, MS Egerton 3143. These do not represent an historical back-reading intended to align an otherwise traditional hermit with the innovations of the poverty movements on the continent. Rather, I suggest that it went the other way around — that Robert was part of a widespread and ascetic reorientation toward the life of poverty, and that this was recognized by later writers who saw in him a forbearer of thirteenth-century mendicancy. While his *vitae* associate Robert with the eremitic tradition, they also witness to the complex ways in which he both affirmed and altered that same culture by expressing in his asceticism an emergent set of attitudes and practices that involved direct association with beggars and the poor.

Novelty and Hermits in the Twelfth Century

One defining feature of twelfth-century religious culture was a deep hostility to perceived novelties, as these exerted pressure on established customs and practices. As demonstrated in Smalley's study and more recently by Stephen Jaeger, that hostility made little distinction between innovations in the social, religious, or intellectual arenas.[8] Orthodox elites and secular authorities resisted such developments in part because of the 'disorder' that supposedly attended new cultural formations.[9] However, what generated such resistance was in fact an inextricable aspect of reform, and few (if any) religious communities, including those involving hermits or would-be hermits, escaped the effects of a rapidly changing and reforming religious culture.[10] These effects included, *inter alia*, a desire for ascetic rigour that drove monks, hermits, and others from otherwise thriving communities to pursue new forms of living; opposition to such developments, including the perception

---

8 Jaeger, *Envy of Angels*, esp. pp. 219–23, 365–66.
9 Smalley, 'Ecclesiastical Attitudes', p. 113.
10 Leyser, *Hermits*, pp. 18–37.

that they amounted to unwelcome novelties, represented, at another level, the 'growing pains' of a culture in transition.[11]

When twelfth-century hermits across Europe left their communities, or groups of monks abandoned one community in order to establish another, that act of relinquishing an established form of living allowed for the emergence of something new, but it was also potentially disruptive.[12] Some traditionalists, however, were at times capable of defending this redrawing of spiritual and cultural boundaries by suggesting a negotiation between the emergent and the familiar, between novelty and authority. Written shortly before the mid-twelfth century in the diocese of Liège, the *Libellus de diversis ordinibus* describes the necessity of relaxing strictures so as to guard tradition and ecclesial unity, and 'ita nova condere, ut ex novitate antiqua partum auctoritas non violetur'[13] (so to establish what is new that the ancient authority of the fathers not be violated through novelty). For the author of the *Libellus*, likely a regular canon, ancient *auctoritas* and contemporary innovation were indeed compatible, indeed were mutual aspects of genuine and ardent spirituality. Despite similar appeals to antiquity, Stephen of Muret (d. 1124) was accused of corrupting tradition in establishing the new order at Grandmont. At times such communities themselves experienced panic and crises of identity, as Caroline Walker Bynum noted.[14] Yet what were decried as novelties in fact represented a creative tension between tradition and innovation, as well as 'changing religious mentalities' across social ranks.[15] Above all, novelty in religious life emanated both from the magnetic allure of a new foundation or guiding figure, as well as from a dissatisfaction on the part of such figures with established institutions.[16]

These patterns are mirrored in the career of Robert of Knaresborough. Pursuing personal and ascetic reform prior to and independent of monastic guidance, and often in association with lay culture, Robert first severed ties with monastic houses before eventually associating with the poor, or *pauperes*, much in keeping with similar movements earlier in the century. In this way, Robert resembles Godric of Finchale (d. *c.* 1170), who pursued the life of renunciation while retaining often close ties with the laity, although Robert would take this association to new heights and extremes.[17] Godric's

---

11 Constable, 'Controversy and Compromise', p. 145.

12 Before the pioneering study by Leyser, *Hermits*, the ways in which the monastic and eremitic traditions in England and abroad mutually shaped each other went largely unexamined; see Knowles, *Religious Orders*; Dauphin, 'L'Érémitisme en Angleterre', pp. 271–303.

13 *Libellus*, ed. by Constable and Smith, p. 36. See also n. 53 in this essay.

14 In a letter addressed to Hildegard of Bingen (d. 1179), the (presumably male) members of a religious community (of canons?) wrote: 'Who are we? We do not follow the Benedictine Rule; we have our own customs; we are being attacked. Can you please tell us what a monk is anyway?' Quoted in Bynum, *Jesus as Mother*, p. 32.

15 Gilchrist, *Contemplation and Action*, p. 157.

16 On this disaffection and the polemical battles that it generated, see Constable, *Reformation*.

17 Reginald, *Libellus de vita et miraculis Vita Godrici*, ed. by Stevenson, p. 33 (cited hereafter as

Benedictine hagiographer Reginald of Durham remarks at the opening to the *Vita* that 'Cunctorum animos novitas aliqua succendit ad stuporem' (Any novelty (*novitas*) inflames the minds of all people with amazement).[18] This emergent lay spirituality also guided the reflections by Bernard of Clairvaux (d. 1153) on the Knights Templar in his *De laude novae militiae*.[19] Indeed, as Beryl Smalley observes, 'the first breakthrough on the question of religious novelties came from Cistercian circles'.[20] That both Reginald and Bernard discovered elements in certain novelties which might nonetheless be praised (rather than criticized) argues once again that at least some within Benedictine and Cistercian monasticism were able to give a positive appraisal of such figures.

Thus as a revision to established religious formations, and a perceived disruption to otherwise secure boundaries, novelty represented a challenge to contemporary means of drawing the lines between lay and clerical (or monastic) culture. At times, that challenge involved the activities that Robert himself pursued, including itineracy and preaching.[21] In this, he resembles another newcomer to the religious life, Norbert of Xanten (d. 1134), founder of the Premonstratensian order, and a figure with whom the author of Robert's *Vita* associates him.[22] Most important, however, was his eventual and close contact with the poor, which represented a radical shift in spiritual and social emphases. Here Robert has much in common with twelfth-century Italian hermit saints, several of whom became figures of voluntary poverty and charity, as Mary Doyno has shown.[23] However, by the close of the twelfth century in England, Yorkshire could boast no such saints — except of course for Robert. In all, as cultural identities destabilized over the course of the twelfth century, the hermit came to rework contemporary realities since he appeared to inhabit a new ascetic space altogether.

Challenging Tradition: Robert among the New Hermits

As innovators in religious life grew largely disaffected with those realities and sought change, they became the subject of opposing judgments that lauded such developments as radically traditional, or maligned them as precisely

---

Vita Godrici). In fact, before living as a hermit, Godric spent decades in secular society as a merchant and effectively had no ties to monastic culture, or its reformist ideals.

18 Reginald, *Vita Godrici*, ed, by Stevenson, p. 17.

19 Bernard, *Opera*, ed. by Leclercq, III, pp. 120–39. He explores the identity of the Knights Templar who were neither laymen nor monks in the strict sense, but represented a new cultural formation. See Smalley, 'Ecclesiastical Attitudes', p. 121; Newman, *Boundaries*, p. 185.

20 Smalley, 'Ecclesiastical Attitudes', p. 123.

21 On the problem of itineracy and regulating the eremitic life, see Hanna, 'Will's Work', pp. 23–66.

22 See below, pp. 227–31.

23 Doyno, *The Lay Saint*. For discussion of religious novelty in twelfth- and thirteenth-century Italian communities, see Rossi, 'Religiones novae', pp. 215–43.

the opposite — corrupt inventions. Defenders found much to praise in the desire for renewed ascetic rigour, for example among the Cistercians. This new solicitude for the disciplined ascetic body, however, was also suspect; it was out of line with traditional customs, potentially excessive, and ostentatious.[24] In brief, it smacked of novelty and elicited calls for moderation.

Robert's disciplines, while praised by his later hagiographers, also brought detractions from his contemporaries and showed a limited toleration for ascetic singularity. The *Life* opens with a description of his ascetic practices prior to entering the monastic life (ll. 67–70). The passage is followed by the intriguing observation and defence of his conduct: 'That tyme nane toke hym wyth trispas; / Off the Haly Gast fulfilled he was' (ll. 70–72). The Middle English term 'trispas' refers to legal or moral violations.[25] The former meaning clearly does not fit the image of his ascetic rigours. On the other hand, the possibility that these constituted a form of moral trespass presupposes that they were (or might be) perceived in a negative light. When undertaken with charismatic vigour, particularly within a monastic context that calls for conformity rather than singularity, ascetic practices are, of course, trespasses in a very real sense. Once Robert enters his first monastic house, the Cistercian foundation of Newminster, his asceticism is decidedly out of place. He is warmly greeted by a fellow brother, who reminds him of this fact:

> Faythfully þan spake the frere
> And sayd, 'Robertt, welcom her.
> The rewle of this religioune
> To proffer ytt wyth perfeccioune,
> Wyth other obseruaunce perfyte,
> Dresse the, Robertt, wyth delyte,
> By the counsayll of collacioune,
> To com to contemplacioune'. (*Life*, ll. 105–12)

Robert is told to assimilate to monastic customs, not to engage in ascetic curiosities that set him apart from the community. He is to follow the local customary ('rewle') and liturgical observances, avoiding practices that might be construed as innovative, singular, or otherwise disruptive of communal life ('collacioune'). Yet this is not to say that Robert is ultimately successful; he pursues 'heghe halynesse' (l. 115) and falls into ascetic extremes that elicit 'marvel' from others (l. 119). Toleration of such extremes clearly has its limits; in the end, Robert survives a mere four months at Newminster before leaving the community.

In one sense, Robert's behaviours are not entirely new, though they witness to a desire to expand beyond mainstream customs, and rank among many transitions during his extraordinary career. From the outset, Robert is caught

---

24 For discussion of this emergence, see Russell, 'Peter Damian's Whip', 20–35.

25 See *MED*, s.v. 'trispas' (sense 1 and 2). See also *Metrical Life*, ed. by Bazire, p. 80 (ll. 1302, 1311).

up in a push-and-pull between renouncing and assimilating to the cultural and religious mainstream. Although he initially intends to take orders as a priest, shortly after becoming a sub-deacon (*Vita*, 1.15–20; *Life*, ll. 89–92) he decides for the monastic life instead. He then joins the Cistercian house at Newminster, which, as we have just seen, he leaves after only a few months (*Vita*, 2.2–16; *Life*, ll. 97–128). He then resides for an unknown period in a cave at Knaresborough (*Vita*, 3.2–5; *Life*, ll. 139–52). After leaving the cave for a chapel dedicated to St Hilda (*Vita*, 3.11–19; *Life*, ll. 173–84), he again enters a monastery, the Benedictine house at Headley, which he later flees (*Vita*, 5.2–23; *Life*, ll. 215–40).[26] Robert's chronic tendency to flee from one monastery and hermitage to another is motivated in large part by a need for greater ascetic rigour, and by a charismatic flair that will eventually attract a devoted following. In this respect, his behaviour reads equally well as repeatedly aborted attempts to pursue a form of living that is neither identical nor entirely at odds with the life of the monk or hermit. It is above all a life of radical renunciation.

> Wyth the Haly Gast this man inspired
> *Nathyng* bott God in erth desyred […]
> *All thynge forsakand* þat he saw,
> *Nathyng* hym liked bott Goddys lawe.
> <div align="right">(<i>Life</i>, ll. 130–38, emphasis added)</div>

By renouncing the world and embracing 'nathyng', Robert left little room for traditional religious structures, which he remodelled in ways that were for the most part culturally uncharted. His behaviour is also noticeably out of alignment with the deep conservatism of English eremitic culture as it appears prior to and throughout the twelfth century.[27] In his actions, Robert is far more strongly reminiscent of the 'new hermits' on the continent, including his namesake Robert of Arbrissel (d. 1116), founder of Fontevrault, among others.[28] Like such reformers, moreover, Robert encounters both resistance as well as the (hagiographical) attempts by others to defend the forms of asceticism to which his life gave expression.

'Tanquam sidus nove claritatis': Resistance and Defence

The objections by traditionalists to emergent religious currents came from contemporaries more or less by definition. In the decades or centuries after movements and charismatic figures first began to flourish, these exemplars of a redefined tradition came to stand within rather than outside of its boundaries.

---

26 See Easterling, 'A Norbert for England', p. 76.

27 Tom Licence has written most extensively on this tradition: *Hermits and Recluses*; on the difficulties of textual survival, see Clayton, 'Hermits and the Contemplative Life', p. 157.

28 For discussion, see Leyser, *Hermits*, esp. pp. 18–20.

A separate Latin prose life, contained in British Library, MS Harley 3775, opens by celebrating its ascetic pioneer, praising Robert as shining forth 'tanquam sidus nove claritatis' (like a star of new radiance).[29] Like Reginald of Durham in his life of Godric, this biographer opens by extolling rather than excusing the newness of Robert's eremitism.

On the other hand, celebrations of the new hermits could only be taken so far, even by their own hagiographers; the charges of hypocrisy fell fast and thick, as these writers openly acknowledged. The accusation ran as follows: spurning or otherwise inhabiting the margins of mainstream (i.e. monastic) religious culture, these ascetic upstarts were mere hypocrites who had arrogated to themselves the name of 'hermit' to justify their corrupt lives and contempt for tradition. In Godric's case, this abuse was internalized and took the form of demonic visions: 'Tu te sanctum facis, cum non sis nisi hypocrita; et heremitam vocari te facis, cum omnis vita tua non sit nisi turpissima' (you make yourself holy, though you are nothing but a hypocrite; you have yourself called (*vocari*) a hermit, though yours is nothing but the filthiest life!).[30] In England as elsewhere, when novelties were not derided as such, the label of hypocrisy served just as well. The demon's point was that Godric's distinctive ascetic life was unrecognizable as a legitimate form of spirituality and so required a venerable designation (*heremita*) as cover.[31]

In Robert's case, the detractions expressed by defenders of the religious and social status quo were not inner and demonic but openly voiced and thoroughly human. At some point in his career, Robert faced persecution from a Yorkshire lord named William of Stuteville (d. *c.* 1203), who called for the hermit's expulsion.[32] In the Latin *vitae*, William's hostility is especially savage: 'O satellites, quantocius hunc Robertum ypocritam expellite; simul eius edificia funditus subvertite. Quod si exire contempserit, ipsum vivum ignibus curate concremare' (O attendants, as quickly as possible expel this Robert, hypocrite; totally destroy his dwellings at once. And if he refuses to leave, see that you burn him alive) (*Vita*, 8.17–19). William was not especially ill-disposed toward hermits. In fact, he would later become reconciled with Robert and even afford him patronage (*Vita*, 10.30–40; *Life*, ll. 439–82).[33] At work instead is the difficulty that William initially experienced in perceiving Robert as leading a viable spiritual vocation. By this point, Robert had long severed his monastic ties, and had begun to associate with *pauperes* and

---

29 *Metrical Life*, ed. by Bazire, p. 129. Bazire describes the Harley *Vita* as 'in a fourteenth-century hand'.

30 Reginald, *Vita Godrici*, ed. by Stevenson, p. 242.

31 Godric was especially prone to such forms of self-abuse. See Reginald, *Vita Godrici*, ed. by Stevenson, p. 269; Licence, *Hermits and Recluses*, esp. p. 20.

32 On William, see *Chronicon*, ed. by Stevenson, p. 26.

33 William was also a loyal patron of Cistercian houses in Yorkshire and supplied Fountains and Kirkstall with materials and land. See Burton, *Monastic Order*, pp. 198, 232; *Chronicon*, ed. by Stevenson, p. 26. That William was eventually buried at Fountains witnesses to his sustained generosity; see Newman, *Boundaries*, p. 35; Hill, *English Cistercian Monasteries*, pp. 67, 76.

ROBERT OF KNARESBOROUGH AND THE POVERTY MOVEMENT 225

beggars — a move for which there was, in fact, no real precedent within the eremitic tradition. Since his affiliations were now with the socially excluded, it is no wonder that William sees in Robert someone who harbours criminals or heretics ('receptour' and 'fautour'), or is otherwise disruptive of cultural norms ('rebellour') (*Life*, ll. 339–45).[34] For William, then, Robert represents a threat to the social or religious order, or indeed to both. These are in fact precisely the terms in which traditionalists ranted and railed against supposed novelties!

Clearly, at least some locals struggled to recognize him as a hermit, and it is nearly an instance of comic relief that others are reduced to insisting on 'hermit' as Robert's identity rather than 'hypocrite', the term that William initially prefers: 'Ane hermet, þat ys full perfytt; / Roberd, þat ys nay rebelloure' (*Life*, ll. 338–39). Robert was fortunate in his supporters; after all, Godric and others struggled to tell the difference between hermits and hypocrites. But again, the very strangeness of Robert's ascetic improvisations, in particular his attachment to what were clearly perceived as social deviants, could easily have rendered such a defence rather hollow and dubious. His turn away from the monastic establishment in this manner may well have been novel in historical terms; however, it was also dangerous, as demonstrated by William's call for Robert's burning. Again, twelfth-century secular and religious elites viewed novelty as disruptive, whether socially or religiously so. From this perspective, William's actions are not especially cruel but serve as a form of vigilance against threats to the social order. For this reason, beyond identifying Robert with a tradition that he was actively transforming, local responses were also potentially defensive; since the strangeness of his manner of living could easily be mistaken as a harbinger of social disorder, the designation of 'hermit' reincorporated him into the familiar and argued that his behaviour was in line with that tradition after all.

Overall, the hypocrite label — a favourite of staunch traditionalists — was one of several responses to cultural transitions and innovations in religious life. Deployed by William against Robert and by Godric of Finchale against himself,[35] the label also appears repeatedly in the twelfth-century poem *De falsis heremitis*, which attacks so-called 'false hermits'. The poem's author, who styles himself Paganus Bolotinus wrote sometime during the 1120s or 30s, although as far as I can tell the poem is not known to have circulated in England.[36] Most likely a secular canon of Chartres, the author had closer affiliations with the black monks and condemns supposed evils, including the

---

34 *MED*, s.v. 'fautour' (sense 1b) and 'receptour'.

35 Reginald reads Godric's self-descriptions as proof of his humility, yet they importantly combine language that was applied to lay society (*immundus* and *rusticus*). Reginald, *Vita Godrici*, ed. by Stevenson, p. 269: 'quantae vir humilitatis fuerit'.

36 Leclercq, 'Le Poème', 52–86. See also Smalley, 'Ecclesiastical Attitudes', p. 119. The author laments as well that, with the rise of this novelty (*vita ... nova*) such hermits are venerated and praised as saints by laypeople. Leclercq, 'Le Poème', p. 84, ll. 325–38.

JOSHUA S. EASTERLING

itineracy of contemporary hermits like Robert.[37] These hermits are figured as uncommitted to spiritual virtue, hypocritical, and too closely associated with lay society. The poem is in fact suffused with a contempt for such innovations — *hec nova res* — from which it also struggles to distinguish hypocrisy.[38] Here novelty and hypocrisy are largely different formulations for describing one and the same social and religious phenomenon as the refusal to assimilate into established institutions. Yet that refusal was also defensible as the resurgence of archaic forms of living that, while out of alignment with contemporary expectations, represented a return to primitive Christianity. It helps to recall that the very notion of 'renewal' suggests newness *and* a return to the past. Robert's own brother Walter approaches him to make this point.

> 'Brother', he sayd, 'me rewes sare
> Þat thou beldes in thes buskes bare,
> And specially in this spelunke
> In wyldernes als dyd a monke.
> Yff thou wyll leue and wend wyth me,
> Whare þat þi liste ys best to be,
> In couent, closter or company
> I sall gar sett the sekerly'. (*Life*, ll. 491–98 [*Vita*, 11.7–16])[39]

The offer to provide Robert with the security ('sekerly') of a monastic life emerges from a perception of his life as thoroughly archaic: Robert dwells 'in wyldernes als dyd a monke'. Walter seeks to draw him out of the 'wilderness', a space that was difficult to reconcile with eremitic culture's otherwise close affiliations with monasticism ('couent, closter or company'). For Walter, Robert's behaviour is not exactly new. It is a renewal of the older asceticism of the Desert Fathers, and thus so thoroughly ensconced in the past that it is out of tune with contemporary expectations.

The emergence of diverse and indeterminate forms of living led many to perceive one and the same phenomenon as either audaciously 'new' or so deeply rooted in past traditions as to bear little resemblance to contemporary reality. And so too was religious novelty defended by appeals to tradition; even if it represented an especially archaic form of eremitism, Robert's choice of a cave afforded security against traditionalists who, with some justification, branded him a fugitive and apostate.[40] However, if his cave provided Robert with 'cover' in more than one sense, his coldness toward the monastic establishment and continued association with the laity relegated this particular asceticism to the cultural and religious margins. It is this pattern that declared itself to

---

37 Leclercq, 'Le Poème', pp. 60–63.
38 Leclercq, 'Le Poème', p. 83, l. 287.
39 Leclercq, '"Eremus" et "Eremita", Pour l'histoire du vocabulaire'; see also Gilchrist, *Contemplation and Action*, pp. 157–208.
40 *Metrical Life*, ed. by Bazire, p. 129: 'Dei famulum ordinis fugitivum apostatamque appellabant'.

contemporaries as disruptive, if not out of control. On the one hand, fears of social disorder would have attended *any* twelfth-century ascetic who not only associated with 'poremen' but also emerged as a focal point for their collective attachment and even devotion. On the other hand, such fears may well have seemed warranted; after all, among English hermits there was no precedent for such behaviour as Robert evinced. Robert alone combined eremitism, itineracy, and active support for the local poor. This was a form of asceticism that was no less radical than innovative. Once again, criticism of hermits by twelfth-century elites was frequently a response to forms of living that represented and operated alongside new and unfamiliar shifts within Europe's social and religious body.

New Orders and the Poverty Movement

The sharpest polemic on innovation in the twelfth century centred on the rise of new religious orders. These proliferated: there were white monks, black and white canons regular, military orders, and hermits, living singly or in groups.[41] Despite Robert's traditionally eremitic cast, he in fact also closely resembles the charismatic pioneers of new religious houses and orders.[42] The innovations brought by those founders, including for example Norbert of Xanten (d. 1134), were often motivated by a mixture of dissatisfaction with the prevailing *ordo* and a commitment to remaining within orthodox boundaries.[43] When Norbert and his order of white canons emerged, they certainly belonged among the 'new monasticism'. This of course meant at least an initial confrontation with reproach and criticism, since such foundations directly raised the grim threat of novelty. Like many of his contemporaries, Norbert belonged to the new 'poor men of Christ' who preached and advanced a new image of religious poverty well before the advent of Francis nearly a century later.[44] It is mostly for these reasons — Norbert's renunciations and his status among the new (eremitical) founders — that the author of Robert's Latin prose *Vita* would incorporate extensive passages from *Vita B* of Norbert.[45] Whether 'real' or actively produced by Robert's later biographer (though probably both), the symmetry between his career and that of Norbert includes a tendency, noted among other twelfth-century figures, to cross institutional and social boundaries, at times dangerously. Norbert ranked among other twelfth-century charismatics whose pursuit of spiritual and ascetic rigour exposed itself to

---

41 Smalley, 'Ecclesiastical Attitudes', p. 119.

42 For discussion here and below, see Easterling, 'Norbert for England', esp. 94–105.

43 On Norbert, see Felten, 'Norbert von Xanten'; Leyser, *Hermits*, esp. pp. 69–77.

44 See Grundmann, *Religious Movements*, esp. p. 9. For a brief and recent discussion of the early contours of the early Franciscan movement alongside other poverty movements, see Elm, 'Francis and Dominic', pp. 33–54.

45 See also Weinfurter, 'Norbert von Xanten', pp. 68–69.

attacks by traditionalists. For this reason, Robert could be seen as courting the very same reproaches in England as Norbert had in Europe; both figures stand as ambivalent toward, if not highly resistant to, traditional religious formations. However, while Norbert brought his innovations well into line with the orthodox establishment, the fact that Robert never managed, or even attempted, to establish an order (the understanding by later generations was that he was in some sense the focal point of an emergent movement), underscored the element of novelty. The comparison with Norbert may well have helped to ease those negative resonances.

That is to say, while Robert almost certainly never intended to institute a religious order or anything like those reforms that mark the twelfth century, he would later become linked with these developments and their turn to poverty as the new form of *imitatio Christi*.[46] Several features of his career are elucidated by the poverty movements of the twelfth and thirteenth centuries, including his turn to preaching and his rejection of the monastic establishment. The bond that he shared with the poor *was* a marked feature of the religious collectives emerging at the close of the twelfth century, most notably the Franciscans and *Humiliati* in Italy.[47] For their part, the *Humiliati* 'stood at the crossroads between tradition and novelty' much like Franciscans in their response to mainstream religious structures.[48] The example of Francis of Assisi (d. 1226) stands as a notable point of comparison. Just as Reginald opens his *Vita* by positively acknowledging Godric's novelty and Robert's biographer describes him as a 'sidus nove claritatis' (star of new radiance), so would Francis's first biographer, Thomas of Celano, proclaim in a hymn later in the thirteenth century: 'Novus ordo, nova vita / mundo surgit inaudita' (A new order and a new life rises, unheard of, in the world).[49] The service to the poor, extreme itinerary, and rejection of the market economy are only a few parallels: both saints suffered persecution from bandits and religious alike (*Life*, ll. 186–200; *Vita prima*, 1.7, p. 194); rejected family and social connections only to return briefly to them (*Life*, ll. 127–30; *Vita prima*, 1.4–6, pp. 188–94 and *Life*, ll. 239–96; *Vita prima*, 1.4, pp. 188–90); submitted to episcopal authority (*Life*, l. 91; *Vita prima*, 1.6, p. 193); resided in a small enclosure only to leave again (*Life*, ll. 173–83; *Vita prima*, 1.5, pp. 190–91); commanded the obedience of animals (*Life*, ll. 122, 589–90; *Vita prima*, 1.21, pp. 234–36); and acquired a local following through preaching (*Life*, ll. 201–14, 229; *Vita prima*, 1.10, pp. 202–04).

However, the linkages between Robert and European poverty movements extend far beyond the resemblance he bears to Norbert or Francis. To begin,

---

46 Leyser, *Hermits*, pp. 52–56.

47 On the *Humiliati*, see Andrews, *Early Humiliati*.

48 Andrews, *Early Humiliati*, p. 1.

49 Quoted in Smalley, 'Ecclesiastical Attitudes', p. 114. For Thomas of Celano's *Vita prima sancti Francisci* (hereafter *Vita prima*), see Armstrong, *Francis of Assisi: Early Documents*, pp. 169–308 (references are to section and page number).

both the *Vita* and the *Life* repeatedly state that Robert had as a primary aim to assist and associate with the poor (*simplices* and *pauperes*), rejecting more established traditions in favour of such a life.[50] Not only socially affiliated with the poor, Robert provides them with food, turning from clerical, monastic, and eremitic models of virtue to one that, at that time, was only in its infancy. The *Life* is replete with descriptions of Robert's solidarity with those subjected to poverty: 'Poremen that war penyles / He fand tham fode of fysshe and flesshe' (*Life*, ll. 247–48); 'To begge an brynge pore men of baile, / Þis was hys purpose principale' (*Life*, ll. 295–96). Eventually, none other than William of Stuteville, Robert's sometime persecutor, would recognize the virtue inherent in his turn to assisting the poor.

Robert's own investment in assisting the poor seemed admirably to recommend him as a religious founder, if not in fact at least in spirit, and the Trinitarian compilers of MS Egerton 3143 clearly wished to see Robert as in *some* indeterminate sense a founding figure, at least for the order's commitment to assisting the poor and captives.[51] Robert is described as intending above all to 'brynge poore men of bayle' (*Life*, l. 295). Traceable here is both Robert's investment in associating with the poor, as well as the Trinitarian order's own commitment to delivering poor, Christian men from captivity. It is not so much that Robert's form of living is being mistaken for a prototype of Trinitarian customs; rather, his hagiographer recognizes a convergence of religious priorities between the English hermit, his contemporaries in France (John de Matha and Felix de Valois, referred to as 'twa heremites' and the order's founders (*Life*, l. 1083)), and later members of the Order of the Holy Trinity.

Like his earlier counterparts, Robert leaves the monastic orbit, and in this way begins a development that would eventually lead to his association with both the Trinitarian and Premonstratensian orders, as well as with the poverty ideal that these promoted and continued. I have argued that for this reason Robert's form of living was, at least initially, largely unrecognizable as a genuine expression of religious piety; it was not an expression with which contemporaries had experience, certainly not in the North. Insofar as Robert and his 'poralles' or poor men (*Life*, ll. 184 and 779) were 'acting collectively for religious purposes' and without the initiation or approval of the church, there were grounds for reproach and detractions.[52] In twelfth-century England, the life of itinerant and ascetic poverty was not a securely orthodox

---

50 On the economic structures of monastic culture in Yorkshire, see Burton, *Monastic Order*, pp. 244–73.

51 The order was founded (1198) by John de Matha, a detail to which the English text obliquely refers (*Life*, ll. 1083–84). See also Flannery, 'Trinitarian Order', 136; *Life*, ll. 1129–64. The tendency to read Robert as the order's founder is also found elsewhere. See *Itinerary*, ed. by Hearne, p. 98, where Robert is assumed to have 'instituted his Companie in the sect of Freres of the Order *de Redemptione Captivorum, alias Sanctae Trinitatis*'. Jones, *Hermits and Anchorites*, pp. 106, 156.

52 Moore, 'New Sects', p. 47.

230 JOSHUA S. EASTERLING

option for anyone committed to 'perfection'. So it is little wonder that such a distinctive form of living generated hostile perceptions of him as a social deviant, as we have seen.

The collective asceticism of Robert and his followers hardly amounted to an order, set of customs, or rule, and precisely for this reason the *Life* defends him by repeated reference to the Gospel (e.g. *Life*, ll. 195–99), the highest authority to which those who introduced novelties into religious life invariably appealed. In Herbert Grundmann's formulation, such 'recourse to the gospels' became 'the driving force behind manifold new forms of orders and communities', and it is this defence that we witness in Robert's biographers (e.g. *Life*, ll. 196, 761–66).[53] In the fragmentary Latin prose *Vita* in Harley 3775, these defences take the form of accusations against traditionalists who supposedly hold merely to a 'sub pretextu vere religionis' (pretext of true religion).[54] Writing to his brothers in response to those who opposed their new community at Grandmont — which again never fully developed into a new order as such — Stephen of Muret expressed the same thought in the following terms:

> Itaque, fratres, a multis vobis dicetur: 'Novitas est hoc quod a vobis tenetur; nec est ordo, nec regula doctorum sanctae Ecclesiae'. Sed quamvis ille qui hoc vobis dixerit, habeat indumenta signumque religionis, dico vobis firmiter quod vitam suam abnegavit, ignorans quid sit ordo vel Regula. Cui vos hoc modo respondete: 'Quandoquidem vitam nostram ac mores reprehenditis, ostendite nobis in quo et libenter emendabimus, si auctoritate evangelica nobis hoc indicare potestis'.
>
> > (And so, brothers, it will be said of you by many: 'this that is practiced by you is novelty; it is not an order, nor a rule of the doctors of holy church'. But although he who will say this to you should have the habit and appearance of religious, I tell you emphatically that he has abandoned its life, not knowing what an order or rule is. Let your response to him be thus: 'inasmuch as you reprehend our life and customs, show to us how, and we will freely correct our ways, if you can prove it to us by authority of the Gospel'.)[55]

As we have seen, Robert faced even more aggressive abuse than was implied in the term 'novelty' — rebel, hypocrite, fugitive, and apostate — and it is worth noting that Stephen's response to the charge of novelty deploys language (*indumenta signumque religionis*) that closely reflects the defensive gesture in Harley 3775: *sub pretextu vere religionis*. The discursive interplay of false and true spirituality, sign and substance, was an integral feature of those cultural

---

53 Grundmann, *Religious Movements*, p. 213.

54 *Metrical Life*, ed. by Bazire, p. 129.

55 Stephen of Grandmont, *Liber*, col. 1086B–C. For discussion of Stephen in a European context, see Grundmann, *Religious Movements*, pp. 211–13; Leyser, *Hermits*, p. 103.

discussions about the risks of novelty. In a similar way Robert's multiple identities as subdeacon, monk, and hermit present his monastic contemporaries, and a religious culture in transition, with that very same dialectic.

Conclusion

In the final decades of the twelfth century, ideals of perfection that called for association with the poor were in full bloom, and would continue to flourish during the coming centuries across Europe and England. The extent to which Robert's radical interventions into the eremitic tradition rested on local inspirations within Yorkshire must remain speculative; it is an important question, though one that I will not pursue here. In any case, the success of such ideals among both approved orders (Franciscans) and those less successfully incorporated into orthodoxy (*Humiliati*) came no less *despite* than because of their initial novelty. For their part, later Trinitarians did not merely set about imposing a mendicant image on an otherwise commonplace hermit: they would hardly have promoted his cult with such devotional and textual effort if Robert had himself reflected none of those ideals that would later guide the order. His life, like the texts that record it, represents an active negotiation between both long-standing and emergent spiritual lineages.

It is for this reason that Robert, rather more noticeably than other hermits, slips the bonds of any *particular* ascetic model. In fact, the designation 'hermit' implies a vocational and motivational identity that the *vitae* themselves undermine. For this reason, it is worth considering how the image of the hermit serves at times to elide otherwise important historical and textual variations in the motivations and religious alignments of particular individuals. It will be the task of a full-length study to provide a more nuanced understanding of the transitions that eremitic culture underwent during the period, say, from the eleventh to the twelfth centuries. Meanwhile, for both medieval and modern readers the (functionally useful) description of Robert and others as 'hermits' serves, among other things, to filter and smooth out the various complexities of their lives and cultural memories. This description also brings within the secure boundaries of the familiar those emergent and even innovative responses to traditional religious formations. Robert confirms above all that the lives of English hermits, too often read in narrowly insular terms, were in many ways in step with contemporary patterns in Europe, particularly the twelfth- and thirteenth-century emergence of new religious collectives. The cultural memory of this Yorkshire figure presents a richly complex and multifaceted image, upon which tradition and novelty marvellously converge.

Works Cited

Manuscripts and Archival Sources

London, British Library, MS Egerton 3143
——, MS Harley 3775

Primary Sources

Armstrong, Regis J., Wayne Hellmann, and William J. Short, ed., *Francis of Assisi: Early Documents*, vol. I (St Bonaventure, NY: Franciscan Institute of St Bonaventure University, 1999)

Bernard of Clairvaux, *S. Bernardi opera*, ed. by Jean Leclercq, C. H. Talbot, and N. M. Rochais, 8 vols (Rome: Editiones Cistercienses, 1957–1977)

Chronicon de Lanercost: 1201–1346, ed. by Joseph Stevenson (Edinburgh: Printing Co., 1839)

The Itinerary of John Leland the Antiquary, ed. by Thomas Hearne, vol. I (Oxford: Fletcher and Pote, 1768)

Libellus de diversis ordinibus et professionibus qui sunt in aecclesia, ed. by Giles Constable and Bernard Smith (Oxford: Clarendon Press, 1972)

The Metrical Life of St Robert of Knaresborough Together with the Other Middle English Pieces in British Museum MS Egerton 3143, ed. by Joyce Bazire, EETS, 228 (Oxford: Oxford University Press, 1953)

The Officium and miracula of Richard Rolle of Hampole, ed. by Reginald Maxwell Woolley (New York: Macmillan, 1919)

Paris, Matthew, *Chronica maiora*, ed. by Henry Richards Luard, 8 vols (London: Longman, 1877–1880 [repr. Cambridge: Cambridge University Press, 2012])

Reginald of Durham, *Libellus de vita et miraculis S. Godrici, heremitae de Finchale*, ed. by Joseph Stevenson, SS, 20 (London: J. B. Nichols and Son, 1847) (cited as *Vita Godrici*)

Stephen of Grandmont, *Liber sententiarum, Patrologia latina*, ed. by Jacques-Paul Migne, CCIV (Paris: Garnier, 1844–1864), cols 1085B–1136C

Two Lives of Saint Cuthbert, ed. by Bertram Colgrave (Cambridge: Cambridge University Press, 1985)

Secondary Works

Andrews, Frances, *The Early Humiliati* (Cambridge: Cambridge University Press, 1999)

Burton, Janet E., 'The Eremitical Tradition and the Development of Post-Conquest Religious Life in Northern England', in *Eternal Values in Medieval Life*, ed. by Nicole Crossley-Holland (Lampeter: Trivium, 1991), pp. 18–39

——, 'Reform or Revolution?: Monastic Movements of the Eleventh and Twelfth Centuries', *Medieval History*, 1.2 (1991), 23–36

——, *The Monastic Order in Yorkshire, 1069–1215* (Cambridge: Cambridge University Press, 1999)

Bynum, Caroline Walker, *Jesus as Mother: Studies in the Spirituality of the High Middle Ages* (Berkeley: University of California Press, 1982)

Clay, Rotha Mary, *The Hermits and Anchorites of England* (London: Methuen, 1914)

Clayton, Mary, 'Hermits and the Contemplative Life in Anglo-Saxon England', in *Holy Men and Holy Women: Old English Prose Saints' Lives and Their Contexts*, ed. by Paul E. Szarmach (Albany: State University of New York Press, 1996), pp. 147–76

Constable, Giles, *Three Studies in Medieval Religious and Social Thought* (Cambridge: Cambridge University Press, 1995)

——, *The Reformation of the Twelfth Century* (Cambridge: Cambridge University Press, 1996)

——, 'Controversy and Compromise in Religious Communities in the Eleventh and Twelfth Centuries', in *Knowledge, Discipline and Power in the Middle Ages: Essays in Honour of David Luscombe*, ed. by Joseph Canning, Edmund King, and Martial Staub, Studien und Texte zur Geistesgeschichte des Mittelalters, 106 (Leiden: Brill, 2011), pp. 145–56

Dauphin, Hubert, 'L'Érémitisme en Angleterre', in *L'Eremitismo in occidente nei secoli XI e XII: atti della seconda Settimana internazionale di studio Mendola, 30 agosto – 6 settembre 1962*, ed. by Societá editrice Via e pensiero (Milan: l'Universitá cattolica del Sacro Cuore, 1965), pp. 271–303

Deslandres, Paul, *L'Ordre des Trinitaires pour le rachat des captifs* (Paris: Privat, 1903)

Doyno, Mary Harvey, *The Lay Saint: Charity and Charismatic Authority in Italy, 1150–1350* (Ithaca: Cornell University Press, 2019)

Easterling, Joshua, 'A Norbert for England: Holy Trinity and Robert of Knaresborough', *Journal of Medieval Monastic Studies*, 2 (2013), 75–107

Elm, Kaspar, 'Francis and Dominic: The Impact and Impetus of Two Founders of Religious Orders', in *Religious Life between Jerusalem, the Desert, and the World: Selected Essays by Kaspar Elm*, trans. by James D. Mixson (Leiden: Brill, 2016), pp. 28–54

Felten, Franz J., 'Norbert von Xanten: Vom Wanderprediger zum Kirchenfürsten', in *Norbert von Xanten: Adiliger, Ordensstifter, Kirchenfürst*, ed. by Kaspar Elm (Cologne: Wienand, 1984), pp. 69–157

Flannery, John, 'The Trinitarian Order and the Ransom of Christian Captives', *Al-Masaq: Islam and the Medieval Mediterranean*, 23.2 (2011), 135–44

Gilchrist, Roberta, *Contemplation and Action: The Other Monasticism* (London: Leicester University Press, 1995)

Gray, Margaret, *The Trinitarian Order in England: Excavations at Thelsford Priory*, ed. by Lorna Watts and Phillip Rahtz (Oxford: Tempus Reparatum, 1993)

Grundmann, Herbert, *Religious Movements in the Middle Ages: The Historical Links between Heresy, the Mendicant Orders, and the Women's Religious Movement in the Twelfth and Thirteenth Century, with the Historical Foundations of German Mysticism*, trans. by Steven Rowan (Notre Dame, IN: University of Notre Dame Press, 1995)

Hanna III, Ralph, 'Will's Work', in *Written Work: Langland, Labor, and Authorship*, ed. by Steven Justice and Kathryn Kerby-Fulton (Philadelphia: University of Pennsylvania Press, 1997), pp. 23–66

Hill, Bennett D., *English Cistercian Monasteries and their Patrons in the Twelfth Century* (Chicago: University of Illinois Press, 1968)

Jaeger, C. Stephen, *The Envy of Angels: Cathedral Schools and Social Ideals in Medieval Europe, 950–1200* (Philadelphia: University of Pennsylvania Press, 1994)

Jestice, Phyllis G., *Wayward Monks and the Religious Revolution of the Eleventh Century* (Leiden: Brill, 1997)

Jones, Edward A., *Hermits and Anchorites in England, 1200–1550* (Manchester: Manchester University Press, 2019)

Knowles, David, *The Religious Orders in England*, 3 vols (Cambridge: Cambridge University Press, 1948–1959)

Leclercq, Jean, 'Le Poème de Payen Bolotin contre les faux ermites', *Revue Benedictine*, 68 (1958), 52–86

——, '"Eremus" et "Eremita", Pour l'histoire du vocabulaire de la vie solitaire', *Collectanea cisterciensia*, 25 (1963), 8–30

Leyser, Henrietta, *Hermits and the New Monasticism: A Study of Religious Communities in Western Europe, 1000–1150* (London: Macmillan, 1984)

Licence, Tom, *Hermits and Recluses in English Society, 950–1200* (Oxford: Oxford University Press, 2011)

Middle English Dictionary (MED) (Ann Arbor: University of Michigan, 2018), <quod.lib.umich.edu/m/med/> [accessed 10 November 2021]

Milis, Ludo J. R., 'Hermits and Regular Canons in the Twelfth Century', in *Religion, Culture, and Mentalities in the Medieval Low Countries*, ed. by Jeroen Deploige, Martin de Reu, Walter Simons, and Steven Vanderputten (Turnhout: Brepols, 2005), pp. 181–246

Moore, R. I., 'New Sects and Secret Meetings: Association and Authority in the Eleventh and Twelfth Centuries', in *Voluntary Religion: Papers Read at the 1985 Summer Meeting and the 1986 Winter Meeting of the Ecclesiastical History Society*, ed. by W. J. Sheils and Diana Wood (Worcester: Ecclesiastical History Society, 1986), pp. 47–68

Newman, Martha G., *The Boundaries of Charity: Cistercian Culture and Ecclesiastical Reform, 1098–1180* (Stanford: Stanford University Press, 1996)

Rossi, Maria Clara, 'Religiones novae e Ordini Mendicanti', in *Storia del cristianesimo. 2: L'età medievale (secoli VIII–XV)*, ed. by Marina Benedetti (Rome: Carocci, 2015), pp. 215–43

Russell, Kenneth C., 'Peter Damian's Whip', *The American Benedictine Review*, 41 (1990), 20–35

Smalley, Beryl, 'Ecclesiastical Attitudes to Novelty, c. 1100–c. 1250', in *Church, Society and Politics*, ed. by Derek Baker, Studies in Church History, 12 (Oxford: Blackwell, 1975), pp. 113–31

Tudor, Victoria, 'Durham Priory and its Hermits in the Twelfth Century', in *Anglo-Norman Durham: 1093–1193*, ed. by David Rollason, Margaret Harvey, and Michael Prestwich (Woodbridge: Boydell, 1994), pp. 67–78

Vauchez, André, *Sainthood in the Later Middle Ages*, trans. by Jean Birrell
(Cambridge: Cambridge University Press, 1997)
Weinfurter, Stefan, 'Norbert von Xanten und die Entstehung des
Prämonstratenserordens', in *Barbarossa und die Prämonstratenser*, ed. by
Karl-Heinz Rueß (Göppingen: Gesellschaft für staufische Geschichte, 1989),
pp. 67–100

CATHERINE SANOK

Hermit Saints and Human Temporalities[*]

The hermit saints of northern England occupy not only asocial spaces but also asocial times. When Cuthbert leaves Coldingham Priory at night to pray immersed in the icy waters of the North Sea, his difference from the monks is most obviously mapped spatially. But his location is above all the forum for a distinct experience of time: instead of the regular schedule of monastic hours, Cuthbert dilates his devotions to last the whole night, a duration rendered miraculous because it also dilates the time a person can remain in the frigid water. John of Beverley, in contrast, experiences time only as structured by bodily necessity — grazing like an animal on all fours in penance for sins so egregious the pope himself is unable to absolve them — until his crimes are undone, as if the recurrent temporalities of basic physical need allow time to run in reverse. While the time of social life rolls inexorably forward, hermit time — unmoored from the collective experience of singular events — can stall, expand, reverse.

This essay explores the contribution that late medieval vernacular legends of these two holy hermits can make to an understanding of premodern temporalities, and so to a historical understanding of how temporal experience has been conceptualized and perhaps also how it has been experienced. The legends of Cuthbert and John of Beverley, on which I focus — a legend of John of Beverley that survives to us only in an early sixteenth-century Dutch text and a sprawling mid-fifteenth-century Middle English Life of St Cuthbert — represent the hermit as removed from the forms of time defined by social structures and experiences, but nevertheless subject to secular temporalities. Complicating any simple binary of sacred and secular time, hermit legends explore embodied temporalities imagined to be outside of social times and ritual devotions. They are, that is, thought experiments about a primary, extra-social, experience of time.

---

[*] This essay has benefitted immeasurably from questions and suggestions from the audience at the Northern Lights conference, the generous feedback offered by Elizabeth Allen, Jessica Brantley, Seeta Chaganti, and Claire Waters to an earlier draft, and the research assistance of Lauren Geiger.

Catherine Sanok (sanok@umich.edu) is Professor of English at the University of Michigan, USA.

Late Medieval Devotion to Saints from the North of England: New Directions, ed. by Christiania Whitehead, Hazel J. Hunter Blair, and Denis Renevey, MCS 48 (Turnhout: Brepols, 2022), pp. 237–259

BREPOLS ❧ PUBLISHERS   10.1484/M.MCS-EB.5.124352

My focus on time may at first seem oblique to the spatial categories of analysis that organize this collection of essays. The regional framework of northern England is, however, an initial warrant for bringing together two quite different texts.[1] More importantly, region is the predicate of the hypothesis at which I hope to arrive: that premodern temporalities — premodern conceptualizations and experiences of time and time systems — take distinct regional forms. Scholarship on the history of time has long taught us that temporal systems and experiences vary by institution, vocation, genre, or domain of practice.[2] They therefore vary, inevitably, across space as well: there is every reason to hypothesize that institutional, vocational, and political cultures, as well as local ecologies, inform regional temporalities. But what is the scale of regional variation? Given its narrow scope and preliminary status, this study cannot answer this question, or the one that follows in the context of this volume: are there temporal systems or experiences characteristic of, even particular to, northern England? This essay aims not to claim that there is a specifically regional temporality; it seeks instead to lay some groundwork for asking whether there might be such a thing by considering how the hermit saint — understood in the late Middle Ages, and today, as a northern figure — represents a particular temporal experience.

Significantly, these legends point to local ecologies as a resource for the hermit's asocial experience of time. The legends imagine the expansion of possible human temporalities especially through the hermit's ability to inhabit an animal temporality modelled by non-human animals, as when John of Beverly determines to graze on all fours as penance for his sins, or through mutual affinity with them, as when Cuthbert is warmed by otters, who chafe his limbs when he finally emerges from the sea. Not all of these episodes can be read as evidence of a specific regional framework: some of the animals may index a northern landscape — as for example Cuthbert's otters — but others, such as the unspecified four-legged herbivores on which John of Beverley models his existence, do not. Nor are the spaces they inhabit — the sea and forest, both familiar topoi in saints' Lives — particularized as northern. Rather than a specific regional landscape, these legends suggest a regional etiology for the hermit's *access* to ecological rather than social temporalities: they trade on an idea of northern England as a place where the social worlds, and social times, of court or cloister exist in proximity to landscapes defined against them, wilderness and wasteland.

---

1 John of Beverley and Cuthbert are linked by the shared interest Bede has in their legends and in the later use of their banners in military contexts. But my approach to them as 'northern' saints relies primarily on the way their identification as hermits aligns with the broader cultural identification of the 'North' with wilderness spaces and so also with the hermit as a figure.

2 Classic studies include Thompson, 'Time, Work-Discipline', and Le Goff, 'Church Time'.

The cultural history of time has received a good deal of recent attention, in what some have called the 'temporal turn'.[3] But it remains riven by opposing historiographic theses that can be traced back to some foundational studies. Scholarship that focuses on, or works back from, modern cultures often argues that premodern ones were dominated by a single eschatological time, and that the fragmentation and diversification of temporal systems and experiences are a hallmark of modernity. This is a basic historiographic premise developed, for example, in Reinhart Kosselleck's *Futures Past* (originally published in 1979), a work that has received renewed attention in Anglophone scholarship with Keith Tribe's 2004 translation.[4] The opposing claim — axiomatic in medieval studies — is that premodern cultures are characterized by multiple temporalities, a variety sometimes understood as a consequence of 'task-oriented' experiences of time, as per E. P. Thompson, or divisions between various forms of secular and sacred temporalities, or the conjunction of natural times — say, the seasons — with social and religious ones in a pre-industrial society. The multiple times of premodern culture, this argument goes, are reduced or resolved into a shared, or homogeneous, abstract temporality as time systems are regularized with the invention of the mechanical clock, or railroad timetables, or Greenwich Mean Time, or modern time zones;[5] or as they dissolve into a monolithic 'secular' age through the wars of religion;[6] or as they are regimented into a normative temporality that serves dominant economic or social regimes.[7]

Scholarship on saints' cults and their affiliated textual traditions has long advanced our recognition of the multiple temporalities in the premodern period by identifying the complex intersections of historical, liturgical, and eschatological times they produce and reflect.[8] Saints' lives are, generally speaking, located in a historical past, however fuzzy or improbable it may be. These narratives are, in turn, affiliated with a feast day through which they are associated with both cyclical seasonal time and liturgical trans-temporality. They also participate in a sacred 'communion' of saints that prefigures eschatological

---

3 The recent historical and theoretical scholarship on time is too voluminous to survey here. Especially important contributions come from the domains of queer theory, ecocriticism, affect studies, and cultural history. The recent surge of interest in time in literary study at large is evidenced by recent handbooks including Allen ed., *Time and Literature*, and West-Pavlov, *Temporalities*.

4 Kosselleck, *Futures Past*, trans. by Tribe.

5 These are taken up by Dohrn-van Rossum, *History of the Hour*; Glennie and Thrift, *Shaping the Day*; Bartky, *One Time Fits All*, and Ogle, *Global Transformation*.

6 Taylor, *A Secular Age*. Walter Benjamin's influential claim in 'On the Concept of History' that modernity is characterized by a 'homogenous empty time' informs many arguments for the emergence of a single normative or dominant temporality: Benjamin, *Selected Writings*, pp. 389–400.

7 For example, Luciano, *Arranging Grief*; Freeman, *Time Binds*.

8 A fuller account of the polytemporality of saints' Lives and especially the legendary as a narrative form is found in Sanok, *New Legends of England*, pp. 31–60.

completion. In England, saints also figure eschatology through the trope of the saint's incorrupt body, which anticipates the resurrected bodies of all the saved. Even this paradigm of secular, sacred, and end time, however, may simplify the plural temporalities of the saint. Some saints are associated with dilated temporalities (as, for example, through the still-flowing spring that spouts when St Wenefrid is decapitated); some enact miraculous synchronicity with other persons (saints whose lives miraculously parallel the life of Jesus); and some make quotidian experience a forum for divine atemporality (saints, say, who find lost objects or restore broken ones). Precisely because saints straddle various secular and religious times, their legends are an important forum for thinking about temporality *per se*.[9]

Regardless of differences between them, most saints' Lives readily exemplify the truism that secular time systems and experiences are social, formed by and informing social experience in some way. My interest in this essay is in an exception to this rule, or perhaps its limit case: I argue that the legends of hermit saints explore an earthly temporal experience outside of social regimes of time. These legends, it may be noted, do not reflect actual eremitic practice.[10] Instead they use the figure of the hermit saint to imagine an escape from social temporalities, including genealogical time, institutional time schedules, and normative temporalities of bodily experience. Cuthbert and John of Beverley, as represented in these legends, cultivate a temporal experience outside of both monastic and mechanical hours, even outside of the cyclical times of liturgy. Their remove from social spaces, that is, is also a rejection of social times. The hermit of these vernacular legends instead inhabits or participates in forms of time correlative of the spaces he inhabits: ecological times, or — more generally — recurrent temporalities characteristic of the natural world and non-human animals.

The hermit's access to these patterns and the temporal experience they enable mark him as exceptional. But because these forms of time are often experienced at the level of the body, they may also be recognized as essentially human, not just proper to the holy hermit. Hermit legends, that is, can be read as explorations of a human experience of a non-social temporality, and in this regard, they may have something to offer recent efforts to theorize and historicize temporal experience. Their interest in a non-social temporality runs athwart most academic conceptualizations of time, both in recent cultural history and in touchstone works of sociology, such as those of Norbert Elias and Eviatar Zerubavel.[11] Recognizing time as a medium of social interaction, such scholarship emphasizes how it is produced by the culturally and historically specific forms that interaction takes. This understanding is

---

9   For a study of the time systems that suggests the contribution of saints' cults, see Champion, *Fullness of Time*.

10 On the communities and institutional structures in which medieval hermits and anchorites participated, see Gunn and McAvoy ed., *Medieval Anchorites*.

11 For example, Elias, *Time: An Essay*; Zerubavel, *Hidden Rhythms*.

especially prominent in recent arguments about the 'acceleration' of time as an effect of digital capitalism and global media.[12] The legends of hermit saints invite us — as perhaps they also invited their first audiences — to imagine a kind of time defined outside of, or against, social times; or, differently put, they invite us to think about *how* temporal experience is social by means of a narrative that imagines the unfamiliar, perhaps impossible, temporality of an asocial human life.

In order to explore how legends of northern hermits imagine this alternative temporality, I adopt as a working hypothesis Norbert Elias's argument that time is a social symbol for the relationship between a regular pattern of recurrent events — whether 'natural', such as the solar day or year, or mechanical, such as the movement of the hands of a clock — and unrepeatable or singular events, which create a sense of sequence insofar as other experiences are known through them as having happened 'before' or 'after'. Recurrent events, on their own, do not create a sense of the past and future, since any particular instance occurs both before and after another from which it is indistinguishable. For this reason, phenomena such as the solar day and year are often conceptualized as forms of cyclical time, a closed pattern in which time does not advance but repeats in a loop defined by its duration. As Elias notes, however, we use such patterns of recurrent events as templates for locating unrepeatable, singular events and orienting other experiences to and by these events, and also for comparing events that occur successively or at a distance from one another in order to apprehend, if not directly experience, them. The apparent flow of unrepeatable events, and the forms of change or temporal difference that they produce, in turn inflects the recurrent phenomena used for time keeping (the regular 'cycle' of the hours, say) with a sense of time passing, and so also with a sense of time's unidirectionality, its orientation toward the future. For Elias, time is neither a 'natural' objective phenomenon, as commonly understood in the physical sciences, nor primarily subjective, either as a Kantian *a priori* or the 'time consciousness' of phenomenology. It is rather a complex social symbol that, again, constructs a relation between recurrent patterns in the physical world and singular events that groups or persons make meaningful by locating them in this pattern in order to orient themselves to and by them.

Hermit legends deconstruct precisely this relation. The hermit has access to patterns of recurrence (such as the biological rhythms of his own hunger or sleep; his regular, perhaps iterative, schedule of devotions; as well as the daily or seasonal cycles he experiences living in a wood or wilderness). But, generally speaking and in theory, he is removed from the flow of unrepeatable events — events that are constitutive of social time, such as the death of a lord, the birth of an heir, or the founding of an institution — and hence from the unilinear experience of time that they produce. This remove from social time

---

12 For example, Wajcman, *Pressed for Time.*

has a surface resemblance to forms of sacred atemporality, which is of course also defined against time as a medium of historical change. But 'hermit time', which is external to ecclesiastical and monastic temporal systems as well as lay ones, is not figured in these legends as an image of divine timelessness: it is a secular temporality, imagined not as the suspension of time but immersion in its cyclical rhythms. Indeed, the hermit's recurrent devotions or penitential practices are defined by their occurrence in the *saeculum*, a temporal forum necessary both in theological terms (there is no need for petition or penance in the realm of divine timelessness) and in ethico-hagiological ones, since *duration* is often what marks these practices, otherwise shared by religious and lay Christians, as extraordinary. Above all, as I suggested above, 'hermit time' — in contrast to sacred temporality — is experienced at the level of the body, as is often underscored through the hermit's affiliation with non-human animals, and so also with the particular ecology he inhabits.

I turn first to the legend of John of Beverley as a 'hairy hermit', to explore how it disaggregates recurrent temporal experiences from the unilinear temporality of social life. I then turn to a few miracles from the late Middle English Life of St Cuthbert to explore further how the saint's access to, or participation in, animal or ecological time stands as an alternative to social times. The animal temporalities that Cuthbert inhabits are marked, in particular, by alternative durations: they rescale the temporal intervals set by social practices and epistemological categories. It is this quality that makes these miracle stories especially provocative in our own historical moment, in the context of recent efforts to extend the timescales we think with, in the context of ethical and social life, in order to recalibrate our own relation to the environments we inhabit.

Recurrent Temporalities in the *Historie van Jan van Beverley*

John of Beverley leaves surprisingly little footprint in vernacular textual culture in late medieval England, especially for a saint with a well-established cult, whose shrine had long been an object of pilgrimage, and who also had an important profile as an English and military saint, especially in the context of English claims to sovereignty over Scotland.[13] St John's banner was carried in royal campaigns against the Scots from the twelfth century, and his status as an 'English' saint was advanced considerably after the victory at Agincourt on his feast day.[14] Brief versions of John's Life appear in vernacular legendaries; it is found in Osbern Bokenham's Abbotsford legendary (fols 102^{r-v}),[15] and the

---

13 The most substantial study of the cult of John of Beverley is Wilson, *Life and After-Life*. See also Baggs, 'Medieval Beverley: Beverley and St John'.

14 See Sharpe, 'Banners of the Northern Saints'.

15 Edinburgh, Advocates Library, MS Abbotsford: Osbern Bokenham, *Legenda aurea*.

Kalendre of the Newe Legende of England.[16] But these are rather perfunctory, especially compared with other vernacular treatments of English saints in the fifteenth century.[17] The thin evidence of John's Life in vernacular textual culture may be a paradoxical index of its importance: so visible a cult, celebrated in a thriving city and throughout England by the knightly class, perhaps had little need for promotion. Or perhaps the Life itself, the story of a capable and virtuous bishop, simply lacked enough narrative interest to advance the cult, which was served instead in the late Middle Ages by the embellishment of the magnificent church that housed the monastery he founded.

Or perhaps it was difficult to reconcile the historical representation of John of Beverley, as for example commemorated by Bede,[18] with a popular legend about him as a 'hairy hermit': a holy man who attracts the malice of the devil and is tricked into committing a linked series of sins — drunkenness, the rape of his sister, and her murder — so egregious that even the pope cannot absolve them, and who thus sets his own penance of living like a four-legged beast. How this story came to be associated with John of Beverley is unclear: the legend is similar to one elsewhere associated with John Chrysostom, and it participates, more generally, in Europe-wide narrative traditions of the 'sins of the hermit' and the 'hairy hermit'.[19] The single extant version of the John of Beverley legend — a Dutch version, first printed by Thomas van der Noot in Brussels in *c.* 1512[20] — may have some connection with Beverley's status as a destination for compulsory penitential pilgrimages set by some Flemish civic courts. Susan Wilson has identified documents from Ghent, Dendermonde, and Aalst that list Beverley as a possible destination.[21] As the only extant version, the Dutch text must stand in for the legend as it circulated in England, for which we have only indirect evidence, the most significant of which is a reference to it by Julian of Norwich in a discussion of the temporality of penance that I address below. The *Historie*'s representation of hermit temporalities may well be inflected by the continental urban culture from which it comes: scholars associate it in particular with dramatic and

---

16 *Kalendre*, pp. 61[r-v].

17 Sanok, *New Legends of England*.

18 Bede, *Ecclesiastical History*, V. 2–6, pp. 237–44.

19 See Deighton, 'The Sins of Saint John of Beverley'. On the motif of the sins of the hermit, see Taylor, 'The Three Sins of the Hermit'; on the hairy hermit, see Williams, *German Legends*. On the proximity of the figures of the hermit and the wild man, see Alexander, 'Godric and the Wild Man'.

20 Other editions followed: that of Jacob van Liesfelt (Antwerp, 1543), Godtgaf Verhulst (Antwerp, 1689), Hieronymus Verdussen (Antwerp, 1698), and two eighteenth-century editions from Ghent. See, *Historie van Jan*, ed. by Boekenoogen, Appendix 1. This edition, to which all citations of the primary text refer, also contains facsimiles of the woodcuts from van der Noot's edition.

21 In addition to Wilson's work, I rely on the essential work of Parsons and Jongenelen, '"In Which Land Were You Born?"'. My discussion is based on their translation of the text. Also useful is Dutton and Haddad, 'The *Historie van Jan van Beverley*'.

rhetorical traditions of lay fraternities.[22] Matthew Champion has recently demonstrated the complex temporalities of the late-medieval Low Countries, and another study might consider the contribution this text makes to his account.[23] I approach it, however, as the single available source of a popular English legend about a hermit who rejects the temporal schedules of social life, first as a devotional and then as a penitential practice.

The legend of John of Beverley as a hermit-wildman is concerned throughout with temporal experience. The story begins with John's determined rejection of social life on the grounds that humans have only 'eenen cleenen tijt hadde te leven op dese allendighe werelt' (a brief time to live in this wretched world). Remote from the 'blivende stadt' (eternal city), social life is 'een sterven al' (all a decline).[24] These are commonplaces of Christian *contemptus mundi*; what is significant is the identification of John's vocation as a response to, even a remedy for, a particular structure of social time: unilinear time, which moves from the past to the future along a steadily downward trajectory. John's father, the Earl of Beverley, also understands social time as unilinear and future-oriented, but in an optimistic vein: dismayed by John's decision, he reminds the young man of all he will have in a near future: the wealth and rulership that are his patrimony, as well as a wife — who represents implicitly John's own future progeny. John's father, that is, offers economic and biological purchase on the future through the structures of patrilinear inheritance and genealogy.

This unilinear social time contrasts sharply with the temporality of the eremitic vocation that John takes up as an alternative to it. Abandoning his father and his social status, John goes to live in the forest, where he determines to serve God 'in allen uren' (through every hour)[25] — presumably a reference to canonical hours, but in any case a temporal system that is segmented into units in order to facilitate repetition — a temporality structured, that is, by recurrence. John will pray 'Nacht ende dach vroech ende spade' (night and day, early and late),[26] language that suggests not timelessness but periodic temporality: repeating temporal units, here on the scale of the solar day, defined by iterations of prayer. It is perhaps significant that the contrast between the forward advance of social time and this alternative mode of recurrence involves a shift in scale: the broad historical view that John offers in his pessimistic assessment of secular time, which is echoed in the generational temporality invoked in his father's optimistic anticipation of the transfer of wealth and privilege to his son, is replaced by the brief, frequent intervals of the hour and the day.

Perhaps John thinks that these units are too short to contain the post-lapsarian experience of decline he seeks to avoid, but they still — of course — participate

---

22 Parsons and Jongenelen, '"In Which Land?"', 33–35.

23 Champion, *Fullness of Time*.

24 *Historie van Jan*, ed. by Boekenoogen, p. 2; Parsons and Jongenelen, '"In Which Land?"', 20.

25 *Historie van Jan*, ed. by Boekenoogen, p. 3; Parsons and Jongenelen, '"In Which Land?"', 20.

26 *Historie van Jan*, ed. by Boekenoogen, p. 3; Parsons and Jongenelen, '"In Which Land?"', 21.

in it, as John learns to his horror, when a moment of temptation leads to a cascading sequence of sins: outraged by John's devotions, the devil tricks him into choosing one of three sins, drinking to the point of intoxication, having sex, or committing murder. Thinking that drunkenness is the least egregious, John asks his sister to bring him wine; when he has drunk it, he rapes her and then murders her to hide his crime.

Drinking, then, is the gateway sin, but the gateway to this gateway, as it were, is John's re-entry into forms of social time, in particular meal times, whose temporal location and duration are set by cultural norms. They are, as Evitar Zerubavel argues, essential 'time maps' of social life. Even the eremitical John assumes them: having acceded to the fiendish trick, he adds his own specifications that make his drinking conform to social time, asking his sister to stay until 'den dach ten avonde quame' (day becomes evening).[27] He adopts, that is, the temporal coordinates — both location and duration — that organize drinking in social life. This social temporality is the forum for the causal chain through which one sin becomes three: John becomes drunk, it inflames his desire and he rapes his sister, and then — in accordance with the social protocols he has introduced via the normative temporality of drinking — he immediately fears the public shame (not the spiritual consequences) his crime will bring, and this prompts him to murder her. The tight causal sequence of these events — drunkenness leads to rape, which leads to murder — bears out John's earlier assessment of social time as a declining unlinear vector, and it sharpens the contrast with the recurrent temporality he had created through a pattern of hourly prayer.

John's crimes are so heinous that they confound even the pope, who is at a loss to suggest appropriate penance or minister any blessing or sacrament. Instead, he advises John to return to England to seek out the holy hermit John of Beverley, unwittingly sending John back to himself — or an earlier version of himself — to receive spiritual guidance. In its (unwitting) recognition and (apparent) misrecognition of the hermit, the pope's advice is the crux of the legend and register of its chronotope: it suggests that John exists *simultaneously* as holy hermit and sinner beyond salvation. This simultaneity is difficult to parse. Does it mark the essential identity of saint and sinner? Or have John's transgressions created a rupture in his identity so profound it creates a temporal ripple? The pope cannot recognize the man before him, guilty of rape and murder, as the famous English hermit, and yet his counsel (that the sinner before him seek the hermit) presents in the most authoritative voice possible a temporal framework in which John persists in his status as a spiritual exemplar. John at once alters to the point of becoming unrecognizable, through an accelerated version of the inexorable process of decline that characterizes the *saeculum*, and he remains self-identical to the holy hermit he vowed to be, a figure who inhabits time through repeating increments — the hour and the day — short enough to approximate stasis.

---

27 *Historie van Jan*, ed. by Boekenoogen, p. 13; Parsons and Jongenelen, '"In Which Land?"', 26.

The pope's inscrutable suggestion, that is, points to two different kinds of time. One is a unilinear temporality whose causal logic of before and after is so absolute that John's former self and current self are split, as it were, into two entirely different persons. The other is, I think, a paradigm special to the hermit, who determines to dwell outside of linear temporality, persisting instead within a constant temporality defined by the iterative schedule of his devotion, entirely separate from the forward-moving flow of time. It is worth noting that this dual temporality, first suggested by the pope's (mis)recognition of John, is also indexed by the legend's form, which alternates prose passages in a third-person narrative voice with verse dialogue.[28] The use of prosimetrum splits the text between narrative time, in which events have already occurred and are presented in linear sequence, and the immediacy of spoken dialogue which creates an abstract present through the 'now' of utterance.

Although the legend is a sensational hybrid of popular motifs, I want to argue for the seriousness of its exploration of these dual temporalities. In doing so, I follow Julian of Norwich, medieval England's greatest theorist of time, whose theology of sin and grace is more deeply informed by this legend than has been recognized.[29] Along with Mary Magdalene, Peter and Paul, and Thomas of India, Julian names John of Beverley as an exemplar of the redeemed sinner, one who is, moreover, 'an hende neybor and of our knowing'. In spite of this familiar acquaintance, Julian sketches his legend:

> in his youngth and in his tendyr age he was a derworthy servant to god, mekyl god lovand and dredand, and nevertheless god sufferyd hym to falle, hym mercifully kepying that he perysschyd nott ne lost no tyme; and afterward god reysed hym to manyfold more grace, and by the contrycion and mekenesse that he had in hys lyuyng, god hath gevyn hym in hevyn manyfold joyes, over passing that he shuld haue had yf he had nott synned or fallen.[30]

Though he falls, Julian claims, John 'lost no tyme', a phrase that identifies the temporal implications of her theory of sin: God 'mercifully ke[eps]' the sinner even in the very act of falling, so that no 'loss' or lapse of time separates sin from redemption. Contrition thus does not restore the sinner, who is always already saved, but rather further increases their spiritual merit. In Julian's theology, sin and salvation are simultaneous: they cannot be charted

---

28 My thinking about this is informed by the workshop performance led by Elizabeth Dutton at the Northern Lights conference, and by questions she posed to participants about their experience of the prose and verse parts as evidence, for or against, the text's status as drama.

29 Julian is the single known witness in Middle English narrative culture to the legend of John as repentant sinner. See Deighton, 'Julian of Norwich's Knowledge'; Reichardt, 'Speciall Sainctes', and Wilson, *Life and After-Life*. Reichardt notes that John's feast day is May 7, and he suggests that this lends weight to the Sloane manuscript reading of 'the viij day of May' as the date on which Julian's visions began, against the BnF, MS fonds anglais 40 reading, 'the xiij daie of May'.

30 Julian, *Shewings*, ed. by Crampton, ll. 1302–8.

in linear time, or distinguished from each other by temporal difference (as 'loss of time').

This simultaneity is initially manifest in the legend of John of Beverley as self-recognition. 'Ick aen mi selven ben ghewijst' (I am dispatched to myself),[31] he observes when the pope directs him to return to England to seek 'John of Beverley': his identity hosts the doubled temporality in which, as holy hermit, he dwells within the recurrent time of his devotions and, as penitent sinner, he moves through the sequencing of sin, repentance, and absolution. To extend the constant temporality of recurrence, in the absence of a sacrament capable of producing the usual sequence of sin and redemption, John determines to live like a four-legged animal, in a temporal order organized only by hunger and its satisfaction. He returns to the spot where he committed his trio of sins, and he determines that he will 'cruypen als een dier / Op handen op voeten als een beeste / Mijn leven lanck in desen foreeste / Ende drincken water ende cruyt eten' (creep like an animal, / on hands and on feet like a beast / my whole life long in this forest / and drink water and eat roots).[32] Further aligning himself with non-human animals, John also vows never to speak again, depriving himself of the temporal experience that may inhere in, or be created by, language use, including the periodicity of repeated prayer that had initially defined his eremitic vocation.[33]

John thus again inhabits a recurrent temporality, one now defined by physical need and ecological affordance rather than the periodic structure of hourly and daily prayer. This temporality is even more absolutely asocial than that of the hermit, in that it lacks a socially determined sense of duration (how long things should last), as well as socially determined temporal locations (when things should happen), two primary coordinates of social time. It is also more categorically identified as recurrent: animal behaviours are understood, in medieval discourses as in many modern ones, as functionally identical actions performed repeatedly, rather than different actions performed in a unidirectional sequence. This is true, too, of John's grazing, recognized as a form of life. John, as a four-legged beast, is fully immersed in the present, engaged in behaviours that have no meaningful relation to events in the past and no particular relation to the future; nor are they dilated by paradigms of ethical or social consequences which would link them to prior or subsequent actions. This time of asocial animal existence is punctuated only by death: hence John's claim that he will live this way his 'leven lanck' (whole life long).

This is apparently contradicted by a second imagined future: John next says that he will live this way until a day-old baby announces that God has forgiven him. His animal existence, on the one hand, imitates a framework of temporal recurrence, in contrast to moral and social models of progress;

---

31   *Historie van Jan*, ed. by Boekenoogen, p. 24; Parsons and Jongenelen, '"In Which Land?"', 34.

32   *Historie van Jan*, ed. by Boekenoogen, p. 26; Parsons and Jongenelen, '"In Which Land?"', 35.

33   Note that language is a paradigmatic image of temporal duration in medieval Christian cultures, from Augustine onward.

on the other, it restores a unilinear temporality (which the pope had been unable to secure through the ritual event of sacrament) in which the present, in which he is unforgiveable, may be followed by a future, in which he will be forgiven. It can do this because John's beast-like existence nevertheless occupies calendar time — we are told it lasts roughly seven years — as a temporal forum of penance (late medieval penance often requires fasting on particular days or for a particular period, or saying a particular number of prayers: temporal location and extension themselves have penitential value). And, as a form of penance, John's animal existence has a causal relation to his (earlier) crime, as the specular relation between his sins and his penance suggest: he now lives, as he sinned, guided by appetite and its satisfaction.

The legend may seem ultimately to privilege the unilinear temporality of sin and redemption over the recurrent temporality of appetite and satisfaction because John is ultimately recognized by a day-old infant who announces that he has been forgiven. But this miracle itself flouts the progressive sequencing on which unilinear temporality depends.[34] Out hunting on the day after his son's birth, the new earl — who has inherited the realm in John's place — encounters John on all fours, so covered in hair that he seems 'een vreemt wilt dier' (a strange wild animal).[35] Brought back to court, John is recognized by the infant, who announces that his sins have been forgiven. Rather than subordinating the recurrent temporality of animal need to the sequential temporality of sin, penance, and redemption, the miracle is identified as such by the fact that the infant himself does not observe expected temporal orders, speaking on his first full day of life. This prolepsis moreover recalls the gap in linear time — specifically the patrilinear temporality of genealogy — produced by John's eremitic vocation, which was intended precisely as a rupture to the forward-moving temporality of secular life. The birth of an heir to the earl who rules in John's place represents a fiction of historical continuity necessary for leaping over this gap in the linear flow of political time.

Unilinear, future-oriented time is challenged still more profoundly by the temporal inversion that John's salvation produces or requires: the un-murdering and, still more surprising, un-raping of his sister Colette, who is discovered in the legend's bizarre denouement to have been unaffected by the crimes against her.[36] She is found alive and also, possibly, a virgin: John's penance

---

34 This miracle echoes the first of St John's miracles narrated by Bede: while bishop of Hexham, John used to retreat to a remote location during Lent; one year, he cured a young man of his dumbness, first blessing his tongue and then teaching him the alphabet and words, all in the space of a day and night (Bede, *Ecclesiastical History*, ed. and trans. by Colgrave and Mynors, V. 2). The hermit legend underscores the miraculous rapidity with which the youth learns language by attributing a similar miracle to the day-old infant, whose recognition of John marks the end of his animal-like penitential regime. More generally, the trope of the speaking infant is found in other hagiographical texts and, perhaps most influentially, in the Merlin legend.

35 *Historie van Jan*, ed. by Boekenoogen, p. 30; Parsons and Jongenelen, '"In Which Land?"', 37.

36 The name Colette, given to John's sister, may bear on the role she plays in the legend: Colette

does not atone for sins so much as undo them, such that the erasure of their consequences for his spiritual identity also erases their effect on his victim. Although the bishop is present as witness when John leads the party to the place where he had buried Colette's body, he says no prayer and performs no rite to restore her. When her grave is opened, Colette simply stands up, as though the crimes against her had never occurred. She claims that she will be rewarded with 'maechdeliken' (maidenhood) despite John's attack on her 'reynicheyt' (purity),[37] suggesting at once that her virginity has been restored and that it was somehow never violated. So, too, she explains that angels comforted her 'alle daghe' (all days),[38] and told her that God forgave John as her soul returned to her body, but leaves out temporal markers that would clarify whether she was recently restored to life or had long been miraculously unaffected by John's crimes.

It is important to recall that a sexualized figure of the female body is often invoked in medieval literature precisely as a figure for the irreversible nature of linear time. As Chaucer's Man of Law has it, lost time is no more recoverable than Malkin's maidenhead: 'lost' virginity is material proof of the impossibility of turning back the clock.[39] Saints' lives are replete with healing miracles that restore some other aspect of bodily wholeness, but the torn hymen is coded as a special category of bodily change that cannot be undone, as exemplified by the fact that it is the one injury from which the virgin martyr is invariably protected. From this ideological perspective, the raped virgin cannot be restored. This legend hesitates between a representation of Colette as restored and as un-raped, both or either figuring a time that can run in reverse. Indeed, her condition provides the strongest suggestion that John's animal existence is to be understood not as a penitential act in the unidirectional, future-oriented time of social life, but instead as a fundamental challenge to it.

Given the inclusion of Beverley on Flemish lists of possible destinations for penitential pilgrimage, we might see this anti-sequential temporality specifically in relation to the city's special sanctuary privileges and its association with absolution — the cancelling of the spiritual consequences of transgressive behaviour. Such an association might identify the legend's temporalities either as local (a function of Beverley's particular status) or regional (a reflection of broader 'northern' sanctuary practices, and in particular of the special visibility and importance of Durham and Beverley as sanctuary cities).[40] But the special

---

of Corbie, who enjoyed a substantial (and newish) cult in Flanders, is credited with the miraculous resurrection of a stillborn baby.

37 *Historie van Jan*, ed. by Boekenoogen, p. 34; Parsons and Jongenelen, '"In Which Land?"', 40.

38 *Historie van Jan*, ed. by Boekenoogen, p. 35; Parsons and Jongenelen, '"In Which Land?"', 41.

39 Chaucer, *Canterbury Tales*, in *Riverside Chaucer*, ed. by Benson, ll. ll. 28–31.

40 *Sanctuarium*, ed. by Raine. Raine includes an account of the history and status of privileges at Beverley from BL, MS Harley 560 (pp. 97–108), as well as the text of the late medieval register recording sanctuary petitions found in BL, MS Harley 4292. The petition for sanctuary — often for murder or unspecified 'felony' — is expressed by the phrase to come 'ad pacem Sancti Johannis'. The register shows both that Beverley was a sanctuary especially

250 CATHERINE SANOK

atemporality of sanctuary, in which the legal and spiritual consequences of sin are suspended through the power of the sacred, is less a concern of the *Historie van Jan van Beverley* than are recurrent temporalities associated with the secular phenomena of animal existence. The legend privileges the non-linear temporality of recurrence, defined above all through basic physical need and its satisfaction, as an alternative to unilinear time and correlative structures of ethical and spiritual consequence. As we have seen, John's eremitic life and, especially, his periodic grazing as a hairy, four-legged animal ultimately provide an alternative not only to the logic of Christian penance that underwrites ecclesiastical authority, and to the forms of patriarchal inheritance predicated on the control of female sexuality (inherited sovereignty and property), but also to the more fundamental Christian temporality of embodiment, and above all its sequencing of feminine embodiment through virginity and its irremediable 'loss'.

Cuthbert and the Duration of Non-human Temporalities

In Caxton's version of his legend, the Irish saint Brendan comes upon an island in the course of his travels where he finds Paul the Hermit, an erstwhile monk of St Patrick's Abbey and warden at the entrance to Purgatory. Brendan acknowledges Paul as his spiritual superior, on the grounds that he 'lyueth more lyke an aungel thenne a man', since he has lived for forty years 'wythout mete and drynke ordeyned by mannes honde'. Paul, in turn, claims that Brendan's privileges exceed his own, since God has shown him more of his 'preuytes' (secrets) (fol. 397^v).[41] His own story is one not of divine secrets but marvellous animality. Sent off in a rudderless boat by a divine vision, Paul arrives on his island in the North Sea to be greeted by 'an otter gooyng on his hyndre feet', carrying a flint and iron in his foreclaws and lugging 'grete plente of fysshe' by his neck (fol. 398^r). Paul boils the fish and lives off it for three days, until the otter returns with a fresh supply. He lived this way, he tells Brendan, for fifty-one years (in Caxton's version), until the age of ninety-one. Assimilated to his environment by the otter who provides for him, Paul ultimately loses the basic daily need of food and inhabits an ecological timescale out of proportion with human temporalities: now 111 years old, he explains, he has lived for the last twenty years without any need for food whatsoever. The primary physical manifestation of his condition is the hair that covers his body: he is so 'forgrowen' — thoroughly grown over — 'that no man myght

---

for those from northern counties (especially Yorkshire, Lincolnshire, and Durham) and that it had a broad appeal, drawing sanctuary seekers from London, Essex, and elsewhere. At Durham, sanctuary men wore a garment with St Cuthbert's cross on the shoulder. See *Sanctuarium*, ed. by Raine, p. xvi.

41 Caxton, *Golden Legende*. Cited by folio number in the main text.

see his body' (fol. 397ᵛ). Covered by luxuriant growth, consuming no ordinary human food, Paul is a feature of the island landscape, and he lives by the temporal categories proper to it — by increments of twenty and forty years, rather than daily rhythms of physical need, such as the patterns of quotidian hunger that had been satisfied by the three-day supply of fish with which the otter provisioned him. So too the human lifespan — often theorized in medieval discourses as lasting seventy years[42] — is eclipsed by an interval, longer than a century, more proper to ecologies than the human organism.

Paul the Hermit suggests a second way that 'hermit's time' is used in this period to theorize temporal experiences outside of the familiar regimes of social time. Where the John of Beverley legend imagines the disruption of unilinear chronologies, this story rescales temporal intervals from familiar human paradigms to marvellous ones set by non-human animals and by a regional ecology. We find this focus on duration rather than order — that is, on temporal units rather than their sequencing — in the Middle English Cuthbert legend as well, where it underscores the saint's miraculous synchrony with non-human animals and the northern environment he inhabits. Rather than merely imitate the temporalities of animal life, as John of Beverley does, Cuthbert inhabits non-human temporalities, often through the help of non-human animals. Cuthbert does not approximate an animal existence in the aftermath of sin; instead, his access to animal temporalities — which is a function of his sanctity — privileges, rather than appropriates, ecological timescales that are external to social time systems.[43]

The sprawling four-book Middle English Cuthbert legend is attested in a single manuscript, now London, British Library, MS Egerton 3309.[44] Once known as the 'Castle Howard couplets' for its provenance and its metrical form, the Life draws on a range of sources, beginning with *Libellus de ortu sancti Cuthberti*, a late twelfth-century northern legend about Cuthbert's early life, and Bede's prose *Vita sancti Cuthberti*, followed by additional materials from miracle collections, hagiography, and chronicle.[45] As the number of sources and the work's length suggest, the legend is notable for its drive to comprehensiveness, the creation of a single dossier in the vernacular, analogous to the sort of compilation that one might find in Latin as part of a bid for canonization. This impulse to a comprehensive assemblage of texts forecloses the narrative shaping we see in other large-scale fifteenth-century vernacular Lives, such as the Wilton *Life of St Edith* or Lydgate's double legend of Alban and Amphibalus. The Cuthbert legend is, in comparison

---

42 Sears, *Ages of Man*.

43 My thinking about the Cuthbert legend has benefitted from conversations with Lauren Geiger, a PhD student at Michigan, who is developing a project on animal miracles and northern ecologies in the Cuthbert legend.

44 *Life of Cuthbert*, ed. by Fowler. Cited in the main text by line number.

45 On the legend's sources, see *Life of Cuthbert*, ed. by Fowler, pp. vi–vii, and Whitehead, *Afterlife of Cuthbert*, which accounts much more fully for the Cuthbert tradition.

to these, conspicuously aggregate in structure, and in this regard seems to suggest an almost antiquarian, rather than devotional, approach to the saint. Where Lydgate's *Life of Sts Alban and Amphibalus* and Lawrence Wade's very late fifteenth-century *Life of Becket*, for example, are divided into books as a formal argument for their cultural value, the Middle English Cuthbert legend is divided into books in order to mark and catalogue its different sources.[46]

I restrict my focus to the first two of the four books: the legendary material concerning Cuthbert's birth and early life derived respectively from *Libellus de ortu* and Bede's Prose *Vita*. Book 1 presents Cuthbert as Irish by birth, an affiliation that, as other scholars have pointed out, is used to foreground his identity as a hermit saint. Indeed, the legend provides a complex etiology for Cuthbert's position outside of social structures in its account of his genealogy, conception, and early childhood. Cuthbert's maternal grandfather, a king named Muriadoc, is murdered by the king of Connaught, who later rapes Cuthbert's mother — the act by which Cuthbert is conceived. These crimes rupture the political and familial frameworks of Cuthbert's social identity, alienating him from them in a way that takes positive institutional shape when his mother goes to live in a nunnery, which is repeatedly identified as a place of remove from 'warldes welthe' (259), where women live in 'in deuocioun / In prayer and conpunccioun' (261–62). Cuthbert begins his life, that is, in a place that is both the remedy for, and an *in bono* version of, his oblique relation to royal genealogy and the social structure organized by it.

The inception of Cuthbert's own monastic vocation creates an even greater breach with his social identity: although the rapist king has promised Cuthbert's mother that he will recognize the child as his heir (309–10), the local bishop tricks the king into granting him the boy. Cuthbert is thus triply positioned outside of social networks: by the circumstances of his birth, by his religious vocation, and by his biological father's inability to secure his kinship relation. Although he descends from two royal lines, Cuthbert's relationship to the social order is structured not by law, custom, blood, intention, consent, or knowledge, but rather by various forms of transgression, trickery, and misapprehension.

In the place of social norms, the legend emphasizes the priority of the law of 'kynde'. The pregnancy of Cuthbert's mother, in particular, is explained with an ironic invocation of the maxim that 'kynde coueyts ay his lawe' (272). In the context of a story about an unmarried pregnant woman in a nunnery, the claim echoes antifeminist tropes that women's nature — that is, their propensity for sexual transgression — will out, even in a nunnery. But Cuthbert's conception via rape is represented as the absence of any sinful sexuality on the part of his mother (198), indeed, as a form of *imitatio Christi*. Untainted by maternal sin, Cuthbert's birth — as an example of the dictum

---

46 On the form of the Lydgate and Wade legends, see Sanok, *New Legends of England*, pp. 173–236.

that 'kynde covets its law' — registers the value of living according to a natural law, outside of social structures that might be seen to permit, even encourage, the forms of violence through which Cuthbert was actually conceived.

Positioned categorically outside of social structures, and within the 'law of kynde', Cuthbert manifests his sanctity in relation to non-human animals: his extraordinary capacity to communicate with, or be cared for by, animals is a correlative, that is, of the asociality that defines him as a hermit saint.[47] His first miracle is paradigmatic: as a young child, Cuthbert accompanies the bishop into the fields to check on some cattle: the bishop sees the boy examining a black cow with curiosity, and asks what 'priue' — secret — thing he sees in the cow's belly (397–98). The cow is with calf, but Cuthbert goes well beyond such a basic observation to demonstrate insights, at once prophetic and scientific, beyond his years. He notes with surprise that the fetal calf is red, not black like its mother, and that it has a snow-white star on its forehead (385–420). The miracle is striking in its lack of consequence: the calf's colour is unimportant, and aside from signalling his sanctity, Cuthbert's prophecy about it has no particular value. There is no miraculous restoration of human health or material value, no demonstrated capacity for suffering or imperviousness to pain. Instead, the miracle serves to align Cuthbert and the cow through the shared or reciprocal way in which Cuthbert's vision transcends the limits of both their bodies: Cuthbert can see the unborn calf because his sight is neither limited by his own sensory capacities nor obstructed by the cow's body, which is thereby identified as the forum — even vehicle — for Cuthbert's sanctity, rather than its antithesis. Moreover, this affiliation opens the saint to an alternative temporality: Cuthbert's knowledge of the calf's colour registers his saintly access to a future moment when the calf will be visible to everyone. And indeed the calf is born before they leave the field. The miracle thus coordinates Cuthbert's uncanny intimacy with the cow (which grants him knowledge unobstructed by the limits either of his body or hers) and an alternative temporality (his access to this knowledge in advance of its availability to others).

Although Cuthbert's prophecy may at first resemble the God-like extra-temporal perspective of other saintly prophecies, it does not announce a future event that cannot otherwise be known: the existence of the calf and a future moment when its colouring will be visible to all can be anticipated by anyone with some knowledge of animal husbandry. In any case, the prolepsis is too short, and the content of this prophecy too banal, to point to special access to a providential perspective. Instead, the miracle identifies gestational time, which we may recognize as a primary unit of animal time, as available to Cuthbert on a schedule that is distinct from human temporal

---

47 We may contrast the hermit's affiliation with animals to the capacity of other saints, who more emphatically embody monastic authority, to control or claim jurisdiction over non-human animals within an abbey's precincts. St Werburge of Chester, for example, banishes geese from abbey lands so that they do not destroy the crops.

experience. Figured as contiguous with other stages of reproduction, the birth of a non-human animal does not create a significant temporal division, an epistemological before and after; so too Cuthbert's knowledge of the calf extends from the observed fact of the cow's pregnancy, coincident with the periodic reproductive time proper to it. The miracle thus exemplifies another way that the saint represents and observes the 'law of kynde', and participates in a temporal order correlative of this law.

It may be remarked that the miracle also underscores a reciprocal relation between the saint and the calf. Following closely the story of Cuthbert's own gestation — especially the discontinuity between the crime by which he was conceived and his spiritual vocation, by which his childhood is marked — the calf's own surprising embodiment (colouring that distinguishes it from its parentage and the white star that suggests exceptionality or election) identifies Cuthbert, just as Cuthbert identifies it. Although distinguished in ways that preserve the difference between human and non-human animals (e.g. linguistic versus symbolic meaning-making), the striking similarities between Cuthbert and the calf suggest that non-human animals, too, are vectors by which the sacred enters the *saeculum*. At the same time, the miracle makes a more general parallel between the saint and the calf as juveniles: Cuthbert's identity with a non-human animal is grounded in their shared life stage.

This parallel is at work, too, in the miraculous rescue of Cuthbert's psalter by a seal calf, an episode that more explicitly coordinates the saint's experience with that of non-human animals on the grounds of timing or duration. After the bishop's death, Cuthbert's mother fears that they are again vulnerable to the rapist king, and she and Cuthbert determine to flee from Ireland. As they embark on a boat headed for Britain, Cuthbert's psalter falls into the water, where it is collected by a seal calf, and when Cuthbert arrives at his destination, the seal delivers the psalter, perfectly preserved, to him (531–76). It is significant that this miracle involves an object that would ordinarily represent the recurrent temporalities of liturgy, and which, in the form of a personal book, makes these recurrent temporalities available as a framework for a life or vocation. The psalter in this way neatly exemplifies Elias's model of time: a symbolic assemblage that synchronizes a recurrent pattern (the liturgy) and a sequence of singular events (an individual spiritual career). At least, that is how we might describe the usual temporality of a private copy of the psalter. The seal-calf miracle, in contrast, coordinates not the temporalities of recurrence and event, but those of human and non-human animal activity, matching the duration of one to the other: Cuthbert's journey by boat, driven by the extraordinary exigency of vulnerability to a corrupted political system, and the seal's unremarkable swimming of this same route are perfectly synchronized with each other. Importantly, this synchronicity is the very ground of Cuthbert's devotions, insofar as it restores his psalter to him. And, as with the miracle of the calf, this one codes parallel stages in lifespan, rather than species, as the grounds for affiliation between two animals. Cuthbert, whose clumsy or careless loss of his psalter may be associated with his youth, is aided by another young animal, whose access to the free time of play, as well as the playful pleasure of a physical challenge, allows it to accompany the boat.

Cuthbert is not only able to synchronize his experience to that of non-human animals, as in these miracles; he is also able to participate fully in the temporality of non-human animals, as is demonstrated most strikingly in his 'custome' of praying at night 'when oþer men slepyd' (1661–1662). In an episode in Book 2, drawn from Bede's Prose *Vita*, the Middle English legend recounts that Cuthbert, while visiting Coldingham Abbey, enters the sea naked during these nightly vigils, remaining in the water for hours.[48] In this miracle, Cuthbert is not just accompanied by a marine mammal, but occupies the northern landscape on the same timescale as one. Although the place of Cuthbert's devotions — the sea — is what initially marks them as exceptional, their duration is the real source of wonder. Being in the sea is not a miracle; the miracle is to remain there. Against the periodic structure of monastic hours — the patterns of prayer and sleep that structure the night in a monastery such as Coldingham — Cuthbert prays across a single continuous span of time, similar to the continuous generational time that informs his first prophecy. Here, however, the miraculous coordination of human and non-human temporalities occurs as a bodily practice, rather than a form of knowledge. Cuthbert's embodiment is affiliated with that of marine mammals for whom the icy waters are a natural habitat. No wonder otters come to warm him when he finally emerges; they are fellow animals who nevertheless recognize the saint's greater physical frailty.

Where the John of Beverley legend uses the figure of the hermit to imagine alternatives to the sequences of linear time (whether those of royal genealogy, penitential practice, or female embodiment), then, the Cuthbert miracles imagine alternative durations and ways of periodizing experience. Where the former legend may be read as a medieval antecedent to the critiques of linear temporality developed, especially, in queer theory,[49] the Cuthbert legend points toward interest in temporality in recent ecocritical scholarship that takes up the possibility and potential of rescaling time categories: that is, of rethinking the priority given to history, agency, environments, and ethics as they are periodized in increments or categories derived from the phenomenology of human embodiment and social life. The late Middle English Cuthbert legend, like some of this work, may be read, I hope to have shown, as an attempt to theorize and represent temporal units proper to other organisms that inhabit the same northern ecology. Cuthbert's sanctity itself is defined by his capacity to participate in these timescales.

---

48 Similar episodes are found in the legends of other northern saints, in particular Godric, in episodes discussed by Anne Mouron, 'The French *Life* of Godric', in this volume, pp. 351–52.

49 Some central contributions include Dinshaw, *How Soon is Now?*; Edelman, *No Future*; Freeman, *Time Binds*; Jagose, *Inconsequence*, and Rohy, *Anachronism and Its Others*.

To be sure, the temporalities of non-human animals and their environments are just some of the many forms of time represented in this sprawling version of the Cuthbert legend. He is also associated with the quasi-atemporality of the monastery, as well as the ambivalent temporalities of England, figured both through founding myths and the vicissitudes of history. The Middle English Cuthbert legend, as a composite text that aims toward comprehensiveness, ultimately places the saint at the centre of a complex system of different temporal orders, including those associated with regional communities, monastic and ecclesiastic institutions, and national histories. But these are grounded, I want to argue, in the initial representation of Cuthbert's immersion in non-human temporalities and his capacity to adapt his bodily experience, and his spiritual life, to their timescales.

* * *

Deviating from the temporal systems that derive from social institutions and the paradigm of human embodiment, the hermit legends of John of Beverley and Cuthbert suggest how imitating or participating in the temporal patterns or experiences of non-human animals might expand human experiences of time. They raise questions about the temporal orientation of ethics — whether and how actions are directed toward the past or the future, for example, or whether their meaning is determined by what comes before or what comes after — and they suggest some of the ethical and epistemological possibilities offered by adopting temporalities scaled to, and by, other species, as ways of inhabiting shared ecologies differently. The legends, that is, provided imaginative models of alternative temporalities for their first audiences to think with. Although they exist at a far remove from the ethical concerns modern readers confront, this very distance — the temporal leap backward we make in the effort to understand them — may add to their value as thought experiments. Precisely because these legends can offer us no immediate lesson for how to rescale the time frames with which we now consider the ethical or environmental stakes of human activity, we are not likely to exaggerate their implications or relevance. But as narratives about a human experience of non-social and animal times, hermit legends might nevertheless help us think about the way we use temporality to distinguish between human communities and the ecologies they inhabit, and about how this sustains a fantasy of a fundamental difference between them. In the hermit's access to the patterns and scale of other times, that is, late medieval saints' Lives imagine the possibility of recognizing ecological time as a human temporality.

Works Cited

Manuscripts and Archival Sources

Edinburgh, Advocates Library, MS Abbotsford (Osbern Bokenham's *Legenda aurea*)
London, British Library, MS Egerton 3309

Primary Sources

Bede, *Bede's Ecclesiastical History of the English People*, ed. and trans. by Bertram Colgrave and R. A. B. Mynors (Oxford: Clarendon Press, 1969)
——, *Ecclesiastical History of the English People*, ed. by Judith McClure and Roger Collins, trans. by Bertram Colgrave (Oxford: Oxford University Press, 1999)
Benjamin, Walter, *Selected Writings, Vol. 4 (1938–1940)*, ed. by Howard Eiland and Michael Jennings, trans. by Edmund Jephcott and others (Cambridge, MA: Harvard University Press, 2006)
Caxton, William, trans., *Golden Legend* [*Legenda aurea sanctorum, sive, Lombardica historia*, by Jacobus de Voragine] (London: William Caxton, 1483) ProQuest, <https://proxy.lib.umich.edu/login?url=https://www.proquest.com/books/legenda-aurea-sanctorum-sive-lombardica-historia/docview/2240950786/se-2?accountid=14667> [accessed 14 Jan 2022]
Chaucer, Geoffrey, *The Riverside Chaucer*, ed. by Larry Benson and others (Oxford: Oxford University Press, 1987)
Historie van Jan van Beverley, ed. by J. G. Boekenoogen, Nederlandsche Volksboeken, 6 (Leiden: Brill, 1903)
Julian of Norwich, *Shewings of Julian of Norwich*, ed. by Georgia Ronan Crampton, TEAMS (Kalamazoo: Medieval Institute, 1994)
Kalendre of the Newe Legende of England (London: Richard Pynson, 1516) <https://proxy.lib.umich.edu/login?url=https://www.proquest.com/books/here-begynneth-kalendre-newe-legende-englande/docview/2240857088/se-2?accountid=14667> [accessed 14 Jan 2022]
Life of St Cuthbert in English Verse, ed. by Joseph T. Fowler, SS, 87 (Durham: Andrews, 1891)
Sanctuarium dunelmense et Sanctuarium beverlacense, ed. by James Raine, SS, 5 (London: J. B. Nichols, 1837)

Secondary Works

Allen, Thomas, ed., *Time and Literature* (Cambridge: Cambridge University Press, 2018)
Alexander, Dominic, 'Godric and the Wild Man: The Resonances of Asceticism in Reginald of Durham's *Vita* of Godric of Finchale', in *Saints of North-East England: 600–1500*, ed. by Margaret Coombe, Anne Mouron, and Christiania Whitehead (Turnhout: Brepols, 2017), pp. 197–218

Baggs, A. P. and others, 'Medieval Beverley: Beverley and St John', in *A History of the County of York East Riding*, vol. VI: *The Borough and Liberties of Beverley*, ed. by K. J. Allison (London: Victoria County History, 1989), pp. 2–11. *British History Online*, <http://www.british-history.ac.uk/vch/yorks/east/vol6/pp2-11> [accessed 17 Dec 2021]

Bartky, Ian, *One Time Fits All: The Campaigns for Global Uniformity* (Stanford: Stanford University Press, 2007)

Champion, Matthew, *Fullness of Time: Temporalities of the Fifteenth-Century Low Countries* (Chicago: University of Chicago Press, 2017)

Deighton, Alan, 'Julian of Norwich's Knowledge of the Life of John of Beverley', *Notes and Queries*, 40 (1993), 440–43

——, 'The Sins of Saint John of Beverley: The Case of the Dutch Volksboek *Jan van Beverley*', *Leuvense Bijdragen*, 82 (1993), 227–46

Dinshaw, Carolyn, *How Soon is Now?: Medieval Texts, Amateur Readers, and the Queerness of Time* (Durham, NC: Duke University Press, 2012)

Dohrn-van Rossum, Gerhard, *History of the Hour: Clocks and Modern Temporal Orders*, trans. by Thomas Dunlap (Chicago: University of Chicago Press, 1996)

Dutton, Elizabeth, and Tamara Haddad, 'The *Historie van Jan van Beverley*', in *Saints and Cults in Medieval England: Proceedings of the 2015 Harlaxton Symposium*, ed. by Susan Powell (Donington: Shaun Tyas, 2017), pp. 381–98

Edelman, Lee, *No Future: Queer Theory and the Death Drive* (Durham, NC: Duke University Press, 2004)

Elias, Norbert, *Time: An Essay*, trans. by Edmund Jephcott (Oxford: Blackwell, 1992)

Freeman, Elizabeth, *Time Binds: Queer Temporalities, Queer Histories* (Durham, NC: Duke University Press, 2010)

Glennie, Paul, and Nigel Thrift, *Shaping the Day: A History of Timekeeping in England and Wales, 1300–1800* (Oxford: Oxford University Press, 2009)

Gunn, Cate, and Liz Herbert McAvoy, ed., *Medieval Anchorites in their Communities* (Cambridge: D. S. Brewer, 2017)

Jagose, Annamarie, *Inconsequence: Lesbian Representation and the Logic of Sexual Sequence* (Ithaca: Cornell University Press, 2002)

Koselleck, Reinhart, *Futures Past: On the Semantics of Historical Time*, trans. by Keith Tribe (New York: Columbia University Press, 2004)

Le Goff, Jacques, 'Church Time and Merchant Time in the Middle Ages', *Social Science Information*, 9 (1970), 151–67

Luciano, Dana, *Arranging Grief: Sacred Time and the Body in Nineteenth-Century America* (New York: New York University Press, 2007)

Ogle, Vanessa, *The Global Transformation of Time, 1870–1950* (Cambridge, MA: Harvard University Press, 2015)

Parsons, Ben, and Bas Jongenelen, '"In Which Land Were You Born?": Cultural Transmission in the *Historie van Jan van Beverley*', *Medieval English Theatre*, 34 (2012), 30–76

Reichardt, Paul, 'Speciall Sainctes: Julian of Norwich, John of Beverley, and the Chronology of the *Shewings*', *English Studies*, 82 (2001), 385–92

Rohy, Valerie, *Anachronism and Its Others: Sexuality, Race, Temporality* (Albany: SUNY Press, 2010)

Sanok, Catherine, *New Legends of England: Forms of Community in Late Medieval Saints' Lives* (Philadelphia: University of Pennsylvania Press, 2018)

Sears, Elizabeth, *Ages of Man: Medieval Interpretations of the Life Cycle* (Princeton: Princeton University Press, 1986)

Sharpe, Richard, 'Banners of the Northern Saints', in *Saints of North-East England: 600–1500*, ed. by Margaret Coombe, Anne Mouron, and Christiania Whitehead (Turnhout: Brepols, 2017), pp. 245–303

Taylor, Archer, 'The Three Sins of the Hermit', *Modern Philology*, 20 (1922), 61–94

Taylor, Charles, *A Secular Age* (Cambridge, MA: Harvard University Press, 2007)

Thompson, E. P., 'Time, Work-Discipline, and Industrial Capitalism', *Past & Present*, 38 (1967), 56–97

Wajcman, Judy, *Pressed for Time: Acceleration of Life in Digital Capitalism* (Chicago: University of Chicago Press, 2015)

West-Pavlov, Russell, *Temporalities* (London: Routledge, 2013)

Whitehead, Christiania, *The Afterlife of St Cuthbert: Place, Texts and Ascetic Tradition, 690–1500* (Cambridge: Cambridge University Press, 2020)

Williams, Charles Allyn, *German Legends of the Hairy Anchorite* (Urbana: University of Illinois, 1935)

Wilson, Susan, *The Life and After-Life of St John of Beverley: The Evolution of the Cult of an Anglo-Saxon Saint* (Aldershot: Ashgate, 2006)

Zerubavel, Eviatar, *Hidden Rhythms: Schedules and Calendars in Social Life* (Chicago: University of Chicago Press, 1981)

11.2 Female Networks and Locations: Coldingham, Ely, Whitby

RUTH J. SALTER

Beyond the *Miracula*: Practices and Experiences of Lay Devotion at the Cult of St Æbbe, Coldingham

Following a demonic attack, Master Merlin's daughter had lost the sight in one eye, hearing in one ear, and the use of her tongue. She was taken to the oratory of St Æbbe to spend the night in vigils:

> Pre tedio dormitans, super altare columbam niueam stare conspexit, quam sibi, soluto statim uinculo lingue, dari peciit. Et in hac uoce euigilans, omnem pariter cum sopore infirmitatem deposuit. Mane facto quibusdam ex nostris a mulieribus, que eam secute fuerant et hec uiderant oblata, se uidere, audire, loqui libera uoce, professa est.

> > (Sleeping through weariness, she saw a snow-white dove standing on the altar, which she begged to be given to her, for the bond of her tongue was immediately released. Awaking at this utterance, she set aside the illness just as she set aside sleep. In the morning some of the women who had accompanied her and seen these blessings declared to some of us that she saw, heard, and spoke with a ready tongue.)[1]

So records the late twelfth-century hagiography, the *Vita et miracula S. Æbbe virginis* (hereafter *Vita Æbbe*), produced *c.* 1190.[2] Æbbe's double monastery had been founded in the Coldingham area in the late seventh century. By the close of the twelfth century, the supposed coffin of the saintly abbess had been translated to the church of the new Durham-dependant Benedictine priory at Coldingham, and an oratory had been established on Kirk Hill, the supposed site of Æbbe's earlier monastery (*Coludi urbs*), approximately two miles north-east.

---

1 *Vita et miracula S. Æbbe virginis* (cited hereafter as *Vita Æbbe*), ed. and trans. by Bartlett, IV.1, pp. 32–33.
2 *Vita Æbbe*, p. xviii.

> **Ruth J. Salter** (r.j.salter@reading.ac.uk) is Lecturer in Medieval History within the Department of History and Graduate Centre for Medieval Studies at the University of Reading.

Late Medieval Devotion to Saints from the North of England: New Directions, ed. by Christiania Whitehead, Hazel J. Hunter Blair, and Denis Renevey, MCS 48 (Turnhout: Brepols, 2022), pp. 263–283
BREPOLS ✠ PUBLISHERS   10.1484/M.MCS-EB.5.124353

The miraculous cure of Master Merlin's daughter at the Kirk Hill oratory site is the first of forty-two reports of successful cure-seeking recorded within the hagiography. Produced by a Durham monk based at Coldingham, Æbbe's hagiography is divided into four books of unequal length: the prologue (an address by the hagiographer to the Durham community); the *vita* (life) containing what little was known about the saint's life and death; the *translatio* (translation) recording the rediscovery of Æbbe's tomb and the events that led to the building of the oratory; and the *miracula* (miracles) in which the accounts of successful miraculous healing are recorded. It is Book IV of the *Vita Æbbe* that this essay is particularly interested in.[3] Through the selected accounts recorded within the *miracula* it is possible to observe wider practices of devotional behaviour that were undertaken and experienced at this borderland cult centre. The *Vita Æbbe* thus presents a fascinating glimpse into devotional interaction with a female saint's cult at the turn of the twelfth to thirteenth century at a monastic institution which, while recently founded, was drawing a connection between itself and an Anglo-Saxon 'Golden Age' of Northumbrian saints.[4]

One key feature of the cult, as highlighted in the *Vita Æbbe*, is the predominance of devotion at the oratory constructed at the site of the abbess's own monastery. However, this is not the only unusual feature which sets Æbbe's cult apart from some of its contemporaries. Indeed, while the production of the *Vita Æbbe* and the development of the oratory site indicates that the late twelfth-century flurry of interest in Æbbe's cult came from both the monks, who acted as the cult's guardians, and the lay cure-seekers who sought out Æbbe's heavenly intercession, it is only the laity who are recorded in the *miracula* as beneficiaries of the abbess's intercession. Intriguingly, women and younger cure-seekers feature heavily amongst Æbbe's devotees, bucking trends seen in other contemporary *miracula* collections.[5] The *Vita Æbbe* also emphasizes that Æbbe and her intercessory powers were perceived to be heavily rooted in the local landscape.[6] This is particularly apparent in the high number of accounts that involve Æbbe appearing to, and physically interacting with, her devotees at the oratory. Æbbe is, in fact, a very hands-on saint who engages readily with her cure-seekers.[7]

The *Vita Æbbe* raises a number of questions regarding the practices and experiences of those who sought out Æbbe's intercession. Does, for example, the presence of so many female cure-seekers in the *Vita* imply that this was a cult particularly promoted to women? Why was there such a strong focus

---

3   *Vita Æbbe*, I, pp. 1–2.
4   Regarding the Northumbrian 'Golden Age', see Cramp, 'The Northumbrian Identity', p. 1; Petts and Turner ed., *Early Medieval Northumbria*, pp. 2–4.
5   Finucane, *Miracles and Pilgrims*, p. 143; Salter, 'Experiencing *Miracula*', pp. 48–99; Salter, *Saints, Cure-Seekers and Miraculous Healing*, pp. 93–94.
6   Powell, 'Pilgrimage, Performance and Miracle Cures'.
7   Whitehead, 'A Scottish or English Saint?', pp. 20–25.

on Kirk Hill? Was Æbbe's presence at the oratory an expected part of the intercessory process? Does her visual and physical presence potentially hint at older practices of lay devotion? Questions such as these provide a gateway through which to consider the practices of lay devotion at Coldingham. In so doing, this essay argues that, despite the *Vita Æbbe*'s focused attention on the oratory, the two sites of Kirk Hill and Coldingham Priory were part of a dual-location pilgrimage process connecting the saint to her pilgrims and to the local landscape: a point subtly woven into the background of the miracle narrative.

In highlighting the practices of Æbbe's cure-seeking pilgrims, this essay also seeks to draw attention to the cult of Æbbe itself and to address a Northumbrian saint who has garnered little scholarly attention by comparison with her other contemporaries, most notably St Cuthbert. With the exception of two nineteenth-century local histories of Coldingham, Robert Bartlett's introduction to the published edition of the *Vita Æbbe*, and articles by Hilary Powell, Christiania Whitehead, and Lauren Whitnah, there has been no modern analysis of Æbbe, meaning that there is still much that can be said about her as both an abbess and a saint.[8] This essay, focusing on Æbbe and her lay cure-seekers, aims to extend that discussion.

Æbbe, *Coludi urbs*, and Coldingham Priory: Æbbe and her Foundation

Æbbe was not only *Coludi urbs*'s founder and first abbess, but, as the sister of kings Oswald and Oswiu she was also Northumbrian royalty. Her move into monasticism, and her posthumous saintly status was mirrored by other women within Æbbe's extended family: Ælfflæd, her niece, was an abbess of Whitby and her niece-in-law, Æbbeldreda, was founder and first abbess of Ely.[9] The latter spent a year at *Coludi urbs* under Æbbe's tutelage, having received her nun's veil from St Wilfrid of Northumbria in *c.* 672.[10] Æbbe was also on good terms with St Cuthbert, whose visit to *Coludi urbs* (while prior of Melrose) provides the backdrop for his famous overnight vigils in the North Sea, and his encounter with the otters the following morning.[11]

Little is known about *Coludi urbs* beyond the fact that it was a royal institution and thus undoubtedly wealthy, and that it was a double monastery (housing both monks and nuns). By the twelfth century, the location for this

---

8 Carr, *A History of Coldingham Priory*, pp. 19–27; King Hunter, *The History of the Priory*; *Vita Æbbe*, pp. xii–xvi; Powell, 'Pilgrimage, Performance and Miracle Cures'; Whitehead, 'A Scottish or English Saint?'; Whitnah, 'Reshaping History'.

9 See Jane Sinnett-Smith's essay in this volume, pp. 285–303 (288–89).

10 *Vita Æbbe*, II, pp. 12–13; *Liber Eliensis*, ed. by Blake, I.10–11, pp. 25–28; *Liber Eliensis*, trans. by Fairweather, I.10–11, pp. 31–36.

11 Bede, *Vita Cuthberti*, ed. and trans. by Colgrave, 10, pp. 188–91.

monastery was believed to be at Kirk Hill, on the promontory known now as St Abb's Head. Despite an arch and chapel surviving into the early nineteenth century, no standing remains survive today of the earlier monastery or the high-medieval oratory, but evidence of underlying groundworks is visible in aerial photography of the site, and they have thus been marked on the Ordnance Survey's map of the St Abb's Head peninsula.[12] What is certain is that Kirk Hill's topography does not lend itself to easy accessibility. The North Sea lies to the east, and there is a sheer drop down to the sea. Inland, to the west, is a low-lying area in which Mire Loch is situated, and, prior to an attempt to drain the valley in the late eighteenth century, this would have been marshy and prone to flooding.[13]

Æbbe's connections to high-status lay and religious individuals suggest that *Coludi urbs* played an important role in late seventh-century northern monasticism. However, following her death (in the 680s), *Coludi urbs* was destroyed in a fire and the monastery was abandoned. According to a passage in Bede's *Historia ecclesiastica*, repeated almost verbatim in the twelfth-century *Vita Æbbe*, the fire was a divine punishment for the community's failure to reform their less-than-monastic behaviour.[14] Bede criticized the religious of *Coludi urbs* for their luxuriant way of life and lustfulness. The nuns in particular were accused of attempting to attract the attention of men through wearing expensive attire.[15] Such criticisms provide a subtle indication of the social standing of *Coludi urbs*'s community (presumably the majority were from a noble background like their abbess) while emphasizing the wealth of this royal foundation.[16]

What is important in Bede's account is the lack of any direct critique of Æbbe for the poor management of her community. Although Bede does state, in recording the monastery's divine fall, that 'praecipue illorum qui maiores' (especially those who were its leaders) were particularly at fault, the abbess herself is not directly named.[17] Nor, as the destruction of the monastery occurs after Æbbe's death, and after the community had relapsed into bad habits, is it clear that Æbbe is the 'authority' in question here. Could this suggest that, following amendments made while Æbbe was still alive, those who succeeded her were unable to retain the improved level of monastic morality? Bede's omission of Æbbe's name creates a certain amount of confusion, thus allowing her to avoid explicit criticism for the monastery's downfall. Indeed, Bede records that Æbbe was disturbed on hearing of her community's misbehaviour, while the *Vita Æbbe* champions

---

12 Carr, *A History of Coldingham Priory*, p. 243.

13 Carr, *A History of Coldingham Priory*, pp. 243–44.

14 Bede, *Historia ecclesiastica* (cited hereafter as *HE*), ed. and trans. by Colgrave and Mynors, IV.25, pp. 420–27; *Vita Æbbe*, II, pp. 12–19.

15 Bede, *HE*, ed. and trans. by Colgrave and Mynors, IV.25, pp. 424–27.

16 Bede, *HE*, ed. and trans. by Colgrave and Mynors, IV.25, pp. 420–27.

17 Bede, *HE*, ed. and trans. by Colgrave and Mynors, IV.25, pp. 420–21.

BEYOND THE *MIRACULA*   267

her devotion to her calling as a point of contrast to the actions of the *Coludi urbs* community.[18]

Despite her good name, the divine destruction of *Coludi urbs* and the consequent abandonment of Æbbe's burial site appear to have had a detrimental effect on her standing among her fellow northern English saints. Both Æbbe and her monastery disappear from the northern religious scene for some 500 years, until the eleventh century.

Æbbe, *Coludi urbs*, and Coldingham Priory: Durham's Dependent Daughter House

Durham's interests in Coldingham began in the early eleventh century when Elfred, son of Westou, a priest of Durham Cathedral, discovered Æbbe's sarcophagus and brought some of her relics back to Durham where they were placed in Cuthbert's tomb.[19] Later, at the end of the eleventh century, King Edgar of Scotland granted the newly established Benedictine priory at Durham the manor of Coldingham, and, by the mid-twelfth century, Durham had founded a dependent daughter house there.[20] It was following the priory's foundation that Durham's interests in Æbbe's cult really developed; her tomb, having been rediscovered, was translated to the new priory church, and, in the 1180s, an oratory was established at Kirk Hill.[21] It is at this point that Æbbe's hagiographer starts to record successful accounts of holy healing, beginning with the cure of Master Merlin's daughter, cited above, who was cured at the new oratory.

That Kirk Hill was definitely the location of Æbbe's seventh-century monastery has been recently questioned, however. Following initial archaeological investigations by Simon Stronach, the company DigVentures spent August 2018 excavating a field near the site of the twelfth-century Coldingham Priory.[22] Both excavations found evidence of boundaries and materials that could be carbon-dated to the seventh or eighth centuries, suggesting that this was the location of *Coludi urbs*.[23] While this is possible, it is worth considering that Bede's eighth-century account of Cuthbert's nocturnal North Sea vigils indicates that the monastery was situated next to, or rather above, the North Sea. Bede comments: 'At ille egressus monasterio [...] descendit ad mare, cuius ripae monasterium idem superpositum'. (Cuthbert left the monastery [...] and went down to the sea, above whose shores the

---

18   Bede, *HE*, ed. and trans. by Colgrave and Mynors, IV.25, pp. 424–25; *Vita Æbbe*, II, pp. 12–13.
19   Symeon, *Libellus de exordio*, ed. and trans. by Rollason, III.7, pp. 160–67.
20   *Early Scottish Charters*, ed. by Lawrie, XV–XXII, pp. 12–18; *The Charters of King David I*, ed. by Barrow, XLIII, LI, LXVIII, LXIX, pp. 75, 77–78, 85.
21   *Vita Æbbe*, III, pp. 20–31.
22   Stronach, 'The Anglian Monastery'; 'Coldingham 2018', *DigVentures*.
23   Stronach, 'The Anglian Monastery'; 'Coldingham 2018', *DigVentures*.

monastery was built).[24] Bede's *Vita sancti Cuthberti* appears to support the clifftop location of Kirk Hill as the site for *Coludi urbs*, especially as there is a small cove to the south of the hill, Horsecastle Bay, that would enable access to the sea. Could the finds in Coldingham, if not those of Æbbe's monastery, be indicative of an early lay community, possibly connected to the monastery? Further excavation at this location, and at Kirk Hill, in the future, may provide additional fascinating insights into the seventh- and eighth-century scene at Coldingham, as well as later medieval pilgrimage practices.

Regardless of the actual location of Æbbe's monastery, it is important to acknowledge that, by the twelfth century, both the monks and Æbbe's lay devotees made a connection to the coastal location, perceiving the oratory at Kirk Hill as the epicentre of her cult and the place where her saintly intercession was manifested most frequently. Second to this was the location of her tomb within the priory's church.

Æbbe's Twelfth-Century Cult: Analysing the *Miracula*

(i)   Gender

Ronald Finucane was an early champion of using statistical analysis to gain insight into patterns of English pilgrimage practice, and his *Miracles and Pilgrims* remains an important and influential study. In discussing the sex of pilgrims recorded in medieval *miracula*, Finucane noted an overall trend of twice as many men as women, although particular shrines did not necessarily follow this pattern.[25] The *Vita Æbbe*'s lay cure-seekers certainly do not follow this common trend. Over half those recorded are female, and younger cure-seekers (identified as either children or youths) also feature prominently, with almost half of the *miracula*'s accounts dedicated to their cures (Table 11.1).

One reason that Æbbe's cure-seeking pilgrims buck general hagiographic trends might be due to the limitations placed upon female access to the cult of St Cuthbert at Durham, Coldingham's motherhouse. A literary construction of Symeon of Durham from the end of the eleventh century, but given a historical precedent in the fall of *Coludi urbs*, Cuthbert was said to vehemently object to the presence of women and, as a result, the majority of the Durham Cathedral complex, including Cuthbert's shrine, was inaccessible to female devotees.[26] It has been suggested that this resulted in female pilgrims being redirected towards Durham-controlled cults away from the cathedral, most notably those of Æbbe and Godric of Finchale, both of whose hagiographies make reference to a large number

---

24 Bede, *Vita Cuthberti*, ed. and trans. by Colgrave, 10, pp. 188–89.
25 Finucane, *Miracles and Pilgrims*, p. 143.
26 Symeon, *Libellus de exordio*, ed. and trans. by Rollason, II.7, pp. 104–08.

of female devotees.[27] Cuthbert's supposed misogyny is certainly a possible explanation for the trends seen at Coldingham, and importantly, it would explain the *Vita Æbbe*'s promotion of female pilgrims. As will be discussed, such attitudes might also offer an explanation for why the Durham monks based at Coldingham appeared keen to promote the external location of the Kirk Hill oratory as a focus of Æbbe's cult.

Table 11.1. Social categorizations of the *Vita Æbbe*'s cure-seekers.[28]

Social categories of cure-seeker	Total
Lay/Religious	
Lay person	42
Religious	0
Male/Female	
Male	18
Female	24
Adult/Child	
Adult	22
Child	20
Adult/Child (male/female)	
Adult (male)	8
Adult (female)	14
Child (male)	10
Child (female)	10
Social Status	
Noble (male)	0
Noble (female)	3
Poor (male)	2
Poor (female)	3
Employment specified (male)	3
Employment specified (female)	0
Status unclear (male)	13
Status unclear (female)	18

---

27 Tudor, 'Reginald of Durham and St Godric of Finchale', p. 301; Whitehead, 'A Scottish or English Saint?', p. 22.

28 The category of 'Child' is used here to cover cure-seekers who are recorded as children or

(ii) Social Status

The majority of Æbbe's cure-seekers are recorded without specific details of their social status. Naturally, the purpose and focus of *miracula* is the fact that divine aid resulted in the cure of a faithful devotee irrespective of status, and that these saints offered their aid to a universal audience was key to their appeal. That said, many hagiographers included personal details on occasion, including references to the status of the cure-seeker in the case of their nobility or extreme poverty.[29] Such references are notable within the *Vita Æbbe*, including one example in which two cure-seekers received healing for similar complaints of paralysis, one devotee being a poor girl, the second a young noblewoman.[30]

Interestingly, the *Vita Æbbe* provides information about the employment of three of its cure-seeking pilgrims: a musician from Lothian; a smith from Lanark, and a youth from Barry, Angus, who sold needles.[31] The work of both the musician and the needle-seller involved travel, and this might have caused or exacerbated the afflictions they sought relief from: gout and paralysis in the knees, respectively.[32] Importantly, the needle-seller only came to Æbbe's shrine because he happened to be staying in nearby Oldcambus on account of his work.[33] The *Vita Æbbe* does not imply that this was a cult with a specific social following, but rather that the saint was ready to assist any and all devotees. Yet, that Æbbe's cult might have attracted those who simply were passing, is indicative of the fact that this was still a developing cult location rather than one that had become a well-established pilgrimage destination.

(iii) Geographic Origin

Considering Coldingham's position on the borders between England and Scotland, it is no surprise to find references to cure-seekers from both countries in the *Vita Æbbe*, although the Durham hagiographer clearly marks out the Scottish cure-seekers as such (Table 11.2). Yet despite the borderland location, the Durham monk who compiled the *Vita* notably presents an Anglo-centric focus to the cult dynamic and includes only eight accounts of Scottish cure-seekers.[34] Of these eight cure-seekers, only the aforementioned 'Scocia' (Scottish) needle-selling youth, and a young man with a swollen throat and stomach who was 'Scocicus nacione' (of the Scottish nation) are specifically recorded as coming from further north than Edinburgh.[35] The term 'Scocia'

---

youths in the Latin.

29 For a discussion of wider practices of reporting, and recording, miracles, see Finucane, *Miracles and Pilgrims*, pp. 100–03.

30 *Vita Æbbe*, IV.13, pp. 52–53.

31 *Vita Æbbe*, IV.6, IV.26, IV.36, pp. 38–41, 58–59, 62–65.

32 *Vita Æbbe*, IV.6, IV.36, pp. 38–41, 62–65.

33 *Vita Æbbe*, IV.36, pp. 62–65.

34 *Vita Æbbe*, IV.5, IV.6, IV.12, IV.26, IV.34, IV.36, IV.39, pp. 36–41, 50–51, 58–67.

35 *Vita Æbbe*, IV.36, IV.39, pp. 62–67.

Table 11.2. Distance between the starting location of the *Vita Æbbe's* cure-seekers and Coldingham.

Distance of cure-seeker from the cult centre	Total
English Cure-Seekers	
Local	
5 miles or under	8
6–20 miles	0
Mid-distance	
21–50 miles	1
Long distance	
51–100 miles	1
101 miles or over	4
Foreign Cure-Seekers	
Scotland	
South of the Forth	5
North of the Forth	2
Distance unknown	1
Wales	
Distance unknown	1
Origin unknown	19

was used with reference to Gaelic-speaking individuals from north of the Forth.[36] The remaining six Scottish cure-seekers lived south of the Forth, and thus might be considered as relative 'locals' to the cult regardless of their nationality.[37] Conversely, among the English cure-seekers are individuals who travel from the far south of the country making journeys of much greater length. There is also one lone Welsh cure-seeker.[38]

The Anglo-centric nature of the *Vita Æbbe* is representative of the cult's borderland location.[39] As Whitehead has highlighted, Æbbe's identity within her literary sources shifts in accordance with geo-political developments in the Scottish Borders.[40] The late-twelfth and thirteenth centuries were a period

---

36 *Vita Æbbe*, IV.39, pp. xxiv–xxv.
37 *Vita Æbbe*, IV.5, IV.6, IV.12, IV.26, IV.34, pp. 36–41, 50–51, 58–63.
38 *Vita Æbbe*, IV.7, pp. 40–43.
39 Whitehead, 'A Scottish or English Saint?', pp. 7–8, 12.
40 Whitehead, 'A Scottish or English Saint?', pp. 5–7, 10–14.

in which Durham controlled Coldingham unproblematically and Æbbe's 'Englishness' was emphasized, in particular, her connection to Cuthbert and Northumbria.[41] This interest in promoting the Englishness of both the saint and the cult centre could well explain why so few Scottish cure-seekers were recorded in the *Vita*, although whether this was a reality of contemporary cult practice remains frustratingly elusive.

As with social status, a number of accounts omit specific details of the cure-seeker's starting location. Again, this reflects the hagiographer's focus on the miraculous cure and the intercessory power of Æbbe. It must also be considered whether this reflects a high level of local interest in the cult. After all, for local devotees it might be that the distance covered in pursuit of Æbbe's aid was not seen to be worthy of note.

(iv)   Nature of the Affliction

What were the causes of the cure-seekers' petitions to Æbbe for her divine intercession? Does the *Vita Æbbe* reveal any trends in the abbess's cure-giving abilities? Although the number of individuals who sought Æbbe's aid, or that of any saint, was greater than the numbers recorded in the hagiographical collections produced, the *miracula* do reveal evidence of trends in the types of affliction that were perceived to have been successfully cured through God's grace and the saint's intercession.

In the *Vita Æbbe*, as in many English saints's cults, cure-seekers requested aid for a range of afflictions, with forms of paralysis and eye complaints (primarily blindness) featuring prominently. Both, as noted by Carole Rawcliffe among others, could be caused by a number of hereditary and environmental factors, including poor diet and malnutrition.[42] Both were often also thought to be incurable unless by divine will, making their remedy somewhat of a saintly speciality. Sicknesses and fevers, which required rapid treatment, also often featured heavily within *miracula*. However, this is not the case in the *Vita Æbbe*, where only one individual is cured of a fever (which had led to temporary insanity due to exhaustion).[43] What *does* feature more prominently than in other contemporary *miracula* are cures of swellings and particularly cures of mutism.[44] In general, these are complaints that appear less frequently among the records of successful miracles, but the *Vita Æbbe* contradicts this (Table 11.3).[45]

---

41   Whitehead, 'A Scottish or English Saint?', p. 5.

42   Rawcliffe, 'Health and Disease', pp. 66–73.

43   *Vita Æbbe*, IV.31, pp. 58–61.

44   Accounts of mutism do not always record fully voiceless cure-seekers, some could still produce sounds but not produce words. Accounts where the cure-seeker was able to make some form of sound are categorized as 'unable to speak'. Accounts categorized as 'mute' record the cure-seekers unable to make any sounds.

45   Finucane, *Miracles and Pilgrims*, pp. 103–12; Salter, 'Experiencing *Miracula*', pp. 273–81; Salter,

BEYOND THE *MIRACULA* 273

Table 11.3. Afflictions suffered by Æbbe's cure-seekers.

Affliction suffered by cure-seeker	Total
Bodily Paralysis	
Whole body	3
Single arm and/or hand only	3
Single leg and/or foot only	2
Both legs and/or feet	1
Half of the body	2
Swellings	
Whole body	2
Back only	1
Side of the body only	1
Stomach	1
Stomach and breast	1
Stomach and throat	1
Knees and legs	1
Gout	1
Eye Afflictions	
Blindness (both eyes affected)	6
Blindness in only one eye	1
Clouded vision	1
Mutism	
Unable to speak	2
Unable to speak (following demonic attack)	2
Mute	2
Madness (and complaints of the mind)	
Demonic possession or attack	3
Mutism with another complaint	
Mute and paralysed	1
Mute and deaf	1
Mute, blind and deaf	1

Saints, Cure-Seekers and Miraculous Healing, pp. 64–65.

Affliction suffered by cure-seeker	Total
Illness	
Fever	1
Injury	
Domestic accident (food related)	1

Why reports of miraculously cured illnesses should be almost entirely absent from the *Vita Æbbe*, and why cures of swellings and mutism should be so prominent, is unclear. Possibly, Æbbe was not considered particularly successful in providing a remedy to sicknesses, or perhaps the answer lies in the fact that the spiritual and geographical focus of Æbbe's cult was primarily the Kirk Hill oratory. As noted, this was not an easily accessible location and, practically, would have proved challenging for those who were weak, let alone bedridden, as a result of their illness or impairment (something the mute were less affected by). Yet, despite these practical issues, the majority of Æbbe's cure-seekers made the difficult journey to the oratory and were rewarded with their desired cure at the Kirk Hill site.

The Dual Locations: Kirk Hill and Coldingham Priory

The oratory was evidently the primary location for requesting Æbbe's intercession. That the location of *Coludi urbs*, despite no longer housing the saint's coffin (which was now two miles away in the priory church) should hold such sway over the patterns of pilgrimage is interesting. But was the focus on the oratory site the result of lay-devotee popularity, or of careful management of the cult by the priory? After all, it is clear that even severely impaired pilgrims were keen to make the journey to the oratory site:

> Fossas ad instar carnis crude sanguine perfusas habebat ubi paulo ante lumen celi uiderat. Erat quidem de amissione desolacio et de humana subuencione grauius urgebat desperacio […] Ab amicis denique admonita, Coldingham, quia ibi sanitates celebrari audierat, uenit et ibi in domo cuiusdam seruientis nostri mansit. Post hec, filia sua paruula eam ducente et gressus cecos regente, ad montem Coludi perrexit et in oratiorium introducta pro sua salute Deo et gloriose uirgini uota precum effudit […] Discussis paululum ex facie eius tenebris, uidit, quamuis ea que uiderat clarius agnoscere non posset. Que mox fontem querere statuit et, circuito monte et hiis que subiecta sunt locis, nullo tandem ducente uel indicante, repperit. Et lauit et, omni penitus decessa caligine, pristinam uidendi graciam recepit.

> > (She had hollows like raw meat [where her eyes should have been], full of blood, where a little time before she had seen the light of heaven. She was desolated by the loss and deeply oppressed by despair of any human help […] On the advice of her friends, she came to Coldingham,

for she had heard that famous cures were occurring there, and lodged there in the house of one of our servants. After this, led by her little daughter who guided her blind steps, she came to St Abb's Head, entered the oratory [...] [And, having been told by Æbbe in a vision to seek out her fountain, she went] around the mountain and places below it without anyone to guide her or show her the way, [and] she found it. She washed and the darkness completely dispersed, and she received the gift of sight.)[46]

The desperation and determination of this unnamed woman is evident within the account. Where the woman began her journey from is unclear, but the *Vita Æbbe* notes that the woman first went to the shrine of St Thomas Becket constructed 'in finibus Londonie' (in the London area): most likely a reference to the early shrine to Becket on London Bridge.[47] Clearly, then, this journey involved a seriously impaired woman travelling almost the length of England, indicating an impressive level of dedication.[48] That she did this with only 'filia sua paruula' (her young daughter) guiding her makes this a yet more impressive feat.[49] The latter part of her cure-seeking is described as a solo undertaking that involved a visually impaired woman navigating the difficult cliffside topography of St Abb's Head. It would appear that the time spent in the oratory, and her vision of Æbbe, provided her with the capability to complete this final aspect of the process independently, even if her blindness persisted until she had washed her eyes. This woman, one of a number of severely impaired devotees within the *Vita Æbbe*, was not alone in making her way to the Kirk Hill oratory: just under four fifths of the cure-seekers in the *miracula* did the same (Table 11.4).

In her study of the performative nature of the pilgrimage route to the oratory, Powell, taking a phenomenological approach, argues that pilgrims' journeys through the landscape mirrored Æbbe's own presence in, and interaction with, the local topography.[50] Æbbe's connection with the local landscape is perhaps most notable in the twelfth-century account of her divine rescue from a hopeful suitor named Aidan 'Scottorum tiranno' (tyrant of the Scots).[51] Having fled to the Berwickshire coast, Æbbe was protected from Aidan's advances when, miraculously, the sea rose around her refuge for three days.[52] She later founded *Coludi urbs* on the site of her protection. That Æbbe herself should be the recipient of a miracle at this site provided further ties between the saint and the devotees who sought her intercession within the same landscape.

---

46 *Vita Æbbe*, IV.2, pp. 32–35.
47 *Vita Æbbe*, IV.2, pp. 32–33, 34 n. 60. See Page ed., *History of the County of London*, I, p. 572.
48 The distance between London and Coldingham is approximately 350 miles.
49 *Vita Æbbe*, IV.2, pp. 34–35.
50 Powell, 'Pilgrimage, Performance and Miracle Cures', pp. 79–80.
51 *Vita Æbbe*, II, pp. 6–9.
52 A similar legend is also connected to Ætheldreda in the *Liber Eliensis*, see Jane Sinnett-Smith's essay in this volume, pp. 285–303 (292–94).

Table 11.4. Location of the *Vita Æbbe*'s cure-seekers at the time of their miraculous cure.[53]

Location of the cure-seeker	Total
Kirk Hill	
Inside the oratory	28
Outside the oratory	1
At the associated spring/fountain	4
Coldingham Priory Church	
At Æbbe's tomb	6
In the churchyard	1
Location unclear	2

That Æbbe's presence could still be felt in the landscape is perhaps most striking in relation to the two springs at Kirk Hill. The *Vita Æbbe* details a higher spring that occasionally dried up in the summer, and a lower spring that 'ad radices eius latice perpetuo madet' (furnishes perpetual moisture with its waters at the roots of the hill).[54] Well Mouth is still marked on the current Ordnance Survey map. Due to the fact that a number of saints were believed to have drunk from these springs in *Coludi urbs*'s heyday, they were thought to have health-giving properties.[55] Other saints associated with the site, and thus with the springs, include Ætheldreda, Cuthbert, and Wilfrid (and possibly Æbbe's brother Oswald), all of whose connections to both Æbbe and *Coludi urbs* were mentioned above. The comments made in the *Vita Æbbe* regarding the springs' thaumaturgic properties could indicate an older, local, association between the springs and the saintly heritage of the area.[56] Indeed, throughout the *Vita* there are other passing comments that hint at a possible earlier, local awareness of Æbbe, if not a full-blown cult.[57] If lay devotion to Æbbe went back further than the monks at Coldingham were willing to recognize explicitly in the *Vita*, then it is possible that there was already lay interest in the Kirk Hill site, thus explaining its popularity in Æbbe's *miracula*.

Although Æbbe might not have completely faded from local legend, there is no evidence of lay devotion or of a cult to her prior to the twelfth century. True, the first oratory constructed on the site was the work of a local layman,

---

53 The two cases marked as 'unclear' both take place during Mass, but whether this was within the Priory church or at the oratory, where a liturgical custom had developed, is uncertain. A reference to services at the oratory can be found in *Vita Æbbe*, IV.7, pp. 42–43.

54 *Vita Æbbe*, II, pp. 8–9.

55 *Vita Æbbe*, II, pp. 10–11.

56 *Vita Æbbe*, II, pp. 8–9.

57 *Vita Æbbe*, I, pp. 1–2, III, pp. 22–25, IV.1, pp. 30–31; Salter, 'Memory, Myth', pp. 39, 42–44.

Henry, but the date of this, as recorded in the *Vita Æbbe*, was 1188, and the priory quickly replaced this oratory with a larger structure.[58] Additionally, it is implied that both the monastic and local lay community were initially doubtful of Henry's construction, presumably because Æbbe's tomb had already been translated to the priory church.[59] Both the date and the initial reaction to Henry's oratory do not support the idea that there was an earlier practice of lay pilgrimage to, and devotion at, Kirk Hill.

Regarding the development of the cult, it must be remembered that both locations associated with it were under the guardianship of Coldingham Priory and thus, theoretically, of Durham Cathedral Priory. As Victoria Tudor and Hilary Powell have highlighted, late twelfth-century Durham was becoming increasingly interested in centralizing the cult of Cuthbert to the cathedral's shrine.[60] For Powell, this centralization had a direct impact on the management of Æbbe's cult, with the priory keen to emphasize her presence in Coldingham in order to defend her from any claims their motherhouse might choose to make on her relics.[61] Did the centralization of Cuthbert's cult also influence other aspects of devotion and pilgrimage to Æbbe's cult? Focusing devotion to Cuthbert on the Durham shrine was, as noted, potentially problematic for female pilgrims whose access to the cathedral was restricted owing to the (supposedly) misogynistic attitude of the saint.[62] Did Æbbe's cult see greater numbers of female cure-seekers as a result of limitations at Durham, and is this also why the priory directed Æbbe's devotees to the external locale of Kirk Hill? The monks based at Coldingham were clearly aware of the attitude at their motherhouse. The *Vita Æbbe* proves as much in reporting *Coludi urbs's* fall.[63] Importantly, and reflecting the eleventh-century invention of Cuthbert's misogyny, the *Vita* goes further than Bede's earlier account of *Coludi urbs's* divine punishment in emphasizing the sexual nature of the sins committed by the monastery's inhabitants, particularly its nuns, identifying this as the reason for Cuthbert's mistrust of women.[64]

The Coldingham monks were clearly aware of the attitudes towards women at their motherhouse, yet to argue that they wished to keep a distance between themselves and Æbbe's lay devotees overlooks the fact that the cure-seeking involved returning to Coldingham to inform the monks of the miracle, as seen in the accounts of Merlin's daughter and the woman from London.[65] The monks were not absent from the oratory either; they witnessed first-hand the

---

58 *Vita Æbbe*, III, pp. 26–31.

59 *Vita Æbbe*, III, pp. 30–31.

60 Tudor, 'The Cult of St Cuthbert in the Twelfth Century', pp. 455–56; Powell, 'Pilgrimage, Performance and Miracle Cures', p. 83.

61 Powell, 'Pilgrimage, Performance and Miracle Cures', p. 83.

62 Symeon, *Libellus de exordio*, ed. and trans. by Rollason, II.7, pp. 104–08; Tudor, 'The Cult of St Cuthbert in the Twelfth Century', pp. 457–58.

63 *Vita Æbbe*, II, pp. 18–21.

64 *Vita Æbbe*, II, pp. 20–21.

65 *Vita Æbbe*, IV.1, IV.2, pp. 30–33, 32–35.

vigils kept by supplicants, and saw and sympathized with Æbbe's cure-seekers. We learn from the *miracula* that the aforementioned musician from Lothian spent four months at the priory recovering from a local famine.[66] The monks also observed the vigils of a woman from Aycliffe, County Durham, who suffered from partial paralysis. The woman spent Monday to Wednesday at the oratory without any food, during which time 'tres uero fratres cenobii Coldynghamenses [...] eam uiderunt et illius miserie quam plurimum condoluerunt' (three brethren of the monastery of Coldingham [...] saw her and deeply sympathized with her misery).[67] On the Thursday, while she slept in front of the altar:

> uidebatur ei quod quedam auis pulcherrima ei super manum egram insideret, uel que auis aut cuius generis esset scire non ualebat. Sed illius decore quam plurimum delectata, manu sana eius complanabat, cui id agenti mulier incomparandi decoris assistens [...] Illa uero et a sompno et ab egritudine surgens, nullo sustentante ad altare accessit, cui oscula crebra impressit. Postera uero die ad Coldyngham peruenit et missam cuiusdam sacerdotis audiuit, cui factum in se miraculum enarrauit.

> (it seemed to her that a very beautiful bird perched on her, or on her diseased hand, though she did not know what bird it was or of what species. But delighted very much by its attractive appearance, she stroked it with her healthy hand. While she was doing this, a woman of incomparable beauty stood before her [...] The woman arose from both her sleep and from her illness, went to the altar without any assistance, and planted many kisses on it. Next day she came to Coldingham and heard the mass of a certain priest, to whom she recounted the miracle that had been performed.)[68]

The actions of the priory's brethren are of course in keeping with St Benedict's *Regula* regarding monastic provision of charity and hospitality to the poor, the sick, and pilgrims.[69] The *Vita Æbbe* emphasizes that the monks were sympathetic towards cure-seekers, and highlights the interaction between the two at both cult locations. Evidently Cuthbert's supposed antipathy toward women did not directly impact the development of Æbbe's cult. While Kirk Hill remained the primary destination for devotees, the priory also played a part in the process of cure-seeking pilgrimage, specifically by recording the miracle. However, Kirk Hill seems to have had a particular connection to the saintly abbess, with Æbbe's presence there functioning as a prominent feature of her *miracula*.

---

66 *Vita Æbbe*, IV.6, pp. 38–41.
67 *Vita Æbbe*, IV.38, pp. 64–65.
68 *Vita Æbbe*, IV.38, pp. 64–65.
69 Benedict, *Rule of St Benedict*, trans. by McCann, 53, pp. 118–19.

Æbbe's Presence at Kirk Hill

For Æbbe's cure-seekers, undertaking vigils at the oratory was an integral part of the cure-seeking process. It is particularly noteworthy that Æbbe was often a present figure at these vigils, appearing in visions as part of the curative process. Not only did the abbess appear to her cure-seekers, for example directing the woman from London to her spring, she also engaged physically with many of them (Table 11.5). A man from the Edinburgh area, who had applied hot irons to himself in the hope of remedying his paralysis, was touched roughly by Æbbe as part of her hands-on treatment of his affliction; a mute youth from Newbattle had his tongue pulled by Æbbe; and a woman with a swollen breast and stomach had the areas of her affliction touched by the abbess while she slept.[70]

In these visions, Æbbe is recorded as having appeared as a nun of incomparable beauty, and in curing the aforementioned needle-selling youth her face also is noted as being 'roseo colore uultum perfusa' (imbued with a rosy hue).[71] Such imagery is not unusual in descriptions of saintly visions, with female saints often described in these terms.[72] However, it is Æbbe's hands-on interaction with her cure-seekers, particularly the mute, that makes her *miracula* stand out from other contemporary collections. A girl from Mersington, who had become mute as a result of a demonic attack, washed her face at the spring and then recovered her speech when Æbbe placed a finger in her mouth.[73] The aforementioned youth from Newbattle, made mute when an evil spirit in the form of a gust of wind blew into his mouth, was cured when Æbbe placed her whole hand into his mouth, 'linguam extraxit et diabolice alligacionis nodum soluit' (pulled forth the tongue, [and] untied the knot that the devil had tied).[74] Æbbe is also described as loosening a knot in the throat of a girl who had been mute since birth, in this instance a 'crepitu' (crack) sounded, indicating that the knot had been broken.[75] Visons of Æbbe and her interaction with pilgrims at the oratory depict the abbess having an almost corporeal presence at Kirk Hill, promoting a sense of her accessibility and willingness to assist those who sought her aid. Æbbe's presence within the local landscape also re-emphasizes Coldingham's claims to her relics and cult, countering other institutions, including Durham, who might have intended to challenge this.[76]

---

70 *Vita Æbbe*, IV.5, IV.12, IV.23, pp. 36–39, 50–51, 56–57.
71 *Vita Æbbe*, IV.36, pp. 64–65; Whitehead, 'A Scottish or English Saint?', pp. 23–24.
72 Ætheldreda is similarly described in the mid-twelfth-century *Liber Eliensis*, see *Liber Eliensis*, ed. by Blake, III.61, p. 313; *Liber Eliensis*, trans. by Fairweather, III.61, p. 387.
73 *Vita Æbbe*, IV.35, pp. 62–63.
74 *Vita Æbbe*, IV.12, pp. 50–51.
75 *Vita Æbbe*, IV.10, pp. 48–49.
76 Powell, 'Pilgrimage, Performance and Miracle Cures', p. 83.

280 RUTH J. SALTER

Table 11.5. Æbbe's appearances to and interactions with her cure-seekers.[77]

Interaction with the cure-seeker	Total
Appearance to cure-seeker	
Vision of Æbbe	16
Vision of Æbbe and the Virgin Mary	2
Vision of Æbbe and Archangel Michael	1
Vision of Æbbe and Margaret of Scotland	1
Vision of Æbbe and a bird	3
Vision of a bird, without Æbbe	2
Interaction between Æbbe and the cure-seeker	
Æbbe talks to, or instructs cure-seeker	7
Æbbe physically engages with the cure-seeker (e.g. through touch)	14
Æbbe talks to and physically engages with the cure-seeker	2

That saints might appear to, and engage with, their devotees is not in itself a surprise, but that this should be such a frequent feature of the *Vita Æbbe*, and that Æbbe should physically interact with her devotees so frequently, sets her hagiography apart from other contemporary *miracula*.[78] It would appear that the abbess's visionary and tactile interaction with her devotees was an accepted and even expected part of the cure-seeking process, just as visiting both the oratory and the priory was. More important still, the physicality of Æbbe's presence at the oratory provides a further explanation for why Kirk Hill was such an important feature, and this must reflect wider practices and experiences of devotional practice within the cult.

Conclusion

The late twelfth-century *Vita Æbbe* offers a rare insight into the high-medieval cult of this little-known Northumbrian saint. The posthumous miracles reveal that this was a cult that stood out from many of its contemporaries. Not only does the cult appear to have been particularly popular with female cure-seekers, perhaps due to the restrictions upon access to St Cuthbert's shrine at Durham Cathedral, but Æbbe seems to have been a potential specialist in the cure of the mute. It is perhaps in the dual location of her cult, however, that St Æbbe

---

77 In three of the five accounts to include a bird in the vision, the bird is named as a dove.
78 For examples of other English late twelfth-century hagiographies, see: Thomas, *The Life and Miracles of St William of Norwich*, ed. and trans. by Jessop and James; Kemp, trans., 'The Miracles of the Hand of St James'.

and her cure-seekers particularly stand out. Separated by approximately two miles, the oratory on Kirk Hill and the priory church not only connected the abbess's cult to the landscape that had housed her own seventh-century foundation of *Coludi urbs*, it also drew a connection between the old and new monasteries, creating a sense of continuity in the landscape despite the disruption of the twelfth-century monastic presence there. For her devotees, Æbbe was seen to remain connected to the site of her own early monastery, and travelling to the oratory was clearly an accepted part of the cure-seeking process. Cure-seekers similarly expected, it would appear, that Æbbe would show herself to them in a vision and quite possibly engage directly with them as part of the miraculous healing process.

Thanks in part to its position and to the successful establishment of Æbbe's cult, Coldingham became Durham's wealthiest daughter house by the mid-thirteenth century.[79] How this cult developed in the later Middle Ages is less well recorded, although it must have been affected by the growing political tensions on the Scottish–English border.[80] While the *Vita Æbbe* cannot reveal these later developments, what we do get from the hagiography is a fascinating insight into the formative years of this unique high-medieval saint's cult, its devotees, and particularly the practices of cure-seeking pilgrimage that were undertaken and experienced at this most northerly of English cult centres.

---

79 Dobson, 'The Last English Monks on Scottish Soil', p. 2; *The Priory of Coldingham*, ed. by Raine, pp. 241–43.

80 Regarding Æbbe and Coldingham in later Middle Ages, see Whitehead, 'A Scottish or English Saint?', pp. 28–42; Carr, *A History of Coldingham Priory*, pp. 7–36; Dobson, 'The Last English Monks on Scottish Soil', pp. 1–25.

Works Cited

Primary Sources

Bede, *Historia ecclesiastica*, in *Bede's Ecclesiastical History of the English People*, ed. and trans. by Bertram Colgrave and R. A. B. Mynors (Oxford: Clarendon Press, 1969) (cited as *HE*)

——, *Vita sancti Cuthberti auctore Beda*, in *Two Lives of St Cuthbert: A Life by an Anonymous Monk of Lindisfarne and Bede's Prose Life*, trans. by Bertram Colgrave (Cambridge: Cambridge University Press, 1940), pp. 141–307

Benedict of Nursia, St, *The Rule of St Benedict: In Latin and English*, trans. by Justin McCann (London: Burns & Oates, 1969)

The Charters of King David I: The Written Acts of David I King of Scots, 1124–53 and of his son Henry Earl of Northumberland, 1139–52, ed. by G. W. S. Barrow (Woodbridge: Boydell, 1999)

Early Scottish Charters prior to 1153, ed. by Archibald C. Lawrie (Glasgow: James MacLehose & Sons, 1905)

Kemp, Brian, trans., '*The Miracles of the Hand of St James*: Translated with an Introduction', *Berkshire Archaeological Journal*, 65 (1970), 1–19

Liber Eliensis, ed. by E. O. Blake, Camden, 3rd series, 92 (Frome: Butler & Tanner, 1962)

Liber Eliensis: A History of the Isle of Ely, from the Seventh Century to the Twelfth, trans. by Janet Fairweather (Woodbridge: Boydell, 2005)

The Priory of Coldingham: The Correspondence, Inventories, Account rolls and Law Proceedings of the Priory of Coldingham, ed. by James Raine, SS, 12 (London: J. B. Nichols and Son, 1841)

Symeon of Durham, *Libellus de exordio atque procursu istius, hoc est Dunhelmensis, ecclesie. Tract on the Origins and Progress of this the Church of Durham*, ed. and trans. by David Rollason (Oxford: Oxford University Press, 2000)

Thomas of Monmouth, *The Life and Miracles of St William of Norwich*, ed. and trans. by A. Jessop and M. R. James (Cambridge: Cambridge University Press, 1896)

Vita et miracula S. Æbbe virginis, in *The Miracles of Saint Æbbe of Coldingham and Saint Margaret of Scotland*, ed. and trans. by Robert Bartlett (Oxford: Clarendon Press, 2006), pp. 1–67 (cited as *Vita Æbbe*)

Secondary Works

Carr, Alexander A., *A History of Coldingham Priory* (Edinburgh: Adam and Charles Black, 1836)

'Coldingham 2018, 19th June–1st July', *DigVentures*, <https://digventures.com/projects/coldingham/> [accessed 17 March 2019]

Cramp, Rosemary, 'The Northumbrian Identity', in *Northumbria's Golden Age*, ed. by Jane Hawkes and Susan Mills (Stroud: Sutton, 1999), pp. 1–11

Dobson, Richard B., 'The Last English Monks on Scottish Soil: The Severance of Coldingham Priory from the Monastery of Durham, 1461–78', *Scottish Historical Review*, 46.1 (1967), 1–25

Finucane, Ronald, *Miracles and Pilgrims: Popular Beliefs in Medieval England* (Basingstoke: Macmillan, 1995)

King Hunter, William, *The History of the Priory of Coldingham* (Edinburgh: Sutherland and Knox, 1858)

Page, William, ed., *A History of the County of London: Volume 1, London Within the Bars, Westminster and Southwark* (London: Victoria County History, 1909)

Petts, David, and Sam Turner, ed., *Early Medieval Northumbria: Kingdoms and Communities, AD 450–1100* (Turnhout: Brepols, 2011)

Powell, Hilary, 'Pilgrimage, Performance and Miracle Cures in the Twelfth-Century *Miracula* of St Æbbe', in *Medicine, Healing and Performance*, ed. by Effie Gemi-Iordanou and others (Oxford: Oxbow, 2014), pp. 71–85

Rawcliffe, Carole, 'Health and Disease', in *A Social History of England, 900–1200*, ed. by Julia Crick and Elisabeth van Houts (Cambridge: Cambridge University Press, 2011), pp. 66–75

Salter, Ruth J., 'Experiencing *Miracula*: Cure-Seekers, Cure-Seeking and Cure-Giving in Twelfth-Century English Hagiography' (unpublished doctoral thesis, University of Reading, 2015)

——, 'Memory, Myth, and Creating the Cult of St Æbbe at Coldingham', *Journal of Medieval Monastic Studies*, 9 (2020), pp. 31–49

——, *Saints, Cure-Seekers and Miraculous Healing in Twelfth-Century England*, Health and Healing in the Middle Ages, 1 (Woodbridge: York Medieval, 2021)

Stronach, Simon, 'The Anglian Monastery and Medieval Priory of Coldingham: *Urbs Coludi* Revisited', *Proceedings of the Society of Antiquaries of Scotland*, 135 (2005), 395–422

Tudor, Victoria M., 'Reginald of Durham and St Godric of Finchale: A Study of a Twelfth-Century Hagiographer and his Major Subject' (unpublished doctoral thesis, University of Reading, 1979)

——, 'The Misogyny of Saint Cuthbert', *Archaeologia Aeliana*, 5th series, 12 (1984), 157–67

——, 'The Cult of St Cuthbert in the Twelfth Century: The Evidence of Reginald of Durham', in *St Cuthbert, His Cult and His Community to AD 1200*, ed. by Gerald Bonner, Clare Stancliffe, and David W. Rollason (Woodbridge: Boydell, 1989), pp. 447–68

Whitehead, Christiania, 'A Scottish or English Saint? The Shifting Sanctity of St Aebbe of Coldingham', in *New Medieval Literatures 19*, ed. by Philip Knox and others (Cambridge: Brewer, 2019), pp. 1–42

Whitnah, Lauren L., 'Reshaping History in the Cult of St Æbbe of Coldingham', in *Medieval Cantors and their Craft: Music, Liturgy and the Shaping of History, 800–1500*, ed. by Katie Ann-Marie Bugyis, A. B. Kraebel, and Margot Fassler (York: York Medieval, 2017), pp. 207–21

JANE SINNETT-SMITH

Ætheldreda in the North

Tracing Northern Networks in the
Liber Eliensis *and the* Vie de seinte Audree

The seventh-century queen and abbess Saint Ætheldreda, also known as Æthelthryth or Audrey (*c.* 630–679), was throughout the Middle Ages intimately linked to the space of Ely in East Anglia. Her Ely shrine, housing her reputedly incorrupt body, drew substantial numbers of pilgrims until its destruction during the English Reformation in 1541.[1] Ely was the site of Ætheldreda's own monastic foundation, and her body's enduring presence asserted a sense of continuity between this saintly foundation and the later medieval monastery.[2] Indeed, throughout the later Middle Ages the Ely monks exploited their possession of Ætheldreda's incorrupt body to interweave the saint tightly with their land and community. The twelfth-century *Liber Eliensis*, compiled by an anonymous Ely monk, stresses the saint's fierce defence of not only her tomb's unviolated integrity, but also the Ely community's territorial and property rights, describing harsh punishments meted out to a Viking invader seeking to open Ætheldreda's tomb (I. 41); monks stealing church goods (II. 138); and local aristocrats cheating Ely out of rent payments (III. 115).[3] As Virginia Blanton has argued, the *Liber* positions the saint's whole, inviolate corpse as a metonym for Ely and its possessions: miraculous protection of Ætheldreda's body is conflated with protection of the monastic community and its property, and seen as a means to assert the Ely monastery's identity and autonomy.[4] The saint, her body, and her *virtus*, are firmly intertwined with her Ely cult centre.

---

1 A description of the twelfth-century shrine is provided in the *Liber Eliensis*, ed. by Blake, III. 50. On Ely's pilgrimage, see Webb, *Pilgrimage in Medieval England*, pp. 40–42.
2 Karkov, 'The Body of St Æthelthryth', p. 402; Ridyard, *The Royal Saints of Anglo-Saxon England*, p. 182.
3 On the *Liber*'s authorship and dating, see *Liber Eliensis*, ed. by Blake, pp. xlvi–xlix.
4 Blanton-Whetsell, '*Tota integra, tota incorrupta*', p. 233.

> **Jane Sinnett-Smith** (janesinnettsmith@gmail.com) recently obtained her doctorate, entitled 'Blood, Bones, and Gold: Rewriting Relics in Medieval French Verse Saints' Lives 1150–1300', in the School of Modern Languages, University of Warwick.

Late Medieval Devotion to Saints from the North of England: New Directions, ed. by Christiania Whitehead, Hazel J. Hunter Blair, and Denis Renevey, MCS 48 (Turnhout: Brepols, 2022), pp. 285–303
BREPOLS ⊛ PUBLISHERS   10.1484/M.MCS-EB.5.124354

Yet versions of Ætheldreda's life produced in the twelfth to thirteenth centuries also display an investment in the saint's activities beyond Ely, and in particular as queen of Northumbria, that renegotiates her cult's centre of gravity. While the rich connections between Ætheldreda and Ely have received substantial scholarly attention, her northern associations have not yet been subject to focused study. This essay explores how tracing Ætheldreda's northern connections can illuminate both the construction of her sanctity, and the treatment of northern saints and spaces in a southern textual context.

I examine Ætheldreda's relationships to the people, artefacts, and spaces of the North in two closely related texts, the aforementioned *Liber Eliensis* (1131–1174) and the *Vie de seinte Audree* (early thirteenth century). Organized into three books, the *Liber* collects a broad range of documents related to the Ely monastery alongside a narrative of its saintly founder's life and numerous posthumous miracles dating from the seventh to the twelfth centuries.[5] The collection is transmitted complete in two manuscripts, and in altered or fragmentary form in a further four, produced from the twelfth to early fourteenth centuries.[6] Those manuscripts with traceable origins are all associated with Ely itself: the *Liber* was produced by and for an Ely monastic audience. The *Liber*'s version of Ætheldreda's life is adapted from Bede's *Historia ecclesiastica*, supplemented by a range of oral and written sources.[7] Born into East Anglian royalty, the *Liber* recounts, Ætheldreda wished to devote her life to Christ, but was reluctantly married off twice, preserving her virginity through both marriages. After her first husband's death, she was married to Ecgfrith, king of Northumbria (r. 670–685). Eventually leaving Ecgfrith to enter monastic orders, she was forced to flee to Ely to escape his pursuit. There, she founded a double monastery, where she was abbess until her death. Her corpse's translation after sixteen years revealed that her body remained whole and incorrupt. Then follow accounts of Ely's ninth-century destruction, its subsequent revival, and the many posthumous miracles Ætheldreda performed there.[8]

The collection's updated version of Ætheldreda's life was the source for several later Latin and vernacular narratives.[9] In particular, in the late twelfth or early thirteenth centuries, a woman identifying herself only as 'Marie' (l. 4624) adapted the *Liber*'s hagiographic material into the Anglo-Norman

---

5   For the *Liber*'s sources, see *Liber Eliensis*, ed. by Blake, pp. xxviii–xlii.

6   Complete manuscripts: Cambridge, Camb. Uni. Lib., MS EDC 1 (s.xiii$^{1/2}$, Ely); Cambridge, Trin. Coll. Lib., MS O.2.1 (s.xii, Ely). Fragmentary versions: Oxford, Bodl. Lib., MS Laud Misc. 647 (s.xiii$^{2/2}$, Ely); BL, MS Cotton Titus A.I (s.xii$^{3/4}$–s.xiii$^{1/4}$, Ely); BL, MS Cotton Domitian A.XV (s.xiii$^{3/4}$–s.xiv$^{1/4}$, Ely); BL, MS Cotton Vespasian A.XIX (1257–1286). *Liber Eliensis*, ed. by Blake, pp. xxiii–xxv.

7   *Liber Eliensis*, ed. by Blake, pp. xxviii–xxxiv.

8   *Liber Eliensis*, ed. by Blake, I. 1–50.

9   These include a late thirteenth-century Latin booklet, John of Tynemouth's fourteenth-century version, and several fifteenth- and sixteenth-century Middle English adaptations. Blanton, *Signs of Devotion*, pp. 9–10, 236, 249–50, 257–58.

octosyllabic verse *Vie de seinte Audree*.[10] June Hall McCash has argued on the grounds of linguistic resemblance that the *Vie* is the work of Marie de France, although some caution must be sounded over this identification.[11] Sharon Kinoshita and Peggy McCracken point to some potential linguistic and organizational dissimilarities between the *Vie* and Marie de France's corpus, while Jocelyn Wogan-Browne has argued that the *Vie*'s language is too late to belong to Marie de France's late twelfth-century period of activity.[12] For this essay's purposes, the enigmatic Marie's individual identity is of less concern than a broader consideration of how her portrayal of Ætheldreda's sainthood is inflected by her status as outside the Ely monastic community. While the *Vie* broadly shares the *Liber*'s contents, it differs in style and perspective from its Latin predecessor, displaying, for example, greater interest in Ætheldreda's subjectivity, and aristocratic women's life experiences.[13] Moreover, the *Vie*'s single extant manuscript was owned by the female religious community at Campsey Ash Priory in Suffolk, where a fourteenth-century inscription indicates it was used for mealtime readings.[14] While this well-known collection of Anglo-Norman verse lives resists any overriding thematic unity, it displays a marked focus on lives of English and female saints, as well as texts written or commissioned by women, providing a range of saintly models for its aristocratic women readers.[15] Written by a woman, and read by a female community, the *Vie* engages with different concerns and communities than those of the monastic *Liber*, showcasing how Ætheldreda's sainthood was transformed beyond her Ely cult centre.

Despite their differences in perspective, both the *Liber* and the *Vie*, I will argue, depict Ætheldreda as embedded in a series of interpersonal and spatial networks that connect her to northern saints and religious institutions. Both

---

10 Marie, *The Life of Saint Audrey*, ed. and trans. by McCash and Barban, p. 9; all translations of the *Vie* are from *The Life of Saint Audrey*, ed. and trans. by McCash and Barban.

11 McCash, 'La Vie seinte Audree', pp. 744–77.

12 Kinoshita and McCracken ed., *Marie de France*, p. 3; Wogan-Browne, 'Wreaths of Thyme', p. 57. Wogan-Browne prefers to identify Marie as a member of the religious house at Chatteris mentioned within the text (*Vie*, ll. 317, 3171), Wogan-Browne, 'Rerouting the Dower', p. 31. As McCash's overview of scholarship on Marie indicates, the question of whether Marie was a nun or laywoman remains unresolved, 'La Vie seinte Audree', pp. 772–74.

13 Blanton, *Signs of Devotion*, p. 174; Wogan-Browne, 'Rerouting the Dower', p. 35.

14 'Ce livre deviseie a la priorie de kanpseie de lire a mangier', BL, MS Add. 70513, fol. 265ᵛ. The *Vie* occupies fols 100ᵛ–134ᵛ. Russell, 'The Campsey Collection'.

15 The manuscript contains ten lives copied in the thirteenth century: Thomas Becket by Guernes de Pont-Sainte-Maxence; Mary Magdalene by Guillaume le Clerc de Normandie; Edward the Confessor by the Nun of Barking; Edmund of Canterbury by Matthew Paris; Ætheldreda by Marie; an anonymous life of Osith; Foy by Simon de Walsingham; Richard of Chichester by Pierre d'Abernon of Fetcham, Catherine of Alexandria by Clemence of Barking; and three lives by Nicolas Bozon added in the fourteenth century, of Elizabeth of Hungary, Panuce, and Paul the Hermit. Edmund's life is dedicated to Isabella of Arundel, who was also the patron of the Latin source of Richard's life. Wogan-Browne, 'Powers of Record', pp. 81, 87; Wogan-Browne, *Saints' Lives*, p. 151.

texts construct a sacred genealogy of saintly women which positions Ætheldreda as spiritual descendant of the northern saints Æbbe of Coldingham and Hilda of Whitby. Ætheldreda also enjoys spiritual friendship with St Cuthbert, materially anchored and memorialized by the gifts she bestows on him. These connections allow Ætheldreda to share in the spiritual authority of northern saints, assimilating them into a narrative of her own sanctity, pointing both to the enduring prestige of these early Northumbrian saints in a later medieval East Anglian context, and to the ways northern sainthood can be reformulated to enhance that of Ætheldreda. Ætheldreda's sainthood is developed, enhanced, and communicated through her participation in northern networks of people, places, and objects, asserting the North's vital role in her saintly formation alongside her well-known Ely associations. Moreover, if Ætheldreda as saint is constructed through northern networks, these texts also envisage the North as indelibly marked by her presence. Ætheldreda's northern networks are repeatedly cemented through material spaces and objects: monastic foundations, miraculous landscapes, and sacred artefacts that leave her material traces across northern England. Ely may be the resting place of Ætheldreda's body, but this textual tradition envisages how her spatial and material networks allow her posthumous presence to be enduringly extended and accessed beyond the confines of her Ely shrine.

Spiritual Genealogies

Both the *Liber* and the *Vie* emphasize Ætheldreda's participation in mobile familial, matrimonial, and spiritual networks that extend far beyond Ely. These networks draw particular attention to the role of inter-regional, even international, genealogies and communities of saintly women. Following the regional alliance forged through the saint's first marriage to the East Anglian Ealdorman Tondberht, her second marriage to Ecgfrith of Northumbria exemplifies the ways in which the circulation of aristocratic women in marriage alliances forges political connections between kingdoms. Both texts describe how Ætheldreda is married against her will, an object of exchange between groups of men, her marriage uniting the lineages of East Anglian and Northumbrian kings (*Liber*, I. 8; *Vie*, ll. 798–813).[16] Yet it also enables her to forge a range of spiritual connections with Northumbrian saintly figures. Her marriage produces a familial connection to St Æbbe, abbess of Coldingham and Ecgfrith's paternal aunt (*Liber*, I. 8). Æbbe plays a foundational role in Ætheldreda's saintly development, overseeing her induction as nun at Coldingham, and enabling her flight south to Ely (*Liber*,

---

16 The *Vie* accentuates Ætheldreda's unwillingness, adapting the *Liber*'s 'quod non speravit' (contrary to her hopes (I. 8)) to 'Tout encontre sa volenté' (Quite against her will, (*Vie*, l. 798)). Wogan-Browne, *Saints' Lives*, p. 57. All translations of the *Liber* are from *Liber Eliensis*, trans. by Fairweather.

I. 10; *Vie*, ll. 1182–86). The *Liber* significantly expands Æbbe's prominence in Ætheldreda's life from its source in Bede's *Historia ecclesiastica*, which only notes briefly that Ætheldreda 'intravit monasterium Æbbae abbatissae, quae erat amita regis Ecgfridi' (entered into the monastery of abbess Æbbe who was aunt to king Ecgfrith).[17] In contrast, the *Liber* underlines the two saints' familial closeness: not only had the abbess 'Ætheldretham in religionem susceperat' (received [...] [Ætheldreda] into the religious life), but she 'in filiam adoptivam nutrierat atque docuerat' (nurtured and educated her as an adopted daughter (*Liber*, I. 14)). Shared devotional activities, in particular the shared religious community at Coldingham, induct Ætheldreda into a spiritual genealogy that positions her as a displaced descendant of this northern saintly woman.

The construction of a northern saintly genealogy for Ætheldreda is emphasized through the treatment of her mother, who the *Liber* and the *Vie* identify as Hereswith, descendant of King Edwin of Northumbria (*Liber*, I. 2; *Vie*, ll. 175–77). This identification positions Ætheldreda as a member of Northumbrian in addition to East Anglian royalty, by birth as well as by marriage, enhancing her northern associations. Moreover, these texts identify Hereswith as the sister of St Hilda of Whitby, allowing Ætheldreda to claim Hilda as her aunt, and projecting a pattern of female sanctity back through Ætheldreda's maternal as well as adoptive genealogy (*Liber*, I. 2; *Vie*, ll. 185–89). Although Bede identifies a woman named Hereswith as Hilda's sister,[18] he does not identify her as Ætheldreda's mother, a figure about whom he provides no information. Instead the *Liber* works to construct a connection between Hereswith and Ætheldreda by drawing on supplementary written sources. The *Liber* notes that a life of St Milburga names Ætheldreda's mother as Hereswith: 'Etheldreth[a], cuius mater Heresuuitha dicebatur' ([Ætheldreda], whose mother was called Hereswith (I. 2)). Through a process of deduction the *Liber* concludes that as there are no records of other women in that period with this name, Ætheldreda's mother must be identified with the Hereswith named by Bede as Hilda's sister: 'Neque alia tunc temporis in tota Anglorum historia [...] repperitur, que tali nomine censeretur' (Nor is there in all the history of the English of that time [...] any other woman found who is enlisted under a name like Hereswith (I. 2)). This passage showcases the ways in which the *Liber* works to enhance and multiply Ætheldreda's spiritual and familial connections with the North. Moreover, by making visible his own work, the *Liber*'s compiler positions his text as a more complete and authoritative rendering of the saint's life that usefully supplements Bede.[19] The *Liber*'s textual authority is generated through the work of the monastic compiler.

---

17 Bede, *Historia ecclesiastica*, ed. and trans. by King, IV. 19.
18 Bede, *Historia ecclesiastica*, ed. and trans. by King, IV. 23.
19 The *Liber*'s compiler declares that he will supplement Bede's life, as 'de ipsa que [...] Beda

Although it often works closely from the *Liber*, the Anglo-Noman *Vie* displays a rather different approach to its narrative sources. Marie similarly recounts Ætheldreda's saintly and royal genealogy, noting her maternal descent from Edwin of Northumbria, and the connection Hereswith forges with Hilda: 'Herswid, | Fu suer [...] | Sainte Hilde' (Hereswith was the sister of Saint Hilda (ll. 185–87)). Yet Marie eliminates any reference to the *Liber*'s supplementary work, ascribing the naming of Ætheldreda's mother as Hereswith directly to the textual and saintly authority of Bede: 'Dist saint Bedes [...] | Ke Hereswidë out a non' ([Saint] Bede says [...] that her name was Hereswith (ll. 170–75)).[20] Indeed, throughout the *Vie* Marie makes no mention of the *Liber* as intermediary, instead consistently citing 'saint Bedes' as her authoritative source (for example ll. 182, 1448, 2898). Marie aligns her text not with the work of the Ely community, but with an older spiritual and textual origin remote from Ely, underlining her lack of interest in the *Liber*'s exploration of monastic identity. The *Vie* retrospectively integrates the *Liber*'s textual additions, including its enhanced portrayal of Ætheldreda's northern ancestry, into Bede's sacred textual authority, which Marie suggests she transmits directly.

Returning to the *Liber*, Ætheldreda's sainthood is not only rooted in, but seems narratively to absorb that of her northern saintly forerunners, as material from Bede's chapters on Hilda and Æbbe is assimilated into Etheldreda's life. The *Liber* repeatedly re-orients Bede's texts from narratives of their own individual protagonists to bolster an overarching narrative of Ætheldreda's sanctity. Material on Hilda's lineage and career from *Historia*, VI. 23 is fragmented and incorporated into descriptions of Ætheldreda's ancestry (*Liber*, I. 2–3). The *Liber* also adapts the entirety of *Historia*, VI. 25, which narrates the destruction of Æbbe's Coldingham Abbey as divine punishment for the nuns' sinfulness.[21] Bede's narrative makes no mention of Ætheldreda, foregrounding the fearsomeness of divine judgement and Æbbe's authority as abbess: the nuns temporarily reform under her rule, but revert to sin after her death. The *Liber* reformulates Coldingham's destruction as a counterpoint to Ætheldreda's piety, describing how the nuns persist in sinning despite not only a heavenly warning, but also their exposure to Ætheldreda's example: the nuns 'nec divino conversi ammonitu nec venerabilis Etheldrethe conpuncti devotione' (had neither been prompted by a divine warning to change their ways, nor pricked by contrition at the devout conduct of the venerable [Ætheldreda] (I. 14)). Coldingham's decline is followed rather pointedly in the *Liber* by a chapter detailing Ætheldreda's flourishing Ely community. The *Liber*'s account

---

disseruit non omnibus eque sufficiunt' (the things which Bede reports about her [...] are not invariably all-sufficient (I. Prologus)).

20 Bede's 'informal' saintly cult was widespread in England by the *Vie*'s date of composition, Rollason, 'The Cult of Bede', p. 198.

21 Bede's *Historia*, VI. 3, on St Chad, is also incorporated into *Liber*, I. 8. See the discussion of the destruction of Coldingham in Ruth J. Salter's essay in this volume, pp. 266–67.

of Coldingham's destruction not only foregrounds Ætheldreda's exemplary holiness, but also hints at how she (and Ely) might supplant the prestige of her northern spiritual pedigree.

Moreover, in both texts Ætheldreda's sainthood is buoyed not only by her northern maternal forerunners, but by an expansive community of holy female relatives who function as her own displaced descendants, ensuring the persistence of her spiritual legacy outside the bounds of marriage and physical procreation.[22] Mapping the places that these texts associate with Ætheldreda's lineage gives a sense of her involvement in an inter-regional geography of which her Northumbrian connections are only one strand: the spiritual careers of Ætheldreda's sisters and nieces draw further links with religious foundations in Kent, East Anglia, the Midlands, and northern France.[23] Æbbe and Hilda's roles as models and foundations for Ætheldreda's sanctity grant Northumbria and its saints a particularly formative place in these genealogical-spatial networks. Ætheldreda's saintly foremothers belong to the North, suggesting the prestige of these early northern saintly women as reference points for Ætheldreda's saintly development. Yet, if Ætheldreda shares in and indeed inherits her northern female saintly ancestry's spiritual authority, she also displaces this northern legacy southwards. The legacy of early northern female sanctity is, these texts suggest, not the exclusive preserve of the North, but rather handed down to Ætheldreda and her spiritual descendants, who expand her sacred, familial networks throughout southern England.

Sacred Landscapes

It is not only Ætheldreda's interpersonal connections that work against a singular association with Ely, as Ætheldreda is herself associated with multiple sacred sites, with a particular concentration in the North. These spatial connections are formed in part through Ætheldreda's role as donor to and founder of multiple religious institutions, an aspect of her holiness the *Vie* particularly accentuates. The foundation of Hexham Abbey is a particularly striking example of the *Vie*'s greater emphasis on Ætheldreda as founder. The *Liber* recounts how St Wilfrid, Ætheldreda's spiritual advisor, founds Hexham after receiving the land from Ætheldreda as queen of Northumbria: 'Nam Augustaldense adepta ab ipsa regina […] Etheldretha,

---

22 Blanton, 'King Anna's Daughters', p. 129; Wogan-Browne, 'Rerouting the Dower', p. 38.

23 Ætheldreda's sister Seaxburga, niece Eormenhild, and great-niece Werburga, all saints, were abbesses at Sheppey before successively inheriting rule of Ely (*Liber*, I. 36; *Vie*, ll. 2383–92). Werburga's relics were housed at Hanbury and Chester (*Liber*, I. 37; *Vie*, ll. 2399–2402). Her youngest sister Saint Withburga was enclosed at Dereham, and her relics housed there then translated to Ely (*Liber*, I. 2, II. 53; *Vie*, ll. 219–28, 4179–4226). Her sister Æthelburga and half-sister Sæthryth, although not sainted, entered monastic orders at Faremoutiers-en-Brie (*Liber*, I. 2; *Vie*, ll. 215–18); her mother retired to Chelles (*Liber*, I. 7; *Vie*, ll. 612–20).

domum Domino [...] fabricavit' (For having received Hexham from [...]
Queen [Ætheldreda] herself, he built a house for the Lord (I. 8)). The *Vie*
eliminates Wilfrid, positioning Ætheldreda as sole founder: 'La gloriuse
seinte Audree | Une noble eglise a fundee' (Glorious Saint Audrey founded
a noble church (ll. 883–84)). If the *Liber* characterizes Ætheldreda principally
as queen (*regina*), enabling but not performing Hexham's foundation, in the
Vie she is already saintly (*seinte Audree*), and enacts the foundation herself.
Ætheldreda converts the distribution of material wealth and land associated
with royalty into saintly action, foregrounding the continuities between her
queenly and saintly identities, and asserting that her tenure as Northumbrian
queen contributes to the development of her sainthood.[24] As Blanton argues,
the *Vie*'s enhanced depiction of Ætheldreda as founder potentially served as
a model for spiritual behaviour for secular aristocratic women.[25] Moreover,
the Hexham foundation stresses that Ætheldreda leaves an enduring physical
trace of her intertwined royal and saintly presence in the northern landscape
that matches her foundation at Ely.[26]

Ætheldreda's flight from Coldingham to Ely to escape Ecgfrith's pursuit
similarly leaves physical traces of her presence behind, materially recording
her passage south with a series of foundations and miraculously transformed
landscapes.[27] In perhaps Ætheldreda's most emblematic miracle, to escape
her husband's soldiers she retreats to a hilltop, around which the waters
miraculously rise in protection, preventing Ecgfrith's approach (*Liber*, I. 11;
Vie, ll. 1271–1424). Blanton has read the *Liber*'s account of this miracle as
conforming to the text's overarching assertion of monastic autonomy: the
encircled hilltop, she argues, becomes analogous to the Isle of Ely itself, the
miraculous protection of the saint's body figuring the protection of the saint's
properties at Ely from external interference.[28] Yet this miracle takes place far
north of Ely, and while it speaks to the protective enclosure of Ely property, it
also gestures to a more expansive understanding of the relationship between
Ætheldreda's saintly presence and sacred spaces beyond Ely. The miracle's
location, named by the *Liber* and the *Vie* as Coldeburcheshevet (I. 11) and

---

24 A sense of the *Vie*'s greater emphasis on Ætheldreda as donor, and the continuities between
her life as queen and religious is further brought out in Marie's version of Ætheldreda's
entry into Coldingham, detailing a long list of donations to the nunnery, including 'ses reals
aorenemenz' (her royal adornments (ll. 1217–21)), significantly expanded from *Liber*, I. 10.
See Blanton-Whetsell, '*Imagines Ætheldredae*', pp. 77–78.

25 Blanton, *Signs of Devotion*, pp. 175, 198. As Blanton notes, the *Vie*'s manuscript was read at
mealtimes at Campsey to an audience that included lay as well as religious women.

26 Hexham maintained a chapel dedicated to Ætheldreda throughout the Middle Ages,
Blanton-Whetsell, '*Imagines Ætheldredae*', p. 97.

27 Ætheldreda performs miracles and founds churches at West Halton (*Liber*, I. 13; *Vie*, ll. 1510–
16) and Stow (*Liber*, I. 13; *Vie* ll. 1532–44) in Lincolnshire. Both maintained dedications to
Ætheldreda in the twelfth century, Goscelin, *The Hagiography of the Female Saints of Ely*,
ed. by Love, p. xlii.

28 Blanton-Whetsell, '*Tota integra, tota incorrupta*', pp. 244–47.

Goldeborch (l. 1332) respectively, and identified as St Abb's Head just outside Coldingham, acts as a lasting material witness to Ætheldreda's miraculous presence.[29] Ætheldreda leaves her footprints imprinted in the hillside rock, 'vestigia pedum illius [...] in latere montis infusa' (the footprints that [Ætheldreda] made [...] were moulded in the side of the cliff (*Liber*, I. 11)): Coldeburcheshevet enduringly displays the traces of Ætheldreda's miraculous body. Moreover, the rock cracks open to provide fresh water to the saint and her companions (*Liber*, I. 11; *Vie*, ll. 1387–98). This water, according to the *Liber*, not only continues to flow, but provides miraculous healing: 'infirmis adhuc saluberrima prestat' (it is available still as a most effective cure for the sick (I. 11)).[30] Following Ætheldreda's posthumous translation, her original burial site at Ely similarly produces a healing spring (I. 31). The miraculous water at Coldeburcheshevet prefigures this later spring, replicating Ætheldreda's sacred space and offering the possibility of miraculous healing far displaced from the saint's Ely shrine. Ætheldreda's role as founder and miracle-worker leaves her mark on the landscape outside of the central locus of Ely, forging an extended network of locations in which proximity to the saint's body, presence, and miraculous intercession might be sought.

Strikingly, a miraculous spring was indeed maintained at St Abb's Head by the Durham monks in the twelfth century, yet these miracles were ascribed locally not to Ætheldreda, but to Æbbe. Æbbe's *Vita* (composed after *c.* 1188 by a Durham monk) narrates a similar miracle in which the sea rises around the hilltop to protect the saint from the pursuit of a tyrannical suitor (here Aidan rather than Ecgfrith).[31] It is unclear which saint's claim to the miracle came first, whether the *Liber* appropriated Æbbe's miracle to extend Ætheldreda's and Ely's influence north into Durham's spiritual territory, or whether Æbbe's *Vita* (which post-dates the *Liber*) conversely assimilated a narrative told about Ætheldreda to bolster a more local cult, or indeed whether the tale was a flexible local legend told about the landscape that became attached to various miraculous women over time. Above all, this institutional competition over sacred space highlights the spiritual and narrative import of the landscape itself as an enduring anchor for a miracle tale that can be adapted to meet shifting (and competing) cult needs.

Indeed, the *Liber*'s account of the Coldeburcheshevet miracle emphasizes the importance of the local landscape. Ætheldreda's miraculous journey from Coldingham is, like the focus on her spiritual genealogy, not found in Bede. The *Liber* explains that it supplements Bede's text with local testimonies: 'Hoc de scriptis Bede non cepimus, sed quicumque locum Coludi norunt cum assertione huius rei testes existunt' (We have not taken this from the writings

---

29 *The Life of Saint Audrey*, ed. by McCash and Barban, p. 276.

30 See *Vie*, ll. 1401–02.

31 *Vita et miracula S. Æbbe virginis*, ed. and trans. by Bartlett, pp. 6–7. My thanks to Ruth Salter for raising this point. For discussion of this episode in relation to Æbbe, and for further discussion of Æbbe's cult, see Ruth J. Salter's chapter in this volume, pp. 275–76.

of Bede, but all those who know the locality of Coldingham are witnesses to this fact (I. 11)). Authoritative knowledge of this miracle is not located in text, but intertwined with Coldingham and its inhabitants.[32] The space around Coldingham generates and legitimates narratives about Ætheldreda's sanctity. Again, the *Vie*'s account of this miracle elides any reference to the *Liber*'s compositional additions to Bede:

> Car saint Bede ne pooit mie
> Par seul conter iceste vie
> Fors tant com il en out enquis
> Par la bone gent del païs (ll. 1421–24)

>> For Saint Bede could never
>> By himself recount this life
>> Unless he had inquired about it
>> From the good folk of the land.

Although Marie eliminates the *Liber* as intermediary, ascribing the collection of local testimony to 'saint Bede', she crucially retains the sense of how the land and its people become a repository for stories about Ætheldreda. The focus in both the *Liber* and the *Vie* on the Coldingham landscape as witness to Ætheldreda's miracle emphasizes the reciprocal relationship between saint and space. Contact with Ætheldreda marks the northern landscape, transforming it into sacred space. In turn, its enduring communication of Ætheldreda's miraculous presence, body, and *virtus* perpetually contributes to the construction of Ætheldreda's sainthood. Without minimizing the important connections between the saint and her Ely shrine, both texts also envisage Ætheldreda's sainthood as embedded in extended geographic, textual, and above all spiritual landscapes.

Object Networks

The depiction of the traces Ætheldreda leaves on the northern landscape points to the ways in which the sense of the saint as mobile and interconnected that she generates during her lifetime is extended beyond her death through material spaces and artefacts. Both texts explore how Ætheldreda's northern networks are posthumously preserved through sacred objects. In another episode with no source in Bede, the *Liber* recounts Ætheldreda's close spiritual friendship with St Cuthbert while still queen of Northumbria, a relationship

---

32 Æbbe's *Vita* also associates this tale with orality and landscape, affirming how local topography generates narrative: 'Quod, quia uulgo tritum est et a maioribus traditum [...] ex loci qualitate uideatur habere uestigium', (This is a familiar story among the populace and has been handed down by our forefathers [...] it seems to have left a trace in the nature of the terrain). *Vita Æbbe*, ed. and trans. by Bartlett, pp. 6–7.

centred on Ætheldreda as gift-giver.[33] Ætheldreda donates plentifully from her royal wealth, and works herself to craft garments for the saintly hermit: 'Stolam […] et manipulum […] ex auro et lapidibus pretiosis propriis […] manibus docta auritexture ingenio fecit eique ob interne dilectionis intuitum pro benedictione offerendum destinavit' (Being skilled in handiwork, she made with her own hands […] by the technique of gold-embroidery […] a stole and maniple […] of gold and precious stones, and she sent this work to be offered to him as a blessing in recognition of a deep-seated affection (i. 9)).[34] The stole and maniple, associated with the creative touch of Ætheldreda's hands, are concrete anchors of the saint's relational network, materially manifesting the affection between her and Cuthbert.

Moreover, Ætheldreda's gift recruits Cuthbert to ensure her enduring commemoration. The stole and maniple are designed for Cuthbert to wear during church services: 'Unde solum […] illius memoriam inter sancta sanctorum misse sollempnia facilius representare posset et pro ea Dominum maiestatis pia postulatione placaret' (So that [Cuthbert] […] would with the greatest of ease be able to display a reminder of her amidst the holiest of holy ceremonies of the mass and placate the Lord of Majesty with pious supplication on her behalf (*Liber*, i. 9)). Ætheldreda's gift allows her to be remembered and represented before God, aiding her salvation and elevating her sanctity. Through wearing her garments, Cuthbert's body is co-opted into the production and performance of Ætheldreda's holiness. This absorption of Cuthbert's body into a display of Ætheldreda's saintly memory is particularly remarkable in the light of his medieval reputation for misogyny.[35] The earliest record of Cuthbert's misogyny, composed by Symeon of Durham *c.* 1104–1107, emphasizes the saint's exclusion of women from his sacred spaces, describing the harsh punishments of women attempting to enter the cathedral or places where his body had lain.[36] Yet far from being excluded from Cuthbert's sacred space, through his wearing of her gift, Ætheldreda is repeatedly made intimately present in the holy space where Mass is performed.[37] The gold embroidery of Ætheldreda's garments was particularly associated with the work of women, not only validating women's craft as divinely oriented, but further highlighting how the *Liber* envisages Cuthbert's body as showcasing female presence.[38] In contrast to depictions of Cuthbert produced at Durham, here his body and

---

33 'Hoc in Beda nequaquam invenimus, sed pro cunctorum usque nunc testimonio scribendum existimavimus' (We do not find any mention of this in Bede, but we have thought it essential for us to write of it in view of all the people who have borne witness to it up to now, (*Liber*, i. 9)).

34 See *Vie*, ll. 1095–1100.

35 Tudor, 'The Misogyny of Saint Cuthbert'.

36 Symeon, *Libellus de exordio*, ed. and trans. by Rollason, ii. 7–9; see p. xlii for dating.

37 On how women's embroidery allows women visibility and participation in church spaces, see Schulenburg, 'Holy Women and the Needle Arts', pp. 84, 108.

38 Schulenburg, 'Holy Women and the Needle Arts', p. 87.

his space are intimately interwoven with celebrating the work, presence, and memory of a female saint.

Indeed, the *Liber* recounts that these sacred gifts enduringly bind Ætheldreda's memory and physical traces into the space of Durham Cathedral. Ely monks reported that the stole and maniple were on display in Durham: 'in signum utriusque venerationis apud ecclesiam Dunhelmi servantur, quibusdam petentibus pro magna adhuc ostenduntur dignitate et de nostris quidam sepius aspexerunt' (These are kept at the church of Durham, as a sign of the pious devotion of both him and her, and they are shown to people on request, as a great honour, and quite frequently some of our number have seen them (1.9)). Ætheldreda's crafted artefacts continue to signify, embody, and commemorate her relationship to Cuthbert long after her death. Again, the *Liber* relies here on contemporary eyewitness testimony as its source, although it locates this authority in the experiences of the Ely community itself, suggesting the ways that the connection commemorated between Ætheldreda and Cuthbert might stimulate similar connections between the saints' respective institutions.[39] Ætheldreda's gifts assert her ongoing participation in the northern spiritual networks she establishes in her lifetime, a material support that offers mediated contact with her erstwhile sacred presence at a distance from Ely, again extending her influence beyond her Ely confines.

The display of stole and maniple in Durham as commemorative objects described by the *Liber* recalls the treatment of relics. In particular, the prolonged contact the garments undergo with both Ætheldreda's and Cuthbert's bodies as they are crafted and worn suggests that they could serve as contact relics of both saints. The possibility that fabric garments created by Ætheldreda may perform the function of relics is supported by the 1383 Durham relic-list compiled by Richard de Segbrok.[40] Alongside a multitude of corporeal relics, reliquaries, and other sacred objects, the list records the presence of a diverse range of textile relics, from fragments to whole garments, associated with saints from the earliest martyrs to Thomas Becket.[41] One of the items listed is indeed a gift from Ætheldreda, although its description diverges from the *Liber*'s account: 'una stola cum ij manipulis quas sancta Etheldreda dedit sancto Wilfrido' (a stole and two maniples that Saint Ætheldreda gave to Saint Wilfrid (fol. 196r)). The list's inclusion of Ætheldreda's garments indicates that they were stored among and considered to be relics.[42] This brief notice not only locates her within the multifarious community of saints included in the Durham relic collection, but records her gift-giving relationship with

---

39 This reference to the Ely community is, as is typical, eliminated in the *Vie*, ll. 1101–04.

40 The list is preserved in a single manuscript, Durham, Durham Cathedral Library, MS B.II.35, fols 192r–198v, although it originally circulated as an independent booklet, Luxford, 'The Nature and Purpose of Medieval Relic-Lists', p. 71. It is printed in *Extracts from the Account Rolls*, ed. by Fowler, II, pp. 425–40.

41 See for example *Extracts from the Account Rolls*, ed. by Fowler, II, pp. 429–30.

42 On the range of objects recorded in relic lists, see Luxford, 'The Nature and Purpose of Medieval Relic-Lists', pp. 65–66.

ÆTHELDREDA IN THE NORTH 297

another saint (here Wilfrid), emphasizing the ways in which Ætheldreda's textile contact relics enduringly embody her saintly connections.

The identification of Ætheldreda's recipient as Wilfrid, rather than Cuthbert, points to the unusual nature of this gift relative to other donations listed. The list records nine donations of relics, reliquaries, and other ornaments to the Durham collection, predominantly donated by Durham bishops and monks, although the list also records two female aristocratic donors.[43] Moreover, the list also records two cloth relics given directly to Cuthbert to clothe his corpse by saintly women: Æbbe and Ælfflæd, abbess of Whitby and another of Æbbe's saintly nieces.[44] The list makes clear that Cuthbert's reputation for excluding women from his sacred spaces did not impede its commemoration of women donors to both the saint and his shrine, and indeed reinforces a connection between the saint, women donors, and textile donations.[45] Yet Ætheldreda's garments stand out as the only recorded gift to neither Cuthbert nor Durham, gifted instead to a saint (Wilfrid) who had little positive association with Durham, prompting the question of why the narratives about the recipient of Ætheldreda's gift differed in twelfth-century Ely and fourteenth-century Durham.

The similarities between the core elements of the *Liber* and the relic-list (a stole and maniple(s) donated by Ætheldreda to a northern male saint) suggest that despite its divergence over time, there was some sort of continuous, if shifting, tradition regarding Ætheldreda's gift at Durham. Yet while the *Liber* asserts that a narrative recounting Ætheldreda's gift to Cuthbert circulated orally in both Durham and Ely in the twelfth century, the *Liber* and the *Vie* appear to be the only extant written witnesses to the tale, which is moreover omitted from Ætheldreda's later lives.[46] Ætheldreda and Cuthbert's friendship, while enriching the *Liber*'s depiction of her interconnected sanctity, does not become an enduring part of her late medieval portrayal, and it is possible that by 1383 it had faded from Durham's collective memory.[47] In contrast to the limited transmission of narratives surrounding Ætheldreda and Cuthbert, Ætheldreda

---

43 Donors in order of recording are: the Countess of Kent; Bishop William; Bishop Thomas Langley (a later addition); Richard of Kirtly, monk of Durham; John of Kellawe; Bishop Thomas of Hatfield; John de Claxton; William Appilby, monk; the Lady of Dalden. *Extracts from the Account Rolls*, ed. by Fowler, II, pp. 426–34.

44 *Extracts from the Account Rolls*, ed. by Fowler, II, pp. 427, 434, 437.

45 The Lady of Dalden's donation, a casket to hold Cuthbert's winding cloth, is also associated with fabric, *Extracts from the Account Rolls*, ed. by Fowler, II, p. 434. On women's donations to monastic shrines, see Luxford, 'Recording and Curating Relics', p. 221.

46 See Note 9 above.

47 Although Durham produced a brief relic-list in the first half of the twelfth century, roughly contemporaneous with the *Liber*'s composition, it does not mention Ætheldreda, giving no indication as to whether her connection to Cuthbert was indeed commemorated in Durham at that time. This list is printed in Battiscombe ed., *The Relics of Saint Cuthbert*, pp. 113–14. Ætheldreda is also not mentioned in an early fourteenth-century Durham list edited in *Historiae Dunelmensis*, ed. by Raine, pp. ccccxxvi–ccccxxx. In both lists, there is a general absence of donor information, and no mention of Æbbe and Ælfflæd's fabric relics, suggesting that Ætheldreda's gift was not targeted specifically for exclusion.

and Wilfrid's relationship was well attested: first noted in Bede (*Historia*, IV. 19), and frequently incorporated into later lives.[48] While speculative, if a connection between Ætheldreda and Cuthbert was indeed forgotten or unrecorded at Durham, and if the presence of a stole and maniple(s) traditionally associated with Ætheldreda required explanation, Wilfrid was certainly a plausible recipient. Ultimately, when read together the *Liber* and the Durham relic-list suggest that perhaps recording the precise identity of Ætheldreda's recipient was of less importance than commemorating her act of donation and the sacred, material connection it inscribes. Indeed, the garments themselves appear to materially anchor the central narrative about Ætheldreda's gift to a saintly compatriot, even as this narrative's details shift over time. Like the Coldingham landscape, Ætheldreda's stole and maniple become a material repository for narrative, enduringly preserving and communicating diverse tales of Ætheldreda's interconnected presence and saintly patronage at this northern location far from Ely.

Conclusion

This essay has explored how, in the *Liber* and the *Vie*, Ætheldreda's sainthood is interwoven with and produced through not only her Ely foundation, but an expansive northern network of people, spaces, and objects. The virtual and material sacred geographies associated with Ætheldreda's sanctity at Ely and beyond are concisely encapsulated in the manuscript illustration that opens the *Vie*. The ways in which the saint might be made present and accessible beyond Ely is particularly important for Marie and for the readers of her text's sole manuscript at Campsey Ash Priory, who — unlike the *Liber*'s monastic audience — did not live in proximity to Ætheldreda's material cult, and thus accessed her principally through the mediation of the text and its manuscript. The Campsey manuscript's readers are presented with a visual representation of the saintly body in a portrait of Ætheldreda in the *Vie*'s opening initial (Fig. 12.1).[49]

The initial reiterates the resonances between Ætheldreda's body, the space of Ely, and the broader geographic networks that thread throughout the *Vie*. The saint gestures towards a church that she holds in her hand, reinforcing the enclosure of her incorrupt body within Ely, but also foregrounding her authority as founder, an authority that encompasses not only Ely itself, but the network of religious houses that stretch across England.[50] She stands on a rocky outcrop, or perhaps rises from a wave of water, recalling Ely's protective landscape.[51] Yet this landscape also recalls the miracle at Coldeburcheshevet,

---

48 For example John of Tynemouth, *Nova legenda Anglie*, ed. by Horstmann, p. 425; the Middle English *Vita S. Etheldredae Eliensis*, ed. by Horstmann, pp. 288–89.

49 Although a number of the manuscript's lives open with a portrait of their titular saint, Ætheldreda's portrait is by far the most visually complex.

50 Blanton, *Signs of Devotion*, p. 190.

51 Campbell, *Medieval Saints' Lives*, pp. 201–02.

FIGURE 12.1. 'Saint Ætheldreda of Ely', London, British Library, MS Add. 70513, fol. 100ᵛ, 1275–1300. Reproduced with permission of the British Library.

the imbrication of Ætheldreda's body and the landscape of a sacred site far from Ely, asserting the foundational importance of northern sacred spaces in her saintly identity. She is encircled by the initial letter 'A', a formal enclosure nevertheless interrupted as the land on which she stands spills over these confines onto the bare page. Like Ætheldreda's networked, mobile body within the text, this visual enclosure enfolds the potential for expansion. This opening image visually associates the saint's body with mobility and a multiplicity of sacred spaces in which she might be accessed.

Ætheldreda in life and death is implicated in extended textual, material, and geographic networks through her foundations, artefacts, and relationships. Both the *Liber* and the *Vie* draw particular connections between Ætheldreda and northern saints and spaces, although Ætheldreda's northern networks do not maintain a similar prominence in her later textual tradition. Many later lives work from Bede (to which the *Liber* added most of Ætheldreda's northern links) rather than the more restrictively circulated *Liber*, while those that adapt the *Liber* routinely omit or de-emphasize Ætheldreda's northern connections.[52] This limited later influence of Ætheldreda's northern scope raises questions about the particular values northern saints and sacred spaces offered to these two twelfth- and thirteenth-century southern hagiographers. In both texts, Ætheldreda's sainthood is constructed in collaboration with northern spaces, saints, and artefacts, highlighting the North's vital role in her sanctity's formation, while also foregrounding how northern authority and sanctity is co-opted into narratives of Ætheldreda's power and prestige. The saintly lineage connecting Ætheldreda to Hilda and Æbbe suggests the North's importance as a source for early models of female sanctity, while allowing this East Anglian saint to claim Northumbria's spiritual legacy, displacing northern saintly prestige southwards. Moreover, these texts assert Ætheldreda's enduring imbrication with the North after her death. The miraculous traces she leaves around Coldingham, and the donated garments displayed at Durham that clothed Cuthbert's body allow the *Liber* to assert Ætheldreda's (and by extension Ely's) presence and influence as extending far north of Ely in a network of sacred spaces and objects. The North — particularly Durham and its dependencies — seems to offer a political and spiritual might that, through its insistence on Ætheldreda's northern connections, the *Liber* seeks to share in, appropriate, or even rival.[53] In contrast, the *Vie*'s treatment of Ætheldreda's northern networks seems less concerned with Ely's institutional authority than the varied models of conventual and secular women's spirituality that elements such as Ætheldreda's northern genealogy or donations while Northumbrian queen might provide, or indeed the possibilities suggested by Ætheldreda's extensive connections for encounters with her presence untethered from Ely's monastic centre. In short, the spiritual and political implications of Ætheldreda's northern networks are multiple and shifting.

Nevertheless, in both texts a sense emerges of the North as particularly holy, dense with saints, sacred spaces, and miracles. The *Liber* and the *Vie* imagine the North as an enviable repository for saintliness and spiritual authority, a sacred past and contemporary institutional prestige in which, they assert, their saint participates. The North imagined by these southern hagiographers is both desirable and malleable, as they reshape northern lineages, landscapes, and narratives at will. Indeed, as the Campsey illumination exemplifies, these texts envisage Ætheldreda's northern connections as mutually transformative. Ætheldreda leaves her material traces behind on northern spaces and bodies; in turn, she is indelibly associated with the transformed landscapes of the North.

---

52 For example, John of Tynemouth's fourteenth-century *Vita* omits Ætheldreda's connections to Hilda, Cuthbert, and Durham, while condensing material on her Northumbrian queenship, relationship with Æbbe, and Coldingham miracle, *Nova legenda Anglie*, ed. by Horstmann, pp. 424–25.

53 Durham's well-established prestige was perhaps particularly enviable in twelfth-century Ely, only recently elevated to a bishopric in 1108.

Works Cited

Manuscripts and Archival Sources

Cambridge, Cambridge University Library, MS EDC 1
——, Trinity College Library, MS O.2.1
Durham, Durham Cathedral Library, MS B.II.35
London, British Library, MS Additional 70513
——, MS Cotton Domitian A.XV
——, MS Cotton Titus A.I
——, MS Cotton Vespasian A.XIX
Oxford, Bodleian Library, MS Laud Misc. 647

Primary Sources

Bede, *Historia ecclesiastica gentis Anglorum*: *Ecclesiastical History*, ed. and trans. by John Edward King, 2 vols (Cambridge, MA: Harvard University Press, 2014)
Extracts from the Account Rolls of the Abbey of Durham, from the Original MSS, ed. by Joseph Thomas Fowler, 3 vols, SS, 99, 100, 103 (Durham: Andrews & Co., 1898–1901), II (1899)
Goscelin of Saint-Bertin, *The Hagiography of the Female Saints of Ely*, ed. and trans. by Rosalind C. Love (Oxford: Clarendon Press, 2004)
Historiae Dunelmensis: scriptores tres, ed. by James Raine, SS, 9 (London: J. B. Nichols and Sons, 1839)
John of Tynemouth, *Nova legenda Anglie*, ed. by Carl Horstmann, 2 vols (Oxford: Clarendon Press, 1901)
Liber Eliensis, ed. by E. O. Blake (London: Royal Historical Society, 1962)
Liber Eliensis, trans. by Janet Fairweather (Woodbridge: Boydell, 2005)
Marie, *La Vie de seinte Audree*, in *The Life of Saint Audrey: A Text by Marie de France*, ed. and trans. by June Hall McCash and Judith Clark Barban (Jefferson: McFarland, 2006)
Symeon of Durham, *Libellus de exordio atque procursu istius, hoc est Dunhelmensis, ecclesie*, ed. and trans. by David Rollason (Oxford: Oxford University Press, 2000)
Vita et miracula S. Æbbe virginis, in *The Miracles of Saint Æbbe of Coldingham and Saint Margaret of Scotland*, ed. and trans. by Robert Bartlett (Oxford: Clarendon Press, 2003), pp. 2–67
Vita S. Etheldredae Eliensis, in *Altenglische Legenden*, ed. by Carl Horstmann (Heilbronn: Henninger, 1881), pp. 282–307

Secondary Works

Battiscombe, C. F., ed., *The Relics of Saint Cuthbert: Studies by Various Authors Collected and Edited with an Historical Introduction* (Oxford: Oxford University Press, 1956)

Blanton, Virginia, 'King Anna's Daughters: Genealogical Narrative and Cult Formation in the *Liber Eliensis*', *Historical Reflections / Réflexions Historiques*, 30.1 (2004), 127–49

——, *Signs of Devotion: The Cult of St Æthelthryth in Medieval England, 695–1615* (University Park: Pennsylvania State University Press, 2007)

Blanton-Whetsell, Virginia, '*Imagines Ætheldredae*: Mapping Hagiographic Representations of Abbatial Power and Religious Patronage', *Studies in Iconography*, 23 (2002), 55–107

——, '*Tota integra, tota incorrupta*: The Shrine of St Æthelthryth as Symbol of Monastic Autonomy', *Journal of Medieval and Early Modern Studies*, 32.2 (2002), 227–67

Campbell, Emma, *Medieval Saints' Lives: The Gift, Kinship and Community in Old French Hagiography* (Cambridge: Brewer, 2008)

Karkov, Catherine E., 'The Body of St Æthelthryth: Desire, Conversion and Reform in Anglo-Saxon England', in *The Cross Goes North: Processes of Conversion in Northern Europe, AD 300–1300*, ed. by Martin Carver (York: York Medieval, 2003), pp. 397–411

Kinoshita, Sharon, and Peggy McCracken, ed., *Marie de France: A Critical Companion* (Cambridge: Brewer, 2014)

Luxford, Julian, 'The Nature and Purpose of Medieval Relic-Lists', in *Saints and Cults in Medieval England: Proceedings of the 2015 Harlaxton Symposium*, ed. by Susan Powell (Donington: Shaun Tyas, 2017), pp. 58–79

——, 'Recording and Curating Relics at Westminster Abbey in the Late Middle Ages', *Journal of Medieval History*, 45.2 (2019), 204–30

McCash, June Hall, '*La Vie seinte Audree*: A Fourth Text by Marie de France?', *Speculum*, 77 (2002), 744–77

Ridyard, Susan J., *The Royal Saints of Anglo-Saxon England: A Study of West Saxon and East Anglian Cults* (Cambridge: Cambridge University Press, 1989)

Rollason, David, 'The Cult of Bede', in *The Cambridge Companion to Bede*, ed. by Scott DeGregorio (Cambridge: Cambridge University Press, 2010), pp. 193–200

Russell, Delbert W., 'The Campsey Collection of Old French Saints' Lives', *Scriptorium*, 57 (2003), 51–83

Schulenburg, Jane Tibbetts, 'Holy Women and the Needle Arts: Piety, Devotion, and Stitching the Sacred, ca. 500–1150', in *Negotiating Community and Difference in Medieval Europe: Gender, Power, Patronage, and the Authority of Religion in Latin Christendom*, ed. by Katherine Allen Smith and Scott Wells (Leiden: Brill, 2009), pp. 83–110

Tudor, Victoria, 'The Misogyny of Saint Cuthbert', *Archaeologia Aeliana*, 5th series, 12 (1984) 157–67

Webb, Diana, *Pilgrimage in Medieval England* (London: Hambledon, 2000)

Wogan-Browne, Jocelyn, 'Wreaths of Thyme: The Female Translator in Anglo-Norman Hagiography', in *The Medieval Translator 4*, ed. by Roger Ellis and Ruth Evans (Binghamton: Medieval and Renaissance Texts and Studies, 1994), pp. 46–65

——, 'Rerouting the Dower: The Anglo-Norman Life of St Audrey of Marie (of Chatteris?)', in *Power of the Weak: Studies on Medieval Women*, ed. by Jennifer Carpenter and Sally-Beth MacLean (Urbana: University of Illinois Press, 1995), pp. 27–56

——, *Saints' Lives and Women's Literary Culture c. 1150–1300: Virginity and its Authorizations* (Oxford: Oxford University Press, 2001)

——, 'Powers of Record, Powers of Example: Hagiography and Women's History', in *Gendering the Master Narrative: Women and Power in the Middle Ages*, ed. by Mary C. Erler and Maryanne Kowaleski (Ithaca: Cornell University Press, 2003), pp. 71–93

DANIEL TALBOT[*]

Conflicting Memories, Confused Identities, and Constructed Pasts

St Hilda and the Refoundation of Whitby Abbey

Whitby Abbey, located by the mouth of the River Esk on the North Yorkshire coast, has long inspired writers. The surrounding town provided the setting for much of Bram Stoker's *Dracula*, and through the fictional diary entry of Mina Murray, Stoker notes that the 'noble ruin' of the abbey is 'full of beautiful and romantic bits', where — local legend has it — 'a white lady is seen in one of the windows'.[1] Likewise, the twelfth-century author of an account known to historians as the *Memorial of the Benefactions of Whitby Abbey*, detailing the foundation of the Benedictine community at Whitby after the Norman Conquest, described how Reinfrid, a soldier in the army of William the Conqueror, was inspired by ruins at Whitby.[2] These were the ruins of the Anglian monastery of Streoneshalh, founded by the Northumbrian abbess Hilda of Whitby *c.* 657 and dedicated to St Peter.[3] The new Norman abbey duly shared this dedication, but was also dedicated to Hilda herself.[4] Unlike Whitby Abbey in *Dracula*, however, Hilda's original monastery does not play a prominent role in the *Memorial*'s narrative. Streoneshalh is referenced only

---

[*] I would like to thank Christiania Whitehead, Denis Renevey, and Hazel Blair for the opportunity to present this paper at the *Northern Lights* conference in Lausanne. I am also grateful to Anaïs Waag for inviting me to speak about this research at *Revealing Records X* in London and am indebted to the helpful questions and comments received on both occasions in the preparation of the final article. I would also like to thank Stephen Church, Tom Licence, Tom Pickles, David Bates, and Gregory Lippiatt for their comments on drafts of this essay.

[1] Stoker, *Dracula*, p. 61. This legend is not original to Stoker, both Lionel Charlton and George Young mention that it is a local tradition, and Walter Scott includes it in *Marmion*. The white lady was, of course, supposed to be Hilda herself. Charlton, *The History of Whitby*, p. 33; Young, *A History of Whitby and Streoneshalh Abbey*, p. 213.

[2] *Cartularium de Whiteby*, ed. by Atkinson, pp. 1–7.

[3] Bede, *Historia ecclesiastica*, ed. and trans. by Colgrave and Mynors, IV. 23.

[4] Bede, *Historia ecclesiastica*, ed. and trans. by Colgrave and Mynors, IV. 26.

Daniel Talbot (mail@dantalbot.co.uk) recently obtained his doctorate from the Department of History at the University of East Anglia.

Late Medieval Devotion to Saints from the North of England: New Directions, ed. by Christiania Whitehead, Hazel J. Hunter Blair, and Denis Renevey, MCS 48 (Turnhout: Brepols, 2022), pp. 305–320
BREPOLS ∰ PUBLISHERS   10.1484/M.MCS-EB.5.124355

once, as a former name for Whitby, and Hilda herself appears only in her role as patron saint of the new community.[5] The story of Whitby Abbey's foundation as told by the *Memorial* has, however, long been recognized as an important source for the history of monasticism in the north-east of England.[6] It touches on events that have come to be known as the 'revival' of northern monasticism, which, within a few decades of the Norman Conquest, saw the (re)foundation of monasteries at Whitby and York, and led to the establishment of the cathedral priory at Durham. These events are well-known and well-documented, both in medieval narratives and modern scholarly discussion, but they are not entirely straightforward. Alongside the *Memorial*, written *c.* 1175, there are two other manuscript witnesses to the events of the 'revival' produced around the turn of the twelfth century. One was authored at Durham by the monk Symeon, and the other — a first-person account by Stephen of Whitby — at St Mary's, York.[7] All three versions disagree, to varying extents, on matters of detail, stress, and narrative force. In contrast to the narrative focus of the Whitby *Memorial*, outlined briefly above and in more detail below, Symeon naturally centres on the events that led to the foundation of the cathedral priory at Durham; his focus is on Aldwin, one of Reinfrid's companions, who would become the first prior at Durham, whom he makes leader of the whole enterprise. Stephen of Whitby's attention is focused on the events which led him to establish St Mary's Abbey, York. He begins with his arrival as a monk at Whitby, explains how he was elected leader, and then explains why — thanks to a combination of piratical raids and the hostility of the new community's patron — he felt obliged to move the community first to a site at Lastingham and then on again to York. Most scholarship has therefore attempted to disentangle the twisted, confused, and, at times, contradictory versions of events given in these three narratives, to try and get to the heart of what happened in the eleventh century.[8]

In contrast to these attempts, there has been little research into the role that these foundation narratives played in the communities' identity building, nor how those constructed identities might influence the way in which the events of the northern revival of monasticism were depicted. Foundation narratives, Amy Remensnyder argues, became a dominant strand in a church's construction of its own identity, allowing a monastery to distinguish itself from other institutions.[9] The point of these stories for

---

5 On the name of Prestby, see Pickles, 'Biscopes-tun, muneca-tun'. Hough, 'Strensall, Streanaeshalch'; Hough, 'Another (ge)streones halh'; and Pickles, 'Streanaeshalch (Whitby)'.
6 Knowles, *The Monastic Order in England*, pp. 165–71.
7 Symeon, *Libellus de exordio*, ed. and trans. by Rollason, pp. 200–11. Dugdale and Dodsworth, *Monasticon Anglicanum*, ed. by Caley and others, III, pp. 544–56. Stephen's authorship is now accepted as authentic, but has been disputed in the past: Bethell, 'Fountains Abbey'. A new version and translation of Stephen's text is being produced by Nicholas Karn.
8 Burton, *Monastic Order in Yorkshire*, pp. 23–44; Burton, 'Monastic Revival in Yorkshire'; Dawtry, 'Benedictine Revival in the North'.
9 Remensnyder, *Remembering Kings Past*, pp. 292–95.

CONFLICTING MEMORIES, CONFUSED IDENTITIES, AND CONSTRUCTED PASTS

Remensnyder was not to record the events as they had happened — whether they did or did not was incidental to their purpose — but to provide, record, or create a memory of the past for the monastery which could give the community status and authority in their present.[10] This memory, once formed, dominated the abbey's identity at every strata, regulating both the community's interactions with the outside world, and the spiritual and liturgical life within the monastery itself.[11]

In my contribution to this volume, I consider the absence of St Hilda from the *Memorial*'s description of the refoundation of Whitby Abbey, offering a re-interpretation of that source in order to demonstrate that rather than providing a consistent, settled, collective memory of the abbey's foundation, the surviving Whitby texts point towards a complex, ongoing, and at times self-contradictory pattern of memorialization, as successive generations of monks grappled with the question of who they were.

The Whitby *Memorial*

The first foundation story with which I am concerned is the *Memorial*, produced around a century after the foundation of the Norman monastery at Whitby. It survives in a twelfth-century gathering of material now bound to the thirteenth-century cartulary codex known as the Abbot's Book — one of two extant cartularies from Whitby.[12] That gathering is now found at the front of the cartulary, but (according to the manuscript's foliation) it was at the rear of the codex before it was rebound in the fifteenth century.[13] The *Memorial* begins on the verso side of the first folio of the gathering. It follows a library catalogue and is succeeded by an account of the resignation of Abbot Benedict in 1148, and a short list of questions put to a new abbot at their blessing ceremony.

The *Memorial* opens by addressing all those serving God and St Hilda. It informs these addressees that William de Percy founded a monastery at Whitby, a place which had once been called Streoneshalh and then Prestby, which he had given to Reinfrid, a monk of Evesham, and his associates to administer.[14] The *Memorial* then specifies William de Percy's original gift — two carucates of land in Prestby — and records that as the number of monks grew, so too did William's generosity. When his brother, Serlo, became prior of the abbey, he gave the abbey vills, lands, churches, and tithes which were approved by his wife, Emma de Port, and his son, Alan.

---

10 Remensnyder, *Remembering Kings Past*, pp. 300–01.

11 Remensnyder, *Remembering Kings Past*, p. 293.

12 The Abbot's Book is now North Yorkshire Record Office, ZCG VI 1; the other surviving cartulary is BL, MS Add. 4715.

13 The gathering is at fols 138ʳ–141ᵛ.

14 *Memorial*, in *Cartularium de Whiteby*, ed. by Atkinson, I, p. 1.

The *Memorial* then changes tack and describes Reinfrid and his arrival at Whitby. Reinfrid, it states, was the strongest soldier in William the Conqueror's army. When he was travelling with William though Northumbria — almost certainly on the campaign known as 'the Harrying of the North' (1069/1070) — he turned aside to Whitby and happened across the ruins of Streoneshalh which had been destroyed by Ingwar and Hubba (identified as dukes of the Alans and the Danes, respectively, and as the beheaders of Edmund, king of East Anglia). Reinfrid was greatly moved by the ruins and decided to travel to Evesham in order to become a monk. Sometime later, he returned to Northumbria with Aldwin, the prior of Winchcombe, and Ælfwig, a fellow monk. He went to William de Percy, who granted him the church of St Peter's, again making reference to William's gift of two carucates of land. The *Memorial* repeats that the number of monks grew, and states that Reinfrid diligently rebuilt the ruined buildings and attracted followers to the monastery. It then moves on to briefly record his death and burial at Hackness; his succession as prior by Serlo, William de Percy's brother; the blessing of William de Percy, nephew to William the founder, as abbot, and the death of William de Percy the founder on crusade at Montjoie.

This narrative is then followed by a list of the abbey's benefactors and their benefactions. This list is roughly three times the length of the narrative section and begins:

> Itaque omnes terras, possessiones, forestas, ecclesias, decimas et libertates, quas saepe nominatus idem Willielmus de Perci, cum Alano de Perci, filio suo, monasterio de Witebi dederat in primis, necnon in ultimis temporibus suis antequam Ierosolimam peteret, vel quique fideles monasterio nostro de Witebi dederunt vel concesserunt in elemosinam perpetuam, ad monimentum, hic breviter annotabimus.[15]

> (In this way we will briefly record here as a memorial all the lands, possessions, forests, churches, tithes and liberties which the same oft-named William de Percy, with his son Alan de Percy, gave to the monastery of Whitby at first, and also in the last of his days before he set out for Jerusalem, and also what other men of faith have given or granted to our monastery of Whitby in perpetual alms for its security.)

This introduction is immediately followed by a lengthy specification of William de Percy's gifts to the abbey, followed by the gifts of Emma de Port, William's wife, their son Richard de Percy, and numerous other benefactors. These last entries vary in length but most are short, simply giving the name of the benefactor and their gift, for example: 'ex dono Roberti de Pichot filii Pichot de Perci ecclesiam de Sutton' (out of the gift of Robert of Pichot, son of Pichot de Perci, the church of Sutton) or 'ex dono Roberti Fossard unam carucatam terre in Roucebi' (out of the gift of Robert Fossard, a carucate of

---

15 *Cartularium de Whiteby*, ed. by Atkinson, p. 2. All translations are my own.

CONFLICTING MEMORIES, CONFUSED IDENTITIES, AND CONSTRUCTED PASTS 309

land in Roxby), before the *Memorial* concludes by stating 'iam numeravimus omnes donationes quas praefati advocati nostri nobis dederunt in elemosinam perpetuam' (now we have accounted for all the donations, which the aforesaid patrons gave to us in perpetual alms).[16] The last gift mentioned in the *Memorial* was granted to the abbey no later than 1175, and it is possible, therefore, that the gathering in which the *Memorial* survives may have been created on (or in the wake of) the succession of Abbot Richard II (1177). There is reason, however, to suggest that some material which may have preceded the twelfth-century gathering has been lost, meaning that the dating and impetus behind its creation remains speculative.

Most studies have treated the *Memorial* text as a *narratio fundationis* of Whitby Abbey. This identification is encouraged by the text itself. The *Memorial* begins by addressing the monks of the abbey directly, exhorting them to learn the events of the monastery's foundation which it goes on to describe. However, Janet Burton has drawn attention to several differences between Whitby's narrative and the versions of events recorded at St Mary's York and Durham in order to argue that the *Memorial* only provides a partial, selective record. In particular, Burton points to the portrayal of Whitby's lay founder, William de Percy, in both accounts. His positive description in the *Memorial* is in sharp contrast to the criticism that he attracts from Stephen of Whitby, who argues instead that he was forced to move the community to York after William had seen how much the monks had improved the land they had been given and wanted to take back his gift. This difference, Burton argues, stems from the *Memorial* author's wish to construct a narrative favourable to the current de Percy patrons of Whitby Abbey. Stephen of Whitby, who, as we have heard, tells us that he began his monastic life at Whitby before being elected leader and moving the community to York, remains unnamed by the Whitby *Memorial*, nor does the author of the text make any reference to a successor community at York which could claim the same origins as Whitby Abbey. Those two omissions, Burton argues, are an attempt by the Whitby monks to write their shared heritage with St Mary's, York, out of their history.[17] In her eyes, they had constructed a version of their own past which erased problematic memories of conflict with lay founders and fellow monks.

This conclusion remains relatively sound, but there are two problems. The first is that this interpretation of the *Memorial* does not adequately explain the narrative's other omissions. These are entirely incidental, if not outright irrelevant, to William de Percy's supposed antagonism to the monastery he endowed and to the schism which led to the foundation of St Mary's, York. By comparison with the two other versions of the story, the *Memorial* fails to reference Reinfrid's desire to live as a hermit, recorded both by Stephen

---

16 *Cartularium de Whiteby*, ed. by Atkinson, I, pp. 5, 7.
17 Burton, *Monastic Order in Yorkshire*, p. 36.

DANIEL TALBOT

of Whitby (who uses it as justification to move to Lastingham) and Symeon of Durham.[18] Similarly, it makes no reference to the fact that Reinfrid had originally gone to Jarrow before settling at Whitby. Second, as noted at the outset, the *Memorial* author provides very little explanation of the importance of Hilda, apparent through the monks' choice of her as a new patron for the monastery, or of the Anglian community of Streoneshalh.

St Hilda, Streoneshalh and the Refoundation Story

The absence of Hilda, and the relative lack of focus on Streoneshalh, are both surprising for a text supposedly reflecting the abbey's identity. These topics are ones that a reader might naturally expect a Whitby *narratio fundationis* to tackle head-on. Saints were a key part of a monastery's identity. Invoking a saint could allow monastic institutions to erase a temporal caesura and stress their continuity with the community they knew had come before them.[19] Moreover, choosing a patron saint and acquiring their relics was itself an important part of the foundation process, which monastic communities felt ought to be recorded. Sometimes the *narratio fundationis* explicitly took the form of a *translatio*, at other times, the saint him or herself was given a role in posthumously dictating events.[20] Within the North East, for example, the monks of both Selby Abbey and the cathedral priory of Durham produced texts which sought to explain the origins of their communities through the intercessory power of their patron saints. Symeon of Durham justified the translation of St Cuthbert from Lindisfarne to Chester-le-Street and then to Durham, by detailing Cuthbert's active involvement in the decision-making process.[21] Similarly, the monks of Selby Abbey, on the banks of the River Ouse, constructed a narrative explaining how St Germanus guided the translation of his finger to Selby to act as the relic around which the community would establish itself.[22] If the author of the Whitby *Memorial* intended to record what he believed to be the most notable things about the foundation of his community, nonetheless, he found no reason to elaborate on its ties to Hilda and her community of Streoneshalh.

Three examples, however, clearly show that the Whitby monks were conscious of their pre-Conquest heritage, casting themselves as the successors of Hilda's community and actively working to promote Hilda's cult.[23] Although this evidence survives in a form more fragmentary and less narratively coherent

---

18 Dugdale and Dodsworth, *Monasticon Anglicanum*, ed. by Caley and others, III, pp. 544–56.
19 Rollason, *Saints and Relics*, p. 197; Bartlett, 'Viking Hiatus in the Cult of Saints'.
20 Remensnyder, *Remembering Kings Past*, p. 76. For *translatio* as a genre, see Geary, *Furta Sacra*.
21 Symeon, *Libellus de exordio*, ed. and trans. by Rollason, pp. 145–47.
22 *Historia Selebiensis* ed. and trans. by Burton and Lockyear.
23 For further evidence of the promotion of St Hilda's cult, see Christiane Kroebel's essay, 'Remembering St Hilda in the Later Middle Ages' below, pp. 321–39.

CONFLICTING MEMORIES, CONFUSED IDENTITIES, AND CONSTRUCTED PASTS   311

than the *Memorial*, it nevertheless attests to Hilda's importance to the Whitby monks before, during, and after the production of the *Memorial*.

The first example comes from the first few decades after the establishment of the Norman community. Around 1086, the monks, now under Serlo's leadership, moved temporarily to a site at Hackness, around eight miles from Whitby, in order to escape from piratical raids and the apparent hostility of their lay founder and patron, William de Percy.[24] The details of this move are contained within a fragment of text copied into the notes of antiquarian Roger Dodsworth, extracted from a Whitby source which otherwise does not survive. The choice of Hackness as a temporary residence was more than a coincidence. It, too, boasted the remnants of an Anglo-Saxon monastery founded by St Hilda, and when the Domesday commissioners completed their circuit of Yorkshire, the land at Hackness was recorded as being 'terra sancte Hilde' (the land of St Hilda).[25] The entry is opaque, even by the standards of the Domesday returns for Yorkshire, but any ambiguity surrounding the meaning was resolved by Alexander Hamilton-Thompson, who noticed that a confraternity agreement between the monks at Durham and Serlo, prior of Hackness, had been added contemporaneously into the Durham *Liber vitae*.[26] The Whitby community had moved to Hackness, a site associated with Hilda, and were styling themselves there as her community. This overt link to the pre-Conquest past is utterly conventional and accords well with the introspection and sense of loss detectable in much historical narrative written after the Conquest. As Anne Dawtry suggests, at least part of the point of the sites chosen by Reinfrid, Aldwin, and Ælfwig was the link they provided to that past.[27] Similarly, Stuart Harrison and Christopher Norton have shown that the restoration work undertaken by Aldwin at Jarrow went beyond simple necessity, and suggests his active desire to live, as much as possible, within the remains of the ruined monasteries there.[28]

The actions of the three southern monks also accord well with international trends. As Remensnyder has shown, the desire of Benedictine monasteries to see their founders as refounders and restorers is the dominant motif of Benedictine foundation narratives in Aquitaine.[29] Although the communities founded by Reinfrid, Aldwin, and Ælfwig were not — strictly speaking —

---

24   Oxford, Bodl. Lib., MS Dodsworth 159, fols 114^r–116^r; MS Dodsworth 118, fols 87^{r-v}. This extract shares two lines of verse with another Whitby source discussed below.

25   *Domesday Book*, ed. by Faull and Stinson, 13N13.

26   Thompson, 'Monastic Settlement'.

27   Dawtry, 'Benedictine Revival in the North', p. 90. The other attraction was that these sites were simply associated with holiness. The importance of the pre-Conquest past could thus be viewed as a backward construction, created to explain retroactively why one particular holy site was more preferable than other options.

28   In particular, they point to the connecting bay constructed between the two Anglo-Saxon churches which converted them into the chancel of Aldwin's new church. Harrison and Norton, 'Lastingham', pp. 70–71.

29   Remensnyder, *Remembering Kings Past*, p, 46.

Benedictine from their inception, the three monks had arrived in the North from Mercian monasteries which were. Fragmentary as the evidence is, it does appear that the community which continued after the death of Reinfrid in the closing decades of the eleventh century believed that they had refounded, and were therefore a continuation of, Hilda's community.

The second example survives in the twelfth-century gathering of material which contains the *Memorial* text. The first folio of this gathering contains a library catalogue in which the monks recorded ninety-one volumes (once duplicate volumes are removed).[30] The catalogue adheres to a loose structure. The list is in three columns, and begins with a mixture of theological, biblical, and patristic works, followed by a section on the lives of saints, a mixture of apparently unrelated works, some from the twelfth century, and finally a list of theological texts. A separate heading in the third column reading 'Liber grammatici' precedes a selection of classical texts and teaching books.[31] The list is not complete and omits standard patristic works and copies of the Bible and the psalms.[32] What is included, however, is a copy of Bede's *Historia ecclesiastica*, a work entitled *De Situ Dunelmensis ecclesie* (most probably Symeon of Durham's *Libellus de exordio*) and an unspecified *Vita Cuthberti*.[33] Whitby was clearly aware of versions of the past emanating from Durham, and their construction of it could not escape the influence of the Durham monks.

In the second column of the catalogue, there is an entry for a life of St Hilda. However, rather than being included with the other hagiographies recorded in the catalogue, it appears amongst the more miscellaneous material at the foot of the second column. More curiously still, the entry is a composite volume for a 'Liber Odonis et Liber Tome de sancta Hilda' (book of Odo and Book of Thomas concerning St Hilda). The 'Liber Odonis' is possibly Odo of Cluny's *Dialogus de musica*, but why it should be bound to a life of Hilda is unclear. Presumably though, the Thomas identified as the author of the work had some local significance to the Whitby community, and it is possible that this work was commissioned by the monks themselves.[34] Although this evidence is slight, it does seem to indicate that by the twelfth century the Whitby monks were actively working to promote Hilda's cult.

The third example begins to pull the Whitby story together. This example consists of a fifteenth-century Latin poem contained in a miscellany produced by a Glastonbury monk who apparently resided in Oxford.[35] Despite its southern

---

30 Lawrence-Mathers, *Manuscripts in Northumbria*, pp. 116–18; Sharpe, *English Benedictine Libraries*, B109, pp. 633–44.

31 Sharpe, *English Benedictine Libraries*, B109, pp. 633–44.

32 For a full discussion of the contents, see Lawrence-Mathers, *Manuscripts in Northumbria*, p. 117.

33 *Cartularium de Whiteby*, ed. by Atkinson, I, p. 341. I follow Sharpe's identification of these texts here: *English Benedictine Libraries*, B109.

34 See Kroebel's essay, 'Remembering St Hilda in the Later Middle Ages', in particular, p. 331, where she discusses the possible theft of this manuscript in the fourteenth century.

35 See Rigg, *A Glastonbury Miscellany*; Rigg, 'Latin Poem on St Hilda'; Rigg, 'Some Notes On Trinity College'.

provenance, this poem must undoubtedly have originated from Whitby Abbey, for it records information unique to the abbey's own understanding of the past.[36] The poem survives in two parts, the first being substantially longer than the second, and has proved impossible to date precisely. A. G. Rigg has suggested a date of the fourteenth or fifteenth century, but neither the rhyme scheme nor events described would preclude a much earlier date.[37] The two parts have different rhyme schemes and the second part begins on the first line of a new folio. It is possible, therefore, that each part may originally have been a distinct poem, but given the lack of any other extant copies for comparison, all that can be said with certainty is that the two parts both came to the attention of the monk who compiled the miscellany in which it survives, probably, although by no means certainly, because they circulated together.[38]

The first part of the poem is a verse life of St Hilda followed by a lengthy section on the poet Caedmon, mostly drawn from Bede's *Historia ecclesiastica*. There are some key differences, though, which suggest that Bede was not the direct source. In particular, the material is ordered slightly differently, and the poem contains three new miracles not found in the *Historia ecclesiastica*.[39] Two of these miracles are firmly located in the Whitby landscape, and one suggests that the work was composed by someone with a close knowledge of Whitby's coastline. That miracle, one of the more famous associated with Hilda, records that she turned snakes into stone. The miracle owes its existence to the thousands of ammonite fossils found along the Jurassic coast of North Yorkshire on which Whitby lies. Hilda, the author says, transformed the poison contained within the snakes, leaving the 'snakestones' with curative properties.[40]

The second part of the poem is a refoundation narrative beginning with the sack of Whitby Abbey by Ingwar and Hubba. The author then states that Hilda's relics were taken to Glastonbury for safe keeping. We can be sure that this part of the text derived from a Whitby source, thanks to the antiquarian notes of Roger Dodsworth who recorded an extract from an otherwise lost Whitby chronicle. As Rigg has noted, the penultimate two lines of the poem are both recorded in the Dodsworth fragment of text in their entirety and the content of the prose which precedes those lines is identical. Unlike the *Memorial* text, the poem places the refoundation of Whitby in the context of the broader revival of northern monasticism, and explicitly ties the new Norman abbey to the old Anglian monastery which had gone before it. In the poem's version of the foundation, all the details that the monks of Whitby

---

36 For an analysis of the poem's source material and arguments in favour of Whitby as the original place of composition, see Rigg, 'Latin Poem on St Hilda', pp. 12–18.

37 Rigg, 'Latin Poem on St Hilda', p. 13.

38 Rigg, 'Latin Poem on St Hilda', p. 13.

39 John of Tynemouth records a life of Hilda, but the order of events in it is different from the Glastonbury poem, and John does not include several events that the poem does. For a discussion of the different versions, see Rigg, 'Latin Poem on St Hilda', p. 14.

40 Rigg, 'Latin Poem on St Hilda', ll. 226–41.

DANIEL TALBOT

supposedly actively wrote out of their foundation story can be found: William de Percy's hostility is recorded, and Stephen of Whitby, who is completely overlooked by the *Memorial*'s narrative, is one of only three people (along with Serlo and Reinfrid) specifically identified as a monk of Whitby.

Even the moment when Reinfrid shuns secular life is different to the *Memorial*'s account. In spite of the fact that the poem begins, or at least circulated, with Hilda's life, and in spite of a clear interest in her relics, the poet rejects the *Memorial*'s assertion that Reinfrid was inspired to become a monk by the destroyed ruins of Hilda's community of Streoneshalh. In the poem's version of the refoundation story, Reinfrid, again named as a soldier in William's army, hears about a cruel woman who ate the limbs of children. He seeks leave from the king, travels to Hackness, where the woman resides, and slaughters her.[41] Whilst there, a maiden appears to him in a vision and tells him to become a monk.[42] He wakes the next morning determined to do so and travels to London to renounce his vows to the king. We might expect this moment to be one where the poet could insert Hilda, but the choice of Hackness and the location of the maiden there may not indicate a curious rejection of Hilda so much as a recasting of the facts of her life, recorded by Bede, to suit this version of the foundation story. Hilda's death, Bede records, was foreseen by a nun of Hackness known as Begu.[43] By the twelfth century, Begu's life had been combined with Bede's description of Heiu, founding abbess of Hartlepool, to create the medieval legend of St Bega.[44] A short vengeance miracle involving Bega also appears at the end of this poem and a surviving missal from Whitby records a feast in albs for her on 31 October.[45] Whilst the author does not mention Bega by name it is difficult to think that he had anyone else in mind other than her for his 'maiden of Hackness'. Rather than foreseeing the death of Hilda, then, the author plays with the known parts of the two saints' lives and recasts Bega as the agent behind the refoundation of Hilda's community.

Fragmentary though the evidence is, these three examples do show glimpses that successive Whitby communities were engaged, as previous study suggests they should be, in an active process of promoting the cult of their saint and portraying themselves as the continuation of the abbey that she had founded at the place they once occupied. The three examples come from both early and late in the abbey's history, and whilst they only permit a snapshot of Hilda's cult spread over a large chronological span, they do suggest that she was important to the monastery.[46] So why does

---

41 Rigg, 'Latin Poem of Hilda', ll. 564–67.
42 Rigg, 'Latin Poem of Hilda', p. 41.
43 Bede, *Historia ecclesiastica*, ed. and trans. by Colgrave and Mynors, IV. 23.
44 On Bega, see Bartlett, 'Bega [St Bega] (supp. fl. late 7th cent.), abbess of Hartlepool', *ODNB*; Downham, 'St Bega'.
45 Oxford, Bodl. Lib., MS Rawlinson, Liturg. B. 1, fol. 8ᵛ.
46 Some of these promotional attempts are explored in more detail below, in Kroebel's essay, 'Remembering St Hilda in the Later Middle Ages', pp. 323–34.

CONFLICTING MEMORIES, CONFUSED IDENTITIES, AND CONSTRUCTED PASTS 315

that importance not come through in the earliest source we have, produced by the Whitby monks themselves? The answer lies in reconsidering exactly what kind of text the *Memorial* is. Most studies have treated the *Memorial's* narrative in isolation from its list of benefactions, but when put together and considered as a whole, the narrative choices the author made begin to make more sense. The *Memorial* is primarily concerned with the abbey's human actors. It begins with the record of William de Percy's original grant, a piece of information it repeats twice, and records that he augmented that gift over the years until his death. Besides William, the only person who is given any extended attention is Reinfrid, as the recipient of William's gift. Viewed in this light, many of the omissions mentioned above from the Whitby *Memorial* become quite understandable. The *Memorial* is simply not a text designed to tell a story about Hilda, the revival of monasticism, or Stephen of Whitby. It is a narrative designed to authenticate and contextualize the actions of those who had given Whitby its possessions.

In this respect the *Memorial* could be defined as a *pancarte*. In its strictest sense, a *pancarte* is a charter which reproduces the text of more than one charter and which 'seeks either in whole or in part to reproduce the diplomatic of its original'.[47] Applied more loosely, however, a *pancarte* could simply be a synthesized record of multiple gifts recorded in a single text which could be presented for confirmation.[48] As David Bates has noted, such documents were effectively narratives which recorded the endowments of a house, and it would not be unusual for them to contain actual narrative elements to preface and buttress the grants claimed within the document.[49] The *pancarte* came to England from Normandy, and there are several concrete examples of abbeys founded in the wake of the Norman Conquest recording their foundation in this format. The monks of St Werburgh's, Chester, also produced a document which served a similar purpose. Their charter, known commonly by its first few words (*Sanctorum prisca autoritate*), contains many of the same features as the Whitby *Memorial*. It begins with a lengthy preamble and a short narrative account of the foundation by Earl Hugh of Chester and Countess Ermentrude, which leads into a specification of the abbey's gift.[50] *Sanctorum prisca* then concludes with a lengthy list of the abbey's early endowments by other benefactors. Despite earlier doubts, *Sanctorum prisca* is now accepted as indisputably genuine, and it appears that the impetus for its creation was to secure a confirmation for the piecemeal grants Chester acquired after the

---

47 *Regesta regum Anglo-Normannorum*, ed. by Bates, pp. 22–23.

48 For a description of the various types of *pancartes*, see Parisse, 'Les Pancartes', pp. 26–35; Bertrand, Bourlet, and Hélary, 'Vers une typologie'; Bates, 'Les Chartes de confirmation'; Bouchard, *Rewriting Saints and Ancestors*, p. 20.

49 For discussion of this point, see Chibnall, 'Charter and Chronicle'; Chibnall, 'Forgery in Narrative Charters'.

50 *Cartulary of St Werburgh*, ed. by Tait, pp. 15–37.

316   DANIEL TALBOT

foundation of the abbey in 1093.[51] The collation of grants into one document became useful far beyond the lifetime of Earl Hugh, and was subsequently presented to his successors as a catch-all charter enabling them to confirm his original gifts.[52]

Interesting as the *Sanctorum prisca* text is in its own right, it is of even greater interest here for its subsequent usage by the monks of Shrewsbury Abbey. They presented charters to Henry I and Stephen for confirmation which bear a striking resemblance to *Sanctorum prisca* (even beginning with the same words). Indeed, Henry I's confirmation of the abbey's lands and liberties replicates the framework of the *Sanctorum prisca* entirely, also beginning with the same words and extensive preamble, to which Shrewsbury added its own narrative. However, even this narrative bears striking similarities to Chester's version, with little more than the proper names changed.[53] Like the Chester version of the *Sanctorum prisca*, the Shrewsbury charter then concludes with a list of grants by other people and, finally, a witness list for Henry I's confirmation.

The *Memorial*'s opening line is reminiscent of the address clause of a *pancarte*, albeit adapted to address the monks, and it is easy to think that the monk who compiled the *Memorial* had such a document either in mind or to hand when he compiled it. It is also quite possible that the *Memorial*, like the *Sanctorum prisca* examples, originally began life as a narrative charter(s) rather than a stand-alone work.[54] There is evidence to suggest that the *Memorial* list of benefactions was compiled in three distinct stages, beginning with a section which carried down to the grant of Toulston.[55] All of these vills, with the exception of the hermitage at Mulgrave which appears to be a later interpolation, were granted before 1140, and there is evidence to suggest that the monks sought to have a version of this list of grants confirmed. A confirmation charter of King Stephen, issued amongst a flurry of confirmations by the king at York in 1136, includes a similar list to the first section of the *Memorial*'s list.[56] Another

---

51 Chibnall, 'Forgery in Narrative Charters', p. 335.

52 For example, *Cartulary of St Werburgh*, ed. by Tait, no. 8, p. 53.

53 *Shrewsbury Cartulary*, ed. by Rees, I, no. 35, pp. 31–40.

54 The *Memorial* begins: 'Notum sit omnibus Deo et Sanctae Hildae Abbatissae servientibus in loco qui olim Streoneshalc vocabatur, deinde Prestebi appellabatur, nunc vero Witebi vocatur, quod Willielmus de Perci, cognomento Asgernus, tempore Willielmi Bastard (nothi), Regis Anglorum, ibi fundaverit monasterium in honore Sancti Petre Apostoli et Sanctae Hildae Abbatissae, atque Reinfrido, monacho de Evesham, cum sociis suis quos sibi adquisiverat, ipsum locum commendaverit' (Know all serving God and St Hilda the Abbess in the place which once was called Streonshalc, then Prestby, and now is called Whitby, that William de Percy, known as Asgernus, in the time of William the Bastard, king of England, founded in that place a monastery in honour of St Peter the Apostle and St Hilda the abbess, and entrusted that place to Reinfrid a monk of Evesham with the associates who he had acquired). *Cartularium de Whiteby*, ed. by Atkinson, I, p. 1.

55 This argument will appear more fully in a forthcoming article by Thomas Pickles. I am grateful to him for sharing his preliminary research on the topic.

56 For a discussion of the context of the grant see King, *King Stephen*, p. 55. Stephen's charter survives only in an *inspeximus* of Edward II: *Cartularium de Whiteby*, ed. by Atkinson, II, p. 531.

CONFLICTING MEMORIES, CONFUSED IDENTITIES, AND CONSTRUCTED PASTS   317

similar list appears again in a bull of Pope Eugene III (1145–1153) in favour of the abbey.[57] Both Stephen's charter and Eugene's bull are genuine, and provide evidence of the existence of a *pancarte* list by the second quarter of the twelfth century which was presented (and accepted) for confirmation.[58] Neither version contains the *Memorial*'s narrative, but neither can have been sent in isolation and, if my argument that there is no break between the list and the narrative is accepted, it is probable that the *Memorial*'s narrative was adapted directly from an extant charter.[59] Whatever the source material though, it is striking that the *Memorial*'s version of events does not appear to have been disseminated or passed down to successive generations of Whitby monks. The first verifiable examples of the *Memorial* text being copied survive from after the dissolution of the abbey, and this version of the foundation story was even absent from John Leland's record of his visit there.[60]

Conclusion

Two distinct strands of the refoundation story can be detected in Whitby's corpus of materials. Both of these strands have much to commend them and both reveal a great deal about certain aspects of the community's identity. The first of these, represented solely in the *Memorial*, tells the story of Whitby's, and more specifically Reinfrid's, relationship to their lay founder, produced, I have argued, to serve the temporary needs of the genre to which the document pertains. In doing so, the Whitby monks downplay or ignore their pre-Conquest past, preferring instead to focus on the immediate events of the abbey's foundation after the Conquest. The second, represented most completely by the Glastonbury poem, but detectable in the earlier fragmentary sources from the abbey, embraces the abbey's pre-Conquest past and links the refoundation story to Whitby's patron saint. In trying to unravel, reconcile, and resolve those divergent strands of the foundational story that the Whitby monks told themselves in pursuit of 'what happened', or in a search for the abbey's 'true' collective memory of the past, there is a risk of privileging certain sources, ordering what is unordered, and distorting the contours, bumps, and rough edges which have been left behind in the surviving material. The evidence suggests that the Whitby monks' identity was complex and multifaceted, and that successive generations of monks wrote and rewrote their foundation story and relationship to Hilda to conform it

---

57 *Cartularium de Whiteby*, ed. by Atkinson, I, p. 117.
58 *Regesta pontificum Romanorum*, ed. by Jaffé, II, p. 83, no. 9645.
59 It is possible too that more than one document underlay the *Memorial*'s narrative, perhaps including an abbey chronicle, which would explain the awkward repetition in the *Memorial* text and the glimpse of narrative flair in its description of the abbey's ruins and Ingwar and Hubba.
60 Leland, *De Rebus Britannicis Collectanea*, IV, p. 39.

to their needs and expectations. In isolation, neither strand of the Whitby past fully encapsulates the monks' sense of who they were. It is only when both strands are bought together and the various foundation stories are considered as part of a greater whole that the Whitby monks' sense of their own identity begins to emerge.

Works Cited

Manuscripts and Archival Sources

London, British Library, MS Additional 4715
Northallerton, North Yorkshire Record Office, ZCG VI 1
Oxford, Bodleian Library, MS Dodsworth 118
——, MS Dodsworth 159
——, MS Rawlinson Liturg. B. 1

Primary Sources

Bede, *Historia ecclesiastica. Bede's Ecclesiastical History of the English People,* ed. and trans. by Bertram Colgrave and R. A. B. Mynors (Oxford: Oxford University Press, 1969)

Cartularium Abbathiae de Whiteby, Ordinis sancti Benedicti fundatae Anno MLXXVII, ed. by J. C. Atkinson, 2 vols, SS, 69, 72 (Durham: Andrews & Co., 1879–1881)

A Cartulary or Register of The Abbey of St Werburgh, Chester, ed. by James Tait (Manchester: Chetham Society, 1920)

Dugdale, William, and Roger Dodsworth, *Monasticon Anglicanum,* ed. by John Caley and others, 6 vols (London: Bohn, 1817–1830)

Domesday Book: Yorkshire, ed. by Margaret Faull and Marie Stinson (Chichester: Phillimore, 1986)

Historia Selebiensis Monasterii: The History of the Monastery of Selby, ed. and trans. by Janet Burton and Lynda Lockyear (Oxford: Oxford University Press, 2013)

Leland, John, *De Rebus Britannicis Collectanea,* ed. by Thomas Hearne, 6 vols (London, 1774)

Regesta pontificum Romanorum ab condita ecclesia ad annum post Christum natum MCXCVIII, ed. by Philippe Jaffé and others, 2 vols (Leipzig: Veit, 1885–1888)

Regesta regum Anglo-Normannorum: The Acta of William I (1066–1087), ed. by David Bates (Oxford: Oxford University Press, 1998)

The Shrewsbury Cartulary, ed. by Una Rees, 2 vols (Aberystwyth: National Library of Wales, 1975)

Stoker, Bram, *Dracula* (Oxford: Oxford University Press, 2011)

Symeon of Durham, *Libellus de exordio atque procursu istius, hoc est Dunhelmensis, ecclesie,* ed. and trans. by David W. Rollason (Oxford: Clarendon Press, 2000)

Secondary Works

Bartlett, Robert, 'The Viking Hiatus in the Cult of Saints as Seen in the Twelfth Century', in *The Long Twelfth-Century View of the Anglo-Saxon Past*, ed. by Martin Brett and David Woodman (Abingdon: Routledge, 2015), pp. 13–25

——, 'Bega [St Bega] (supp. fl. late 7th cent.), abbess of Hartlepool', *Oxford Dictionary of National Biography*, <https://doi.org/10.1093/ref:odnb/1956> [accessed 22/03/2019]

Bates, David, 'Les Chartes de confirmation et les pancartes normandes du règne de Guillaume le Conquérant', in *Pancartes monastiques des XIᵉ et XIIᵉ siècles: Table ronde organisée par l'ARTEM, 6–7 juillet 1994, Nancy*, ed. by Michel Parisse, Pierre Pégeot, and Benoit Michel Tock (Turnhout: Brepols, 1998), pp. 95–109

Bertrand, Paul, Caroline Bourlet, and Xavier Hélary, 'Vers une typologie des cartulaires médiévaux', in *Les Cartulaires méridionaux*, ed. by Daniel Le Blévec (Paris: Publications de l'École nationale des Chartes, 2006), pp. 7–20

Bethell, Dennis, 'Fountains Abbey and the State of St Mary's', *Journal of Ecclesiastical History*, 17 (1966), 11–27

Bouchard, Constance Brittain, *Rewriting Saints and Ancestors: Memory and Forgetting in France, 500–1200* (Philadelphia: University of Pennsylvania Press, 2014)

Burton, Janet, 'The Monastic Revival in Yorkshire: Whitby and St Mary's York', in *Anglo-Norman Durham: 1093–1193*, ed. by David Rollason, Margaret Harvey, and Michael Prestwich (Woodbridge: Boydell, 1994), pp. 41–51

——, *The Monastic Order in Yorkshire 1069–1215* (Cambridge: Cambridge University Press, 1999)

Charlton, Lionel, *The History of Whitby and of Whitby Abbey* (York: A. Ward, 1779)

Chibnall, Marjorie, 'Charter and Chronicle: The Use of Archive Sources by Norman Historians', in *Church and Government in the Middle Ages: Essays presented to C. R. Cheney on his 70th Birthday*, ed. by Christopher Brooke (Cambridge: Cambridge University Press, 1976), pp. 1–17

——, 'Forgery in Narrative Charters', in *Fälschungen im Mittelalter. Internationaler Kongreß der Monumenta Germaniae Historica München, 16.-19. September 1986 Teil IV Diplomatische Fälschungen (II)* (Hanover: Hahn, 1988), pp. 331–46

Dawtry, Anne, 'The Benedictine Revival in the North: The Last Bulwark of Anglo-Saxon Monasticism?', *Studies in Church History*, 18 (*Religion and National Identity*) (1982), 87–98

Downham, Clare, 'St Bega – Myth, Maiden, or Bracelet? An Insular Cult and its Origins', *Journal of Medieval History*, 33.1 (2007), 33–42

Geary, Patrick, *Furta Sacra: Thefts of Relics in the Central Middle Ages* (Princeton: Princeton University Press, 1978)

Harrison, Stuart, and Christopher Norton, 'Lastingham and the Architecture of the Benedictine Revival in Northumbria', in *Anglo-Norman Studies 34: Proceedings of the Battle Conference 2011*, ed. by David Bates (Woodbridge: Boydell, 2012), pp. 63–104

Hough, Carola, 'Strensall, Streanaeshalch and Stronsay', *Journal of the English Place-Name Society*, 35 (2002–2003), 17–24

——, 'Another (ge)streones halh', *Journal of the English Place-Name Society*, 36 (2003–2004), 61–62

King, Edmund, *King Stephen* (New Haven: Yale University Press, 2010)

Knowles, David, *The Monastic Order in England: A History of its Development from the Times of St Dunstan to the Fourth Lateran Council 940–1216* (Cambridge: Cambridge University Press, 1940)

Lawrence-Mathers, Anne, *Manuscripts in Northumbria in the Eleventh and Twelfth Century* (Woodbridge: Boydell, 2003)

Parisse, Michel, 'Les Pancartes. Etude d'un type d'acte diplomatique', in *Pancartes monastiques des XIe et XIIe siècles: Table ronde organisée par l'ARTEM, 6–7 juillet 1994, Nancy*, ed. by Michel Parisse, Pierre Pégeot, and Benoit Michel Tock (Turnhout: Brepols, 1998), pp. 11–62

Pickles, Thomas, 'Biscopes-tun, muneca-tun and preosta-tun: Dating, Significance and Distribution', in *The Church in English Place-Names*, ed. by Eleanor Quinton, Journal of English Place-Name Society, extra series, 4 (Nottingham: English Place-Name Society, 2009), pp. 39–108

——, 'Streanaeshalch (Whitby), its Satellite Churches and Lands', in *Making Christian Landscapes in Atlantic Europe*, ed. by Tomas Ó Carragáin and Sam Turner (Cork: University of Cork Press, 2016), pp. 265–76

Remensnyder, Amy, *Remembering Kings Past: Monastic Foundation Legends in Medieval Southern France* (London: Cornell University Press, 1995)

Rigg, A. G., 'Some Notes on Trinity College, Cambridge, MS. O.9.38', *Notes and Queries*, 13.9 (1966), 324–30

——, *A Glastonbury Miscellany of the Fifteenth Century: A Descriptive Index of Trinity College, Cambridge, MS. O.9.38* (London: Oxford University Press, 1968)

——, 'A Latin Poem on St Hilda and Whitby Abbey', *The Journal of Medieval Latin*, 6 (1996), 12–43

Rollason, David, *Saints and Relics in Anglo-Saxon England* (Oxford: Blackwell, 1989)

Sharpe, Richard, *English Benedictine Libraries: The Shorter Catalogues*, Corpus of Medieval Library Catalogues, 4 (London: British Library, 1996)

Thompson, Alexander Hamilton, 'Monastic Settlement at Hackness', *Yorkshire Archaeological Journal*, 27 (1924), 388–405

Young, George, *A History of Whitby and Streoneshalh Abbey* (Whitby: Clark and Medd, 1817)

CHRISTIANE KROEBEL*

Remembering St Hilda
in the Later Middle Ages

Introduction

St Hilda was known to late eleventh-century readers through the pages of Bede's *Historia ecclesiastica* but was that the sole means of transmitting her memory or is there other evidence in the landscape? This essay examines the origins of the churches dedicated to St Hilda, including Whitby Abbey church, together with the role played in these dedications by the founders of the Benedictine abbey, enabling us to understand the extent to which Norman patrons showed an interest in St Hilda and the Anglo-Saxon past. The essay will also consider how Whitby Abbey promoted devotion to St Hilda, and enquire whether its activities influenced other monastic institutions to recognize her in their liturgical practices.

It is necessary to state some initial provisos. A major part of this essay concerns churches dedicated to St Hilda. These dedications can be problematic to date and should not be taken for granted even when the existence of a church is certain. Often the church or chapel is mentioned without the saint's name. However, in the absence of any reference to re-dedications in the archbishops' registers, the dedications to St Hilda have been presumed to be original. Pre-Conquest stones found within churches present further difficulties: many are funerary monuments, but while they indicate the presence of a churchyard, they do not necessarily prove the existence of a church as well, although some focus around the funeral ceremony is likely to have existed in the form of a chapel or mortuary.

---

* I would like to thank Professor David Rollason, Durham University, for reading earlier versions of this essay and for his comments that shaped and improved my arguments; any errors remain mine.

Christiane Kroebel (christiane.kroebel@gmail.com) is curator of Whitby Abbey collection, a Whitby Museum volunteer, and a retired librarian.

Late Medieval Devotion to Saints from the North of England: New Directions, ed. by Christiania Whitehead, Hazel J. Hunter Blair, and Denis Renevey, MCS 48 (Turnhout: Brepols, 2022), pp. 321–339

BREPOLS ❧ PUBLISHERS   10.1484/M.MCS-EB.5.124356

The Role of St Hilda in the Monastic Foundation at Whitby

St Hilda and the memory of her Anglo-Saxon monastic foundation played a central role in the revival of monasticism at Whitby in the late eleventh century. Writing *c.* 1100, Symeon of Durham noted that the impetus to revive monastic observance in the North came from the prior of Winchcombe, Aldwin, who was inspired after reading Bede's *Historia*. He was joined by Ælfwig and Reinfrid, monks at Evesham, and the three travelled north 'to lead a life of poverty' on the deserted monastic sites. They arrived in Durham 1073–1074 and after some years at Jarrow, their group of followers had grown so large that they decided to part company. Aldwin went to Melrose, Ælfwig stayed in Durham, and Reinfrid, probably in 1078, 'ad *Streoneshalch* (quod Hwitebi appellatur) secessit, ubi aduenientes suscipiens monachorum habitationem instituere cepit' (went to *Streoneshalch* (now called Whitby). There he received people coming to him and he began to establish a dwelling of monks).[1] The Whitby tradition adds that Reinfrid had been a soldier in the Conqueror's army and that when he passed through Northumbria he took a detour to visit Whitby and saw the Viking destruction caused by Ingwar and Ubba.[2] Although this first visit to Whitby contains some fabulous aspects, Reinfrid clearly had long-standing interests in the Anglo-Saxon past, nurtured during his time at Evesham, which must have inspired him to return to Whitby to imitate St Hilda's life of piety. Upon his return, he was given land by William de Percy at Prestebi, thought to be the site of the abbey. Within a few years, renewed Viking attacks forced a split of the monks, with one group moving to Hackness, where Reinfrid died in an accident, while the other under Stephen moved to Lastingham to re-establish a monastery there before settling in York and founding St Mary's Abbey.[3] Hackness was held by William de Percy by 1086 and included 'Land of St Hilda', presumably a Percy land grant to the Whitby monks.[4] Reinfrid's companions eventually returned to Whitby where William de Percy's brother, Serlo, became prior.

Charter evidence indicates that the monastic church at Whitby adopted dedications to St Peter and St Hilda before the end of the eleventh century. The earliest, an undated charter purporting to be a confirmation from Hugh, Earl of Chester, granting the church of St Peter at Whitby to Prior Reinfrid, seems to suggest that the addition of St Hilda came after Reinfrid's death. This corresponds to the foundation memorial stating that William de Percy gave Reinfrid the ancient monastic church of St Peter.[5] However, before William

---

1 Symeon, *Libellus de exordio*, ed. and trans. by Rollason, pp. 200–01, 204–07.
2 *Cartularium de Whiteby*, ed. by Atkinson, I, p. 3.
3 Burton, 'The Monastic Revival'.
4 *Domesday Book*, ed. by Faull and Stinson, fol. 323ᵃ; Thompson, 'The Monastic Settlement'.
5 *Cartularium de Whiteby*, ed. by Atkinson, I, p. 1, p. 28 n. 7; introduction pp. xliii–xlviii; *Early Yorkshire Charters*, ed. by Farrer II, p. 193 (cited hereafter as *EYC*).

de Percy's departure for the Holy Land, in a charter dated 1090–1096, he granted land and the port to Serlo's monastic community, naming the church of St Peter and St Hilda at Whitby as the recipient of this grant. William de Percy's son, Alan, gave additional land and tithes of grain early in the next century. Four charters dated 1100–*c*. 1115 again refer to the church of St Peter and St Hilda at Whitby, which became an abbey under William de Percy, nephew of the founder and Alan's cousin.[6] It seems then that by the early twelfth century the dedication to St Peter and St Hilda was well established, and that the Percy family promoted St Hilda specifically. This fits well with Susan Ridyard's analysis which challenges the perception that the Normans suppressed Anglo-Saxon saints.[7]

St Hilda in Church Dedications

As already mentioned, medieval church dedications provide evidence for the commemoration of St Hilda. In the following discussion, these dedications are grouped by chief land holder to see if some patterns emerge.

William de Percy's role as patron and donor of Whitby Abbey was examined above. The earliest church associated with William de Percy and dedicated to St Hilda is in Hinderwell, where he acquired the manor at the Conquest (see Fig. 14.1 (1)). The church has a late eleventh-century cross-head and there was said to be a hogback in the cemetery in the nineteenth century which has since been lost.[8] The place-name may derive from Scandinavian feminine *Hildr*, probably replacing Old English (OE) *Hild*, but it could be also the OE *hylder* or *hyldre* meaning 'elder-tree', as plants and trees are often combined with *wella* in England.[9] Therefore, either the cross with the holy well inspired the foundation of a church after the Conquest and the place-name reminiscent of St Hilda provided the dedication, or there may already have been a church and cemetery at the well before the Conquest, in which case Percy found the dedication when he acquired the manor.

Other churches that can be associated with Percy, his family, or his tenants followed in the succeeding centuries. A chapel dedicated to Hilda in Sneaton (Fig. 14.1 (5)) is first mentioned amongst Percy's donations to Whitby monastery in the late eleventh century. This township was a berewick (demesne farm) to the manor of Whitby in 1086, hence it was dependent on the manor and located within Whitby parish. The foundation date of the chapel is

---

6 *Cartularium de Whiteby*, ed. by Atkinson, I, pp. 31–35, p. 223; II, pp. 361–62; *EYC*, II, pp. 197–202.

7 Ridyard, '*Condigna Veneratio*'.

8 *Domesday Book*, ed. by Faull and Stinson, fols 322^d, 305^a, 305^b; *Victoria History: North Riding*, ed. by Page, II, pp. 365–71 (cited hereafter as *VCH-NR*); Lang, *Corpus of Anglo-Saxon Stone Sculpture, Vol. 6*, pp. 280, 295.

9 Fellows-Jensen, *Scandinavian Settlement Names*, pp. 256–57.

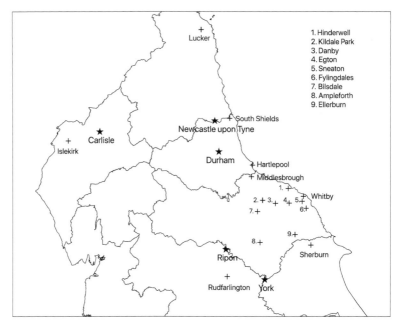

FIGURE 14.1. Churches and hermitages dedicated to St Hilda within pre-1974 county boundaries. This work is based on data provided through www.VisionofBritain.org.uk and uses historical material which is copyright of the Great Britain Historical GIS Project and the University of Portsmouth. In addition, it contains OS data © Crown copyright and database right 2019.

uncertain and only an early twelfth-century font remains.[10] Another chapel in Whitby parish was in Fylingdales, a large moorland township (Fig. 14.1 (6)). Contemporary records mention (1) an unnamed church in Saxeby, South Fyling, given to Whitby Abbey by Robert de Ayketon, an under-tenant of Percy, 1177x1181, and (2) an indulgence granted to those visiting on certain feast days and contributing to the repairs of the monastic church and the chapel of St Hilda near Fyling, 1431–1437.[11] These may refer to the same chapel or to different ones. Witnesses in 1588 recalled a number of chapels, one then used as a hay-house and another as a barn or private chapel, with a further reference to a disused chapel named St Iles. The location of the chapel of St Iles is remembered in a field named Chapel Garth at the adjacent St Ives Farm.[12] It is tempting to equate the two chapels, but it is only certain that there was once a chapel dedicated to St Hilda near Fyling in the fifteenth century.

---

10 *Cartularium de Whiteby*, ed. by Atkinson, I, p. 3; *Domesday Book*, ed. by Faull and Stinson, fol. 305ᵃ; Wood, *Romanesque Yorkshire*, p. 199.
11 *Cartularium de Whiteby*, ed. by Atkinson, I, pp. 51–53 and notes; *Original Papal Documents*, ed. by Sayers, p. 37.
12 *VCH-NR*, II, pp. 534–37.

A chapel of St Hilda in Rudfarlington, near Knaresborough (Fig. 14.1), is named in the life of St Robert of Knaresborough, at the point when Robert is offered this chapel by a noblewoman, along with some land, to use as a hermitage in the late twelfth century. The Victorian editor of the *Memorials of Fountains*, John Walbran, summarizes the story and interpolates that this benefactor may have been a Plumpton or a Percy. A hundred years earlier, Percy had acquired one of two manors there, and, in 1166, Nigel de Plumton (Plumpton) held the knight's fee of Percy.[13] St Robert's benefactor may have been Nigel de Plumton's wife or his mistress, Juliana de Warewic, and the chapel an earlier Percy foundation.

St Hilda's, a proprietary chapel for a branch of the Percy family in Kildale Park, Kildale parish (Fig. 14.1 (2)), is only referred to between the thirteenth and early fourteenth centuries, when a William de Percy granted it with some land and a mill to Healaugh Park Priory with the proviso that the monks find two priests to celebrate divine service. Within a generation, they returned the grant to William's son, Arnald, who installed Crutched Friars, but Archbishop William Greenfield forbade the use of the chapel because these friars were not an officially recognized order and were not allowed to hold divine services for local people.[14] This is a late reference to the chapel; however, another Arnald de Percy held Kildale from Robert de Brus as early as 1119, and this de Percy can be identified as the same Arnald who witnessed a Whitby foundation charter. The site of the chapel may have been near a close in the parish called 'Saynt Yld's Garth', remembered by this name in the sixteenth century.[15]

The chapel in Kildale Park raises several interesting points. On the one hand, if it was a late and short-lived foundation, it demonstrates that the Percy descendants continued to be devoted to St Hilda, even though they apparently let it fail when they installed unsuitable friars after the monks of Healaugh Park returned the grant. On the other, if it was an early twelfth-century foundation, then there is a definite link to the Whitby dedication. The chapel was also the vehicle for an interaction between Arnald de Percy and Robert de Brus, whose connections with St Hilda churches are discussed below, a possible indication of the role played by a network of Norman landholders in the transmission of Hilda's cult.

The only example of a chapel that can be proven to have a late foundation is in Lucker, Bamburgh parish, Northumberland, a distinct manor in the barony of Alnwick (Fig. 14.1). Here, it would appear that the chapel of St Hilda was built on the site of St Peter's Church at some point after the latter was

---

13 *Memorials of Fountains*, ed. by Walbran, pp. 166–67; *Domesday Book*, ed. by Faull and Stinson, fols 322ᵃ, 327ᵃ.

14 *Cartularium de Gyseburne*, ed. by Brown, II, pp. 389–90.

15 *VCH-NR*, II, pp. 249–53; *Domesday Book*, ed. by Faull and Stinson, fols 331ᵇ, 332ᵈ 380ᶜ; *Cartularium de Whiteby*, ed. by Atkinson, I, p. 32; II, p. 698. 'Saynt Yld's Garth' is noted in *VCH-NR*, II, p. 253, quoting Kew, TNA, Exchequer: King's Remembrancer: Miscellaneous Books series I, E164/37, date 12 Eliz I, fol. 241d.

mentioned in 1242. The barony of Alnwick came to the Percy family in 1309.[16] This suggests that the dedication arose out of the Percy family's long-standing interest in Hilda rather than as a distant memory of their Whitby connection; more on this below.

Robert de Brus (I), who acquired his land from Henry I, probably in 1106, or his son, also Robert (II), made the following donations during the twelfth century. The earliest is recorded in a charter which Farrer has dated *c.* 1120, whereby Brus granted the church of St Hilda the abbess at Middlesbrough (Fig. 14.1) to Whitby, on condition that the monks establish a cell there. During the 1130s, the monks of Whitby and canons of Guisborough finally settled a dispute over the tithe and customs from the twelve carucates of land belonging to this Middlesbrough chapel, because Brus had given the church of Stainton, in whose parish St Hilda's was, to his new foundation of Guisborough. The houses agreed to divide the land so that the tithe, customs, and burial fees from six carucates would go to each monastery and St Hilda's would become a mother church. John Atkinson believed Brus's grant was a confirmation of the Earl of Chester's earlier donation.[17] Although there is some question about the authenticity of the Earl of Chester's grant because the charter refers to the church of Flamborough instead of Middlesbrough, the mention of such an early dedication could place the origins of this church within the pre-Conquest period. In addition, Robert de Brus was a witness to the Earl's charter.

The churches dedicated to St Hilda in Danby, on the North York Moors (Fig. 14.1 (3)), and Sherburn, in Ryedale on the south side of the Vale of Pickering and not to be confused with Sherburn-in-Elmet (Fig. 14.1), are considered together because they have a number of similarities. Before the Conquest, Danby was one of four berewicks in the manor of Crunkly held by Ormr, while Sherburn was one of five berewicks in the manor of Langton also held by Ormr; both came to Hugh, son of Baldric, after the Conquest. The manor of Langton had two churches and two priests but their location is unspecified. Most of Hugh's lands were granted to Robert de Stuteville after the Domesday Book was compiled; Sherburn must have been one of these, but there is no information on Danby. Stuteville forfeited his lands in 1106, and Sherburn came to Roger de Mowbray while de Brus received Danby from Henry I. Robert de Stuteville (III) became an under-tenant of Mowbray and claimed Sherburn amongst the other lands which were restored to him by Henry II.[18]

The church of St Hilda at Sherburn, originally in the East Riding of Yorkshire, has significant pre-Conquest stone monuments comprising fourteen

---

16 Bateson, *History of Northumberland, 1*, pp. 99–100, 234, 237–38; Tate, *History of Alnwick*, I, p. 110.

17 *Domesday Book*, ed. by Faull and Stinson, fols 332^c–333^a, and appendix 3.3: 'Robert of Brus'; *Cartularium de Whiteby*, ed. by Atkinson, I, pp. 28, 95, 214–16, pp. xliii–xlviii; *EYC*, II, pp. 193–97, 203, 221–22; Burton, *Monastic Order in Yorkshire*, p. xviii.

18 *Domesday Book*, ed. by Faull and Stinson, fols 327^c, 328^b, 333^a; in addition, the archbishop and the Count of Mortain had land in Sherburn, fol. 382b; *EYC*, IX, pp. 73–74.

cross-shafts and grave cover parts ranging in date from the late-ninth to the tenth century, along with further undated monuments, which were probably made from sandstone from the Whitby area. Additionally, the church has some elements of twelfth-century architecture: part of a doorway reused at the entrance, the chancel arch, and font.[19] It seems likely that this church existed before the Conquest, especially when it transpires that the same Ormr was responsible for rebuilding St Gregory's minster in Kirkdale *c.* 1055–1065.[20] Both Sherburn and Danby were given to Guisborough Priory, Sherburn by Peter de Cordanville with the permission of Robert de Stuteville (the charter was confirmed 1150–1153), and Danby by de Brus.[21] Nothing further can be said about Danby church until more information becomes available, so it is impossible to ascribe it to either Ormr or de Brus. The reason for Cordanville's donation of Sherburn to Guisborough is unclear, but it may be that the canons were actively looking to acquire churches with St Hilda dedications.

It is safe to link de Brus to the chapel of St Hilda in Hartlepool (Fig. 14.1). The church has architectural stonework from the early twelfth century but the current church is mostly from the late-twelfth to the early thirteenth century. It seems that remains from the Anglo-Saxon monastery did not survive and therefore did not influence the layout of the post-Conquest new town. Robert de Brus II gave the church of Hart and its chapel of Hartlepool to Guisborough Priory in the mid-twelfth century and the first mention of the dedication that can be authenticated is mid-thirteenth century.[22] The manorial centre was at Hart and the church there had parochial rights over a significant territory, remaining the parish church throughout the Middle Ages. Hart itself has significant eighth- to eleventh-century Anglo-Saxon stone sculpture, the majority from the ninth to tenth centuries, while sculpture from Hartlepool dates from the seventh and eighth centuries, although one cross, now lost, may derive from the Anglo-Norman overlap period.[23] Lacking documentary sources, the cemetery evidence points to de Brus founding St Hilda's chapel.

The remaining churches dedicated to St Hilda are:

1. Ampleforth chapel (Fig. 14.1 (8)). Here, the link may be through Roger de Mowbray, whose mother, Gundreda, had given land to Whitby Abbey in the 1130s while her relative Robert D'Auney was master of the leper hospital there, before he became a hermit at Hood.[24]

---

19 Lang, *Corpus of Anglo-Saxon Stone Sculpture, Vol. 6*, pp. 201–06, 227–28; Wood, *Romanesque Yorkshire*, pp. 193–94.

20 *Domesday Book*, ed. by Faull and Stinson, appendix 3.4: 'Ormr', 23N17.

21 *English episcopal acta, Vol. 5*, ed. by Burton, 118 p. 91; *EYC*, IX, pp. 94–95; Burton, *The Monastic Order in Yorkshire*, pp. 77–78.

22 Daniels, *Hartlepool*, pp. 26, 29; *Cartularium de Gyseburne*, ed. by Brown, I, p. 16; *English episcopal acta, Vol. 29*, ed. by Hoskin, pp. 62–65.

23 Cramp, *Corpus of Anglo-Saxon Stone Sculpture, Vol. 1*, pp. 93–97, 97–101, 153.

24 Roger de Mowbray granted the church of Coxwold with its chapels to Newburgh Priory in the mid-1150s. This was followed by a dispute between the Priory and York Minster regarding the prebend of Ampleforth, which was settled 1164x1180, probably after 1171. The church

2. Bilsdale chapel, Helmsley parish (Fig. 14.1 (7)). This chapel is thought to have been founded in the early twelfth century by William Spech, Walter Espec's father and then given by the latter to the Augustinian priory of Kirkham in 1122 as part of his grant of the church of Helmsley.[25] Rather curiously, Walter Espec appears in the miracles of St Bega, see below, and is named in Henry I's confirmation charter of (Great) Ayton church to Whitby Abbey. However, as he was Henry I's justiciar in the North and received the barony of Wark on Tweed from Henry, he was undoubtedly a well-known figure.[26]

3. Ellerburn chapel, Pickering parish (Fig. 14.1 (9)). This chapel appears to be of early Norman date but has an unusually high nave and significant tenth-century stone sculpture, which could indicate a pre-Conquest origin.[27]

4. Egton chapel (Fig. 14.1 (4)). This is considered traditionally to have been a chapel to St Oswald's Church, Lythe. It is mentioned for the first time in 1291 in Pope Nicholas's grant of an indulgence to those visiting the church of St Hilda at Egton, which is likely to have been instigated by Stephen de Mauley, deacon and papal chaplain, who also held the church of Lythe, and must have been related to Peter de Mauley, lord of Mulgrave manor in Lythe parish. Later, in 1349, a cemetery was commissioned at Egton chapel for victims of the Black Death.[28]

5. South Shields chapel, Jarrow parish in County Durham (Fig. 14.1). This chapel was well established as a possession of Durham Priory by 1204. Earlier charters linking this chapel to Durham exist but are unfortunately forgeries. What is not in doubt are the existence of St Hildeyere and Ebbeyere (weirs), fisheries on the south side of the Tyne, belonging to St Cuthbert's church in Durham in the reign of Henry I.[29] Since Aldwin, Ælfwig, and Reinfrid had settled at Jarrow from Evesham in the 1070s, it is conceivable that their influence can be seen here.

---

has Romanesque architecture surviving in the south doorway and the font. Mowbray also granted Hood to Newburgh Priory. *EYC*, IX, pp. 206–07; *VCH-NR*, I, pp. 463–64; *English episcopal acta, Vol. 20*, ed. by Lovatt, 131, pp. 146–48; Wood, *Romanesque Yorkshire*, pp. 36–37.

25 'Early Inscription in Bilsdale Church', pp. 237–38; *English episcopal acta, Vol. 5*, ed. by Burton, 91, pp. 72–74.

26 *Vita Bege*, ed. by Wilson, pp. 513–14; *Cartularium de Whiteby*, ed. by Atkinson, I, p. 291; Sanders, *English Baronies*, pp. 52–53, 149.

27 *VCH-NR*, II, p. 440; Lang, *Corpus of Anglo-Saxon Stone Sculpture, Vol. 3*, pp. 126–30. It may be one of the unnamed chapels in a confirmation to the Deanery of York Minster, 19 October 1119xc.1129, of the Pickering churches given to them by King Henry I: *English episcopal acta, Vol. 5*, ed. by Burton, 78, pp. 63–64.

28 *VCH-NR*, II, pp. 343–48; *Calendar of Entries*, ed. by Bliss, I, p. 537; Dixon, *Fasti eboracenses*, ed. by Raine, I, p. 444.

29 *English episcopal acta, Vol. 29*, ed. by Hoskin, 69, p. 62, *Inspeximus* dated Durham, 13 April 1253; Hodgson, *Borough of South Shields*, pp. 37–38.

The research into the history of these churches and chapels has shown that Hinderwell, Sherburn, Middlesbrough, and Ellerburn were almost certainly founded before the end of the eleventh century and likely before the Conquest. The twelfth century saw a programme of new foundations; some of these were apparently churches but most were chapels. The evidence for familiarity with Hilda from Bede's *Historia* seems strongest in the case of William de Percy, and for the church dedication from Hinderwell. De Percy's support of Reinfrid's hermitage and his subsequent funding of a monastery suggest his belief in the monastic revival, while the dedication to St Peter and St Hilda shows that he remembered Hilda's history. Succeeding generations continued to remember St Hilda and probably not only because they were encouraged by the monks at Whitby. The chapels in Rudfarlington and Lucker, at a considerable distance from Whitby, give an indication that some Percy family memories were involved in these dedications.

The Brus family were founders or supporters of monasteries, churches, and chapels, but only in Hartlepool does it seem clear that knowledge of St Hilda's seventh-century monastery must have been the impetus for dedicating the chapel to her. The motivation of the patrons involved in the foundation of the remaining churches, except for South Shields, is more difficult to fathom. The locations of these churches have no known association with seventh-century Hilda; their foundation, therefore, points to a more generic twelfth-century interest in saints from the Anglo-Saxon past. However, the fact that several of the landholders witnessed one another's grants demonstrates that connections existed between them.

Other Evidence of Lay Interest in St Hilda

There are a few references to Hilda that indicate interest in her by other, probably lay, people. St Hilda's hermitage in Islekirk or Hildekirk, in the king's forest of Inglewood in Cumbria (Fig. 14.1), was established in the twelfth century by the hermit Roger Goki. After his death, King John granted it to the Cistercian abbey of Holm Cultram in 1215. It must have been a substantial holding because the king agreed to let the monks have a vaccary (dairy farm) for forty cows and their calves there. Although Roger Goki's antecedents are unknown, Robert de Brus (II) made donations to Holm Cultram in the twelfth century, including a house in Hartlepool,[30] suggesting that there were people moving between the two locations. A further connection between the two may arise from Holm Cultram's involvement in the cult of St Bega (centred at the local Benedictine Priory of St Bees), since Bega's Life, preserved in a thirteenth-century manuscript in Holm Cultram's library, claims that she was the founding abbess of Hartlepool instead of Heiu, as Bede recounted.[31]

---

30 *Register and Records of Holm Cultram*, ed. by Grainger and Collingwood, pp. 43, 76, 126.

31 *Vita Bege*, ed. by Wilson, p. 505; Bede, *Ecclesiastical History*, ed. by Collins, McClure, and

A different type of dedication comes in the form of a guild dedicated to St Hilda, established before 1369 at St Michael Le Quern, in Farringdon Ward Within, in London, built at or over the corn market and close to the Shambles and Smithfield market.[32] There is only one mention of this guild in the London will of Geoffrey Bonere, a 'paternoster maker' with numerous tenements in London and Bruges, Flanders, who left a bequest 'to the brethren of the Guild of S. Hilda'. No link to Whitby is apparent, but the guild may have had its origin amongst merchants from Whitby who sought friendship and cooperation through such a fraternity to replace more localized kinship ties.[33]

Cynthia Turner Camp's current research into Books of Hours and the laity's devotion to northern English saints is also relevant to this essay, since these Books provide clues about whom late medieval lay readers may have prayed to and give some idea of the frequency of those prayers. She has generously shared the references she has collected to those Books that name St Hilda; the saint only appears in two calendars and four litanies, and can therefore be considered a rare inclusion.[34]

Two of these Books have associations with the Percy family however: (1) the early fifteenth-century 'Percy Hours', from Warkworth in Northumberland, where the litany includes Hilda last among the virgins; and (2) the Percy Psalter from the late thirteenth century, only recently acquired by the British Library, where St Hilda is included in the calendar on the August page.[35] More Percy interest may be evident in an early fifteenth-century book, now in Durham, that apparently belonged to a Percy family member later in the same century, which includes the tale of St Hilda turning snakes into ammonites in an expanded version of the story given in John of Tynemouth's Life of St Hilda in his fourteenth-century *Sanctilogium Angliae*.[36] This, together with the late church dedication in Lucker, provides evidence for the continuing appeal of St Hilda to Percy family members.

St Hilda and the Whitby Monks

In this section, I will consider the ways in which the Whitby monks promoted St Hilda to further the standing of the monastery. It is likely that they initiated the fair on the feast of St Hilda, 25 August, held next to the abbey church,

---

Colgrave, IV. 23; Rollason, *Saints and Relics*, p. 197. See also Christiania Whitehead's essay on the saints' lives of Holm Cultram in this volume, pp. 53–74, esp. 66.

32 Hoffman, *Guilds and Related Organisations*, I, p. 10; Newcourt, *Repertorium ecclesiasticum parochiale Londinense*, I, p. 488.

33 Unwin, *Gilds and Companies*, pp. 116, 369; *Calendar of Wills*, ed. by Sharpe, pp. 123–34.

34 See Cynthia Turner Camp's essay in this volume, pp. 99–125, and personal communication of 9 May 2019.

35 BL, MS Harley 1260, fols 96–102ᵛ, catalogue; BL, MS Add. 70000, fol. 10ʳ.

36 Durham, Durham University Library, MS Cosin V.IV.9; Doyle, 'A Miracle of St Hilda', pp. 243–47.

which was recorded in 1122 and later confirmed by Henry I.[37] This is the first mention of the feast of St Hilda on 25 August; there is no foundation for this date in Bede or any other pre-Conquest source.

The Whitby Cartulary includes the catalogue of the abbey library thought to be from the late twelfth century. This catalogue lists a volume on St Hilda, although whether it was written by one of the monks is unclear, as well as books on other saints, showing the monks' interests and their devotional reading one hundred years after their foundation.[38] It is conceivable that this may be the 'Life of S Hilda worth 10s' that was stolen from the chamber of the Prior of Whitby in 1375, by one John del Hole, along with a bowl, some napkins and a ewer.[39] Del Hole was brought before the local magistrate, Thomas Ingelby, in 1378, and it is possible that he may have had to return the volume since, when John Leland visited the monastery before its dissolution, he made a note of this or a similar book, together with the tale of St Hilda turning the snakes to stone.[40] Although no copy is extant, it therefore seems likely that the monastery originally possessed and/or produced a *Vita* of Hilda combining the relevant chapters from Bede's *Historia* with two additional miracles. The first of these miracles relates that Hilda banished snakes that were infesting the site of the monastery and forced them towards the clifftop, where they then turned into stones (ammonites) and could be found fallen at the bottom. The second relates that she asked wild fowls, later specifically geese, not to return to her lands because they had eaten all her corn. This *Vita* seems likely to have been used by John of Tynemouth for his fourteenth-century *Sanctilogium Angliae*, later published in 1516 by Wynkyn de Worde as the *Nova legenda Anglie*.[41]

These two additional miracles are not unique to Hilda, and they also occur in the *Vita* of Keyne, a Cornish saint whose life follows Hilda's closely, and in the *vitae* of Milburgh, and Werburgh.[42] Whether they originated or were copied at Whitby cannot be determined, but the ammonite tale was incorporated into the abbey's arms, which show three ammonites with snake's heads in a shield with the head of a crosier and a mitre above.[43] The two stories would have resonated with a local audience: ammonites are common in the cliffs along the coast from Whitby. Native greylag geese were once common in Britain

---

37 Letters, *Online Gazetteer of Markets and Fairs*, Yorkshire: Whitby.
38 *Cartularium de Whiteby*, ed. by Atkinson, I, pp. x, 341, and n. 1, where Atkinson states that the catalogue is in the same hand with the same glossy ink as the *Memorial*, and should therefore be dated to the late twelfth century. See Dan Talbot's discussion of this catalogue entry in his essay in this volume, p. 312.
39 Kew, TNA, JUST 3.79.3.014. My thanks to Michael Collinson, retired local archivist and former co-editor of the Yorkshire Archaeological Journal, who kindly shared this reference with me and provided supplementary contextual information.
40 Leland, *Itinerary*, III, pp. 39–40.
41 Bede, *Ecclesiastical History*, ed. by Collins, McClure, and Colgrave, IV. 23; *Nova legenda Anglie*, ed. by Horstmann, II, pp. 29–30.
42 *Kalendre of the Newe Legende*, ed. by Görlach, pp. 101, 118, 153.
43 Tonge, *Heraldic Visitation of the Northern Counties*, p. 22.

and were known in the Cleveland area in the early Middle Ages but gradually disappeared, becoming extinct in England by the early nineteenth century.[44]

The *Whitby Missal*, dated to *c.* 1400, is of significant interest but has not been published nor digitized, and the following incomplete information is reliant on the summary in the Bodleian Library catalogue and a personal communication. The calendar in the *Missal* shows the translation of St Hilda's relics on 25 August, and her obit on 17 November; similarly in the *sanctorale*, which contains the offices proper for saints' days, her translation is in August and her feast in November.[45] Other northerners commemorated in the calendar with particularly close ties to Whitby or Hilda are the saints Aidan, Cuthbert, Wilfrid, and Bega/Begu. Also noteworthy are the calendar entries for St Egwine of Evesham and St Indract of Glastonbury. The connection with Evesham is unsurprising since a confraternity agreement between the two monasteries was in place before 1125,[46] and St Hilda is also in calendars and litanies from Evesham dating from the 1250s to the 1370s.[47] By contrast, the inclusion of the Irish saint, Indract, seems surprising until it is remembered that Glastonbury claimed Hilda's relics and apparently placed them in a shrine with Indract and Guthlac. However, St Hilda does not appear in any surviving calendars at Glastonbury, and she is only invoked in one litany.[48] Besides the calendar entry, the *Whitby Missal* also includes an office for Indract. Michael Lapidge's research on Indract and David Rollason's comments may offer clues as to the reasons for this inclusion. Glastonbury collected relics of Irish saints during the late Anglo-Saxon centuries to enhance its prestige and antiquity by claiming historical continuity with early Irish Christianity.[49] It seems far-fetched for the Whitby monks to connect Indract with anyone associated with the Anglo-Saxon monastery, but their veneration of a Glastonbury saint may have attracted southern pilgrims, increasing the national standing of the abbey.

The Whitby monks' promotion of St Bega/Begu is also interesting. Her translation was commemorated by them on 20 June, and her death on 31 October.[50] St Bega is a conflation of a mythical Irish princess and two seventh-century nuns, Heiu from Hartlepool and Begu from Hackness, both

---

44 Teesmouth Bird Club, *The Breeding Birds of Cleveland*, p. 59–60.

45 Oxford, Bodl. Libr., MS Rawlinson Liturg. B.1, fols 7ᵛ, 9ʳ, 233ʳ, 245ᵛ, details regarding northern saints remembered at Whitby were supplied with thanks by Dr Michael Carter, English Heritage, personal communication of 10 February 2018; further details from Bodleian Library Catalogue. For a discussion of other saints in the *Whitby Missal*, see Winterbotham, 'The Mediaeval Settlement at Hackness', pp. 7–10.

46 Thomas, *History of Evesham*, ed. by Sayers and Watkiss, pp. lxi–lxii.

47 *English Monastic Litanies*, ed. by Morgan, using BL, MS Add. 44874; 1 Evesham, Almonry Museum, Psalterium; Oxford, Bodl. Lib., MS Barlow 41.

48 William, *The Deeds of the Bishops of England*, p. 132; *English Monastic Litanies*, ed. by Morgan, using BL, MS Add. 64952, and vol. III, p. 136. For Glastonbury's interest in early northern saints, see also David Thornton's essay in this volume, pp. 387–408, esp. 398–402.

49 Lapidge, 'The Cult of Indract at Glastonbury', pp. 419–52; Rollason, *Saints and Relics*, pp. 204–05.

50 Oxford, Bodl. Libr., MS Rawlinson Liturg. B.1, fols 6ᵛ, 8ᵛ, 216ᵛ, 248ᵛ.

associated with Hilda. Having left Ireland to avoid a forced marriage and landed at Copeland in Cumberland, where St Bees Priory was later established from St Mary's Abbey, York, Bega is then reputed to have travelled east and founded the monastery at Hartlepool. The early thirteenth-century *Vita S Bege* elaborates on Bega's friendship with Hilda during her lifetime and claims that, some centuries after her death, the Whitby monks miraculously found her coffin at Hackness and translated her bones to Whitby. This story is clearly designed to strengthen Whitby's links with Hackness and the abbey's claims to land there. During the Middle Ages, Whitby and Hackness parishes formed Whitby Strand wapentake under the jurisdiction of the abbey.[51] A number of miracles follow the *Vita S Bege*, including one which refers to Walter Espec, mentioned earlier with regard to Bilsdale chapel (Fig. 14.1 (7)). Although the *Vita* was probably written at Holm Cultram Cistercian abbey or St Bees Priory, both in Cumberland, this suggests an author familiar with the topography of the North Riding of Yorkshire.[52] At the beginning of the fifteenth century an ambulatory dedicated to St Bega existed at Whitby Abbey.[53] So far, none to St Hilda has been found.

The appearance of St Hilda in missals from York is to be expected and, indeed, she is named in missal manuscripts dating from the twelfth to the fifteenth centuries, together with early sixteenth-century printed editions.[54] The missal of the geographically close Augustinian foundation of Guisborough, which has been mentioned already in connection with the donation of churches, names St Hilda in its *sanctorale*, litany, and calendar on 25 August with a nine-lesson feast, but the priory does not appear to have been exceptionally active in commemorating her, although its cartulary contains a reference to a now lost spring called St Hilda.[55] Similarly, St Hilda appears in a number of Durham Cathedral Priory manuscripts: she is invoked in a litany from the late thirteenth-century Coldingham breviary, and in both a calendar and litany in another manuscript from the late fifteenth century.[56] However, bearing in mind the links through Reinfrid at Jarrow with St Hilda's chapel, and Hilda's own early foundations on the Wear and at Hartlepool, one would have expected memorialization to have taken place very early and in more numerous manuscripts. It may be that Durham had few direct links with Whitby while York had close ones through their fraternity agreement.

---

51 *VCH-NR*, II, p. 502.

52 With thanks to Christiania Whitehead for pointing me towards this *Vita*: *Vita Bege*, ed. by Wilson, pp. 513–14; Todd, 'St Bega'. See also Whitehead's essay in this volume, pp. 53–74.

53 *Testamenta Eboracensia*, ed. by Raine, II, p. 77, '1436. Ego Willelmus Salvayne, Armiger Monasterii de Whitby - sep. in Monasterio de Whitby in deambulatorio Sanctæ Begæ'.

54 *Missale ad usum insignis ecclesiae Eboracensis*, ed. by Henderson; *Breviarium ad usum insignis ecclesie Eboracensis*, ed. by Lawley.

55 BL, MS Add. 35285; *Cartularium de Gyseburne*, ed. by Brown, I, pp. 48, 49, 66, appears as *ad fontem S. Hildæ* and *at Hildekelde*.

56 *English Monastic Litanies*, ed. by Morgan, using BL, MS Harley 4664; BL, MS Harley 1804; *Horae Eboracenses*, ed. by Wordsworth, pp. 13, 94.

Other Benedictine monasteries where Hilda's name appears in missals but which cannot be explained through known links to Whitby are Westminster, Chester (Abbey of St Mary and St Werburgh), and Bury St Edmunds.[57]

There are noteworthy references to St Hilda in calendars and martyrologies associated with the Birgittine Order.[58] Somewhat reminiscent of the early double monasteries in Gaul and England, including of course Whitby, Birgittine monasteries were double foundations where nuns, monks, deacons, and lay brothers were ruled by an abbess.[59] A fifteenth-century calendar from Naantali/Nådendal Abbey in Finland marks Hilda's translation, 25 August, while a twelfth-century litany to Hilda from Bury St Edmunds became incorporated into a manuscript of fifteenth-century devotional texts that may have belonged to Vadstena Abbey in Sweden, the first Birgittine house, although quite how is unknown.[60] The English martyrology from the Birgittine house at Syon, founded by Henry V in 1415, was published shortly before the abbey's suppression in 1539. It contains two dates for St Hilda: 17 November for her feast day celebrated in Ireland, and 18 November for her feast in England.[61] A connection to Whitby cannot be shown but there was a strong following of the Birgittines in Yorkshire.[62]

Conclusion

The memorialization of St Hilda appears to have been simultaneously limited and widespread. Her cult never became as famous as those of Cuthbert and Oswald, nonetheless, she was remembered from England to the Baltic. Although this essay makes a distinction between lay and religious commemoration, there was of course a great deal of interaction and overlap. However, the lay opportunities to promote a local saint seem to have been different. Founding a church or chapel afforded an opportunity for the laity to demonstrate their devotion, although it would have had to meet with the approval of the bishop responsible for dedicating the church.

The Whitby monks, under the leadership of the Percy family, started to celebrate St Hilda soon after the monastery's refoundation. The unique double dedication of their church to St Peter and St Hilda shows that they wanted to create a sense of place and give their abbey a distinct identity. Following on from that, they promoted 'their saint' in similar ways to other monasteries

---

57 *Missale ad usum ecclesie Westmonasteriensis*, ed. by Legg, I, p. xv; *English Benedictine Kalendars*, ed. by Wormald, I, p. 99.

58 *English Saints*, ed. by Toy, pp. 138–39; *English Monastic Litanies*, ed. by Morgan, Stockholm, Kungliga Biblioteket Holmiensis A 49; *Martiloge in Englysshe*.

59 Patricia, 'Birgitta Birgersdotter', I, p. 17.

60 *English Monastic Litanies*, ed. by Morgan, III, p. 13.

61 *Martiloge in Englysshe*, pp. 179–80, 233.

62 Morris, 'St Birgitta', p. 223.

through fairs and papal indulgences. Some links to other monasteries can be shown, such as Evesham's initial role in the monastic revival and later in the confraternity agreement with Whitby and liturgical veneration of Hilda,[63] and suggest scope for further investigations.

Neither the Percy nor the Brus families appear to have 'exported' the cult beyond the North East of England, suggesting that the local laity identified with St Hilda on the basis of a sense of place which could not be transferred elsewhere easily. Religious, on the other hand, identified with saints more generally, lighting on Hilda as someone whom Bede had revered; their interest was not based solely upon geographical location but also focused on their exemplary lives.

---

63 See pp. 322, 332 above.

Works Cited

Manuscripts and Archival Sources

Durham, Durham University Library, MS Cosin V.IV.9
Kew, The National Archives, Exchequer: King's Remembrancer: Miscellaneous
    Books series I, E164/37, date 12 Eliz I
——, The National Archives, JUST 3.79.3.014
London, British Library, MS Add. 35285
——, MS Add. 44874
——, MS Add. 64952
——, MS Add. 70000
——, MS Harley 1260
——, MS Harley 1804
——, MS Harley 4664

Oxford, Bodleian Library, MS Barlow 41
——, MS Rawlinson Liturg. B.1 (The *Whitby Missal*)
Stockholm, Kungliga Biblioteket Holmiensis A 49

Primary Sources

Bede, *The Ecclesiastical History of the English People*, ed. and trans. by Roger Collins,
    Judith McClure, and Bertram Colgrave (Oxford: Oxford University Press, 1994)
Breviarium ad usum insignis Ecclesie Eboracensis, Vol. 2, ed. by S. W. Lawley, SS, 75
    (Durham: Andrews, 1883)
Calendar of Entries in the Papal Registers Relating to Great Britain and Ireland:
    Papal Letters 1198-[1513], ed. by William Henry Bliss, 19 vols (London: HMSO,
    1893–1999)
Calendar of Wills Proved and Enrolled in the Court of Husting, London: Part 2,
    1358–1688, ed. by Reginald Sharpe (London: John C. Francis, 1890)
Cartularium Abbathiae de Whiteby, Ordinis S. Benedicti, ed. by John C. Atkinson,
    2 vols, SS, 69, 72, (Durham: Andrews & Co., 1879–1881)
Cartularium prioratus de Gyseburne, Ebor. dioeceseos, ordinis S. Augustini, ed. by
    William Brown, 2 vols, SS, 86, 89 (Durham: Andrews & Co., 1889–1894)
Dixon, William, H., *Fasti eboracenses: Lives of the Archbishops of York, Vol. 1*, ed. by
    James Raine (London: Longman, 1863)
Domesday Book: Yorkshire, ed. by Margaret L. Faull and Marie Stinson, 2 vols
    (Chichester: Phillimore, 1986)
Early Yorkshire Charters, being a Collection of Documents Anterior to the Thirteenth
    Century made from the Public Records, Monastic Chartularies, Roger Dodsworth's
    Manuscripts and other available Sources, ed. by William Farrer, 3 vols
    (Edinburgh: Ballantyne, Hanson & co., 1914) (cited as *EYC*)

Early Yorkshire Charters, vol. IX: *The Stuteville Fee*, ed. by Charles Travis Clay (Leeds: Yorkshire Archaeological Society, 1952) (cited as *EYC* IX)

English Benedictine Kalendars after A.D. 1100, ed. by Francis Wormald, 2 vols, Henry Bradshaw Society, 77, 81 (London: Henry Bradshaw Society, 1939–1946)

English episcopal acta, Vol. 5: York, 1070–1154, ed. by Janet E. Burton (Oxford: Oxford University Press, 1988)

English episcopal acta, Vol. 20, York, 1154–1181, ed. by Marie Lovatt (Oxford: Oxford University Press, 2000)

English episcopal acta, Vol. 29: Durham, 1241–1283, ed. by Philippa M. Hoskin (Oxford: Oxford University Press, 2005)

English Monastic Litanies of the Saints after 1100, ed. by Nigel J. Morgan, 3 vols, Henry Bradshaw Society, 119, 120, 123 (London: Henry Bradshaw Society, 2012–2018)

English Saints in the Medieval Liturgies of the Scandinavian Churches, ed. by John Toy, Henry Bradshaw Society, Subsidia, 6 (London: Boydell, 2009)

Horae Eboracenses: The Prymer or Hours of the Blessed Virgin Mary According to the Use of the Illustrious Church of York, ed. by Christopher Wordsworth, SS, 132 (Durham: Andrews & Co., 1920)

The Kalendre of the Newe Legende of Englande, from Pynson's printed edition, 1516, ed. by Manfred Görlach, Middle English Texts, 27 (Heidelberg: C. Winter, 1994)

Leland, John, *The Itinerary of John Leland the Antiquary*, 9 vols (Oxford: Thomas Hearne, 1770)

The Martiloge in Englysshe after the Use of the Chirche of Salisbury and as it is Redde in Syon with Addicyons (Printed by Wynkyn de Worde in 1526), Henry Bradshaw Society, 3 (London: Harrison & Sons, 1893)

Memorials of the Abbey of St Mary of Fountains, ed. by John Richard Walbran, SS, 42 (Durham: Andrews, 1863)

Missale ad usum ecclesie Westmonasteriensis, ed. by John Wickham Legg, 3 vols, Henry Bradshaw Society, 1, 5, 12 (London: Harrison & Sons, 1891–1897)

Missale ad usum insignis ecclesiae Eboracensis, ed. by William G. Henderson, 2 vols, SS, 59, 60 (Durham: Andrews & Co., 1874)

Nova legenda Anglie: as collected by John of Tynemouth, John Capgrave, and Others, and First Printed, with New Lives, by Wynkyn de Worde a.d. mdxui [1516], ed. by Carl Horstmann, 2 vols (Oxford: Clarendon Press, 1901)

Original Papal Documents in Lambeth Palace Library: A Catalogue, ed. by Jane Sayers (London: University of London Press, 1967)

Register and Records of Holm Cultram, ed. by Francis Grainger and W. G. Collingwood, Cumberland and Westmorland Antiquarian and Archaeological Society, record series, 7 (Kendal: Titus Wilson, 1929)

Symeon of Durham, *Libellus de exordio atque procursu istius hoc est Dunhelmensis, ecclesie: Tract on the Origins and Progress of this Church of Durham*, ed. and trans. by David Rollason (Oxford: Clarendon Press, 2000)

Testamenta Eboracensia, or, Wills Registered at York: Illustrative of the History, Manners, Language, Statistics, &c. of the Province of York, from the year MCCC downwards, ed. by James Raine, 6 vols, SS (London: J. B. Nichols, 1836–1902)

Thomas of Marlborough, *History of the Abbey of Evesham*, ed. and trans. by Jane Sayers and Leslie Watkiss (Oxford: Clarendon Press, 2003)

Tonge, Thomas, *Heraldic Visitation of the Northern Counties in 1530*, ed. by W. Hylton Dyer Longstaffe, SS, 41 (Durham: Francis Le Keux, 1863)

Vita S Bege, in *The Register of the Priory of St Bees*, ed. by J. Wilson, SS, 126 (Durham: Andrews & Co., 1915), pp. 497–520

William of Malmesbury, *The Deeds of the Bishops of England = Gesta Pontificum Anglorum*, trans. by David Preest (Woodbridge: Boydell, 2002)

Secondary Works

Bateson, Edward, *A History of Northumberland, Vol. 1: The Parish of Bamburgh* (Newcastle: Andrew Reid, 1893)

Burton, Janet, 'The Monastic Revival in Yorkshire: Whitby and St Mary's, York', in *Anglo-Norman Durham, 1093–1193*, ed. by David Rollason, Margaret Harvey, and Michael Prestwich (Woodbridge: Boydell, 1994) pp. 41–51

——, *The Monastic Order in Yorkshire, 1069–1215* (Cambridge: Cambridge University Press, 1999)

Cramp, Rosemary, *Corpus of Anglo-Saxon Stone Sculpture, Vol. 1: County Durham and Northumberland* (Oxford: Oxford University Press, 1984)

Daniels, Robin, *Hartlepool: An Archaeology of the Medieval Town* (Hartlepool: Tees Archaeology, 2010)

Doyle, A. I., 'A Miracle of St Hilda in a Migrating Manuscript', in *Crossing Boundaries*, ed. by Eric Cambridge and Jane Hawkes (Oxford: Oxbow, 2017), pp. 243–47

'Early Inscription in Bilsdale Church', *Yorkshire Archaeological Journal*, 17 (1903), 237–40

Fellows-Jensen, Gillian, *Scandinavian Settlement Names in Yorkshire* (Copenhagen: I kommission hos Akademisk forlag, 1972)

Hodgson, George B., *The Borough of South Shields: From the Earliest Period to the Close of the Nineteenth Century* (Newcastle-upon-Tyne: Reid, 1903)

Hoffman, Tom, comp., *Guilds and Related Organisations in Great Britain and Ireland: A Bibliography*, 4 vols (unpublished draft, 2011) <http://www.bbk.ac.uk/library/archives-and-special-collections> [accessed 5 October 2018]

Lang, James, *Corpus of Anglo-Saxon Stone Sculpture, Vol. 3: York and Eastern Yorkshire* (Oxford: Oxford University Press, 1991)

——, *Corpus of Anglo-Saxon Stone Sculpture, Vol. 6: Northern Yorkshire* (Oxford: Oxford University Press, 2001)

Lapidge, Michael, 'The Cult of Indract at Glastonbury', in Michael Lapidge, *Anglo-Latin Literature, 900–1066* (London: Hambleton Press, 1993), pp. 419–52

Letters, Samantha, *Online Gazetteer of Markets and Fairs in England and Wales to 1516* <http://www.history.ac.uk/cmh/gaz/gazweb2.html> [Yorkshire] (16 December 2013) [accessed 19 May 2019]

Morris, Bridget, 'St Birgitta of Sweden's *Revelationes* (1492) in York Minster Library', *Journal of the Early Book Society*, 13 (2010), 221–36

Newcourt, Richard, *Repertorium ecclesiasticum parochiale Londinense: An Ecclesiastical Parochial History of the Diocese of London*, 2 vols (London: Motte, 1708–1710)

Patricia, Sr. O.SS.S., 'Birgitta Birgersdotter', in *Studies in St Birgitta and the Brigittine Order*, 2 vols (Salzburg: Institut für Anglistik und Amerikanistik, Universität Salzburg, 1993), I, pp. 7–28

Ridyard, Susan J., '*Condigna Veneratio*: Post-Conquest Attitudes to the Saints of the Anglo-Saxons', in *Proceedings of the Battle Conference, 1986*, ed. by R. Allen Brown, Anglo-Norman Studies, 9 (Woodbridge: Boydell, 1987), pp. 179–206

Rollason, David W., *Saints and Relics in Anglo-Saxon England* (Oxford: Basil Blackwell, 1989)

Sanders, Ivor J., *English Baronies: A Study of their Origin and Descent, 1086–1327* (Oxford: Clarendon Press, 1960)

Tate, George, *The History of the Borough, Castle and Barony of Alnwick*, 2 vols (Alnwick: H. H. Blair, 1866–1869)

Teesmouth Bird Club, *The Breeding Birds of Cleveland* ed. by Graeme Joynt, Ted Parker, and Vic Fairbrother (n. p.: Teesmouth Bird Club, 2008)

Thompson, A. Hamilton, 'The Monastic Settlement at Hackness and its Relation to the Abbey of Whitby', *Yorkshire Archaeological Journal*, 27 (1924), 388–405

Todd, John M., 'St Bega: Cult, Fact and Legend', *Transactions of the Cumberland and Westmorland Antiquarian and Archaeological Society*, 80 (1908), 23–35

Unwin, George, *The Gilds and Companies of London* (London: G. Allen & Unwin, 1938)

The Victoria History of the County of York: North Riding, ed. by William Page, 3 vols (London: Constable, 1914–1925) (cited as *VCH-NR*)

Winterbotham, J. J., 'The Mediaeval Settlement at Hackness', *Transactions of the Scarborough Archaeological and Historical Society*, 24 (1982), 7–10

Wood, Rita, *Romanesque Yorkshire* (Leeds: Yorkshire Archaeological Society, 2012)

II.3 Beyond the North:
Southern, European, and
Post-Medieval Perspectives

ANNE MOURON

The French *Life* of St Godric of Finchale, or Adventures for Thirteenth-Century Nuns

Introduction: Reginald of Durham

Miri Rubin, in her introduction to her recent translation of Thomas of Monmouth's *Vita et passio sancti Willemi martyris Norwicensis*, an account of William's alleged kidnapping and killing by Jews in 1124, writes that the twelfth century was, 'a dynamic period of literary innovation [which] produced a great deal of hagiographical writing and displayed a strong interest in history'.[1] One of these hagiographical texts is Reginald of Durham's *Libellus de vita et miraculis sancti Godrici*, a huge work in excess of 480 pages in Joseph Stevenson's edition.[2] Reginald of Durham, or of Coldingham in Berwickshire in the Scottish Borders where he was perhaps born, was a monk in the Benedictine monastery in Durham where he died around 1190.

As Reginald explains in the prologue, he was encouraged to write the saint's life and miracles by the famous Cisterican author and abbot, Aelred of Rievaulx.[3] This should not be surprising, for Aelred was not only a 'child of the North of England',[4] but he also personally knew Godric and visited him a number of times, which Reginald records in his text.[5] Aelred, as a writer of a number of saints' lives, had a keen sense of their role and function. Indeed, in the prologue to his *Vita sancti Ædwardi confessoris* he explains:

---

1 Thomas, *The Life of William of Norwich*, trans. by Rubin, p. xxix.
2 Reginald, *Libellus de vita et miraculis S. Godrici*, ed. by Stevenson (cited hereafter as Reginald, *Vita Godrici*). Margaret Coombe is preparing a new edition of the text to be published by Oxford University Press. A shorter version of Godric's life by 'Walter' (otherwise unidentified) is to be found alongside Thomas's *Vita S Willemi Norwicensis* in Cambridge, Camb. Uni. Lib., MS Additional 3037, fols 119ᵛ–68ʳ, which also contains John of Ford's *Vita Wulfrici*, fols 81ʳ–119ᵛ. See Thomas, *The Life of William of Norwich*, trans. by Rubin, p. liii.
3 Reginald, *Vita Godrici*, p. 19.
4 Aelred, *The Lives of the Northern Saints*, trans. by Freeland, p. 1.
5 See, for example, Reginald, *Vita Godrici*, chap. 77, pp. 175–77. For the translation into medieval French, see *Reginald of Durham's Life of St Godric: An Old French Version*, ed. by Coombe, Hunt, and Mouron, pp. 107–09 (cited hereafter as *French Life*).

Anne Mouron (Anne.mouron@regents.ox.ac.uk) is an associate member of Regent's Park College, University of Oxford.

Late Medieval Devotion to Saints from the North of England: New Directions, ed. by Christiania Whitehead, Hazel J. Hunter Blair, and Denis Renevey, MCS 48 (Turnhout: Brepols, 2022), pp. 343–360

BREPOLS ❧ PUBLISHERS   10.1484/M.MCS-EB.5.124357

Nichil enim magis ad aemulationem perfectionis animum humanum prouocat et accendit quam quorumlibet perfectorum legere uel audire uirtutes, mores addiscere, gloriam aestimare, cum impossibile sibi nullus debeat arbitrari, quod alium fecisse cognouerit.

> (Nothing encourages and incites the human mind to the emulation of perfection more than reading and hearing the virtues of any of the perfect, learning of their way of life, and considering their renown, for no one should think impossible for himself what he knows another has done.)[6]

Whatever agenda, religious or political, Reginald may have had in writing such a monumental work, the French translation of his *Vita Godrici* certainly fulfils the aims of the saint's life as described by Aelred. It perpetuates the memory of Godric in a wealth of detail and it gives ample examples of how to live a religious life in such a way that the reader may think it possible to do 'quod alium fecisse cognouerit' (what he knows another has done).

After a short summary of Godric's life, this essay briefly examines Paris, Bibliothèque Mazarine, MS 1716 which contains the only surviving copy of the *French Life* of Godric along with other saints' *legendae*. We next turn our attention to the *French Life* itself to consider it first as a didactic text, then as a work enchanting its aristocratic reader with various instances of the 'merveilleus' (the wonderful), and finally as a rare example of a 'real' saint's life and not one re-packaged and sanitized by a church cleric to conform to the conventional model saint's life. Finally, we conclude with a question: was Godric all too 'real' to be an enduring saintly example?

Godric: An English Peasant Saint

Godric of Finchale was born *c.* 1070 in Norfolk to poor Anglo-Saxon farmers. Around 1085 he became a pedlar in Lincolnshire, but soon extended his commercial enterprise to Scotland, Denmark, and Flanders, buying a half-share in a merchant vessel and becoming a skilled sailor. In 1101 he made his first pilgrimage to Jerusalem, coming back to England via Santiago de Compostela, and subsequently made pilgrimages to Rome and to St Giles in Provence. In 1105 Godric joined the hermit Ælric in a forest near Carlisle until the latter's death in 1108, and after a second pilgrimage to the Holy Land, he became a hermit in Finchale just outside Durham for the next sixty years where he died on 21 May 1170.[7]

---

6 Aelred, *Vita sancti Ædwardi*, ed. by Marzella, p. 87. Aelred, *The Life of Edward the Confessor*, trans. by Freeland, p. 125.

7 For a longer account of Godric's life and bibliographical references, see Tudor, 'Godric of Finchale'. For a modern, fictional rendering of the saint's life see Buechner, *Godric*.

THE FRENCH *LIFE* OF ST GODRIC OF FINCHALE   345

Although no Middle English account of his life has survived, Godric was still venerated in the North of England in the fifteenth century. In one of the extant manuscripts of *The Desert of Religion*, a short northern poem on vices and virtues, Godric features visually in the company of two other northern saints: St Hilda and Richard Rolle (but interestingly, not St Cuthbert). The illustration in question depicts Godric kneeling and praying to an image of the Virgin and Child with the words 'Goderyke heremit' underneath. The illustration is framed by the following rhyming couplets:

> In wasterne and in wildernes / whare nane wont bot wilde, / I went and in halines / a heremitage I plylde. / The fendes with faindinges of my flesche / fayne walde me have filede, / bot Gode his grace to me gune dres, / elles hade I bene [be]gilde.[8]

These words may indicate an acquaintance with the lyric the Virgin Mary allegedly taught Godric, which has survived separately,[9] as well as with the hermit's harsh life in the wilderness and his successful overcoming of many temptations from 'li Anemi' (the Enemy).[10]

Godric's *French Life*: Paris, Bibliothèque Mazarine, MS 1716

Notwithstanding the absence of a Middle English *Life*, a translation into Anglo-Norman was made in England in the late twelfth or early thirteenth century by the chaplain of Ase of Montferrant. As Margaret Coombe has recently discovered, Ase was 'the daughter of a prominent Durham family' who had links with 'the nearby Cistercian Abbey of Meaux in Holderness, also in East Yorkshire'.[11] It is possible, therefore, that the translation, which Anthony Hunt dates from internal evidence to within the period 1160–1196, originated at Meaux, but if so that manuscript has not come down to us.[12]

The *French Life* of Godric survives in a unique thirteenth-century manuscript, Paris, Bibliothèque Mazarine, MS 1716.[13] This is a large legendary volume of 368 folios in which the *Life* of Godric is accompanied by forty-eight other prose texts, most of them saints' lives.[14] Although a number of these texts have been

---

8 Mouron, 'An Edition of the Desert of Religion', II, p. 295; BL, MS Cotton Faustina B VI, pars ii, fol. 16ᵛ.

9 For example, BL, MS Royal 5 F VII, fol. 85ʳ. For a printed edition, see Godric, 'A Cry to Mary', in *Medieval English Lyrics*, ed. by Davies, p. 51.

10 For example, Reginald, *Vita Godrici*, chap. 114, pp. 234–35; for the French translation, see *French Life*, pp. 145–46.

11 *French Life*, pp. 7–8.

12 *French Life*, p. 8.

13 'The date of the manuscript cannot be refined beyond its assignment to the turn of the thirteenth century', *French Life*, p. 4.

14 For a description of the manuscript, see Molinier and d'Artois, *Catalogue des manuscrits*, II,

edited, there is no study of the manuscript as a whole.[15] Anthony Hunt notes that 'some soundings undertaken so far [in the *Lives* of Mazarine, MS 1716] suggest a widespread Franco-Picard colouring'.[16] On the verso of the first flyleaf there is an eighteenth-century inscription by the discalced Augustinian brother Leonard who bought the manuscript in 1704, indicating that the manuscript is 500 years old and comes from the Abbey of Longchamp.[17] This most likely refers to the Franciscan convent of Poor Clares founded at Longchamp in 1255 by Isabelle of France, the daughter of Louis VIII of France and Blanche of Castille, and the sister of Saint Louis.[18]

A medieval note in the manuscript reads: 'Madame est bonne dame; — Madame Ysabaus, fille le roy de France, est bonne dame; — Madame de Navarre; — Marguerite escrit bien' (Madame is a good lady; — Madame Isabelle, the daughter of the king of France, is a good lady; — My Lady of Navarre; — Margaret writes well).[19] The catalogue of the Mazarine Library states that Isabelle of France here alludes to the wife of Edward II of England.[20] Victoria Tudor agrees with this attribution, but Margaret Coombe in her more recent thesis believes that Isabelle refers instead to the daughter of Louis VIII and Blanche mentioned earlier.[21] The former Isabelle was notorious for her beauty, her involvement in English politics, and her liaison with Roger Mortimer (first Earl of March) with whom she effectively ruled after the deposition of Edward II.[22] In contrast, the latter Isabelle, sister to Louis IX, was known for her fervent piety and rigorous asceticism, making her a much more likely recipient of Mazarine, MS 1716.[23] However, the mention of 'Navarre' in the inscription may hint at a third Isabelle, Louis IX's daughter (1242–1271), who married Thibaud V, 'comte de Champagne et roi de Navarre' in 1255. Like all Louis IX's children she received a 'bonne éducation religieuse et morale'.[24] She was also the recipient of *Li enseignement ke li bons rois Sains Loÿs escrist*

---

pp. 193–94. See also 'Contenu' in *Section romane*, notice de 'PARIS, Bibliothèque Mazarine, 1716'; *French Life*, pp. 2–3.

15 See 'Bibliographie' in *Section romane*, notice de 'PARIS, Bibliothèque Mazarine, 1716'.

16 *French Life*, p. 3.

17 Molinier and d'Artois, *Catalogue des manuscrits*, II, pp. 193–94.

18 Although she never became a nun, Isabella took a vow of chastity and retired at the Abbey of Longchamp but lived separately from the nuns. She died in 1270 and was buried at the Abbey. Cambridge, Fitzwilliam Museum, MS 300, an 'exquisite prayer book', is believed to have been made for Isabelle. The Abbey of Longchamp was situated just outside Paris in what is now known as the Bois de Boulogne, but it was completely destroyed at the French Revolution.

19 Molinier and d'Artois, *Catalogue des manuscrits*, II, p. 194.

20 Molinier and d'Artois, *Catalogue des manuscrits*, II, p. 194.

21 See Tudor, 'Reginald of Durham and Godric of Finchale', pp. 331–33; Coombe, 'Reginald of Durham's Latin Life', p. 85.

22 See Parsons, 'Isabella [Isabella of France]'.

23 For examples of her piety and ascetism, see Agnès d'Harcourt, *Vie d'Isabelle de France*, ed. by Allirot.

24 Le Goff, *Saint Louis*, pp. 734–42.

THE FRENCH *LIFE* OF ST GODRIC OF FINCHALE   347

de sa main a ma Dame Ysabel.[25] Regardless of the identity of the recipient of Mazarine, MS 1716, it seems likely that the manuscript was intended for a French royal princess.

The *Life* of Godric stands out in the manuscript, not only because it is by far the longest text (sixty-four folios), but more specifically because Godric is the only English saint represented in the legendary, and one of only three near-contemporary saints.[26] As was the case with the majority of medieval translations, there are additions, omissions, and variants in the French rendering, but on the whole it follows Reginald's work, the greatest exception being that the vernacular text does not include the miracles Reginald narrates after Godric's death.[27] Although the *French Life* of Godric relies heavily on its source text, it is nevertheless considered here as a work in its own right and with its own audience. One may ask, for example, why the Franciscan nuns of Longchamp would have enjoyed reading the saint's *Life*, although it is unlikely that they had any prior knowledge of the northern English hermit. Some of these reasons may perhaps also account for the survival of only one manuscript of the French text.

Godric's *French Life*: A Didactic Text Containing Good Examples to Imitate

Unfortunately, Mazarine, MS 1716 has suffered substantial damage, as some folios have been torn out, and the very beginning of the *Life* of Godric is now missing. Nevertheless, the opening remarks of some of the other lives have survived in part. The *Life* of St Giles begins thus:

> A ceuls qui volentiers entendent et cuer ont du retenir, ce est qui en nostre seingneur croient, vueil je raconter la vie d'un saint homme qui Saint Gyles a non que maintes genz requirent de pluseurs contrees loingtainnes là où son cors gist en Provance por avoir de lors pechiez remission.

---

25 This text has survived in many manuscripts (often with the *Enseignemenz que Monseigneur saint Loys fist a son ainsné fils Phelippe*). Louis IX, 'The French *Enseignemenz a Phellippe* and *Enseignement a Ysabel* of Saint Louis', ed. by Ashley, p. 5; for the edition and translation into English of the 'Enseignement … a ma Dame Ysabel', see pp. 17–22. The 'Marguerite' of the inscription could refer either to Louis IX's wife, Margaret of Provence (1221–1295) or to another daughter of Louis IX, Margaret (1254–1271) who married 'Jean I, Duke of Brabant' (Le Goff, *Saint Louis*, tableaux généalogiques (no pagination)). Note that in BnF, MS français 11662, which contains several documents referring to the Abbey of Longchamp, there is a letter about the foundation of the abbey mentioning that, if Louis IX laid the first stone and his sister Isabella the fourth one, his wife, Margaret, 'y mist la seconde pierre' (laid the second stone there) (fol. 40ᵛ).

26 The other two are St Theobald of Provins who died in 1066 and St Elisabeth of Hungary who lived from 1207 to 1231, Mazarine, MS 1716, fols 255ᵛᵇ–58ʳᵃ and 296ʳᵃ–311ᵛᵇ respectively.

27 Reginald, *Vita Godrici*, pp. 333–481. See also *French Life*, p. 6. This article does not examine the French text as a translation, something that has been discussed elsewhere. See Mouron, '"Help thin Godric in Francrice"'.

> (To those who willingly hear and are determined to remember these things, that is those who believe in our Lord, I want to tell the life of a holy man whose name is St Giles and whom many people sought from numerous far regions — where his body lies in Provence — in order to have forgiveness for their sins.)[28]

Similarly, the *Life* of St Anastasia begins:

> ceulz qui nostre seingneur aiment et criement et cil qui volentiers les oient et entendent i pevent mout de bien aprendre et retenir par les bonnes examples qu'il oient conter et dire.

> (those who love and fear our Lord and those who willingly hear and pay attention to them [saints' lives?] there may learn and remember many good things from the good examples they hear related and narrated.)[29]

Since these opening remarks occur elsewhere, they may not have originated in Mazarine, MS 1716, but the compiler obviously thought them worth including. These introductory words, like Aelred's, point out the benefits to the spiritual life that such texts offer.

The *French Life* of Godric, perhaps unsurprisingly, is full of such 'bonnes examples' and the text frequently calls attention to their exemplary nature. Chapter 82, for example, shows Godric facing an illness in which his flesh starts to decay and emits a foul odour. In order to recover health, Godric rubs his body forcibly with salt until it bleeds. The chapter begins:

> *Merveilleuses* et pluseurs sont les ovraingnes Nostre Seingnur que sa grant pitié de misericorde parfait par divers ordres en .i. de ses esliz. Car il renovelle chascun jor signes *merveilliex* par ses sers que nous bien poons connoistre par cest saint home, se nous dignement voulons encerchier ses euvres et ses paroles.[30]

> (*Wonderful* and many are the works of our Lord which by the great pity of his mercy are accomplished by various ways in one of his elect. For every day he repeats *marvellous* signs through his servants which we can well recognise by this holy man, if we want to examine his deeds and his words worthily.)

---

28 The *Life* of St Giles, Paris, Mazarine, MS 1716, fol. 187ᵛᵃ. All translations from Mazarine, MS 1716 are my own. Although such initial remarks do not accompany all prose lives of St Giles and St Anastasia, a version of these occur in other manuscripts. For example, BnF, MS Français 23117 (s. xiii–xiv), see fol. 353ʳ (beginning of the *Life* of Giles), fol. 465ʳ (*Life* of Anastasia). See also, BnF, MS français 413, a *Vie des Sains* (s. xv), fol. 288ᵛ (beginning of the *Life* of Giles), fol. 434ʳ (*Life* of Anastasia).

29 The *Life* of Anastasia, Mazarine, MS 1716, fol. 318ʳᵃ. The very beginning of the text is missing. Note here the emphasis on 'hearing' (rather than reading) which may confirm Paul Meyer's suggestion that saints' lives in prose were written to be read during meals in convents for female religious. Meyer's words are cited in Perrot, *Le Passionnaire français*, p. 1.

30 *French Life*, p. 112, my italics in all quotations; Reginald, *Vita Godrici*, chap. 82, pp. 183–84.

THE FRENCH *LIFE* OF ST GODRIC OF FINCHALE   349

And it ends with the following words not in the original:

> Seingnurs, qui la durté avez oïe que cil saint hom fesoit a sa propre char, aprenez a horer et a plourer que tel chose ne pouez emprendre por voz pechiez. Car lermes de pius courage levent pechié mortel, et almosne et oroison l'engetent aprés du tout. Amendez vostre vie par l'example de cestui, car Diex le commande et dist: 'Pluseurs profiteront et ateindront a mon resgne par l'example des bons.' […] et Diex par sa grace nous doint tel example prendre en ceste sainte vie que vous avez oïe, que vous vostre char, qui anemie vous est, puisiez dampter au proffit de l'ame et par l'aide saint Godric entrer [au regne pardurable?, MS damaged here].[31]

> > (My lords, you who have heard about the harshness with which this holy man treated his own flesh, learn to pray and to weep that you cannot undertake the same for your sins. For tears from a pious heart wash deadly sin away, and almsdeeds and prayer drive them out completely afterwards. Amend your life by the example of this holy man, for God commands it and says: 'Many will profit and gain the kingdom of heaven through the example of good men.' […] and may God by his grace enable us to take such example from this holy life which you have heard, that you may master your flesh (which is your enemy) to the profit of your soul, and by the help of St Godric enter [the kingdom of heaven].)

Thus preceding, concluding (and elsewhere interrupting) the flow of the narrative with sermon-like exhortations, the text appeals to the reader at the very least by using a first-person plural pronoun, 'nous' (we) and sometimes by directly addressing them as 'Seignurs' (Lords).[32] In this way, sometimes adding remarks of his own, sometimes retaining observations already made by Reginald, the translator enhances the didactic nature of Godric's *Life* for the reader.

On another occasion Godric describes to Reginald how a saint (possibly St Peter) visits him in a vision to celebrate his Mass. The chapter concludes:

> Et je, tresliez de cel miracle, louai Dieu *en toutes ses merveilles* et commançai la messe de Nostre Dame par son commandemant. Estrange vertu resplandi en cest saint home qui einsi de ses eulz veoit Dieu et Nostre Dame et ses sainz et ne mie par autre vision. Loez soit li sainz hons a qui Nostre Sires revela tantes *merveilles* et doint que nous en ses visions puissions partir qui memoire de lui fesons. Amen.[33]

---

31   *French Life*, pp. 113–14. Note that using salt in this way was a recognized remedy against suppurating wounds, see Astrup, *Salt and Water*, p. 146.

32   The plural first-person pronoun 'nous' is used throughout, for example, *French Life*, p. 30, l. 52; p. 134, ll. 188–89; p. 50, l. 776; p. 54, l. 933; p. 63, ll. 1267–68, etc. The address 'Seignurs', occurs on p. 120, l. 3334; p. 141, l. 4098; p. 203, l. 6372; and p. 210, l. 6658. Note that some (but not all) of these pronouns are already part of the Latin original, but the address 'Seigneurs' is not. For a discussion of 'Seignurs' in Mazarine, MS 1716, see *French Life*, pp. 14–17.

33   *French Life*, p. 135; Reginald, *Vita Godrici*, chap. 99, p. 211.

(And I [that is Reginald], very happy because of this miracle, praised God *in all his wonderful deeds* and began to say the mass of our Lady by his commandment. An extraordinary virtue shines in this holy man who in this way sees God and our Lady and his saints with his bodily eyes rather than through a ghostly vision. Praised be the holy man to whom our Lord revealed so many *wonders* and would that we could share in the visions of him whom we commemorate. Amen.)

Perhaps with such repeated sermon-like interventions throughout, the *French Life* of Godric more than most such texts, 'profite[s] mych to þe conversion and amendment of feythfull peple', to use the words of another text written for thirteenth-century nuns.[34] Note in passing the continued emphasis on the 'merveilleux' (the marvellous).

Godric's Adventures: Two Sides of a Coin

(i) A Sense of the Merveilleux

As a royal foundation, the nuns of Longchamp were mostly aristocratic ladies who may have enjoyed tales of knights and ladies and other such subjects before joining the abbey.[35] If they were then told: 'Vous qui prenes plaisir a lire / Les romans d'armes et d'amours / Leissez les et veilles eslire / Cieulx qui enseigne[n]t bonnes meurs' (you who take delight in reading romances of war and love, leave them alone, and choose instead works which will teach you how to behave well), they could not have chosen a better text than the *French Life* of Godric.[36] Although the text may not provide them with adventures of secular knights, it certainly offers them 'la bataille au saint home' (the holy man's battle), that is, the battles and tribulations of Godric, the knight of Christ, 'li chevaliers Dameldieu' or 'chevaliers Nostre Seingneur'.[37]

Some of these adventures, such as temptations by the Devil disguised as a beautiful woman, may even remind one of Perceval's temptations in the *Queste del Saint Graal*.[38] Indeed a sense of the 'merveilleux' (the marvellous) which pervades such knightly adventures is omnipresent in the *Vita Godrici*,

---

34 Bernard (pseudo-), *Manere of Good Lyvyng*, ed. by Mouron, p. 77.

35 One of these aristocratic ladies was Agnès of Harcourt who was abbess at Longchamp (1263–1279, 1281–1286) and died in 1289. She is the author of the *Vie d'Isabelle de France* mentioned above (see n. 23). For a list of the nuns of Longchamp, see BnF, MS français 11662.

36 *Floret de S. Bernard*, Prologue, ll. 1–4.

37 *French Life*, pp. 140, 47, 145, respectively. The Latin reads in both cases: 'miles Christi', Reginald, *Vita Godrici*, chaps 21, 114, pp. 67, 234. 'La bataille au saint home' has no equivalent in the Latin.

38 *French Life*, p. 150. Reginald, *Vita Godrici*, chap. 119, p. 242. In the *Queste del saint Graal*, when Perceval is left without a mount, a beautiful lady tempts him and offers him a horse. Realizing that both were sent by the Enemy, Perceval crosses himself and the horse vanishes

and even more so in the French text which repeats the words 'merveilleus' and 'merveilles' where the Latin prefers a more varied vocabulary.[39]

'Wonderful hystoryes and adventures' of a different kind occur on a winter's night.[40] Godric not only fasted, chastised his body by wearing a 'haire' (hair-shirt) and 'hauberc' (coat of mail) and devoted his nights to vigils and prayers, but he also spent time in cold water:

> Les nuiz d'yver es granz gelees et es nois aloit li *chanpions Dameldieu* a la rive de Wer, si ostoit ses dras et entroit en l'eue engelee, et sacrefioit a Dameldieu toute nuit en cele froide eue sa char. Il avoit trouvee en cele eue une pierre naturelment cavee sanz entaille a la maniere d'un vessel faitiz, où il ens se baingnoit, et torjors en l'eue trusques au col, et illuec disoit ses sepsiaumes et ses oroisons en lermes et en jemissemenz. [...] Por ce que li Malignes Esperiz a torjors envie seur les bons, se demostra il illuec visablement en laide forme et horrible de tabor, jetant flamble, rechignant des denz, trop lez et espoentables de toz membres. [...] Lors s'en venoit aus vestemenz au saint ami Dieu dont il s'estoit despoilliez seur la rive — son hauberc et sa haire et autres dras — si les prenoit et s'en aloit. Et quant il estoit .i. pou esloingniez, si s'aparcevoit li sainz hons et li escrioit: 'Ha! ha!' Lors retornoit li Anemis espoantez et confus, et remetoit la vesteure arrieres la où il l'avoit avant prise, puis s'en departoit.[41]

> (In winter nights when there was snow and a hard frost, God's champion went to the bank of the River Wear, took off his clothes and entered the frozen water, and all night in this cold water he sacrificed his flesh to God. He had found in this water a rock naturally formed into a well-made container in which he bathed, always with the water up to his neck, and there he recited his psalms and prayers weeping and moaning. [...] Because the Fiend is always envious of the just, he showed himself there visibly in an ugly form and with a horrible noise, throwing flames, gnashing his teeth, very big and frightening in all his limbs. [...] Then he would go to the place where the holy friend of God had disrobed himself of his clothes on the bank — his hauberk and his hair-shirt and his other garments — and he took them and left. And when he had gone a few steps, the holy man would notice and shouted: 'Ha, ha!' Then the Enemy would come back frightened and vanquished and put his clothes back where he had previously taken them from, and then leave.)

---

from under him (*La Queste del saint Graal*, ed. by Pauphilet, pp. 91–93). For a similar temptation later in the text, see pp. 104–10.

39   See Reginald, *Vita Godrici*, chap. 39, p. 96 and *French Life*, p. 62; Reginald, *Vita Godrici*, chap. 70, p. 157 and *French Life*, p. 97. A search for 'merveille', the adjective 'merveilleux', and the verbs 'se merveiller' and 'esmerveillier' in the whole text produces 122 hits.

40   Caxton, 'Preface to Malory's *Morte*', ed. by Vinaver, p. xv.

41   *French Life*, pp. 57–58. Reginald, *Vita Godrici*, chaps 33–34, pp. 85–88.

This appearance of the 'Malignes Esperiz' is only one among many, and the episode concludes: '*Merveilleuse* vertu a ci et bele, que li Anemis fu si tost chaciez par la voiz de l'ami Dameldieu, ne que par nul *enchantement* nel pot espoanter nel faire remuer de s'oroison ne seulement esmaier' (*Wonderful and beautiful is his virtue that the Enemy was so quickly driven away by the voice of the friend of God, and that he could not frighten him or stop him in his prayer or even in any way worry him by any *enchantment*).[42] Godric, like Perceval or Galahad, easily vanquishes his Enemy and is not taken in by his 'enchantement'.

Nevertheless, there is nothing unique about Godric chastizing his flesh in this way, as other saints endured similar things. In his *Vita Wulfrici anchoretae Haselbergiae*, a text contemporary with the *French Life* of Godric, the Cistercian John of Ford says of Wulfric:

> Procedit itaque miles loricatus ad spirituale certamen [...] At vero noctibus in frigore et nuditate in vas quoddam frigida aqua infusum descendebat in quo et Daviticos psalmos ex integro [...] Domino offerre consuevit, in tympano et psalterio psallens ei.
>
> > (The soldier newly harnessed advanced to the spiritual battle [...] At night he plunged himself cold and naked in a tub filled with cold water and there [...] would offer to the Lord the psalms of David from start to finish, singing to him with drum and psaltery.)[43]

The actions depicted are identical, but the *French Life* of Godric stands out as it exudes a sense of reality, almost plunging its reader in the cold water with Godric. We know precisely where Godric goes and what the place looks like. We are not simply told that he often recited the psalms immersed in cold water, rather the episode is described at length ending with Godric's clothes stolen by the 'Malignes Esperiz', most probably some poor folk passing by. Presented in such a realistic way, the marvellous becomes perhaps more tangible for the reader and therefore less impossible to emulate.

Godric's Adventures: Two Sides of a Coin

(ii) A Sense of Reality

This extraordinary sense of reality is encountered throughout the work and is without doubt due to Reginald's talent as a writer and his personal and intimate knowledge of Godric. Another telling example occurs at the end of

---

42 *French Life*, p. 59.

43 John of Ford, *Wulfric of Haselbury*, ed. by Bell, p. 19. John of Ford, *The Life of Wulfric*, trans. by Matarasso, p. 104. Note that the *Vita Wulfrici* mentions Godric. See John of Ford, *The Life of Wulfric*, trans. by Matarasso, p. 96. Catherine Sanok's essay in this volume examines a similar cold-water immersion in the Middle English *Metrical Life of St Cuthbert*, pp. 237, 255.

THE FRENCH *LIFE* OF ST GODRIC OF FINCHALE   353

Godric's life when he is weak and bedridden and requires constant care. Godric is sleeping in the church alone, when Reginald hears him calling for help:

> Je getai ce que j'avoie entre mains et ving a lui, si le trovai tout nu enmi l'aire du moustier. Lors commençai a plourer tendremant de pitié. Si l'envelope de dras tant que je oy son lit refait. Puis le pris entre mes bras et le recouchai, de de ce me merveillai mout que je le poi porter qui foibles estoie. […] Lors m'asis devant lui et le reconfortoie au plus que je pouoie par paroles. Une piece aprés, quant il fu auques reconfortez, li demandai tout en plourant comment ce fu et par qui il fu getez loing de son lit el pavement de l'eglyse. Il me dist: 'Beau fuilz, cil venimeus chiens, mes anemis li Deables, fu ci a moi, si ot envie de ce que reposoie. Et quant je oy .i. pou remué ce qui seur moi estoit, qui moistes est de sueur, et je m'apoia[i] .i. pou vers cest ais, si sailli avant et me sacha hors de mon lit enmi cele aire, si que mon chief feri a cel eschemel qui ci est estastez, car je sui auques bleciez'. Je mis ma main et trovai une boce en son chief grosse levee comme .i. oef de coulon. […] Lors l'asolz je et toutesvoies por ceste aventure remuai je l'eschamel qui devant lui estoit et fis ma peneance por ce que je li avoie mis.[44]

> (I threw down what I had in my hands and went to him and found him naked on the floor of the church. I then began to weep tenderly out of pity. I enveloped him in some clothes until I had remade his bed and then took him in my arms and laid him back in his bed, and marvelled much that I could carry him as I was a weak person. […] Then I sat down in front of him and comforted him as much as I could by my words. Sometime later, when he was comforted, weeping I asked him how this happened and by whom he had been thrown out far from his bed onto the pavement of the church. He told me: 'My son, this venomous dog, my enemy the Devil, was here with me and was irritated that I was resting. And when I moved slightly what was covering me, which was wet with sweat, and I leaned a bit on this board, he jumped ahead and snatched me and pulled me out of my bed onto the middle of the floor, so that my head hit this stool which was placed here for I am somewhat hurt'. I put my hand on his head and found a bump raised on his head as big as the egg of a pigeon. […] Then I absolved him and nevertheless because of this adventure moved away the stool which was in front of him and did penance because I had put it there in the first place.)

The scene described is uncommonly realistic.[45] Again the translator concludes the chapter with additional words of his own, seeing Godric as an example of the need to chastise one's flesh:

---

44   *French Life*, pp. 143–44. Reginald, *Vita Godrici*, chap. 112, pp. 231–32.
45   It may perhaps indicate that Godric suffered from some kind of dementia.

Seingneurs, par example de cestui, aviez aspre vesteure por la char dampter, que vous par vesteure mole n'encourez es forz temptations de l'Anemi agaitant. Car or poez veoir et entendre con nous sommes agaitié. Quant cil qui touz fu espirez ne pot onques pes avoir, gardez, bonnes genz, que vous oiez cest escrit, que je en vain ne travail de fere le vous entendre, mes que vous puissiez par l'example de cest preudomme vostre vie amender, et si eschiver les felons agaiz, que la bone dame par qui ceste vie est trestiee en romanz, et vos qui par li l'entendez et le latin ne savez, puisiez par amandement digne guerredon recevoir, Amen.[46]

> (My lords, by the example of this holy man, have rough clothes in order to tame the flesh that you do not by soft clothing expose yourself to the strong temptations of the Enemy setting traps for you. For you can see and hear how he is waiting to attack us. When he who was completely inspired could not have peace, good people, ensure that you take note of this writing, so that I do not work in vain to make you understand it but that you may by the example of this wise man amend your life and thus avoid the cruel traps, and so that the good lady through whom this *Life* is translated into French and you who thus hear it and cannot read Latin, may receive a worthy reward by amending your life. Amen.)

This sense of encountering real, if exemplary, events in the *French Life* of Godric is enhanced by the constant use of dialogue which is unusual for a saint's life.[47] Also unusual is the extent to which Godric's personality comes to the fore.[48] He may be a model saint, adopting extreme asceticism,[49] seeing things at a distance,[50] being granted divine revelations,[51] practising prophecy,[52] resisting temptations (mostly lust),[53] and performing miracles whilst alive.[54] But he is

---

46 *French Life*, pp. 144–45. For a brief discussion of the lady responsible for the translation, Ase of Montferrant, see *French Life*, pp. 7–8.

47 For example, 'How Godric saw the soul of the Abbot and of a woman', *French Life*, pp. 106–07 (Reginald, *Vita Godrici*, chap. 76, pp. 173–75); 'How Godric heard Mass from a saint of God', *French Life*, pp. 134–35 (Reginald, *Vita Godrici*, chap. 99, p. 211), etc.

48 Reginald includes a detailed physical description of Godric: *Vita Godrici*, chap. 100, pp. 212–13.

49 He regularly spends nights in cold water, eats rotten bread, and uses a stone for a pillow. See, respectively, *French Life*, pp. 57–58 (Reginald, *Vita Godrici*, chaps 33–34, pp. 85–88; *French Life*, pp. 54–55 (Reginald, *Vita Godrici*, chaps 29–30, pp. 79–81); *French Life*, pp. 55–56 (Reginald, *Vita Godrici*, chap. 31, pp. 81–82).

50 Godric describes places he has never visited. See *French Life*, pp. 124–25 (Reginald, *Vita Godrici*, chap. 87, pp. 192–93).

51 For example, the Virgin Mary teaches Godric the famous lyric 'A Cry to Mary': *French Life*, pp. 74–76 (Reginald, *Vita Godrici*, chap. 50, pp. 117–20).

52 *French Life*, p. 111 (Reginald, *Vita Godrici*, chap. 80, pp. 180–81).

53 For example, *French Life*, pp. 52–53 (Reginald, *Vita Godrici*, chap. 27, p. 76).

54 The saint brings back to life a little girl. See *French Life*, pp. 83–85 (Reginald, *Vita Godrici*, chap. 57, pp. 132–35).

THE FRENCH *LIFE* OF ST GODRIC OF FINCHALE 355

also adventurous,[55] very strong physically,[56] intelligent and keen to learn,[57] shy with other people,[58] generous,[59] hard with himself but tender to animals and to women,[60] not to mention showing concern and care for members of his own family.[61] He not only copes with visits from devils,[62] and angels and saints,[63] but also battles against the elements,[64] and is attacked by marauding soldiers who kill his cow.[65] He meets local people as well as the monks of Durham, and a number of foreign and English ecclesiastics including Aelred of Rievaulx.[66] It has been said about Chaucer's portraits of pilgrims in his General Prologue to *The Canterbury Tales* that 'much of [their] depth [...] lies in the interplay between the type and the individual'.[67] The convincing power of the *French Life* perhaps lies in a similar mixture of saintly pattern and real characteristics which would have appealed to the nuns of Longchamp.

---

55 As a child, he ventures alone onto the beach and is caught up by the returning tide. See *French Life*, pp. 30–31 (Reginald, *Vita Godrici*, chap. 3, pp. 26–27). Later Godric goes on pilgrimage to Rome and to Jerusalem twice. See *French Life*, pp. 34–36 (Reginald, *Vita Godrici*, chaps 7–8, pp. 37–40 (Rome); *French Life*, pp. 41–44 (Reginald, *Vita Godrici*, chaps 13–16, pp. 52–58 (Jerusalem, twice).

56 Godric fells and carries huge trees. See *French Life*, pp. 56–57 (Reginald, *Vita Godrici*, chap. 32, p. 84).

57 Whilst in Durham, Godric goes to the 'mostier sainte Marie' (the church of St Mary) to join children in learning. See *French Life*, p. 44 (Reginald, *Vita Godrici*, chap. 16, pp. 58–60).

58 Godric hides to avoid meeting people. See *French Life*, pp. 49–50 (Reginald, *Vita Godrici*, chap. 23, p. 71).

59 Godric assists a poacher in getting away with a stolen fish. See *French Life*, pp. 142–43 (Reginald, *Vita Godrici*, chap. 111, pp. 230–31).

60 He releases animals caught in traps and rebukes a visitor for hitting his wife. See respectively *French Life*, pp. 63–64 (Reginald, *Vita Godrici*, chap. 40, pp. 98–99); *French Life*, pp. 175–76 (Reginald, *Vita Godrici*, chap. 153, p. 291). One has only to think of the Wife of Bath who is hit so hard on the ear by her fifth husband that she becomes deaf to recognize how uncommon Godric's concern was.

61 Godric's mother, brother, sister, and nephew come to live with him. For the first three, see *French Life*, pp. 86–87 (Reginald, *Vita Godrici*, chaps 60–61, pp. 139–41); for the nephew, see *French Life*, pp. 76–77 (Reginald, *Vita Godrici*, chap. 51, pp. 120–21). Godric sees the spirits of his mother and sister and does penance for his brother's soul. See *French Life*, pp. 79–80, 88–91 (Reginald, *Vita Godrici*, chaps 54, 63–64, pp. 125–27, 143–47).

62 See above pp. 350–53. There are numerous other examples throughout the text.

63 St Cuthbert, the Virgin Mary, Mary Magdalene, and angels all appear to Godric. See *French Life*, pp. 41–42, 74–76, 128–29 (Reginald, *Vita Godrici*, chaps 13, 50, 93, pp. 52–53, 117–20, 202–03).

64 See *French Life*, respectively, pp. 67–68 (flood), pp. 102–03 (fire), pp. 130–31 (drought) (Reginald, *Vita Godrici*, chaps 45, 73, 96, pp. 105–06, 166–68, 206–07).

65 *French Life*, pp. 73–74 (Reginald, *Vita Godrici*, chap. 49, pp. 114–16).

66 Godric sees the soul of a woman called 'Edgithe', *French Life*, pp. 106–07; he catches a salmon for Durham monks who come 'por le servise fere' (to celebrate Mass), pp. 98–99; he heals the servant of a foreign monk, pp. 152–53; he talks to Prior Cuthbert of Gisburn, p. 118 and to Aelred, pp. 107–09, etc. (Reginald, *Vita Godrici*, respectively, chaps 76, 71, 122, 138, 77, pp. 173–75, 159–61, 245–46, 267, 175–77).

67 Cooper, *Oxford Guides to Chaucer*, p. 31.

Conclusion: Godric, an All-Too-Real Saint?

If the compiler of Mazarine, MS 1716 believed that the *French Life* of Godric would fit nicely along other more conventional saints lives, it may seem surprising that there are no more surviving manuscripts of the vernacular life. Although this must remain speculation, there may be a number of reasons for this. The length of the text may have worked against it, but this could have been abbreviated as many saints' lives were. Rather, the overwhelming presence of the North of England, in the geography, names, and ecclesiastical politics of the text may have become something of an impediment for an audience living on the French side of the channel in the later Middle Ages, while on the English side, with Anglo-Norman on the wane, the audience for such texts became increasingly limited. But most of all, the sense of reality which suffused the text is perhaps too unusual for a saint's life to ensure a sustained readership. Indeed, at times, the *French Life* of Godric may reveal too much of a human, rather than a saintly, nature. For example, on one occasion when one of his visitors is about to leave, Godric wants to give him some food to take home with him and he asks one of his attendants to go to the 'peescherie' (fish pond) to find some fish to give his visitor. The 'serjant' refuses as he has just been there and there was nothing. Godric asks him to go again:

> 'Biaus filz, alez i encore, car Diex nous en porra envoier ainz que vostre repaire aucun [poisson]'. Li serjant li dist: 'Voirement vous est pou de nostre travail, qui toute jor nous faites corre ça et la por neant'. Li amis Dieu se tu .i. pou, et puis li dist: 'Alez delivrement, si nous aportez les poissons que Dieu nous a donnez'. *Lors se recorrouça li serjanz* et dist qu'il n'iroit ja, que ce seroit en vain. *Adont se corrouça .i. pou li sainz hons* et dist: 'Vous grondrilliez torjors contre la pitié Dieu, et desesperez de sa porvoiance. Sachiez qu'il a .ii. poissons qui vous atendent. Li uns est bien refez et vient a nous de la mer. Li autres n'a mie encore muees ses eschardes. Mes bons amis qui ci est enportera le refet en sa meson a ma fillole et vous avrez le piour por vostre grouceiz. Or alez, si ne vous desesperez mie autre foiz du don Dieu, que vous ne soiez autre foiz noiant dignes du recevoir'.[68]

> ('Dear son, go back there for God may have sent us a fish in the meantime'. His servant said to him: 'truly you care little about our work for you make us run here and there the whole day long for nothing'. God's friend said nothing for a while and then told him: 'go quickly and bring us the fish God has given us'. *Then the servant became angry again* and said that he would not go for it would be in vain. *The holy man therefore became somewhat angry* and said: 'You always grumble against God's pity and despair of his providing food for us. You should know that there are two fish waiting for you in our pond. One is quite

---

68 *French Life*, pp. 78–79 (Reginald, *Vita Godrici*, chap. 53, pp. 123–24).

THE FRENCH *LIFE* OF ST GODRIC OF FINCHALE   357

fat and comes to us from the sea. The other has not yet changed its scales. My good friend who is here will take the fat one home to my god-daughter and you will have the less good one for your grumbling. Go presently, and another time do not despair of the gift of God so that another time you may not be deemed unworthy to receive it'.)

The exchange perhaps suggests that Godric is at times a difficult person to deal with. In this instance the saint himself 'se corrouça' (became angry), and saints are not supposed to give in to sins (here wrath), even if only '.i. pou' (for a while). Note that the Latin text is here more neutral: 'vir vero Dei ad talia aliquantisper *commotus*' (truly the man of God was somewhat *roused* to say the following things).[69]

It is, of course, impossible to know what the nuns of Longchamp thought of the *French Life* of Godric, nevertheless it certainly offered them 'best sentence and moost solaas'.[70] To the modern reader, the *Life* also provides an unparalleled vivid sense of twelfth-century eremitical life in the north of England in the vernacular. We can be grateful, therefore, as Aelred stated in his life of another, much earlier northern saint, Ninian, Apostle of the Southern Picts (*c.* 360–*c.* 432), that 'multis uirorum sapientium qui fuerunt ante nos studio fuit sanctorum uitam, mores, uerba [...] litteris dare [...] obliuioni subducere, et perpetuare memoria' (many of the wise men who lived before us were zealous to put into writing the lives, practices, and words of the saints, [...] to save [them] from oblivion and perpetuate [their] memory).[71]

---

69 Reginald, *Vita Godrici*, chap. 53, p. 124.
70 Chaucer, 'The General Prologue', in *The Canterbury Tales*, ed. by Benson, p. 36, l. 798.
71 Aelred, *Vita sancti Niniani*, ed. by Pezzini, p. 113. Aelred, *The Life of Ninian*, trans. by Freeland, p. 35.

Works Cited

Manuscripts and Archival Sources

Cambridge, Fitzwilliam Museum, MS 300 <https://www.fitzmuseum.cam.ac.uk/illuminated/manuscript/discover/the-psalter-hours-of-isabelle-of-france/section/undefined> [accessed 8 June 2019]

——, Cambridge University Library, MS Additional 3037

London, British Library, MS Cotton Faustina B VI, pars ii

——, British Library, MS Royal 5 F VII <https://www.bl.uk/catalogues/illuminatedmanuscripts/ILLUMIN.ASP?Size=mid&IllID=39480> [accessed 13 January 2020]

Paris, Bibliothèque Mazarine, MS 1716 (cited as Mazarine, MS 1716)

——, Bibliothèque nationale de France, MS français 413 <https://gallica.bnf.fr/ark:/12148/btv1b90076543> [accessed 24 July 2019]

——, Bibliothèque nationale de France, MS français 11662 <https://gallica.bnf.fr/ark:/12148/btv1b9061726x> [accessed 24 July 2019]

——, Bibliothèque nationale de France, MS français 23117 <https://gallica.bnf.fr/ark:/12148/btv1b90639749> [accessed 24 July 2019]

Primary Sources

Aelred of Rievaulx, *Vita sancti Niniani*, in *Aelredi Rievallensis, Opera historica et hagiographica*, ed. by Domenico Pezzini, CCCM, 3 (Turnhout: Brepols, 2017), pp. 111–34

——, *The Life of Ninian, Apostle of the Southern Picts*, in *The Lives of the Northern Saints*, trans. by Jane Patricia Freeland, intro. and notes by Marsha L. Dutton, Cistercian Fathers Series, 71 (Kalamazoo: Cistercian Publications, 2016), pp. 35–63

——, *Vita sancti Ædwardi regis et confessoris*, in *Aelredi Rievallensis Vita sancti Ædwardi regis et confessoris; Anonymi Vita sancti Ædwardi versifice*, ed. by Francesco Marzella, CCCM, 3A (Turnhout: Brepols, 2017), pp. 85–181

——, *The Life of Saint Edward, King and Confessor*, in *The Historical Works of Aelred of Rievaulx*, trans. by Jane Patricia Freeland, Cistercian Fathers Series, 56 (Kalamazoo: Cistercian Publications, 2005), pp. 123–243

Agnès d'Harcourt, *Vie d'Isabelle de France*, in Anne-Helene Allirot, 'Isabelle de France, soeur de Saint Louis, la vierge savante: étude de la *Vie d'Isabelle de France* écrite par Agnès d'Harcourt', *Médiévales: Langue, Textes, Histoire*, 48 (2005), 55–98 (pp. 76–98)

Bernard of Clairvaux (pseudo-), *The Manere of Good Lyvyng*, ed. by Anne Mouron (Turnhout: Brepols, 2014)

Caxton, William, 'Preface to Malory's *Morte d'Arthur*', in *Malory: Complete Works*, ed. by Eugène Vinaver, 2nd edn (Oxford: Oxford University Press, 1971), pp. xiii–xv

Chaucer, Geoffrey, *The Canterbury Tales*, in *The Riverside Chaucer*, ed. by Larry D. Benson, 3rd edn (Oxford: Oxford University Press, 1987; repr. 1990), pp. 23–328

Floret de S. Bernard en franczoys (Rennes, 1485), Paris, Bibliothèque nationale de
France, département Réserve des livres rares, RESM-YC-993 <https://gallica.
bnf.fr/ark:/12148/btv1b8625630v> [accessed 6 August 2019]

John of Ford, *Wulfric of Haselbury*, ed. by Maurice Bell, Somerset Record Society,
47 (London: Printed for subscribers only, 1933)

——, *The Life of Wulfric of Haselbury, Anchorite*, trans. by Pauline Matarasso,
Cistercian Fathers Series, 79 (Collegeville: Cistercian Publications, Liturgical
Press, 2011)

Louis IX, 'The French *Enseignemenz a Phellippe* and *Enseignement a Ysabel* of Saint
Louis', ed. by Kathleen Ashley in *Medieval Conduct Literature: An Anthology
of Vernacular Guides to Behaviour for Youths, with English Translations*, ed. by
Mark D. Johnston, Medieval Academy Books, 111 (Toronto: University of
Toronto Press, 2009), pp. 3–22

Medieval English Lyrics: A Critical Anthology, ed. by Reginald Thorne Davies
(London: Faber and Faber, 1963; repr. 1988)

La Queste del Saint Graal, ed. by Albert Pauphilet, Les Classiques Français du
Moyen Age, 33 (Paris: Honoré Champion, 1967; repr. 1999)

Reginald of Durham, *Libellus de vita et miraculis S. Godrici, heremitae de Finchale*,
ed. by Joseph Stevenson, SS, 20 (London: J. B. Nichols and Son, 1847) (cited as
Reginald, *Vita Godrici*)

——, *Life of St Godric: An Old French Version*, ed. by Margaret Coombe, Tony Hunt,
and Anne Mouron, Anglo-Norman Text Society Occasional Publications Series,
9 (Oxford: Anglo-Norman Text Society, 2019) (cited as *French Life*)

Thomas of Monmouth, *The Life and Passion of William of Norwich*, trans. by Miri
Rubin, Penguin Classics (London: Penguin, 2014)

Secondary Works

Astrup, Poul, *Salt and Water in Culture and Medecine*, trans. by K. Skovbjerg and
Andrew L. Cameron-Mills (Copenhagen: Munksgaard, 1993)

Buechner, Frederick, *Godric* (London: Chatto & Windus, 1981)

Coombe, Margaret, 'Reginald of Durham's Latin Life of St Godric of Finchale: A
Study' (unpublished doctoral thesis, University of Oxford, 2011)

Cooper, Helen, *Oxford Guides to Chaucer: The Canterbury Tales* (Oxford: Oxford
University Press, 1989; repr. with corrections, 1991)

Le Goff, Jacques, *Saint Louis* (Paris: Gallimard, 1996)

Molinier, Auguste Marie, and Armand d'Artois, *Catalogue des manuscrits de la
Bibliothèque Mazarine*, 4 vols (Paris: E. Plon, Nourrit et cie, 1885-[98])

Mouron, Anne, 'An Edition of the Desert of Religion and its Theological
Background', 2 vols (unpublished doctoral thesis, University of Oxford, 1996).
The thesis was written under the name A. McGovern-Mouron

——, '"Help thin Godric in Francrice": An Old French *Life of St Godric*', in
Translation and Authority – Authorities in Translation, ed. by Pieter De Leemans
and Michèle Goyens, The Medieval Translator, 16 (Turnhout: Brepols, 2016),
pp. 215–27

Parsons, John Carmi, 'Isabella [Isabella of France] (1295–1358)', *Oxford Dictionary of National Biography* (Oxford: Oxford University Press, 2004), vol. XXIX, pp. 419–23

Perrot, Jean-Pierre, *Le Passionnaire français au Moyen Age* (Geneva: Droz, 1992)

Section romane, notice de 'PARIS, Bibliothèque Mazarine, 1716' dans la base Jonas-IRHT/CNRS <http://jonas.irht.cnrs.fr/manuscrit/44498> [accessed 15 June 2019]

Tudor, Victoria, 'Reginald of Durham and St Godric of Finchale: A Study of a Twelfth-Century Hagiographer and his Major Subject' (unpublished doctoral thesis, University of Reading, 1979)

——, 'Godric of Finchale [St Godric of Finchale] (*c.* 1070–1170), trader and hermit', *Oxford Dictionary of National Biography* (Oxford: Oxford University Press, 2004), vol. XXII, pp. 601–02

JAMES G. CLARK

The Reception of St Oswine
in Later Medieval England

At the end of its medieval history the cult practice of the northern church was still sometimes prompted by the passing of a popular king. In September 1513, a self-consciously unobtrusive burial party set out from the castle at Berwick-upon-Tweed to make the sixty-mile journey due south to Newcastle-upon-Tyne. It may have made a stop at Alnwick, where the canons of the Augustinian priory would have kept a watch over the body in its workaday coffin. But there is a stronger likelihood that before it was seen safely into the city it was sheltered at another monastery church, the most ancient in all that coastal country. On its approach the 'secret conveyance' came under fire from 'some Scottes that appered on a hyl'. There was 'great jeoparde', dispelled only after 'ordynaunce shott suche a peale'.[1] The body was that of James, the fourth Stewart king of Scotland, cut down at the Battle of Flodden three weeks before by the army of the Tudor king of England, whose ally he once was and whose brother-in-law he remained.[2] The church was that of the Benedictine priory of Tynemouth, whose origins reached perhaps as far as another monarch dead in battle, Edwin, king of Northumbria (d. c. 632).[3]

King James was not the first fallen monarch who may have briefly found a safe harbour in the sea-swept church. Five centuries before, Malcolm III of Scotland (1058–1093) had been buried at Tynemouth by his murderer,

---

1 *Hall's Chronicle*, p. 564.

2 For James IV of Scotland and Flodden see Goodwin, *Fatal Rivalry*. The earliest record of the transit of his body is dated 9 September and refers only to its first stopping-place at Berwick: Kew, TNA, SP 49/1 fol. 18[r]. A little over a week later Queen Katharine of Aragon wrote from Woburn (Surrey) of receiving a trophy off-cut of James's coat: BL, MS Cotton Vespasian F III, fol. 33[r]. According to Hall his remains had been ordered from the battlefield to Newcastle, 'with all effectuall deligence'. Tynemouth men had taken part in the battle but had 'fledd', at 'the furstt schott of the Scottish gonnys': BL, MS Cotton Caligula B VI, fol. 48[r].

3 For a comprehensive and still authoritative account of Tynemouth Priory, see Craster, *History of Northumberland*.

James G. Clark (j.g.clark@exeter.ac.uk) is Professor of History at the University of Exeter, UK.

Late Medieval Devotion to Saints from the North of England: New Directions, ed. by Christiania Whitehead, Hazel J. Hunter Blair, and Denis Renevey, MCS 48 (Turnhout: Brepols, 2022), pp. 361–386

BREPOLS ❦ PUBLISHERS   10.1484/M.MCS-EB.5.124358

the Mowbray earl of Northumberland.[4] Four hundred years before that, the body of another murdered prince, Oswine, king of Deira (*c.* 644–51), had been placed in the custody of the colony of monks settled a quarter-century before by Edwin. Oswine was the son of Osric (d. 634), Edwin's kinsman, who had ruled Deira in the wake of the king's death. He had been his father's chosen successor but his authority was challenged by the Bernician Oswiu (d. 670) who aimed at hegemony in the north of Britain. Refusing to give battle, Oswine withdrew to a church of his own foundation at Gilling, where he was betrayed and lynched by Oswiu's men.[5]

Oswine's remains did not suffer the instability of other early prince and prelate saints of the North, although it may have been because they were undisturbed that his name and distinction were not always readily recalled. Yet among the sacred sites of the northern borderland it was Tynemouth perhaps above all that was imprinted with the image of Christian kingship, as an exemplum of steadfast piety to the community of the faithful.

For the Tudors it seems, Tynemouth's symbolism was as strong as for any of England's royal families since the Norman Conquest. The dispatch of the defeated Scottish king was not the only moment that the church set the scene on their displays of imperial authority. Ten years earlier in August 1503, the priory had been incorporated into the progress of the marriage party of Margaret, daughter of Henry VII, and the same King James. Taking in the most celebrated churches on both sides of the border, the progress began at Durham and reached as far as Coldingham, almost a hundred miles to the north. When they came to Tynemouth they were met by the prior with as grand a train as any monastic had showed in public in the shadow of the dissolution: 'well apoynted, and in hys company xxx horseys. Hys folke in hys livery'; although not noticed in this account, the advance guard from the church may have carried with them relics from Oswine's shrine.[6]

Tudor interest in Tynemouth endured. Cardinal Wolsey's capture of the abbacy of St Albans, the priory's parent monastery, fixed it on the political as well as the devotional horizons of the Henrician court.[7] When a protégé of the cardinal was removed from the priorate, his replacement drew the attention of the royal household. The most influential meddler was Lady Mary Carey (née Boleyn), King Henry's former mistress, whose father, Sir Thomas, was

---

4   For near-contemporary notice of Malcolm's end see William of Malmesbury, *Gesta regum Anglorum*, ed. and trans. by Mynors, Thomson, and Winterbottom (hereafter *GR*), III. 250. For an account of his murder founded on Durham sources, see Aird, *St Cuthbert and the Normans*, pp. 240–41.

5   The only Saxon account of Oswine's brief reign, betrayal, and burial was made by Bede, *Ecclesiastical History*, ed. and trans. by Colgrave and Mynors (cited hereafter as *HE*), III. 14.

6   The ceremonies are described in Kew, TNA, SP 58/1/27, fols 122^r–42^r. Excerpts were noted by John Leland and printed by Thomas Hearne in *De rebus Britannicis collectanea*, IV. 277.

7   Thomas Wolsey, Cardinal legate *a latere*, Archbishop of York and Bishop of Durham was appointed to hold the abbacy of St Albans *in commendam* in December 1521: Smith, London, and Brooke ed., *Heads of Religious Houses*, III, p. 64.

the convent's chief steward.[8] Her candidate, Thomas Gardiner, was a monk of Westminster Abbey who also happened to be the grandson of Jasper Tudor, great uncle of the king. For almost a millennium Tynemouth had been associated with regal Christianity; now its pastor held the blood of the king.[9]

These sixteenth-century scenes naturally prompt a question about the fortunes of the north country's cult history in later medieval and pre-Reformation generations when it is generally assumed the centre of devotional gravity in England had shifted decisively to the south. The northern pantheon of missionaries, convert kings, and monastic pioneers suffered a steady attrition until the names and reputations of only one of each — Oswald, Cuthbert, Bede — were still recognizable nationwide. The dominant (if not quite, domineering) Sarum calendar carried the festivals of these three alone and it may be it reflected what was already a local reality even before it spread its influence across the country. In fact the Christian legend of the North was not so much erased as overwritten. The early advance of the friars — arriving at Newcastle as early as 1237 — propagated forms of popular religion, pastoral and sacramental, that were the polar opposite of the traditions of monastic suffrage centred on an ancient shrine. The mendicant mission complemented a growing vernacular spirituality that drew much of its strength from the distinctive terrain of the northern province, of small populations widely dispersed which found their religious focus in charismatic people and places — such as Richard Rolle at Hampole — as much as in the institutional church.[10]

Yet the early history of faith in the north country was not entirely eclipsed in the later Middle Ages. It is true that its textual tradition faded fast after 1200. But its narrative outline and some of its leading characters endured long enough to be taken up into new accounts of the early history of the church in England. Moreover, the material culture of the first northern cults was unusually well preserved, providing visible and tangible proofs of a legendary past even in an age of print and proto-Protestantism. The reception of Oswine, which can be traced into the Tudor period brings this story of change and continuity clearly into focus. It is a reminder that alongside the *avant garde* theology of Hampole, the older habits of devotion remained. For all its novel features, late medieval religion still carried the imprint of its first beginnings.

Oswine was the last of the Saxon legends of the North to be made the subject of a cult. He was remembered well enough for the date of the commemoration of his martyrdom to be found in the calendar associated with the northern European missionary, Willibrord (d. 739), and in the martyrology of Tallaght

---

8   Sir Thomas Boleyn is identified as steward in a petition which Craster dated to between 1528 and 1536: Craster, *History of Northumberland*, pp. 107–08.

9   For Thomas Gardiner see Smith, London, and Brooke ed., *Heads of Religious Houses*, III, p. 153; Smyly, 'Thomas Gardiner's History'; Boffey and Payne, '*Gardyner's Passetaunce*'. I am grateful to Julia Boffey and Matthew Payne for their further insights into Gardiner's career.

10   For these developments, see Freeman, 'Priory of Hampole'; Lutton, 'Bridlington Priory'; Sanok, 'John of Bridlington'; Hughes, *Pastors and Visionaries*, pp. 82–88, 90–100.

(Co. Dublin). The significance of Tynemouth was still recognized at the end of the eighth century when the remains of another fallen ruler, Osred II (d. 792), were carried there.[11] But veneration of Oswine did not develop deep roots, and the monastic church itself proved poor defence against the piracy of the Danes. It was only at the end of the eleventh century that a monastic colony was contemplated again. The monks of Durham Priory told the story of the old Saxon church being granted to their forebears at Jarrow by the last English earl of Northumbria, Waltheof (d. 1076), from which an outpost was established, while Oswine's relics they transferred with them to Durham. The incoming Norman earl, Robert de Mowbray (d. 1125), was said to have violently expelled them (*violenter expelleretur*) and offered the church to Paul of Caen, abbot of St Albans (1077–1093).[12] There is no corroboration for Durham's tale of Tynemouth and the building remains strongly suggest that what St Albans gained was no rich plunder but a site that was still derelict.[13] Probably there was no observant community in place before at least 1110.

Sustained cult interest in Oswine came only after there was a settled community at Tynemouth and even then it came from outside the region. It was the monks of St Albans Abbey, making Mowbray's gift into a distant cell, who led the revival of the early relic shrine. Tynemouth presented the southern monastery with the means of protecting its position as a proprietor in the northern province from the imperial ambition of Durham. It was a seignorial manoeuvre that locked St Albans and Durham into a conflict that continued for almost two centuries.[14] But it assured Tynemouth an independent profile in the northern church and it allowed the name of Oswine to be broadcast through two channels, north and south.

The monks of St Albans set about the cult history they inherited, together with a distant church, with a creative energy and a commitment greater than they showed towards their own patron saint. Oswine may have been all but eclipsed in his own northern heartland at the beginning of the twelfth century by the reinvigorated devotion to Cuthbert and Oswald, but he and his history held attributes conspicuously absent in Alban: the preservation of his relics was undisputed and his identity, his English nationhood and royalty, was attested by the best known of indigenous authorities. For the Norman leadership of the refounded St Albans, the matter of Oswine was the most valuable of all their northern acquisitions. They filled the mother church with the relics of saints from an Anglo-Norman repertory that was already taking shape when Lanfranc was archbishop, one drawn from the strongest of the insular cults as well as those that were dominant, or newly current, in the

---

11 Hayward, 'Sanctity and Lordship', pp. 107–08, 112; Rollason, 'Cults of Murdered Royal Saints', pp. 3, 13–15.

12 Symeon, *Historia regum*, ed. by Arnold, 201, pp. 260–61.

13 The St Albans annalist gave only a bald account of its acquisition: *Gesta abbatum monasterii sancti Albani*, ed. by Riley (cited hereafter as *GASA*), I. 56–57.

14 Hayward, 'Sanctity and Lordship', pp. 113–16.

THE RECEPTION OF ST OSWINE IN LATER MEDIEVAL ENGLAND   365

churches of northern France.[15] Cuthbert was such a focus for the community, and when the church was rededicated it was claimed he had cured the afflicted abbot, Richard d'Aubigny (1100–1119).[16] The earliest extant calendars, which date from the second quarter of the century, display a mix of English and mainland European devotions, among them several still relative rarities on this side of the Channel such as Leodgar, Ruf, and Vincent of Saragossa.[17] Alban, meanwhile, was left at the margins. The Norman abbey church was three decades old before there was any inclination to (re)create a shrine for his relics, and it remains uncertain if indeed there had been anything there before.[18] Even then the investment was tentative and the work was stopped and the materials recycled before it was eventually finished.[19] No original history of Alban was written until well into the second half of the century, and a comparatively modest cycle of miracle stories was collected only after 1172, more than fifty years after other leading abbeys had fixed the textual traditions of their patron saints.[20]

Oswine was therefore a surrogate. Abbot Richard brought relics of the king to St Albans, perhaps following his attendance at the translation of Cuthbert in 1104.[21] He may have also presented relics to the dependent priories of Hertford and Wymondham (Norfolk); there are signs of a strong devotion to Oswine at both houses across the twelfth century and beyond. Richard also assumed responsibility for the reconstruction of the principal shrine at Tynemouth itself, which with a narrative neatness was said to have been ready to receive the relics on the day of the feast, in 1110, even though the monastery church itself remained under construction.[22] In fact, an earlier date was sometimes claimed: the king martyr's feast in the year 1103, significantly perhaps the year preceding the translation of Cuthbert at Durham.[23] The competing veneration of the Durham saint surely pressed on the monastic community. One miracle story told of Oswine's intercession, delivering a prisoner from certain death, on the feast of the translation of his Durham rival.[24]

The form of Oswine's shrine is not described in any surviving source but a passing reference of the thirteenth or fourteenth centuries spoke of rich decoration in gold, silver, and gemstones ('in theca argentea auro et gemmis

---

15 *GASA*, I. 58, 69–70, 94.

16 *GASA*, I. 70.

17 For example, BL, MS Egerton 3721, fols 2ʳ, 5ᵛ, 6ᵛ; BL, MS Royal 2 B VI, fols 4ᵛ, 10ʳ. See also Thomson, *Manuscripts from St Albans*, I, pp. 28–30.

18 Crook, *English Medieval Shrines*, p. 141.

19 *GASA*, I. 83, 96, 109.

20 McLeod, 'Alban and Amphibal', p. 409. The miracles survive as a sequence in two manuscripts of *c.* 1200 and *c.* 1400, respectively BL, MS Cotton Faustina B IV, fols 19ᵛᵇ–40ᵛᵃ and BL, MS Cotton Claudius E IV, fols 59ʳᵃ–70ᵛᵇ.

21 *GASA*, I. 70.

22 *Vita Oswini*, ed. by Raine (hereafter *Vita Oswini*), XI, p. 24.

23 *Vita Oswini*, IV, p. 15.

24 *Vita Oswini*, XLII, pp. 55–57 (56).

venustissime decorata').[25] For successive generations of monks of St Albans, schooled in the deeds of their first abbots, the contrast between this object and the unfinished platform for their own patron saint must have been stark. They may have stage-managed the translation of 1110 to play upon the symmetry with the recent ceremony for the relics of Cuthbert at Durham. At Tynemouth, the bishop of Durham presided; at Durham, Abbot Richard of St Albans had been guest of honour.[26]

The earliest of the (only) two surviving manuscript copies of the *Vita Oswini* gives the impression of a cult church setting out its stall for its 'prince and father of the land', as the antiphon named him. It opens with a liturgical calendar based on the customs of the (far older) monastery of Hexham, adapted for Tynemouth use. It fills an opening leaf with a list of the relics already collected at the church, recording vestments of Oswine as well as his remains, and complements the text of the life and miracles with an extensive liturgy of the festive office, lections, votive prayers, and two sermons, which together take up four quires.[27]

In the quarter-century from the completion of the new shrine, the cult was successfully syndicated across the St Albans territory. The abbey had forged a chain of eight dependent cells before 1146 and from the outset their discipline and observance was bound closely to the mother house.[28] No calendar from any of them survives of a date earlier than 1200 but given that two of the miracle stories of Oswine were set at Hertford and Wymondham it may be assumed that the principal calendar feasts celebrated at St Albans had also been adopted there.[29] The formation of a domestic repertory of feasts may itself have been a product of the growth of the abbey's network and even in the mid-twelfth century it was still in flux. When a fine psalter was commissioned by Abbot Geoffrey de Gorron (1119–1146) for the anchoress-turned-abbess, Christina of Markyate in the mid-1140s, it carried a calendar lacking the feast of Oswine; it was added later, albeit in the same century.[30]

The dependent cells did not amount merely to lesser franchises of the St Albans brand; rather they acted as annexes of the senior convent, a point of entry, education and formation for monks of the whole network, and a proving ground for the abbey's future leadership. Consequently, it seems that there was more than lip-service paid to the devotional priorities of the parent house. The miracle story set at Hertford features a monk of Westminster, Henry, a visitor in the entourage of Abbot Gervase, whose failing eyesight is

---

25 Cambridge, Camb. Uni. Lib., MS Ee 4.20, end flyleaf; Craster, *History of Northumberland*, pp. 71–72 (72).

26 *GASA*, I. 70–71.

27 Oxford, Corpus Christi College, MS 134, fols viii^r–ix^v, xi–xii^v, xiv$^{r–v}$ (calendar), 2^r (relics), 19^r–29^v (sermons), 63^r–104^v (office: antiphon at 78^r). See also Thomson, *Descriptive Catalogue*, pp. 66–67; <http://mlgb3.bodleian.ox.ac.uk/mlgb/book/5528> [accessed 30 November 2021].

28 *GASA*, I. 67–69.

29 *Vita Oswini*, XXVI (Wymondham); XXXII (Hertford), pp. 40, 47.

30 Hildesheim, Dombibliothek, MS St Godehard 1, p. 10.

THE RECEPTION OF ST OSWINE IN LATER MEDIEVAL ENGLAND 367

restored by a codex containing the life of Oswine in the possession of one of his hosts.[31] For the tale to hold any interest in the St Albans network, Oswine's name, and devotional significance, was surely already known.

The monastic community at Wymondham were certainly consumers of the cult; perhaps they also contributed to its textual tradition. The project to compose a life of Oswine and to collect his miracles may have been initiated by Abbot Richard but in two of the miracle stories the writer identifies himself as a former prior of Wymondham.[32] One is set at the Norfolk priory, and concerns the misfortune of a secular clerk for choosing to harvest his barley crop on Oswine's feast day.[33] The other story tells of the writer's own sojourn 'per annum integrum et eo amplius' (for upwards of a year) as a cloister monk (*in claustro*) at Tynemouth.[34]

Wymondham was a new house, the foundation of William d'Aubigny, kinsman of the St Albans Abbot Richard. It seems likely that a lively interest in Oswine was introduced there, like the anonymous compiler, from the mother house.[35] It has been assumed that the same writer was responsible for the full sequence of miracle stories, and for the *Vita Oswini*, but neither can be certain. The first-hand narration of the miracles is found only in the two stories related above, and the story sequence and the *vita* give different dates to the translation of the relic. It is worth noting that the sequence of miracle stories of St Alban carries echoes of more than one narrator and editor.[36] Hagiography was not necessarily the result of a coordinated campaign; rather it was an accretion of manifold responses to a cult, in this case a cross-current created by the busy traffic passing around the St Albans network.

St Albans in the twelfth century achieved a sphere of influence that extended even beyond its own vast dominion. Perhaps the principal vehicle was the monastery's own personnel, who passed on to the headship of other houses. Looking back from the thirteenth century Matthew Paris claimed the abbey had become 'quasi schola aliarum magistralis' (a school that was master to others).[37] From the moment of its refoundation, the abbey also sponsored and supervised workshops for the production of manuscripts which from the second quarter of the twelfth century transmitted books in wider monastic circles.[38] By these means, it seems the name of Oswine was carried to other monastic churches in south-east England, Westminster and perhaps Canterbury

---

31   *Vita Oswini*, XXXII, p. 46.

32   *Vita Oswini*, XXV–XXVI, pp. 39–40.

33   *Vita Oswini*, XXVI, p. 40.

34   *Vita Oswini*, XXV, p. 39. The text does not identify him as a prior of Tynemouth, as suggested by Janet Burton in her introduction to the *Historia Selebiensis*, p. xcii.

35   *GASA*, I. 67.

36   For the miracles associated with St Alban and his shrine see above, n. 20. See also, Clark, 'Miracles of Saint Alban'.

37   *GASA*, I. 59.

38   The finest outputs and their furthest reach were seen under the abbacies of Geoffrey de Gorron (1119–1146) and Simon (1166–1183): Thomson, *Manuscripts from St Albans*, I. 37–42, 52–62.

JAMES G. CLARK

(Christ Church) and Ramsey; possibly, by the witness of a later calendar reference, also Norwich.[39] Abbot Gervase of Westminster featured in Miracle 27, a walk-on part which would only have been accepted by the readership if it was plausible for there to be a following for Oswine at his abbey, where at least two prominent St Albans monks had progressed their careers.[40] German, a St Albans monk who had served as prior of Tynemouth, was chosen to be abbot of Selby in 1160 and it seems he took the tradition of Oswine with him.[41] The Yorkshire monastery's stories of miracles attributed to its own relics of St Germanus bear some resemblance to those in the Oswine collection, as well as those in Reginald of Durham's *Libellus Cuthberti*.[42] A mid-twelfth century psalter manuscript whose scriptorial features strongly suggest it originated in the St Albans workshop and which shows the influence of its own calendar and litany passed into the possession of the Benedictine nunnery at Wherwell, Hampshire, before 1200.[43] Neither monks nor books from St Albans passed into the western half of the kingdom. There was no trace of either Alban or Oswine at Malmesbury, Gloucester, Glastonbury, Tewkesbury, or Worcester. But on its eastern side from as far south as the Pays-de-Calais, to the lowlands of Yorkshire, in the years before the canonization of Thomas Becket, its principal calendar feasts were widely known, with Oswine among them.

After Becket, and the colliding consequences of Interdict (1208–1214), the fourth Lateran Council (1215), and the First Baronial War (1215–1217), St Albans lost its leadership position. The recession of the abbey also retracted its cultural influence, not least because it appears to have arrested the activity of its manuscript workshops which had remained productive for more than a century. The devotional distinctions of St Albans and its family of churches did not fade from view entirely but it does seem that recognition of them no longer reached as far. The only witness to the miracles of St Alban from outside the abbey itself is a codex made at the Cistercian abbey of Holm Cultram around 1200.[44] The manuscript also carries a copy of the text of the late twelfth-century Latin life of the saint, itself rarely seen beyond St Albans.

---

39 Stories concerning Canterbury and the monks of Westminster feature in the miracle collection: *Vita Oswini*, pp. 46–47, 50–51. Awareness, if not appreciation of the cult at Ramsey, may be inferred from the exchange of feasts with the St Albans family which is apparent in the St Albans psalter: Collins, 'Pictures and the Devotional Imagination', p. 21. For the Norwich reference see n. 79 below. Yet if there was a familiarity outside the St Albans network it did not transpose Oswine's name into the calendar of feasts. Francis Wormald's concordance of high medieval Benedictine calendars records entries only for St Albans and Durham: *English Benedictine Kalendars*, ed. by Wormald, I. 41, n. 175.

40 *Vita Oswini*, XXXII, pp. 46–47. The sequence of miracles begins at VI; *GASA*, I. 108, 133.

41 *GASA*, I. 120.

42 *Historia Selebiensis*, ed. and trans. by Burton, XV; XXII. See also Burton's introduction, pp. lv, lxxix, lxxxvii, xcii; *GASA*, I. 120.

43 Cambridge, St John's College, MS C 18, fols 1ʳ–6ᵛ. See also Thomson, *Manuscripts from St Albans*, I. 56–60.

44 BL, MS Cotton Faustina B IV, fols 19ᵛᵇ–40ᵛᵃ. See the discussion of this manuscript in Christiania Whitehead's essay in this volume.

THE RECEPTION OF ST OSWINE IN LATER MEDIEVAL ENGLAND 369

Oswine's profile receded in parallel with the proto-martyr's own. There is no surviving copy of the Latin life or the miracles later than 1200, nor is any attested. It was not included in the Holm Cultram collection; it is certainly possible that the exemplar for its Alban-*alia* had come to Cumbria from Tynemouth, and it may be that any text associated with Oswine was overlooked because the cult was little known on the north-west coast. Clearly the *Vita Oswini* was still available at St Albans since Roger Wendover copied it almost verbatim to give an account of the martyrdom, the rediscovery of the relics, and the memorable miracle of the martyr's indestructible hair, as testified by Countess Judith of Northumbria.[45] Yet there are also indications that attitudes to the old saints had begun to shift even at St Albans itself. In the wake of the civil war, Matthew Paris depicted a church in recovery, determined to recapture the devotional interest, and investment, of lay society. He scarcely touched on the fortunes of the patron saints of the house but he is positively expansive about the monastery's personal affiliations to present-day figures on the threshold of sainthood: Stephen Langton, Robert Grosseteste, Edmund Rich, and Richard Wych.[46] His alternative devotional interests were matched by other annalists within the St Albans network. Roger Wendover was excited by the wonders reported of the Holy Rood at the Cluniac priory of Broomholm.[47] John of Wallingford reached back into pre-Conquest church history to reflect on the witness of monastic saints, Guthlac, Dunstan, and Kenelm.[48]

The feast of Oswine surely retained its place in the liturgical regime of each one of the nine St Albans churches, but not perhaps with the same emphasis which had been seen a century before. It seems there was some uncertainty as to its standing in the hierarchy of feasts. Each one of the surviving calendars from thirteenth-century St Albans ascribes it a different status: two that are bound with manuscripts associated with Matthew Paris (*c.* 1235–1260) record the feast and its octave, but one shows it standing outside of the principal feasts (Alban, Amphibalus, and Edward the Confessor), while the other shows that it shared the same rank as forty-five other feasts throughout the year.[49] In a third calendar, the feast of Oswine was added as an afterthought.[50]

The only witness to the observance of the feast at this time is found in a manuscript neither from St Albans nor Tynemouth but from Wymondham.

---

45 Roger, *Chronica sive Flores historiarum*, ed. by Coxe, I. 504–07. See also *Vita Oswini*, IV, pp. 11–15.

46 Matthew Paris, *Chronica majora*, ed. by Luard (hereafter *CM*), V. 420, 496–97.

47 Roger, *Chronica sive Flores historiarum*, ed. by Coxe, II. 194–95.

48 Vaughan, 'Chronicle attributed to John of Wallingford', pp. 4–8, 39, 58, 66–67. Kenelm was also the subject of a Latin couplet composed by Abbot John of the Cell (1095–1214); an invocation of him was also scribbled on the flyleaf of a book of Bede's hagiography: *Three Eleventh-Century Latin Saints' Lives*, ed. by Love, p. cxviii; Cambridge, Pembroke College, MS 82, fols xii, xiii, 130^v–137^v.

49 Cambridge, Corpus Christi College, MS 26, fol. vi^v; BL, MS Royal 14 C VII, fol. 7^v.

50 BL, MS Royal 2 B VI, fols 2^r–7^v.

An anthology of invocatory prayers for thirty-two saints, presumably taken from their festal liturgies, includes one in the name of Oswine. Written in a script of the second half of the thirteenth century that lacks the polish of a professional, the book has the look of a manual prepared independently by a monk for personal use in and outside of the choir. The Oswine prayer is the penultimate in the sequence, separated from two in the name of Alban, that are clustered together with Edmund, Edward the Confessor, Cuthbert, and Benedict of Nursia. Perhaps the placement is indicative of the position of Oswine in the Wymondham litany.[51]

There is no equivalent manuscript evidence to give a comparative view of the status of the feast at Tynemouth itself. An anonymous letter found in a St Albans cartulary of *c.* 1400 but dated to the thirteenth century since it refers to the church 'de novo constructa', describes a conflicted scene: observant monks the very model of a fraternal community, 'cum consensu et ore et corde alacriter decantavant', but marooned, living in a spartan condition, deprived of any comfort or charm ('omni amenitate privatum, omni solacio et jocunditate carentem'), and surrounded by a people beaten a Moorish brown (*mauri*) by the weather.[52] The implication that priory's exposed position dampened its spiritual mood is reinforced by Matthew Paris who told of a visiting monk who was woken one night by the ghost of King John.[53]

Given the growing interdependence of the St Albans monasteries it is not impossible that the cult faded at Tynemouth and the mother house while at Wymondham it still held its ground. The disordered state of the surviving office book (Oxford, Corpus Christi College, MS 134) may tell its own story. The historical tradition of Oswine may have been more secure. In the course of the thirteenth century the community of Tynemouth became accustomed to identify their domain as the liberty of St Oswine.[54] The mid-century prior, Germanus, depicted the king martyr on his seal.[55] When the dispute between St Albans and Durham was finally settled through the intercession of the papal curia, it may be that the confidence of the community in its original identity was steadily restored.[56] Matthew Paris's close observation of the wedding banquet convened at York for the marriage of Alexander II and Henry III's daughter, Margaret, in 1251, may reflect the presence of St Albans representatives from Tynemouth.[57] Perhaps the burial at the priory in 1248 of Patrick, earl of Dunbar, grandson of the Scots' king William I, which required the return of his remains from Marseille, represented some acknowledgement

---

51 BL, MS Arundel 201, fol. 96[v].

52 Cambridge, Camb. Uni. Lib., MS Ee 4. 20, end flyleaf; Craster, *History of Northumberland*, pp. 71–72 and nn.

53 *CM*, III. 112–13.

54 Alnwick Castle, MS D XI, fol. 116[r]; Horwood and others, ed., *Sixth Report of the Royal Commission*, p. 225.

55 Craster, *History of Northumberland*, p. 121, citing an example subsequently lost.

56 *GASA*, I. 389–94; *CM*, V. 8–12.

57 *CM*, V. 266–70 (269).

THE RECEPTION OF ST OSWINE IN LATER MEDIEVAL ENGLAND   371

of its regal legend. It marked, Matthew Paris mused, a reconciliation with the blessed Oswine.[58]

Certainly, in the second half of the thirteenth century there are slight signs of rising devotional interest. Transactions recorded in the cartulary of the St Albans sacrists, which date from 1208 to 1380, include several donations targeted at Tynemouth and its shrine. During the priorate of Ralph (probably de Dunham, who held office from 1252 until the mid-1260s), Robert Russell presented 3s of rent from a plot at St Albans (Dagenhall Street) to be administered by the prior and convent to provide for a candle at the altar of St Oswine in the abbey church.[59] Agnes, wife of William Le Mirie quitclaimed a plot in the same street to the sacrist at Tynemouth, receiving a security of 5s by the hand of one of their monks, Roger de Hertford, presumably when he travelled from the priory. No doubt, the interest of the St Albans neighbourhood in the northern cult reflected its continued curation at the abbey itself although the sacrists' charters suggest another reason: St Albans was a community of migrants, some of whom originated in the north country. Gilbert de Mora, steward of Tynemouth, appears as witness to an undated charter concerning the St Albans parish of St Stephen. Adam de Selby is also found both as a witness and as a one-time reeve of the town.[60] Perhaps they carried their cult interests with them when they came south; perhaps they found the abbey's ties to the northern saint a compelling reason to stay.

Yet Tynemouth now also attracted patronage closer to home. From the reign of Edward II to that of Richard II, the surviving cartulary shows frequent traffic in grants and the profitable assertion of rights within Tynemouth and its environs.[61] These transactions were framed by the devotional tradition of the patron saint. Tenants presented themselves at the high altar, still the location of Oswine's shrine; the service of bondmen was rendered on the patronal feast itself.[62] An echo of this carried as far as St Albans, where the annalist identified as John de Trokelowe dramatized for his own brethren the defeat of one of the priory's oppressors, Gilbert de Middleton, 'pro damnis et injuriis Sancto Oswino.'[63]

The cross-border campaigning of Edward I reinforced Tynemouth's strategic importance and although the attraction was more circumstantial than devotional it did bring royal patronage. The king and his second queen between them took the priory's hospitality on six occasions from 1292 to 1304

---

58 'ut Deo et beato Oswino reconciliaretur': *CM*, v. 41; Craster, *History of Northumberland*, pp. 74–75.

59 BL, MS Cotton Julius D III, fols 15ʳ–16ʳ. For Prior Ralph de Dunham see Craster, *History of Northumberland*, p. 123.

60 BL, MS Cotton Julius D III, fols 56ʳ⁻ᵛ.

61 For example, Alnwick Castle, MS D XI, fols 51ʳ, 77ʳ–82ᵛ; Horwood and others, ed., *Sixth Report of the Royal Commission*, pp. 224–25.

62 See, for example, Alnwick Castle, MS D XI, fol. 35ᵛ; Craster, *History of Northumberland*, pp. 222–23.

63 *Trokelowe*, ed. by Riley, p. 101.

for a total period of almost eight months.[64] There is no account of Edward or Margaret at the shrine, although they are known to have witnessed the conventual Mass and the king commanded a search of the book collection to contribute to the dossier of proofs for his claim to the Scottish crown.[65] Edward was inclined to favour the church so much as to free it from St Albans's rule. This was robustly resisted but the interest of the royal couple did secure the monastery's right to a two-day market on the feast of St Oswine which had been fiercely challenged by the traders of Newcastle. The resumption of war under Edward's son saw king, queen, and favourite (Gaveston) at Tynemouth. Their presence was reported at St Albans and although it was not explicit that they visited the priory, the language 'apud ... existente', and 'recepit' does suggest it.[66]

Prominent patrons at Tynemouth may have persuaded the cathedral monastery at Durham to make a place for Oswine in their calendar and their litany. The king's natal date (20 August) was among many of British saints added into the margins of the cantor's copy of Usuard's martyrologium; the script is perhaps a generation later than the main text but still before 1200,[67] passing the same recognition also to their dependent priory at Coldingham.[68] The manuscript now known as the Coldingham breviary was written and decorated at Durham around the last quarter of the thirteenth century, the time at which the dispute with St Albans and Tynemouth was finally settled.[69] It received many additions on arrival at Coldingham but the feast of Oswine remained untouched in the red ink of a major feast, the same status ascribed to the feast of the dedication of the local altar of St Æbbe and the feast of Queen Margaret of Scotland.[70]

The assertive administration of a succession of priors together with the defensive stewardship of St Albans led Tynemouth towards something of a rebirth in the fourteenth century. The number of monks rose to a level not seen since the end of the twelfth century; and for the first time since then the leadership of the house was held to be a prize within the St Albans network. Between 1320 and 1380, the priory was in the hands of men from the south country, Richard of Tewing (1315–1340), a Hertfordshire man born to be a

---

64 *GASA*, II. 19–21; *Itinerary of King Edward I*, ed. by Gough, II. 100, 241; Craster, *History of Northumberland*, pp. 83–84.

65 *Rishanger*, ed. by Riley, p. 188.

66 *Trokelowe*, ed. by Riley, p. 75; Haines, *Edward II*, p. 84.

67 Durham, Cathedral Chapter Lib., MS B IV 24, fol. 30ʳ.

68 There were already relics of the saint at Durham before 1200. The configuration of the Coldingham calendar may also be a reflection of the Durham regime given its subjection. However, Paul Haywood has argued on the evidence of one surviving manuscript that the feast was not recognized at the cathedral before the fifteenth century: Haywood, 'Sanctity and Lordship', p. 120.

69 Pfaff, *Liturgy*, pp. 223–24. See also <http://www.cursus.org.uk/ms/coldingham> [accessed 30 November 2021].

70 BL, MS Harley 4664, fols 126ʳ–131ᵛ (129ᵛ, 131ʳ).

member of the St Albans hierarchy; Thomas de la Mare (1340–1349), kinsman of Plantagenet nobility; and Clement Whethamstede (1350–1378x1379), son of a gentry family steadily rising in influence.[71] Under their direction the church was remodelled so far as to detach it entirely from its recent past. Prior Tewing created a Lady Chapel, a natural response perhaps to the relative buoyancy of lay interest in the church.[72] De la Mare turned his attention to the shrine of Oswine, removing it from the position at the high altar that it had held for more than two hundred years to a site (unspecified) which his biographer described as better for his devotees since it was quieter, more open and spacious ('ut advenientes quietius, liberius et capacius possen [...] suas devotiones continuare').[73] Whethamstede is thought to have built on this recasting of the cult centre of the conventual church, inserting perpendicular windows above the high altar.[74]

These changes might well be read as a conscious effort to erase any lingering impression that the church was merely an ancient pilgrim chapel by emphasizing its capacity for the forms of Marian worship which the laity now demanded from any Benedictine foundation deserving of their patronage. This appears to have been the view of the St Albans author of De la Mare's biography who did not think to specify the new home for Oswine's shrine.[75] It may indeed have been the ambition of the priors. If the visual identity of their chancery can be taken as indicative of their devotional inclinations, it may be significant that at the turn of the fourteenth century the design of the priory seal evolved, giving prominence to the figure of the Virgin Mary, shown either with the Christ child and a figure perhaps intended to be Oswine or a stylized prelate.[76] Prior De la Mare opened the church and its monks to public and popular religion. His biographer recalled his own vernacular sermons and his encouragement of clerks and friars passing through 'secum detinuit semper clericos et magistros tam saecularis habitus quam ordinis mendicantium' (ever he drew around him clerks and scholars, both seculars and mendicants).[77]

Yet while there is no written witness to their worship at the shrine, there are signs that the cult of Oswine continued to be a central feature of their observant life. A psalter, fronted with a calendar, both written (first) in a hand of the second half of the fourteenth century, was, from its festive preferences, prepared for a monk of the priory. It is the only original Tynemouth calendar

---

71 Smith, London, and Brooke ed., *Heads of Religious Houses*, II, pp. 132–33.

72 A grant of property for its maintenance was made in 1338: Alnwick Castle, MS D XI, fol. 172ᵛ; Craster, *History of Northumberland*, p. 91.

73 *GASA*, II. 379.

74 Craster, *History of Northumberland*, p. 101.

75 *GASA*, II. 379.

76 *Catalogue of Seals*, ed. by de Gray Birch, I. 783; Craster, *History of Northumberland*, pp. 121–22, examples (4) and (6).

77 *GASA*, II. 380.

374   JAMES G. CLARK

to survive from any period of the priory's history. It identifies the patronal feast and the feast of the invention as principals to be celebrated in copes; the octave of the primary feast is marked for observance 'in albs'. The surrounding entries give some impression of the context of these celebrations. The feasts of three other saints of their northern region are recognized, Bede, Cuthbert, and Oswald, but of these only the latter is a second order feast, to be celebrated in albs, while the other two are third order dates to be marked unvested. Of the remaining English saints of the Sarum repertory, Edward the Confessor, Edmund, king and martyr, and Thomas Becket, each is classified also of the second rank. The special significance of the feast of the invention was perhaps deliberately enhanced by the placement of the conventual anniversary for the parents of the professed brethren two days later.[78]

The curation of the cult at this time might be confirmed, obliquely, by the compilation of a compendium of the histories of saints of England's calendar by the secular clerk named in contemporary manuscripts as John of Tynemouth. John's connection with the place or the priory remains uncertain: perhaps he held the benefice of the parish church, although perhaps the association is nothing more tangible than a toponym. What is more certain is that in preparing his *Sanctilogium* he consulted texts at a number of monasteries at least in the eastern counties of England, perhaps from north to south. St Albans Abbey itself appears to have secured an early exemplar of the *Sanctilogium*, since a copy was among the deluxe manuscripts commissioned by the former Prior De la Mare after he had taken the abbacy at St Albans. The collection captured the interest of a cross-section of monastic England: certainly, it was known in whole or in part at Durham and Bury St Edmund's before 1400, since manuscript witnesses survive. Perhaps it was also at Thetford's Dominican Friary, where in 1479 William Worcestre made a note of Oswine's martyrdom from a text he described as 'Lives of the Saints of England'.[79]

John's text is credited with reinvigorating interest in the root lives of the English legendary. It was his repertory that was the most familiar source of reference for vernacular hagiography in the fifteenth century and an interpolation of his original Latin became the basis of the *Newe Legende of Englande* printed by Richard Pynson in 1516.[80] For the life of Oswine in fact John offered nothing new. His text was substantially that of the *Vita Oswini*, incorporating Bede within it; a reflection it seems, of the practice of the festive office itself.[81] John did not use Roger Wendover's version of the *Vita* text taken up in to the *Flores historiarum*, and in his own synthesis of histories, *Histora*

---

78 Oxford, Bodl. Lib., MS Gough Liturg. 18, fols xviii[r]–xxviii [ult.] at xx[r], xxii[r], xxv[r–v].

79 For surviving copies see Sharpe, *Handlist of Latin Writers*, pp. 333–34 (334). For Thetford see Worcestre, *Itineraries*, ed. by Harvey, pp. 164–65.

80 The early antiquarians Johns Leland and Bale mistakenly believed John Capgrave to have been the agent of transmission between John of Tynemouth's text and the *Newe Legende*: Lucas, 'John Capgrave and the *Nova legenda Anglie*'; Lucas, 'John Capgrave (1393–1464)'.

81 *Nova legenda Anglie*, ed. by Horstmann, II. 269–73.

aurea, he ignored Oswine entirely and gave no notice to the priory church of Tynemouth.[82] Yet his closing summary of miracle stories culminated in a tale of a woman haunted by visions of hairy, horned and tailed demons (cornute, hispidi et caudate) not found in the twelfth-century collection.[83] Still, the reach of John's historical compendia does appear to have encouraged an association of the place-name, if not the priory itself, with a fount of historical lore. Writing his *Scalachronica* in the mid-century, Sir Thomas Gray declared, 'Douce amy, ceo disoit Sebille, cesti est le vikeir de Tilmouth [...] de ditz de qy, tu poez auoir graunt enformacioun' (Dear friend, said the Sybil, this is the vicar of Tillmouth [i.e. Tynemouth], from whose saying you will be able to gain much information).[84] The St Albans manuscript of the *Sanctilogium* does carry additional material, the text of two votive prayers which it may be assumed also belonged to the liturgy of the festive office. However, these are written into the wide lower margin of the manuscript leaf. The script is in the same hand as the main text of the book but this in itself does not challenge the most plausible conclusion that the prayers were incorporated at St Albans to facilitate local use.[85]

The recognition given to Oswine at Tynemouth still radiated through the St Albans network. Raised to the abbacy itself (1349), the former Tynemouth prior Thomas de la Mare reconstructed (*de novo aedificata*) the altar dedicated to Oswine, also adding an image (presumably a panel painting); now the martyr was to share the dedication with Benedict, patron of the monastic order, and other doctors of the church.[86] Surely this was seen to raise his status since at the same time (1351) he created a new sequence of commemorations, of the Virgin, St Benedict, Alban, Amphibalus, and Oswine, to be performed daily at the abbey; in the same constitutions he called on Tynemouth to observe a daily commemoration for their patron after that of the Virgin.[87] He also presented a copy of John of Tynemouth's *Sanctilogium* to the nearest cell at Redbourn.[88] The priory was used as vacation residence for monks from the mother house although there was an expectation that an observance routine was maintained.[89] Since the book was a large folio written in an upright textura script, it seems possible it was intended for the choir lectern, where John's text could supply readings for the festal offices. In the *Gesta abbatum* De la

---

82 John's *Historia aurea* remains unprinted. For copies see Sharpe, *Handlist of Latin Writers*, p. 334.
83 *Nova legenda Anglie*, ed. by Horstmann, II. 271–22; BL, MS Cotton Tiberius E I/1, fols. 51rb–52vb at 52va. See also the version in the Latin *Legenda* which was the source-text for Pynson, Oxford, Bodl., MS Tanner 15, pp. 461–64, at 464.
84 Gray, *Scalacronica*, ed. and trans. by King, p. 7.
85 Harper, 'Traces of Lost Late Medieval Offices', pp. 7–8.
86 *GASA*, II. 362.
87 *GASA*, II. 424–28 (427).
88 Now, BL, MS Cotton Tiberius E I (1–2), bound in two volumes. *Ex dono* inscription at fol. 6^r, *Vita Oswini* at fols 52^v–54^v.
89 *GASA*, I. 202–05 (203).

Mare's biographer commented that the Legenda that he gave the priory was for the commemoration of the saints 'year round' (*per anni circulum*).[90] In support of this, in the margins of the leaves carrying Oswine's history there is a schematic genealogy of the martyr and a sequence of three suffrages, making confession to the father of Deira (*pater Deirorum*); seeking his guidance to the glory of heaven (*duc ad celi gloriam*); and praying that God Almighty will see him glorified (*facis beatissimi Oswini martiris tui commemoracione gloriari*).[91]

Abbot De la Mare also carried the cult to the abbey's patrons. Perhaps it was his personal influence that persuaded Edward III, whose close counsels he was said to enjoy, to secure for himself a relic of Oswine. The king is not recorded at Tynemouth, but Newcastle was a frequent stop in his early years of campaigning.[92] Perhaps it was to reinforce the image of particular royal patronage that led an unnamed abbot — quite possibly De la Mare given the date and the detail of the record — to allow William Whethamstede to take an amber chalice, given by Edward's daughter-in-law, Princess Joan of Kent, to adorn the shrine. It was recorded that the cup was used for a dole of wine, a commemorative act that was perhaps also De la Mare's coinage.[93]

There are glimpses of interest at two other of the dependent cells. The monks of Wymondham Priory, it appears, did not forget the particular affinity of their house to the cult. In a fourteenth-century manuscript fragment that carried the obit of their founder, a verse was written recalling the date of Oswine's death, the recovery of his relics (here given as 1055) and their translation to a new shrine (here, 1103).[94] A Wymondham calendar, preceding a missal, written in a script of *c*. 1400, recognized the feast. It is a pocket-book, surely prepared for the personal reference of a member of the community, perhaps an aide memoire for their choir duties but as likely a source of reading, or at least reference, in their independent hours.[95]

A manuscript also made at the beginning of the fifteenth century for a prior of the St Albans dependency of Hatfield Peverel, more than fifty miles to the east of St Albans close to the Essex coast, certainly points to the presence of Oswine in the private reading of the monks. The prior's book holds a version of Bede's *Historia ecclesiastica*. The text has been heavily excerpted, removing the greater part of its secular history of kings and kingdoms, to leave a concentrated chronicle of the pioneering pastors of the English church. In the

---

90   *GASA*, I. 399–400 (399).

91   The texts were printed in the *Nova legenda Anglie*, ed. by Horstmann, II. 268, 273.

92   Ormrod, *Edward III*, p. 100.

93   Cambridge, Corpus Christi College, MS 7, fol. 104[rb].

94   Dublin, Trinity College, MS 496, fol. 125[v].

95   Oxford, Bodl. Lib., MS Lat. Liturg. g 8, fols x[r]–xv[v] at xi[r] (invention), xiii[v] (principal). A prayer for all saints names Oswine alongside St Alban and Amphibalus, fols 57[r]–60[v] at 58[v]. The rear flyleaf carries the signature of Robert Blakeney, the last prior of Tynemouth. Perhaps his office led to his acquisition of a book that acknowledged Oswine in the triumvirate of St Albans saints.

THE RECEPTION OF ST OSWINE IN LATER MEDIEVAL ENGLAND 377

Bedan original, the story of Oswine is told at the centre of Book III (chapter fourteen of thirty). But here at Hatfield the book was wholly reorganized. The core now concerns Bishop Aidan but the climax of the final chapter is the relocated account of the betrayal and murder of Oswine. The condition of the leaf at which this final chapter begins suggests that it drew more attention from its readers than might usually be expected at the end of the third book of a four-book text. The top left-hand corner of the leaf is rubbed and grease stained markedly more than preceding or following leaves; the name of Oswine in the chapter heading has itself been rubbed to the extent that the capital letter is very faint indeed. At the very least, these signs of use point to a pattern of use in which readers passed over the reordered book three to arrive at Oswine's martyrdom; perhaps also the written name prompted a votive response.[96]

Oswine remained a focus for private devotion into the fifteenth century. John Whethamstede, first elected abbot in September 1420, who held the office on two occasions before his death in 1465, adopted Oswine as personal and familial patron. He was the kinsman of those who had served as cellarer and prior of Tynemouth in the years either side of 1400.[97]

In the middle years of the century, perhaps on his return to abbatial office in 1452, Whethamstede commissioned a mural for the west vault of the presbytery ceiling featuring the arms of his abbey, the saltire of St Alban, of Tynemouth, the three crowns of Oswine, and the royal standard, flanked by the dove and the eagle that were the customary symbols of the two Apostolic Johns, the Baptist, and the Evangelist. The imagery spoke of his institutional position under the patronage of the crown, and the pastoral and doctrinal responsibilities of his office; yet the figures could also speak of himself, and his dynasty, and their devotion to the cult of the St Albans domain.

During his first period in office, at a visitation of the monastic community at Tynemouth in 1423, Whethamstede issued injunctions concerning the observant customs of the house. These made no reference to the veneration of Oswine but instead scolded the monks for their neglect of the feast of St Cuthbert.[98] Perhaps here, and in his presbytery mural, Whethamstede was inclined to make a distinction between the obligation of his church to reflect, and respond to, the cult interest of its principal patrons, and the devotional traditions inside the monastic enclosure. Amid more homogenized patterns of public worship, it may be that the historic figure of Oswine (and possibly others) was reserved for the professed.

---

96 Oxford, Bodl. Lib., MS Rawlinson B 189, fols 119ʳ–179ᵛ, Book III of *HE* beginning at fol. 134ʳ, with the re-positioned final chapter of Oswine's death, at fols 151ᵛ–152ʳ. The soiled corner and rubbed name is at fol. 151ᵛ.

97 William Whethamstede, cellarer, fl. 1384–1405; John Whethamstede, prior, 1393–1418: Craster, *History of Northumberland*, p. 100 & n.

98 *Annales monasterii S. Albani a Johanne Amundesham*, ed. by Riley, I. 62, pp. 212–21 (214, 221).

Later devotional interest in Oswine was not confined to the St Albans family. The primary feast now became a feature of the calendar at York Minster and Durham Cathedral Priory. Durham also retained relics of the king-martyr, recorded in an inventory of 1383.[99] It is possible that there was contact between Tynemouth and Durham: the opening leaf of the Coldingham breviary contains annotations in the hand of an identified monk of Tynemouth, John Westwick.[100] Such interaction may not have been innocuous. Perhaps from Tynemouth itself, the St Albans family appears to have acquired a recension of the *Meditatio devota* of the Durham monk, John Uthred of Boldon, which closes with an invocation of Cuthbert. A new recension was prepared replacing Cuthbert with Alban, perhaps with the intention of an independent transmission in the southern province.[101]

The primary feast was not incorporated into the Sarum calendar which was widespread in the southern province soon after 1300. Yet still it retained some profile at least on the eastern side of the country, north and south. There are glimpses of a popular cult in the diocese of Norwich. Portraits of the saint survive in stained-glass schemes in two churches, one urban, the other rural, St Peter Mancroft in the cathedral city, and All Saints, Catfield, nearly twenty miles to the north-east. Since the latter was a long way from either of the St Albans cells, Binham (35 miles) and Wymondham (30 miles), where the cult was surely maintained, it may be that it was now independent of monastic influence.[102] Three liturgical books, two apparently originating in the south-east, and one from northern England, hint at a late resurgence of the feast. A fine, illuminated breviary perhaps made in London in the first quarter of the fifteenth century carries a prayer added perhaps seventy-five years later invoking Oswine, 'rex gentis Anglorum, miles'.[103] A calendar, probably of Norwich origin, apparently in the possession of the Scrope family by 1384, was amended in crayon in the early sixteenth century to record Oswine's feast-day.[104] On a blank leaf of the Coldingham breviary, a sixteenth-century hand copied out the lections for Oswine and added the feast of the invention to the calendar at the front of the book.[105]

The mutable character of liturgical calendars in the later Middle Ages is a valuable reminder that there was no sudden subjection either to Sarum or

---

99 *Missale*, ed. by Henderson, I, pp. xxix, xxxvii; a Durham calendar of early date was amended to accommodate the feast of Oswine after 1400: Cambridge, Jesus College, MS Q B 6, fols 2ᵛ–7ʳ; *Extracts from Account Rolls*, ed. by Fowler, II, p. 430.

100 I am grateful to Seb Falk for this identification.

101 For this copy see Cambridge, Camb. Uni. Lib., MS Gg 4.11.

102 For the Toppes windows at St Peter Mancroft see King, *Medieval Stained Glass of St Peter Mancroft*, pp. cxlcccix, cxcv, 100, fig. 22. For the screen at Catfield see Luxford, 'Sacred Kingship', pp. 113–14.

103 BL, MS Harley 7398, fol. 359ᵛ.

104 BL, MS Stowe 12, fol. 159ʳ.

105 BL, MS Harley 4664, fols 324ᵛ–325ᵛ.

THE RECEPTION OF ST OSWINE IN LATER MEDIEVAL ENGLAND 379

to any agenda of national reformation devised either by the Lancastrians, or
the early Tudor regime. Surely it was also a very visible effect of the dynamic,
multilingual hagiography that entered circulation between the Black Death
and the Break with Rome. This discourse returned the sacred history of
early England to a general, clerical and lay readership for the first time since
the end of the twelfth century. Its vehicles were not only discrete Latin and
vernacular lives, but also repertories of (Latin) lives, or digests of lives, some
of which were so brief that as a reader they were more akin to an elaborated
form of a litany. The transmission of these texts would appear to have been
across a wide front, since the subjects and style of the surviving examples
are very varied. Oswine is frequently featured, although not always. There is
no geographical pattern to his appearance: one can be connected with the
London Charterhouse; another appears to be associated with a religious
house in Berkshire, perhaps Reading Abbey.[106]

It would be wrong to infer from these sources that Oswine, among
others in the early English tradition, had been consigned to a subject of only
antiquarian interest. Generally, these texts have only held the attention of
scholars of historical writing whose instinct has been to classify them among
the jumble of annals, date lists, and excerpts from classic histories that late
medieval clerks liked to collect in their commonplace books in homage to
a tradition of chronicling that fascinated, but to which they were incapable
of making an original contribution. Yet closer attention to their manuscript
context shows that they were charged with a different purpose. The sequence
in Lambeth Palace Library, MS 99 is introduced as a catalogue of the saints
that originated in England and whose relics still remain there ('Cathalogus
sanctorum in anglia pausancium et oriundorum').[107] It is a demonstration of the
sacred foundation of this insular Christianity, of its antiquity, and its continuity.
In a monastic context — as is possible for this particular manuscript — this
might be read as a reach for an identity distinct from the traditions of the
continental congregations to which, in their governance, they were aligned.
A statement of devotional values, within it there was surely also an intention
to instruct. The Lambeth repertory is arranged according to the calendar,
and it is explained to the reader 'quorum deposicionum dies consequenter
annotantur' (the sequence of days is annotated accordingly).[108] The placement
of these repertories among other texts recording the history and customs of
the church does seem to suggest that they formed part of a syllabus of readings
for monastic formation. It may not be coincidental that the last generations
of monks recruited in pre-Reformation England were inclined to change the
first or second name at their solemn profession, and, frequently, they chose

---

106 Oxford, Trinity College, MS 46, fols 165ᵛ–166ʳ (London Charterhouse); Lambeth Palace
     Library, MS 99, fols 187ʳ–193ʳ (Reading Abbey?).
107 Lambeth Palace Library, MS 99, fol. 187ʳ.
108 Lambeth Palace Library, MS 99, fol. 187ʳ.

one from England's sacred legend. St Albans was affected and the earliest list of monks to show evidence of it (1524–1525) features one John Oswyn.[109]

Beyond these repertories and outside of the handful of religious houses well-stocked with early hagiography, Oswine still held a place in the historical imagination. The legend of the king and the enduring presence of his relics at Tynemouth was conveyed to a general readership by the annals of Britain's history that achieved a wide circulation after 1300. Roger Wendover's summary version of the invention of the relics, derived from the *Vita Oswini*, was incorporated into the *Flores historiarum* which was transmitted through a chain of Benedictine abbeys in the century after 1265.[110] There were faint echoes of the *Flores* in otherwise independent accounts of Oswine's story given space in two chronicles of the mid-fourteenth century: the compiler of *Eulogium historiarum* pictured his tomb 'in quodam rupi super mare honorifice humatus' (honourably buried on a rock by the sea), and reported his many miracles ('colitur multis miraculis coruscando').[111] Another chronicle known only by the names of those that owned a copy — the Fitzhugh family and John Brompton, abbot of Jervaulx (1436–1466) — reflected that the martyr became a figure beloved by all ('ab omnibus dilectus'), frequently visited by the great and the good of diverse provinces ('frequenter a nobilibus cuiuscumque provincie visitatus').[112] In his *Speculum historiale*, perhaps compiled in the last quarter of the century, the Westminster monk, Richard of Cirencester, was satisfied to reproduce the *Flores* in full.[113]

In Northumberland it seems to the end of the Middle Ages the king martyr was understood to express the identity of the region. An early Tudor burgess of Newcastle, Oswine Ogle, was not perhaps the only one of his generation to be so named.[114] The arms of the three crowns were added to the glass of the city's parish church of St Nicholas, and retained at the Reformation, not, surely, to honour the priory with which the merchant community had so often warred. Indeed, at this late date it may be that Oswine and the ancient sanctity of Tynemouth became increasingly detached from the monastic community that occupied the site. After the Black Death there is no doubt that the incidence of substantial benefactions to the monastery steadily declined. The interest of the Newcastle magnate, William Sire, in 1353, conspicuously challenged the contemporary pattern of investment in the city and its satellite parishes to the north, west and south.[115] Other than Sire, the priory was recognized

---

109 Oxford, Jesus College, MS 77, fol. 323^r. Only one other monk in this cohort adopted such a name: Thomas Amphabel. See further, David E. Thornton's essay on monastic hagionyms in this volume.

110 *Flores historiarum*, ed. by Luard, I. 582–84.

111 *Eulogium historiarum*, 79, ed. by Haydon, III. 2.

112 Cambridge, Corpus Christi College, MS 96, fol. 25^v.

113 *Ricardi de Cirencestria speculum historiale*, ed. by Mayor, I. 162–67.

114 Baggs, Brown, and others, 'The Sixteenth Century: Achievement of Self-Government', pp. 63–65.

115 *Early Deeds Relating to Newcastle*, ed. by Oliver, pp. 174–75 (175); Holford and Stringer, *Border Liberties*, p. 56.

by testators recorded in the Durham and York registers only on the relatively rare occasions they assigned token sums to each of the principal monastic and mendicant houses.[116] However, when those on the wrong side of the law looked to escape local and royal authority out of Newcastle, they were still conscious of the claim of a Tynemouth sanctuary on the coast. The last time a murderer is known to have fled there was in 1523.[117]

In the first generation of printing in England, the independent profile of Oswine, Tynemouth, and early Christianity in England was propagated by histories and liturgical aids that targeted a new readership of translations from the Latin. 'Oswyn was discomfited & slaine and lyeth at Teynmouth' recalled the *Cronycles of the londe of Englond*. 'A kynge of englond that for y[e] welth of his people wylfully put hymselfe in the handes of his enemyes', reflected the *Martiloge* of 1526.[118] The *Kalendar of the Newe Legend of Englande* reproduced John of Tynemouth's digest of Bede, describing Oswine, 'buryed at Tynemouth [...] a place in suche reverence'.[119] Perhaps in anticipation of renewed attention, it appears that the shrine was well maintained. It led the list of venerated objects compiled by the king's visitors in 1535. There may be just a hint of a shift in its status, from cult object to historical artefact, in their description as 'feretrum sive monumentum' (shrine or tomb).[120]

It was this same profile that the Tudor regime sought to appropriate in 1503 and 1513. Surely it also made the priorate such a resonant opportunity for the courtier champions of Thomas Gardiner. Of course, this was not a significant departure from the impulses that had caused the creation of the shrine and the priory church four and a half centuries before, even if the relics and the rhetoric of their miraculous power were, for reasons of changing taste, no longer centre-stage. Oswine was a precious fragment of an original Christian England that might still lend history to a new dynasty and sanctity to its novel headship of the church.

---

116 For Tynemouth to benefit from this tokenism was itself rare. See, for example, the will of John Rodum: *Testamenta Eboracensia*, ed. by Raine, p. 137.

117 *Letters and Papers*, ed. by Brewer and others, 3/2, 3095. The cartulary records the case of another fugitive almost two centuries before (1342): Alnwick Castle, MS D XI, fol. 212[r]; Horwood and others, ed., *Sixth Report of the Royal Commission*, p. 226.

118 *Cronycles of the londe*, CI; *Martiloge in Englysshe*, fol. 91[v].

119 *Here begynneth the kalendre of the newe legend of Englande*, fols 84[v]–85[r].

120 Kew, TNA, SP 1/109, fol. 99[v].

Works Cited

Manuscripts and Archival Sources

Alnwick Castle, MS D XI
Cambridge, Corpus Christi College, MS 7
——, Corpus Christi College, MS 26
——, Corpus Christi College, MS 96
——, Jesus College, MS Q B 6
——, Pembroke College, MS 82
——, St John's College, MS C 18
——, Cambridge University Library, MS Ee 4.20
——, Cambridge University Library, MS Gg 4.11
Dublin, Trinity College, MS 496
Durham, Cathedral Chapter Library, MS B IV 24
Hildesheim, Dombibliothek, MS St Godehard 1 <https://www.albani-psalter.de/>
    [accessed 21 December 2021]
Kew, The National Archives, SP 1/109
——, SP 49/1
——, SP 58/1/27
London, British Library, MS Arundel 201
——, MS Cotton Caligula B VI
——, MS Cotton Claudius E IV
——, MS Cotton Faustina B IV
——, MS Cotton Julius D III
——, MS Cotton Tiberius E I (1–2)
——, MS Cotton Vespasian F III
——, MS Egerton 3721
——, MS Harley 4664 (Coldingham Breviary) <http://www.cursus.org.uk/ms/
    coldingham>
——, MS Royal 2 B VI
——, MS Royal 14 C VII
——, MS Stowe 12
London, Lambeth Palace Library, MS 99
Oxford, Bodleian Library, MS Gough Liturg. 18
——, MS Lat. Liturg. g. 8
——, MS Rawlinson B 189
——, MS Tanner 15
Oxford, Corpus Christi College, MS 134
——, Jesus College, MS 77
——, Trinity College, MS 46

Primary Sources

Annales monasterii S. Albani a Johanne Amundesham monacho ut videtur conscripti (AD 1421–1440), ed. by Henry Thomas Riley, 2 vols, Rolls Series, 28 (London: HMSO, 1870–1871)

Bede, *Historia ecclesiastica gentis anglorum. Bede's Ecclesiastical History of the English People*, ed. and trans. by Bertram Colgrave and R. A. B. Mynors, Oxford Medieval Texts (Oxford: Clarendon Press, 1969) (cited as *HE*)

Catalogue of Seals in the British Museum Department of Manuscripts, ed. by Walter de Gray Birch, 6 vols (London: Trustees of the British Museum and others, 1887–1900)

Chronica monasterii sancti Albani. Johannis de Trokelowe et Henrici de Blaneforde monachorum S. Albani necnon quorundam anonymorum chronica et annales, ed. by Henry Thomas Riley, Rolls Series, 28/3 (London: HMSO, 1866) (cited as *Trokelowe*)

——, *Willelmi Rishanger, quondam monachi S. Albani, et quorundam anonymorum, chronica et annales*, ed. by Henry Thomas Riley, Rolls Series, 28 (London: Longman, 1865) (cited as *Rishanger*)

Cronycles of the londe of Englond (Antwerp: Gerard de Leew, 1493), STC (2nd edn), 9994

Early Deeds Relating to Newcastle upon Tyne, ed. by A. M. Oliver, SS, 137 (Durham: Andrews & Co., 1924)

English Benedictine Kalendars after AD 1100, ed. by Francis Wormald, 2 vols, Henry Bradshaw Society, 77, 81 (London: Harrison & Sons, 1939–1946)

Eulogium (historiarum sive temporis): Chronicon ab orbe conditio usque ad annum domini MCCCLVI a monacho quodam Malmesburiensi exaratum, ed. by Frank Scott Haydon, 3 vols, Rolls Series, 9 (London: Longman, 1858–1863)

Extracts from the Account Rolls of the Abbey of Durham, ed. by James Fowler, 3 vols, SS, 99, 100, 103 (Durham: Andrews & Co., 1899)

Flores historiarum, ed. by Henry Richards Luard, 3 vols, Rolls Series, 95 (London: HMSO, 1890)

Gesta abbatum monasterii sancti Albani, ed. by Henry Thomas Riley, 3 vols, Rolls Series, 28 (London: HMSO, 1866–1869) (cited as *GASA*)

Gray, Thomas, *Scalacronica*, ed. and trans. by Andy King, SS, 209 (Woodbridge: Boydell, 2005)

Hall's chronicle, containing the history of England during the reign of Henry IV and the succeeding monarchs to the reign of Henry VIII, collated with the editions of 1548 and 1550, published under the superintendence of Sir Henry Ellis and others (London: J. Johnson, 1809)

Historia Selebiensis monasterii. The history of the monastery of Selby, ed. and trans. by Janet Burton with Lynda Lockyer, Oxford Medieval Texts (Oxford: Oxford University Press, 2013)

The Itinerary of King Edward I Throughout his Reign, AD 1272–1307, ed. by Henry Gough, 2 vols (Paisley: Alexander Gardener, 1900)

Here begynneth the kalendre of the newe legend of Englande (London: Richard Pynson, 1516), STC (2nd edn) 4602

Leland, John, *De rebus Britannicis collectanea*, ed. by Thomas Hearne, 6 vols (Oxford: n. pub., 1715)

Letters and Papers Foreign & Domestic of the Reign of Henry VIII, ed. by John S. Brewer and others, 23 vols in 35 (London: Longman, 1862–1932)

The Martiloge in Englysshe after the use of the chirche of Salisbury (London: Wynkyn de Worde, 1526), STC (2nd edn), 17532

Matthaei Parisiensis monachi sancti Albani Chronica majora, ed. by Henry Richards Luard, 7 vols, Rolls Series, 57 (London: HMSO, 1872–1883)

Missale ad usum isignis ecclesiae Eboracensis, ed. by William G. Henderson, 2 vols, SS, 59–60 (Durham: Andrews & Co., 1874)

Nova legenda Anglie: as collected by John of Tynemouth, John Capgrave and others and first printed with new lives by Wynkyn de Worde ad mdxvi, ed. by Carl Horstmann, 2 vols (Oxford: Clarendon Press, 1901)

Ricardi de Cirencestria speculum historiale de gestis regum Angliae, ed. by John E. B. Mayor, 2 vols, Rolls Series, 30 (London: Longman, 1863–1869)

Roger de Wendover, *Chronica sive Flores historiarum*, ed. by Henry O. Coxe, 16 vols (London: English Historical Society, 1842)

Symeon of Durham (attrib.), *Historia regum*, in *Symeonis monachi opera omnia*, ed. by Thomas Arnold, 2 vols, Rolls Series, 75 (London: Longman & Co., 1880–1885), II

Testamenta Eboracensia, or Wills Registered at York, ed. by James Raine, SS, 2 (London: J. B. Nichols and Son, William Pickering, 1836)

Three Eleventh-Century Latin Saints' Lives. Vita S. Birini, Vita et miracula S. Kenelmi, Vita S. Rumwoldi, ed. by Rosalind C. Love, Oxford Medieval Texts (Oxford: Clarendon Press, 1996)

Vita Oswini, in *Miscellanea biographica. Oswinus rex Northumbriae. Cuthbertus episcopus Lindisfarnensis. Eata episcopus Haugustaldensis*, ed. by James Raine, SS, 8 (London: J. B. Nichols and Son, William Pickering, 1838), pp. 1–59 (cited as *Vita Oswini*)

William of Malmesbury, *Gesta regum Anglorum. The History of the English Kings*, ed. and trans. by R. A. B. Mynors, Rodney Thomson, and Michael Winterbottom, 2 vols (Oxford: Clarendon Press, 1998–1999) (cited as *GR*)

Worcestre, William, *Itineraries, Edited from the Unique MS. Corpus Christi College Cambridge, 210*, ed. by John Harvey (Oxford: Clarendon Press, 1969)

Secondary Works

Aird, William D., *St Cuthbert and the Normans: The Church of Durham, 1071–1153* (Woodbridge: Boydell, 1998)

Baggs, A. P., L. M. Brown and others, 'The Sixteenth Century: The Achievement of Self-Government', in *A History of the County of York East Riding: Volume 6, the Borough and Liberties of Beverley*, ed. by Keith John Allison, Victoria County Histories (London: Institute for Historical Research, 1989), pp. 63–65

Boffey, Julia, and Matthew Payne, 'The *Gardyner's Passetaunce*, the *Flowers of England*, and Thomas Gardyner, Monk of Westminster', *The Library*, 18.2 (2017), 175–90

Clark, James G., 'The Miracles of Saint Alban', (forthcoming)

Collins, Kristen, 'Pictures and the Devotional Imagination in the St Albans Psalter' in *The St Albans Psalter: Painting and Prayer in Medieval England*, ed. by Kristen Collins, Peter Kidd, and Nancy K. Turner (Los Angeles: J. P. Getty Museum, 2013), pp. 9–64

Craster, H. H. E., *A History of Northumberland. VIII: The Parish of Tynemouth* (Newcastle upon Tyne: Andrew Reid, 1907)

Crook, John, *English Medieval Shrines* (Woodbridge: Boydell, 2011)

Freeman, Elizabeth, 'The Priory of Hampole and its Literary Culture: English Religious Women and Books in the Age of Richard Rolle', *Parergon*, 29.1 (2012), 1–25

Goodwin, George, *Fatal Rivalry: Henry VIII, James IV and the Battle for Renaissance Britain: Flodden 1513* (London: Weidenfeld & Nicholson, 2013)

Haines, Roy Martin, *Edward II: Edward of Caernarfon, His Life, His Reign and Its Aftermath, 1284–1330* (Montreal: McGill University Press, 2003)

Harper, Sally, 'Traces of Lost Late Medieval Offices? The *Sanctilogium Angliae, Walliae, Scotiae et Hiberniae* of John of Tynemouth (fl. 1350)', in *Essays in Honour of John Caldwell: Sources, Style, Performance, Historiography*, ed. by Emma Hornby and David Maw (Woodbridge: Boydell, 2010), pp. 1–21

Hayward, Paul Anthony, 'Sanctity and Lordship in Twelfth-Century England: Saint Albans, Durham and the Cult of Saint Oswine, King and Martyr', *Viator*, 30 (1999), 105–44

Holford, Matthew L., and Keith L. Stringer, *Border Liberties and Loyalties: North-East England, c. 1200 to c. 1400* (Edinburgh: Edinburgh University Press, 2010)

Horwood, A. J., H. T. Riley, J. C. Jefferson, and R. B. Knowles, ed., *The Sixth Report of the Royal Commission on Historical Manuscripts: Part I Report & Appendix* (London: HMSO, 1877)

Hughes, Jonathan, *Pastors and Visionaries: Religious and Secular Life in Late Medieval Yorkshire* (Woodbridge: Boydell, 1988)

King, David, *The Medieval Stained Glass of St Peter Mancroft, Norwich* (Oxford: Oxford University Press, 2006)

Lucas, Peter J., 'John Capgrave and the *Nova legenda Anglie*: A Survey', *The Library*, 5th Series, 25 (1970), 1–10

——, 'John Capgrave (1393–1464)', *Oxford Dictionary of National Biography* (Oxford: Oxford University Press, 1970)

Lutton, Rob, 'Bridlington Priory in Late Medieval England and the Cult of John Thweng', in *Celebrating the Heritage: Bridlington Priory in its Historical Context, 1113–2013*, ed. by Penelope Weston and David Weston (Bridlington: Bridlington Priory, 2015), pp. 19–32

Luxford, Julian, 'Sacred Kingship, Genealogy and the Late Medieval Rood Screen: Catfield and Beyond', in *The Art and Science of the Church Screen in Medieval Europe: Making, Meaning, Preserving*, ed. by Spike Bucklow, Richard Marks, and Lucy Wrapson (Woodbridge: Boydell, 2017), pp. 100–22

McLeod, W., 'Alban and Amphibal: Some Extant Lives and a Lost Life', *Mediaeval Studies*, 42 (1980), 407–30

Ormrod, W. M., *Edward III* (New Haven: Yale University Press, 2011)

Pfaff, Richard, *The Liturgy in Medieval England: A History* (Cambridge: Cambridge University Press, 2009)

Rollason, David W., 'The Cults of Murdered Royal Saints in Anglo-Saxon England', *Anglo-Saxon England*, 11 (1983), 1–22

Sanok, Catherine, 'John of Bridlington, Mitred Prior and Model of the Mixed Life', in *Religious Men and Masculine Identity in the Middle Ages*, ed. by P. H. Cullum and Katherine J. Lewis (Woodbridge: Boydell, 2013), pp. 143–59

Sharpe, Richard, *A Handlist of the Latin Writers of Great Britain and Ireland before 1540* (Turnhout: Brepols, 1997)

Smith, David M., Vera C. M. London and C. N. L. Brooke, ed., *The Heads of Religious Houses England & Wales, 940–1540*, 2nd edn, 3 vols (Cambridge: Cambridge University Press, 2001–2008)

Smyly, J. G., 'Thomas Gardiner's History of England', *Hermathena*, 19.43 (1922), 235–48

Thomson, Rodney, *Manuscripts from St Albans Abbey, 1066–1235*, 2 vols (Woodbridge: Brewer, 1982)

——, *A Descriptive Catalogue of the Medieval Manuscripts of Corpus Christi College, Oxford.* (Cambridge: Brewer, 2011)

Vaughan, Richard, 'The Chronicle attributed to John of Wallingford', Camden Miscellany, 21 (London: Royal Historical Society, 1958), pp. 1–67

DAVID E. THORNTON

Northern Saints' Names as Monastic Bynames in Late Medieval and Early Tudor England

The study of the veneration of saints by monastic communities in late medieval and early modern England is facilitated by a variety of extant written and visual sources: the composition and transmission of saints' lives; relic lists; references to individual saints in monastic calendars, litanies, and martyrologies; and the survival of artistic material, including stained glass and paintings. Taken together, these and other sources can provide a detailed insight into the interest in and promotion of the cults of individual saints by houses of monks and regular canons before the Dissolution. One conclusion that may be drawn from such evidence is the fact that the cults of saints were not always merely 'local' in their extent — for instance, associated only or largely with the church or churches founded by the particular saint. Some saints and their cults were of course truly international: in the case of medieval England, the cult of Thomas Beckett is the best known and most widely studied example. However, even within England, the cults of less well-known saints can be traced beyond the obvious reach of the churches and monasteries that housed their relics or penned their hagiographies. Thus, devotional interest in saints of northern English origin and focus may be readily found in the south of the country. One possible means of studying devotion to saints within monastic communities that has hitherto been largely neglected by historians are the surnames or 'bynames' adopted by monks and regular canons on entering religion, that were also the names of saints. These saintly or hagionymic bynames were relatively common in the late fifteenth and early sixteenth centuries: examples include John Aidan, Benedictine monk of Glastonbury, between 1518 and 1539; Thomas Bede, Augustinian canon of Keynsham, in Somerset from 1521 to 1539; and John Cuthbert, Cluniac monk of Bermondsey in Surrey from 1526 to 1540.[1] This essay will seek to show how hagionymic

---

1 Watkin, *Dean Cosyn*, p. 163; Taunton, Somerset Rec. Off., MS D/D/B. Reg. 11 (Wolsey);

> **David Thornton** (tdavid@bilkent.edu.tr) is Assistant Professor in the Department of History, Bilkent University, Ankara, Turkey.

Late Medieval Devotion to Saints from the North of England: New Directions, ed. by Christiania Whitehead, Hazel J. Hunter Blair, and Denis Renevey, MCS 48 (Turnhout: Brepols, 2022), pp. 387–408
BREPOLS ☙ PUBLISHERS   10.1484/M.MCS-EB.5.124359

bynames, especially for the period *c.* 1490–1500, may be employed to study the cults of northern English saints, both in the southern part of the country as well as north of the Humber. Firstly, the existence of the late medieval practice of adopting monastic bynames will be demonstrated and the general distribution pattern of these bynames will briefly be outlined, drawing on data from twenty monasteries in the southern diocese of Worcester. Thereafter, the essay will examine the distribution and nature of the hagionymic bynames, and will then focus more specifically on the bynames seemingly derived from the names of saints of northern English provenance.

What Were Monastic Bynames?

The basic argument of this essay rests upon the indirect evidence that, from at least *c.* 1300 until the Dissolution, the majority of monks and regular canons in England, and to a lesser extent in Wales, ceased to be known generally by their family or hereditary surnames and instead assumed or were given another name, probably following formal admission to their monasteries.[2] Thus, according to Dom David Knowles:

> The modern practice of taking a new name [forename] from a patron saint on entering religion had not begun in the true medieval period. The monk was known by his Christian name, and as the number of these in common use was extremely limited, the toponymic or surname of provenance was by no means superfluous [...] Round about the year 1500 a sudden change of fashion is noticeable. Many of the brethren now bear names which were clearly assumed on entering religion and in some cases follow their Christian names. These names are of two types. The one is made up of the names of saints, usually either fathers of the Church or national figures [...] More curious is another group of names found at Westminster, harbinger of Puritan taste: Goodhaps, Vertue, Charity, Goodluck.[3]

Knowles argues that for most of the late Middle Ages, members of monastic orders assumed a new surname which was derived from a place-name and which, he suggests, indicated their place of origin. Furthermore, towards the end of the period, some monks and canons took on alternative types of surname: either the name of a saint or of a virtue. This new name 'in religion'

Kew, TNA, E322/112; London, Metropolitan Archives, DL/A/A/004/MS09531/010, second series, fols 1ʳ–12ʳ; Kew, TNA, E315/233.

2 I examine the question of monks' and regular canons' names in more detail in Thornton, 'Locus, Sanctus et Virtus'. Also see Thornton, 'How Useful are Episcopal Ordination Lists?'; Thornton, 'The Prosopography of English Monastic Orders'.

3 Knowles, *The Religious Orders*, II, pp. 231–32. See also Greatrex, *The English Benedictine Cathedral Priories*, p. 42; Cross and Vickers, *Monks, Friars and Nuns*, p. 3.

was not hereditary: it had not been inherited from the monk's or canon's father and, prior to the dissolution of the religious orders in England and Wales in the late 1530s, it was not passed on to any offspring. As such, I will hereafter use the phrase 'monastic byname' to distinguish such names from surnames proper. Furthermore, following Knowles, I will refer to place-name bynames as 'toponyms', and I will designate the saintly bynames as 'hagionyms'. It is worth noting at the outset that this apparent pattern of adopting a byname on admission seems to have been restricted to male monastic orders in particular. Preliminary investigation of the names borne by friars and by female religious during the same period would suggest that mendicants, nuns, and canonesses generally retained their family surnames on entering religion.[4] Similarly, the pattern would seem to have been most prevalent in England and, to a lesser extent, in Wales: monks and canons in Scotland and Ireland do not appear to have adopted this onomastic practice.

There is, to my knowledge, no contemporary direct evidence that describes the existence of, and logic behind, this apparent naming practice, but there is sufficient indirect evidence to support its existence. Very rarely, additional biographical information is preserved that throws light upon the naming of individual monks and canons. For example, the Durham *Liber vitae* records a number of fifteenth- and sixteenth-century monks of the cathedral priory alongside members of their families, who often had a surname different from that of the monk. Thus, brother William 'Wylom' (perhaps a toponym referring to Wylam, a village west of Newcastle), monk from *c.* 1513 until the surrender, is recorded among the relatives — presumably children — of John *Watson* and his wife Alice. He occurs later however as William Watson, prebendary of the cathedral (1541–1556).[5] In addition, material from the period of the Dissolution sometimes provides insights into the names of former religious. Thus, many monks and canons are recorded in the deeds of surrender or in the pension lists, either with a completely different surname to the one they had used while an active religious, or with two surnames.[6] For example, brother Walter Bede, monk of Winchcombe Abbey around 1534, occurs in post-Dissolution documents as

---

4 The documentary evidence for studying the prosopography of nuns and canonesses is of course more restricted than that for male religious, as women were not ordained. Although there is a growing consensus that late medieval English nuns were not as exclusively aristocratic in origin as had been previously assumed, it does seem likely that even those of more middling social status retained their family surname on admission. However, a more general survey of what evidence is available for nunneries may throw up some clearer patterns. In particular, I wonder whether Gilbertine nuns may have adopted toponyms, like the canons: in 1379/80, over seventy-five per cent of nuns of Ormsby and Watton had toponymic surnames, about seventy per cent at Alvingham, Bullington, and Sixhills, and over sixty per cent at Catsby and Shouldham: Kew, TNA, E179/35/7, E179/45/9, E179/68/11; Stephenson, *The Gilbertine Priory of Watton*, pp. 34–35.

5 *The Durham Liber vitae*, ed. by Rollason and Rollason, III, pp. 420–21.

6 On this, see Thornton, 'The Prosopography of English Monastic Orders', pp. 45–49.

Walter Turbott.[7] Some brethren are mentioned in documents at the time of the Dissolution with an additional surname or 'alias'. For instance, Thomas Oswald, monk of Worcester Cathedral Priory (1534–1540), occurs in a list of stipendiary priests in 1540 as 'dom. Thomas Webbe *alias* Oswald',[8] and we may assume that Webbe had been his surname prior to entering religion.

In addition, the evidence of wills made after the Dissolution by former religious, now secular clerks, would support the view that many adopted bynames. From the south of England, for instance, I have identified the wills of seven former Benedictine monks of St Peter's Abbey, Gloucester; in each case, the individual in question continued to use the same name that he had borne in religion, both at the surrender of the abbey and when making his will.[9] In a number of cases, bequests were made to relatives whose surname was different from that of the former monk.[10] It seems likely therefore that the last generation of monks of Gloucester adopted bynames on admission and continued to be known by these bynames after the surrender of their abbey. The patterns for other monasteries, especially in the north of England, are less consistent, however. For Kirkstall Abbey, Yorkshire, of the ten monks whose later wills may be identified with some degree of certainty, half occur as testators with a surname *different* from the name they used while in religion, and some make bequests to relatives who also have this different surname.[11] This suggests that these monks changed their names on admission but resumed using their surnames at the Dissolution. A number of monks however do not seem to have

---

7 Kew, TNA, E25/120/1; London, Lambeth Pal. Lib., MS Cart. Ant. et Misc. XI/56; Kew, TNA, E315/494/1, pp. 75–76, E315/245, fol. 154; BL, MS Add. 8102; Kew, TNA, E164/31.

8 Thornton, 'The Last Monks', p. 14.

9 *A Calendar of Wills*, ed. by Phillimore and Duncan, pp. 4 (Edward Bennett), 14 (Walter Stanley), 15 (Philip Oxford), 17 (William Augustine), 19 (Richard Frocester), 35 (Thomas Kingswood); Kew, TNA, PROB 11/28/221 (Thomas Bisley).

10 Thus, Edward Bennett, ordained 1527–1528 and later prebendary canon of Gloucester Cathedral, whose will is dated 29 August 1545, made a bequest to his brother named William Mychell. More telling, Richard Frocester, ordained 1508–1510, and later minor canon at the cathedral, made his will on 18 July 1554 in which he called himself 'Richard Frowcetter alias Smarte' and made bequests to his brothers Thomas Smart and William Smart, and to the latter's son Thomas Smart. See also, Thornton. 'The Last Monks', pp. 14–15; and Thornton, 'The Prosopography of English Monastic Orders', pp. 56–57.

11 For example, the monk Robert Preston, ordained *c.* 1527, may be identified with Robert Hemsworth in the Kirkstall pension list of 1539, and in turn is probably the Robert Hemsworth who in his will of 23 March 1553 termed himself 'of Preston in the parish of Kippax, clerk' and who made bequests to relatives surnamed Hemsworth: Cross and Vickers, *Monks, Friars and Nuns*, pp. 141–42, 146; York, Borthwick Inst. for Archives, Prob. Reg. 13/2, fol. 974ᵛ. Even more likely, his former confrère Edward Pountfrete, ordained 1505–1507, may be identified with the Kirkstall pensioner Edward Heptonstall and thus with the testator Sir Edward Heptonstall 'otherwise called Sir Edward Pomfret', priest, who requested burial in the parish church at Leeds and whose beneficiaries include relatives surnamed Heptonstall: Cross and Vickers, *Monks, Friars and Nuns*, pp. 140, 142, 146; York, Borthwick Inst. for Archives, Prob. Reg. 15/3, fol. 59ᵛ.

ceased using their surnames in the first place, when entering the Kirkstall community.[12] A similarly mixed onomastic pattern can be found at other monasteries in the north of England: of the twelve ex-monks of Durham Cathedral Priory whose wills can be identified, nine occur as testators with the same name they had borne in religion and at least five of these make bequests to relatives who also bear the same surname.[13] Thus, while many sixteenth-century monks and regular canons in the south of England would seem to have maintained the late medieval tradition of adopting a monastic byname on admission, a number of their contemporaries in the North appear simply to have continued using their family surnames when entering religion. The question of the varying usage of monastic bynames in the North c. 1490–1540 will be examined in more detail below, as it will have a bearing upon our analysis of the northern hagionyms.

Previous studies of monastic naming have generally focused on the evidence from one monastery, usually as part of a broader examination of the history of that house.[14] How far such evidence from a single religious house may be representative of broader trends is not clear, however. Thus, to gain a more comprehensive understanding of naming patterns, I have collected the names of monks and regular canons of multiple religious houses from a broader locality within the south of England where, as noted above, the use of bynames would seem to have continued into the sixteenth century. To date, 4256 brethren have been identified from twenty monasteries in the diocese of Worcester between 1300 and 1540, and the names of 3876 of these monks and canons have been analysed according to type.[15] The results are summarized in Table 17.1.[16]

---

12 Thus, John Lister, ordained 1533–1535, occurs in the pension list with the same name and is possibly the secular clerk John Lister, of Hollym in Holderness, who in his will of 7 July 1562 bequeathed various items to his godson Christopher Lister: Cross and Vickers, *Monks, Friars and Nuns*, pp. 142, 147; York, Borthwick Inst. for Archives, Prob. Reg. 17/1, fols 238[r–v]. Kirkstall Abbey, we might note, had earlier appropriated the chapel in Hollym.

13 *Wills and Inventories*, ed. by Raine, pp. 130–31 (Ralph Blaxston), 172–73 (Robert Bennett), 217–21 (John Binley), 269 (William Todd), 283 (Alexander Durham alias Woodmons), 288–89 (John Duckett), 312 (John Forster), 407 (Richard Foster); Raine, ed., *History and Antiquities*, pp. 128–29 (Thomas Spark); Durham Univ. Lib., Archives and Spec. Coll., MSS DPR/1/1/1584/B6/1 (William Bennett), DPR/1/1/1574/W3/1 (William Maurice alias Watson), and DPR/1/2/2, fols 17[v]–18[r] (Roger Bell alias Watson).

14 For a notable exception, see Cross and Vickers, *Monks, Friars and Nuns*.

15 For this data-set, see Thornton, 'How Useful Are Episcopal Ordination Lists?'

16 I have not yet been able to determine the origin/meaning of some of the missing 380 names. In addition, those names that are first attested after 1537 are also not included, because many monks and canons resumed using their family surnames at this time.

Table 17.1. Distribution of surnames of monks and canons before 1537.

Surname Type	Percentage
French	2.6%
Hagionymic	2.3%
Nickname	1.9%
Occupational	2.3%
Patronymic	4.2%
Toponymic	80.1%
Topographical or toponymic	6.5%
Virtue	0.1%

About eighty per cent of the monks and canons had toponymic bynames, and this increases to eighty-six per cent if we include topographical names such as Lee, Pool, and Stone, which might equally have been place-names. These figures agree with what historians have observed at some other monasteries in late medieval England.[17] Such a high percentage of toponymic bynames stands in contrast to evidence for the types of surnames borne by the laity during the same period, where locative surnames, though relatively common, rarely exceed thirty per cent.[18] Furthermore, if the data from the diocese of Worcester is arranged chronologically, by decade of first attestation of the bearer (Figure 17.1), then it can be seen that toponyms consistently account for between eighty and ninety per cent of monastic bynames until the early sixteenth century, falling to about fifty per cent by the second half of the 1530s.

On the other hand, Figure 17.1 also indicates that bynames which, with varying degrees of certainty, may be categorized as hagionymic, show the opposite trend: such saintly names hover at around one or two per cent for most of the period, and then begin to increase during the 1490s, reaching a peak of over twenty per cent in the 1520s. The data from the diocese of Worcester thus suggests that, in the south of England, most monks and regular canons adopted toponymic bynames on admission, though by the late fifteenth century the alternative use of hagionymic bynames began to develop. As we have seen above however, evidence from the North indicates that, by the

---

17 For example, Dobson, *Church and Society*, p. 56; Dobson, 'Recent Prosopographical Research', pp. 188–89; Dobson, 'The Monks of Canterbury', p. 118. Not all studies agree with this pattern however. For Torre Abbey, for example, only fifty-five per cent of the Premonstratensian canons attested there during the fourteenth century had toponyms, and this declined further to thirty-nine per cent in the fifteenth century and thirty-four per cent in the sixteenth: Jenkins, 'Torre Abbey', pp. 232–33.

18 For example, McKinley, *Surnames of Lancashire*, pp. 77–79; Postles, *The Surnames of Devon*, pp. 110–11; Postles, *The Surnames of Leicestershire and Rutland*, pp. 130, 134; McKinley, *A History of British Surnames*, pp. 22–23; Reaney, *The Origin of English Surnames*, pp. 22–23.

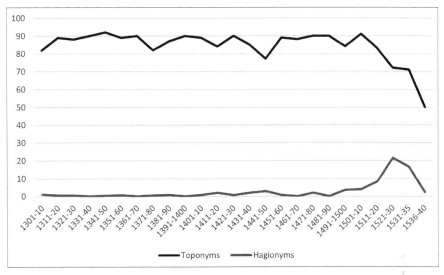

FIGURE 17.1. Toponymic/topographical and hagionymic surnames in the diocese of Worcester (as percentage by decade).

period of the Dissolution at least, male religious in that part of the country were adopting monastic bynames — of any type — less frequently than in the south, and this fact means that fewer hagionyms are attested at northern monasteries (see below).

Analysing Hagionymic Data: The Challenges

In order to understand the distribution and possible function of hagionymic bynames as evidence for monastic interest in saints' cults, and especially those from the North, ordination lists from most English dioceses between c. 1300 and 1540 have been consulted.[19] The result is a database of over 1150 monks and regular canons whose names may refer to saints. Of these 1150 or so monks and canons, about one fifth (twenty-one per cent) bore hagionymic bynames that may refer to insular saints and other British or Irish figures active before the eleventh century. These include about seventy monks and canons who bore up to fifteen different hagionymic bynames that may refer to so-called 'northern' English saints. A sample of northern hagionyms is given in Table 17.2.

---

19 To date, I have consulted episcopal ordination records, published and unpublished, from most dioceses except the diocese of Norwich and the unpublished registers for Exeter. See Smith, *Guide to Bishops' Registers*.

394   DAVID E. THORNTON

Table 17.2. Some English hagionymic bynames of northern provenance.

Name	Order	Monastery	Dates
Robert Aidan	OSB	Bardney, Lincolnshire	1521–1522
Thomas Bede	OSA	Keynsham, Somerset	1521–1534+
Bryan Bee	OCart.	Axholme, Lincolnshire	1537–1540
John Cuthbert	OSA	Southwark, Surrey	1539
John Cuthbert	OClun.	Bermondsey, Surrey	1526–1540
William Oswald	OSA	Bristol, Gloucestershire	1492–1504
Thomas Wilfrid	OSB	Canterbury Christ Church, Kent	1507–1519

As is often the case with analyses of onomastic data, the exact explanation and interpretation of individual hagionymic bynames are not always certain. For instance, there is strong evidence to suggest that most of the apparently saintly bynames attested before the last decades of the fifteenth century may not actually be hagionymic as such. The byname of Roger de Sancto Botulpho, Cistercian of Vale Royal, Cheshire, in 1332, may not be a direct reference to St Botulph but rather to Boston, Lincolnshire, which took its name from the saint. Indeed, brother Roger occurs later as de Botulfston, that is 'of Boston'.[20] In other cases, seemingly saintly surnames such as Francis, James, and Lawrence were used — though relatively rarely — as forenames in the late Middle Ages, and so could here be patronymic surnames. Consequently, the following analyses will focus mostly on those saintly bynames which are attested in the late fifteenth and early sixteenth centuries and which, therefore, are more likely to have been hagionymic in origin. Furthermore, the exact identity of the eponymous saint is not always apparent for every hagionymic byname. Thus, for instance, the frequently attested byname 'Benet' and the less common form 'Benedict' — on which, see below — may have been a reference to St Benedict of Nursia, but an alternative identification could be the northern English monastic founder and saint Benedict Biscop.

Based upon the representative, but admittedly not exhaustive, database of 1150 hagionym-bearing monks and canons, it would seem that the practice of adopting hagionymic bynames was more common in certain religious houses than others and, by extension, among the Benedictines than the other monastic orders, as shown in Figure 17.2.[21]

Although the Benedictines made up about a third of the male monastic population in the period 1500–1534 (thirty per cent), they account for more than fifty per cent of the hagionymic — and 'possibly hagionymic' — bynames in the database. The Augustinian canons, in contrast, who comprised a similar

---

20 Stafford, Staffs. Rec. Off., MS B/A/1/2, fols 166ᵛ, 169ᵛ.
21 Figure 17.2 is based on data from Knowles and Hadcock, *Medieval Religious Houses*, pp. 489–92.

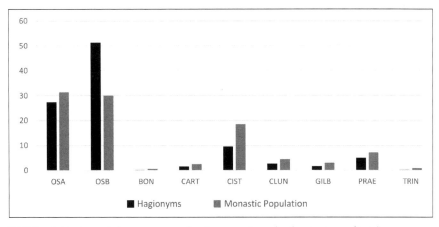

FIGURE 17.2. Hagionymic bynames according to monastic order (percentage of total).

proportion of the monastic population (31.5 per cent), account for only 27.5 per cent of the saintly names. This is partly due to the fact that there are a small number of monasteries, all Benedictine, for which vastly more brethren with hagionyms are attested: the front-runner by far is Glastonbury Abbey with eighty-one monks; this is followed well behind by Christ Church Canterbury (fifty-eight), St Albans (thirty-eight), Winchcombe (thirty-three), and Westminster Abbey (thirty-one). Taken together, these five Benedictine houses account for about twenty per cent of the total.

Similarly, certain individual saints' names are far more common than others, as illustrated in Figure 17.3. The overall winner is Benet (occasionally 'Benedict') with ninety attestations, followed by Martin (with sixty), Alban (forty) and Augustine (or 'Austin') with thirty-eight. Benet, of course, may not always be a hagionym but instead a patronymic, and many of the cases of Alban — especially those of the earlier form de Sancto Albano — may be toponymic in origin. Lastly, it should be noted that very few female saints are attested as hagionymic bynames; those that are mostly occur before the late fifteenth century and are also probably toponymic in origin.[22]

Northern Saints and Hagionymic Bynames

With the foregoing provisos in mind, there were a number of monks and regular canons who had hagionymic bynames that may, with varying degrees of certainty, refer to saints of northern English provenance: that is, saints

---

22 For example, William *de St Radegund*, monk of Rochester in 1333–1335; Thomas *de Sancta Ositha*, canon of Colchester, in 1379; and Robert *de Sancta Ositha*, canon of St Osyths, in 1386: Greatrex, *Biographical Register*, p. 633; London Metropolitan Archives, DL/A/A/004/MS09531/003; London, Lambeth Pal. Lib., Archb. Reg. Sudbury, fols 145^r–150^v.

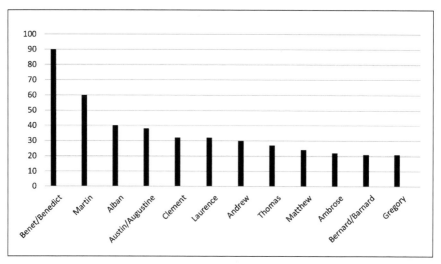

FIGURE 17.3. Most common hagionyms (total numbers).

and other holy men who originated from and/or were active in the region encompassed by the Anglo-Saxon kingdom of Northumbria. As demonstrated by Table 17.3, not all northern hagionyms are found associated with religious houses in the north of England (where the cults of the relevant saints would have been most widespread).

Here we see that, as already noticed, the distribution of hagionyms overall is mostly in the southern part of England and that, for Somerset in particular, there is a very high absolute number of hagionyms of northern and possible northern English origin. However, if the same figures are analysed as percentages, then the English counties with a higher percentage of northern hagionyms are those in the North: Northumberland, Durham, Cumberland, and Yorkshire, as well as Derbyshire. This would suggest that, while the use of monastic bynames in general, and hagionymic bynames in particular, was mainly popular in the south of England, the use of northern saints for monastic hagionyms was still significant in the North.

Of the hagionyms of northern English saints, the most frequently attested is Cuthbert: fourteen monks and canons who had this byname have been identified, as summarized in Table 17.4.[23] It should be noted that the four canons of Alnwick Abbey and two of the monks of Durham with the byname Cuthbert all date from the early to mid-fifteenth century, a little before the trend for hagionymic bynames is thought to have taken off. It is possible that

---

23 I am assuming that the Gilbertine canon Christopher Cuthbert ordained in 1505/7 when at Bullington is the same man as the canon of that name who was at Sixhills Priory in 1539: Lincoln, Lincs. Archives, Episc. Reg. XXIV [no pagination], *sub dat.* 22 March 1504/5 and 3 April 1507; *Faculty Office Registers*, ed. by Chambers, p. 172.

NORTHERN SAINTS' NAMES AS MONASTIC BYNAMES   397

Table 17.3. Distribution of northern hagionymic bynames by county, c. 1300–1540.

County	Hagionyms (total)	North. Hagionyms (total)	North. Hagionyms (%)	County	Hagionyms (total)	North. Hagionyms (total)	North. Hagionyms (%)
Beds.	18	1	5.5	Lancs.	10	1	10
Cumb.	6	1	16.6	Lincs.	51	4	7.8
Derby.	3	1	33.3	Nhumb.	10	4	40
Devon	47	2	4.3	Som.	144	15	10.4
Durh.	13	4	30.8	Staffs.	11	1	9.1
Essex	38	1	2.6	Surrey	44	2	4.5
Gloucs.	77	5	6.5	Sussex	58	3	5.2
Hants.	56	1	1.8	Warws.	15	1	6.6
Herts.	47	1	2.1	Worcs.	18	2	11.1
Kent	123	4	3.2	Yorks.	34	6	17.6

Table 17.4. The hagionymic byname Cuthbert.

Monastery	Order	Name	Dates
Alnwick	OPraer.	John Cudberde	1419–1435
Alnwick	OPraer.	John Cuthbert	1433
Alnwick	OPraer.	Robert Cuthbert	1437
Alnwick	OPraer.	Robert Cuthbert	1472
Athelney	OSB	Ludovicus Cuthbert	1516
Battle	OSB	Thomas Cutbert	1538–1539
Bermondsey	OClun.	John Cutberte	1526–1540
Bullington/Sixhills	Gilb.	Christopher Cutbert / Cuthberde	1505–1539
Durham	OSB	George Cuthbert	1528–1558
Durham	OSB	William Cuthbert *senior*	1440–1474
Durham	OSB	William Cuthbert *junior*	1460–1496
Meaux	OCist.	Robert Cuthbert	1488–1489
Southwark	OSA	John Cuthbert	1539
Winchcombe	OSB	John Cuthbert	1534

398   DAVID E. THORNTON

at least some of these men bore family surnames. On the other hand, the monks of Athelney, Battle, Bermondsey, and Winchcombe, and the canon of Southwark, all date from the sixteenth century. What encouraged these brethren of southern religious houses to adopt a seemingly northern hagionym?

To explore this question further, we may examine the well-documented case of Glastonbury Abbey. As noted above, Glastonbury generated the largest group of hagionymic bynames collected to date and this partly accounts for the relatively high number of northern hagionyms in Somerset. This group of bynames has accordingly drawn the attention of historians who have noted that the relevant eponymous saints are also associated with the abbey in other ways.[24] Indeed, if we only consider those monks who are first attested *after* 1450 (sixty-two in total), then about ninety-seven per cent (sixty in total) had bynames of saints and other figures associated in some way with the history and liturgy of the abbey.[25] This data is summarized in Table 17.5: the first column gives the forms of the relevant byname; the second, the number of monks who bore that byname; the third column suggests probable identifications of the relevant eponymous saint(s); and the final column summarizes the nature of the saint's association with Glastonbury.

Identification of the most likely saintly source for particular bynames is relatively straightforward in some cases: for example, it is probable that the four monks Thomas *Dunstone* (1495–1539), John *Dunstan* (1513–1524), William *Dunstane* (1515–1539), and Robert *Dunstone* (1523–1526), all derived their common byname from the tenth-century ecclesiastical reformer Dunstan, archbishop of Canterbury and *quondam* abbot of Glastonbury. On the other hand, some identifications are less certain: the byname of brother William *Edmond*, ordained 1469–1471, has up to four possible saintly sources associated with Glastonbury.[26]

---

24   Carley, *Glastonbury Abbey*, p. 75; Dunning, 'Revival at Glastonbury', pp. 218–19; Watkin, 'Glastonbury 1538–9'. I am very grateful to Mark Hutchinson, doctoral student at the University of Exeter, for kindly sharing his thoughts and prosopographical data on Glastonbury Abbey with me.

25   The sources for, and modern literature on, Glastonbury are vast. The following have been used to prepare Table 17.5: William of Malmesbury, *Early History*, ed. and trans. by Scott; John of Glastonbury, *Chronicle*, ed. and trans. by Carley and Townsend; Carley and Howley, 'Relics at Glastonbury'; Howley, 'Relics at Glastonbury Abbey'; Krochalis, '*Magna Tabula*'; Blows, 'A Glastonbury Obit-List'; *English Monastic Litanies*, ed. by Morgan, I, pp. 164–66; III, pp. 33–34.

26   The possible sources are Edmund the Martyr, king of East Anglia (d. 869/870) if he was the St Edmund whose *camisia* the abbey claimed to possess and for whom prayers are invoked in BL, MS Add. 64952; Edmund 'Senior', king of the English (d. 946), who donated relics to the abbey and was said to have been buried there himself; Edmund Ironside, king of the English (d. 1016), another benefactor, also allegedly interred at Glastonbury; and Edmund Rich, archbishop of Canterbury (d. 1240) whose bones and skin were held by the abbey.

NORTHERN SAINTS' NAMES AS MONASTIC BYNAMES

Table 17.5. Monastic bynames at Glastonbury, derived from saints and other figures (first attested *after* 1450).[27]

D: Donor of property and/or relics to Glastonbury Abbey
H: Figure recorded in history or legends of Glastonbury Abbey
L: Name recorded in calendars and litanies of Glastonbury Abbey, and the obit list
R: Saint whose body or relics were allegedly housed within Glastonbury Abbey

Forms of Byname	Monks (no.)	Saint/Figure	Glast. link
Elphege, Elpegus	1	1. Ælfheah, ealdorman	DL
		2. Ælfheah, mk Glast, archb Cant	HLR
		3. Ælfheah, bish Winchester	L
Alwynus, Alvernon	1	Ælfwine, ealdorman, mk Glast	DHLR
Adelwoldus, Athelbold, Ethelwold	2	Æthelwold, mk Glast, bish Winchester	DHLR
Albane	1	Alban, proto-martyr	LR
Aldelme, Adelam	1	Aldhelm, abb Malmesbury	L
Ambrose	2	Ambrose, St	LR
Andrew, Andrewe, Androw	2	Andrew, St, apostle	LR
Anselm	1	Anselm, St, archb Cant	
Appollynar, Appollyneer	1	Apollinarius of Ravenna, martyr	LR
ab Arimathy, ab Aramathia	2	Arimathea [Joseph of]	HLR
Arthur	1	Arthur, king	HR
Athelstan, Athelstone	1	Athelstan Half King, ealdorman, mk Glast	DLR
Aydan, Aydane, Aydanus	2	Aidan, bishop Lindisfarne	LR
Baptista, Baptyst	1	Baptist [John the]	LR
Barnard	1	Bernard of Clairvaux, St	
Basill, Besill, Besyll	1	1. Basilus, St	L
		2. Besilius, martyr	R
		3. Boisil, prior Melrose	R
Bede	1	Bede, mk Jarrow	LR

27 In addition, the forms (in print) of the name of a monk variously called John Allendo(r)/ Allendot and John Alrude, 1534–39, may derive from 'Ailnoth' (Æthelnoth). If so, there are at least three possible Glastonbury sources: a Glastonbury monk who went on to be archbishop of Canterbury (1020–1038), mentioned by William of Malmesbury; an abbot of Glastonbury deposed by Lanfranc in 1078; and an ealdorman who donated relics to the abbey.

Forms of Byname	Monks (no.)	Saint/Figure	Glast. link
Benett	1	1. Benedict Biscop, abb	LR
		2. Benedict of Nursia, St	LR
Bennynge, Bynnyne, Benygne	2	1. Benignus, disciple of St Patrick	HLR
		2. Benignus of Dijon, St	LR
Britwolde, Brytwold	1	1. Beorhtwald/Beorwald, abb Glast	DH
		2. Brihtwold, mk Glast, bish Ramsbury	DHLR
Kentwyne, Kentwinus	1	Centwine, king Wessex	DR
Ceolfryde, Ceolfrede	1	Ceolfrith, abb Wearmouth	LR
Crosse	1	1. The Cross of Jesus	R
		2. Arthur's Cross	R
		3. Lesser crosses	R
Deruvian, Deryvyan, Dyrwyan	1	Deruvian, St, missionary	HR
Dunstan, Dunstane, Dunston, Dunstone	4	Dunstan, St, abb Glast, archb Cant	HLR
Edgar, Edgare	2	Edgar, king	DLR
Edmond	1	1. Edmund I, king East Anglia	DLR
		2. Edmund Ironside, king	DLR
		3. Edmund, king, martyr	LR
		4. Edmund, archb Cant	R
Gilde, Gylde, Glyde	1	Gildas, St	HLR
Herstanus, Herstane, Herstone, Hirstane	1	Heorstan, father of St Dunstan	H
Indract, Indracte, Endracte, Yndratte	2	Indracht, martyr	HLR
Ine, Yne, Yeve, Iva	1	Ine, king of Wessex	DL
Joseph, Yosephe	2	Joseph of Arimathea	HLR
Marke, Merke	2	Mark, St, evangelist	LR
Marten, Martyn	1	Martin, bish Tours	LR
Mathow	1	Matthew, St, evangelist	LR
Maure, Mawre, Mare, Mary	2	Maurus, St	L
Neot, Neott	1	Neot, St, mk Glast	HL

Forms of Byname	Monks (no.)	Saint/Figure	Glast. link
Oswolde, Eswolde	1	1. Oswald, king Northumbria, martyr	LR
		2. Oswald, bish Worcester, archb York	L
Pantaleon, Pantalion, Pantales	1	Pantaleon, St, martyr	LR
Patrick, Patricius	1	Patrick, St	DHLR
Pawlyn, Pauly, Pallye	1	Paulinus, bish York, bish Rochester	HLR
Phagan, Phegan	1	Phagan, St, missionary	HR
Ultan, Woltane	1	Ultan, bishop	R
Urban, Urbane, Urbayn	2	Urban, pope, martyr	LR
Walter	1	1. Walter de Cantilupe, bish Worcester	R
		2. Walter de Cowick	R
Wylfryd	1	Wilfrid, bish York	L
Ider, Yder, Ydar	1	Yder/Eder ap Nudd, Arthurian knight	HR

As Table 17.5 demonstrates, late fifteenth- and early sixteenth-century monks of Glastonbury who bore hagionyms rather than toponyms as their monastic bynames would seem to have used saints and royal figures who formed part of the liturgy and history of their abbey as it came to be formulated during the High and later Middle Ages and/or whose relics the abbey claimed to possess. Thus, for instance, the feast day of St Paulinus (10 October), missionary bishop of York and later bishop of Rochester, was recorded in the pre-Conquest calendars at Glastonbury; by the twelfth century at least, there was a tradition that Paulinus had undertaken building improvements at the abbey church; and finally, most later relic lists claim that the monastery possessed the relics of this saint. The bynames of brother William *Josephe*, attested 1525–1539, and of his contemporaries Robert *ab Aramathia*, 1505–1526, and John *ab Arimathy*, 1524–1539, would all seem to refer to Joseph of Arimathea, another figure closely linked to Glastonbury legends. Non-ecclesiastical figures include royal patrons of the abbey, such as King Arthur, whose legend is inextricably tied with Glastonbury where he was allegedly buried, and the early kings of Wessex, Ine and Centwine. Lastly, the byname of William Crosse, attested 1498–1501, could, at a pinch, refer to one of a number of crosses that are recorded in the Glastonbury relic lists.[28]

---

28 On the Cross of Arthur, see Rahtz and Watts, *Glastonbury: Myth and Archaeology*, pp. 58–59. There was also a John *Crosse*, prior of Glastonbury (1445–1459) but his byname is too early to be included in the data presented in Table 17.5.

This link between monks' bynames and saints associated with the same monastery can be paralleled at other religious houses, including a number located in the north of England. For example, Table 17.6 shows eight different hagionymic bynames borne by monks of Durham, of which five may be linked to saints associated with the cathedral priory.[29]

Table 17.6. Hagionymic bynames from Durham, c. 1420–1540.

Name	No. of bearers	Associated cult/relics?
Benet	2	Y
Cuthbert	3	Y
Daniel	1	
Dennis	1	Y
Edward	1	Y
Mark	1	
Matthew	1	
Patrick	1	Y

Apart from the obvious association with St Cuthbert and his cult, thirteenth- and fourteenth-century relic lists claim that, like other major Benedictine houses, the priory had hundreds of relics, including those of Sts Dionysius and Edward the Confessor, the vestments of St Benedict, and the bones and other relics of St Patrick.[30] The monastic promotion of saints' cults in England during the late Middle Ages, through preservation of hagiographical legends and the collection of relics, was especially associated with the older Benedictine houses — the larger abbeys and cathedral priories that in many cases could trace their foundation before 1066. It is probably not coincidental therefore that it is mostly, though not exclusively, at these same Benedictine houses that the majority of the recorded hagionymic bynames are found, as we have seen above. However, the new monastic orders were not to be outdone, although the evidence is often less forthcoming. For example, at the Cistercian house at Meaux, Yorkshire, in 1488–1489, we find a monk called Robert Cuthbert, and the abbey did claim to possess relics of St Cuthbert, including clothing, skin, hair, and his handkerchief.[31]

It is notable that as many as nine monks of Glastonbury appear to have derived their hagionyms from the names of saints of northern England: Aidan

---

29 Not surprisingly, the evangelists Mark and Matthew also occur in the Durham litanies: *English Monastic Litanies*, ed. by Morgan, I, pp. 100–01.

30 *Historiae Dunelmensis scriptores tres*, ed. by Raine, pp. ccccxxvi–ccccxxx; *Extracts from the Account Rolls*, ed. by Fowler, pp. 425–35.

31 Cross and Vickers, *Monks, Friars and Nuns*, p. 153; Thomas, 'The Cult of Saints' Relics', pp. 517, 520.

NORTHERN SAINTS' NAMES AS MONASTIC BYNAMES   403

(2), Bede, Benedict Biscop, Boisil (possibly), Ceolfrith, Oswald, Paulinus, and Wilfrid. The first five of these were part of a specific group of Northumbrian saints whose relics the abbey claimed to possess.[32] There were two traditions of how these northern relics reached Glastonbury. One, recorded in the *De antiquitate* of William of Malmesbury (ch. 21), attributed their translation to an eighth-century Northumbrian cleric Ticca who, fleeing from Viking raids in the North, allegedly came south with the relics to Glastonbury where he became abbot.[33] An alternative account, also mentioned in passing in the *De antiquitate* (ch. 52) but elaborated in later sources, including John of Glastonbury, claims that the northern relics — to which are added those of Oswald, king of Northumbria — were given to Glastonbury by Edmund I, king of the English (d. 946).[34] Regarding these northern relics, we possess additional early evidence that relics of St Aidan and Abbot Ceolfrith were housed at Glastonbury before 1066, and a number of the other northern saints were also recorded in pre-Conquest Glastonbury calendars.[35] The acquisition by Glastonbury Abbey, by whatever alleged means, of the relics of northern English saints, including those of some less popular saints, and the development of the cult of those saints at the abbey, must surely explain the occurrence of many of these northern saints as likely sources for hagionymic bynames at Glastonbury during the late fifteenth and early sixteenth century.

In fact, Glastonbury was by no means unique. As we have seen, northern saints may also be identified as bynames at other, less well-documented southern Benedictine houses, though not to the same extent. Research into monastic names at nearby Winchcombe Abbey has produced up to thirty-three hagionymic bynames to date, of which four may refer to northern saints. These include Bede, Cuthbert, and two instances of Oswald — though, in this case, it is probably more likely that the name refers to the tenth-century monastic reformer Oswald, bishop of Worcester and archbishop of York, who founded Winchcombe. The occurrence here of Bede and Cuthbert is interesting, because we know that the penultimate abbot of Winchcombe, the learned Richard Kidderminster (1488–1525), while on a visit to northern Benedictine monasteries in 1513, had been delighted to discover that Durham Cathedral Priory ultimately owed its (re)foundation in 1083 to Ealdwine, prior of Winchcombe, much to the local monks' chagrin apparently.[36] The bynames Bede and Cuthbert are both relatively late at Winchcombe — neither bearer is attested before 1534 — and it may be possible that interest in these

---

32 Krochalis, '*Magna Tabula*' (1997), pp. 106–07.
33 William of Malmesbury, *Early History*, ed. by Scott, p. 21.
34 John of Glastonbury, *Chronicle*, ed. and trans. by Carley and Townsend, p. 122; Carley and Howley, 'Relics at Glastonbury', pp. 112–13.
35 Rollason, 'Lists of Saints' Resting-Places', pp. 71, 92; Gransden, 'The Growth of the Glastonbury Traditions', p. 345 n. 3.
36 Knowles, *Religious Orders*, III, p. 93.

northern saints at Winchcombe had been inspired by Abbot Kidderminster's 'discovery' of his abbey's links with Durham.[37]

Conclusion

This essay has argued there is evidence that, between *c*. 1300 and 1540, many monks and regular canons in England adopted new surnames or 'monastic bynames' on entering religion. For the most part, these bynames were toponymic in character and were probably derived from the place of birth or recent provenance of their bearers. From the late fifteenth century onwards, however, some monks and canons, especially Benedictine monks, alternatively took on a byname that was the name of a (male) saint. In a number of well-documented cases, it is possible to associate the relevant saint with the monk or canon's respective monastery, for example, in relic lists and litanies. Thus, at Glastonbury, the names of a number of saints of northern English origin whose relics rest within the abbey, occur as hagionyms borne by its monks. Accordingly, it might be argued that the occurrence of hagionymic bynames at other, less well-documented religious houses may suggest the possible existence of a cult of, or devotion to, the relevant saints at those houses. More generally, the occurrence of northern hagionymic bynames at monasteries throughout England during the late fifteenth and early sixteenth centuries may provide an additional means of tracing the cults of the northern saints.

---

37 On the other hand, Cuthbert occurs in the twelfth-century litany of Winchcombe, though Bede does not: *English Monastic Litanies*, ed. by Morgan, II, p. 103. Unfortunately, no relic list survives from Winchcombe. Furthermore, Nigel Morgan has highlighted the popularity of the cult of Cuthbert throughout medieval England: *English Monastic Litanies*, III, p. 97. Both Bede and Cuthbert also occur as bynames at Battle Abbey.

Works Cited

Manuscripts and Archival Sources

Durham University Library, Archives and Special Collections,
MS DPR/I/1/1584/B6/1
——, MS DPR/I/1/1574/W3/1
——, MS DPR/1/2/2
Kew, The National Archives, E25/120/1
——, E164/31
——, E179/35/7
——, E179/45/9
——, E179/68/11
——, E315/233
——, E315/245
——, E315/494/1
——, E322/112
——, PROB 11/28
Lincoln, Lincolnshire Archives, Episcopal Register XXIV
London, British Library, MS Additional 64952
——, MS Additional 8102
London, Lambeth Palace Library, Archbishops Registers, Register Sudbury
——, MS Cart. Ant. et Misc. XI/56
London, Metropolitan Archives, DL/A/A/004/MS09531/003
——, DL/A/A/004/MS09531/010
Stafford, Staffordshire Record Office, MS B/A/1/2
Taunton, Somerset Record Office, MS D/D/B. Reg. 11
York, Borthwick Institute for Archives (BIA), Probate Register 13/2
——, Probate Register 15/3
——, Probate Register 17/1

Primary Sources

*A Calendar of Wills Proved in the Consistory Court of the Bishop of Gloucester,
1541–1650, with an Appendix of Dispersed Wills and Wills proved in the Peculiar
Courts of Bibury and Bishop's Cleeve*, ed. by W. P. W. Phillimore and Leland L.
Duncan (London: British Record Society, 1895)
The Durham Liber vitae: London, British Library, MS Cotton Domitian A. VII, ed.
by David Rollason and Lynda Rollason, 3 vols (London: British Library,
2007)
English Monastic Litanies of the Saints after 1100, ed. by Nigel Morgan, Henry
Bradshaw Society, 119–20, 123 (Woodbridge: Boydell, 2012–2018)
*Extracts from the Account Rolls of the Abbey of Durham, from the Original MSS,
Vol. II*, ed. by J. T. Fowler, SS, 100 (London: Surtees Society, 1899)

Faculty Office Registers 1534–1549: A Calendar of the First Two Registers of the Archbishop of Canterbury's Faculty Office, ed. by D. S. Chambers (Oxford: Clarendon Press, 1966)

Historiae Dunelmensis scriptores tres, Gaufridus de Coldingham, Robertus de Graystanes, et Willielmus de Chambre, ed. by James Raine, SS, 9 (London: Surtees Society, 1839)

John of Glastonbury, *Chronicle of Glastonbury Abbey: An Edition, Translation and Study of John of Glastonbury's Cronica sive antiquitate*, ed. and trans. by James P. Carley and David Townsend (Woodbridge: Boydell, 2009)

William of Malmesbury, *The Early History of Glastonbury: An Edition, Translation, and Study of William of Malmesbury's De antiquitate Glastonie ecclesie*, ed. and trans. by John Scott (Woodbridge: Boydell, 1981)

Wills and Inventories Illustrative of the History, Manners, Language, Statistics, &c., of the Northern Counties of England, from the Eleventh Century downwards. Part 1, ed. by James Raine, SS, 2 (London: Surtees Society, 1835)

Secondary Works

Blows, Matthew, 'A Glastonbury Obit-List', in *The Archaeology and History of Glastonbury Abbey*, ed. by Lesley Abrams and James P. Carley (Woodbridge: Boydell, 1991), pp. 257–69

Carley, James P., *Glastonbury Abbey: The Holy House at the Head of the Moors Adventurous* (Woodbridge: Boydell, 1988)

Carley, James P., and Martin Howley, 'Relics at Glastonbury in the Fourteenth Century: An Annotated Edition of British Library, Cotton Titus D.vii, fols 2^r–13^v', *Arthurian Literature*, 16 (1998), 83–129

Cross, Claire, and Noreen Vickers, *Monks, Friars and Nuns in Sixteenth-Century Yorkshire*, Yorkshire Archaeological Society Record Series, 150 (Leeds: Yorkshire Archaeological Society, 1995)

Dobson, R. B., 'Recent Prosopographical Research in Late Medieval English History: University Graduates, Durham Monks, and York Canons', in *Medieval Lives and the Historian: Studies in Medieval Prosopography*, ed. by Neithard Bulst and Jean-Philippe Genet (Kalamazoo: Medieval Institute, 1985), pp. 181–200

——, 'The Monks of Canterbury in the Later Middle Ages, 1220–1540', in *A History of Canterbury Cathedral*, ed. by Patrick Collinson, Nigel Ramsay, and Margaret Sparks (Oxford: Oxford University Press, 1995), pp. 69–153

——, *Church and Society in the Medieval North of England* (London: Hambledon, 1996)

Dunning, Robert W., 'Revival at Glastonbury', in *Renaissance and Renewal in Christian History*, ed. by Derek Baker, Studies in Church History, 14 (Oxford: Blackwell for the Ecclesiastical History Society, 1977), pp. 213–22

Gransden, Antonia, 'The Growth of the Glastonbury Traditions and Legends in the Twelfth Century', *Journal of Ecclesiastical History*, 27.4 (1976), 337–58

Greatrex, Joan, *Biographical Register of the English Cathedral Priories of the Province of Canterbury, c. 1066 to 1540* (Oxford: Clarendon Press, 1997)

——, *The English Benedictine Cathedral Priories: Rule and Practice, c. 1270–1420* (Oxford: Oxford University Press, 2011)

Howley, Martin, 'Relics at Glastonbury Abbey in the Thirteenth Century: The Relic List in Cambridge, Trinity College R.5.33 (724), fols 104^r–105^v', *Medieval Studies*, 71 (2009), 197–234

Jenkins, John Christopher, 'Torre Abbey: Locality, Community, and Society in Medieval Devon' (unpublished doctoral thesis, University of Oxford, 2010)

Knowles, David, *The Religious Orders in England*, 3 vols (Cambridge: Cambridge University Press, 1948–1959)

Knowles, David, and R. Neville Hadcock, *Medieval Religious Houses: England and Wales*, 2nd edn (London: Longman, 1971)

Krochalis, Jeanne, '*Magna Tabula*: The Glastonbury Tablets', *Arthurian Literature*, 15 (1997), 93–183, and 16 (1998), 41–82, reprinted in *Glastonbury and the Arthurian Tradition*, ed. by James P. Carley (Woodbridge: Boydell and Brewer, 2001), pp. 435–567

McKinley, Richard, *Surnames of Lancashire*, English Surnames Series, 4 (London: Leopard's Head, 1981)

——, *A History of British Surnames* (London: Longman, 1990)

Postles, David, *The Surnames of Devon*, English Surnames Series, 6 (London: Leopard's Head, 1995)

——, *The Surnames of Leicestershire and Rutland*, English Surnames Series, 7 (Oxford: Leopard's Head, 1998)

Raine, James, ed., *History and Antiquities of North Durham, as Subdivided into the Shires of Norham, Island, and Bedlington, which from the Saxon Period until the Year 1844, Constituted Parcels of the County Palatine of Durham, but are now United to the County of Northumberland* (Durham: J. B. Nichols and Son, 1852)

Rahtz, Philip, and Lorna Watts, *Glastonbury: Myth and Archaeology* (Stroud: Tempus, 2003)

Reaney, Percy H., *The Origin of English Surnames* (London: Routledge & K. Paul, 1967)

Rollason, David W., 'Lists of Saints' Resting-Places in Anglo-Saxon England', *Anglo-Saxon England*, 7 (1978), 61–93

Smith, David M., *Guide to Bishops' Registers of England and Wales: A Survey from the Middle Ages to the Abolition of Episcopacy in 1646* (London: Royal Historical Society, 1981)

Stephenson, Michael, *The Gilbertine Priory of Watton* (York: Borthwick Institute, 2009)

Thomas, Islwyn Geoffrey, 'The Cult of Saints' Relics in Medieval England' (unpublished doctoral thesis, University of London, 1974)

Thornton, David E., '*Locus, Sanctus et Virtus*: Monastic Surnaming in Late Medieval and Early Tudor England Reviewed', *Journal of Medieval Monastic Studies*, 10 (2021), 211–46

——, 'How Useful are Episcopal Ordination Lists as a Source for Medieval English Monastic History?', *Journal of Ecclesiastical History*, 69 (2018), 493–530

——, 'The Last Monks of Worcester Cathedral Priory', *Midland History*, 43 (2018), 3–21

——, 'The Prosopography of English Monastic Orders at the Dissolution: Evidence from The National Archives Assessed', *Archives: The Journal of the British Records Association*, 54 (2019), 33–58

Watkin, Aelred, *Dean Cosyn and Wells Cathedral Miscellanea* (Frome: Somerset Record Society, 1941)

——, 'Glastonbury 1538–9 as Shown by Its Account Rolls', *Downside Review*, 67 (1949), 437–50

CLAUDIA DI SCIACCA*

Northern Lights on Southern Shores

Rewriting St Oswald's Life
*in Eighteenth-Century Friuli**

Seventh-century Northumbria bestowed upon the English church two of her most popular saints: Oswald, king of Northumbria from 634 to 642,[1] and Cuthbert, the monk-bishop of Lindisfarne (d. 687).[2] Apart from their shared geographical background, and although Cuthbert and Oswald (or, at least, Oswald's skull) came to share their final resting place and a distinctive iconography at Durham,[3] however, the circumstances of their life do not seem to have much in common and neither do their subsequent cults. While Cuthbert was raised from the calibre of Northumbrian holy man[4] to that of pan-English saint in the late Anglo-Saxon period,[5] Oswald, whose life was firmly rooted in Northumbria and its dynastic controversies,[6] and whose cult began through the active promotion of his lineage, went on to become a truly European saint and found his most enduring fame on the continent.

This essay will trace the diffusion of Oswald's devotion to north-east Italy, particularly the region of Friuli, where from the fifteenth to the mid-nineteenth century a remote village in the Carnian Alps, Sauris, was a major cult centre and a popular pilgrimage resort especially in time of plague.

---

* My warmest thanks to Lucia Protto for her bibliographical help and a very enlightening tour of Sauris, and to the editors for their stimulating comments. Throughout this essay 'Anglo-Saxon' is used to refer specifically to the history and culture of pre-Conquest England.

1 Holdsworth, 'Oswald'; Whatley, 'Oswaldus Rex'.

2 Thacker, 'Cuthbert'; Whatley, 'Cuthbertus, vita'; Di Sciacca, '"concupita, quaesita"'.

3 Rollason, 'St Oswald', pp. 174–77; Stancliffe and Cambridge, 'Introduction', pp. 8–9. On the posthumous partnership between Oswald and Cuthbert, see Cambridge, 'Archaeology', pp. 128–29, 148–54, 160; Whitehead, 'Translating the Northern English Saints', pp. 27–31.

4 Thacker, 'Bede's Ideal of Reform', pp. 148–49; Thacker, 'Lindisfarne', p. 115.

5 Gretsch, *Ælfric and the Cult of Saints*, pp. 66–101; Simpson, 'The King Alfred/St Cuthbert Episode'; Rollason, 'St Cuthbert and Wessex'; Rollason, 'Relic-Cults', pp. 102–03; Jolly, *The Community of St Cuthbert*, pp. 4–14.

6 Cramp, 'The Making of Oswald's Northumbria'.

Claudia Di Sciacca (claudia.disciacca@uniud.it) is Professor of Germanic Philology at the University of Udine, Italy.

Late Medieval Devotion to Saints from the North of England: New Directions, ed. by Christiania Whitehead, Hazel J. Hunter Blair, and Denis Renevey, MCS 48 (Turnhout: Brepols, 2022), pp. 409–432
BREPOLS ✠ PUBLISHERS   10.1484/M.MCS-EB.5.124360

Sauris features prominently in the *vita* authored by the eighteenth-century Friulan hagiographer, Giampietro della Stua, still heavily indebted to Bede's account of Oswald. This study will review the unfolding of Oswald's legend from the original Bedan narrative to the Italian *vita*, in order to highlight the key steps in the appropriation of the Northumbrian saint in such a distant context. Thus, I hope to contribute a pertinent albeit modest case-study of hagiography as a culturally specific and context-bound genre, as well as of the impactful relationship of the medieval with the modern.

The Anglo-Saxon Tradition of St Oswald

The Anglo-Saxon hagiographical tradition of St Oswald consists of no fewer than four texts, that is, Bede's account of the king's life, death, and early spread of his cult in the *Historia ecclesiastica*,[7] Alcuin's *Versus de patribus regibus et sanctis euboracensis ecclesiae*,[8] the entry for Oswald's feast day (5 August) in the *Old English Martyrology*,[9] and Ælfric's 'Life of St Oswald'.[10] Our key and virtually only early source on Oswald, however, is Bede,[11] and the other three texts — indeed, all Oswald's hagiographies in general — ultimately depend on Bede.

Bede concocts a 'carefully contrived portrait' of Oswald,[12] quietly sidestepping the less edifying features in his military career and dynastic dealings.[13] In Bede's grand scheme of the English as a chosen people achieving salvation under the leaders of his native Bernicia, Oswald plays a prominent role as the ruler who managed institutionally to merge kingship with sainthood, military prowess with heartfelt devotion, by championing the Gregorian principle of *iustum bellum* aimed at protecting the Church against its enemies, whether pagans or heretics.[14] The enthusiastic epithets that Bede repeatedly bestows on Oswald (*vir Deo dilectus, sanctissimus ac uictoriosissimus rex, christianissimus rex, reuerentissimus rex, rex mirandae sanctitatis, Deo dilectus rex*)[15] perfectly

---

7 *Bede's Ecclesiastical History of the English People*, ed. and trans. by Colgrave and Mynors (cited hereafter as *HE*), III.1–6, 9–13; IV.14.

8 Alcuin, *Versus de patribus regibus*, ed. and trans. by Godman, ll. 236–506, 1600–48 (pp. 24–45, 130–33).

9 *Old English Martyrology*, ed. and trans. by Rauer, pp. 154–55.

10 Ælfric, 'Life of St Oswald', ed. by Needham.

11 A few crucial facts about Oswald's youth are mentioned in a source predating Bede, the *Vita sancti Columbae* (I. 1.8a–9b) by Adomnán of Iona (d. 704), ed. and trans. by Anderson and Anderson, pp. 14–17; see also Stancliffe, 'Oswald, "Most Holy and Most Victorious King"', pp. 50–51.

12 Thacker, '*Membra Disiecta*', p. 97.

13 Stancliffe, 'Oswald, "Most Holy and Most Victorious King"', pp. 33–46, 61–75.

14 Thacker, '*Membra Disiecta*', pp. 111–12; Thacker, 'Bede's Ideal of Reform'; Clemoes, *The Cult of St Oswald*, p. 590; Lazzari, 'Kingship and Sainthood', pp. 29–35; Stancliffe, 'Oswald, "Most Holy and Most Victorious King"', pp. 66–71, esp. 63–64.

15 *HE*, III.1, l. 30; III.7, l. 14; III.9, l. 1; III.11, l. 23; III.13, ll. 7 and 34; IV.14, l. 41.

epitomize the twin attributes of secular power and spiritual authority that make him a veritable Northumbrian Constantine.[16]

For all his enthusiasm for Oswald, however, Bede never goes so far as to call him a martyr, nor does he include Oswald in the original version of his *Martyrologium*.[17] Alcuin (d. 804) follows suit, but the ninth-century *Old English Martyrology* features the saint, and Oswald's definitive attainment of martyrial status was sanctioned by the tenth-century Benedictine Reform, when he is expressly styled 'king and martyr' in calendars and litanies, probably as a result of the reformers' interest in royal martyr cults (a preoccupation connected with the murder of the young king Edward in 978),[18] and of the increasing formalization of saintly categories in litanies.[19] Given the standardized four-tiered sequence of apostles, martyrs, confessors, and virgins, Oswald could hardly have fitted any other category than the martyrs.[20] (That the matter must long have been somewhat controversial is attested by our eighteenth-century Friulan hagiographer, who still felt it necessary to review the case and restate Oswald's martyrial status.[21])

In his vernacular take on the life of St Oswald, Ælfric, like Bede, presents the king's death fighting against Penda at Maserfelth as the demise of a military leader on the battlefield, rather than a martyrdom proper, although the rubric heading the life qualifies Oswald as king and martyr.[22] Ælfric follows Bede closely, though with some substantial editing or with additions from other sources (such as Cuthbert's vision of angels carrying the soul of Aidan heavenward, which derived from Bede's prose *Vita S. Cuthberti*).[23] Alterations concerning the chronology of some events give greater emphasis to Oswald's spirituality than to political details that were no longer topical in Ælfric's day.[24] '[Unlike Bede, Ælfric] places the existence of the holy King in a wider spatial-temporal context' which spans from the arrival of the Gregorian mission in Kent to Ælfric's days, and encompasses virtually the whole of England.[25]

---

16 Cramp, 'The Making of Oswald's Northumbria', p. 30; Wallace-Hadrill, *Bede's Ecclesiastical History*, pp. 88–89; Rollason, 'The Cult of Murdered Royal Saints'; Ridyard, *Royal Saints*, pp. 92–93. See also Folz, *Les Saints Rois*, pp. 53–54; Klaniczay, *Holy Rulers*, pp. 82–86.

17 Quentin, *Les martyrologes historiques*, pp. 20–23, 48. See also Gunn, 'Bede and the Martyrdom'; Thacker, '*Membra Disiecta*', pp. 112–17.

18 Miller, 'Edward the Martyr'.

19 Thacker, '*Membra Disiecta*', pp. 124–25.

20 It has also been suggested that 'there seems to have been a greater readiness on the continent to regard Oswald as a martyr, [...] than we find in England': Stancliffe and Cambridge, 'Introduction', p. 6.

21 See below, pp. 423–24.

22 'he ofslagen wearð for his folce ware' (he was killed in defence of his people): Ælfric, 'Life of Oswald', ed. by Needham, ll. 122–23 (p. 35). All translations from Latin, Italian, and Old English are my own.

23 Thacker, '*Membra Disiecta*', p. 125; Lazzari, 'Kingship and Sainthood', pp. 46–60.

24 Lazzari, 'Kingship and Sainthood', pp. 56–57.

25 Lazzari, 'Kingship and Sainthood', p. 51.

412   CLAUDIA DI SCIACCA

Ælfric's Lives of Saints were written in the 990s,[26] a decade of renewed Viking incursions, in response to the requests of two powerful ealdormen, Æthelweard and his son Æthelmær, much involved on the military front.[27] Against this background of a country at war, warrior martyrs like Oswald proved pivotal to the overall scheme of the collection, showing that spiritual war could coexist with earthly war in the name of God and that a *rihtlic gefeoht*, a just war, was possible.[28] Indeed, according to J. Cross, Ælfric's Lives of Saints contain the most explicit statement there is on the Christian vision of the just war.[29]

The Relics and Beginnings of the Cult

However widespread the circulation of the *Historia ecclesiastica* may have been and however authoritative Bede's endorsement, the success of Oswald's cult — extraordinary both for its geographical and chronological extent, as well as for its spread through different layers of society — was principally triggered by his violent death at the hands of the pagan Mercians at Maserfelth[30] and the eventual spread of his dismembered body in the guise of highly cherished relics.[31]

In its earliest phase, Oswald's cult was 'primarily a secular and dynastic affair', indeed almost a family affair.[32] Oswald's body had been hacked to pieces at the behest of the Mercian king Penda, and the head and arms affixed to stakes.[33] Oswiu, Oswald's brother and successor in Bernicia,[34] recovered the head and arms and took them to the Bernician stronghold of Bamburgh,[35] where the *right* arm was enshrined, still uncorrupted in accordance with the

---

26 On the somewhat shifting chronology of Ælfric's Lives of Saints, see Clemoes, 'Chronology', p. 56; Kleist, 'Ælfric's Corpus', pp. 131–32; and Kleist, *The Chronology and Canon*, pp. 135–44 and 279–80.

27 Lazzari, 'Kingship and Sainthood', pp. 39–45; Miller, 'Æthelweard'. Æthelweard was also the cousin of Matilda († 1011), abbess of the imperial abbey of Essen and grand-daughter of Edith, half-sister of Æthelstan, and eventually wife of Otto the Great. Like Edith, Matilda too could have promoted Oswald's devotion: see Ó Riain-Raedel, 'Edith, Judith, Matilda', p. 211, and below, pp. 414–15.

28 Passions of warrior martyrs make up a third of the Lives of Saints: Lazzari, 'Kingship and Sainthood', pp. 42–45.

29 Cross, 'The Ethic of War', pp. 272–73. While Oswald's military merits remain a constant feature of late medieval Latin hagiography, in the vernacular legendaries they are downplayed in favour of milder traits: see Whitehead, 'Translating the Northern English Saints', pp. 31–33.

30 On the Maserfelth site, see Stancliffe, 'Where Was Oswald Killed?'.

31 For a convenient synopsis, see Bede, *Historia ecclesiastica*, ed. by Plummer, II, pp. 157–58.

32 Thacker, '*Membra Disiecta*', pp. 105–07, quotation at 109.

33 Thacker, '*Membra Disiecta*', p. 97 n. 8.

34 Holdsworth, 'Oswiu'.

35 The skull was later buried at Lindisfarne and ultimately placed in St Cuthbert's coffin: Thacker, '*Membra Disiecta*', pp. 101–04; Bailey, 'St Oswald's Heads', pp. 195–201, 208–09.

famous prophecy uttered by Bishop Aidan after witnessing Oswald's gift of a silver tray and its contents to the poor during an Easter banquet.[36] This imperishable right arm apparently remained at Bamburgh at least until the 1050s when it was allegedly stolen by a monk of Peterborough and eventually translated to Ely.[37]

Some fifty years after Oswald's death, his other remains were discovered and translated to the monastery at Bardney, Lindsey, by Osthryth, Oswald's niece, eventually ending up in Gloucester in 909.[38] Whereas the tradition concerning the skull and right arm is more stable, Oswald's other remains were subject to a veritable 'relic-mongering': they apparently multiplied and scattered far and wide in both the British Isles and the continent.[39]

Finally, besides the relics, Oswald's cult could also count on the sites of the two major battles fought by the king, Heavenfield and Maserfelth, with which miraculous healings were associated from an early date.[40]

Oswald's Cult on the Continent

Oswald's cult soon spread outside English boundaries, flourishing in the Low Countries, Germany, Austria, Bohemia, Switzerland, Scandinavia, including Iceland, and, last but not least, northern Italy.[41]

Crucial agents of the diffusion of Oswald's cult in this second phase were prominent Anglo-Saxon and Irish ecclesiastics — the latter's enthusiasm presumably a reflex of the Ionan connections of the king — as well as aristocratic devotees. Among the ecclesiastical figures, the Northumbrian missionary Willibrord (658–739) deserves pride of place.[42] After spending part of his youth in Ireland with the English community at Rath Melsigi, he eventually moved to the continent to convert the Frisians, where he became Archbishop of Utrecht and founded the monastery of Echternach, bringing with him some of Oswald's relics which were installed there.[43] Another early sponsor of Oswald's cult on the continent may have been Virgil, the Irish bishop of Salzburg for over forty years (743–784).[44] Some while later, the king's cult

---

36 *HE*, III.6, ll. 19–21.

37 Thacker, '*Membra Disiecta*', p. 119; Tudor, 'Reginald's *Life of St Oswald*', pp. 191–92; Rollason, 'St Oswald', pp. 168–69.

38 Thacker, '*Membra Disiecta*', pp. 104–05.

39 Bede, *Historia ecclesiastica*, ed. by Plummer, II, pp. 159–60; Thacker, '*Membra disiecta*'.

40 On Heavenfield, see *HE*, III.2, ll. 15–16 (but cf. Stancliffe, 'Oswald, "Most Holy and Most Victorious King"', p. 64 n. 145). On Maserfelth, see *HE*, III.2, ll. 9–10.

41 See *HE*, III.13, ll. 1–3; Thacker, '*Membra disiecta*', pp. 113–19, esp. 118; Clemoes, *The Cult of St Oswald*; Jansen, 'The Development of St Oswald's Legends'; Baker, 'St Oswald and His Church'; Baker, 'The Cult of St Oswald'.

42 Mostert, 'Willibrord'.

43 *HE*, III.13; Thacker, '*Membra disiecta*', pp. 114–17; Bailey, 'St Oswald's Heads', p. 201.

44 See Baker, 'The Cult of St Oswald', p. 193. Some of the earliest surviving paintings of

in Switzerland and southern Germany benefitted from the sponsorship of Gregory, the English reformed abbot of Einsiedeln (960/964–990),[45] and of the Irish Benedictine monastery of St James at Regensburg (founded *c.* 1080).[46]

Amongst the aristocratic devotees, a key role was played by the dynastic interrelations established through matrimonial bonds between continental high nobility and English ladies of royal descent after the Northumbrian king was appropriated by the Mercian and West Saxon leadership. Oswald's niece, Osthryth, responsible for the translation of most of Oswald's remains to the royal foundation of Bardney in Lindsey, an area instrumental in the propagation of his cult, was married to the Mercian king Æthelred (d. *c.* 716).[47] In 909, at the behest of Æthelred, lord of the Mercians (d. 911), and his wife Æthelflæd, daughter of Alfred the Great (d. 918), these relics were moved from Bardney to the minster of new St Peter's, later known as St Oswald's, founded in Gloucester by the royal couple in the 890s, their new headquarters in the aftermath of the Viking invasions and their final resting place.[48]

At the time of the translation, Æthelstan, the future king of the West Saxons (924/925–927) and of the English (927–939), was being fostered at the Mercian court.[49] The many miracles attributed to Oswald must have had an impact on the young king, a great sponsor of saints and collector of relics, all the more so since he could claim a (tenuous) dynastic relationship with Oswald via the latter's wife, whom Bede presents as the daughter of Cynegils, king of the West Saxons.[50] Æthelstan was the first southern king to extend his authority over Northumbria and his promotion of Oswald's cult as a means of furthering political ambition may have been followed in Saxony, where his half-sister Edith married Otto the Great in 929/930 and

---

Oswald are the frescoes from the Stift Nonnberg in Salzburg: see Vizkelety, 'Oswald König von Northumbrien'. In an eleventh-century Salzburg missal St Oswald is grouped with St Gregory and St Benedict, who also figure in the Nonnberg paintings: Baker, 'St Oswald and His Church', p. 115 n. 1. Interestingly, in Æthelwold's Benedictional, Gregory, Benedict, and Cuthbert, the other Northumbrian saint with whom Oswald is often associated, form a distinctive triptych within the miniature of the Choir of the Confessors, which is in turn mirrored in Ælfric's Second Series of the *Catholic Homilies*: see Di Sciacca, '"concupita, quaesita"', pp. 172–74.

45 Gregory represents an important continental offshoot of the English Benedictine reformers' penchant for Oswald: Thacker, '*Membra Disiecta*', pp. 123–24.

46 Ó Riain-Raedel, 'Edith, Judith, Matilda', pp. 225–29. On the Benedictine order's promotion of Oswald's cult in general, see Folz, 'Saint Oswald', p. 60.

47 Thacker, '*Membra Disiecta*', pp. 114–15.

48 Keynes, 'Æthelred'; Blair, 'Gloucester'; Rollason, 'St Oswald', pp. 168–69 esp. n. 20.

49 Miller, 'Æthelstan'; Thacker, '*Membra Disiecta*', pp. 120–21.

50 *HE*, III.7, ll. 16–17. See also Ó Riain-Raedel, 'Edith, Judith, Matilda', pp. 214–16. In his *Vita S. Oswaldi regis et martyris* (*BHL*, no. 6365), Reginald of Durham (d. *c.* 1190) names the queen Kyneburga: *Vita Oswaldi*, 11, ed. by Arnold, I, p. 349; Tudor, 'Reginald's *Life of St Oswald*'. However, Kyneburga may, in fact, have been the name of Penda's daughter: *HE*, III.21, ll. 13–14; Bede, *Historia ecclesiastica*, ed. by Plummer, II, p. 142.

was generously provided by Æthelstan with a dowry which in all probability included precious relics.[51]

Again by means of high-ranked matrimonial arrangements, Flanders became a veritable hub in the dissemination of Oswald's cult on the continent. Before marrying Count Baldwin I of Flanders, the Carolingian princess Judith was wife of the West Saxon kings Æthelwulf (839–855) and Æthelbald (855–860), and her son, Count Baldwin II, established Saint-Winnoc at Bergues in 900.[52] By about the mid-eleventh century, Saint-Winnoc had become a centre of Oswald's cult, hosting some of his relics, and by 1058 a young monk of Saint-Winnoc, Drogo (d. 1084),[53] authored a *vita* of St Oswald, heavily dependent on Bede[54] except for Drogo's unequivocal designation of Oswald as a martyr.[55] Such an upsurge in Oswald's devotion could have benefitted from the return to her native Flanders of Judith (*c.* 1027–1094), stepdaughter of Baldwin IV of Flanders, and widow of Tostig (d. 1066), earl of Northumbria and brother of King Harold.[56] In 1071, Judith married Welf IV, first duke of Bavaria (d. 1101), and in all probability she procured the relics of Oswald that feature prominently in the couple's rich endowment to the monastery of St Martin at Weingarten, near Lake Constance, founded by Welf in 1056 and elected as their burial place.[57] Through marital arrangements with noble ladies with English ancestry or connections, the powerful Welfs and their favourite foundation of Weingarten continued to play a key role in the diffusion of Oswald's cult in south-west Germany and Switzerland.[58]

---

51 In her *Gesta Ottonis Imperatoris* (*c.* 965), Hrotsvitha of Gandersheim celebrates Edith as 'natam de stirpe beata Oswaldi regis' (born from the blessed kin of King Oswald): ed. and Italian trans. by Pillolla, ll. 95–96 (p. 14).

52 Ó Riain-Raedel, 'Edith, Judith, Matilda', pp. 217–18.

53 Huyghebaert, 'Un moine hagiographe'.

54 *BHL*, no. 6362; Drogo, *Vita S. Oswaldi*.

55 Drogo, *Vita Oswaldi*, §§ 2, 25 (pp. 94, 99). Two sermons on the saint were also attributed to Drogo: *BHL*, nos 6363–64; Drogo, *Sermones*, ed. by Huyghebaert, pp. 105–07, 107–08, respectively. A Latin office for Oswald's feast day, formerly attributed to Drogo, is now considered to date from s.xii[med]: Clemoes, *The Cult of St Oswald*, pp. 592–93.

56 During her stay in Northumbria, Judith had become a devotee to two local saints, Cuthbert and Oswine, king of Deira (d. 651): see Ó Riain-Raedel, 'Edith, Judith, Matilda', pp. 220–22; Dockray-Miller, *The Books and Life of Judith of Flanders*, pp. 13–47.

57 Dockray-Miller, *The Books and Life of Judith of Flanders*, pp. 82–84; Ó Riain-Raedel, 'Edith, Judith, Matilda', pp. 217–20.

58 Ó Riain-Raedel, 'Edith, Judith, Matilda', pp. 223–24; Baker, 'St Oswald and His Church', pp. 105–07; Baker, 'The Cult of St Oswald', pp. 188–91; Clemoes, *The Cult of St Oswald*, pp. 593–95.

Regensburg and the South German Tradition of St Oswald

The principal seat of the Welf family was the imperial city of Regensburg, a centre 'where various strands of devotion to the saint seem to have converged'.[59] From about the mid-twelfth century the above-mentioned monastery of St James in Regensburg was home to a very active scriptorium, the hagiographical production of which betrays an obvious interest in Oswald's legend.[60] Such an interest may be put down not only to Oswald's many Irish connections, but also (yet again) to the pervasive Welfs and their role as generous benefactors of Irish monastic foundations in Germany.[61]

Regensburg also played a role in the development of the prolific and often extravagant vernacular elaborations of Oswald's legend in the German speaking area.[62] Here, the historical saint-king becomes the hero of a chivalric romance centred on the familiar theme of the *Brautentführung*, the abduction of a bride from a pagan father, a feat in which Oswald is assisted by a raven through which the couple exchanges messages, and the mutual gift of a ring.[63] The popularity and diffusion of the Middle High German take on Oswald's legend can be gauged from its impact on the saint's iconography, with the raven (with or without a ring in its beak) becoming a regular attribute by the mid-fifteenth century.[64]

---

59 Ó Riain-Raedel, 'Edith, Judith, Matilda', p. 224. Regensburg was also a point of departure from Germany in the first three Crusades (1096–1099, 1145–1149, and 1187–1192) and Oswald's cult intertwined with the military spirit awakened by the Crusades, as the king perfectly embodied a prototype Crusader: Ó Riain-Raedel, 'Edith, Judith, Matilda', pp. 223, 229; Clemoes, *The Cult of St Oswald*, p. 596.

60 Ó Riain-Raedel, 'Edith, Judith, Matilda', pp. 225–28.

61 Ó Riain-Raedel, 'Edith, Judith, Matilda', pp. 228–29.

62 Bowden, *Bridal-Quest Epics*, pp. 102–36; Curschmann, *Der Münchner Oswald*; Jansen, 'The Development of St Oswald's Legends'; *Ósvalds saga*, ed. by Kalinke, pp. 31-69; Weitbrecht, 'Haüsliche Heiligkeit'. The early-sixteenth century Icelandic *Ósvalds saga* can be considered a spin-off of the German legend and a key witness to its idiosyncratic development: Wolf, *The Legends*, pp. 300–01, and *Ósvalds saga*, ed. by Kalinke, pp. 9–30 and 69–103.

63 Bowden, *Bridal-Quest Epics*, pp. 122–26.

64 On the changing image of St Oswald and on the different iconographic traditions in England and on the continent, see Stancliffe and Cambridge, 'Introduction', pp. 4–12; Jansen, 'The Development of St Oswald's Legends', pp. 237–40; Vizkelety, 'Oswald König von Northumbrien', cols 102–03; Vizkelety, 'Der Budapester Oswald', pp. 131–40; Curschmann, *Der Münchener Oswald*, pp. 169–93. On Oswald's iconography in north-east Italy, see Bergamini and Bianco, 'Introduzione', pp. 15–23. It has also been suggested, however, that the ultimate origin of the raven may have been much older, deriving from an association between Oswald and Odin in popular tradition: Clemoes, *The Cult of St Oswald*, p. 597; Stancliffe and Cambridge, 'Introduction', pp. 2–3; Jansen, 'The Development of St Oswald's Legends', pp. 237–40.

St Oswald in the Alpine Regions and in Friuli

Oswald's cult in north-east Italy can be considered as a distinctive and vigorous spin-off of the South German penchant for the saint,[65] initiated when German-speaking immigrants started to move down the valleys of south Tyrol and Friuli between the twelfth and fourteenth centuries.[66] In the process Oswald was divested of his kingly and martial qualities, becoming instead the patron saint of cattle, the harvest, and the weather.[67] Even more relevant for the present study is the fact that, since the Black Death, Oswald had become popular as a protector against infectious diseases.[68] This efficacy against disease derives from the *Historia ecclesiastica*, where, with one exception,[69] the miracles attributed to Oswald are all healing miracles.[70] In particular, two are miraculous healings from plague, either through the direct agency of Oswald's relics or his intercession.[71] (Interestingly, in the second miracle, Oswald's intercession is revealed in a vision to a dying boy by the apostles Peter and Paul, the same who apparently flank Oswald in the renowned *Flügelaltar* in Sauris.[72]) Furthermore, in the twelfth century, Reginald of Durham reports the story, apparently derived from an unspecified Latin source, of an outbreak of plague during Oswald's reign. The king, himself ill with the disease, received a vision prophesying the end of the epidemic thanks to his prayers, and his future martyrdom, and henceforth lived even more virtuously, observing a vow of chastity with his wife.[73]

Devotion to Oswald in Friuli and Veneto similarly centred on the saint as a healer, and its chief hub was Sauris, a village founded in a secluded valley of the Carnian Alps around the mid-thirteenth century by German-speaking settlers coming from Tyrol and Carinthia.[74] In the downhill area of the village, Sauris di Sotto or Dörf, a church dedicated to St Oswald hosting the king's

---

65 'Clearly southern Germans made Oswald their own': Clemoes, *The Cult of St Oswald*, p. 598.

66 Clemoes, *The Cult of St Oswald*, pp. 596–97; Baker, 'The Cult of St Oswald', pp. 179–81. On the German-speaking communities in the eastern Alps, see Hornung, 'Die Osttiroler Bauernsprachinseln'; Prezzi, ed., *Isole di cultura*; Bidese, Dow, and Stolz, ed., *Das Zimbrische*; Caria, 'Le isole linguistiche germanofone'.

67 Jansen, 'The Development of St Oswald's Legends', p. 237. The power to control the weather could probably be a corollary of the syncretic merging of Oswald's cult with the pagan cult of Odin: see above, n. 64.

68 Baker, 'The Cult of St Oswald', p. 179 n. 1.

69 *HE*, III.10.

70 *HE*, III.2; III.9; III.10, ll. 22–25; III.11, ll. 28–31; III.11, ll. 40–42; III.11, ll. 44–74; III.12.

71 *HE*, III.13; IV.14.

72 The wooden altar is the work of the famous sixteenth-century sculptor Michael Parth from Brüneck: see Perusini, 'L'altare'. Whereas St Peter can be identified with certainty by his most typical attribute, the key, the identification of the other statue with St Paul is disputed.

73 Reginald, *Vita Oswaldi*, I. 10–11, ed. by Arnold, I, pp. 346–49. See also Tudor, 'Reginald's *Life of Oswald*', pp. 186–87.

74 The German place-name is Zahre and a distinctive German dialect is still spoken there. On Sauris, its history and language, see Cozzi, Isabella, and Navarra, ed., *Sauris/Zahre*.

(supposedly left) thumb[75] was officially consecrated as a parish church on 28 September 1470 after having been rebuilt, but local devotion to Oswald can be dated back to the thirteenth century and flourished in spite of the difficult access to the village and inadequate spiritual provision offered by the understaffed sanctuary.[76] Thanks to the healing powers attributed to the king's relic, the Sauris sanctuary established itself as a major cult centre from the fifteenth up to the mid-nineteenth century, attracting a constant flux of pilgrims from Venice and its provinces, an area periodically subject to outbreaks of plague and fevers.[77]

Alongside the Sauris relic, Oswald's cult in Friuli was also fostered by the circulation of a considerable number of hagiographies. No fewer than six manuscripts, all associated with either Aquileia or Cividale and dated between the late twelfth and the mid-fifteenth century, attest to at least three different textual traditions of Oswald's life.

First, Cividale MS XV (s.xiii*med*, probable origin Aquileia; provenance Cividale), and the derivative MSS X (s.xv, Cividale) and XI (s.xiv, Cividale), are three passionaries that attest to a composite text combining the twelfth-century *vita* by Reginald of Durham with a *vita* derived from the one by Drogo,[78] and included in the great South German collection, *Magnum legendarium Austriacum*, circulating in Austria and Bavaria since the end of twelfth century.[79] Second, Udine MS Joppi 142, one of the earliest Friulan hagiographic collections (s.xii²), attests to a Bedan version circulating in southern Germany and included in the *Windberg Legendary*.[80] Finally, Cividale MS XVI and Gorizia MS 9, two thirteenth-century passionaries from Aquileia, contain a rare version of the *vita* attested in a French witness.[81] Notably, Cividale MS XVI contains the lives of two other Anglo-Saxon and Irish saints, Cuthbert and Columba, and it is possible that their lives, together with Oswald's, may have reached Aquileia in a booklet specifically devoted to insular saints, which was eventually copied into a larger local legendary.[82]

---

75 On the hazy route of the relic to Sauris, see below, pp. 421–22.

76 For a detailed description of St Oswald's church and its history, see Bucco, *Le chiese*, pp. 6–29. The uphill area of the village, Sauris di Sopra or Plotzn, had its own church dedicated to St Lawrence, like Oswald, a martyr saint venerated in Carinthia, and both St Oswald's and St Lawrence's were originally established as churches of the same parish, sharing one priest, though the latter was stationed at St Lawrence's, creating competition between the two communities. St Oswald's was established as a chaplaincy in 1637 and became the seat of the parish in 1809; finally, the two churches were established as two independent parishes in 1960: see Tilatti, 'La parrocchia', pp. 64–71; Bucco, *Le chiese*, pp. 36–54; Baker, 'The Cult of St Oswald', pp. 174–79; Bergamini and Bianco, 'Introduzione', pp. 7–11.

77 Baker, 'The Cult of St Oswald', pp. 167–79; Tilatti, 'La parrocchia', pp. 82–86.

78 *BHL*, no. 6365; *BHL*, no. 6370.

79 Scalon and Pani, *I codici*, pp. 99–109, 120–23.

80 *BHL*, nos 6361–61b. Merlino, 'Oswald', pp. 65–67, 69–70; Chiesa, 'Il re', p. 49.

81 This version corresponds to *BHL*, no. 6367. Scalon and Pani, *I codici*, pp. 123–26, esp. 126; Merlino, 'Oswald', pp. 67–69, 71–72; Chiesa, 'Il re', pp. 49–50; *Acta S. Oswaldi*, ed. by Du Sollier and others, § 51, p. 93.

82 Chiesa, 'Il re', pp. 49–50.

Later, the long period of peace enjoyed by Friuli under Venetian control, from the early sixteenth century up to the fall of the Republic at the end of the eighteenth century, continued to favour the spread of Oswald's cult in the region.[83] Within the span of a century, from the 1660s to the 1760s, three lives of Oswald were written by Venetian and Friulan hagiographers. The earliest, the *Vita di S. Osvaldo* was published in Udine, the 'capital' of Friuli, by a local nobleman, Pietro C. Soardo, in 1667 and dedicated to the Venetian governor of Friuli, Alvise Foscari.[84] Its chief source text, Bede, is complemented with a German one, probably derived from the late medieval prose life featuring within the hagiographic collection *Der Heiligen Leben*.[85] Nearly half a century later, the *Vita di S. Osvaldo* was published by the Franciscan Stefano Pace, dedicated to the abbess and nuns of a convent in the Venetian town of Vicenza,[86] and heavily dependent on Soardo. Sauris and its sanctuary are not given much space in Soardo and Pace's works, although Pace attests to the popularity of Sauris as a pilgrimage destination attracting devotees not only from Friuli and Veneto but also from Germany.[87]

The *Vita* by Giampietro della Stua

Giampietro della Stua, an ecclesiastic of Udine, was the first local hagiographer to focus on Sauris and to offer a detailed, if not always reliable, account of its development as a cult centre for St Oswald. His work was apparently commissioned by the very Rector of the Sauris sanctuary, Andrea Antongiacomi, whom della Stua calls *mio singolare amico* (my special friend).[88]

Della Stua is a writer with some pretension to scholarship, and in his preface he presents a vast set of sources ranging from Bede to Adrien Baillet (1649–1706), from William of Malmesbury to Lorenz Sauer (1522–1578), from Drogo to Soardo and Pace, and from the Jesuit English missionary Michael Alford (1587–1652) to the Bollandists and an unnamed hagiographer of the late seventeenth century.[89] However, della Stua explicitly prefers the earliest

---

83 Several dedications of churches in Friuli date from that period: Baker, 'The Cult of St Oswald', p. 192; Bergamini and Bianco, 'Introduzione', pp. 14–15; Rettori, 'Un re taumaturgo'.

84 Soardo, *Vita di S. Osvaldo.*

85 *Der Heiligen Leben*, ed. by Rüttgers, II, pp. 287–94. A detail traceable to this German prose life is the overtly Christian interpretation of the raven as the heavenly bearer of the chrism for Oswald's coronation. In his preface, della Stua hints that the factual errors of both Soardo and Pace can ultimately be put down to a shared German source: della Stua, *Vita di Sant' Osvaldo re di Northumberland*, (cited hereafter as *VSO*), p. 12.

86 Pace, *Vita di S. Osvaldo.*

87 Pace, *Vita di S. Osvaldo*, p. 89.

88 *VSO*, p. 11 n. (b).

89 *VSO*, pp. 9–12. Baillet, author of *Les vies des saints*, is referred to as 'un severo scrittor Franzese' (a stern French writer), and criticized by della Stua for his many omissions, including, crucially, Oswald's martyrdom, and for considering the king just a confessor. The

sources,[90] especially Bede and Drogo, as well as Alford, whom he repeatedly refers to, while he programmatically distances himself from his immediate predecessors, Soardo and Pace, taking the opportunity to correct them, rather pointedly at times, on various issues in the course of his narrative.[91]

Correctly identifying the common derivation of Soardo and Pace's accounts, della Stua blames them for relying on an unspecified German source, to which Soardo's interpretation of the raven can most likely be put down.[92] Dismissing this interpretation as *varie fanfaluche* (various fiddlesticks), della Stua proposes instead that the raven is derived from a dove,[93] which should be traced to St Columba whom Oswald reputedly saw in a vision before the battle of Heavenfield, while the ring it carries should be construed as a hieroglyph. While the auspicious vision can indeed be traced as far back as Adomnán's *Vita sancti Columbae*,[94] the wordplay between St Columba and the dove (Lat. *columba*), as well as the metamorphosis of the latter into a raven and of the hieroglyph into a ring, seem to be della Stua's own constructs, although he purportedly bases them on Bede's and Alford's accounts.[95]

This idiosyncratic interpretation apart, della Stua's life of St Oswald generally abides by its author's proposition of resting on the authority of his (early) sources and of being as factual as possible. The life is preceded by a historical and geographical introduction, providing contemporary readers with what we can suppose was welcome background information (§ I). Oswald's biography is then narrated following the familiar Bedan progression, namely the dynastic vicissitudes preceding Oswald's ascent to the throne and his formative years during his youthful exile in Dál Riata (§ II), his crucial victory at Heavenfield against the Briton Ceadwalla (§ III), his active engagement in the evangelization of his people and cooperation with Aidan (§§ IV–V), the expansion of his lordship well beyond Northumbria, his involvement in the conversion of the king of Wessex and his marriage with the latter's daughter Kineburga (§§ VI–VII), the enthusiastic description of his many virtues as both secular and spiritual leader (§ IX), up until his violent death at the hands of the pagan Penda (§ X). The only substantial non-Bedan addition concerns the bout of plague during

---

German hagiographer Lorenz Sauer put together the collection of saints' lives *De probatis Sanctorum historiis*, while Alford authored the *Fides regia Britannica siue annales ecclesiae Britannicae*: see Toussaint, 'Baillet Adrien'; Du Moustier, 'Surius, Lawrence'; Edwards, 'Alford, Michael'. Finally, the unnamed hagiographer is simply described as an elderly author, criticized by della Stua for having concocted a work of fiction rather than a reliable report of the saint's life: *VSO*, p. 10.

90 'nulla avanzi che non sia appoggiato all'autorità degli antichi' (nothing that rests on the authority of the ancient writers will be left out): *VSO*, p. 12.

91 See *VSO*, p. 22 nn. (a) and (c); p. 23 n. (b); p. 29 n. (b); p. 34 n. (a); p. 35 n. (a); p. 41 n. (b); p. 42 n. (b). Soardo, in particular, is attributed a rather creative, fictional treatment of the narrative: *VSO*, p. 12.

92 *VSO*, p. 12 and above, n. 85.

93 *VSO*, p. 29.

94 See above, n. 11.

95 *VSO*, p. 29 n. (b).

Oswald's reign (§ VIII). As mentioned above, this anecdote is first attested in Reginald of Durham, although the source acknowledged by della Stua is the late medieval English hagiographer John Capgrave (1393–1464).[96]

The second section of della Stua's work consists of a detailed account of the development of Oswald's cult, from the recovery of his remains and early diffusion of his relics both in England and on the continent (§§ X bis, XI, and XIII), to a discussion of the origin of the Sauris relic, the history of the local sanctuary, and its enduring popularity as a pilgrimage resort (§ XII). Della Stua goes to great lengths to identify the Sauris relic not just generically as a finger but as the left thumb, in particular. Firstly, the shape and size of the relic is that of a thumb, as della Stua himself often had the opportunity to see close up and as attested by both Soardo and the Rector of the Sauris sanctuary, the above-mentioned Antongiacomi.[97] Secondly, it must necessarily be the left thumb because, as della Stua himself had previously reported, the right hand with the arm, originally enshrined in Bamburgh, was eventually moved to Ely in 1175, where he surmises it is still kept.[98] And while the right hand must undoubtedly be incorrupt, according to Aidan's prophecy and as attested by sources from William of Malmesbury to William Camden (d. 1623),[99] the Sauris thumb is instead *nudo affatto e spolpato* (completely stripped bare of any flesh).[100]

As to the route followed by the relic to Sauris, della Stua dismisses the tradition that it was brought to Sauris by a German huntsman and proposes instead that it was collected straight from the battlefield and brought to Sauris by a local serving in St Oswald's army.[101] Della Stua admits that this (rather questionable) theory cannot ultimately be proven due to lack of historical records,[102] but insists that it is supported by a time-honoured tradition passed on through generations,[103] as well as by the travelling and entrepreneurial spirit of the Carnians apparently embodied by the putative soldier.[104]

It is somewhat puzzling that della Stua does not mention another (more credible) itinerary of the Sauris relic attested in one of his contemporary sources, Giusto Fontanini, Archbishop of Ankara and a celebrated Friulan historian and bibliophile, whom della Stua names in his introduction and to whom he gives

---

96 *VSO*, pp. 43–46, esp. 43 n. (e). This Life of St Oswald (*BHL*, no. 6366) is quoted via the *Acta Sanctorum* (cf. *Acta S. Oswaldi*, §§ 11–14, p. 85), but Capgrave's authorship has now been discredited: see De Meijer, 'Capgrave, John'.

97 *VSO*, p. 59.

98 *VSO*, p. 54.

99 *VSO*, p. 53.

100 *VSO*, p. 60.

101 *VSO*, pp. 60–61.

102 'Il difetto di monumenti non ci lascia rischiarare, siccome vorremmo, questo punto' (Much as we would like to clarify this point, the lack of documents doesn't allow us to do so): *VSO*, p. 61.

103 'è tradizion costante passata dagli Avi ai Nipoti' (It is a long-standing tradition passed down from the forebears to their offspring): *VSO*, p. 60.

104 'Il genio viaggiatore e industre della Nazion Carna pare che ci renda anche più certi e sicuri del fatto' (The travelling and entrepreneurial spirit of the Carnian nation seems to make us more certain and positive of this circumstance): *VSO*, pp. 60–61.

pride of place at the opening of the chapter devoted to Sauris.[105] In his life of
St Colomba of Aquileia (d. 524) published in 1726,[106] Fontanini included the
Sauris thumb in a large gift of relics by Patriarch Paulinus of Aquileia to Angilbert,
during the latter's embassy to Pope Leo III on behalf of Charlemagne in 796.
Together with most of these relics, Oswald's thumb would then have been
part of a donation by Pope Eugene III to the abbey of St Matthias in Trier in
1148.[107] Interestingly, in the work of a local historian, Niccolò Grassi, published
in 1782, both the theory of the Carnian soldier and that of Angilbert as agents
of transmission of the Sauris relic are reported, though merely juxtaposed.[108]
However, unlike Fontanini, Grassi mentions a further step: that Angilbert would
in turn have donated the relics to the north French Abbey of St Riquier during
his abbacy there. Be that as it may, the circumstances of the subsequent arrival
of Oswald's thumb, whether from Trier or St Riquier, to Sauris are not explained
by either Fontanini or Grassi. More recently, Baker has suggested that the Sauris
relic could instead be traced back to Salzburg, which may well have been a centre
of Oswald's cult in the Alpine regions thanks to its Irish connections, but in the
current state of knowledge it remains a matter of speculation.[109]

Similarly, della Stua ultimately has to rely on tradition when it comes to
the authenticity of the Sauris thumb, since the definitive certification has
become lost.[110] Hence, indirect but no less sound proof of the authenticity
of the relic is afforded by the antiquity of the church hosting the relic, and
of official documents recording the indulgences granted by high prelates,
including popes Clement X, Clement XI, and Benedict XIV, to devotees
and pilgrims since 1328, as well as by the frequent and uninterrupted series
of miracles attested both by the *ex voto* tablets hanging from the sanctuary
walls and by the esteemed clerics.[111] (Della Stua duly collects extracts from
relevant records spanning from 1328 to 1750 in a final appendix.[112])

The nature of the (many) miracles allegedly accomplished by Oswald's
relics or through Oswald's intercession, both in Sauris and elsewhere, is
rarely specified,[113] but when it is, they tend to be miraculous healings.[114]
Notably, della Stua reports the three healings from plague ascribed to
Oswald by Bede and Reginald of Durham.[115] However, while della Stua
repeatedly attributes many miracles to Oswald and strongly defends their

---

105 *VSO*, pp. 7, 59.
106 Fontanini, *Di Santa Colomba* [...] *commentario*. On St Colomba, see Villa, 'Colomba, Santa'.
107 Fontanini, *Di Santa Colomba* [...] *commentario*, pp. 44–48, esp. 47–48.
108 Grassi, *Notizie storiche*, pp. 170–74, esp. 170–71.
109 Baker, 'The Cult of St Oswald', pp. 175, 190; Tilatti, 'La parrocchia', p. 83. On Salzburg, see
      above, pp. 413–14, esp. n. 44.
110 *VSO*, pp. 61–65.
111 *VSO*, pp. 62–68.
112 *VSO*, pp. 81–83.
113 *VSO*, pp. 51, 58, 69.
114 *VSO*, pp. 31, 55–56, 64–66, 69–70, 82.
115 *VSO*, pp. 69–73, 43–46.

truth against the disbelief of Protestant authors,[116] he seems somewhat unwilling to dwell on them. This reluctance is probably in keeping with della Stua's own proposition of being as factual as possible, but also with the contemporary more cautious, rationalistic approach to saints' cults endorsed by Pope Benedict XIV (1740–1758) in his meticulous and extensive treaty on the process of canonization and beatification,[117] and by L. A. Muratori (1672–1750) with his appeal to a *regolata divozion* (disciplined devotion).[118] Indeed, at one point, della Stua claims that, however great the miracles wrought by Oswald, the chief proof of his sanctity doesn't rest on them but on the virtues that consistently inspired his life,[119] even though he reasons that it is to *sì fatti prodigi* (such wonders) that Oswald ultimately owes his great reputation.[120] Thus, although della Stua is not always explicit or particularly emphatic about Oswald's healing powers, it can be concluded that what constantly drew flocks of pilgrims to Sauris,[121] in spite of the remoteness of its sanctuary,[122] was Oswald's fame as a thaumaturge, especially effective against plagues and pandemics.[123]

The case della Stua is most determined to argue concerns Oswald's classification as a martyr, presumably as a way of enhancing the prestige of his subject, given that martyrs are second only to the apostles in the hierarchy of saints' categories, as well as of rebutting Protestant attempts to disprove the king's sanctity and miracles.[124] Moreover, della Stua's vindication of Oswald's martyrdom should be read in light of the contemporary debate on saints' devotion,[125] not to mention the revised edition of the Roman Martyrology overseen by Pope Benedict XIV.[126]

Oswald is presented by his joint official qualification of king and martyr in the title of della Stua's work (*Vita di S. Osvaldo re di Nortumberland e*

---

116 *VSO*, pp. 73–74.

117 Benedict, *De servorum Dei beatificatione*.

118 Muratori, *Della regolata divozion*.

119 'Ma per risplendenti che fossero questi miracoli, può dirsi che le principali prove della sua santità consistevano nelle virtù che la componevano' (However shining these miracles had been, it can be said that the chief pieces of evidence of his sanctity consisted of the virtues that constituted it): *VSO*, p. 51.

120 *VSO*, p. 51.

121 'i Divoti, che più di cento miglia lontani da Venezia, dal Territorio Vicentino e Padovano, e dalla Marca Trivigiana, e da molte altre parti vengono a prosciogliere i loro voti' (The devotees that come to fulfil their vows from further away than one thousand miles, from Venice, the region of Vicenza and Padua, from the province of Treviso, and from many other regions): *VSO*, p. 65. See also Fontanini, *Di Santa Colomba* [...] *commentario*, p. 48; Grassi, *Notizie storiche*, pp. 171–72.

122 The road leading to the sanctuary was apparently 'aspra, montuosa, erta, ed appena capace di qualche cavalcatura, non già di alcuna sorta di Calessi' (harsh, mountainous, steep, and just wide enough for a horse to pass but not for any sort of barouche): *VSO*, p. 67.

123 Baker, 'The Cult of St Oswald', pp. 167–68, 178–79.

124 *VSO*, pp. 4, 74.

125 See above, nn. 117, 118.

126 Benedict, *Martyrologium romanum*.

martire), in the dedication to the Archbishop of Udine, and three times again in the course of the narrative,[127] as well as in three of the official documents pertaining to the sanctuary quoted by della Stua.[128] Della Stua also picks up on Oswald's mistaken classification as a confessor rather than a martyr in one of his sources.[129] Moreover, della Stua reviews and discusses extensively the 'evidence' in favour of Oswald's martyrdom in the third and final section of his work.[130] He acknowledges that neither Bede nor the earliest martyrologies identify Oswald as a martyr, and relies instead on later calendars and martyrologies as well as, once again, the devotional tradition. Furthermore, he rests his argument on the patristic authority of St Augustine, reaffirmed by Pope Benedict XIV, according to whom what makes a martyr is first and foremost the *cause* of their death, i.e. the upholding of the Christian faith, rather than the *manner* of it, as expressed in the famous Augustinian motto *non poena sed causa*.[131]

On a final note, it is striking that, as for Bede and Ælfric, for della Stua too, Oswald still epitomizes the ideal of Christian kingship, being compared to Hezekiah, Constantine, and Theodosius.[132] Oswald is credited with creating an *ante litteram* United Kingdom by joining under his crown the whole of England with Wales, Scotland, and Ireland, countries which apparently submitted voluntarily *en masse* to his enlightened, charitable rule.[133] A further aspect of Oswald's outstanding leadership was, apparently, his love of learning and instigation of a programme of instruction, including the foundation of state schools where children could be instructed both in letters and the Christian faith. This characterization, unparalleled in Bede, probably reflects contemporary preoccupations and the appropriate sensibilities of a man of the Enlightenment.[134]

---

127 *VSO*, pp. 5, 9, 43–46, 59, 66.
128 *VSO*, pp. 67, 81, 82.
129 See above, n. 89.
130 *VSO*, pp. 77–80.
131 *VSO*, pp. 78–79. On Augustine's argument, see Łazewski, 'La sentenza agostiniana'.
132 *VSO*, pp. 29–31.
133 *VSO*, pp. 48–49. Here della Stua expands rather enthusiastically on *HE*, III.6, ll. 5–7, where it is stated that Oswald held under his sway all the peoples and kingdoms of Britain; this claim, however, should be interpreted conservatively in the sense of some overlordship by Oswald over the Anglo-Saxon kingdoms and some of the British nations: see *HE*, pp. 230–31 and n. 1; Stancliffe, 'Oswald, "Most Holy and Most Victorious King"', pp. 46–61. Bede may be echoing some earlier tradition (cf. Adomnán, *Vita S. Columbae*, ed. and trans. by Anderson and Anderson, I. 1.9a, pp. 16–17), and Alcuin and Ælfric, in turn, reiterate Bede's statement: Alcuin, *Versus de patribus regibus*, ed. and trans. by Godman, ll. 499–502 (pp. 42–43); Ælfric, 'Life of St Oswald', ed. by Needham, ll. 87–89 (p. 32).
134 *VSO*, pp. 37–39; cf. *HE*, III.3, ll. 38–40.

Conclusion

Many centuries and miles away from its original setting, in eighteenth-century Friuli Oswald's life is still narrated as a politico-religious success story, exemplifying that collaboration between church and state by which alone society can thrive. Like his Anglo-Saxon predecessors, however, della Stua goes beyond the political implications and portrays Oswald as an all-round figure of sanctity, encompassing wholehearted devotion, remarkable charity, missionary zeal, as well as an important bonus of the post-Bedan tradition, the martyrial sacrifice. Hence, he further strengthens the tradition inaugurated by Bede of a cult figure of universal appeal, capable of being 'absorbed into the devotional symbolism of the universal church'.[135] At the same time, Oswald and the narrative of his political and evangelizing mission, healing powers, and martyrdom are adopted and adapted to make him the identitarian symbol of an idiosyncratic, secluded Alpine community, as well as the embodiment of contemporary, more exacting paradigms of Catholic sanctity and modern ideals of enlightened kingship. This adoption of the early medieval, northern English king-saint centuries and miles away from the original setting of his life demonstrates the relevance of the all too often overlooked medieval past in the shaping of the modern, as well as opening a new window onto the vast and complex interweave making up the cultural fabric of Europe.

---

135 Clemoes, *The Cult of St Oswald*, p. 592.

Works Cited

Manuscripts and Archival Sources

Cividale, Museo Archeologico Nazionale, MS X
——, MS XI
——, MS XV
——, MS XVI
Gorizia, Biblioteca del Seminario, MS 9
Udine, Biblioteca Civica 'V. Joppi', MS Joppi 142

Primary Sources

Acta S. Oswaldi: De S. Oswaldo rege ac martyre in Anglia commentaries prævius, ed. by Joannes Pinius, in *Acta Sanctorum Augustii* [...] *Tomus II*, ed. by Jean B. Du Sollier, Jean Pien, Guillaume Cuypers, and Pieter van den Bosch (Antwerp: van der Plassche, 1735), pp. 83–93

Adomnán, *Vita S. Columbae*, ed. and trans. by Alan O. Anderson and Marjorie O. Anderson, Oxford Medieval Texts, rev. edn (Oxford: Clarendon Press, 1991)

Ælfric of Eynsham, 'Life of St Oswald' [*Non. Ag. Natale Sancti Oswaldi regis et martyris*], in *Lives of Three English Saints*, ed. by Geoffrey I. Needham, rev. edn (Exeter: Exeter University Press, 1976), pp. 27–42

Alcuin, *Versus de patribus regibus et sanctis euboracensis ecclesiae*, ed. and trans. by Peter Godman (Oxford: Clarendon Press, 1982)

Bede, *Historia ecclesiastica gentis Anglorum; Historia abbatum; Epistola ad Ecgberctum una cum Historia abbatum auctore anonymo*, ed. by Charles Plummer, 2 vols (Oxford: Clarendon Press, 1881–1896)

——, *Historia ecclesiastica gentis anglorum. Bede's Ecclesiastical History of the English People*, ed. and trans. by Bertram Colgrave and Roger A. B. Mynors (Oxford: Clarendon Press, 1969) (cited as *HE*)

Benedict XIV, *De servorum Dei beatificatione et beatorum canonizatione*, 4 vols (Bologna: Longhi, 1734–1738)

——, *Martyrologium romanum Gregorii XIII jussu editum* [...] *editio nouissima* [...] (Rome: Typographia Balleoniana, 1748)

Della Stua, Giampietro, *Vita di Sant'Osvaldo re di Northumberland e martire colla storia del suo culto* (Udine: A. del Pedro, 1769) (cited as *VSO*) <https://books.google.it/books?id=AE9iAAAAcAAJ&printsec=frontcover&hl=it&source=gbs_ge_summary_r&cad=0#v=onepage&q&f=false> [accessed 10 July 2019]

Drogo of Saint-Winnoc, *Sermones primus et secundus in festo pretiosi regis et martyris Oswaldi*, in 'De twee sermoenen van Drogo van Sint Winnoksbergen over de konig-martelaar St Oswald', ed. by Nicolas-N. Huyghebaert, *Ons Gestelijk Erf*, 56 (1982), 97–108

——, *Vita S. Oswaldi regis ac martyris*, in *Acta Sanctorum Augustii*, pp. 94–103

Fontanini, Giusto, *Di Santa Colomba vergine sacra della città di Aquileia* […] *Commentario* […] (Rome: Bernabò, 1726)

Grassi, Niccolò, *Notizie storiche della provincia della Carnia* […] (Udine: Gallici, 1782)

Der Heiligen Leben und Leiden: anders gennant das Passional, ed. by Severin Rüttgers, 2 vols (Leipzig: Insel, 1913)

Hrotsvitha of Gandersheim, *Gesta Ottonis Imperatoris*, ed. and trans. by Maria P. Pillolla, Per verba, 20 (Tavarnuzze: SISMEL-Edizioni del galluzzo, 2003)

Muratori, L. A., *Della regolata divozion de' cristiani* (Venice: Albrizzi, 1747)

The Old English Martyrology. Edition, Translation and Commentary, ed. and trans. by Christine Rauer, Anglo-Saxon Texts, 10 (Cambridge: Brewer, 2013)

Ósvalds saga, in *St Oswald of Northumbria: Continental Metamorphoses. With an Edition and Translation of 'Ósvalds saga' and 'Van sunte Oswaldo deme konninghe'*, ed. and trans. by Marianne E. Kalinke, Medieval and Renaissance Texts and Studies, 27 (Tempe, AZ: ACMRS, 2005)

Pace, Stefano, *Vita di S. Osvaldo, re di Nortumbria, dedicata al merito dell'eccellentissima suor Regina Ghesina abbadessa, suor Verginia Cividale Vicaria e di tutte le altre monache del Monasterio d'Araceli di Vicenza* (Bassano: n. pub., 1712)

Quentin, Henri, *Les martyrologes historiques du moyen âge: étude sur la formation du martyrologe romain* (Paris: Lecoffre, 1908); repr. in Uomini e mondi medievali. Reprints Centro italiano di Studi sull'Alto Medioevo, 5, I (Spoleto: Centro italiano di Studi sull'Alto Medioevo, 2002)

Reginald of Durham, *Vita S. Oswaldi*, in *Symeonis monachi opera omnia*, ed. by Thomas Arnold, 2 vols, Rolls Series, 75 (London: HMSO, 1882–1885), I, pp. 326–85

Soardo, Pietro C., *Vita di S. Osvaldo Re di Northumbria, specchio e esempio de' Principi e Soldati Christiani: corrota del Venerabile Beda e di altri approvati Autori*, (Udine: G. A. Re, 1667; 2nd edn Udine and Bassano, 1689)

Secondary Works

Bailey, Richard N., 'St Oswald's Heads', in *Oswald: Northumbrian King to European Saint*, ed. by Clare Stancliffe and Eric Cambridge (Stamford: Paul Watkins, 1995), pp. 195–209

Baker, E. P., 'St Oswald and His Church at Zug', *Archaeologia*, 93 (1949), 103–23

——, 'The Cult of St Oswald in Northern Italy', *Archaeologia*, 94 (1951), 167–94

Bergamini, Giuseppe, and Furio Bianco, 'Introduzione', in *Un santo inglese a Sauris. Il culto e il mito di Sant'Osvaldo nei territori alpini e in Europa*, ed. by Giuseppe Bergamini and Furio Bianco (Udine: Forum, 2006), pp. 7–25

Bidese, Ermenegildo, James R. Dow, and Thomas Stolz, ed., *Das Zimbrische zwischen Germanisch und Romanisch*, Diversitas Linguarum, 9 (Bochum: Brockmeyer, 2005)

Blair, John, 'Gloucester', in *The Wiley Blackwell Encyclopedia of Anglo-Saxon England*, ed. by Michael Lapidge, John Blair, Simon Keynes, and Donald Scragg, 2nd edn (Chichester: Wiley Blackwell, 2014), p. 215

Bowden, Sarah, *Bridal-Quest Epics in Medieval Germany: A Revisionary Approach* (London: Modern Humanities Research Association, 2012)

Bucco, Gabriella, *Le chiese del Comune di Sauris* (Udine: Deputazione di Storia Patria per il Friuli, 2017)

Cambridge, Eric, 'Archaeology and Cult of St Oswald in Pre-Conquest Northumbria', in *Oswald: Northumbrian King to European Saint*, ed. by Clare Stancliffe and Eric Cambridge (Stamford: Paul Watkins, 1995), pp. 128–63

Caria, Marco, 'Le isole linguistiche germanofone in Italia: la realtà plurilingue della Valcanale nei suoi aspetti sociolinguistici' (unpublished doctoral thesis, University of Sassari, 2014)

Chiesa, Paolo, 'Il re che divenne martire. Oswald di Northumbria fra storia e leggenda', in *Un santo inglese a Sauris. Il culto e il mito di Sant'Osvaldo nei territori alpini e in Europa*, ed. by Giuseppe Bergamini and Furio Bianco (Udine: Forum, 2006), pp. 27–54

Clemoes, Peter, 'The Chronology of Ælfric's Works', in *The Anglo-Saxons. Studies in Some Aspects of their History and Culture Presented to Bruce Dickins*, ed. by Peter Clemoes (London: Bowes & Bowes, 1959), pp. 212–47; repr. with addenda, in *Old English Prose: Basic Readings*, ed. by Paul E. Szarmach (New York: Garland, 2000), pp. 29–72

——, *The Cult of St Oswald on the Continent*, Jarrow Lecture, 1983 (Tyne and Wear: St Paul's Church, 1983); repr. in *Bede and His World: The Jarrow Lectures 1958–1993*, ed. by Michael Lapidge, 2 vols (Aldershot: Variorum, 1994), II, pp. 590–610

Cozzi, Donatella, Domenico Isabella, and Elisabetta Navarra, ed., *Sauris/Zahre. Una comunità delle Alpi Carniche*, 2 vols (Udine: Forum, 1998–1999)

Cramp, Rosemary, 'The Making of Oswald's Northumbria', in *Oswald: Northumbrian King to European Saint*, ed. by Clare Stancliffe and Eric Cambridge (Stamford: Paul Watkins, 1995), pp. 17–32

Cross, James E., 'The Ethic of War in Old English', in *England Before the Conquest: Studies in Primary Sources Presented to Dorothy Whitelock*, ed. by Peter Clemoes and Katharine Hughes (Cambridge: Cambridge University Press, 1971), pp. 269–82

Curschmann, Michael, *Der Münchener Oswald und die deutsche spielmännische Epik*, Münchener Texte und Untersuchungen zur deutschen Literatur des Mittelalters, 6 (Munich: Beck, 1964)

De Meijer, Alberic, 'Capgrave, John', in *NCE*, III, col. 83

Di Sciacca, Claudia, '"concupita, quaesita, ac petita solitudinis secreta": The Desert Ideal in Bede's *Vita S. Cuthberti* and Ælfric's *Life of St Cuthbert*', in *Hagiography in Anglo-Saxon England: Adopting and Adapting Saints' Lives into Old English Prose (c. 950–1150)*, ed. by Loredana Lazzari, Patrizia Lendinara, and Claudia Di Sciacca, TEMA, 73 (Barcelona: Brepols, 2014), pp. 121–81

Dockray-Miller, Mary, *The Books and the Life of Judith of Flanders* (Farnham: Ashgate, 2015)

Du Moustier, Benoît, 'Surius, Lawrence', in *NCE*, XIII, pp. 628–29

Edwards, Francis O., 'Alford, Michael', in *NCE*, I, pp. 278–79

Folz, Robert, 'Saint Oswald Roi de Northumbrie: étude d'hagiographie royale', *Analecta Bollandiana*, 98 (1980), 49–74

——, *Les Saints Rois du moyen âge en occident (VIᵉ-XIIIᵉ siècles)*, Subsidia Hagiographica, 68 (Brussels: Société des Bollandistes, 1984)

Gretsch, Mechthild, *Ælfric and the Cult of Saints in Late Anglo-Saxon England*, Cambridge Studies in Anglo-Saxon England, 34 (Cambridge: Cambridge University Press, 2005)

Gunn, Victoria A., 'Bede and the Martyrdom of St Oswald', in *Martyrs and Martyrologies*, ed. by Diana S. Wood, Studies in Church History, 30 (Oxford: Blackwell, 1993), pp. 57–66

Holdsworth, Philip, 'Oswald, King of Northumbria', in *The Wiley Blackwell Encyclopedia of Anglo-Saxon England*, ed. by Michael Lapidge, John Blair, Simon Keynes, and Donald Scragg, 2nd edn (Chichester: Wiley Blackwell, 2014), p. 355

——, 'Oswiu', in *The Wiley Blackwell Encyclopedia of Anglo-Saxon England*, ed. by Michael Lapidge, John Blair, Simon Keynes, and Donald Scragg, 2nd edn (Chichester: Wiley Blackwell, 2014), pp. 356–57

Hornung, Maria, 'Die Osttiroler Bauernsprachinseln Pladen und Zahre in Oberkarnien', *Osttiroler Heimblätter*, 98 (1960), 1–14

Huyghebaert, Nicolas-N., 'Un moine hagiographe: Droge de Bergues', *Sacris Erudiri*, 20 (1971), 191–256

Jansen, Annemiek, 'The Development of St Oswald's Legends on the Continent', in *Oswald: Northumbrian King to European Saint*, ed. by Clare Stancliffe and Eric Cambridge (Stamford: Paul Watkins, 1995), pp. 230–40

Jolly, Karen L., *The Community of St Cuthbert in the Late Tenth Century: The Chester-le-Street Additions to Durham Cathedral Library A.IV.19* (Columbus: Ohio University Press, 2012)

Keynes, Simon, 'Æthelred', in *The Wiley Blackwell Encyclopedia of Anglo-Saxon England*, ed. by Michael Lapidge, John Blair, Simon Keynes, and Donald Scragg, 2nd edn (Chichester: Wiley Blackwell, 2014), p. 16

Klaniczay, Gábor, *Holy Rulers and Blessed Princesses: Dynastic Cults in Medieval Central Europe* (Cambridge: Cambridge University Press, 2002)

Kleist, Aaron J., 'Ælfric's Corpus: A Conspectus', *Florilegium*, 18 (2001), 113–64

——, *The Chronology and Canon of Ælfric of Eynsham*, Anglo-Saxon Studies, 37 (Cambridge: Brewer, 2019)

Łazewski, Wojciech, 'La sentenza agostiniana *martyrem facit non poena sed causa*' (unpublished doctoral thesis, Pontificia Universitas Lateranensis, 1987)

Lazzari, Loredana, 'Kingship and Sainthood in Ælfric: Oswald (634–42) and Edmund (840–69)', in *Hagiography in Anglo-Saxon England: Adopting and Adapting Saints' Lives into Old English Prose (c. 950–1150)*, ed. by Loredana Lazzari, Patrizia Lendinara, and Claudia Di Sciacca, TEMA, 73 (Barcelona: Brepols, 2014), pp. 29–64

Merlino, Chiara, 'Oswald di Northumbria in due passionari meddioevali', in *Un santo inglese a Sauris. Il culto e il mito di Sant'Osvaldo nei territori alpini e in Europa*, ed. by Giuseppe Bergamini and Furio Bianco (Udine: Forum, 2006), pp. 65–73

Miller, Sean, 'Æthelstan', in *The Wiley Blackwell Encyclopedia of Anglo-Saxon England*, ed. by Michael Lapidge, John Blair, Simon Keynes, and Donald Scragg, 2nd edn (Chichester: Wiley Blackwell, 2014), pp. 17–18

——, 'Æthelweard', in *The Wiley Blackwell Encyclopedia of Anglo-Saxon England*, ed. by Michael Lapidge, John Blair, Simon Keynes, and Donald Scragg, 2nd edn (Chichester: Wiley Blackwell, 2014), p. 20

——, 'Edward the Martyr', in *The Wiley Blackwell Encyclopedia of Anglo-Saxon England*, ed. by Michael Lapidge, John Blair, Simon Keynes, and Donald Scragg, 2nd edn (Chichester: Wiley Blackwell, 2014), pp. 167–68

Mostert, Marco, 'Willibrord', in *The Wiley Blackwell Encyclopedia of Anglo-Saxon England*, ed. by Michael Lapidge, John Blair, Simon Keynes, and Donald Scragg, 2nd edn (Chichester: Wiley Blackwell, 2014), p. 499

Ó Riain-Raedel, Dagmar, 'Edith, Judith, Matilda: The Role of Royal Ladies in the Propagation of the Continental Cult', in *Oswald: Northumbrian King to European Saint*, ed. by Clare Stancliffe and Eric Cambridge (Stamford: Paul Watkins, 1995), pp. 210–29

Perusini, Teresa, 'L'altare di Sant'Osvaldo a Sauris di Sotto', in *Un santo inglese a Sauris. Il culto e il mito di Sant'Osvaldo nei territori alpini e in Europa*, ed. by Giuseppe Bergamini and Furio Bianco (Udine: Forum, 2006), pp. 75–85

Prezzi, Christian, ed., *Isole di cultura: Saggi sulle minoranze storiche germaniche in Italia* (Lucerne: Centro di documentazione, 2004)

Rettori, Stefania, 'Un re taumaturgo. Il culto di Sant'Osvaldo a Sauris e in Friuli' (unpublished MA dissertation, University of Udine, 1995–1996)

Ridyard, Susan J., *Royal Saints of Anglo-Saxon England: A Study of West Saxon and East Anglian Cults* (Cambridge: Cambridge University Press, 1988)

Rollason, David, 'The Cult of Murdered Royal Saints in Anglo-Saxon England', *Anglo-Saxon England*, 11 (1983), 1–22

——, 'Relic-Cults as an Instrument of Royal Policy c. 900–c. 1050', *Anglo-Saxon England*, 15 (1986), 91–103

——, 'St Cuthbert and Wessex: The Evidence of Cambridge, Corpus Christi College MS 183', in *St Cuthbert, His Cult and His Community to AD 1200*, ed. by Gerald Bonner, David Rollason, and Clare Stancliffe (Woodbridge: Boydell, 1989), pp. 413–24

——, 'St Oswald in Post-Conquest England', in *Oswald: Northumbrian King to European Saint*, ed. by Clare Stancliffe and Eric Cambridge (Stamford: Paul Watkins, 1995), pp. 164–77

Scalon, Cesare, and Laura Pani, *I codici della Biblioteca capitolare di Cividale del Friuli* (Florence: SISMEL — Edizioni del Galluzzo, 1998)

Simpson, Luisella, 'The King Alfred/St Cuthbert Episode in the *Historia de sancto Cuthberto*: Its Significance for Mid-Tenth-Century English History', in *St Cuthbert, His Cult and His Community to AD 1200*, ed. by Gerald Bonner, David Rollason, and Clare Stancliffe (Woodbridge: Boydell, 1989), pp. 397–411

Stancliffe, Clare, 'Oswald, "Most Holy and Most Victorious King of the Northumbrians"', in *Oswald: Northumbrian King to European Saint*, ed. by Clare Stancliffe and Eric Cambridge (Stamford: Paul Watkins, 1995), pp. 33–83

——, 'Where Was Oswald Killed?', in *Oswald: Northumbrian King to European Saint*, ed. by Clare Stancliffe and Eric Cambridge (Stamford: Paul Watkins, 1995), pp. 84–96

Stancliffe, Clare, and Eric Cambridge, 'Introduction', in *Oswald: Northumbrian King to European Saint*, ed. by Clare Stancliffe and Eric Cambridge (Stamford: Paul Watkins, 1995), pp. 1–16

Thacker, Alan, 'Bede's Ideal of Reform', in *Ideal and Reality in Frankish and Anglo-Saxon Society. Studies Presented to J. M. Wallace-Hadrill*, ed. by Patrick Wormald, Donald Bullough, and Roger Collins (Oxford: Blackwell, 1983), pp. 130–53

——, 'Lindisfarne and the Origins of the Cult of St Cuthbert', in *St Cuthbert, His Cult and His Community to AD 1200*, ed. by Gerald Bonner, David Rollason, and Clare Stancliffe (Woodbridge: Boydell, 1989), pp. 103–22

——, '*Membra Disiecta*: The Division of the Body and the Diffusion of the Cult', in *Oswald: Northumbrian King to European Saint*, ed. by Clare Stancliffe and Eric Cambridge (Stamford: Paul Watkins, 1995), pp. 97–127

——, 'Cuthbert', in *The Wiley Blackwell Encyclopedia of Anglo-Saxon England*, ed. by Michael Lapidge, John Blair, Simon Keynes, and Donald Scragg, 2nd edn (Chichester: Wiley Blackwell, 2014), pp. 134–35

Tilatti, Andrea, 'La parrocchia di Sauris: le chiese, gli uomini, i santi', in *Sauris/ Zahre. Una comunità delle Alpi Carniche*, ed. by Donatella Cozzi, Domenico Isabella, and Elisabette Navarra (Udine: Forum, 1998–1999), I, pp. 63–90

Toussaint, C., 'Baillet Adrien', in *Dictionnaire de théologie catholique*, ed. by Alfred Vacant and Eugène Mangenot, 15 vols (Paris: Letouzey et Ané, 1915–1950), II, cols 36–37

Tudor, Victoria, 'Reginald's *Life of St Oswald*', in *Oswald: Northumbrian King to European Saint*, ed. by Clare Stancliffe and Eric Cambridge (Stamford: Paul Watkins, 1995), pp. 178–94

Villa, Luca, 'Colomba, Santa', in *Nuovo Liruti: Dizionario biografico dei friulani. I: Il Medioevo*, ed. by Cesare Scalon, 2 vols (Udine: Forum, 2006) <http://www.dizionariobiograficodeifriulani.it/colomba/> [accessed 10 July 2019]

Vizkelety, András, 'Der Budapester Oswald', *Beiträge zur Geschichte der deutschen Sprache und Literatur*, 86 (1964), 107–88

——, 'Oswald König von Northumbrien', in *Lexicon der christlichen Ikonographie. Ikonographie der Heiligen*, ed. by Engelbert Kirschbaum and Wolfgang Braunfels, 8 vols (Rome: Herder, 1968–1976), VIII, cols 102–03

Wallace-Hadrill, John M., *Bede's Ecclesiastical History of the English People: A Historical Commentary*, Oxford Medieval Texts (Oxford: Clarendon Press, 1993)

Weitbrecht, Julia, 'Häusliche Heiligkeit: Zur Transformation religiöser Leitbilder in der Oswaldlegende', *Beiträge zur Geschichte der deutschen Sprache und Literatur*, 137/I (2015), pp. 63–79

Whatley, E. Gordon, 'Cuthbertus, vita', in Frederick M. Biggs and others, ed., *SASLC AAS: Sources of Anglo-Saxon Literary Culture. vol. I: Abbo of Fleury, Abbo of Saint-Germain-des-Prés, and Acta sanctorum* (Kalamazoo: Medieval Institute Publications, 2001), pp. 157–60

——, 'Oswaldus Rex', in Frederick M. Biggs and others, ed., *SASLC AAS: Sources of Anglo-Saxon Literary Culture*. vol. I: *Abbo of Fleury, Abbo of Saint-Germain-des-Prés, and Acta sanctorum* (Kalamazoo: Medieval Institute Publications, 2001), pp. 366–68

Whitehead, Christiania, 'Translating the Northern English Saints Within Late Medieval Vernacular Legendaries: Oswald, Cuthbert, Ninian', *Viator*, 49.2 (2018), 25–45

Wolf, Kirsten, *The Legends of the Saints in Old Norse-Icelandic Prose* (Toronto: University of Toronto Press, 2013)

Manuscript Index

Aberdeen, Aberdeen University
Library, MS 25 (Burnet Psalter):
110
Alnwick Castle, MS D XI: 370–71,
373, 381

Cambridge, Cambridge University
Library, MS Additional 2604: 70
MS Additional 3037: 61, 343
MS EDC 1: 286
MS Ee.4.20: 370
MS Ff.1.27: 136
MS Gg.4.11: 378
MS Ii.6.2: 112
Cambridge, Corpus Christi
College, MS 7: 376
MS 26: 369
MS 96: 380
MS 161: 65
Cambridge, Fitzwilliam Museum,
MS 300: 346
Cambridge, Jesus College,
MS Q.B.6: 378
MS Q.B.7: 37
Cambridge, Pembroke College,
MS 82: 369
Cambridge, St John's College,
MS C.18: 368
MS E.26: 103, 105, 108, 110, 113, 115
Cambridge, Trinity College,
MS O.2.1: 286
MS R.3.29: 56
Cambridge, MA, Harvard College,
MS Lat. 27: 58

Cividale, Museo Archeologico
Nazionale, MS X: 418
MS XI: 418
MS XV: 418
MS XVI: 418

Dijon, Bibliothèque publique,
MS 657: 206, 210
Dublin, Trinity College, MS 496: 376
Durham University Library,
Archives and Special
Collections, MS DPR/1/2/2: 391
MS DPR/I/1/1574/W3/1: 391
MS DPR/I/1/1584/B6/1: 391
Durham, Cathedral Chapter
Library, MS B II 35: 210
MS B IV 24: 372
Durham, Durham University
Library, MS Cosin B III 30: 179
MS Cosin V IV 9: 330

Edinburgh, Advocates Library,
MS Abbotsford (Osbern
Bokenham's *Legenda aurea*): 242

Gloucester Cathedral, MS 1: 61, 65
Gorizia, Biblioteca del Seminario,
MS 9: 418

Hildesheim, Dombibliothek,
MS St Godehard 1: 366

Kew, The National Archives,
E25/120/1: 390
E101/44/26: 188
E164/31: 390

E164/37 (Exchequer: King's Remembrancer: Miscellaneous Books series I, date 12 Eliz I): 325
E179/35/7: 389
E179/45/9: 389
E179/68/11: 389
E315/233: 388
E315/245: 390
E315/494/1: 390
E322/112: 388
JUST 3.79.3.014: 331
PROB 11/28: 390
SP 1/109: 381
SP 49/1: 361
SP 58/1/27: 362

Leeds, Leeds University, Brotherton Collection, MS Additional 18: 103, 111, 112
Lichfield Cathedral, MS o.1: 210
Lincoln Cathedral, MS 149: 61
MS 150: 61
Lincoln, Lincolnshire Archives, Episcopal Register XXIV: 396
London, British Library, MS Additional 4715: 307
MS Additional 8102: 390
MS Additional 17511: 56
MS Additional 28946: 103, 109, 112, 115
MS Additional 35110: 56
MS Additional 35285: 333
MS Additional 42130: 188
MS Additional 44874, 332
MS Additional 50001 (Hours of Elizabeth the Queen): 103, 108
MS Additional 64952: 332, 398
MS Additional 70000: 330
MS Additional 70513: 287, 299
MS Additional 74236: 187

MS Additional 89379 (The Percy Hours): 102, 111
MS Arundel 201: 370
MS Cotton Caligula B.VI: 361
MS Cotton Claudius A.V: 26, 58–70
MS Cotton Claudius D.IV: 202, 204
MS Cotton Claudius D.VII: 87
MS Cotton Claudius E.IV: 64, 210, 365
MS Cotton Cleopatra A.XIII: 107
MS Cotton Domitian A.XV: 286
MS Cotton Faustina B.IV: 26, 58–70, 365, 368
MS Cotton Faustina B.VI, pars ii: 345
MS Cotton Galba A.XVII: 206
MS Cotton Julius D.III: 371
MS Cotton Nero A.V: 55
MS Cotton Tiberius D.III: 65
MS Cotton Tiberius E.I: 60, 375
MS Cotton Titus A.I: 286
MS Cotton Vitellius C.V: 210
MS Cotton Vitellius D.XX (V): 136
MS Cotton Vespasian A.XIX: 286
MS Cotton Vespasian F.III: 361
Egerton Charter 523: 183
MS Egerton 3143: 80, 218–19, 229
MS Egerton 3309: 251
MS Egerton 3721: 365
MS Harley 322: 61, 206–07
MS Harley 955: 103, 108, 110, 112–13
MS Harley 1260: 330
MS Harley 1804: 333
MS Harley 3775: 78, 224, 230
MS Harley 3776: 210

MANUSCRIPT INDEX 435

MS Harley 4664 (Coldingham
Breviary): 333, 372, 378
MS Lansdowne 436: 206
MS Royal 2 A XVIII (Beaufort-
Beauchamp Hours): 103,
107–08, 112, 115–17, 187
MS Royal 2 B VI: 365, 369
MS Royal 5 F VII: 206, 345
MS Royal 14 C VII: 369
MS Stowe 12: 378
London, Lambeth Palace Library,
Archbishops Register, Register
Sudbury: 395
MS 99: 379
MS Cart. Ant. et Misc. XI/56:
390
MS Lambeth 51: 210
London, Metropolitan Archives,
DL/A/A/004/MS09531/003:
395
DL/A/A/004/MS09531/010:
388
Los Angeles, Huntington Library,
MS HM 19915: 56

New Haven, Beineke Library,
MS Osborn a44: 112
New York, Pierpont Morgan
Library, MS M.105 (Porter
Hours): 99, 103, 117
Northallerton, North Yorkshire
Record Office, ZCG VI 1: 307
Nottingham, University of
Nottingham, MS WLC/
LM/LL: 112

Oxford, Bodleian Library,
MS Auct. D. inf. 2.11: 112
MS Barlow 41: 332
MS Dodsworth 118: 311
MS Dodsworth 159: 311
MS Fairfax 6: 206

MS Gough Gen. Top. 16,
(Gough map): 167
MS Gough Liturg. 18: 374
MS Hatton 101: 56
MS Lat. Liturg. F. 2: 102, 105,
109, 113, 116
MS Lat. Liturg. G. 8: 376
MS Laud Misc. 647: 286
MS Rawlinson A 416: 65
MS Rawlinson B 189: 377
MS Rawlinson Liturg. B.1 (The
Whitby Missal): 314, 332
MS Tanner 15: 375
Oxford, Corpus Christi College,
MS 134: 366, 370
Oxford, Jesus College, MS 77: 380
Oxford, Magdalen College, MS 53:
64
Oxford, Trinity College, MS 46:
379
Oxford, University College,
MS 82: 181–82

Paris, Bibliothèque Mazarine,
MS 1716: 209, 344–49, 356
Paris, Bibliothèque nationale de
France, MS français 413: 348
MS français 11662: 347, 350
MS français 23117: 348
MS latin 11784: 206
MS latin 17294: 185

Rennes, Bibliothèque Municipale,
MS 22: 107

Salisbury, Salisbury Cathedral
Library, MS 148: 210
Stafford, Staffordshire Record
Office, MS B/A/1/2: 394
Stockholm, Kungliga Biblioteket
Holmiensis A 49, 334

MANUSCRIPT INDEX

Taunton, Somerset Record Office,
MS D/D/B. Reg. 11: 387

Udine, Biblioteca Civica 'V. Joppi',
MS Joppi 142: 418

Winchester, Winchester Cathedral
Library, MS 10: 206

York, Borthwick Institute for
Archives, Probate Register
13/2: 390
Probate Register 15/3: 390
Probate Register 17/1: 391
York, Borthwick Institute of
Historical Research, Register
19: 159
York, York Minster Library, MS
Additional 2 (Bolton Hours):
103, 105, 109, 112, 115
MS Additional 54: 102, 105, 112,
115
MS Additional 67: 103, 105,
110–11, 113
MS M2(1)f: 113, 158
MS XVI.I.12: 210
MS XVI.K.6 (Pavement Hours):
103, 105

Index

Acca, bishop of Hexham, saint, *see also* Hexham bishop-saints: 37, 43–47, 178
  relics: 46–47
Aberdeen breviary: 186, 189
Adam of Dryburgh, theologian: 18
Adomnán, abbot of Iona Abbey, hagiographer: 56, 69, 420
  Vita sancti Columbae [*Life of Columba*]: 56
Æbbe of Coldingham, abbess, saint: 15, 18, 24, 28, 170, 186, 263–81, 288–91, 297
  cult, dual-location: 263, 267–68, 274
  locality: 264, 276–78
  mute, healing: 264, 268–74, 278–81; *see also*, healing, miraculous
  pilgrimage: 265
  relic: 186, 267, 270
  translation: 264, 286
Ælfflæd, abbess of Whitby: 170, 186, 265, 297
Ælfric, abbot of Eynsham, hagiographer: 410–14, 424
  Natale sancti Oswaldi regis et martyris [*Life of St Oswald*]: 410–11, 424; *see also* Oswald, King of Northumbria
Ælfwig: 308, 311, 322, 328
Ælfwold II, bishop of Sherbourne: 25, 131–35, 141
Aelred of Rievaulx, saint, abbot of Rievaulx: 26, 35–49, 56–57, 343–44

De miraculis Hagustaldensis ecclesiae: 36–37; *see also* Hexham, saint-bishops
Eulogium Davidis: 36; *see also* David I, King of Scotland
Genealogia regum Anglorum: 36
Speculum caritatis: 36
Vita sancti Ædwardi regis et confessoris [*Life of Saint Edward*]: 36, 65, 343–44; *see also* Edward 'the Confessor'
Vita sancti Niniani, [*Life of Ninian*]: 41–42, 57, 357; *see also* Ninian, saint
see also Walter, Daniel; *Vita Aelredi*
Ætheldreda of Ely, Queen of Northumbria, saint: 24, 28, 43, 112, 285–300,
  donor, gifts: 291, 295–99
  founder, role of: 292
  miracles: 292–94
  northern, saintly genealogy: 286, 288–91, 298–300
  pilgrimage to: 291
  shrine: 293
  see also Liber Eliensis (anon)
  see also Vie de Seinte Audree (anon)
Æthelred, Lord of the Mercians: 414
Æthelstan, King of the West Saxons: 181, 414–15
Æthelwine, bishop of Durham: 46
Æthelwold, bishop of Lindisfarne, 55, 138, 170, 399

INDEX

Affreca, wife of Sir John de
Courcy: 54
Agincourt, Battle of: 99, 109, 158–59
Aidan of Lindisfarne, saint,
bishop: 138–39, 170, 186–87, 377,
399, 403, 413
Alchmund, bishop of Hexham,
saint: 170, 37, 45, 47, *see also*
Hexham bishop-saints
relics: 47
Alban, saint, marytr: 58, 61–64,
188, 251–52, 395
*see also Gesta abbatum monasterii
sancti Albani* (anon)
see also The Boke of Saint Albans
(anon)
Alcuin, theologian, *Versus de
patribus regibus et sanctis
euboracensis ecclesiae*: 410–11;
see also Oswald, King of
Northumbria
Aldhelm of Malmesbury, saint,
abbot of Malmesbury, bishop of
Sherborne, scholar: 58, 61–65,
68, 399; *see also* Faricius of
Arezzo; *Vita sancti Aldhelmi*
Aldwin, prior of Durham and of
Winchcombe: 306, 308, 311, 322,
328
Alexander I, pope: 201
Alexander II, King of Scotland: 53,
68, 370
Alexander III, pope: 209
Alnwick, Northumbria: 18, 325–26,
361, 396–97
Ampleforth Chapel, *see* Hilda of
Whitby; dedications to
*Annales monasterii S. Albani a
Johanne Amundesham monacho
ut videtur conscripti*: 187, 377
architecture, northern: 42, 55,
129–43, 165–69

Arnald de Percy: 325
Augustinian (order)
canons: 43–44, 57, 85, 106, 109,
116, 174, 207, 211, 361, 387, 394
friars: 48, 112, 210, 346

Bamburgh, Northumbria: 325,
412–13, 421
Basingwerk Cistercian Abbey:
62–64
Bardney, Lindsey: 394, 413–14
Beauchamp, Margaret: 108
Becket, Thomas, saint, archbishop
of Canterbury: 84–85, 102,
149–54, 159–60, 174, 180, 209, 211,
275, 368, 374
model: 150
translation: 149
water: 150
Bede, saint, monk of Jarrow,
scholar: 27, 37–39, 41, 119,
138–40, 168, 186–87, 266–68,
289–90, 293–94, 298–99, 335,
403, 410–12, 419–20, 424–25
Conversion-era saints: 119, 331
*Historia ecclesiastica gentis
anglorum*: 111, 137, 140, 137,
166, 266, 286, 289, 298, 312–13,
321–22, 329–31, 376, 410, 412, 417
relics: 39
Vita sancti Cuthberti (prose):
140, 180, 251–52, 255, 268, 411
Bega of Copeland, saint, hermit,
abbess: 17, 23–24, 61–68, 187–88,
314, 329, 332–33; *see also Vita
sancti Bege* (anon)
miracles: 67–68, 328
Benedict XIV, pope: 422–24
*De servorum Dei beatificatione et
beatorum canonizatione*: 423
*Martyrologium romanum
Gregorii XIII jussu editum*: 423

INDEX 439

Benedict of Nursia, saint: 179, 370, 375, 394, 400, 402–03
  Regula sancti Benedicti [the Rule of Saint Benedict]: 278
Benedictine (order): 29, 58, 61, 179, 221, 311–12
  hagionyms, *see* bynames
Bernard of Clairvaux, abbot of Clairvaux, saint, theologian: 35–36, 63, 221; *see also Floret de S. Bernard en franczoys*
  relics: 174
Bernard of Clairvaux (pseudo-), *The Manere of Good Lyvyng*: 350
Beverley, Yorkshire: 24, 27, 107, 109–111, 113, 118, 150, 156–60
Bilsdale Chapel, *see* Hilda of Whitby; dedications to
Black Death, *see* plague, the
Boisil of Melrose, saint, prior: 138, 170–71
Book of Hours: 19, 99–119,
  Beaufort-Beauchamp: 103, 107–08, 112–13, 115–17
  Bolton: 101, 103, 105, 109–11, 113, 115–16
  Elizabeth the Queen: 103, 108, 115, 117
  northern sanctity in: 19, 99–119
  Sarum: 102–103,105, 108–09, 112
  Tabram: 103, 108, 112–13, 115, 117
  York: 102–03, 105, 109–10, 111–13, 115
borders: 18–19, 53–55, 68–69, 362
  Anglo-Scottish: 18, 42, 55, 89, 167, 270–71, 281
  cross-: 18–19, 54, 69, 371
  northern: 18–19, 53–55, 68–70, 89, 138, 167–68, 260–71, 343, 362, *see also Polychronicon*
Brendan, saint: 250; *see also* Caxton, William; *Golden*

Legende [Legenda aurea sanctorum, sive, Lombardica historia]
Bridlington Priory, Yorkshire: 107
Breviarium ad usum insignis ecclesiae Eboracensis, see York; breviary
Breviarium ad usum insignis ecclesiae Sarum, see Sarum; breviary
bynames, monastic
  hagionyms
    Benedictine: 394–95, 402–04
    Glastonbury: 398–404
    religious house, link with: 391, 394, 396
  northern: 395–404
  post-dissolution, use of: 389
  practice of using: 387–89, 394
  southern: 386, 390–93, 396–98, 403
  toponyms: 389, 392, 395, 401, 404

Campsey Ash Priory: 287, 298
Canterbury: 149, 152–53, 160, 170, 186, 207, 367–68
Canterbury Tales, see Chaucer, Geoffrey
Cartularium Abbathiae de Whiteby: 28, 305, 307–10, 312, 316–17, 322–28, 331, *see also Memorial of the Benefactions of Whitby Abbey*; Whitby Abbey; foundation
Capgrave, John, hagiographer: 421
Carlisle, Cumbria: 19, 53, 68–69, 168–69, 177, 344
  cathedral: 25
  paintings: 177, 179–80
Catherine of Alexandria, saint: 148–49, 179

Caxton, William: 20, 250
 Golden Legende [Legenda aurea sanctorum, sive, Lombardica historia]: 250; see also Brendan, saint
Celtic sanctity: 63–64
Ceolfrith, saint, abbot: 171, 186, 403
Ceolwulf, saint, King of Northumbria: 170, 179
Chad, saint, bishop: 178, 188
charters, 315–17, 322–23, 326, 328, 371
 of Durham: 201–02, 207
 of Finchale Priory: 204
 of King David I: 267
 of Yorkshire: 322
 Scottish: 267
Chaucer, Geoffrey, Canterbury Tales: 249, 355, 357
Chester-le-Street: 169, 183, 310
Chillingham, Northumbria: 180–81
Christian, bishop of Whithorn, 41, 57, 67, 69
Chronica Johannis de Oxenedes: 210
Chronica monasterii sancti Albani. Johannis de Trokelowe et Henrici de Blanforde, see St Alban's Abbey
Chronica monasterii sancti Albani, Willelmi Rishanger, quondam monachi S. Albani, et quorundam anonymorum, chronica et annales, see St Alban's Abbey
Chronica maiora, see Matthew Paris
Chronicle of St Mary's Abbey, York: 68
Chronicon de Lanercost (anon.): 86–88, 211; see also Godric of Finchale
Chrysostom, John, saint, archbishop of Constantinople: 151, 243

Cistercian (order): 26, 35–37, 49, 54–70, 78–81, 174, 204, 209, 221
 desert: 79
 eremitic: 79–81
 missionary saints: 42
Clare Priory, cartulary: 173
Claxton, William, Rites of Durham: 27, 134, 176, 178, 188; see also Durham
Clement of Alexandria, theologian, Stromateis: 153
Clement Whethamstede, prior of Tynemouth: 373, 376–77
Cockersand, Lancashire: 18
Coldingham: 18, 23, 28, 255, 265–71, 280–81, 288–94, 298–300, 372
 breviary: 333, 372, 378
 priory: 237, 263, 267, 274–79
Collan, guardian of Cuthbert's shrine: 47
Coludi urbs monastery: 263, 265–68, 274–77, 280–81
 punishment, divine: 277
Columba, saint: 263, 418, 420; see also Vita sancti Columbae
Compendium compertorum (anon.): 172, 174–76
continental sanctity: 17, 65, 82–83, 148–49, 218–19, 223, 231, 241, 363, 365, 413–15
Coquet, the (river): 141
Coverham Abbey: 154
counties, northern: 21, 99, 107
Chronica magistri Rogeri de Houedene, see Roger of Hoveden
Chronica sive flores historiarum, see Roger de Wendover; see also Oswine, King of Deira
Chronicle of Glastonbury (Cronica sive Antiquitate), see John of Glastonbury

Chronicle of Walter
of Guisborough,
see Walter of Guisborough
Cronica maiora of Thomas
Walsingham, *see* Walsingham,
Thomas
Cronycles of the londe of Englond
(anon): 381
cults
appropriation: 29, 183, 410
development: 17, 152, 219, 221,
228– 29, 277, 403, 416, 419–21
episcopal: 23, 150–54, 160
Cumbria: 18, 22–23, 26, 53–58,
61–62, 67–70, 168–69, 174
Cuthbert, saint, monk, bishop of
Lindisfarne: 21–28, 38–39, 45–47,
49, 84, 88, 170–71, 267–69,
409–11
asociality: 253
cult of: 36, 46–47, 277,364–66
donations to, *see* Ætheldreda;
donor
ecological temporality, *see*
temporality
figure: 23, 55, 66
hermit: 84, 237–56
in Book of Hours: 100, 103–04,
110–11, 114–19
mist: 129–30, 137
misogyny, supposed: 269, 277,
295
pilgrimage: 133–43
prophecies: 253
shrine: 36, 47, 176, 280
see also, Bede, *Vita sancti*
Cuthberti (prose)
see also, Libellus de ortu sancti
Cuthberti (anon)
see also, Life of Saint Cuthbert
(anon), metrical Middle
English

see also, Reginald of Durham;
Libellus de admirandis beati
Cuthberti virtutibus

Danby Church, *see* Hilda of
Whitby; dedications to
Daniel, Walter, monk,
hagiographer, *Vita Aelredi,*
37–38, 42; *see also* Aelred of
Rievlaux
David I, King of Scotland: 36, 39,
53; *see also Eulogium Davidis*
De antiquitate Glastonie ecclesie, see
William of Malmesbury
De falsis heremitis (anon.): 225,
see also hermit; hypocrisy,
accusations of
De miraculis Hagustaldensis
ecclesiae, see Aelred of
Rievaulx
De principis instructione,
see Gerald of Wales
De rebus Britannicis collectanea,
see Leland, John
De servorum Dei beatificatione et
beatorum canonizatione,
see Benedict XIV
De situ Dunelmi (anon.), poem,
Old English: 27, 135–39, 141;
see also Durham
De vita et conversacione sancti
Roberti iuxta Knaresburgum,
(anon.): 78–79, 89; *see also*
Robert of Knaresborough
Della Stua, Giampietro: 410, 419–25
Vita di sancti Osvaldo re di
Nortumberland e martire:
423–24; *see also* Oswald, King
of Northumbria
Dempster, Thomas, historian,
Historia ecclesiastica gentis
Scotorum: 56

442   INDEX

devotions, northern: 17–29, 36, 46, 100–14, 153–60, 166, 169–89, 263–65, 276–77, 330–35, 362–79, 387

Der Heiligen Leben und Leiden: anders gennant das Passional (anon): 419

Di Santa Colomba vergine sacra della città di Aquileia, see Fontanini, Giusto

divisions, northern: 20, 77

Domesday Book (anon.): 322–27; *see also* Hilda of Whitby

donations: 17, 155, 177, 292, 297, 300, 309, 326, 329, 371; *see also* William de Percy

Drayton, Michael, poet, *Poly-Olbion:* 92–93; *see also,* Robert of Knaresborough

Drogo of Saint-Winnoc: 415, 418–20

Sermones primus et secundus in festo pretiosi regis et martyris Oswaldi, 415

Vita sancti Oswaldi regis ac martyris, 415; *see also* Oswald, King of Northumbria

Dryburgh, Berwickshire: 18

Dundrennan, Galloway: 18, 41 Abbey: 35

Dunstan, saint, bishop: 65, 170, 369

Durham: 18–23, 36, 43, 45–48, 129–43, 179, 200–12, 267–69, 364–66

bosses: 175

cathedral: 27, 39, 114, 131–135, 139–124, 166, 170, 175–76, 183–85, 277

disputes (monks and bishops): 201–04

Familia of saints: 23, 61

hagiographies: 56

priory: 18, 22, 111, 183, 391, 403

relics: 139, 170–71, 173–76, 296–98, 306, 378

rivalries: 46–48, 67

topography: 135–138

see also, De situ Dunelmi (anon.)

see also, Historiae Dunelmensis scriptores tres, Gaufridus de Coldingham, Robertus de Graystanes, et Willielmus de Chambre

see also, Claxton, William, *Rites of Durham*

see also, Symeon of Durham; *Libellus de exordio atque procursu istius, hoc est Dunhelmensis, ecclesie*

see also, The Durham Liber vitae (anon)

Durham Episcopal Charters, see charters

Eadfrith, bishop of Lindisfarne: 170

Eata, bishop of Hexham, saint: 37, 43–44, 48, 171, 178, 187; *see also* Hexham bishop-saints

East Anglia: 165, 288–89

Echternach monastery: 413

Edgar, King of Scotland: 267

Edmund, King of East Anglia, saint, martyr: 24, 99, 104, 112, 370, 374, 403

Edmund of Abingdon, saint, Archbishop of Canterbury: 82–83

Edward I 'the Hammer of the Scots', King of England: 69, 371

Edward 'the Confessor', saint, King of England: 24, 65, 170, 370, 374, 402; *see also Vita sancti Ædwardi regis et confessoris*

Edward IV, King of England: 107, 167

Edwin, King of Northumbria, saint: 111, 170, 186, 289–90, 361–62

Egton Chapel, *see* Hilda of Whitby; dedication to

Ellerburn Chapel, *see* Hilda of Whitby; dedication to

Elizabeth of Hungary, princess, saint: 25, 181

Ely, Cambridgeshire: 28, 186, 285–300
 monastery: 285–92, 300
 relics: 413, 421

episcopal acts
 of Durham, 1153–95: 208
 of Durham, 1241–1283: 327–28
 of York, 1070–1154: 327–28
 of York, 1154–1181: 328–28

eremitic sanctity: 23, 27, 61, 63, 65–67, 79–81, 84, 141, 217–31, 239–56

Erkenwald, saint, bishop of London: 63, 65, 69, 105, 113

Espec, Walter, founder of Rievaulx: 43 328, 333

Eulogium Davidis, see Aelred of Rievaulx

Eulogium (historiarum sive temporis): Chronicon ab orbe conditio usque ad annum domini MCCCLVI a monacho quodam Malmesburiensi exaratum, (anon): 380; *see also* Oswine, King of Deira

evangelism: 37, 41–42, 58, 363, 425

Everard, first Abbot of Holm Cultram, hagiographer: 56–57, 67

Evesham, Worcestershire: 24, 83–85, 322, 332, 335

Faricius of Arezzo, Benedictine monk, hagiographer, *Vita sancti Aldhelmi* [*Life of Aldhelm*]: 58, 61, 64–65

Farne Islands, the: 27, 55, 140, 169

Faversham, Kent: 65

Fergus, Lord of Galloway: 35, 41

female sanctity: 23, 28, 148–49, 179–81, 263–335

Finchale priory: 207
 charters of, *see* charters

Flambard, Ralph, bishop of Durham: 142–43, 200, 207

Floret de S. Bernard en franczoys (anon.): 350; *see also* Bernard of Clairvaux

Folcard, monk, hagiographer, *Vita sancti Johannis Episcopi Eboracensis,* [*Life of St John of Beverley*]: 58, 61, 64–65, *see also* John of Beverley

Fontanini, Giusto, Archbishop of Ankara, historian: 421–22
 Di Santa Colomba vergine sacra della città di Aquileia: 422–23, *see also* Oswald, King of Northumbria; relics

Forth, the: 18, 68, 271

foundation narratives: 285, 291–92, 298–335
 relics: 332

Fountains Abbey: 209

Francis of Assisi, saint: 217, 219, 228, *see also Vita prima sancti Francisci*

French Life of Godric (anon.): 343–57, *see also* Godric of Finchale
 didactic nature: 344, 347–50, *see also* hagiography
 merveille: 350–52

444 INDEX

realism: 352–57

Frethbert, bishop of Hexham, saint: 37, 44, *see also* Hexham; saint-bishops

Fylingdale Chapel, *see* Hilda of Whitby; dedications to

Galloway: 18, 36, 40–42, 54, 67
  barbarity: 40, 67–68

Gemma ecclesiastica, see Gerald of Wales

Genealogia regum Anglorum, see Aelred of Rievaulx

Geoffrey of Burton, *Vita sancte Moduenne virginis,* [*Life and Miracles of St Modwenna*]: 137

Geoffrey of Coldingham, also known as Geoffrey of Durham, monk, chronicler: 203
  Vita sancti Bartholomaei Farnensis: 56
  Vita sancti Godrici: 204, *see also* Godric of Finchale

Geoffrey of Monmouth, historian, *Historia regum brittanniae*: 21

Gerald of Wales, historian: 209–10
  De principis instructione: 210
  Gemma ecclesiastica: 210, *see also* Godric of Finchale

Gesta abbatum monasterii sancti Albani (anon), *see* St Alban's Abbey

Gesta Ottonis Imperatoris, see Hrotsvitha of Gandersheim

Gesta pontificum Anglorum, see William of Malmesbury

Germanus, prior of Durham: 204, 207, 370

Girona Cathedral, Catalonia: 185

Glastonbury Abbey: 395, 398–99, 403
  hagionyms, *see* bynames

relics: 26, 186, 313, 332, 403
  see also, John of Glastonbury; *Cronica sive Antiquitate*
  see also, William of Malmesbury; *De antiquitate Glastonie ecclesie*

Godric of Finchale, saint, hermit: 17, 27, 171, 174, 186, 198–212, 220, 225, 343–57
  Cistercian associations: 204, 207, 209, 211–12
  Durham Benedictine associations: 199–208, 211–12
  national appeal: 209–10
  versatility (figure): 205
  see also Chronicon de Lanercost (anon)
  see also French Life of Godric (anon.)
  see also Gerald of Wales; *Gemma ecclesiastica*
  see also Geoffrey of Coldingham; *Vita sancti Godrici*
  see also Reginald of Durham; *Libellus de vita et miraculis sancti Godrici, heremitae de Finchale*

Golden Legende [*Legenda aurea sanctorum, sive, Lombardica historia*], *see* Caxton, William

Gough Map: 167

Grassi, Niccolò, historian, *Notizie storiche della provincia della Carnia*: 422–23, *see also* Sauris; relic

Gray, Thomas, *Scalacronica*: 375

Greenfield, William, archbishop of York: 153, 325

Grosseteste, Robert, bishop of Lincoln, philosopher: 24, 147, 155, 369

Guisborough Priory: 327

INDEX 445

Hackness, Yorkshire: 66, 308, 311, 314, 322, 332–33
  priory: 23, *see also* Hilda of Whitby
hagiographies: 26, 56–58, 64, 65–66, 75–82, 90–92, 148, 200–05, 263–64, 268–72, 280–81, 343–57, 409–11, 418–19
  didactic nature: 344, 347–50, *see also French Life of Godric*
  political agenda: 199–200, 344
  rewriting, translation as: 345–47, 381
hagionyms, northern, *see* bynames
Haltemprice Priory: 173
Haliwerfolc: 170, 200
Hartlepool: 54, 332–33
  chapel: 327, 329
Headley Benedictine Priory: 78, 223
healing, miraculous: 84–85, 148, 152, 249, 263–81, 293, 417–18, 422–23, 425
  affliction, type of: 272–74, *see also* Æbbe of Coldingham; mute, healing
  laity: 264–66, 268–69, 274, 276–77
  locality: 264–65, 271–72, 275–79
  plague, the: 409, 417–18, 422–23, *see also* Oswald, King of Northumbria; healing
  social status: 269–70
  women: 268–69
Henry, sub-prior of Durham: 203
Henry II, King of England: 53, 85, 211, 326
Henry IV, King of England: 104, 106, 109, 158
Henry V, King of England: 25, 99, 106–10, 118, 159, 186, 188, 334
Henry VI, King of England: 107, 176

heraldry: 188
hermits: 26–29, 61, 75–93, 137, 154, 199, 203–05, 217–31, 237–56, 344–45
  animal, non-human: 238, 240, 242, 247, 250–56
  ascetic practices: 79, 218–24
  charity: 88, 221
  desert: 79, 81
  ecological temporality, *see* temporality
  hypocrisy, accusations of: 224–26, 230, *see also De falsis heremitis* (anon.)
  poverty: 86, 88, 217–19, 227–31
  sins of: 243
  wilderness: 79, 82, 141, 226, 238, 241, 244, 345
Hexham, Northumberland (town): 36–37, 42–47
Hexham Abbey: 35–49, 178–79, 291–92
  bishop-saints: 26, 37, 43–49, 182
  independence: 43, 46, 48–49
  panels: 178–79
  relics: 45–49, 170
  see also Acca, bishop of Hexham
  see also Aelred of Rievaulx; *De miraculis Hagustaldensis ecclesiae*
  see also Alchmund, bishop of Hexham
  see also Eata, bishop of Hexham
  see also Frethbert, bishop of Hexham
  see also Tilbert, bishop of Hexham
Higden, Ranulf, author, *Polychronicon*: 20, 165, 167, *see also* northern; borders

446   INDEX

Hilda of Whitby, saint, abbess
  of Whitby: 23–24, 28, 66, 290,
  305–17, 321–335
  chapel: 223, 305, 321, 323–29
  dedications to
      Ampleforth Chapel: 327
      Bilsdale Chapel: 328, 333
      Danby Church: 326–27
      Egton Chapel: 328
      Ellerburn Chapel: 328–29
      Fylingdale Chapel: 324
      Hinderwell Church: 323, 329
      Kildale Park Chapel: 325
      Lucker Chapel: 325, 329–30
      Middlesbrough Church:
        326, 329
      see also Robert de Brus
      see also William de Percy
  feast: 314, 330–32, 334
  founder: 307, 310–12, 322
      see also Hackness
      see also Whitby Abbey
  Latin poem about: 312–14
  miracles: 313–14, 328, 331
  missals: 314, 332–33
  relics: 310, 313–14, 332
  see also Domesday Book (anon.)
Hildegard of Bingen, saint,
  Benedictine abbess, prophetess:
  83
Hinderwell Church, see Hilda of
  Whitby; dedications to
Historia anglorum, see Paris,
  Matthew
Historia ecclesiastica gentis
  anglorum, see Bede
Historia ecclesiastica gentis
  Scotorum, see Dempster, Thomas
Historia regum brittanniae,
  see Geoffrey of Monmouth
Historia rerum Anglicarum, see
  William of Newburgh

Historia Selebiensis monasterii,
  see also Selby Abbey
Historie van Jan van Beverley
  (anon.), Dutch: 242–50,
  see also John of Beverley
Historiae Dunelmensis scriptores
  tres, Gaufridus de Coldingham,
  Robertus de Graystanes, et
  Willielmus de Chambre: 202, 297,
  402, see also Durham
Holford, Matthew: 18–19, 76–78,
  84, 89
Holm Cultram, Cumbria: 18,
  53–70, 329
  abbey: 18, 26, 53–56, 69–70, 329,
    368–69
  Celtic hagiographies: 55, 62–65,
    69
  cross-border affiliation: 54
  economy: 54–55, 68
  European influence: 55, 70
  library: 55–56, 58–61
  north-western hagiographies: 55,
    58, 60, 62, 68
  south-western hagiographies: 55,
    62, 65, 67–70
Hrotsvitha of Gandersheim
  Gesta Ottonis Imperatoris, 415
Hugh, saint, bishop of Lincoln: 24,
  147, 154–55
  myroblyte: 154–55
Hugh du Puiset, bishop of
  Durham: 200, 202, 204
Humber, the (river):18, 168, 388
Humiliati (Italian religious order):
  219, 228, 231

iconography: 25, 164–187, 409, 416
  northern: 25, 27, 165–87, 409
  saint's attributes: 181–82, 188, 416
identity, northern: 24–27, 76–77,
  88–93, 172, 306–07, 379–80

Ireland: 54, 58, 62, 137, 254, 333–34, 389, 413, 424

Isleham, Cambridgeshire: 105–06

Islekirk, Cumbria: 28, 329,

Jarrow Abbey: 39, 111, 171, 186, 310–11, 322, 328, 333, 364

Jerome, saint: 174, 179

Jocelin of Furness, hagiographer, *Vita sancti Waldevi*: 57

John, King of England: 21, 68, 85, 86, 329, 370

John Beaufort, English nobleman: 107–08

John of Beverley, saint, hermit, bishop of Hexham and York: 58, 61, 63–66, 99–101, 103–04, 108–19, 146–47, 156, 171, 178, 181, 186–87, 237–56

ecological temporality, *see* temporality

feast: 109, 158–59

hermit: 237–56

myroblyte: 154–60

redemption: 246–48

sinner: 245–47

wildman: 243–44

see also Folcard; *Vita sancti Johannis Episcopi Eboracensis* [*Life of St John of Beverley*]

see also Historie van Jan van Beverley (anon.)

see also Ketell, William; *Miracula sancti Johannis* [*Miracles of John of Beverley*]

John (Thweng) of Bridlington, saint: 24–25, 99–119, 159, 170–71,

Augustinian canon: 106, 109, 112, 116

House of Lancaster: 109

northerness: 109

shrine: 107

John of Ford, abbot, hagiographer: 61–63, 209

Vita Wulfrici anchoretae Haselbergiae [*Life of Wulfric*]: 58, 61–63, 352, *see also* Wulfric of Haselbury

John of Glastonbury, Benedictine monk, chronicler, *Cronica sive Antiquitate*: 403, *see also* Glastonbury

John of Tynemouth, hagiographer, historian: 60, 330–31, 374–75, 381

Sanctilogium Angliae, Walliae, Scotiae et Hiberniae: 60, 330–31, 375, 381

Julian of Norwich, mystic: 243, 246

Shewings of: 246

Kalendre of the Newe Legende of Englande: 243, 381

Kempe, Margery, mystic: 170

Ketell, William, hagiographer, *Miracula sancti Johannis* [*Miracles of John of Beverley*]: 58, 61, 64, *see also* John of Beverley

Knaresborough: 75, 87, 154

castle: 92

Priory: 80, 90

Kildale Park Chapel, *see* Hilda of Whitby; dedications to

kingship, Christian: 172, 362–63, 410–11, 424–25

Kirkham, Lancashire: 57, 328

Kirk Hill: 28, 265–69, 274–81

oratory: 263–64, 267–69, 274–76, 280–81

springs: 276, 279

La Queste del Saint Graal: 350–51

Lancaster, House of: 108

448 INDEX

Langley, Thomas, bishop of
Durham: 118, 134
landscapes, sacred: 169, 288,
291–94
Lastingham, Yorkshire: 306, 310, 322
*Le livere de Reis de Brittaine e Le
livere de Reis de Engletere* (anon):
210
Le Morte D'Arthur,
see Malory, Sir Thomas
Leland, John: 171, 317, 331
De rebus Britannicis collectanea:
362
legendary, of saints: 22, 24, 59–61,
70, 242–43, 252, 345–47, 363,
374, 418
Lanercost Chronicle (anon.):
85–88, *see also* Robert of
Knaresborough
*Libellus de admirandis beati
Cuthberti virtutibus*,
see Reginald of Durham
*Libellus de diversis ordinibus
et professionibus qui sunt in
aecclesia* (anon.): 220, *see also*
monasticism, new
*Libellus de exordio atque procursu
istius, hoc est Dunhelmensis,
ecclesie*, *see* Symeon of Durham
Libellus de ortu sancti Cuthberti,
(anon): 251–52, *see also* Cuthbert
*Libellus de vita et miraculis sancti
Godrici, heremitae de Finchale*,
see Reginald of Durham
Liber Eliensis (anon): 265, 279,
285–300, *see also* Ætheldreda
of Ely
Liber revelationum,
see Peter of Cornwall
Liber sententiarum, *see* Stephen of
Muret [also known as Stephen
of Grandmont]

Life and Miracles of St Modwenna,
see Geoffrey of Burton, *Vita
sancte Moduenne virginis*
Life of Aldhelm, *see* Faricius of
Arezzo; *Vita sancti Aldhelmi*
Life of Columba, *see* Adomnán;
Vita sancti Columbae
Life of Neot, *see Vita sancti Neoti*,
'later' Latin *Life of St Neot* (anon)
Life of Ninian, *see* Aelred of
Rievaulx; *Vita sancti Niniani*
Life of Saint Cuthbert (anon),
metrical Middle English: 237,
242, 352, *see also* Cuthbert
Life of Saint Nicolas, Old English,
see Nicolas de Myra
Life of St John of Beverley,
see Folcard; *Vita sancti Johannis
Episcopi Eboracensis*,
Life of Wenefred, *see Vita sancti
Wenefrede*, (anon.)
Life of Wulfric, *see* John of Ford;
*Vita Wulfrici anchoretae
Haselbergiae*
Lincoln: 23, 27, 154–56, 159–60
cathedral: 147
Lindisfarne, Northumberland: 22,
45, 111, 140, 170–71, 179, 183
locality of saints: 26–27, 42–43,
48–49, 55, 76–82, 91–93, 150, 154,
158–59, 172–74, 205, 218, 264–65,
275–76, 293–94, 391
Louis IX, King of France: 346–47
*Li enseignement ke li bons rois
Sains Loÿs escrist de sa main a
ma Dame Ysabel*: 346–47
Lucker Chapel, *see* Hilda of
Whitby; dedications to

Magnum legendarium Austriacum:
418, *see also* Oswald, King of
Northumbria

Malcolm III, King of Scotland:
53, 361
Malcolm IV, King of Scotland: 209
Malmesbury, Wiltshire: 62–64,
67, 368
Malory, Sir Thomas, author: 21, 351
Le Morte D'Arthur: 351
Margaret of Scotland, saint, queen
consort of Malcolm III: 170–71,
180–81, 372
*Martiloge in Englysshe after the use
of the chirche of Salisbury*: 334,
381
Martin of Tours, saint: 41, 49, 395
martyrdom, debate: 410–11,
423–24
*Martyrologium romanum
Gregorii XIII jussu editum,
see* Benedict XIV
Martyrology, Old English: 410–11,
see also Oswald, King of
Northumbria
Maurice, Abbot of Rievaulx: 38–39
Melrose, Roxburghshire: 18, 53–57,
63, 68–69, 170, 322
Abbey: 53–57, 68–69, 210
Chronica de Mailros: 210
*Memorials of the Abbey of St Mary
of Fountains* (anon): 209, 325
*Memorial of the Benefactions of
Whitby Abbey*: 28, 305, 307–10,
312, 316–17, 322–28, 331, *see
also Cartularium Abbathiae de
Whiteby*
*Metrical Life of St Robert of
Knaresborough* Middle English
(anon): 75–80, 88–93, 218,
222–27, 230, *see also* Robert of
Knaresborough
Micklegate, Yorkshire: 105
Midlands, the (region): 85, 118,
168, 291

Middlesbrough Church, *see* Hilda
of Whitby; dedications to
Miracles of John of Beverley, see
Ketell, William, hagiographer;
Miracula sancti Johannis
Miracula, see Healing, miraculous
Miracula sancti Johannis [*Miracles
of John of Beverley*],
see Ketell, William
Miracula Symonis de Montfort
(anon.), *see also* Simon de
Montfort
*Missale ad usum insignis ecclesiae
Eboracensis, see* Hilda of Whitby;
missals
missionary: 41–42
model: 37, 55, 57–58, 137
vision: 41–42, 425
Modwenna, saint: 137, *see also
Vita sancte Moduenne virginis*
[*Life and Miracles of St
Modwenna*]
monastic litanies, English: 169, 186,
332–34, 398, 402, 404
monasticism, new: 227–31,
*see also Libellus de diversis
ordinibus et professionibus qui
sunt in aecclesia* (anon.)
northern revival: 305–07, 313–18,
322–23, 329, 334–35
monuments, pre-conquest: 130,
311, 317, 321, 326

*Natale sancti Oswaldi regis et
martyris, see* Ælfric of Eynsham
national sanctity: 24–26, 76–78,
82–83, 88–92
Neot, saint: 61–65, 69,
see also Vita sancti Neoti
networks of saints, northern: 17,
19, 23–25, 28, 36, 46, 285–300
Neville family: 108

450 INDEX

Newminster, Northumberland, Cistercian Abbey: 78, 80–81, 87, 207, 222–23

Nicholas of Myra, saint: 148–52, 154 160,
Old English *Life of Saint Nicolas*: 150

Nidd, the (river): 75, 87

Ninian of Whithorn, saint: 18, 23, 26, 36–37, 41–42, 49, 57, 169, 180, 357, *see also Vita sancti Niniani*

Norbert of Xanten, saint, bishop, founder of the Premonstratensian order: 221, 227–29

Norroy: 19, 167

northerners: 21, 41, 92, 332

Northumbria, Anglo-Saxon kingdom of: 18, 20, 43, 49, 87–88, 137, 168, 286, 288–91, 308, 396, 409–10, 414–15

Notizie storiche della provincia della Carnia, see Grassi, Niccolò

odour of sanctity: 148, 155

oil: 147–60
ampullae: 152–53
canons: 149, 152–54, 156–57, 160
cult promotion: 150, 152, 160
devotional function: 152–53, 156, 160
episcopal authority: 148, 150–54, 160
northern English: 149, 159
translation: 147–49, 152–55, 160
Whitweek: 151–52, 155–56

Osthryth, queen of the Mercians, wife of king Æthelred: 413–14

Ósvalds saga (anon): 416, *see also* Oswald, King of Northumbria

Oswald, King of Northumbria, saint, martyr: 17, 22, 26, 29,

100, 110–11, 114, 138–39, 169–72, 182–88, 204–05, 403, 409–25
continental imagery: 413–15
cults: 209–10, 412–19, 421–22, 425
continental: 413–15
secular: 410–12
dynasty: 409–10, 412, 414, 420
martyrdom: 410–12, 415, 417, 423–25
miracles: 414, 417, 422–23,
see also healing, miraculous; plague, the
relics: 412–15, 418, 421–22, *see also Di Santa Colomba vergine sacra della città di Aquileia*
thumb, left, *see* Sauris
see also Ælfric of Eynsham; *Natale sancti Oswaldi regis et martyris*
see also Alcuin; *Versus de patribus regibus et sanctis euboracensis ecclesiae*
see also Drogo of Saint-Winnoc; *Vita sancti Oswaldi regis ac martyris*
see also della Stua, Giampietro; *Vita di sancti Osvaldo re di Nortumberland e martire*
see also Magnum legendarium Austriacum (anon)
see also Ósvalds saga (anon)
see also Reginald of Durham; *Vita sancti Oswaldi*
see also Soardo, Pietro; *Vita di sancti Osvaldo Re di Northumbria, specchio e esempio de' Principi e Soldati Christiani*

Oswine, King of Deira, saint, martyr: 17, 23, 29, 170, 186–88, 361–81
cult: 363–64, 366–67, 370–71, 373–74, 376–78

calendar, presence in: 363,
365–66, 368–74, 376, 378–79
feasts: 365–69, 372, 378
identity, regional, expression of:
379–80
miracles: 365–69, 380
patron saint: 364–65, 371, 377
relics: 362, 364–65, 376, 380–81
shrine: 362–66, 371–73, 376, 381
translation: 367, 376, 381
see also Eulogium (historiarum
sive temporis): Chronicon ab
orbe conditio usque ad annum
domini MCCCLVI a monacho
quodam Malmesburiensi
exaratum (anon)
see also Roger de Wendover;
Chronica sive flores historiarum
see also Vita sancti Oswini (anon)
Oswiu, King of Bernicia: 265, 362,
412
Pace, Stefano,Vita di
sancti Osvaldo, re di Nortumbria:
419–20, see also Oswald, King of
Northumbria
Paris, Matthew, Benedictine
monk, chronicler: 25, 75, 82–83,
147, 149, 210, 217, 367, 369–71
Chronica maiora: 147, 210, 217
Historia Anglorum: 82
Paul the hermit: 250–51
Paulinus, saint: 178, 187, 401, 403,
422
Pennines, the (mountain range):
20, 55, 65, 67, 168, 172
Peter of Cornwall, Augustinian
prior, Liber revelationum: 210
pilgrimage: 24, 64, 113–14, 132–34,
158, 172–73, 243, 267–78, 280–81
female: 268–69
royal: 106–07, 119
plague, the: 409, 417–18, 420, 422–23

Polychronicon, see Higden, Ranulf
Poly-Olbion, see Drayton, Michael
Porter, William: 99–101, 111, 116–19
Porter Hours: 103, 108, 110–11,
113, 116, 119

Reginald of Durham, Benedictine
monk, hagiographer: 23, 27,
84, 130, 133, 135, 174, 199–212,
221, 224, 343–44, 347, 349–50,
352–53, 368, 417–18, 421–22,
ambitions: 200–01, 204
Libellus de admirandis beati
Cuthberti virtutibus [Libellus
Cuthberti]: 130, 133, 201, 368,
see also Cuthbert
Libellus de vita et miraculis
sancti Godrici, heremitae de
Finchale [Vita sancti Godrici]:
199–212, 343, see also Godric of
Finchale
Vita sancti Oswaldi: 417–18,
421–22, see also Oswald, King
of Northumbria
writing style: 203–04, 208 212
regional sanctity: 20, 24–25, 36–37,
54–55, 76–78, 80–82, 88–93, 112,
149–53, 156–60, 165–72, 238
Regula sancti Benedicti, see
Benedict of Nursia
Reinfrid, soldier of William the
Conqueror, monk, prior of
Whitby, hermit: 23–24, 305–11,
314–15, 317, 322, 328–29, 333
Richard of Cirencester, monk,
Speculum historiale: 380
Richard II, King of England:
107–08, 371
Richard of Tewing, prior of
Tynemouth Abbey: 372–73
Rievaulx Abbey: 18, 35, 37–39, 43,
172, 207

Ripon Minster: 24 150, 158, 171
Rites of Durham, William Claxton: 27, 134, 176, 178, 188, *see also* Durham; Claxton, William
Robert de Brus: 325–27, 329, *see also* Hilda of Whitby
Robert de Stuteville: 326–27
Robert of Knaresborough, saint, hermit: 17, 24–27, 75–93, 147, 171–72, 217–31, 325
   ascetic rigour: 79, 91, 219–23, 226–27
   charity: 86–88, 221
   knightly figure: 89–91
   miracles: 82–85, 248–49
   myroblyte: 82, 147, 154
   northern figure, 76–78, 84–85, 88–90, 92
   relics: 79–80
   see also De vita et conversacione sancti Roberti iuxta Knaresburgum, (anon.)
   see also Drayton, Michael; *Poly-Olbion*
   see also Lanercost Chronicle (anon.)
   see also Metrical Life of St Robert of Knaresborough, Middle English (anon)
   see also Trinitarians
   see also Vita sancti Roberti heremiti, (anon) 'Cistercian *vita*'
   see also Vita sancti Roberti iuxta Knaresburgum, (anon) 'Trinitarian *vita*'
Robert de Molesme, founder of the Cistercian order: 58
Rolle, Richard, hermit: 22, 93, 171, 345
Roger de Wendover, *Chronica sive flores historiarum*: 210

Roger (Niger) of Beeleigh, bishop of London, saint: 83
Roger of Hoveden, *Chronica magistri Rogeri de Houedene*: 209
rood: 134, 176, 187, 369
Rudfarlington, Knaresborough: 28, 78, 329
   chapel, *see* Hilda of Whitby; dedications to
Rule of Saint Benedict, the, *see* Benedict of Nursia, saint; *Regula sancti Benedicti*

Scalacronica, see Gray, Thomas
Sanctilogium Angliae, Walliae, Scotiae et Hiberniae, see John of Tynemouth
Sanctorum prisca autoritate, see St Werburgh's Abbey, Chester
Sanctorum prisca: 315–16, *see also* Whitby abbey
   pancarte: 315–17
Saint-Winnoc Abbey, Berguesy: 415
Sartis Abbey: 38
Sarum: 22, 102–03, 105, 108–09, 112, 117–18, 185–86, 363, 374, 378
   Book of Hours: 105, 108–09, 112
   breviary: 117–18, 185
   Breviarium ad usum insignis ecclesiae Sarum: 117–18
   calendar: 22, 186, 363, 378
Sauris, Friuli, Italy: 409–10, 417–23
   relics: 418, 421–22, *see also Notizie storiche della provincia della Carnia*
   sanctuary: 418–19, 421
Scotland: 21, 36, 54–55, 67, 137, 165, 167–68, 186, 209, 242, 289, 424
   border: 18, 42, 55, 89, 167, 270
   Picts: 41
   wars: 21, 25, 69, 109

INDEX 453

Scrope, Richard, archbishop of York, saint: 17, 24, 100–06, 109–10, 112–13, 115, 119, 158, 171, 177

Selby Abbey, Yorkshire: 174, 310, 368, *see also Historia Selebiensis Monasterii*

Serlo de Percy, Prior: 307–08, 311, 322–23

Sermones primus et secundus in festo pretiosi regis et martyris Oswaldi, see Drogo of Saint-Winnoc

Sherborne, Dorset: 62, 131, 134–35, 187

Sherburn church, *see* Hilda, dedications to

Shrewsbury Abbey: 62–63, 316, *see also Cartularium Abbathiae de Whiteby, pancarte*

Simon de Montfort, baron: 83, *see also Miracula Symonis de Montfort* (anon.)

Soardo, Pietro: 419–21
  Vita di sancti Osvaldo Re di Northumbria, specchio e esempio de' Principi e Soldati Christiani: 419, *see also* Oswald, King of Northumbria

Solway Firth, estuary: 53–54, 67–68

Song of Songs: 63

Soulseat, Galloway: 18

South Shields chapel, *see* Hilda; dedications to

Speculum caritatis, see Aelred of Rievaulx

Speculum historiale, see Richard of Cirencester

spirituality, vernacular, northern: 363

St Abb's Head, *see* Kirk Hill

St Albans Abbey: 23, 25, 29, 60, 362, 364–78, 395

Chronica monasterii sancti Albani. Johannis de Trokelowe et Henrici de Blanforde: 371–72

Chronica monasterii sancti Albani. Willelmi Rishanger, quondam monachi S. Albani, et quorundam anonymorum, chronica et annales: 372

Gesta abbatum monasterii sancti Albani: 364–68, 370, 372–73, 375–76

influence, sphere of: 363, 367–68, 378

recession: 368

stained glass: 378

St Andrews cathedral: 150

St Bees Priory, Cumbria: 18, 62–64, 66–68, 155, 169, 187, 329, 333

St James' Monastery, Regensburg: 414, 416

St Martin's Monastery, Weingarten: 415

St Mary's Abbey, York: 18, 62, 66, 68, 178, 188, 306, 309, 322, 333
  Chronicle of St Mary's Abbey: 66, 68

St Peter Mancroft: 187, 378

St Werburgh Abbey, Chester: 169, 315–16
  cartulary of: 315–16

Stephen of Muret [also known as Stephen of Grandmont], saint, hermit, founder of the Order of Grandmont: 220, 230
  Liber sententiarum: 230

Stephen of Whitby: 306, 309, 314–15

Stromateis, see Clement of Alexandria

Streoneshalh: 305, 307–08, 310–17
  monastery ruins: 305, 308, 311, 314
  see also: Whitby Abbey

suffrages: 24–26, 99–119, 363, 376

Sutton, Oliver, bishop of Lincoln: 147, 155

Swithun, saint: 65, 170

Symeon of Durham, Benedictine monk, historian: 139–41, 170, 268, 295, 306, 310, 322
  Capitula de miraculis et translationibus sancti Cuthberti: 135
  Libellus de exordio atque procursu istius, hoc est Dunhelmensis, ecclesie: 46–47, 139–41, 170, 200, 322, *see also* Durham

Syon Abbey, Brigittine convent: 108, 334

Tees, the (river): 141, 171

temporality: 19, 21, 28, 237–56,
  asociality: 252–53
  ecological: 238–42, 247, 250–56
  (non-) linearity: 241–42, 244–51, 255
  regionality: 238, 249
  virginity: 249–50

The Boke of Saint Albans: 188, *see also* Alban, saint

The Manere of Good Lyvyng, see Bernard of Clairvaux (pseudo-)

The Desert of Religion (anon), Middle English poem: 345

The Durham Liber vitae (anon): 311, 389, *see also* Durham

Thomas II, Archbishop of York: 43

Thomas de la Mare, prior of Tynemouth, abbot of St Albans: 188, 373, 375

Thomas of Celano, hagiographer, *Vita prima sancti Francisci*: 228, *see also* Francis of Assisi

Thomas of Lancaster: 171, 174, 188

Thomas of Monmouth, *Vita et passio sancti Willemi martyris*

Norwicensis: 343, *see also* William of Norwich

Tilbert, bishop of Hexham, saint: 37, 44, 178, *see also* Hexham bishop-saints

tombs: 17, 82, 104, 106, 112–13, 131, 133–34, 147–60, 172–73, 180–82, 264, 267–68, 285, 380

Tongland, Galloway: 18

topography: 20, 23, 78–84, 141, 168, 266, 275, 333
  northern: 28, 136–39, 166–69, 238, 298–94

Tractatus de regimine principum ad Regem Henricum Sextum (anon): 107

Trent, the (river): 19–22, 84, 88, 137, 167–68

Trinitarians: 26, 80–82, 87–91, 218–19, 229, 231, *see also* Robert of Knaresborough

Tudor, House of: 21, 29, 360, 362–63, 379–81

Tweed, the (river): 18, 53, 168

Tyne, the (river): 20, 45, 328

Tynemouth Benedictine Priory: 29, 170, 172, 174, 188, 361–72, 375–78, 380–81
  Oswine, liberty of: 370
  rebirth, fourteenth century: 372–73
  rivalry, *see* Durham
  Tudor interest: 362–63

universal sanctity: 25, 70, 82–83, 174–84

Versus de patribus regibus et sanctis euboracensis ecclesiae, see Alcuin

Virgin and Child: 176–78, 345

Vie de seinte Audree, (attrib. Marie de France): 28, 285–300

Vita Aelredi, see Daniel, Walter

INDEX 455

Vita et passio sancti Willemi
  martyris Norwicensis,
  see Thomas of Monmouth
Vita et miracula sancti Æbbe virginis
  (anon): 263–81, 293, *see also*
  Æbbe of Coldingham
Vita sancti Ædwardi regis et
  confessoris, see Aelred of Rievaulx
Vita sancti Aldhelmi, see Faricius of
  Arezzo
Vita sancti Bartholomaei Farnensis,
  see Geoffrey of Coldingham
Vita sancti Bege (anon): 62–63, 333,
  see also Bega of Copeland
Vita sancti Columbae, see Adomnán
Vita sancti Cuthberti (prose), *see* Bede
Vita sancti Cuthberti (anon): 79,
  see also Cuthbert
Vita prima sancti Francisci, see
  Thomas of Celano
Vita sancti Godrici, see Reginald of
  Durham; *Libellus de vita et miraculis*
  sancti Godrici, heremitae de Finchale
Vita sancti Godrici, see Geoffrey of
  Coldingham
Vita sancti Johannis Episcopi
  Eboracensis [*Life of John of*
  Beverley], *see* Folcard
Vita sancti Moduenne virginis [*Life*
  and Miracles of St Modwenna],
  see Geoffrey of Burton
Vita sancti Neoti, 'later' Latin Life
  of St Neot (anon): 59, 61–62, 64,
  see also Neot, saint
Vita sancti Niniani, see Aelred of
  Rievaulx
Vita di sancti Osvaldo Re di
  Northumbria, specchio e esempio
  de' Principi e Soldati Christiani,
  see Soardo, Pietro
Vita di sancti Osvaldo re di
  Nortumberland e martire,
  see della Stua, Giampietro

Vita di sancti Osvaldo, re di
  Nortumbria, see Pace, Stefano
Vita sancti Oswaldi regis ac martyris,
  see Drogo of Saint-Winnoc
Vita sancti Oswaldi, see Reginald of
  Durham
Vita sancti Oswini, (anon): 366–69,
  374, 380, *see also* Oswine, King
  of Deira
Vita sancti Roberti heremiti, (anon)
  'Cistercian *vita*': 78–80, *see also*
  Robert of Knaresborough
Vita sancti Roberti iuxta
  Knaresburgum, (anon)
  'Trinitarian *vita*': 80–82, *see also*
  Robert of Knaresborough
Vita sancti Waldevi, see Jocelin of
  Furness
Vita sancti Wenefrede, (anon)
  [*Life of Wenefred*]: 62, 64,
  see also Wenefred
Vita sancti Willelmi, (anon)
  [*Life of William*]: 150–51,
  see also William of York
Vita Wulfrici anchoretae
  Haselbergiae, see John of Ford

Wake, Thomas, knight: 173–74
Wales: 62, 67, 165, 167, 209, 388–89,
  424
Walsingham, Thomas, *Cronica*
  maiora: 106–07
Wardon Abbey, *see* Sartis
Wear, the (river): 129, 135–36, 139,
  169, 333, 351
Welf, House of: 415–16
Welf IV, duke of Bavaria: 415
Wenefred, saint: 59, 61–62, 64–65,
  69, 108, 110, 112, *see also Vita*
  sancti Wenefrede (anon.)
Wessington, John, prior of
  Durham: 179

456 INDEX

West Riding of Yorkshire: 78–80, 88
Westou, Elfred, sacristan of
Durham: 39, 46–47
Wetheral priory, Cumbria: 18, 174
Whitby Abbey, Yorkshire: 28, 66,
305–18, 321–35
cartulary: 307, 331, 333
foundation: 304, 306–07, 309,
310–11, 313–18, 322–23, 325–26, 329
missals: 333–34
see also *Cartularium Abbathiae
de Whiteby* (anon)
see also Hilda of Whitby
see also *Memorial of the
Benefactions of Whitby Abbey*
see also Streoneshalh
see also Stephen of Whitby
see also Symeon of Durham;
Libellus de exordio
Whithorn, Galloway: 18, 41–42, 49,
67, 69
Whitsun: 150–52
wilderness, topos: 79–82
Wilfrid of Ripon, bishop of
Hexham, saint:48, 113, 159
William de Percy: 307–09, 311,
314–15
donations 308–09,
see also Hilda of Whitby
William de Stuteville: 78, 89
William of Malmesbury, historian:
20, 59, 61, 64, 131, 135, 142, 403,
419, 421
De antiquitate Glastonie ecclesie:
403, see also Glastonbury
Gesta pontificum Anglorum:
58–59, 131–33, 142
William of Newburgh, *Historia
rerum Anglicarum*: 209
William of Norwich, saint: 185,
see also *Vita et passio sancti
Willemi martyris Norwicensis*

William of Saint-Calais, bishop of
Durham: 36
William of St Alban, Benedictine
monk, hagiographer: 61, 64
William of Ste Barbe, bishop of
Durham: 200
William of Stuteville: 78, 86, 89,
224, 229
William of York, archbishop
of York, saint: 17, 24, 43, 84,
99–104, 109–15, 118–19, 149–59,
171, 177–78, 185, 209
episcopal-pastoral: 150–54
feast: 151–52
myroblyte: 149–54
see also *Vita sancti Willelmi
(Life of Saint William)*, (anon)
William, Abbot of Rievaulx: 172
Willibrord, Northumbrian
missonary: 363, 413
Windberg Legendary: 418
Wulfric of Haselbury, saint: 209,
see also *Vita Wulfrici anchoretae
Haselbergiae*

York: 18–19, 24–27, 42–49, 76–78,
80–82, 87, 89–93, 102–06, 108–19,
146, 149–160, 167–68, 171–74,
177–78, 306, 309, 333
breviary: 114, 118
*Breviarium ad usum insignis
ecclesiae Eboracensis*: 114–15,
118, 333
canons: 149, 152–53
diocese: 18–19, 87, 155, 160, 168
episcopal sanctity: 48–49
Minster: 20, 25, 27, 100, 102–06,
110–11, 113, 115, 118–19, 152,
157–59, 178, 378
northerness: 42–43, 77, 89–93
treaty: 53

Medieval Church Studies

All volumes in this series are evaluated by an Editorial Board, strictly on academic grounds, based on reports prepared by referees who have been commissioned by virtue of their specialism in the appropriate field. The Board ensures that the screening is done independently and without conflicts of interest. The definitive texts supplied by authors are also subject to review by the Board before being approved for publication. Further, the volumes are copyedited to conform to the publisher's stylebook and to the best international academic standards in the field.

Titles in Series

Megan Cassidy-Welch, *Monastic Spaces and their Meanings: Thirteenth-Century English Cistercian Monasteries* (2001)

Elizabeth Freeman, *Narratives of a New Order: Cistercian Historical Writing in England, 1150–1220* (2002)

The Study of the Bible in the Carolingian Era, ed. by Celia Chazelle and Burton Van Name Edwards (2003)

Text and Controversy from Wyclif to Bale: Essays in Honour of Anne Hudson, ed. by Helen Barr and Ann M. Hutchison (2005)

Lena Roos, *'God Wants It!': The Ideolog y of Martyrdom in the Hebrew Crusade Chronicles and its Jewish and Christian Background* (2006)

Emilia Jamroziak, *Rievaulx Abbey and its Social Context, 1132–1300: Memory, Locality, and Networks* (2004)

The Voice of Silence: Women's Literacy in a Men's Church, ed. by Thérèse de Hemptinne and María Eugenia Góngora (2004)

Perspectives for an Architecture of Solitude: Essays on Cistercians, Art and Architecture in Honour of Peter Fergusson, ed. by Terryl N. Kinder (2004)

Saints, Scholars, and Politicians: Gender as a Tool in Medieval Studies, ed. by Mathilde van Dijk and Renée Nip (2005)

Manuscripts and Monastic Culture: Reform and Renewal in Twelfth-Century Germany, ed. by Alison I. Beach (2007)

Weaving, Veiling, and Dressing : Textiles and their Metaphors in the Late Middle Ages, ed. by Kathryn M. Rudy and Barbara Baert (2007)

James J. Boyce, *Carmelite Liturgy and Spiritual Identity: The Choir Books of Kraków* (2008)

Studies in Carthusian Monasticism in the Late Middle Ages, ed. by Julian M. Luxford (2009)

Kevin J. Alban, *The Teaching and Impact of the 'Doctrinale' of Thomas Netter of Walden (c. 1374–1430)* (2010)

Gunilla Iversen, *Laus angelica: Poetry in the Medieval Mass*, ed. by Jane Flynn, trans. by William Flynn (2010)

Kriston R. Rennie, *Law and Practice in the Age of Reform: The Legatine Work of Hugh of Die (1073–1106)* (2010)

After Arundel: Religious Writing in Fifteenth-Century England, ed. by Vincent Gillespie and Kantik Ghosh (2011)

Federico Botana, *The Works of Mercy in Italian Medieval Art (c. 1050–c. 1400)* (2011)

The Regular Canons in the Medieval British Isles, ed. by Janet Burton and Karen Stöber (2011)

Wycliffite Controversies, ed. by Mishtooni Bose and J. Patrick Hornbeck II (2011)

Nickiphoros I. Tsougarakis, *The Latin Religious Orders in Medieval Greece, 1204–1500* (2012)

Nikolaos G. Chrissis, *Crusading in Frankish Greece: A Study of Byzantine-Western Relations and Attitudes, 1204–1282* (2012)

Demetrio S. Yocum, *Petrarch's Humanist Writing and Carthusian Monasticism: The Secret Language of the Self* (2013)

The Pseudo-Bonaventuran Lives of Christ: Exploring the Middle English Tradition, ed. by Ian Johnson and Allan F. Westphall (2013)

Alice Chapman, *Sacred Authority and Temporal Power in the Writings of Bernard of Clairvaux* (2013)

Religious Controversy in Europe, 1378–1536: Textual Transmission and Networks of Readership, ed. by Michael Van Dussen and Pavel Soukup (2013)

Ian Johnson, *The Middle English Life of Christ: Academic Discourse, Translation, and Vernacular Theology* (2013)

Monasteries on the Borders of Medieval Europe: Conflict and Cultural Interaction, ed. by Emilia Jamroziak and Karen Stöber (2014)

M. J. Toswell, *The Anglo-Saxon Psalter* (2014)

Envisioning the Bishop: Images and the Episcopacy in the Middle Ages, ed. by Sigrid Danielson and Evan A. Gatti (2014)

Kathleen E. Kennedy, *The Courtly and Commercial Art of the Wycliffite Bible* (2014)

David N. Bell, *The Library of the Abbey of La Trappe: A Study of its History from the Twelfth Century to the French Revolution, with an Annotated Edition of the 1752 Catalogue* (2014)

Patronage, Production, and Transmission of Texts in Medieval and Early Modern Jewish Cultures, ed. by Esperanza Alfonso and Jonathan Decter (2014)

Devotional Culture in Late Medieval England and Europe: Diverse Imaginations of Christ's Life, edited by Stephen Kelly and Ryan Perry (2014)

Matthew Cheung Salisbury, *The Secular Liturgical Office in Late Medieval England* (2015)

From Hus to Luther: Visual Culture in the Bohemian Reformation (1380–1620), ed. by Kateřina Horníčková and Michal Šroněk (2016)

Medieval Liège at the Crossroads of Europe: Monastic Society and Culture, 1000–1300, ed. by Steven Vanderputten, Tjamke Snijders, and Jay Diehl (2017)

Episcopal Power and Local Society in Medieval Europe, 900–1400, ed. by Peter Coss, Chris Dennis, Melissa Julian-Jones, and Angelo Silvestri (2017)

Saints of North-East England, 600–1500, ed. by Margaret Coombe, Anne Mouron, and Christiania Whitehead (2017)

Tamás Karáth, *Richard Rolle: The Fifteenth-Century Translations* (2017)

Late Medieval Devotional Compilations in England, ed. by Marleen Cré, Diana
Denissen, and Denis Renevey (2020)

Episcopal Power and Personality in Medieval Europe, 900–1480, ed. by Peter Coss,
Chris Dennis, Melissa Julian-Jones, and Angelo Silvestri (2020)

*Inwardness, Individualization, and Religious Agency in the Late Medieval Low
Countries: Studies in the* Devotio Moderna *and its Contents*, ed. by Rijcklof
Hofman, Charles Caspers, Peter Nissen, Mathilde van Dijk, and Johan
Oosterman (2020)

Late Medieval Devotional Compilations in England, ed. by Marleen Cré, Diana
Denissen, Denis Renevey (2020)

Episcopal Power and Personality in Medieval Europe, 900-1480, ed. by Peter Coss,
Chris Dennis, Melissa Julian-Jones, Angelo Silvestri (2020)

Bishops' Identities, Careers, and Networks in Medieval Europe, ed. by Sarah Thomas
(2021)

*Wycliffism and Hussitism: Methods of Thinking, Writing, and Persuasion
c. 1360–c. 1460*, ed. by Kantik Ghosh and Pavel Soukup (2021)